Charlotte Brontë's Thunder

The Truth Behind
The Brontë Sisters' Genius

MICHELE CARTER

Library and Archives Canada Cataloguing in Publication

Carter, Michele,
    Charlotte Brontë's thunder: the truth behind the Brontë sisters' genius / Michele Carter.

Includes bibliographical references. Issued also in electronic format.

ISBN 978-0-9682728-5-5

1. Brontë, Charlotte, 1816-1855.   2. Brontë, Charlotte, 1816-1855—Authorship.
3. Brontë, Emily, 1818-1848—Authorship.
4. Brontë, Anne, 1820-1849—Authorship.
5. Novelists, English—19th century—Biography.   I. Title.

PR4168.C37 2011   823'.809   C2011-907553-9

CONTENTS

ILLUSTRATIONS

ACKNOWLEDGMENTS

No book of this kind can be written without citing other scholars, biographers, and historians. Two of the sources that were most invaluable were Juliet Barker's detailed biography *The Brontës*. Barker was a curator of the Brontë Parsonage Museum and had access to extensive documentation surrounding the entire Brontë family. During the seven years spent writing and researching this book, her 800-page text was never far from my desk. The three volumes of *The Letters of Charlotte Brontë* edited by Margaret Smith provided not only Charlotte's letters but also detailed annotations that made this an equally important research tool.

INTRODUCTION

Recognize what is before your eyes,

and what is hidden will be revealed to you.

—The Gospel of Thomas

The three Brontë sisters, Charlotte, Emily, and Anne, and one brother, Branwell lived in a vicar's residence with their father Reverend Brontë in a village in Yorkshire, England during the mid-nineteenth century. In 1846, while Emily and Anne were still in their twenties and Charlotte was just 30, the three Brontë sisters self-published, under the male pseudonyms of Currer Bell, Ellis Bell, and Acton Bell, a book of poetry entitled *Poems*, which sold only two copies. In 1845, their brother Branwell had begun a novel that remained unfinished at his death in 1848, but between 1841 and 1848 he published approximately 18 poems in various newspapers in Yorkshire (*Oxford* 77). In 1847, the 'Bell brothers' acquired two separate publishers who handled the publication of Currer Bell's *Jane Eyre*, Ellis Bell's *Wuthering Heights,* and Acton Bell's *Agnes Grey*. Currer Bell's other fiction *The Professor* was rejected nine times, but published posthumously two years after Charlotte's death.

By the end of 1848, Emily had also died, so only two sisters remained with their father in the parsonage. In 1849, Acton Bell's novel *The Tenant of Wildfell Hall* and Currer Bell's new fiction *Shirley* were accepted and published. By mid-1849, the youngest sibling Anne had died. The final Currer Bell novel *Villette*, which was also the last 'Bell brother' book, came out in 1853. During this time, two years before her death, Charlotte started 'The Story of Willie Ellin,' and an unfinished novel called 'Emma.' Collectively, the three Bell brothers had written seven novels, and the response from the public was an interesting one: the readership noted a striking similarity in the subject matter and tone of the novels; some critics went so far as to suggest the 'brothers' were one person, Currer Bell, and that, perhaps, *he* was actually a woman.

Did Charlotte Brontë write all the Brontë sisters' novels? A few brave souls have entered this controversial territory in the past. Sidney Dobell, a highly respected, Victorian literary critic read the Brontë novels when they were first published under the pseudonyms of Currer, Ellis, and Acton Bell. He believed that Currer (Charlotte), not Ellis (Emily), wrote *Wuthering Heights* due to the similarities he found between it and *Jane Eyre*, but scholars have dismissed Dobell as "eccentric." George Saintsbury, another Victorian literary critic, believed Acton Bell (Anne Brontë) had written *Wuthering Heights*, and he was called "wrong-headed." According to Lucasta Miller, author of *The Brontë Myth*, John Malham-Dembleby was "an obsessive enthusiast" who existed on the fringes of a kind of "Brontëmania" that bordered on "pathological:" he, too, believed that Charlotte wrote *Wuthering Heights*. Miller writes that he "offers an extreme example" of a "conspiracy theorist" when he asserts "that there was nothing in Charlotte's novels that was not a direct copy from life." Miller contends that his conclusions begin "with a sane or semi-sane hunch" and then digress into statements that show "he is wholly incapable of distinguishing fact from fiction," especially when it concerns his "mad views" that Charlotte and Monsieur Heger, her instructor in Brussels, had a love affair that was never consummated, and that Charlotte wrote *Wuthering Heights* (116).

As Miller states, Malham-Dembleby makes a number of claims that simply cannot be true. In *The Confessions of Charlotte Brontë* he attributes Branwell's work to Charlotte and states with absolute certainty that to have given credit to the brother for Charlotte's work "was one of the most absurdly deluding affectations in the annals of falsely assigned authorship ever known" (2). Scholars admit confusion arises over authorship of some of the Brontë poems, but Malham-Dembleby believes the confusion is groundless, asserting that Charlotte wrote all the poetry and that her sisters merely made fair copies on her behalf. His hyperbole borders on rude when referring to Emily and Anne, but respectful when speaking of Charlotte: Emily was a "simpleton," and "a slovenly illiterate, with the copyist mentality belonging a dull child of eight, little Charlotte, we shall see, was a cunning mock philologist, a brilliant essayist and satirist, a gifted poet, and a promising young dramatist at thirteen or fourteen" (14). Reproductions of Anne's poetry "plainly disclose Anne not only as her sister Charlotte's transcriber, but also as a very childishly illiterate copyist." Her mentality is inane and simplistic and "failure to recognise this glaring truth can be the result only of absolute unacquaintance with Charlotte's work, and of a complete ignoring of the redundant evidence of Anne Brontë's literary ineptitude," and any assumptions that Anne wrote good poetry are "farcical" (80-81).

His comparison of the Brontë novels for similarity of words and phrases has some merit in a few cases, but his unwavering certainty, rude tone, and dangerous pronouncements that rumours are facts make him an unreliable interpreter of the most persistent Brontë mysteries. The other difficulty with his opinions is that he casts them in a convoluted and opaque syntax. For instance, he believes he has exact matches in real life for the characters in *Wuthering Heights* and that these were "all sequently transmuted to her novel with such a flagrant indifference to the liberty of simple allocation and patent adaptation, that after the book's being published Charlotte must have been tortured with a constant terror lest a sensational literary exposure of the extraordinary facts were made before the reading public" (5).

His prose is decidedly tortuous, which makes his claims all the more outrageous but, in the spirit of full disclosure, I also compared two texts that I later discovered he had analyzed, and my conclusions are similar and will be dealt with in chapter thirty.

Elizabeth Rigby in the December 1848 issue of *Quarterly Review* also recognized a similarity in the Brontë sisters' work but, at the time of her writing, they were still called the Bell brothers. She suggests that the author of *Jane Eyre* "combines a total ignorance of the habits of society, a great coarseness of taste, and a heathenish doctrine of religion. And as these characteristics appear more or less in the writings of all three Currer, Acton, and Ellis alike . . . we are ready to accept the fact of their identity or of their relationship with equal satisfaction," but when comparing *Jane Eyre* with *Wuthering Heights* "purporting to be written by Ellis Bell," she acknowledges "there is a decided family likeness between the two." Rigby echoes other reviewers when she notes that the Bell brothers seem to write with one sensibility: the books contain "singularly unattractive" protagonists and the writing shares a coarseness and brutality that combines "genuine power with such horrid taste."

The questions surrounding authorship, therefore, are not new but, as another "conspiracy theorist" that dares to step outside the prescribed view of three genius sisters, I must prepare myself for the derision and ridicule. Will I be classed as dreadfully wayward or simply another crack-brained eccentric? A fear of mockery should not stifle a person's opinion, however, and until the questions are finally resolved to everyone's satisfaction—which may never happen—theories should be allowed the light of scrutiny and argument. In my case, I never set out to challenge the *status quo*, but as I studied the novels for a shared symbolic design, I found an odd set of words that I intuitively surmised might lead into deeper truths. I knew little of the Brontë family—only that there were three sisters—and I knew nothing of Haworth, the village where the family lived for most of their lives. As I read *Jane Eyre*, I noticed Brontë's descriptions incorporate religious symbols, and after closer analysis found she was borrowing heavily from the rituals and symbols of Freemasonry. I later discovered she had a brother Branwell who was a Mason, but that was all I knew. The next step in solving the clues came when I saw that, like the Freemasons, she was using signs and secret codes to construct a separate narrative. Gradually, I blundered through the crests and valleys of the story until I accidentally tripped over the possibility that Charlotte may have been the sole genius in her family. This theory is not absolute proof but, after several years of studying the Brontës, I am convinced of its reliability; thus, I have decided to share my views and risk aligning myself with the wrong-headed and the pathological.

The purpose of this book is not to change hearts and minds, but to offer an alternative reading of Charlotte Brontë. As I unravelled threads to Brontë's intricate system of code, puns, and clues, I discovered a shocking story of unimagined and diabolical horrors. Through these clues, Brontë unveils examples of criminal activity that either friends or family members must have conveyed to her and, in some cases, she directly experienced. As far as she was concerned, the underlying and constant threat of violence was grounds for anonymity in her writing; she was convinced that these crimes were being committed in her township, and if she were to ever divulge the pattern of these crimes in her novels, she had best cloak herself in the disguise of a male pseudonym. If she were the sole author in the family, she would want to protect her sisters from any negative repercussions following her actions, so in order to guarantee her two sisters enjoyed financial freedom if she died, either naturally or under suspicious circumstances, she would list them as authors; thus, Emily and Anne (now Ellis and Acton) would receive royalties for life. Why not simply name them in her will? As the story emerges, we uncover why Brontë believed a last will and testament would have been the least favoured way to ensure her sisters' financial security.

The professional surprises uncovered in my research led directly to Brontë's personal revelations. The biographical and historical facts supported many of these new revelations, but the method of exposing them is certainly open to cynicism and criticism. The newly discovered secret I found in my investigation of her wordplay is that Charlotte Brontë was an avid anagrammatist. She left hundreds among her novels, letters, and poems. In several of the anagrams, she explains that she, not her sister Emily, wrote *Wuthering Heights*. Brontë's rules about the anagrams remain consistent: she transforms each 'surface' prose phrase in the sentence into a 'hidden' anagram phrase; if commas separate the surface phrases, the anagram word is limited to that phrase and cannot be moved to another place within the sentence, but if no commas separate the phrases, an anagram word or two can be shifted to another spot in order to make sense. If a word in the surface prose is enclosed in two commas, it cannot be altered; it stays as is and makes sense when included with the rest of the anagrams.

An example of her skill occurs in the opening sentence of an 1850 disclaimer she wrote after critics suggested she was the sole author of all the writings. The anagrams refer to symbolic terms found in Freemasonry. These elements are covered in chapter nine and in later chapters to show how Brontë uses Masonic rituals and symbols in her fiction. She includes hints of her process in the disclaimer, which reads as follows: "It has been thought that all the works published under the names Currer, Ellis, and Acton Bell, were, in reality, the production of one person." (Currer, Ellis, and Acton were the pen names attributed to Charlotte, Emily, and Anne.)

The natural divisions occur between the words "works" and "published," leaving "in reality" separate because it lies between the two commas, and the last section would be, "were the production of one person." In this anagram, she omits articles, so without "the" or "a" the sentence has an odd syntax, but the added punctuation helps clarify her message. Also, as mentioned before, when portions of words are not contained within commas, Brontë allows for a word or two to be moved from one place to the next to provide clarity. The completed anagram makes sense with the small shift. First, the completed anagram is written out, followed by each separate phrase to show where the break occurs. The entire anagram with all the adjustments comes at the end. (*Noah* and *wolf* are her terms for a Mason.)

Below heath heights' tort talk, bold Catherine haunts Noah dullard. Fill pen. Use secret numbers. Tiny Ariel. Hood on pen. Now free to recite spur.

These are the splits as explained above. First her surface prose is written out and then the anagram.

"It has been thought that all the works" / *Below heath heights' tort talk haunts.*

"published under the names of Currer Ellis and Acton Bell" / *Bold Catherine Noah dullard. Fill pen. Use secret numbers.*

"in reality" / *tiny Ariel*

"were the production of one person." / *Hood on pen. Now free to recite spur.*

She refers to *Wuthering Heights* and its torts or civil actions, a reference that coincides with the analysis of the novel in its delineation of the law of entail in chapter twenty-seven. As is discussed in chapter eighteen, the anagram in *Wuthering Heights* of Lockwood's words "I was over head and ears" could be "*I rove as dead Earnshaw.*" This "*dead Earnshaw*" would most likely refer to Catherine's ghost haunting the dull "*Noah*" Lockwood. The act of filling a pen with ink would be an accurate term for the activity at that time. The "*secret numbers*" are the Masonic landmarks that signify the rules of Freemasonry and are discussed later.

Brontë writes in the first person singular with "*fill pen*" and "*use secret numbers,*" as in "I fill pen," and "I use secret numbers," so she is not describing her sister's actions, which would need a different subject verb agreement and would read as, "she fills pen;" consequently, Brontë is writing about herself, not her sister. Plus, Charlotte is the small sibling in the family, so her "*tiny Ariel*" indicates she wrote the book, not Emily who was the tallest sister. This anagram also alludes to the mischievous sprite in Shakespeare's *The Tempest*. Like the Mason initiate, Charlotte wears a hood, but on her pen not her head and, because of her anagram cover, she can freely tell us what motivated her to write the novel with her Masonic symbols and allusions to their rituals and rules.

The next line, with its natural breaks, reads, "This mistake I endeavoured to rectify / by a few words of disclaimer / prefixed to the third edition of *Jane Eyre*." The anagrams that fit with the breaks come first but are stilted. The final anagram, with its words repositioned and marked with a number, clarifies the meaning.

"This mistake I endeavoured to rectify" / *Inked rude emotive Cathy satire. Foist*

"by a few words of disclaimer" / *Wry maid. Describe wolf oaf's*

"prefixed to the third edition of *Jane Eyre*" / *profit. Jeer fetid hero. Need identity hoax.*

The anagram with the words shifted slightly within the anagram sentence are:

1) *Inked rude, emotive Cathy satire. Foist oaf's profit. Wry maid. Describe wolf. Jeer fetid hero. Need identity hoax.*

Chapter twenty-eight provides a complete analysis of this and subsequent anagrams found in her disclaimer. Other chapters show how the anagrams enabled Brontë the freedom *to recite* all her secrets to her readers.

Charlotte Brontë's *Thunder* is designed to explore one specific theory regarding the authorship of the Brontë works. The resulting narrative tries to introduce the biographical and historical facts together with an analysis of the Brontë writings to assess the viability of this theory. Without absolute proof, however, the assumptions are necessarily based on limited knowledge. Nonetheless, the speculations and the possibilities warrant disclosure.

The book is also presented for educational and entertainment purposes. Together with clues, puns, narratives, and facts, the anagrams provide a glimpse into the real life behind the professional and personal myths, and allow Brontë's readers to view the hidden thunder of her denunciations. By transcribing these anagrams and declaring their accuracy, I do not necessarily concede their veracity, but I do accept that Brontë believed she was telling her readers the truth, as she knew it; therefore, I made every effort to support her claims with external evidence.

Not everything she states in her anagrams can be proved at this time, so the crimes that she outlines are only alleged crimes and must be viewed as such. Her powerful imagination could have just as easily constructed these tales of apparent brutality, or she may have exaggerated the rumours of corruption to fulfil her creative drive, so readers should try to remember that a number of her claims are her opinion only and not necessarily factually supported.

Other claims she makes, however, do coincide with historical facts. In one or two cases, I was not prepared for the uncomfortable truth, and it took some time to absorb the impact of her anagrams, but rather than avoid the controversy surrounding these unusual disclosures, I chose to put the findings in front of readers to let them decide what is fact or fiction. At the very least, the contents of this book may bring fresh insight into this fascinating family, and introduce Brontë's novels to a whole new audience.

PROLOGUE

The human heart has hidden treasures

In secret kept, in silence sealed.

—Charlotte Brontë

On a warm afternoon in early autumn, I climbed to the top of the cobbled Main Street in Haworth, observing the serried ranks of shops and homes whose grim stone faces still wear the grey stain of nineteenth century industrial smoke, and I paused at the crest of that steep, winding hill to steady my excitement before turning up the lane that leads to the Brontë parsonage museum.

To my left stood the imposing front entrance to the church of St. Michael's and all Angels where the Reverend Patrick Brontë began his duties in 1820 as perpetual curate. After following a slight bend in the lane onto Church Street, the famous Brontë home came into view. A few tall trees masked the full glory of the two-story structure, as did a high stone wall that enclosed the grounds. Set between the church and the parsonage was a cemetery with its oblong gravestones and large, stone boxes that resembled forgotten coffins still waiting to be interred. Strips of persistent grass crept along the edges of stone, growing among flattened slabs that designated burials of men, women, and children honoured and loved from centuries long past. To my right was a house built around 1830 by John Brown, a stone mason, church sexton, and friend of the Brontës. Attached to the house is the old school room where Charlotte Brontë had once taught the village boys and girl.

I made my way to the opening in the stone wall and stepped onto the front garden of the parsonage museum. My first impression was that the grounds were smaller than I had imagined, but neatly kept with varied shrubs and trees providing a peaceful setting. I walked along the path and faced the museum with its five windows along the second story, its two windows on either side of the front door, and the two story extension on the right, added after the Reverend Brontë had died. The white curtains contrasting with the grey stone suggested a civilized and gracious façade had merged with the darker substance of life.

Here was the home where great works of literature were imagined and penned: *Wuthering Heights, Agnes Grey, The Professor, Jane Eyre, The Tenant of Wildfell Hall, Shirley,* and *Villette.* Hundreds of pages written behind those windows during windstorms and endless rainy nights when the Brontë sisters would light candles, and the silhouettes of their bodies bent over the table would fade with the embers in the fire's grate. In the imagined silence and stillness of a foggy dawn, brown moors and icy streams visited a corner in my mind's eye where I saw nature's elemental power igniting the Brontë soul to speak of passion and truth, and fuelling the mysterious yearning of a lonely spirit determined to unite with her invisible readers.

The building had been constructed in 1778. The windows and the front door all faced east toward Brow Moor, and the north gate entrance led onto Church Street toward St. Michael's. Inside the parsonage museum, the rooms were dressed in the furnishings of the Brontë era, which spanned from 1820 to 1861 when Reverend Brontë died at the age of eighty-four, having outlived his wife and six children (two of the eldest girls had died young). To the left was the sitting room where the family received visitors, ate their meals, and enjoyed their writing. Recollections of Charlotte's lifelong friend Ellen Nussey are documented in Margaret Smith's first volume of Brontë letters:

"There was not much carpet any where except in the sitting room, and on the centre of the study floor. The hall floor and stairs were done with sand stone, always beautifully clean as everything about the house was, the walls were not papered but coloured in a pretty dove-coloured tint, hair-seated chairs and mahogany tables, book-shelves in the Study but not many of these elsewhere. Scant and bare indeed many will say, yet it was not a scantness that made itself felt—mind and thought, yes, I had almost said elegance, but certainly *refinement* diffused themselves over all, and made nothing really wanting" (599).

As I took my place behind the corded rope that prevented visitors from wandering freely throughout each room, I joined a proud membership in the society of pilgrims from all over the world who made this journey each year, in the thousands, to see the Brontë shrine. The

Brontë name alone conjures a charming, collective image of isolated, genius writers living in a remote village surrounded by romantic moorland, far from the literary lights of London, and where they kept their talents veiled in secrecy. When the novels appeared under the male pseudonyms of Currer, Ellis, and Acton Bell, conjecture and curiosity groomed the mystery surrounding authorship: who were these men? Evocative imaginings reached mythic proportions after the brothers became sisters who the public learned not only suffered great family tragedy but had also died young.

The family began in 1812 when Patrick Brontë married Maria Branwell. They had six children: five girls and one boy. By 1825, the Reverend's wife and two eldest daughters had died. Cancer claimed their mother, and Maria and Elizabeth aged twelve and ten died from tuberculosis, a disease that would later take the lives of Emily and Anne, but in 1825, at nine years of age, Charlotte was now the eldest of the four remaining children. Branwell was eight, followed by Emily who was seven, and Anne, the youngest, who was only five when their mother died. The deaths continued. In September of 1848 at the age of thirty-one, Branwell died, followed in December of that year by Emily. Reverend Brontë, Charlotte, and Anne were still grieving their loss when Anne succumbed to tuberculosis a few months later in May of 1849. The combination of female genius, enigmatic characters revealed in the novels, and early deaths helped generate the mythic ethos of these three legendary sisters.

Dozens of representations of the novels, including films, television movies, musicals, operas, ballets, and plays keep the Brontë works alive in the hearts and minds of generations of readers and give us visual depictions of such powerful characters as Heathcliff, Catherine, Rochester, Jane, and Bertha Mason, the mad wife in the attic of gothic Thornfield manor. Now after so much reading and watching, I had finally arrived at the source of all that creativity and was standing inside the four walls where talent and productivity had surpassed most storytellers published during the Victorian era.

To the right of the hallway was Reverend Brontë's study. The Reverend, a tall, erect man with a distinguished head of white hair, a broad brow, and high cheekbones, was a commanding figure. He carried himself with a justifiable pride, having been a graduate of Cambridge, and later an ordained minister in the Church of England. I pictured him at his desk, his head of white hair receding from a large forehead, his round glasses perched securely on his strong Irish nose, and his lips pursed as he read through the pages of his own book entitled *Cottage Poems*, written in 1811 when he was a young Anglican curate in Shropshire. In his book of poetry, he introduces himself to the reader and then says that his religious duties should not curtail his desire to write: "a religious field" could certainly be one "favourable for a poet to range through." He adds that if "the Author has not succeeded as a poet, he will not blame his subject, but will readily acknowledge the fault to be entirely his own; nor will he be able to offer, as an excuse, that he was not interested. He certainly was interested, and that in no small degree." He had composed moral verses which he hoped would "be rendered useful to some poor soul" (qtd. in Lock 98). Thankfully, the man who believed in education and poetry had passed down his interest in literature to his children.

Next, I stood at the kitchen door and imagined Tabby, the Yorkshire woman who, at the age of fifty-four, began work as a servant a few years after the Brontës had arrived in Haworth. She remained their faithful servant for over thirty years, dying in February 1855 a few weeks before Charlotte's death at the end of March. Tabby had her practical side but, with her broad accent, could easily spin a yarn sprinkled with the supernatural and the superstitious, or recount tales of the local families and their histories. She took charge of the children with kindness and a no-nonsense approach to life. Her "childers" soon regarded her as a loved member of the family.

I stared into the small space of a kitchen and imagined four children sitting round the blazing fire on a cold, snowy night. I recalled Charlotte's rendering of a particular scene in her 'Tales of the Islanders,' and soon saw the stocky frame of Tabby settled at the table to sew the sleeve on one of Anne's frocks. The flames in the grate beamed across the hearth and glittered over the copper kettle that Tabby had set on the hob to keep the tea warm. The glow of the ruddy fire barely stretched far enough to discern a tea tray with its teapot, cream ewer, and sugar basin nestled beside Tabby's elbow.

Outside, flakes dropped fast, and the white storm blew cold and thick over grass and moor. The wind moaned and howled with such a high piercing squeal, the children requested the heartening addition of candlelight. Tabby, being a frugal and practical Yorkshire woman, saw no sense in wasting candles when the peat from the fire provided plenty of light. She lectured the children on the propriety of being wasteful when they had nothing to fear and no need to see. In fact, they might prefer the darkness of sleep in their beds to the peaceful enjoyment of a cheery fire. The children acknowledged Tabby's victory over the candle question when they witnessed none being produced.

A silence ensued until their brother Branwell sighed and said, "I don't know what to do." Emily and Anne echoed his sentiment.

Tabby offered a solution: "Wha ya may go t'bed."

"I'd rather do anything than that," said Branwell.

Charlotte weighed in with her impressions: "You're so glum tonight, Tabby." The woman continued her dressmaking without comment. Charlotte then suggested they imagine something exciting. "Suppose we had each an Island."

Branwell's eyes perked up. "If we had, I would choose the Island of Man."

"I would choose the Isle of Wight," said Charlotte.

"The Isle of Arran for me," said Emily.

"And mine should be Guernsey," added Anne.

Charlotte declared, "The Duke of Wellington should be my chief man."

Branwell chose Colonel Herries, the Commandant of the Light Horse Volunteers of London and Westminster. Emily wanted the novelist Walter Scott to be her chief man, and Anne decided on Hans William Bentinck, the 1st Earl of Portland who had been England's ambassador to France in 1698 (Gaskell 53-54).

The children's loud voices overpowered the wild tumult of the tempest outside. Their excitement grew as they planned how their chief men would inhabit these new islands. Soon they would begin writing down their tales but, for now, on this night, only their voices were recording their heroes' adventures. Their fervour could not stop time, and soon the dismal sound of the grandfather clock striking seven alerted them to their fate.

Tabby ordered they march straight up to bed, and the sound of her voice faded into the creak of footfalls on the floor above.

After this brief reverie in the kitchen, I crossed the hall to Arthur Bell Nicholls' studio and remained only a short time to study his portrait. He had been born in Ireland of Scottish parents and attended Trinity College in Dublin. He became curate to Reverend Brontë in 1845 and in 1854 married Charlotte. His Irish features and grim face with its bushy beard and stern mouth conveyed a certain pride, and his dark eyes lacked humour and suggested an earnest deportment that could be intimidating. Charlotte's father was outraged when his curate was bold enough to propose to his daughter and supported Charlotte's refusal. He said "the match would be a degradation." In December of 1852, Charlotte wrote to Ellen Nussey to explain her refusal to marry Nicholls: "My own objections arise from a sense of incongruity and uncongeniality in feelings, tastes [and] principles" (*Letters, Vol.III* 95). By 1854, she felt something quite different.

Her father thought his curate lacked prospects and was not good enough for his daughter. He also enjoyed his living situation and did not wish it to change with the inclusion of another man, but Nicholls persevered and assured Reverend Brontë that following the marriage, the aging Reverend's "convenience and seclusion were to be scrupulously respected" (242). Nonetheless, on June 29, 1854, her father refused to make the short walk to the church to attend his daughter's wedding. Charlotte Brontë, now Charlotte Nicholls remained married for nine months, until her death in March of 1855.

Nicholls remained in the parsonage until the Reverend's death in 1861. The church trustees declined the curate's offer to take over the Reverend's position, so he left Haworth to return to Ireland where he married his cousin, became a farmer, and died in 1906 at the age of eighty-nine.

On the second floor of the parsonage were the bedrooms and the children's study. This small room was tucked between their father's bedroom and their Aunt Branwell's room. In 1821, the mother's sister Elizabeth Branwell had moved in when Maria was dying. After her sister's death, Aunt Branwell remained to assist the Reverend with the raising of the children.

Miss Branwell was a small, middle-aged lady with light auburn curls who preferred to dress in silk. She had come from Cornwall in the south and needed a few months to brace herself for the close, sultry days of summer, as well as the damp, sombre nights and slashing rain of winter. For the majority of the twenty-one years remaining in her life, she stayed inside the parsonage, avoiding Main Street entirely, but stepping out on Sunday mornings to walk the short distance across the churchyard, into St. Michael's, and up the aisle to the front pew. At home, she read the newspapers, took her meals in her room, and indulged in her bit of snuff. While she was well read and able to discuss the news of the day with her brother-in-law, she was also proficient in sewing and needlework and passed these skills on to her nieces. She wanted the girls to learn proper manners and the household arts, which coincided with the Reverend's desire that they take instruction in painting and music.

I peeked into the children's study and thought I heard the soft tinkling sound of distant laughter. The scent of lilacs floated overhead and my stomach gave a subtle flip as I imagined an event made famous in Charlotte's writings. One evening in 1826, the children's father had brought home a box of twelve wooden soldiers for Branwell. Reverend Brontë went up the stairs to the room behind his own and quietly placed the box beside the sleeping boy's bed. These soldiers would replace previous troops who had suffered the indignities of beheadings, chopped limbs, and burned bodies, as well as ignoble exiles into the marshy bogs. The recruits would be a welcome gift.

The Reverend recognized the precocious intelligence and fiery exuberance of his son and envisioned great success for his heir. Perhaps his boy would be a scholar, or a painter, or a brilliant poet worthy of the eminence of a Horace or a Virgil. Before leaving the boy in his tranquil repose, the father gently smoothed his son's unruly red hair.

The next morning, the boy showed his sisters his latest treasure. The wooden uniforms had been carefully applied with paint. The soldiers were dressed in tall black boots, white pants, and white waistcoats under bright red jackets. They wore black hats, and some had white sashes across their chests and thick moustaches painted above their serious mouths. On seeing their brother's gift, Charlotte and Emily immediately jumped from their bed. Charlotte quickly reached into the box and took out the tallest, proclaiming, "This is the Duke of Wellington! This shall be the duke!" Emily's choice had a grave expression painted across his face, so they called him Gravey. Anne's pick was a small soldier that they christened Waiting-boy. Branwell studied those remaining and lifted out the one with a commanding stature and called him Bonaparte. By December of the following year, during that snowy night in the kitchen with Tabby, the children's soldiers became islanders, and in this cozy children's study, they sat on the floor plotting their latest adventures. (Beer 182)

The interest in these two great military leaders, the Duke of Wellington and Napoleon Bonaparte arose from recent events in history. Since 1789, France had been entangled in a bloody Revolution that lasted ten years before its citizens witnessed major political shifts in their system of government. A democratic republic, led by General Bonaparte, replaced the monarchy and aristocratic rule and, with each successful battle across Europe, Napoleon grew in military might, declaring himself Emperor of France. Despite his initial victories, the Duke of Wellington, the commander of the British forces, defeated Napoleon in 1815 at the Battle of Waterloo.

The children's father enjoyed reading over the details of military campaigns and regaling them with tales of battle scenes. His fondness for the stratagems of war and the exploits of generals heightened their interest in playing soldiers and in acting out attacks against the enemy, as they embroiled their imaginary soldiers in rebellion, revolution, and war. Charlotte saw herself in the strong, male persona of Wellington, leading her own personal rebellion against her sibling adversary, Branwell, who, as an only son would have wielded the power over his sisters in their more mundane roles as girls. For Charlotte and Branwell, the real life models of military leaders and emperors fused perfectly with the fictional lives of their wooden soldiers to create volumes of tales that grew to staggering proportions.

The minimal research I had done at this point enabled me to absorb and appreciate the impact this family has had on those who have enjoyed the novels and the films of the books. Readers from all over the world also find the legends and myths that abide round this family worth the journey to the parsonage museum where they can bask in the magic of their personal view of the Brontës.

During those brief years in the mid-nineteenth century, the air of Haworth was electric with acts of genius that resonate today. The aftermath of those creative outbursts has lasted through decades of scholarship and study that analyze and admire the Brontës' contribution to literature. Terms like "masterpiece," "Shakespearean," and "classic" are attached to *Jane Eyre* and *Wuthering Heights* as they consistently appear on the top ten lists of novels written in the English language. Those who read the works simply for pleasure and entertainment connect on an emotional level with the temperamental characters and wild landscape and become part of the Brontë phenomenon.

When I left the parsonage and began a short walk along the moors, the late afternoon sun had slipped behind a few grey clouds. I passed mounds of heather, low shrubs, and scrubby bushes as I strolled along paths beside brown fields and grassy knolls. Along the horizon, green hills dipped towards darker hills, some bordered with a dark band of trees and others with low cloud. The shadows among the trees were slightly undulating from a northerly breeze and the tall grasses leaned to the south. Drawn by the image of the Brontë children running ahead of me, I continued along a barren stretch of moors until I halted on a rise to glance down upon the serene landscape with its ribbons of gravel paths cutting through miles of heather. The land, while desolate and vast, was not gloomy or bleak, and prompted a moment's contemplation of nature's endurance and splendour.

Within moments, the weather changed and a mist drifted toward me. The darkening sky lingered as the wind gave a blast that sent the mist fleeing over the hills. I had just stepped around a watery bog and was coming to the tip of another rise when a sight yards ahead startled me. The sudden shock almost compelled me to lose my balance. As the mist swept past, clearing a patch on the moor, I noted a strange form on the edge of a ridge, and my quiet contemplation banished when the dark shape moved. In the shadow of a black cloud it loomed like a frightful spectre.

Fortunately, its back was to me and had not observed my presence. I froze and stirred not a muscle. The wind had picked up its force, and I feared the cold in my blood would still my heart, but the greater fear surfaced in my throat when the moan of the wind altered to a dreadful cry. The anguish in my chest exploded into a frightened sigh, my breath panting, and my body stiff with dread. I wished I had never come alone onto the moors. What foolish prompting had led me to wander this sparse heath so late in the day? The ghastly shrieks wakened every urge to flee. I waited for the precise moment to twist around unseen and run.

The daylight had all but disappeared, but my eyes suddenly beheld that the form and its wretched cry had come from a shape that seemed human. A man it was, and he stood rigid on the moors, head back, weeping his misery beneath the desolate sky. His cloak blew open and whipped behind him and still he did not move. The doom of twilight fast approached, and his shrieks subsided with the dimming light. The wind that beat against his face burned mine with the same harsh chill. I prayed his torment would soon end.

I imagined his face and recognized that ghostly countenance. In all the lonely landscape, no lonelier aspect existed. Here was Heathcliff, doomed lover of Catherine, landlord of Thrushcross Grange, and inhabitant of that infamous dwelling Wuthering Heights. I had read that he still haunts the moors, and now I was witness to his ghoulish mien. Alone we remained, I mesmerized by his mysterious power, he oblivious to his uninvited intruder. His head bowed to the weight of his sorrow, his hands wiped back the tears, and his fingers pressed into his brow. I asked myself if any man in literature had ever felt such grief.

His cries on the bleak moor and the howl of the wind had fallen mute. The smouldering mist crept on as the wind lost its force. Only the cold remained. The misery was over for now. I stepped toward the ridge and saw that the man would never take his inner tempest home. He had no earthly dwelling.

He was gone, but he would remain connected to these moors forever, haunting the crags and hills as he searched for his beloved Catherine. The alarm had passed. The space where his body had been shrank back to its natural state. The wild birds fluttered over my head in search of warm nooks. Faint streaks of sunlight strained between the dark clouds and, from far away, I heard the sighs of a breeze as it headed toward the sea. The man had been an illusion, of course, a melancholy fantasy brought on by the effects of both the Brontë's mystique and an active imagination, but the leaves of a stunted elm tree moping in the distance had charged the atmosphere with possibility.

My immersion in the culture of the Brontës had evidently coloured my view of the moors and affected my perception of what was truly before my eyes. For a moment, I had lost my objectivity and allowed my mind to drift with the romance inherent in the Brontë culture. I believed I had seen something that was not actually there but, as we all know, if we hear stories of hauntings and ghostly sightings enough times, we begin to believe spirits may indeed exist and, perhaps, one day we will actually see a lone figure roaming the moors. In a similar manner, if we are told all three Brontë sisters were genius writers, we accept this assertion as fact, even though objective reality may dispute this long-held belief, but the image is too strong and the romance too deep to encourage us to take a closer look; the assertion colours our view, and we naturally ignore evidence that suggests our perception of the Brontës may be an illusion.

What if the mythology of three genius sisters is an illusion, a fantasy perpetrated by Charlotte, and that only she wrote everything? Scholars, who agree Charlotte manufactured a specific mythology around her sisters, are troubled over the inconsistencies and are unable to reconcile the discrepancies, but accept that these mysteries will never be solved. Understandably, they would certainly be unwilling to support the "one Brontë genius" theory without substantial evidence, but what if things are not what they seem and overlooked evidence exists?

The historical and biographical facts are undisputed except when linked to the actual writings themselves. Scholars and critics admit, that on a number of issues, contradictory facts and inexplicable mysteries abound. Most enthusiasts of the Brontës know the story of the sisters' lives; less ardent fans may only be aware of a few facts, while a large population of readers simply enjoys the books without delving further into the intricacies of family or village life during the Brontë era. Some of those readers may not know that brother Branwell was an alcoholic and drug addict, or that the Reverend Brontë, although President of the Haworth Temperance Society (Branwell was also a member) drank as well, as did a significant number of the men in their village.

Nor will they be aware that no manuscripts with Emily's or Anne's handwriting have ever been found, or that their publisher, who would have seen the original manuscripts, declared that Charlotte was the sole author, or that diary papers written by the younger sisters and later discovered in the 1890s are examples of childish musings, and in Emily's case, of such poor craftsmanship that she shows no discernable aptitude for writing at all.

By 1849, a few critics were deducing that the three Bell brothers were actually one author who wrote all the works, but in 1850, they let their suppositions go. In that year, after her sisters were both dead, the second edition of *Wuthering Heights* came out, and included a "Biographical Notice of Ellis and Acton Bell," in which Charlotte rejected the one-author theory. Also, however, as Lucasta Miller states in her preface to *The Brontë Myth*, the Notice contained "ambiguous and contradictory comments". Charlotte underplayed her sister's ability: "Instead of acknowledging Emily's intellectual sophistication, she presented her as a simple country girl, who was not 'learned'". Charlotte gave the impression that the novel came from "a childish mind"; consequently, her remarks "led to the apocryphal claim that Branwell Brontë . . . had written it". Reviewers and scholars were left to explain unresolved mysteries surrounding the book and its author: "rather than offering unvarnished facts, she created a legend. Like many who came after her, she responded to the discomfort created by *Wuthering Heights* by taking refuge in myth" (viii-ix). Why would Charlotte equivocate when the Biographical Notice provided an excellent opportunity to inform her readers about the book and its author? Rather than clarify misconceptions, she fuelled them. Her choice made no sense, unless she felt compelled to mask the truth in an extraordinary and excessive way.

When the mist of mythology lifts and the novels are read as one body of work, the discrepancies begin to fade. Charlotte left clues to direct her readers to her detailed explanations as to why she might have lied, and she provided a view of her world that is unlike anything her readers could ever imagine. The reality, not the vision of her life, can be seen with the aid of clues and covert messages that she hid throughout the Brontë novels, poems, and letters and will provide a new and startling depiction of the Brontë story. Her reality involved a belief that a few rogue men in her community, with their greed and desire for vengeance, had planned and perpetrated the early deaths of many prominent citizens.

Due to film and television images, however, some readers may view the Brontës in a more romantic light, picturing tempestuous winds circling isolated moors and medieval manors. They may think of Haworth during the Brontë years as a grim and lonely place, unlike the quaint villages of cozy mysteries where neighbours in their ivy-covered cottages welcome visitors with a pot of tea, or leisurely wander Main Street trading pleasantries with shopkeepers. The factual reality renders a much darker vision of an early, nineteenth-century, industrial village mired in grime, with its inhabitants suffering from the effects of poor sanitation, disease, and high mortality rates.

In order to understand why Charlotte Brontë felt it necessary to orchestrate a hoax of three writing sisters, we must examine her village and the inhabitants of her Township, not with a blind sentimentality but with a clear perception of how a small population of wealthy and powerful men may have seen financial possibilities in the misfortunes of others, and how they could have exploited the frequent incidences of sickness and death to their advantage in the pursuit of greater wealth and power. According to Brontë, this vicious element ran the village, like a modern day criminal syndicate, and flourished unchecked with the aid of alcohol, guns, violence, and fear, but their strongest weapon in their successful campaigns of thievery and murder was their shared oath of secrecy. No member of their select brotherhood would ever divulge the crimes unless he wanted his throat cut, but occasionally their macabre plots would slip from lips loosened by alcohol just when an inquiring mind, with a writer's ear for story, was lurking and listening to their boastful admissions of guilt.

From childhood, the Brontë children were familiar with the local Freemasons who met at the Three Graces Lodge on Newell Hill. Charlotte's younger brother Branwell was initiated into the fraternity in February of 1836 when he was only nineteen. A few months later he was raised to Master Mason. His creative imagination and curious intellect entertained his fellow Masons with his lengthy recitations of poetry and Shakespearean soliloquies. That same imagination and intellect would have taken delight in the rituals and symbolic dramas played out in their ceremonies, and his desire to impress his sisters, particularly Charlotte, with his knowledge of ancient mysteries would have motivated him to share the strange nature of this secret club.

Secrets and myths can conceal reality, but truth can release their grip. Charlotte Brontë believed these men were committing crimes, and she was terrified of the criminals, but she was equally determined to reveal their brutal tale. Her methods are stunning, surprising, and so ingenious that they have remained hidden for over a hundred and sixty years, but with the key to her code now found, her revelations can finally erase years of supposition.

For those who prefer the myth that Brontë fabricated, this adventure may prove disappointing and upsetting, but if we allow her other side to guide us, we might learn to accept a more believable reality. The myth-maker herself wrote in chapter thirty-nine of her final novel *Villette* an alternative sentiment: "I always, through my whole life, liked to penetrate to the real truth;" therefore, perhaps we should follow her lead and penetrate the fiction to resolve the mysteries that fuel the myths.

1 VILLAGE OF HAWORTH

The name means hedged enclosure, but the Brontë sisters' village of Haworth, in the gently sloping Upper Worth Valley, never got an Enclosure Act. Instead of landowners setting borders with fences, ditches, stone walls or hedgerows, the men left the uncultivated stretches of moorland to grow wild. Major wars against the French during the late 1700s and early 1800s prevented open trade between Britain and France, which created a shortage of cereal and caused an increase in the price of grain; consequently, the richer proprietors of the land perceived the old grazing practices on the commons as a waste of valuable property. Crops could provide food for a growing population and increase revenue for the owners, so supply and demand motivated the landowners to cultivate the land, plant crops, charge tenants higher rents, and earn bigger profits. Labour increased in arable areas when farmers hired men to plough, sow, hoe, and harvest crops. This new economy gave rise to industries like brewing and milling, and a surge in beer and ale consumption, as did the construction of small mills and, later, the cottages to provide shelter for the workers until, gradually, larger textile mills emerged among the surrounding farmland.

The Haworth Township covers approximately 10,500 acres and includes the villages of Near and Far Oxenhope and Stanbury. To better industrialize the partitioned topography, owners cleaned up the land. They cleared the heather and bracken, drained the soggy soil, and added fertilizer and lime for healthy crops. The sheep had already settled in the grasslands, so the wool was handy for the warp, woof, shuttle, and weave of the textile workers busy inside the cottages scattered on various farms.

Horses chewed oats or worked the ploughs, and birds called twites circled under sunny skies. These small, brown songbirds flew to this southern edge of the Pennine mountain range to feast on the red berries of the mountain ash and on the arable weeds growing in the oat fields. Food was plentiful for flocks of lapwings and curlews that gorged in the hay meadows while keeping an eye out for predators like wrens, peregrine falcons, and shorthaired owls.

Unlike the industrialized lands, the moors remained uncultivated and unimproved, just like Mother Nature had devised. The rise and fall of heath provided not only wild scenery in its heather and ferns, but also stone and shale byways for the Brontë children to scramble over, past nettles and prickly hedges, or to splash through mud and marsh. One can imagine bees stirring in a bilberry shrub as the three sisters carefully picked daisies and bluebells, humming in tune with the birdsong.

This vast moorland would provide the children with a physical playground that would nourish their spirits and fuel their imaginations. The pastures and fields were frequent pathways to the freedom of their long walks during genial weather. They could spend all day on the edge of the heath under a hazy sky that would suddenly threaten showers, or they might run barefoot over swells of heather, then lie in the sweet, warm grass.

On darker days, the moors could seem a solitary, gloomy wilderness with its shadows and cold winds. The penetrating sound of those melancholic moans would blow past the trees and descend among the distant crags. Grey hills would sweep into misty valleys that could chill a rambler to the bone. The crimson twilight would deepen, and the children would gaze with awe as the streaks of light dappled through barren branches onto the hard ground.

Far and wide, the scenery that informs the novels enabled their spirits to expand with the same pleasure their bodies enjoyed from their outdoor exercise. The moors, their beautiful moors could be threatening, frightening, consoling, and peaceful, but never dull.

Their South Pennine village of Haworth is not only surrounded by fields and moors but also overlooks a tributary of the Aire called the River Worth. Its surface water ripples at the first indication of an approaching spring breeze. In summer, during the Brontë era, nothing was dreamier than the scent of stocks and wallflowers wafting along in the warm air. As the breeze intensified, a weakened formation of scattered trees provided scant resistance to the autumn winds, and the peat bogs and moorland grasses failed to correct the mounting blasts of winter's south-westerlies, whirling like avenging Furies across the moors. The winds lost steam and dipped momentarily into the quarry hollows where men extracted flagstones for the roads and smoothed blocks of masonry for the buildings.

Then the winds reached Main Street and the idyllic pastoral scents and fragrances floating on the breeze withered from the smell of sewage and death.

In 1850 Benjamin Herschel Babbage, the superintending inspector for the Board of Health, filed a report regarding the sanitation and water supply in the village; he concluded that Haworth was a town of deadly microbes, much in need of purification. His observations contribute to the facts and statistics in this chapter with respect to sanitation and health (see Babbage Report). When he first arrived, he would have seen a Main Street much like today, one that ran three-quarters of a mile up an incline as steep as a pitched roof, with grey stone houses hugging the road's edge from bottom to top. He would also have noted that the close range between road and windows provided an easy reach for throwing garbage onto the street. This practice and other shocking observations formed the basis of his report.

The open sewers streamed down the gutters and joined the flow of household refuse that mixed with the waste from the pigsties and chicken coops, and with the offal from the slaughterhouse. Behind the butcher's shop, pig's blood, green meat, and rotting chicken entrails littered piles of sloppy human waste, politely referred to as "night soil." These dunghills or "middens" extended their putrid bounty in high and wide mounds on street corners or behind houses, and were left to ooze their revolting odours for months. One midden near the road measured sixteen square yards, and its fumes spread twice that distance. Dung heaps from the stables leaned against the outside of shops and beside kitchen doors where children played. Fifty middens and twenty-three manure and refuse-heaps helped create a community cesspit that discharged an offensive and continuous stink, and abetted the spread of disease.

Water closets had been patented in the previous century, but indoor toilets remained a mystery for most British citizens in the mid 1800s. Inhabitants in villages and towns preferred the ash pit privy, a type of commode, usually a one-seater, with a wooden door for privacy. Haworth built sixty-nine of these to accommodate approximately 2,500 people. At each end of Main Street, twenty-four homes shared the use of one privy, while seven houses had none in their vicinity. A common condition was eight families sharing one privy.

The waste from this outdoor convenience was often layered with the ashes from the fireplaces. Ideally, it would be collected at night, on a regular basis, to be distributed as fertilizer for gardens and farmland. Farmers were less inclined to haul away Haworth's manure because when the ash diluted its nitrogen content it made terrible fertilizer, so the night soil could be left for months before a man, with his cart and spade, worked alone after dark to remove it. In the meantime, with an annual rainfall of thirty-five inches, the probability of the flow of waste fluids escaping and percolating through dwelling walls was high.

The placement of these outdoor toilets contributed to the indignity of public exposure. The two privies that served twenty-four homes each were located on the well-trod main avenue in full view of pedestrians and peering neighbours. A third privy, on a rise that overlooked the entire street like a throne, contained a small door underneath that would burst open from the burden of ashes and night soil, and spill its excess waste down the busy street. A few feet from this sewage pit was a tap that provided water for the homes nearby.

Most of the inhabitants had access to two public wells and nine pumps for their water. They wisely avoided drinking or cooking with pump water, which had underground seepage from the middens. A large number used a well at the bottom of the hill, but in summer the source would quickly dry up; consequently, the poorer women would leave their cottages before dawn on Monday mornings to obtain enough water from the stream to fill their buckets. After patiently waiting their turn, they would haul the heavy containers back up the steep hill for the Monday morning wash. Occasionally, the water from this well would be so foul that the cows would prefer thirst to drinking a single brown drop. The quality of the second well was equally suspect.

Haworth village could claim ownership to seventy-three mounds of filth and waste, but two other sources of contamination contributed to the impurities. In 1820, nineteen textile mills prospered in the Haworth Township, three of which were inside the village itself (Greenwood 3). The dark smoke from the numerous high chimneys belched out black clouds to the heavens and swirled downwind until the murky air stained the buildings' stonework a dingy grey. The mills also emptied their refuse into the streams and the River Worth.

The second source of pollution came from the cemetery, several yards from Main Street's summit. The village had adopted the unhealthy practice of covering entire graves with long slabs of stone. Rather than installing a headstone upright at the burial site, the stonemason would place a heavy, flat, carved stone over the full length of the grave. The weighty cover blocked the air from circulating through the soil, and impeded the body's decomposition.

The villagers had no idea that remains of loved ones languished unnaturally a few feet below ground. On warm mornings, the large flat stones provided a perfect surface for women to stretch their washing out to dry and who, after years of enduring the smell, had become impervious to the odour of miasma casting its noxious pall over the burial ground and its vicinity. The graveyard was also a well-trod byway for the men as they passed through the labyrinth of tombs on their walks to and from the village. Children even played among the monuments. Rain or shine, the graveyard was active, not only with two or three burials a week, due to the rise in infectious diseases, but also with the shifting of vapours underground. During the rainy season, long-standing gases emanating from the corpses would be flushed through the town to permeate the water supply.

The Brontë sisters lived next to the cemetery and were unable to avoid its close proximity, but they rarely ventured down Main Street. They were shy and preferred their own company to that of the villagers, and found the moors offered them the beauty of streams and vast patches of land far removed from the filth of close quarters and restricted walkways. The villagers, on the other hand, lacked the luxury of choice: they needed to earn a living that, for the most part, kept them in their homes, and while the outdoors proved hazardous, the indoor trade also posed a threat to one's health.

Haworth had been an industrialized Township for some years, but "while Haworth's mills were significant in 1820" when Reverend Brontë and his family arrived, "they did not dominate the local economy until [the] 1860s." Over the course of those forty years, the spinning mills introduced power looms, and the cottage industry of woolcombing became mechanized (Greenwood 3).

Before and during this time, a large portion of Haworth's population worked in the worsted wool industry. Inside a weaver's cottage, the woman sat downstairs at the spinning wheel, making yarn for her husband upstairs where he worked the loom and wove the fabric. His job required an abundance of light accessible only from the upper floor windows. The wife twirled the wheel and guided the thread, her legs cramped under a wooden stool, and her head aching from the monotonous bang, bang, bang from the floor above, as her husband's foot operated the treadle that lifted and lowered alternate threads. Over time, the factories employed women and children to work the spinning machines, and the men left the home to run the power looms.

A third of the inhabitants of Haworth earned their living as wool combers for the factories, an occupation that kept them inside their homes. Since the work involved upper body strength, only the men were employed in this function. Usually, the father worked on his own with the help of his sons, but in some instances three or four men worked together and called their combing room a shop. The shop could be in a small upper room or bedroom where, due to the method used to comb the wool, windows remained closed or jammed shut with no ventilation. In a family of six or seven, one room would be set aside for wool combing and the second would be for eating and living, but often the bedroom would house the shop, so the family would be crammed into that one room with usually only two beds.

The process required more stamina than skill and could involve the entire family. A cloth merchant delivered to the cottage the sheared wool in bags of sackcloth. The women and children washed the wool in a trough to remove the dirt, dried perspiration, and the yolk or greasy secretion that naturally covers the sheep's wool. After soaking the wool for a few hours, the mother or child guided the wool through the rollers in the scouring machine to squeeze out excess water from the fleece. The wool was often treated with oil to give it increased manageability and to allow the fibres to slip past each other when combed. If the wool were especially gritty, they would repeat the washing process. After the final scouring, they poured the grimy water onto the street. The rank smell of dirty wool would remain inside the cottage for days, especially since the process of wool combing required all windows be closed.

Before the wool could be spun into yarn, the father and his sons combed the fleece to straighten the worsted fibre. The resulting sliver was then ready to be spun in the spinning machines at the factory. The combing consisted of forcibly pulling wool through two heavy iron or metal spiked toothcombs, but the process had one drawback: the combs had to be heated at a proper temperature or the fibres would break and the oil would become sticky. The main apparatus in the shop, therefore, would be an iron stove fuelled by wood, peat, or coal that could maintain a stifling ninety-degree temperature inside the room all day and all night, in winter or summer. Only during the summer would a window be opened to supply a little relief. In the small shops, the men, while dressed in corduroy trousers and wool shirts rolled to their elbows, worked with as many as three combing pots at one time. After heating the comb, one man would firmly attach it to a pole at about chest height. He carefully applied the cut end of the lock in a smooth continuous motion to the teeth of the hot comb. He then pulled the wool with another heated comb until the fibres lay parallel to each other.

The conditions indoors were as deplorable and dangerous to health as those outside. The men combed wool in small spaces with rotting timbers overhead, plaster peeling from the walls, and the infusion of privies and middens seeping in under their feet. The lack of proper ventilation, the constant fumes from the combs, the heat, and the physical exertion contributed to the air smelling of sweat, grease, oil, and dirt, which increased the probability of ill health and an early death. In Gauger's Croft, off of Main Street, a family's wool combing shop and living space comprised two rooms in a damp cellar dwelling. Four feet from the front door was a privy. The cellar dwellings, with their inoperable windows, forced the confined stale air to occupy the living rooms and settle on the sewage that seeped through walls and flooded the stone floors. The filthy lane, a manure heap, and a contaminated water supply added to the risk of catching a fever or dying from disease.

In another cottage off Main Street, a dung heap leaned against a dwelling that housed wool combers and quarrymen. In a room approximately twenty-four feet in length and six feet wide with a seven-foot ceiling, eight quarrymen slept in four beds. In an adjacent room, six men and boys slept in a similar state, and carried on their wool combing

7

work in a third room. The shut windows may have kept out the stench of the dung heap, but the heat of the stove and the number of male bodies created a disgusting and harmful atmosphere conducive to sickness.

The mortality rate of Haworth was forty-four percent higher than the normal rate in neighbouring hamlets. The average age at death for the villagers was twenty-five years. Forty-one percent of the population died before reaching the age of six years. Twenty-five persons out of every thousand died each year. According to the figures from the British Parliament, Haworth exceeded the lawfully accepted national average by 10.5%, which indicated the village was in as unhealthy a state as three of London's worst slums.

Two of the Brontë children died young, but Emily was thirty, Anne was twenty-nine, and Charlotte was a month shy of her thirty-ninth birthday when she died. The sisters, therefore, were above the average age of mortality in Haworth.

Over the years, the villagers had complained about the poor sanitation to the wealthy wool manufacturers and to the men of the cloth. The Reverend Patrick Brontë, as perpetual curate of St. Michael's and All Angels Anglican church, listened to their complaints and tried to help. The parsonage, like two dozen other homes, enjoyed the use of a private privy, a two-seater located out back. The home also came supplied with one of the five private wells in the village and was safely situated above the burial ground. The Reverend's personal comforts, however, had not dissuaded him from petitioning the General Board of Health in London to send an authorized agent to assess Haworth's lack of clean water. Following the cholera epidemic in 1847, the British government passed the Public Health Act in 1848, thus enabling Reverend Brontë to gather a petition signed by over one-tenth of the population, or two hundred and twenty-two inhabitants, which he attached to his request for an examination of the village water supply.

Benjamin Herschel Babbage, the health inspector, arrived in Haworth in the spring. Inside the national schoolroom across the lane from the parsonage, he met with a large contingency of interested men, including Reverend Grant from the neighbouring Oxenhope who explained that the hamlets in his parish suffered bouts of typhus fever, and asked if Babbage could include his area in the inspection. Baggage advised him that his present duties were limited to Haworth, but he would take this request to the Board when he returned to London. Before the meeting ended, Joseph Redman, the parish clerk, offered to accompany Babbage on his inspection.

Redman guided the health inspector through the warren of streets and lanes to familiarize him with the layout of the village. Babbage noted that the total number of inhabited houses in the town was three hundred and sixteen, which included twenty-five cellar dwellings. Twenty-three of the ninety-four properties located on Main Street were wool comber cottages, with other shops making up an additional thirty-three dwellings, leaving thirty-eight that were simply private homes. Many of the shops had gas lamps, the gas being supplied from a mill a mile away.

A blacksmith, shoemaker, draper, grocer, and clockmaker were some of the businesses on Main Street (Whitehead 53). Four of the seven inns were at the summit of the hill, one of which—the Cross Inn—the wine and spirit merchant William Thomas had purchased in 1846. William Thomas also owned all the properties on the north side of the summit. His brother Enoch had run the King's Arm from1830 until he took over the Black Bull Inn as manager in 1840. The inn owners brewed their own beer, and the gin palaces and beer shops supplied more alcohol but, with the aid of Enoch Thomas's calculations, Babbage found that the annual consumption of 14,244 gallons of beer or ale for a population of approximately 2,500 was below the national average, but still represented a large quantity, especially without the inclusion of the figures for illegal alcohol sales. Since only a few families were brewing their own beer, and the men had informed him that there was little drinking of spirituous liquors, Babbage reported that consumption of these products was also below the average of other towns.

Babbage was impressed with the "enterprising" wine and spirit merchant William Thomas in his efforts to supply water to his own properties. Thomas had built a cistern in a field not far from his establishment and then laid leaden pipes back to a spring of water called Sowden's spring. From the cistern to his properties he built pipes made out of earthen pottery, which caused considerable leakage and loss of water, but villagers simply put buckets and cans under the leaks to collect what they could. Unfortunately, if those above turned on their taps, the ones below would lose pressure and their taps would yield only one or two drops. Despite this inconvenience, Thomas' tenants told Babbage they were satisfied with their water supply. Thomas paid rent to use the spring, but he recouped his losses after charging his tenants an annual rate of three to five shillings.

After Babbage examined Thomas' waterworks, Redman, the parish clerk, continued the tour and showed him the direction of the existing drains. The drainage water flowed in ditches to the fields below Main Street, as a form of irrigation. Villagers told Babbage that this drainage water also ended up in a watercourse that supplied homes with their drinking water, and that in warm weather it was as unhealthy as the water at the pumps. He calculated that each house would require fifty gallons of water daily or approximately 15,800 gallons every day for the entire town. He concluded that the springs would not be sufficient.

He recommended that Haworth implement immediate improvements. Water could be brought into town through a piped system from a reservoir on the moors. The graveyard should not inter any more bodies; only one public slaughterhouse should be allowed; privies should be converted to water closets; and sewers must be built if the inhabitants, especially the poorer classes, were to enjoy the comforts of better health.

Several men told Babbage that the diseases were not prevalent in any one place or section of the town, so their impressions were that, aside from the poor water supply, the sanitary conditions in town were satisfactory. Babbage disagreed with the men and stated as much in his report: "I am now in a condition to show that this idea of the inhabitants of Haworth is entirely a delusion."

He also noted that, in considering the high mortality rate, a second danger lurked inside the Township. People were dying without "any person to certify the cause of death, excepting the ignorant, or perhaps interested relatives." Lacking the proper medical means to determine cause of death afforded a "very great acuity for the concealment of crime." His concerns included "ill treatment, starvation and neglect," but his greatest fear was that, without any systematic examination of bodies, men could conceal the worst crime of all: "murder in its naked form."

2 FIGHT FOR CLEAN WATER

Reverend Brontë took seriously his responsibility for his parishioners, especially in his efforts to reduce crime and decrease the number of deaths. His attempts to improve the village water supply would draw him into a battle waged by the wealthy landowners against the proponents of health, and would introduce him to a different kind of criminal element.

The Reverend was under no delusions that the government in London would take its time assisting Haworth with its water problems. He understood the role of patience in achieving an objective, no matter how urgent, and prepared for delays. Several months of inconvenience could easily be offset by the end result: the installation of a clean water system would save countless lives. He even expected minor snags along the course of construction, but what he never anticipated was the unkindest cut of all.

He had been the curate at St. Michael's since 1820 when, at forty-three, he accepted the position and moved his wife and six children to Haworth. As perpetual curate, he would live in this village for the rest of his life. In 1823, two years after his wife died, he wrote a letter to Mary Burder, his first love, with an offer of marriage. She declined, but in his letter he had stated, "my salary is not large; it is only about two hundred a year. But in addition to this two hundred a year, I have a good House, which is mine for life also, and is rent free. No one has anything to do with the Church but myself, and I have a large congregation" (qtd. in Lock 238). In terms of religious matters, he was an independent preacher, but the trustees of the parsonage and church lands, mostly wealthy landowners, had held the deed to the property since 1559, and they controlled his living arrangement. They also paid his annual salary, which was not two hundred pounds but only £170 (approximately $270), an amount much larger than that earned by most of the villagers, and one that placed him in the middle class, but his salary paled in comparison to the landowners who, according to the Brontë Parsonage Museum website, were making from £10,000 to £20,000 a year. Two years after writing his letter to Mary Burder, his opinion had changed: he wrote to the governors of Queen Anne's Bounty describing his salary as an insufficient sum to support his family, "even with the most rigorous economy," especially when faced with shouldering the cost of household improvements, repairs, medicine, and schooling for his daughters (qtd. in Barker 87).

When his wife and two eldest daughters died from disease, he found his grief as onerous as the financial challenges. The trustees could not legally evict their perpetual curate at will, but they could adjust his salary in either direction, or not pay it at all depending on their inclination, so Reverend Brontë drew on his Irish imagination to find additional relief through charitable donations. He had faced disappointments and hardship, but he was brave and daring, although some would say impetuous, so his moral inclinations compelled him to fight for the villagers and attempt to abolish the squalour, even if it meant offending the landowners.

Ten months after the health inspector Benjamin Babbage visited Haworth and recommended vast improvements to the unsanitary water conditions, Reverend Brontë had still received no correspondence from London. He wrote to the Secretary of the General Board of Health in London on February 12, 1851 reminding him that he had made application to the Board some time ago to procure a pure water supply, and was surprised and "grieved that nothing has yet been done towards the furtherance of this desirable end." He referred the Secretary to Mr. Babbage who knew the severity of the situation, and could "give them, the requisite information" (qtd. in Lock 433). Joseph Redman, clerk for both the parish and the Haworth Health Committee also wrote letters to the Board, and the first response from London seemed encouraging.

Reverend Brontë organized a meeting in which he hoped to ensure that the villagers would support the Babbage recommendations. The inhabitants were concerned about the closure of the graveyard, which the Reverend noted in his next letter to London: "to shut it up, before new burial ground shall have been procured would be the cause of great confusion, and seriously evil consequences." The wealthy landowners were loath to contribute funds to construct drains that would have no impact on their land and would, therefore, be a waste of money; consequently, Reverend Brontë attached an amended plan of the area that differed from the boundaries in the original petition. This altered plan would not include outlying farms "which do not require, our proposed improvements, and consequently could not be reasonably demanded to pay for what would go only to the benefit of others." He hoped "this alteration, which we petition for, will not render it necessary, for the Board, to make another Survey—and that they will proceed, as soon as practicable in the execution of the laudable end in view, as Summer is approaching, and all that we petition for, and have petitioned for, will be most urgently needed" (434). Clean water during a hot summer would be a dire necessity.

The Reverend remained hopeful that the wheels of progress would continue to turn, but his optimism was short-lived. Several days after the meeting, he received shocking information: the churchmen and merchants, who had signed the original petition, were now deserting the cause. The news that they would definitely have to pay increased water rates brought on a wealth of apoplexy. Already in possession of their own water supply on their lands, they stood their ground and refused to pay for improvements that they did not require. They went over the Reverend's head and put their opinions in print when they wrote their objections directly to the Board of Health in London (435).

The Reverend should not have been surprised. A few years earlier in 1843, he had written a letter to the National Society, an organization founded in 1811 that promoted "the education of the poor in the principles of the established church." He requested funds to build an Anglican school in the village and received enough money to open one in 1844. He believed education could help break the lasting affliction of ignorance. "I have resided in Yorkshire above 30 years and have preached and visited in different parishes—I have also been in Lancashire and from my reading, personal observation and experience I do not hesitate to say that the populace in general are either ignorant or wicked. . . . Some exceptions no doubt there are, but they are few and far between" (qtd. in Barker 430). His opponents to clean water appeared to be not only ignorant, wicked, and greedy, but also indifferent to the impact of their betrayal. Mercenary beings always reckon the costs. They were men of few words, but they could think and act if they felt needy fingers looting their pockets.

The first prominent men to write to London were the Merrall brothers of Ebor Mill. The mill, a three-storey water-powered spinning mill in Haworth, was built in 1819 by Hiram Craven, a stone mason and architect. Over the years, two of Craven's sons rented the mill from the executors of their late father's will, until Hiram Junior died in 1848 and the mill suffered losses, which forced the Cravens to cease occupancy in 1849. In 1851, the four Merrall brothers rented Ebor Mill before buying it from the executors a year later. The brothers also owned Lees Syke Mill just outside of the Haworth Township, but less than a stone's throw from Ebor Mill inside the boundary, and they rented Springhead Mill, also outside the boundary, but nearby. Their business was profitable enough to add a weaving shed and extra power looms shortly after acquiring Ebor Mill (Greenwood 29).

The Merrall brothers wrote to London to make their objections clear. "We hereby give notice that we object to the Sanitary Measures proposed for the Hamlet of Haworth being applied to Ebor, as shown in the map accompanying the Superintending Inspectors Report—the property is already well supplied with good water, for which according to the terms of purchase it is chargeable with an annual rent for Ebor—the Sanitary condition is also in other respects satisfactory" (qtd. in Lock 435). They employed men, women, and children from Haworth, but they were not willing to absorb minor additional costs that would contribute to the sanitation of the poorer classes.

William Thomas, the wine and spirit merchant, also wrote to the Board. He owned several properties in the village as well as farms and mills, and had already built the cistern and attached earthen pot pipes that led water to several of his cottages. He wanted his buildings at Hollings Cottages at Rough Nook, at Gaugers Croft, and at Lower Brow Land at Hawkcliffe excluded from the improvement plans "as all the Property is well supplied with water." His son, Richard Robert Thomas also objected to his properties, "the White Lion Inn and the 8 Cottages adjoining" being subject to the costs of improvement since these buildings were well supplied with their own water. Tobias Lambert, a worsted manufacturer, rented six acres at the bottom of Main Street that were supplied with water from Hough Spring and, therefore, did not need water from the new system. Joseph Hartley, a farmer living at the top of Main Street, did not want his other house at Sowdens, a property just beyond the Brontë parsonage, included in the improvements because he had his own water supply. The Board of Health decided to send Babbage back to Haworth to sort out the confusion (435).

Reverend Brontë realized that the entire venture would drag on for months if they were meant to endure further investigations and another application for assistance. After calling a second meeting to discuss the water issue and the attendant delays, he sent a letter to the Board on July 10, 1851 to request immediate action. As predicted, the summer had exacerbated the need for water, and the conditions were desperate: "There has already been long, and tedious delay—there has been a deal of sickness amongst us, and there is now a great want of pure water, which ills might have been prevented, or palliated, had the remedial measures we hope for, been duly applied. A few interested individuals, might try to throw difficulties in the way, but by the large majority, consisting chiefly of the working people, there is an anxious desire that the work should on the earliest opportunity be done." The Methodists and the Baptists joined forces with the Anglican Reverend's cause against the wealthy landowners, but their efforts continued to meet with obstruction (436).

A significant part of the problem lay with the Central Board of Health. The government in London had been aware, for years, of the appalling health conditions in most villages and towns in England, where families routinely shared contaminated wells. The wealthier classes assumed the filth and wretched conditions among the working poor were simply inborn deviations, not problems resulting from a lack of money needed to pay for proper sanitation and cleanliness. Throughout the 1840s, due to the outbreak of fatal diseases, the government commissioned reports to investigate the cause of deadly illnesses and to implement reforms. Proper drainage of sewage and a clean water supply were two of the recommended measures. Unfortunately, the immense costs to correct the problem stirred businessmen to object, and the government acquiesced to the wealthy voters and did nothing. After a series of protests from the investigating committee, the government, although hesitant to get involved, agreed in 1844 to the formation of a Royal Commission on the Health of Towns.

The Commission concluded that local boards, such as the one in Haworth, should deal with their own issues of health. It also stipulated that a central board in London act as senior administrator and oversee all findings and procedures. The Central Board would, therefore, make all the decisions, but the government would place the bulk of responsibility for dealing with sanitation on local boards in the towns and villages. In 1848, the three-member Central Board of Health began its operations. Local boards were not permitted to perform their own investigations, so, in the case of Haworth, after petitioning the Central Board, Mr. Babbage had arrived from London to examine the sanitary conditions. This complete lack of power rendered the local town administrators dependent on the men in London and restricted their ability to determine how to allocate funds obtained from ratepayers. The inexorable process slowed to a frustrating pace while the illness and death continued unabated.

In September of 1851, the Secretary of the Board in London received another letter from the Haworth Reverend who signed each letter, "Your most obedient servant." Always the diplomat, he tried not to complain too harshly, but impatience began to leak into his letters. Reverend Brontë was stymied as to why the men of the Board were still moving so slowly when they had ample legal right to proceed. ". . . after tedious delay, they have as far as we know done almost nothing—We might have thought that this arose from a press of more urgent business had it not been that we have learned from good authority that their salutary rules have been adopted and enforced in various other places where there was less necessity for them, and from whence application was made at a date long after ours. What we have to request, therefore, is that you will be so kind as to inform us as soon as you conveniently can—whether our case has been entirely given up—and if not, at what time we may expect a decisive and final arrangement." The Secretary responded that a request had been initiated but that the recent property exclusions to the water system required amendments to the original boundaries. The landowners, through the introduction of their counter claims, were effectively sabotaging the hope of improvements (436).

In December, several more water ratepayers joined the fight against the Reverend. They forwarded a signed petition to the Board asking London to send another representative. They stated that because cottagers, and not property owners, were the only members elected to the local Health Committee, the elections were illegal. Mr. Butterfield, a wealthy mill owner in Haworth, informed London that another election would soon be held and asked that the London representative, Mr. Ranger, visit him personally to discuss the possibility of an increase in the sum of the rate qualification to limit the range of people who could be elected. After assessing the electoral system, Ranger suggested that in order to stand for election, the property owners who paid a minimal annual water rate of £10, and not the previous rate of only £5, be the men qualified to run for membership on the Health Committee. This meant that the wealthy owners of forty-three properties, which included five inns, would qualify for seats on the Committee, effectively eliminating poorer cottagers (437).

Joseph Redman, the parish clerk, complained to the Board. The owners of the springs together with the property owners were causing unnecessary delays. He asked the Secretary if they had a legal right to obstruct the process. London responded that, "there is no power of compulsory purchase," that the owners were under no obligation to participate in the improvements, so they were not liable for any illegal impropriety and could, therefore, continue to inquire into matters, such as election qualifications, as long as they wished. He advised Redman that the Board would be able to proceed as soon as it received a fresh survey (437).

The Haworth surveyor, Mr. Brierley, drew up the new plans, but made the design measurements to the wrong scale. This created a further delay (437).

The public water supply continued to trickle out of the springs. Thomas Parker, a Baptist and a member of the temperance society, witnessed increased consumption of beer as the water became less potable. He and several other concerned citizens wrote to London, but to no avail: the current process slowed to a crawl. No reservoirs or springs were approved on land that contained wells. The wealthy ratepayers already paid their dues and had no intention of increasing their payments no matter how serious the conditions of health became in their community. The Board recommended implementation of drains, but the mill owners demanded such a high compensation for the use of their water that the plan collapsed. By 1854, nothing had been done to improve the village water supply (437).

In an attempt to calm the rivers of discontent, the Health Committee laid a sewer at the bottom of Main Street "172 yards in length" (438). The plan was to bill the owners at that end of the street for the entire cost. Redman tried to convince the owners that their financial contribution would greatly reduce the refuse and filth being dumped onto the street. The owners listened with half an ear. During the day, they posted their complaints to London, while at night they took matters into their own hands and put things to right.

The owners exulted in their power to kick like stallions at legal obstacles. They were not a folk easily frightened, and they had said there would be mischief if the committee brought them trouble. They were bound only by the Blessed Book, and gave not a farthing for village decrees. Outside, at the bottom of the street, the men gripped their spades. With blades freshly sharpened and ready for wielding, their axes lay waiting against a muck heap.

Inside the sealed rooms off Main Street, a mass of coughs and sneezes sprayed germs throughout the stifling air. As the working poor slept four and five to a bed, and their snores drowned the cries from neighbouring babies, the wealthy owners executed their plan. The children's dreams of custard and sweets popped in and out of their heads like fleas. The parents dreamed of looms banging in a distant land. The odd sounds of digging and scraping drifted into their dreams, but the cottagers were too exhausted to open their eyes or investigate.

In the morning, the poorer inhabitants woke to find their sewer had been exhumed. The owners, in their unbridled wisdom, had destroyed every newly set drain.

Years later, Charlotte Brontë's close friend Ellen Nussey refers to the "Passing-bell" that would toll for each death, when she commented on the situation: "Mr. Brontë was frequently making efforts, and trying to stir up his Parishioners to efforts, for the sanitary improvement of the village, but for years all he could *do* appeared to be unavailing; the needful outlay was not to be thought of: Haworth like many other places refused to acknowledge the real remedy for prevalent sickness and epidemic—the inhabitants persisted in ignoring evils which necessitated a free use of their money; they would not listen to the wisdom of a reform which Mr. Brontë's higher intelligence would fain have obtained by friendly persuasion—The Passing-bell was *often* a dreary accompaniment to the day's engagements, and must have been trying to the sensitive nervous temperaments of those who were always within sound of it as the Parsonage inmates were . . . as you issued from the Parsonage gate, you looked upon the Stone-cutter's chipping shed which was piled with slabs ready for use, and to the ear there was the incessant sound of the *chip, chip* of the recording chisel as it graved in the In Memoriams of the departed" (*Letters, Vol.I* 604).

The situation had seemed hopeless but, in 1856, Reverend Brontë won a major battle. The Health Committee borrowed £800 to construct a small reservoir. After more resistance from the landowners, the reservoir was completed in 1858, and the cottages were receiving fresh water through stand-taps in the street (Lock 438).

The Reverend had achieved his ends through borrowed funds, and the citizens were paying the rates. The wounds incurred from selfish landowners were still fresh, but the fight earned him respect from the poorer villagers who understood that the Reverend had challenged the very men who controlled the purse strings of the parsonage. The issue had become greater than the man: during the wrangling with the wealthy landowners, more deaths had occurred from inadequate sanitation.

Charlotte would have witnessed her father's struggle to help his parishioners and would have been equally frustrated at their wealthy citizens' reluctance to help those less fortunate, but she would have realized that diplomacy ruled in this particular battle: she must never confront or criticize powerful men whose reach of control extended into her home.

With conflicts like these, she learned from an early age that, even with the tenuous protection of her father's position as a respected Anglican minister, any bold challenges aimed at ruthless men would unleash the wrath of devils, especially if those acts of defiance threatened their finances. The inequality between wealthy landowners and poor villagers would always be a fact of life, but her awareness that the motivation behind preventing the poorer neighbours from acquiring clean water arose from the landowners' greed would have certainly stirred her anger at the injustice.

She had known these men all her life, and could see that they were not wise, sensible, or caring individuals when their money was part of the social equation. They could be unrelenting in their efforts to retain their wealth and in their quest for more riches. Her writer's instincts to tell a story would soon awaken as she heard more tales of their activities, but her woman's brain would caution her to be discrete, especially when it concerned revealing her name.

3 ROUGH HEATHENS

Reverend Brontë's accounts of the darker elements in his village rarely appeared in the public press, so he was under no serious threat from the criminals. He had been writing articles in the *Bradford Observer* on the subject of church rates when, in 1841, he included an interesting anecdote in one of those articles:

"Not long since, I met with a man who objected to the payment of Church-rates, under the plea that to do so would violate the dictates of his conscience. Well knowing his circumstances, I said to him, 'James, do you pay your rents without any such religious scruple?' 'Yes,' said he, 'I do, and why not?' 'Do you know,' I observed, 'that part of these rents go towards keeping beer shops and part, I fear, towards upholding a gambling house?' 'Yes,' he observed, with rather a downcast countenance, conjecturing, as I suppose, what I was after. 'Well,' I remarked, 'how can you conscientiously do this; do you really think, that even, according to your way of thinking, Church-rates would go to so bad a purpose?' He only observed—'I have been wrong, but I trust that, by Divine grace, I shall be right for the future, and that no one shall ever mislead me any more by false arguments.' He went home and I heard no more of his opposition to Church rates" (qtd. in Barker 356-7).

Apparently, the habit of wealthy landowners spending their rental profits on alcohol and gambling was common knowledge among the inhabitants of Haworth. Gambling and the consumption of alcohol also occur on the pages of *Wuthering Heights*, as does the portrayal of violence.

The first reviews of *Wuthering Heights* focused on its depiction of brutal cruelty. One critic, Douglas Jerrold, wrote in January of 1848 that "the reader is shocked, disgusted, almost sickened by details of cruelty, inhumanity and the most diabolical hate and vengeance" (Allott 43). A reviewer in *Britannia* states that the "characters are a commentary on the truth that there is no tyranny in the world like that which thoughts of evil exercise in the daring and reckless breast" (42). G.H. Lewes adds that the novel is "sombre, rude, brutal, yet true. The fierce ungoverned instincts of powerful organizations, bred up amidst violence, revolt, and moral apathy, are here seen in operation." He deduces that most men would easily indulge in similar brutality "were our lives as insubordinate to law; were our affections and sympathies as little cultivated, our imaginations as undirected" (64-5). D.G. Rossetti comments on the novel's power, but says, "The action is laid in hell,—only it seems places and people have English names there" (67). A critic from *Eclectic Review* calls it "one of the most repellent books we ever read," one that contains a "monster," a "fool," and an "ignorant and brutish" boy: "Such a company we never saw grouped before; and we hope to never meet with its like again" (66).

In her preface to the 1850 edition of *Wuthering Heights*, Charlotte explains that Haworth men could exhibit "harshly manifested passions," and that the rough men depicted in the novel are actually based in reality. These uneducated men were weaned on the whip and the rod—tools of discipline passed down from fathers to sons and used against wives and children with impunity. A stranger could certainly find these men frightful and believe them capable, if presented with the opportunity, of bending their minds toward theft and murder.

Were the men of Yorkshire's West Riding dangerous and deadly criminals? Were they "sleuth-hounds in pursuit of money" (8) as Elizabeth Gaskell, the novelist and biographer, states in *The Life of Charlotte Brontë*?

In 1857, two years after Charlotte Brontë's death, Gaskell's biography helped generate more interest in the late author's work. She was a friend who had spent time at the parsonage visiting Charlotte and meeting Reverend Brontë. She describes the inhabitants of the West Riding as people who "seldom show themselves on the surface. Indeed, there is little display of any of the amenities of life among this wild, rough population. Their accost is curt; their accent and tone of speech blunt and harsh." She classifies some of the inhabitants of Haworth as "savage yeomen" with an "eager desire for riches." These "wild, rough" men were capable of intense hate: grudges were not easily forgotten and could be "bequeathed from generation to generation" as "revenge was handed down from father to son as an hereditary duty." She adds, "Their feelings are not easily roused, but their duration is lasting." Charlotte shared with her a well-known saying in Haworth: "Keep a stone in thy pocket seven year; turn it, and keep it seven year longer, that it may be ever ready to thine hand when thine enemy draws near" (7-13).

Gaskell also remarks on the poetic view of West Riding "when the classical impression is left, and the details forgotten." She heard stories "of coarseness—of the uncouthness of the rustic mingled with the sharpness of the tradesman—of irregularity and fierce lawlessness." These images "mar the vision of pastoral innocence and simplicity," but their accuracy is no less real (8).

Gaskell's depiction of the men makes it clear that they were shrewd and purposeful in their pursuit of both good and evil and that abuse did occur. She could easily be referring to the men who waged a battle against Reverend Brontë over water rates when she writes that their "dislike of authority," their "hereditary spirit of independence" together with a dogged "indifference to human life" created fear among the weaker men: "the roads were so notoriously bad . . . that there was little communication between one village and another," and because of the isolation of the lonely houses, "crimes might be committed almost unknown, certainly without any great uprising of popular indignation calculated to bring down the strong arm of the law" (8-11).

Through the course of his employment as curate in Yorkshire churches, Reverend Brontë had witnessed enough violence to arm himself against any unpremeditated attack from a few thugs. He had been a curate at Hartshead during the Luddite riots when the cottage weavers attacked the wagons with cudgels, hatchets, hammers, and axes, and disabled the new machinery allocated for the factories and brought in to replace their jobs. Even though he was not afraid of hooligans, he carried a loaded pistol for protection on his long walks across the moors (25). A tailor once had Reverend Brontë as a customer and noted that his "coat always bore, in the parson's own rough sewing, two pockets designed to accommodate the two pistols which he invariably carried with him" (qtd. in Lock 284).

He also had a strong grasp of the workings of a musket. For years the Reverend had practiced target shooting and bird hunting with firearms and knew enough about their mechanisms to write a letter to the weapons branch of the British military, offering his assistance because he believed he had devised a better musket. The Master General thanked him for his papers outlining the alterations to the Musket, but wrote that the Select Committee assembled for discussions on this particular instrument of war had concluded that his ideas "did not appear desirable to them," and that his alteration not be "adopted into the Service" (306).

Since arriving in Yorkshire and witnessing violence that could occur at any time, the guns and his expertise were a comfort. He could protect himself, but others less prepared and more vulnerable would be at risk, especially since the lone constable, elected to keep the peace, found policing such a large jurisdiction an exercise in futility.

Gaskell points out that no rural police force existed in the region, and the magistrates were usually related to the perpetrators, so they were most likely "inclined to tolerate eccentricity, and to wink at faults too much like their own." Her descriptions of these men could be taken from the pages of *Wuthering Heights*. They enjoy hunting, shooting, fighting, drinking, and gambling. Their addiction to rum or ale or a mixture of both was considered "one of the manly virtues," as was the horsewhipping, gouging, and biting in their frequent "up and down fights." During Charlotte's time, one could hear about their "rough heathen ways," and be shocked by "details of coarseness—of the uncouthness of the rustic mingled with the sharpness of the tradesman—of irregularity and fierce lawlessness" (9-15). A Vicar from a neighbouring town described Haworth as "a very wild and rough part of this extensive parish" (qtd. in Lock 457). Mix ignorance with a little alcohol and lawlessness, and one can only imagine "what strange eccentricity—what wild strength of will—nay, even what unnatural power of crime was fostered by a mode of living in which a man seldom met his fellows" (Gaskell 12). The moors cover a vast area and are dotted with infrequent cottages, so few people would be aware of their neighbour's lawless pursuits, but if they were aware, they would be unwilling to accuse the hooligans and thugs of any violent or criminal acts, charges that could drag them, not into a court of law, but into the muck of a shallow, wet bog.

Gaskell even refers to the ancestral dwellings as if she has taken the description from the pages of *Wuthering Heights*. Inside these dwellings, the same families have lived for generations. When "the possessor falls into idle, drinking habits," he loses the family property in much the same way as the character of Hindley Earnshaw: "drunkenness and dissipation occasioned the ruin of many respectable families." Come too close to some of these houses, and a stranger would face the "inhospitable custom" of a blast of buckshot aimed at his head. She concludes by stating, "these tales of positive violence and crime that have occurred in these isolated dwellings . . . still linger in the memories of the old people of the district." The Brontë vision of cruelty, revenge, and thievery could not have been written in a vacuum nor been the precise reproduction of a distant memory: crimes were still occurring in the community, and a Brontë pen was chronicling that criminality without the knowledge of the perpetrators or the other inhabitants. The men and women of the village were mostly illiterate farmers or workers in the trades, labouring to put food on the table. Uneducated, hard working villagers would keep their heads down when talk of gambling and drinking circulated through town (12-19).

Reverend Brontë himself was not immune to the lure of alcohol. He suffered from poor eyesight and bouts of bronchial attacks, but he enjoyed his regular drinks of port wine and sherry—for medicinal purposes—that he ordered from William Thomas. The villagers had once claimed that he smelled of alcohol, but he explained to the church trustees that the alcohol was in the drops he had been prescribed for his eyes: "they keep propagating false reports—I mean to single out one or two of these slanderers, and to prosecute them, as the Law directs. I have lately been using a lotion for my eyes, which are very weak, and they have ascribed the smell of that to a smell of a more objectionable character" (qtd. in Lock 375).

The Reverend owned a 562-page medical book entitled *Modern Domestic Medicine* by Thomas John Graham, M.D., and it showed his interest in alcohol. In pencil and ink, he inscribed on almost all of the pages a few comments regarding the effectiveness of the prescribed cures for ailments ranging from cancer to toothache and from snakebite to intoxication. Under the heading "Ether," he writes: "I tried Ether, and found it to be rather too heating, and irritating, like fiery spirits," and adds, "A teaspoonful of Ether in a little Brandy and water is good for flatulency" (qtd. in Lock 379).

Under the heading, "Wine," he includes more notes. "As a wine merchant told me, dealers often mix brandy, and other articles of a pernicious kind with the ordinary sorts of port, sherry, and other similar wines—and the most salutary wines are genuine sherry, not less than three, or four years old—which costs from 38s [shillings] to 48s a dozen—the inferior kinds cost only 30s—and Madeira, sent to the Indies, to be rendered mellow by the voyage: this costs 60s a dozen, but—Madeira made from grapes which grow on vines transplanted from Persia is the best of all and costs 80s a dozen." He ends by writing, "champagne and port are not salutary—Burgundy Hermitage . . . are the dearest of all wines and are sold at from 80s to 90s a dozen" (379-80).

The Reverend's alcohol consumption did not interfere with his role as President of the Haworth Temperance Society, nor was it detrimental to his health—he lived to be eighty-four, but his efforts to curtail the drinking habits of others failed to meet the levels of success he had imagined.

Alcohol, guns, gambling, and a police force of one allowed the sinister machinations of men in positions of power to remain safely concealed, especially when, those engaged in the crimes, swore to keep their plots secret. Anecdotal reminiscences make for interesting tales of possible corruption, but documented facts provide evidence that Reverend Brontë was aware of the crimes as soon as he arrived in Haworth.

4 THE CRIMINAL ELEMENT

Reverend Brontë was a vicar and, as such, was also Chairman of the vestry meetings held at the church. The minutes of those meetings provide a clearer picture of the village and its problems (See Lock 317-19).

At the vestry meeting held in January of 1822, almost two years after the Brontë family's arrival, the members discussed measures to eliminate crime: they said, "a number of ill-behaved and disorderly persons have for a long period colleagued together, not only to destroy the property but to endanger the lives of the peaceable inhabitants of this township." The afternoon meeting had been called to "adopt such measures as may be conducive to Peace and tranquility."

The men formed "An Association for the Suppression of Vice," and resolved that "its operations shall extend to all who shall be guilty of Murder, or of assaulting unoffending Individuals or of robbing and stealing, or committing any depredation." Unfortunately, the lone constable elected to keep the peace, even with his best efforts, was unable to protect the public. Too often, he found himself dealing with the rabble on his own, and he could hardly contain and imprison all the men engaged in acts of public drunkenness and debauchery in their one-room jail, so, in early 1827, members at the vestry meetings decided to help the constable. They voted to disband one of the sources of the violent behaviour.

The householders and inhabitants had requisitioned a special meeting at the vestry to discuss the excessive intake of beer. The participants were to find the means to suppress "the notorious practices of selling illicit Beer, the which practices are productive of every imaginable Evil." If they wanted to secure their property and maintain "the well-being of society," the villagers would have to close down the ubiquitous "whist" shops "which abound in the Parish of Haworth, and the surrounding neighbourhood," where the men played the popular card game and sold and drank beer illegally while engaged in the destructive practice of gambling.

In 1818, Reverend Brontë had written a novel entitled *The Maid of Killarney,* in which a character states his opinion of Whist. Not only do cards take up valuable time from one's life, they encourage men to play for money: "this gives a taste for gaming, and gaming produces covetousness, dissimulation, malice, and sometimes even worse effects" (qtd. in Lock 362).

The men at the vestry meeting agreed that these shops could create major social problems. They "have a constant and direct tendency to lower and vitiate the minds both of those who keep them and those who frequent them, and from their unseasonable hours—to sow the seeds of various diseases and greatly to injure the body as well as the soul." The shops also catered to the exchange and "disposal of articles of every kind and however got," and "in consequence of the inward pollution they naturally produce," offered "a great variety of strong temptations to licentious conduct—to outrage—and to theft and robbery of every description." Outrage could take the form of beatings, fights, rape, and murder.

The men in the vestry saw these activities as a blight on their community, so they resolved to assist the village's only constable as best they could in the detection and prosecution of the perpetrators. They reported to the owners of the dwellings where tenants engaged in these illegal sales, and asked the owners to demand these activities desist immediately. They also spoke to the employers of the offenders and requested they "turn them out of their employ unless they give satisfactory proof of their repentance and amendment by immediately desisting from their illegal practices." Their efforts never attained the goal of complete suppression of vice. The gambling, violence, and drinking continued.

One faction of the community that contributed to the drinking and gambling was the Freemasons. According to "The History of Freemasonry in Haworth," in the early nineteenth century, the men of Haworth began meeting as Freemasons in a local tavern. In 1831, they connected with other "brothers" from the outlying areas to join England's United Grand Lodge. Two years later, the Haworth Freemasons rented a room for approximately $8 a year in a building on Newell Hill owned by William Eccles. To celebrate the move from the public Black Bull Inn to their own private meeting room, the Masons organized a procession of 120 brethren from neighbouring Lodges, and paid the Reverend Brontë ten shillings to solemnize the occasion with a sermon. The Three Graces Lodge was now officially open.

Three years later, Charlotte's younger brother Branwell became a Mason. He was proposed as a brother, and accepted on the 1st of February, 1836, initiated February the 29th, passed March the 28th, and raised April the 25th to the status of Master Mason. He was only eighteen, not the required age of twenty-one, so he received special dispensation from John Brown, the Worshipful Master who was also his father's friend, church sexton, and stone mason. Branwell had been party to their activities before that day in February 1836 when he became an Entered Apprentice at eighteen, but had he actually witnessed any crimes? More importantly, if he had, would he ever directly reveal them to his older sister, or would he simply describe them in print?

From an early age, Branwell had been a precocious, intelligent child who, under his father's tutelage, had learned Latin and Greek. According to Brontë biographer Winifred Gerin, he "wrote equally fluently with both hands—at times with both hands at once, and in moments of bravado in Greek with his right and in Latin with his left" (vi). This feat is almost impossible to imagine when one tries to write two different names with both hands at the same time, but for Branwell it was a parlour trick that amazed his Mason brothers, as did his ability to recite from memory Shakespeare's soliloquies and lines of poetry by Wordsworth and Byron. These uneducated men would have been entertained by his gregarious personality, and with an ample supply of alcohol at their fingertips, been happy to reward Branwell with a glass or two. His early writings suggest he witnessed a great deal under their tutelage. He was also a participant at a boxing club in the village "which met in an upper room of one of the public houses" (Barker 196). This sport would give him a certain confidence when faced with a challenge to fight, as he records in his prose.

His depiction of life in his fictional city of Verdopolis mirrors the social problems Reverend Brontë was encountering in Haworth. In Branwell's poetry and prose, he writes about "anxious faces" on "a silent crowd" as men gamble and drink in pothouses (the cheaper pubs). His characters are stabbed, suffocated, throttled, drowned in a bog, or filled with gunpowder, and they steady themselves with "a draught of brandy" while playing "a rubber of whist for a few guineas" (Collins 187). In his poem 'Interior of a Pothouse By Young Soult' he writes of a man buried under the flagstones in the floor of an inn. The fellow loses at cards and, now ruined, stabs himself. The men continue to gamble while he breathes his dying breath, but they "promise to aid his orphans dear." They allow him to die on the floor unhindered, but if "they find him in their way / . . . they'll kick him all awry." Their other option is to pull up a flagstone: "in the neatly sanded floor / they'll throw him in and leave him there / and think of him no more" (Neufeldt *Works* 1.37).

Two years before his initiation into Freemasonry, at the age of sixteen, in his story, "Real Life in Verdopolis," Branwell describes a young lad's adventure in Glass Town, where he wanders the streets late at night to show that "he is game and will ere long be a passable glass town youngster." He walks down a damp, dirty lane and stops at a door, worn and rotten, and sees the town's elite entering a private gambling club. Could this be a Masonic haunt that Branwell had visited, and is he actually providing a glimpse into the sordid activities inside their club?

The "uninitiated hero" follows the men into a large candlelit hall. The doors and walls are covered with thick matting. The soundproofing makes it impossible to hear the men on the other side of the wall. He enters the windowless, interior room and stares with amazement at the grandeur of the furnishings: the oak and marble, the chandeliers, the velvet sofas, and rich carpets. He waits near a sideboard heaped with goblets and bottles of liquor, and watches the crowds of men sitting or standing around tables, concentrating on their gambling.

A man notices the young hero and brings him closer to the tables. "Gents. Ho. Waiter a glass of something. Gentlemen, a young sprig here lately sprouted wants to be planted in the gardens of Paradise." The men make fun of the lad, but he punches one in the mouth, threatens to fill their bones with his pistol's shot, and brandishes a "brace of firearms" to prove his intent. The men laugh and admire his "pluck," and immediately usher him into a small room equipped with an altar where he kneels while they "initiate" him into Elysium, a secret men's club in Verdopolis. He must promise that he will "never under any pretence whatsoever violate the rules of this society, abscond from or disclose the least matter connected with it." He swears his allegiance and is told the names of the officers of the club.

After the initiation, the men return to their card games, but some look over their portfolios or read the newspapers. Several play Hazard, a dice game for "1 or 2 guinea points," while others plot mischief in the corners. One man after experiencing financial ruin from his gambling, "with trembling hand snatched a pistol and blew his brains out." The other men "at the report turned their heads round but most of them with a scornful laugh turned again to their absorbing enjoyment." Their leader shouted, "off with him," and two men picked up the "lamentable victim to gambling," while the young, newly initiated man laid down his cards and shuddered at the incident. He looked at the others, "but not in one could he see an emotion answering to his own. All were absorbed in the hopes, fears or despairs of their tremendous occupation," occupations which included cards, dice, and the counting of gold (289-293).

Branwell's depictions of fighting and gambling also involve his alter ego Percy and his officers who regularly go out on the town to get drunk. They spend their nights "half floated," "quaffing large draughts," stirring "stiff rummers of punch," or emptying, in one gulp, "a whole bottle of brandy." Branwell's man likes his cognac neat and his brandy with water, but at times the alcohol makes him sick. His rendering of this experience ends with a muddled brain drifting off the subject.

"I called for a tumbler and a bottle of brandy. I poured the spirits into it, neat brandy you know, and neat it was, and so I drank it. Oh, but it only made me sicker, so then I ordered in a bowl and some bread and some water, I put them onto the fire and made a tremendous large bowl of stirabout. It was a tremendous basin. I took it but it only made me sicker. I vomited, Oh, I vomited sir—I'll just take a glass of mixture then I'll be back to that church, I'll settle down and I can see there's an opening for his genius who although a prodigy for musical talent is the most wandering and easy minded being extant" (*Brother in the Shadow* 4).

Branwell's stories contain images of large oak tables covered with fresh killed game and "mighty jugs and casks and bottles of brandy, rum, whisky, arrack, and beer." Men, with "sinister and reckless aspect, evidently given up to the vilest dissipation and perhaps the most lawless courses," sit and drink with weapons clearly exposed: "huge pistols were seen sticking in every belt" and "knives and daggers" were used for "assaulting with eager fury" (Collins 142). Two men who are known to quarrel with each other "set in to profound drinking. For a long time they continued to pour down amazing quantities of the 'lush' in perfect silence," but soon the name-calling begins: "dog," "hound," "villain," "beast! Wretch! Scavenger." One man lets out "a loud execration," and "amid repeated draughts of brandy, continued roars of imprecation, and incessant shouts of cursing," they drunkenly crash into each other and fall among bottles, glasses, tables, and chairs until the servants cart them off to bed (139).

One unlucky nobleman fares worse. His friends find him "grovelling in a black, musty hole, behind a heap of casks, drunk, miserably drunk, his head wounded in last night's revel now bound up, his face pale and ghastly, and himself so weak as to be unable to lift himself or sit upright" (186). In an earlier episode, alcohol not only acts as the lubricant for a fight, it also cures this same friend after another bloody encounter: one man pours down his throat "a bottle of mixed gin and brandy, which draught mightily revived the nobleman. He sat upright and took another tumbler and a third of wine that effectually strengthened him" (176).

Branwell preferred this exciting, masculine life. The Reverend's son discovered his Mason brothers governed a rough world that was far removed from the dull, feminine universe of the parsonage, and he delighted in writing shocking episodes in the tales he wrote with his sister. From their close camaraderie in their early years, we can see where his confident narrative voice influenced Charlotte's work and gave her permission to write like a man. We can also deduce the origins for the criticisms levelled at *Wuthering Heights* for its "savages ruder than those who lived before the days of Homer," situated "far from the haunts of civilised men" where we witness "wickedness" and the "brutalising influence of unchecked passion" and "the fierce ungoverned instincts of powerful organisations bred up amidst violence, revolt, and moral apathy . . . such brutes we should all be, or the most of us, were our lives as insubordinate to law; were our affections and sympathies as little cultivated, our imaginations as undirected" (Allott 40-65). Branwell's influence should not be underestimated, not only for his realistic scenes, but also for his very probable supply of story material to Charlotte about the Masons and their secret plots.

During those carefree years when they were partners in prose, her woman's voice was gaining strength and, in her early writing, we begin to hear the subtle strains of her ingenious declaration of war against the men.

5 THE EARLY TALES

The Brontë parsonage and its interior life contained a much healthier atmosphere than that experienced on Main Street. The weathered, outside walls of the parsonage contrasted with the tidy, clean rooms. Inside and to the right of the parsonage front door was the father's study with its desk, a hair-seated chair, and stacks of bookshelves. Across the hall was the dining room or sitting room, with a table and chairs in front of the fireplace, and a sofa against the wall. Behind the dining room was a storeroom entered from the back, and behind Reverend Brontë's study was the kitchen. Upstairs were three bedrooms, the children's study, and a room for the servants. The children preferred to play in their study or out on the moors rather than wander over to Main Street where their aversion to odours, middens, and open sewers kept them away.

The daily routine consisted of family prayers, meals, lessons, and play. The children ate their breakfast in the dining room with their father, but he ate his dinners alone. Branwell stayed home and studied the classics from their father. The girls also had morning lessons with their father and afternoon walks with Tabby, followed by tea in the kitchen, sewing and frequent reading of the newspapers with Aunt Branwell. The rest of the day was available for music, painting, and writing pursuits when they had finished their chores (Lock 263).

Charlotte and her two younger sisters, Emily and Anne, rarely ventured toward the village, but not just because of the unhealthy environment. They preferred the comforts of their home, and their shy, reserved natures inhibited them when meeting strangers or familiar acquaintances, but their adventurous brother Branwell tolerated the unsanitary conditions and the displays of public intoxication in his pursuit of excitement.

For their games out on the moors, the sisters would seek the path that wound away from the village, and far from the glances of the quarrymen, to hike long distances across the heath. In spring and autumn, when Branwell would join them, the four siblings scampered over bare masses of stone under a cold, clouded sky streaked with grey, and huddled together while a high wind blustered round stunted trees. Or in summer they lay for hours on the banks of the moors surrounded by the bloom of harebells, listening to the sounds of nature in the far off hills. The winter frost and snow forced them to bundle up in their woollen coats as they ran through chilly mists, past the frozen fog circling icy creeks where they would imagine themselves as kings and queens, explorers and politicians, all proclaiming their greatness to the wind and the sky.

Their schooling in the parsonage included the wondrous world of their father's library. All four children had access to the many stories, and soon discovered allegorical books like *The Pilgrim's Progress* and the epic poem *Paradise Lost*. The Reverend nurtured their joy of reading from an early age, and took particular care to teach Branwell Greek and Latin, but Charlotte listened and watched and soon acquired a comfortable understanding of the classics as well as a respectable knowledge of French.

When Charlotte and Branwell began weaving their own tales that began on that snowy evening with their wooden soldiers ruling over their respective islands, the brother and sister peppered the pages with allusions from classical literature. They also followed the warring exploits of their military heroes, the Duke of Wellington, Commander of the British forces, and Napoleon Bonaparte, Emperor of France.

Charlotte and Branwell took the lead over the two younger siblings in the creation of their fictional world. They placed their characters in a land called Angria and wrote poetry, short stories, and articles in little magazines. They composed tales of adventures in tiny hand-made books, sewn together with the same care that went into the construction of the characters and their rebellions.

The majority of the tales involve insurrection and war. Leaders form alliances and engage in political intrigues involving Reformers, Republicans, Revolutionists, and Constitutionalists vying for power and territory. These sagas usually end in betrayal and wars. Threats, attacks, united forces, rivalries, defeats, and victories later enabled the military and political professionals to establish the kingdom of Angria where Branwell enlisted thousands of soldiers to fight in dozens more bloody campaigns led by heroic men. Charlotte drafted page after page of machinations between Angria's first King, the Duke of Wellington, and his political rivals, but she also described the men and women circulating the halls of the royal palace.

In the Angria saga, Branwell's Napoleon becomes Alexander Sneaky, then Alexander Percy who is also called Rogue, Lord Ellrington, and the Duke of Northangerland. The exploits of Percy or Rogue or Northangerland as a pirate inform his actions: his ruthless individualism and his corrupt exploits prove Percy/Northangerland answers to no one but himself. As Branwell's alter ego, Percy's bravado and pride echo his own. Branwell also used the pseudonym of Northangerland on the several poems he published later in his twenties and even in his correspondence with friends.

The study of the juvenile writing provides a glimpse into the minds of Charlotte and Branwell and shows how they work closely, influencing each other's narratives. During those early playful years, Branwell's characters provided fodder for Charlotte's wit as demonstrated in 1829 when she describes Percy/Northangerland.

"His countenance is handsome, except that there is something very startling in his fierce grey eyes and formidable forehead. His manner is rather polished and gentlemanly, but his mind is deceitful, bloody, and cruel. His walk (in which he much prides himself) is stately and soldier-like, and he fancies that it greatly resembles that of the Duke of Wellington. He dances well and plays cards admirably, being skilled in all the sleight-of-hand-blackleg tricks of the gaming table. And, to crown all, he is excessively vain of this (what he terms) accomplishment" (Alexander 1.128).

She describes another of Branwell's pseudonyms, Young Soult, as a "great poet." He dresses in a shoddy manner, and "his countenance is wild and haggard," but she believes he will make a name for himself in the future. "In his disposition he is devilish but humane and good natured. He appears constantly labouring under a state of strong excitement occasioned by excessive drinking and gambling, to which he is unfortunately much addicted. His poems exhibit a fine imagination, but his versification is not good" (127). She really does seem to be describing her brother and gives a clue to his developing temperament. Her criticism of his poetry may be warranted, but Branwell's ability improved sufficiently for his works to be published in newspapers and magazines. Stories of debauchery contained in their favourite *Blackwood's Magazine* may have influenced Charlotte's reference to Young Soult's drinking and gambling but, in 1829, at the time of the writing, Branwell was twelve, an age when boys have been known to experiment with alcohol and to play cards.

Another pseudonym of Branwell's is Sergeant Bud. Charlotte describes him as "a clever lawyer and a great liar," and such a scoundrel that he deserves a brutal beating. She revels in the grisly details: "I would first duck him in water, next I would give him 70 stripes with a cat-o-nine-tails, then I would make him ride through the Glass Town on a camel with his face turned to the tail, and lastly I would hang him on a gallows 60 feet high. When he was dead, he should be cut down and given to the surgeons for dissection" (128).

Her description of Alexander Percy includes his external and internal characteristics. He has regular features and a handsome face, but "there was in the expression of his blue, sparkling, but sinister eyes and of the smile that ever played round his deceitful looking mouth, a spirit of deep, restless villainy which warned the penetrating observer that all was not as fair within as without, while his pallid cheek and somewhat haggard air bespoke at once the profligate, the gambler, and perhaps the drunkard" (*The Early Writings* 99-100).

In her prose tale, *My Angria and the Angrians*, written in 1834, Charlotte's narrator Lord Charles Albert Florian Wellesley meets Patrick Benjamin Wiggins, another representation of her brother, red-haired Patrick Branwell Brontë. She describes him as a small man in a black vest and grey pants, with his hat pushed to the back of his head "revealing a bush of carroty hair so arranged that at the sides it projected almost like two spread hands, a pair of spectacles placed across a prominent Roman nose, black neckerchief adjusted with no great attention or precision." He carries a black rattan cane that he "flourished" in his hand as he walked "tolerably upright" with an "indescribable swing always assumed by those who pride themselves on being good pedestrians" (Alexander ii, pt ii 245).

Her brother, as Wiggins, echoes a description that Charlotte's friend, Ellen Nussey, wrote after first seeing Branwell in a horse-drawn cart with his sisters. "His shock of red hair hangs down in somewhat ragged locks behind his ears, for Branwell Brontë esteems himself a genius and a poet, and, following the fashion of the times, has that abhorrence of the barber's shears which genius is supposed to affect." His clothes were "countrified," but he was not a "bumpkin," and his face "is a handsome and a striking one, full of Celtic fire and humour, untouched by the slightest shade of care, giving one the impression of somebody altogether hopeful, promising, even brilliant." His sisters enjoyed his exuberance and were his best audience as he recited lines of poetry while steering their chariot with panache and daring (Reid 30).

Charlotte was an equal opportunity narrator who permitted Patrick Benjamin Wiggins to swing his rattan cane in the direction of his sisters and voice his view of the three girls. Charles Wellesley asks Wiggins "Are they as queer as you?"

"Oh they are miserable silly creatures not worth talking about. Charlotte's eighteen years old, a broad dumpy thing, whose head does not come higher than my elbow. Emily's sixteen, lean and scant with a face about the size of a penny, and Anne is nothing, absolutely nothing."

"What! Is she an idiot?"

"Next door to it" (Alexander 250).

Their tiny manuscripts exceeded the output of the adult published fiction. Charlotte catalogued her "books," which did not include the original three plays, for a period of approximately fifteen months from early 1829 to mid-1830 and lists twenty-two volumes of romantic tales, adventures, magazines, dramas, songs, and poetry that contain an average of sixty to one hundred pages in each volume, all of which have survived. These twenty-two volumes are written in such minute lettering that a reader requires a magnifying glass to view the work.

Branwell's imaginative scribbles outlining his penchant for fighting also fill several volumes. His spelling errors and lack of punctuation fail to weaken his passion for the written word as his breathless writing races across the page avoiding the inconvenience of full stops.

A great deal of Branwell's writing deals with war. He addresses the preparation for war among soldiers and officers, the fighting of war with swords and swagger, and the lengthy proclamations from the victorious generals and emperors. He pits his alter ego, Rogue (which Branwell spells R-o-u-g-u-e) against Charlotte's man Arthur, the Marquis of Douro, so they can engage in Branwell's favourite sport of boxing. A ring of bystanders watch as the two men roll up their sleeves, and Rougue immediately lands "a tremendous facer" on his opponent.

The fight is on. "Arthur beautifully parried and like lightning popped Rougue a dig at the ribs which made them sing like a bell. Rougue staggered but threw his shot right and left ending with a blow upon Arthur's collar that dashed him onto the ground with the victor over him. Arthur scorned this and began round second by a cautious guard of his person and a toucher on Rougue's smeller which brought out a beautiful stream of claret. First blood was cried for the Marquis and the Odds for him were 3 to 2. Rougue with much malice aimed always at Arthur's face which malice was returned by his Antagonist with interest. Soon their eyes became black as the Midnight, their lips red as coral, their cheeks like those of a Milkmaid." They fight for over three hours, and by the "91st round" they both collapse on the floor as "the bell of St. Michael's tolled Four in the morning" (Neufeldt 294-5).

The close ties between Charlotte and Branwell would have extended to his confiding in her, and his sharing of eye-witnessed reports of the drinking and gambling. Like most siblings close in age, she would have been more aware of Branwell's mischievous involvement with the men than would the Reverend Brontë. Her brother was her link to that boisterous and dangerous world, especially when he joined the Freemasons, a fraternity whose secret rites and rituals would have ignited both their imaginations and, even though he had taken an oath of secrecy, the thrill of divulging the ancient mysteries presented too strong a temptation to ignore. Moreover, since both siblings were competitive with each other, he would certainly enjoy the superiority of being a member of a group that his sister would never be allowed to join.

The younger siblings Emily and Anne had also written in those early years. Unfortunately, the written narrative of their imaginary world of Gondal survives in the form of only a few fragments contained in their diary papers and provides sparse details of the Gondal story. Like the manuscripts and drafts of their novels, nothing remains of the Gondal tales. Charlotte kept all of Branwell's writing, including the inferior works of his early years. Was the Gondal saga lost or never written at all? Or had Charlotte destroyed any evidence of her sisters' writing because it would have proven that the younger sisters had never been writers at all?

6 THE DIARY PAPERS

The only surviving evidence of the younger sisters' prose appears in their diary papers and birthday papers. The main material on Gondal is also found in a few references in these scraps of paper, which they would write on a sibling's birthday and then open four years later. These diaries are little scraps of paper that were tucked up in a tiny, tin box and left in a desk drawer for years after Charlotte died. Her husband Arthur Bell Nicholls found them in the 1890s and sent them to Clement Shorter, a Brontë biographer, along with "some of the minute childhood writings wrapped in newspaper at the bottom of a drawer" (Bentley 127).

Emily and Anne's papers record life at the parsonage, and report on the Gondal story. Two of the papers are written when they are both living at home in 1834 and 1837 and are called the diary papers. The birthday papers are written in 1841 and 1845. Life at home in 1834 seems mundane but busy with domestic chores.

In the first diary notation written on November 24, 1834, Emily provides an intimate peek into life at the parsonage, but the writing contains several spelling and punctuation errors. As one Brontë biographer notes: "Emily's entry at the age of sixteen—poorly spelt, abominably punctuated and covered with blobs—gives no sign that thirteen years later she would produce *Wuthering Heights* or her visionary poems" (Fraser 94). Another biographer echoes this sentiment: "the dreadful handwriting and spelling are scarcely credible as the work of a highly intelligent sixteen-year-old" (Barker 221). The diary reads as follows:

"I fed Rainbow, Diamond, Snowflake Jasper phesant (alias this morning Branwell went down to Mr Drivers and brought news that Sir Robert peel was going to be invited to stand for Leeds Anne and I have been peeling Apples Charlotte to make an apple pudding and for Aunt nuts and apples Charlotte said she made puddings perfectly and she was of a quick but limited intellect. Taby said just now come Anne pillopatate (ie pill a potato Aunt has come into the Kitchen just now and said where are you feet Anne Anne answered On the floor Aunt papa opened the parlour Door and gave Branwell a Letter saying her Branwell read this and show it to your Aunt and Charlotte—The Gondals are discovering the interior of Gaaldine. Sally Mosley is washing in the back Kitchin.

"It is past Twelve o'clock Anne and I have not tid[i]ed ourselves, done our bed work or done our lessons and we want to go out to play. We are going to have for Dinner Boiled Beef, Turnips potato's and applepudding the Kitchin is in avery untidy state Anne and I have not Done our music exercise which consists of b majer Taby said on my putting a pen in her face Ya pitter pottering there instead of pilling a potate I answered O Dear, O Dear, O Dear I will derictly With that I get up, take a Knife and begin pilling (finished pilling the potatos papa going to walk Mr Sunderland expected.

"Anne and I say I wonder what we shall be like and what we shall be and where we shall be if all goes on well in the year 1874—in which year I shall be in my 57th year Anne will be going in her 55th year Branwell will be going in his 58th year And Charlotte in her 59th year hoping we shall all be well at that time We close our paper. Emily and Anne November the 24 1834" (Barker 221).

The biographer Juliet Barker notes that Emily's "reference to Sir Robert Peel being invited to stand as Member of Parliament for Leeds was an indication of a revived interest in politics which swept the family" (221). When Charlotte was sixteen, the same age as Emily at the time of the above diary paper, she too was interested in politics, but her ability to express herself contrasts sharply with her sister's in that it demonstrates the writing of "a highly intelligent sixteen-year-old." In May of 1832, while away at school in Roe Head, she writes to Branwell about her renewed interest in politics:

"Lately I had begun to think that I had lost all the interest which I used formerly to take in politics but the extreme pleasure I felt at the news of the Reform-bill's being thrown out of the House of Lords and of the expulsion or resignation of Earl Grey, etc etc convinced me that I have not as yet lost *all* my penchant for politics. I am extremely glad that Aunt has consented to take in Frazer's Magazine for though I know from your description of its general contents it will be rather uninteresting when compared with 'Blackwood' still it will be better than remaining the whole year without being able to obtain a sight of any periodical publication whatever, and such would assuredly be our case as in the little wild, moorland village where we reside there would be no possibility of borrowing, or obtaining a work of that description from a circulating library" (*Letters, Vol.I* 112).

In June 1837, Branwell's twentieth birthday, Emily would have been almost nineteen when she wrote the following lines from the two younger sisters' diary paper. Anne was seventeen and a half.

"A bit past 4 o'Clock Charolotte working in Aunts room Branwell reading Eugene Aram to her Anne and I writing in the drawing room. Anne a poem beginning 'fair was the evening and brightly the sun—I Agustus Almedas life 1st vol—4th page from the last a fine rather coolish thin grey cloudy but Sunny day. Aunt working in the little room papa gone out. Tabby in the Kitchin. The Emperors and Empresses of Gondal and Gaaldine preparing to depart from Gaaldine to Gondal to prepare for the coranation which will be on the 12th of July Queen Victoria ascended the throne this month. Northangerland in Monceys Isle—Zamorna at Eversham. All tight and right in which condition it is to be hoped we shall all be on this day 4 years at which time Charollote will be 25 and 2 months—Branwell just 24 it being his birthday—myself 22 and 10 months and a piece Anne 21 and nearly a half I wonder where we shall be and how we shall be and what kind of a day it will be then let us hope for the best" (Barker 271-2).

By the age of eighteen, Emily has forgotten how to spell Charlotte's name, and her writing, has hardly evolved into the complex style necessary for a novelist who is about to emerge in ten years to write a literary masterpiece. This is part of the reason scholars say *Wuthering Heights* came out of nowhere.

At this time, Charlotte is twenty-one, and her writing still stands in stark contrast to Emily's. The example below is from Charlotte's school journal in 1837 where she writes about her room back home at the parsonage. Her more polished prose emits the voice of a born novelist, and the words and tone are reminiscent of a later work.

"Remembrance yields up many a fragment of past twilight hours spent in that little unfurnished room. There have I sat on the low bed-stead my eyes fixed on the window, through which appeared no other landscape than a monotonous stretch of moorland, a grey church tower, rising from the centre of a church-yard so filled with graves, that the rank-weed and coarse grass scarce had room to shoot up between the monuments. Over these hangs in the eye of memory a sky of such grey clouds as often veil the chill close of an October day and low on the horizon glances at intervals through the rack the orb of a lurid and haloed moon" (Gordon 60).

"The grey church looked greyer, and the lonely churchyard lonelier. I distinguished a moor sheep cropping the short turf on the graves. . . . In winter, nothing more dreary, in summer, nothing more divine, than those glens shut in by hills, and those bluff, bold swells of heath. . . . all that remained of day was a beamless, amber light along the west; but I could see every pebble on the path, and every blade of grass by that splendid moon."

This latter quotation is a compilation of three sentences from two short paragraphs in *Wuthering Heights* (305-7), sentences that have a remarkable resemblance in tone, word choice, and syntax to the excerpt from Charlotte's journal. The sentiment is similar in remembrance and in observation, and the objects of contemplation resemble each other: the grey church tower, the grey church, the churchyard, the lonely churchyard, graves, coarse grass, short turf, every blade of grass, a haloed moon and a splendid moon. Could two unique voices, such as Charlotte's and Emily's be so alike?

Another example of Emily's writing occurs in the diary paper from 1841. Now twenty-three years old, she begins, "A Paper to be opened when Anne is 25 years old or my next birthday after—if—all be well— Emily Jane Brontë July the 30th 1841. It is Friday evening—near nine o'clock—wild rainy weather. I am seated in the dining room 'alone'— having just concluded tidying our desk-boxes—writing this document— Papa is in the parlour. Aunt up stairs in her room—She has been reading Blackwood's Magazine to papa—Victoria and Adelaide are ensconced in the peat-house—Keeper is in the Kitchen—Nero in his cage—We are all stout and hearty as I hope is the case with Charlotte, Branwell, and Anne, of whom the first is at John White Esq- upperwood House, Rawden The second is at Luddenden foot and the third is I beleive at—Scarborough— enditing perhaps a paper corresponding to this.

"A Scheme is at present in agitation for setting us up in a school of our own as yet nothing is determined but I hope and trust it may go on and prosper and answer our highest expectations. This day 4—years I wonder whether we shall still be dragging on in our present condition or established to our heart's content Time will show—

"I guess that at the time appointed for the opening of this paper—we (i.e.) Charlotte, Anne and I—'shall' be all merrily seated in our own sitting-room in some pleasant and flourishing seminary, having just gathered in for the midsummer holydays our debts will be paid off and we shall have cash in hand to a considerable amount. papa Aunt and Branwell will either have been— or be coming—to visit us—it will be a fine warm summery evening very different from this bleak look-out Anne and I will perchance slip out into the garden a few minutes to peruse our papers. I hope either this [o]r something better will be the case—

"The Gondalians are at present in a threatening state but there is no open rupture as yet—all the princes and princesses of the royal royaltys are at the palace of In-struction—I have a good many books on hand but I am sorry to say that as usual I make small progress with any—however I have just made a new regularity paper! and I mean—verb sap—to do great things—and now I close sending from far an exhortation of courage courage! to exiled and harassed Anne wishing she was here" (*Letters, Vol.*I 262-3).

Anne wrote her diary paper on July 30, 1841 while she was a governess with the Robinson family. Although younger, she demonstrates a more developed skill with the pen than does Emily:

"July the 30th, A.D. 1841. This is Emily's birthday. She has now completed her 23rd year, and is, I believe, at home. Charlotte is a governess in the family of Mr. White. Branwell is a clerk in the railroad station at Luddenden Foot, and I am a governess in the family of Mr. Robinson. I dislike the situation and wish to change it for another. I am now at Scarborough. My pupils are gone to bed and I am hastening to finish this before I follow them.

"We are thinking of setting up a school of our own, but nothing definite is settled about it yet, and we do not know whether we shall be able to or not. I hope we shall. And I wonder what will be our condition and how or where we shall all be on this day four years hence; at which time, if all be well, I shall be 25 years and 6 months old, Emily will be 27 years old, Branwell 28 years and 1 month, and Charlotte 29 years and a quarter. We are now all separate and not likely to meet again for many a weary week, but we are none of us ill that I know of and all are doing something for our own livelihood except Emily, who, however, is as busy as any of us, and in reality earns her food and raiment as much as we do. How little know we what we are. How less what we may be!

"Four years ago I was at school. Since then I have been a governess at Blake Hall, left it, come to Thorp Green, and seen the sea and York Minster. Emily has been a teacher at Miss Patchet's school, and left it. Charlotte has left Miss Wooler's, been a governess at Mrs. Sidgwick's, left her, and gone to Mrs. White's. Branwell has given up painting, been a tutor in Cumberland, left it, and become a clerk on the railroad. Tabby has left us, Martha Brown has come in her place. We have got Keeper, got a sweet little cat and lost it, and also got a hawk. Got a wild goose which has flown away, and three tame ones, one of which has been killed. All these diversities, with many others, are things we did not expect or foresee in the July of 1837. What will the next four years bring forth? Providence only knows. But we ourselves have sustained very little alteration since that time. I have the same faults that I had then, only I have more wisdom and experience, and a little more self-possession than I then enjoyed. How will it be when we open this paper and the one Emily has written? I wonder whether the Gondalian will still be flourishing, and what will be their condition. I am now engaged in writing the fourth volume of *Solala Vernon's Life*.

"For some time I have looked upon 25 as a sort of era in my existence. It may prove a true presentiment, or it may be only a superstitious fancy; the latter seems most likely, but time will show" (*Letters, Vol.I* 264-5). Scholars infer that Anne Brontë's Gondal character, Solala Vernon, left Gondal and the palace to become the character of a governess in her novel *Agnes Grey*.

The following recollections are from Emily's diary of July 30th 1845, very near the time she would have been writing *Wuthering Heights*. "Haworth—Thursday—July 30th 1845. My birthday—showery—breezy—coo—I am twenty-seven years old to day—this morning Anne and I opened the papers we wrote 4 years since on my twenty third birthday—this paper we intend, if all be well, to open on my 30th three years hence in 1848—since the 1841 paper, the following events have taken place.

"Our school scheme has been abandoned and instead Charlotte and I went to Brussels on the 8th of Febrary, 1842 Branwell left his place at Luddenden Foot C and I returned from Brussels November 8th 1842 in consequence of Aunt's death—Branwell went to Thorpgreen as a tutor where Anne still continued—January 1843 Charlotte returned to Brussels the same month and after staying a year came back again on new years day 1844 Anne left her situation at Thorp Green of her own accord—June 1845 Branwell left—July 1845.

"Anne and I went our first long Journey by ourselves together—leaving Home on the 30th of June—monday sleeping at York—returning to Keighley Tuesday evening sleeping there and walking home on Wedensday morning—though the weather was broken, we enjoyed ourselves very much except during a few hours at Bradford and during our excursion we were Ronald Macelgin, Henry Angora, Juliet Augusteena, Rosobelle Esualdar, Ella and Julian Egramon Catherine Navarre and Cordelia Fitzaphnold escaping from the palaces of Instruction to join the Royalists who are hard driven at present by the victorious Republicans— The Gondals still florish bright as ever I am at present writing a work on the First Wars—Anne has been writing some articles on this and a book by Henry Sophona—We intend sticking firm by the rascals as long as they delight us which I am glad to say they do at present" (*Letters, Vol.*I 407-8).

Neither the character Solala Vernon nor Henry Sophona appears in the novel *Agnes Grey*. Emily's reference to a work about "the First Wars" suggests a story about the Gondals, not a novel about Heathcliff and Catherine whose conflicts have nothing to do with Republicans or the palaces of Instruction.

Emily continues her paper on a cheerful note. "I should have mentioned that last summer the school scheme was revived in full vigor— We had prospectuses printed, despatched letters to all acquaintances imparting our plans and did our little all—but it was found no go—now I dont desire a school at all and none of us have any great longing for it. We have cash enough for our present wants with a prospect of accumolation— we are all in decent health—only that papa has a complaint in his eyes and with the exception of B who I hope will be better and do better, hereafter. I

45

am quite contented for myself—not as idle as formerly, altogether as hearty and having learnt to make the most of the present and hope for the future with less fidgetness that I cannot do all I wish—seldom or ever troubled with nothing to do ie and merely desiring that every body could be as comfortable as myself and as undesponding and then we should have a very tolerable world of it—

"By mistake I find we have opened the paper on the 31st instead of the 30th Yesterday was much such a day as this but the morning was devine—

"Tabby who was gone in our last paper is come back and has lived with us—two years and a half and is in good health—Martha who also departed is here too. We have got Flossey, got and lost Tiger—lost the Hawk. Nero which with the geese was given away and is doubtless dead for when I came back from Brussels I enquired on all hands and could hear nothing of him—Tiger died early last year—Keeper and Flossey are well also the canary acquired 4 years since.

"We are all now at home and likely to be there some time—Branwell went to Liverpool on 'Tuesday' to stay a week. Tabby has just been teasing me to turn as formerly to— 'pilloputate.' Anne and I should have picked the black currants if it had been fine and sunshiny. I must hurry off now to my turning and ironing I have plenty of work on hands and writing and am altogether full of buisness with best wishes for the whole House till 1848 July 30th and as much longer as may be I conclude E.J. Brontë" (408-9).

At twenty-seven, she is still not demonstrating the necessary facility with words nor the great mental powers required to write *Wuthering Heights*, and her "undesponding" mood contrasts significantly with the fury and passion contained in the novel. The gloomy and profound mystic has been replaced by "a surprisingly cheerful figure, insensitively lost in a world of her own and blind to the troubles of her family" (Winnifrith 6).

Branwell's decline into alcoholism and drug addiction fails to garner her deep displeasure or frustration. Charlotte, on the other hand, expresses her disappointment to her former teacher in a letter:

"You ask about Branwell; he never thinks of seeking employment and I begin to fear that he has rendered himself incapable of filling any respectable station in life, besides, if money were at his disposal he would use it only to his own injury—the faculty of self-government is, I fear almost destroyed in him" (*Letters, Vol.I* 447-8). Unlike Charlotte, Emily appears less affected by Branwell's deterioration. She acknowledges he has a problem but refers to it only briefly with the hope that he "will be better and do better, hereafter."

The following excerpt from Anne's 1845 paper is equally informative concerning the whereabouts of the inhabitants at the parsonage, which also included the pets, and she refers to Branwell with the same hopes as Emily:

"Branwell has left Luddendenfoot and been a Tutor at Thorp Green and had much tribulation and ill health he was very ill on Tuesday but he went with John Brown to Liverpool where he now is I suppose and we hope he will be better and do better in future—This is a dismal cloudy wet evening we have had so far a very cold wet summer—Charlotte has lately been to Hathersage in Derbyshire on a visit of three weeks to Ellen Nussy—she is now sitting sewing in the Dining Room Emily is ironing upstairs I am sitting in the Dining Room in the Rocking chair before the fire with my feet on the fender Papa is in the parlour Tabby and Martha are I think in the Kitchen Keeper and Flossy are I do not know where little Dick is hopping in his cage—When the last paper was written we were thinking of setting up a school—the scheme has been dropt and long after taken up again and dropt again because we could not get pupils— Charlotte is thinking about getting another situation—she wishes to go to Paris—Will she go? she has let Flossy in by the bye and he is now lying on the sopha—Emily is engeaged in writing the Emperor Julius's life she has read some of it and I want very much to hear the rest—she is writing some poetry too I wonder what it is about—I have begun the third volume of passages in the life of an Individual. I wish I had finish-ed it—This afternoon I began to set about making my grey figured silk frock that was dyed at Keigthley—What sort of a hand shall I make of it? E. and I have a great deal of work to do—when shall we sensibly diminish it? I want to get a habit of early rising shall I succeed? We have not yet finished our Gondal chronicles that we began three years and a half ago when will they be done? The Gondals are at present in a sad state the Republicans are uppermost but the Royalists are not quite overcome—the young sovereigns with their brothers and sisters are still at the palace of

Instruction—The Unique Society 'above' half a year ago were wrecked on a dezart Island as they were returning from Gaaldin—they are still there but we have not played at them much yet—The Gondals in general are not yet in first rate playing condition—will they improve? I wonder how we shall all be and where and how situated on the thirtyeth of July 1848 when if we are all alive Emily will be just 30 I shall be in my 29ᵗʰ year Charlotte in her 33ʳᵈ and Branwell in his 32ⁿᵈ and what changes shall we have seen and known and shall we be much changed ourselves? I hope not—for the worse at least—I for my part cannot well be *flatter* or older in mind than I am now—Hoping for the best I conclude Anne Brontë" (*Letters, Vol.I* 410-11).

In this diary paper Anne misspells Keighley, the town near Haworth pronounced Keithley, so she records it as Keigthley. She mentions having "a great deal of work to do." The word "work" usually refers to needlework at this time, so both sisters are busy with their household chores.

Her "third volume of passages in the life of an Individual" is considered to be the novel *Agnes Grey*, but her writing suffers, like Emily's, from a lack of sophistication and style and, again, like her sister she is preoccupied with discussing the Gondal characters and their exploits. This reasoning suggests her "Individual" may not have been the novel depicting Agnes Grey's experiences as a governess, but simply a story based on a Gondal character.

The two sisters share a fascination for the Gondal saga, and Anne explains why their creations are in "a sad state": the Royalists have not yet been beaten, the princes and princesses are still at the palace, and some characters continue to be stranded on a desert island. Both Emily and Anne show considerable interest in events and characters from their fantasy world, a world that they enjoy playing at and acting out, so the possibility that Emily is composing a masterpiece while writing "the Emperor Julius's life" and that Anne is completing the third volume of *Agnes Grey*, a character based on the real world, is highly unlikely.

The two sisters are neither exceptionally creative nor inventive, and both lack any significant signs of accomplishment in language that one would expect from genius writers. Anne's writing is plain, almost formal at times, and nothing in her observations or subject matter distinguishes it as masterful prose.

Their letter writing is also sparse. Whereas Charlotte wrote letters that would fill three volumes, only four of Anne's letters have survived and Emily's comprise just over three hundred words. Anne's letter-writing skill is better than what we see in the birthday diary papers, but they fail to show any of the talent necessary to construct novels. In fact, she admits her weakness in a letter to Charlotte's friend Ellen in 1848: "you must know there is a lamentable deficiency in my organ of language which makes me almost as bad a hand at writing as talking" (*Letters, Vol.II* 19). Why would she lie about her writing skill? Perhaps she never wrote *Agnes Grey* or *The Tenant of Wildfell Hall*, and is being sincere when she says her writing is inadequate.

Emily's letter writing output is slim and scarce. Her three surviving letters are all short, which creates further mystery around her: "Emily left so little behind her that it is not surprising she remains enigmatic. Unlike many Victorian girls, she was not a letter-writer" (Drabble x). Emily writes to Ellen Nussey in May of 1843:

"All here are in good health so was Anne according to the last accounts—the holydays will be here in a week or two and then if 'she' be willing I will get her to write you a proper letter—a feat that I have never performed" (*Letters, Vol.I* 318).

In her own words, Emily disputes the genius writer myth: writers write, whether they write letters, books, essays, or poems—they write, just like Charlotte, who penned three books of letters and was always dreaming of composing when her circumstances restricted her time to write. Emily admits that even letter writing is a feat that she has never performed. A Brontë biographer agrees that she had an "unwillingness to write long letters" and "it does seem that her 'taciturnity' extended as much to the written word as the spoken. It may appear all the more remarkable that she eventually wrote a full-scale novel, and less amazing that she never wrote a second one" (Chitham 159).

After Charlotte convinced her critics that Emily and Anne were authors, scholars tried to find value in the diary papers, but an objective reading should have communicated the truth that these girls were, as Anne admits, lamentably deficient in the art of writing.

The diary papers have always dismayed the scholars, but they try to reconcile Emily's immature style and Anne's straightforward epistles with the brilliance of *Wuthering Heights, Agnes Grey,* and *The Tenant of Wildfell Hall* by saying the girls were pretending to be childish; consequently, the bad writing was just a game.

Margaret Drabble, the novelist, biographer, and critic acknowledges that the authorship of *Wuthering Heights* is still an unsolved riddle. Part of the problem comes from "how little we know of Emily" and that the "main sources of information are Charlotte herself, Ellen Nussey, Charlotte's descriptions of her to Mrs. Gaskell, and the gossip and recollections of neighbours—none of which are necessarily impartial or accurate." She believes that Elizabeth Gaskell's account of Emily reading a German book while making bread has "given rise to the idea that Emily was a keen scholar, which she probably was not, and that she read German, which is again in doubt." Without any drafts of her work, "there is not much first-hand literary evidence of her character and development."

She refers to Emily's poems about the Gondal characters as "inferior, and in a very recognizable way," and asserts that the Gondal poems and Emily's diary papers "do not reveal her as a novelist." She adds, "There *is* something awkward and freakish about a girl of twenty-seven playing nursery games. The absence of the awkward in *Wuthering Heights* is stunning," so how did the writer of adolescent tales "write a solid, elegant, original, beautifully constructed and firmly Yorkshire novel like *Wuthering Heights,*" especially when Emily's life was known to be "outwardly uneventful"?

Drabble wonders where Emily learned "a narrative technique that makes most other English novelists look amateur, a prose style that makes them look verbose and rhetorical, and a sense of deeply-rooted physical reality of place and person unique in the language." She agrees with other scholars that the book "is the work of a master," and concludes that Emily must have heard strange tales from Tabby and Reverend Brontë "that impressed themselves on her growing mind." Unfortunately, the "dearth of information" on Emily enables the book's authorship to "remain a mighty enigma," and elicits efforts to solve the riddle of who really wrote this "work of genius" (ix-xx).

The Brontë scholar Lucasta Miller blames Charlotte for the confusion. She notes that Emily "never seems to have made a single significant friend outside her immediate family . . . and left little behind her." Also, people who knew her said she ran away "at the sight of strangers," so we only have Charlotte's words to provide information about her sister.

Miller believes, however, that "if anyone is responsible for exacerbating the mystery surrounding her" it would have to be Charlotte: Emily never had an Elizabeth Gaskell to write her biography, so we must acquire our impressions from the information Charlotte left behind and, as Miller points out, Charlotte makes this a difficult exploration because of her tendency to protect and control her sister's legacy: she "is a slippery authority whose comments tell us more about her own attitude toward her sister than about the inner workings of Emily's mind. They betray ambivalent feelings: protectiveness tipping over into an urge to dominate, admiration tinged with condescension." These ambivalent feelings "reveal conflicting impulses on Charlotte's part: immense admiration for Emily's genius coupled with a tendency to infantilise her, and an urge to protect which merges ambivalently into a desire to control" (170-71). No one denies Charlotte controlled the family's image, and the diary papers understandably add to the confusion.

Biographers explain the dearth of material from Emily and Anne is due to pages of prose being either lost or destroyed. The only possible person living in the home at the time of Emily's and Anne's deaths who would have had control of those papers is Charlotte, but why would she destroy her sisters' prose works when Branwell's writing has survived and never went missing? The diary papers, hidden inside a tin box, were never actually lost. They were recovered and shown to the public. Even Charlotte's husband chose not to destroy them.

If Emily and Anne had left extensive records of their Gondal prose, Charlotte would have saved it. The fact that no such papers survived suggests the third possibility: they were neither lost nor destroyed; they simply never existed.

If the early reviewers had seen the diary/birthday papers, would they have discounted the story of three separate authors and continued to voice their suspicions that only writer produced the novels? How would those publishers and reviewers in 1847 have judged the writing in the diary papers? Their objectivity, unhampered by years of mythology built up around the Brontë sisters, would have dismissed the writing as inferior. They would have expected a great deal more from the two authors. The best example of the kind of quality fiction publishers required at that time, and the calibre of prose they sought comes in the response from the publishing company Smith, Elder and from the critics when they first read *Jane Eyre*.

7 *JANE EYRE* ARRIVES

On August 24, 1847, plain brown paper concealed an unknown author's remarkable story, now on its way by train from the wild moors in the north of England to one of the principal streets in the heart of London. The journey ended several hours later at a large bookseller's shop, situated at 65 Cornhill where the publishers, Smith, Elder & Company had occupied the premises since 1824. Inside, several young men sat at a long table reading and editing sheets of manuscript while a few younger lads hurried back and forth filling inkwells, sharpening quills, or opening the post. The recently delivered packet lay on the front counter among a display of first editions of Smith, Elder publications. A boy's small hand lifted the brown package and tore off the paper before placing it beside one of the company's readers.

For the next two days, the story remained nestled among soon to be published works due out in early 1848. By Thursday afternoon, the 26th of August, a young reader had found the opportunity to begin reading the newly arrived manuscript. He completed it the following morning and was so powerfully moved by the central character that he rushed into Mr. Smith's office to declare, in the strongest possible language, that the company must publish this novel.

Smith laughed at the young man's enthusiasm. "You seem to have been so enchanted that I do not know how to believe you."

George Smith was an attractive young man with dark hair and an ambitious nature. He had begun his apprenticeship at the age of fourteen and had taken over the running of his father's publishing business at twenty-one. Now at the age of twenty-three, with his father's recent death, he had assumed full responsibility for the company. He was an enterprising, but fair and cautious man, so he decided to solicit a second opinion of this new novel. He chose an older, clear thinking employee who would be less susceptible to enchantment. He told the young man to give the manuscript to William Smith Williams, the company's most experienced reader.

William Smith Williams began his publishing career with Taylor and Hessey who in 1818 had published a book of poems by John Keats.

Reports find Smith Williams among a select few in 1820 who witnessed Keats departure to Italy, the country where the poet died less than a year later. After a few years of writing articles, William Smith Williams became a literary editor at Smith, Elder. From early childhood, he had loved reading literature, and in later years became a friend to writers, but being a modest man had neither required nor desired recognition for his contribution to the world of letters.

He had recognized the name of Currer Bell. A year earlier, the author had sent a different manuscript to Smith, Elder, and while Williams had rejected that particular work, he could see the talent in the writing and offered to read Bell's next novel.

Smith Williams removed his handkerchief and wiped his brow and neck. The sultry August heat had expanded to every corner of the shop and was slipping beneath his collar. His pale face affirmed that he had passed the majority of the summer indoors, and his stooped shoulders hinted at a profession spent bending both his body and mind to the promise of discovering great books. He was in his late forties, a quiet man with mild eyes and a relaxed mouth that suggested a contemplative temperament, but the strong brow marked a large intellect hidden behind. He put this new manuscript into his bag to read at home. He gripped the bundle long enough for the damp tips of his fingers to leave a faint imprint on the last sheet. That evening he began reading and continued reading well into the night.

The next day, Smith Williams showed the manuscript to George Smith. He hesitated before handing it to him, and when he reluctantly let it go, cleared his throat, still searching for the right words to express his deep conviction that they had in their possession a writer of great literary power. Not a man prone to ebullient expression, he put one hand in his pocket and simply said, "I'd like you to read this."

George Smith knew something was up, so he took the manuscript home with him on Saturday night. On Sunday morning, a warm breeze carried the perfume of blooming honeysuckle through his open study window. After a light breakfast and cup of black coffee, he began reading the story. Summer tints glowed among the furniture as a ray of sunshine traversed the small room, casting rosy reflections on the walls. A dog's bark and the loud peals of a nearby church bell gradually lost distinction as

Smith ventured deeper into the novel. At midmorning, darker hues crept in when the sun disappeared beyond the house. The cooing of doves on his windowsill had stopped and a multitude of shadows gathered round his chair. By the end of chapter nine, he felt a sense of deep solitude.

Just before noon, his groom brought Smith's horse round to the front door, saddled and ready to go. Smith stared at the bridle in the man's hand and tried to recall why he had ordered his horse at this time. His man reminded him of an appointment he had made with a friend to take a ride together in the country. Before Smith could respond, a woman's voice, echoing from the novel, summoned him back to the story, so he scribbled out a quick note to his friend apologizing for not being able to see him that day, explaining that circumstances had arisen to prevent his meeting him. He handed the note to his groom and asked him to deliver the message to his friend.

Back inside the comfort of his study, Smith continued to read about this remarkable Jane Eyre. An hour later, a servant rapped at the door to announce that his luncheon was on the table. He tried to soften his displeasure at the interruption.

"I'll be eating in my study today. Just bring me a sandwich and a glass of wine." He lowered his dark eyes and returned to the young heroine's plight.

By the dinner hour, he was compelled to eat and to rest his eyes. He put the manuscript down and hurried through the meal, wondering if the heroine's spirit would survive the tempest of her emotions. Would she indulge her feelings and return to Rochester?

The clock in the hall struck once. The candlelight dimmed. Smith read the last page and placed both hands on the sheet of paper. His brain worked restlessly, calculating publishing terms for this new author. He would offer £100 conditional upon Smith, Elder obtaining the right of first refusal on the next two books. Thoughts of subsequent editions, foreign rights, and future payments circled round the image of words on a cover. A slight alteration needed there. Not quite so dry a title. Better to suggest a true story, one told to an objective party by the governess herself. Yes, that would do well. The book would be called, *Jane Eyre. An Autobiography* edited by Currer Bell. (Smith 'Recollections')

The novel jumped the queue ahead of other expectant Smith, Elder manuscripts and faced the public in October of 1847. The opinions of the press were immediate (See Allott *Jane Eyre* 50-73).

"There can be no question but that *Jane Eyre* is a very clever book. Indeed it is a book of decided power. The thoughts are true, sound, and original; and the style, though rude and uncultivated here and there, is resolute, straightforward, and to the purpose. There are faults, which we may advert to presently; but there are also many beauties, and the object and moral of the work is excellent. . . . There are, it is true, in this autobiography (which though relating to a woman, we do not believe to have been written by a woman), struggles, and throes, and misgivings, such as must necessarily occur in a contest where the advantages are all on one side; but in the end, the honesty, kindness of heart, and perseverance of the heroine, are seen triumphant over every obstacle."—*The Examiner*.

"Almost all that we require in a novelist the writer has: perception of character and power of delineating it; picturesqueness, passion, and knowledge of life. The story is not only of singular interest, naturally evolved, unflagging to the last, but it fastens itself upon your attention, and will not leave you. The book closed, the enchantment continues: your interest does not cease. Reality—deep, significant reality is the great characteristic of this book. It *is* an autobiography—not, perhaps, in the naked facts and circumstances, but in the actual suffering and experience. This gives the book its charm: it is soul speaking to soul: it is an utterance from the depths of a struggling, suffering, much enduring spirit: *suspiria de profundis*."—G.H. Lewes.

"The style of *Jane Eyre* is peculiar . . . although by no means a fine style, it has the capital point of all great styles in being personal—the written speech of an individual, not the artificial language made up from all sorts of books."—*Fraser's Magazine*.

"From the first page to the last, it is stamped with the same vitality, and there is a minuteness and detail in every point, which makes this picture of a life true and interesting beyond any other work that has appeared for very many years."—*Weekly Chronicle*.

"We know not whether this powerful story is from the pen of a youthful writer; there is all the freshness and some of the crudeness of youth about it, but there is a knowledge of the profoundest springs of human emotions, such as is rarely acquired without long years of bitter experience in the troubled sea of life."—*Atlas*.

When the second edition appeared, Currer Bell was no longer listed as the editor of the story. The title had been amended to *Jane Eyre. An Autobiography* by Currer Bell. The reviews continued but were now addressing the identity of the book's author.

"Indeed, the public taste seems to have outstripped its guides in appreciating the remarkable power which this book displays. For no leading review has yet noticed it, and here we have before us the second edition. The name and sex of the writer are still a mystery. Currer Bell . . . is a mere *nom de guerre*—perhaps an anagram."—*Christian Remembrancer*, April 1848.

"There seem to have arisen in the novel-reading world some doubts as to who really wrote this book; and various rumours, more or less romantic, have been current in Mayfair, the metropolis of gossip . . . though we cannot pronounce that it appertains to a real Mr. Currer Bell and to no other, yet that it appertains to a man, and not, as many assert, to a woman, we are strongly inclined to affirm." —*Quarterly Review*, December 1848.

Currer Bell's first novel became the subject of much conversation and debate. The famous novelist William Makepeace Thackeray hailed the book as "the masterwork of great genius." Others found the book coarse and harsh in its dealings with the upper classes, while some referred to the unseemly depiction of love affairs, the unconventional locales, and the unusual casting of a plain, poor, assertive orphan as the heroine instead of the more acceptable beautiful woman who submits to her handsome hero. A few felt the passionate individualism Jane Eyre expresses bordered on vulgarity. Many questions perplexed the readers: was Currer Bell a man or a woman? Was he using a pseudonym, a *nom de guerre*? Did he live in Yorkshire? (One suggested he was a weaver living in Lancashire.) Who was the governess that gave him her story? And had he written any other works? But the question most wanted answered was "why all the secrecy?"

In his reminiscences, George Smith states that he presumed Currer Bell was a pen name and had little doubt about gender: "I had the advantage over the general public of having the handwriting of the author before me. There were qualities of style, too, and turns of expression, which satisfied me that 'Currer Bell' was a woman, an opinion in which Mr. Williams concurred." Like all the readers of *Jane Eyre*, Smith and Williams were curious about the identity of their new writer, but "were bound, however, to respect the writer's anonymity." After the initial excitement of the reviews, George Smith and William Smith Williams returned to their labours and left the mystery of Currer Bell for others to solve (Smith 'Recollections').

The controversy, analysis, and questions did not go unnoticed by Currer Bell. William Smith Williams kindly sent the mix of reviews and several copies of the novel's latest editions to his author via train from the heart of London to the wild moors of Haworth in the north of England. The sensational success of *Jane Eyre* provoked the London literary establishment into accepting Currer Bell as a fellow male member. Two years later they would meet a shy, tiny lady the size of an eleven-year-old girl, who had soft, brown hair, spectacles, and an unassuming plain face, but the mind of a literary giant.

The mysteries and questions persisted. Charlotte had carefully crafted her literary legacy as well as shaped the mythic drama of three writing sisters living in an isolated Yorkshire village, so, for years to come, scholars and biographers would continue grappling with the inconsistencies between diary papers and novels as well as over Charlotte's claims that contrasted with recorded factual evidence. Her clues and careful use of words pointed her readers to an alternate drama hidden beneath the surface, but her assertions were so convincing that they understandably muted that other voice.

8 A POETIC ENIGMA

The Brontë experts have questioned but mostly accepted Charlotte's contradictory version of her family, but not all are convinced of their veracity: "Her words, because of their persuasive power, have ever since been taken to be written on tablets of stone, handed down from the Great Author; absolute and unquestionable truths" (Barker 654). But just as Charlotte had played fair and allowed Branwell to "speak" as Wiggins in one of her juvenile stories, she gave her readers a chance to find the truth. An exploration of her hints and editorial changes to her sisters' works offers a useful glimpse into her method and her mind, and shows why the scholars have searched for but never found probable explanations to resolve the discrepancies between Charlotte's accounts and the actual evidence.

Between September 1848 and May of 1849, three of Charlotte Brontë's siblings were gone. Branwell, Emily, and Anne had died within months of each other, and now the surviving sister felt the gloom of loneliness. In the early decades of the twentieth century, Brontë biographers embraced the dark tragedy of this gloom and loneliness to generate excitement about the Brontë sisters and their mournful end. The facts were an inconvenience when narratives about death and poetry circling innocent lives like a tempestuous wind could arouse feelings of pity and sorrow in the readers. If facts were unavailable, the biographers would imagine scenes and then interpret from their fictionalized version of events how the sisters must have felt. Emily's poetry especially influenced this "Purple Heather" school of biography and criticism.

In Romer Wilson's 1928 book, *All Alone: The Life and Private History of Emily Jane Brontë*, she imagines Emily making the beds and sweeping the floors, when a short burst of vision interrupts Emily's reverie: "Flash! I am myself in my pride, dark, lonely, marvellous. The thing is gone before the thought is quite complete, and leaves one staring at a vision not perfectly clear to the mind's eye, leaves one dreamy and vague. The bed-making or sweeping in hand at the time gets done with somewhat trembling limbs, and there is a craving in the pit of the stomach to get off alone and dream things over or to rush out on a hill-top and run wildly about" (91). She continues, "These moments are not frequent. They often happen in solitude. As the years pass Emily becomes partly conscious *of* them though not *in* them, and keeps them under control: but she never sees what beauty she reveals, even though she keeps herself as still as a toad under a rock" (92-3).

Another example of imagining the workings of Emily's consciousness comes from Virginia Moore in her book *The Life and Eager Death of Emily Brontë*. Emily "craved heightened emotion, and, failing great love, rejected a small loneliness as insufficient, opening her cloak to a loneliness so great it devoured her" (78). Moore also conjures up the depth of Emily's soul: "Emily's inner life was 'luminous with intense realization' to a degree seldom vouchsafed to or achieved by a mortal: at times she could step aside from the stream of circumstances and let it flow past. But at other times she could not—she could not" (153). Moore's book is noted for these examples of the "Purple Heather" school of biography, and for "the fact that she misread the untidy title in a poetry manuscript by Emily, 'Love's Farewell,' as 'Louis Parensell', and jumped to the conclusion that this must have been the name of Emily's secret lover" (Dinsdale 147).

The trend continued when Emily's birth inspired a moment of veneration in Reverend Brontë's biographer: "Was there a violent storm on Thursday, 30th July 1818? Did the lightning fork its way across the Yorkshire sky? Did the thunder, locked in the Pennine Hills, roar a wild greeting from dawn to dusk? At night did the stars seem brighter and nearer to earth? . . . The head of the budding heather and ling nodded in expectancy and homage; the curlew flew lower and called in greeting; the lapwings hovered lovingly over Thornton and flew with the good news to their haunts on Haworth moor" (Lock 179).

This kind of subjective attachment to Emily's personality creates a distorted image of the actual person. The biographers "use the poetry as a means of gaining insight into the life of the author rather than into the poetry itself" and this interpretation "adds to the ever-increasing store of elegiac criticism, so familiar in Brontë studies," especially when the analysis concerns Emily: "many sensibilities have been affected by her work to a degree that scrutiny as to the ways and means of its production seems nothing short of sacrilege" (Peeck-O'Toole 133-4).

Lucasta Miller's book *The Brontë Myth* examines this phenomenon and its origins. Mrs. Gaskell's biography of Charlotte kept its focus on three lonely sisters wandering the isolated, wind-swept moors, oblivious to their approaching, untimely deaths: "Gaskell shaped the evidence" (64). According to Miller, a later writer, May Sinclair presents Emily "as an ideal figure who raises herself above the external, phenomenal world and achieves realisation of the divine within herself" (222). This form of adoration leads to Emily being transformed into "a being of rare spiritual gifts;" a woman, "who half a century before, had been dismissed as dog-like and repellent had become instead a symbol of the divine within the human. The mystic of the moors was born" (223).

Miller refers to Henry James and his critique of this type of sentiment: "This is exactly the sort of confused attitude Henry James had in mind when he complained that the Brontë story had become a beguiled infatuation": James believed the mystical idealism confuses the facts, "'with the result that we cease to know, in the presence of such ecstasies, what we have hold of or what we are talking about'" (63). His concern with the romantic, "Purple Heather" critiques is that each story "'embodies, really, the most complete intellectual muddle, if the term be not extravagant, ever achieved, on a literary question, by our wonderful public'" (58).

Miller also examines offshoots of this "intellectual muddle." She writes that E. F. Benson, who wrote a 1932 biography of Charlotte, "hero-worshipped Emily" and was determined "to seek out the less pleasant aspects" of Charlotte. This search for her character flaws "was a reaction against what he saw as Victorian sentimentality" (135). His "excessively fault-finding nature" displays his own "supremely judgemental" nature, which was "in its own negative way, as moralistic as the Victorian eulogies. Charlotte remained detached from her works in that the biographer's purpose was not to gain a deeper understanding of her literary imagination but to sit in judgement on her private life, as if higher personal standards were expected of a great novelist than of mere mortals" (138).

Another writer Miller notes that "vilified" Charlotte is the novelist Charlotte Cory who concludes that Brontë "was so embittered by her lack of physical attractions that her novels became a mere channel for pent-up bile and viciousness" (138). The fascination with personality had usurped the literary accomplishments.

One aspect of Brontë mythology has been the question of authorship of *Wuthering Heights*, which is the subject of this book. One theory proposes Branwell as the creator. Miller writes, "the supposed 'problem' of *Wuthering Heights*'s authorship would eventually become established as one of the most alluring mysteries of the Brontë cult. (It is telling that this insubstantial theory would find a particularly welcoming niche in the fictional biographies of the 1930s)." The author in the "insubstantial theory" is always Branwell: a theory "rooted less in factual evidence than in nineteenth-century prejudices about women's writing" (206).

Evidently, an acquaintance of Branwell who was also a poet reported that he had seen portions of Branwell's manuscript and recalled a character resembling Heathcliff. Miller explains how this misconception could surface: "All the Brontës were subject to the same literary influences, and all their fiction had its ultimate roots in the shared literary experience of their childhood and adolescence." She adds about the acquaintance that, "One suspects that his desire as a poet to be seen to be connected with Yorkshire's most famous literary family fuelled his inspiration as much as his views on the authorship of *Wuthering Heights*" (207).

These examples demonstrate that impressions of the Brontës are not necessarily based in reality. The challenge, therefore, in writing a biography that could be relegated to the conspiracy theorists' dustbin, is to break through the "muddle" of impressions and try to present both a new understanding of Charlotte Brontë's work and an appreciation of her literary imagination without shaping her into a set pattern of victim, saint, feminist, or overbearing sibling. No matter what the application, however, scholars and biographers seem to adhere to one conflicting argument that forms the basis for this kind of study.

A contradiction that restricts discussion of authorship is that while the scholars agree the Brontë sisters were distinct individuals, they explain the similarity in the writing by saying the siblings shared literary works and grew up in the same environment. Charlotte, the plain, shy, big sister; Emily, the reserved mystic; and Anne, the pretty but frail youngest sister lived together in the parsonage and had 'played' at their early plots together, so their writing would understandably be alike. Or would it?

Perhaps this argument suits their poetry, which shares the same rhyming scheme and, at times, sentiments and sensibilities, but that same argument lacks credibility in the presence of the novels. Why would these three, unique women write novels that share a coarseness of tone, a powerful liberty with language, an equally strong passion for violence that shocked Victorian readers, and a seemingly perverse tendency to depict the actions of crude, vulgar men?

The Brontë sisters were separate and unique, but their writing is at times indistinguishable. Common sense might suggest one woman wrote all the books, the same woman who had control of the family's literary legacy, and who herself was a master at crafting convincing fiction. Understandably, the task of removing Emily's name from *Wuthering Heights* is fraught with controversy, but is not borne from a desire to "be connected with Yorkshire's most famous literary family," to vilify Emily and Anne, nor to canonize Charlotte, but to explore the evidence and arrive at a clearer understanding of how Charlotte's fertile imagination constructed her novels.

In the cool summer of 1849, after all those deaths, Charlotte would have taken her cloak from the hook near the door of the Haworth parsonage, called to the two dogs Keeper and Flossy, and crossed through the eastern gate in the garden to the churchyard. At the cemetery, the wind still uttered its low howl. A shroud of solitude circled those stone and marble monuments, intensified by a shadow passing overhead, signalling the arrival of heavy rain clouds leaning toward the heath. The first signs of growling thunder carried the remnants of sorrow. Soon the wind would blow strong from the northeast and the rain would usher in a misty afternoon. Charlotte continued along the path onto the brown moors where the wind flipped the hem of her cloak, chilling her limbs. She ached for that wind to carry her above her misery and lead her towards a brighter future as she found a favourite bench near the wreck of a chestnut tree and wrote to her friend and editor William Smith Williams.

"A year ago had a prophet warned me how I should stand in June 1849—how stripped and bereaved—had he foretold the autumn, the winter, the spring of sickness and suffering to be gone through—I should have thought this can never be endured. It is over. Branwell, Emily, Anne are gone like dreams, gone as Maria and Elizabeth went twenty years ago.

One by one I have watched them fall asleep on my arm and closed their glazed eyes. I have seen them buried one by one and, thus far, God has upheld me. From my heart I thank Him. . . .

"Haworth parsonage is still a home for me, and not quite a ruined or desolate home either. Papa is there, and two most affectionate and faithful servants, and two old dogs, in their way as faithful and affectionate— Emily's large house-dog which lay at the side of her dying bed, and followed her funeral to the vault, lying in the pew couched at our feet while the burial service was being read—and Anne's little spaniel. The ecstasy of these poor animals when I came in was something singular. At former returns from brief absences they always welcomed me warmly, but not in that strange, heart-touching way. I am certain they thought that, as I was returned, my Sisters were not far behind, but here my sisters will not come no more. Keeper may visit Emily's little bed-room—as he still does day by day—and Flossy may look wistfully round for Anne. They will never see them again, nor shall I—at least the human part of me.

"I must not write so sadly, but how can I help thinking and feeling sadly? In the day-time effort and occupation aid me, but when evening darkens something in my heart revolts against the burden of solitude—the sense of loss and want grows almost too much for me. I am not good or amiable in such moments—I am rebellious—and it is only the thought of my dear Father in the next room, or the kind servants in the kitchen, or some caress from the poor dogs which restores me to softer sentiments and more rational views.

"As to the night—could I do without bed—I would never seek it— waking—I think—sleeping—I dream of them, and I cannot recall them as they were in health—still they appear to me in sickness and suffering. Still my nights were worse after the first shock of Branwell's death—they were terrible then—and the impressions experienced on waking were at that time such as we do not put into language. Worse seemed at hand than was yet endured—in truth worse awaited us.

"All this bitterness must be tasted—perhaps the palate will grow used to the draught in time and find its flavour less acrid—this pain must be undergone—its poignancy—I trust—will be blunted one day" (*Letters, Vol.II* 220, 224).

After an hour's walk, she returned home in the late afternoon with the two dogs trotting along to the back step. She replaced her cloak on the hook by the door, entered the parlour, and took her place at the table where she normally had sat with her sisters. There, she continued to write.

"Lonely as I am, how should I be if Providence had never given me courage to adopt a career, perseverance to plead through two long, weary years with publishers till they admitted me? How should I be with youth past, sisters lost, a resident in a moorland parish where there is not a single educated family? In that case I should have no world at all: the raven, weary of surveying the deluge and without an ark to return to, would be my type. As it is, something like hope and motive sustains me still. . . . The fact is, my work is my best companion—hereafter I look for no great earthly comfort except what congenial occupation can give. For society— long seclusion has in a great measure unfitted me—I doubt whether I should enjoy it if I might have it. Sometimes I think I should, and I thirst for it, but at other times I doubt my capability of pleasing or deriving pleasure. The prisoner in solitary confinement—the toad in the block of marble—all in time shape themselves to their lot. . . .

"The two human beings who understood me and whom I understood are gone . . . but I must have my own way in the matter of writing. The loss of what we possess nearest and dearest to us in this world, produces an effect upon the character: we search out what we have yet left that can support, and when found, we cling to it with a hold of new-strung tenacity.

"The faculty of imagination lifted me when I was sinking, . . . its active exercise has kept my head above water since. Its results cheer me now for I feel they have enabled me to give pleasure to others. I am thankful to God who gave me the faculty, and it is for me a part of my religion to defend this gift and to profit by its possession. . . .

"Whatever now becomes of the work—the occupation of writing it has been a boon to me. It took me out of dark and desolate reality to an unreal but happier region. The worst of it is my eyes are grown somewhat weak and my head somewhat weary and prone to ache with close work. You can write nothing of value unless you give yourself wholly to the theme, and when you so give yourself, you lose appetite and sleep. It cannot be helped" (227, 232, 261, 241).

She finished her letters and looked over the collection of poems lying in front of her on the table. Her life was different now with her sisters forever gone, but the work would continue. She reread the poem 'No Coward Soul is Mine' and jotted down a few words in the margin: "The following are the last lines my sister Emily ever wrote."

Those sombre words still grace the edge of the poem, but what if that line is not what it seems? What if those words hold a clue to a mystery?

The date of the poem's completion is January 2, 1846. Charlotte says those are the last lines Emily wrote, but that statement may be inaccurate because Emily Brontë's apparent last poem, 'Often rebuked, yet always back returning,' is dated nine months later—September 14, 1846. What could account for Charlotte's obvious error? Had she forgotten that Emily had written a final poem in September, or was there another reason for her choice of words? Perhaps this brief notation was an example of her tendency to prevaricate.

In order to explain the discrepancy between the existence of the January and September poems and Charlotte's recollection, scholars believe that she might have written the September poem herself and included it with Emily's poetry. No original manuscript exists to verify if it had been written in Emily's or Charlotte's hand. But why would she misrepresent the work and say the poem was one of her sister's when it was actually one of her own? And why would she add her poem to a group of poetry that was designated as Emily's?

Edward Chitham and Victor Neufeldt believe that Charlotte merely edited the poem, while Charles Hatfield, the editor of *The Complete Poems of Emily Jane Brontë* believes that the feelings expressed in the poem sound more like Charlotte's: "The poem seems to express what may well be Charlotte's thoughts about her sister, but . . . not what Emily would write about herself" (4-5). Janet Gezari, author of *Emily Jane Brontë: The Complete Poems* gives credit for the poem to Charlotte: the poem "may be the product of Charlotte's not incompetent attempt to write a poem that her sister might have written." (See 'Gezari's Commentary' and the 'BrontëBlog' March 22, 2008)

Edward Chitham also refers to another poem attributed to Emily but with Charlotte's words. The poem entitled 'The Prisoner' dated October 9, 1845 speaks of a "nocturnal visitant." Chitham cautions the reader: "we have to be very careful in commenting on the latter passage. At least one well-known Brontë commentator quotes Charlotte's 1850 additions to explain the nature of the visitant. . . . These well-known lines are *not* by Emily Brontë. They show, once again, what Charlotte thought Emily might be feeling" (209).

In 1895, Clement Shorter bought the poetry manuscripts from Charlotte's husband on behalf of Thomas James Wise. Wise became confused over who wrote what because the tiny script was similar and also because some of the poems had no signatures; consequently, "we find Emily's name on the binding of unsigned poems in the handwriting of her sisters and brother" (Hatfield 6).

The confusion around authorship continues when we study Charlotte's editorial changes made in 1850 on, not only Emily's poems, but also on Anne's poetry.

The Brontë biographer Juliet Barker describes Charlotte's edits of her sisters' works as "curious in the extreme," "unnecessary and capricious," and "cavalier." Charlotte selected specific poems, supposedly by Anne, and made changes to them, changes which comprised improvements in rhyme and metre, tenses, titles, and even the inclusion of four to eight lines of her own creation. She made alterations to the originals of the poetry manuscripts, substituting her own lines for Anne's, and created new versions that completely transform the original meaning.

According to Barker, Charlotte removed the saddest parts of the poem and replaced them with less longing. For instance, in a poem that begins, 'I have gone backward in the work,' Charlotte deleted one whole stanza and changed the last line 'And hear a wretch's prayer' to 'Christ, hear my humble prayer.' Barker believes that in one poem the "resulting substitution is a misinterpretation of the original."

She also believes that both Emily and Anne "would have been infuriated by Charlotte's unwarranted interference in their work." This is a completely understandable response. Why would a writer alter not one but two writers' poetic works? Why would Charlotte not respect her sisters' choices and, instead, take seven poems credited to Anne, and eighteen of Emily's and "in virtually every one" make "substantial editorial changes" (654-657)?

The issue of respecting authorship intensifies when she makes her own edits to *Wuthering Heights*, once published as an Ellis Bell book and later as Emily Brontë's masterpiece. Charlotte corrected the novel's typographical errors and punctuation. She also combined short paragraphs to create larger ones and adjusted the style and diction, especially in the speech of Heathcliff's servant Joseph, whose strong, northern, Yorkshire dialect in the first edition proved difficult for southerners to understand.

Charlotte wrote to the publisher remarking on the importance of incorporating these changes into the 1850 edition: "It seems to me advisable to modify the orthography of the old servant Joseph's speeches—for though—as it stands—it exactly renders the Yorkshire accent to a Yorkshire ear—yet I am sure Southerns must find it unintelligible—and thus one of the most graphic characters in the book is lost on them" (*Letters, Vol.II* 479). In a recent edition of *Wuthering Heights*, Helen Small makes reference to these edits: Charlotte seems to alter the Northern dialect "to soften an uncouthness of tongue lest it prove intractable and/or alienating for non-Northern readers," and that her "emendations reflect a comparatively 'normative' or conventionalizing view of style" (xxiii). Perhaps Charlotte thought her poetic and novelistic skills were superior to both younger sisters, but is that sufficient reason to alter her sisters' work?

The question of authorship with regards to *Wuthering Heights* has recurred over the years. Early speculations by some scholars had Branwell writing the novel because of his close affiliation with the men of the village. Emily was essentially a reserved recluse who avoided contact with men, especially the kind whose thick, regional dialect and speech patterns the character of Joseph mimics. She would have needed to be among these men and interested enough to listen in order to learn not only the unschooled speech, but also the brutal and coarse language contained in the novel's dialogue. Perhaps those scholarly instincts of a substitute author were accurate but misdirected.

The confusion intensifies with the mysterious disappearance of the drafts and original manuscripts of only Emily's and Anne's work. While all of Charlotte's manuscripts have survived (and Branwell's writings), papers with early attempts at *Wuthering Heights* and the manuscripts of the Anne Brontë novels *Agnes Grey* and *The Tenant of Wildfell Hall* have never been found. The manuscripts would enable scholars to review the handwriting to resolve the question of authorship once and for all, but the papers have never been recovered. Did Charlotte destroy all her sisters' work, even the manuscripts of their published novels? If she had, why would she feel compelled to do such an extreme act? One question leads to another: How much should one sister modify another's work? Without the original manuscripts can we really be certain of their authorship? With all of Charlotte's amendments, had she in fact written the poetry? And were the edits on *Wuthering Heights*, as Barker says of her changes to the poetry, "curious in the extreme" or was she, as the author, simply amending her own novel?

There had also been a rumour that a first edition copy of *Wuthering Heights* could be traced to Charlotte's husband, Arthur Bell Nicholls, and that it contained alterations in Emily's handwriting. When Sotheby's, the auctioneers, sold the edition in 1969, they reported that the handwriting was Charlotte's not Emily's (Lathbury 'English Matters'). Again, Charlotte's pen crosses paths with the book.

This confusion over Charlotte's words and deeds continually stymied scholars. They concluded that, like a public relations manager, Charlotte carefully controlled the information about Emily and Anne, and agree with Lucasta Miller when she says Charlotte "set the agenda which would turn the Brontës into icons" (25). Certain changes to the works would be in keeping with Charlotte's plan to present a particular reality of her family, but what were her criteria when making those alterations? How did those specific changes satisfy her vision for the Brontë myth? The poems are in Emily's and Anne's handwriting. Charlotte says her younger sisters were the poets, but when placed beside the diary papers, one may wonder if they actually wrote at all. If they merely copied out the lines of her creations, why would they sign them, and why would Charlotte lie and say the poems were theirs?

Charlotte had given misinformation before. Between 1834 and 1846 Emily appears to have written close to two hundred poems. This number includes fragments as well as short poems. By February of 1844, she had copied thirty-one 'personal' poems into a notebook, and into a second notebook had transcribed forty-four Gondal poems. The literary critic Denis Donoghue recognized a discrepancy in Charlotte's words: she "speaks of one volume, but the first printed poems come variously from both sources, the personal poems as well as the Gondal pieces; no distinction is announced. This has caused some confusion" (*Critical Essays* 77).

Charlotte also muddied the waters in relation to the novels and their completion dates. In 1846, a year before *Jane Eyre* appeared, the sisters, using the male pseudonyms of Currer, Ellis, and Acton Bell paid to publish a book of their poetry entitled *Poems*, the "first printed poems" referred to above. Charlotte had submitted the poems to Aylott and Jones, without success; consequently, she offered an alternative method of seeing the work in print: "If you object to publishing the work at your own risk— would you undertake on the Author's account?" (*Letters, Vol.I* 445). All the correspondence relating to the publication is between the editor and Charlotte.

She organized and designed the entire project from beginning to end: "I should like it to be printed in I octavo volume of the same quality of paper and size of type as Moxon's last edition of Wordsworth. The poems will occupy—I think from 200-250 pages" (449).

She continued to oversee the specifications: "I select the long primer type for the poems—I do not think it would be necessary to adopt a stouter paper nor would lines round the pages be required" (453).

She later wrote, "There will be no Preface to the Poems—the blank leaf may be filled up by a table of contents which I suppose the Printer will prepare—It appears the volume will be a thinner one than was calculated on" (464).

When the book came out, she sent Aylott and Jones the money to pay for advertisements in various publications, and by July of 1846 wondered about the book's sales: "Will you favour me with a line, stating whether *any*, or how many copies have yet been sold." One thousand copies were printed, and in 1848 when Charlotte's publisher Smith Elder bought the remaining stock, only two copies had been sold (486).

Charlotte's attention to detail is apparent when dealing with her work, but she suffered a lapse in accuracy in a letter to Aylott and Jones dated 6 April 1846. After they had published *Poems*, Charlotte wondered if Aylott and Jones might be interested in further works by the Bells. She wrote that the "relatives" were now working on three novels: "C.E. & A. Bell are now preparing for the Press a work of fiction—consisting of three distinct and unconnected tales which may be published either together as a work of 3 vols. of the ordinary novel-size, or separately as single vols—as shall be deemed most advisable" (461). In this case, the editors were not interested and declined.

Charlotte suggests that the Bell works were in progress, but the novels had already been finished by then. According to later editors: "All three novels must have been well on the way to completion by the date of this letter," even though, no one can say with certainty when *Wuthering Heights* was started. In Charlotte's 'Biographical Notice of Ellis and Acton Bell' in the 1850 edition of *Wuthering Heights*, she "misleadingly implies that the novels were begun only after the failure of the *Poems*" (461). In both cases, she gave inconsistent dates of completion.

Was she trying to set up believable timelines to fit her future version of events? As it is, scholars can only guess at the months when *Wuthering Heights* was probably written, but their calculations could be years off the actual date, especially if Charlotte was rearranging the chronology.

No one disputes that Charlotte carefully crafted a mythology around the Bell brothers. Not until 1850 did she reveal their true gender. *Wuthering Heights* and the Anne Brontë novel *The Tenant of Wildfell Hall* received harsh criticism for their coarse language, violence, and rough depiction of uncultivated Yorkshire men. In her 'Biographical Notice,' Charlotte tries to soften the critics' impression of her sisters when she explains that they were both uneducated, village girls who lived in a remote area where their limited experience exposed them to "rugged moorland squires who have grown up untaught and unchecked, except by mentors as harsh as themselves."

Their depiction of unbridled, passionate natures and rough speech came from witnessing rustic temperaments let loose through drink and aggression, but were her sisters really observing this behaviour or was Charlotte? The village of Haworth in Yorkshire's west riding, Charlotte explains, "is moorish, and wild, and knotty as the root of heath," so her sisters simply wrote what they knew, but the diary papers show two young women who would have avoided that wild world of drunk and aggressive men, and who were absorbed in their Gondal saga.

Apparently, according to Charlotte, they were simple country girls who wrote from instinct, not design, when they created horrors of darkness and, in the case of Emily, a masterpiece both vivid and bleak that still required the assistance of Charlotte's correcting hand. Perhaps the younger sisters were simple country geniuses whose older sister felt it her duty to fuss with their literary works or, perhaps, Charlotte's intrusion into the poetry and novels is consistent with a deeper truth.

The questions continue when confronted with the unusual circumstance of Emily's and Anne's missing manuscripts. Charlotte was diligent and responsible about controlling most of the details surrounding the writings, which included saving Branwell's and her own work, so how could she have been careless enough to misplace a significant body of writing? Nothing exists of these works to help clear up the mystery of authorship. Was this a careless or jealous act, or an intentional strategy?

Could Charlotte's note in the margin of the January poem be a clue? It reads, "The following are the last lines my sister Emily ever wrote." Charlotte is fully aware of her words and chooses the exact term to express her meaning. She does not say, this is the last poem, but that "the following are the last *lines*."

What if Emily wrote out lines of poetry for Charlotte? If so, the note would be accurate: Emily never actually composed the poetry, only wrote out lines. Charlotte's poems but Emily's lines. The poetry manuscripts have survived and show Emily's ink-smudged papers and awkward penmanship and Anne's, at times, illegible hand. Had Charlotte assigned poems with particular themes to each sister? Poetry would certainly be easier to copy than would an entire novel.

Edward Chitham notes that Emily's output of poems in 1843 decreases substantially: "One reason for Emily's low poetic output during parts of 1843-4 must have been her involvement in domestic chores" (159). Another explanation could be that this period coincides with the months when Charlotte was in Brussels. Perhaps the poems Emily wrote out sporadically in 1843 were the ones that Charlotte had left for her to transcribe.

Charlotte returned to Haworth in January of 1844, and Barker points out that Emily began writing poetry again at that time: "In February 1844, she began to collect her poems together . . . and copying them out into one notebook which she entitled 'Gondal Poems' and another which she left untitled. In fact, there was no hard and fast distinction between the two, for Emily does not appear to have stuck to her intention to include only personal poems in the second notebook." Barker adds that this period of time "was a fruitful one, inspiring some of her most lyrical poetry."

It could be a coincidence that Emily's writing had decreased while Charlotte is away and then starts up again upon her sister's return, but one could argue that Emily's "copying" involved writing down Charlotte's poetry. Emily's lines but Charlotte's poems: "Throughout 1844 she continued to produce a steady stream of poems" (435) that were some of her best work, but was it Emily's "lyrical poetry" or Charlotte's?

The notebook contains 31 poems dated from November 5, 1838 to January 2, 1846. The last poem 'No Coward Soul is Mine' is mentioned above, regarding Charlotte's claim that these were the last lines Emily wrote. Of these poems numbers 20-30 are included in the Bell book *Poems*. Number 22 dated February 10, 1844 entitled 'My Comforter' is shown below. The speaker addresses a loving spirit that resides within her imaginative world and brings solace and calm to her "resentful mood." She relies on this source of peace to comfort her when she feels most alone:

My Comforter

Well has thou spoken—and yet not taught
A feeling strange or new;
Thou hast but raised a latent thought,
A cloud-closed beam of sunshine brought
To gleam in open view.

Deep down—concealed within my soul
That light lies hid from men,
Yet glows unquenched—though shadows roll,
Its gentle ray cannot control—
About the sullen den.

Was I not vexed, in these gloomy ways
To walk unlit so long?
Around me, wretches uttering praise,

Or howling o'er their hopeless days,
And each with Frenzy's tongue—

A Brotherhood of misery,
With smiles as sad as sighs;
Their madness daily maddening me,
And turning into agony
The Bliss before my eyes

So stood I, in Heaven's glorious sun
And in the glare of hell
My spirit drank a mingled tone
Of seraph's song and demon's moan—
What my soul bore my soul alone
Within its self may tell.

Like a soft air above a sea
Tossed by the tempest's stir—
A thaw-wind melting quietly
The snowdrift on some wintery lea:
No—what sweet thing can match with thee,
My thoughtful comforter?

And yet a little longer speak,
Calm this resentful mood,
And while the savage heart grows meek,
For other token do not seek,
But let the tear upon my cheek
Evince my gratitude.

During 1844, after Charlotte had returned from Brussels, she "remained stupefied by low spirits" (Barker 437). The despondent tone of 'The Comforter' certainly matches someone in low spirits.

Charlotte wrote to her friend Ellen Nussey that she could not leave Haworth to seek a life of her own because her father, now aging, depended upon her: "he is losing his sight. I have felt for some months that I ought not to be away from him, and I feel now that it would be selfish to leave him (at least so long as Branwell and Anne are absent) in order to pursue selfish interests of my own. With the help of God I will try to deny myself in this matter and to wait."

She was also upset over leaving Monsieur Heger who had been her kind and non-judgmental instructor in Brussels: "I suffered much before I left Brussels. I think however long I live I shall not forget what the parting with Mons Heger cost me. It grieved me so much to grieve him who has been so true and kind and disinterested a friend."

She continues to express her sadness to Ellen: "there are times now when it appears to me as if all my ideas and feelings except a few friendships and affections are changed from what they used to be— something in me which used to be enthusiasm is tamed down and broken—I have fewer illusions—what I wish for now is active exertion—a stake in life. Haworth seems such a lonely, quiet spot, buried away from the world. I no longer regard myself as young, indeed I shall soon be 28, and it seems as if I ought to be working and braving the rough realities of the world as other people do. It is however my duty to restrain this feeling at present and I will endeavour to do so" (*The Letters, Vol.I* 341).

At the same time, Emily was also in low spirits due to the death of her cat Tiger, and her mood may have inspired her to write 'The Comforter,' but the contrast in tone in both sisters' writing and the depth of emotion displayed in Charlotte's letter suggest otherwise. Emily refers to Tiger's death in her diary paper: "We have got Flossey, got and lost Tiger—lost the Hawk. Nero which with the geese was given away and is doubtless dead for when I came back from Brussels I enquired on all hands and could hear nothing of him—Tiger died early last year—Keeper and Flossey are well also the canary acquired 4 years since." The loss of a pet can be traumatic and cause a significant period of grief, but Emily's brief recollection of her pet is only to record its death. We learn nothing of its personality, its physical appearance, or its activity while alive.

On the other hand, Charlotte's sadness in her letter comes from her realization that her life is at a crossroads and coincides with deep yearning for a "thoughtful comforter." The poet who wrote in 1844, "What my soul bore my soul alone / Within its self may tell" had suffered deeply and was harbouring the kind of sorrow that comes from the loss of a human relationship recently severed.

The question arises again. Did Charlotte write all the novels and the poetry? Was the creation of the Bell brothers an elaborate hoax Charlotte conjured and if so, why? And why has it lasted over a hundred and sixty years without being discovered?

9 FREEMASONRY

In order to know what motivated Charlotte to create this hoax, we need to look closely at her language. Her subterfuge began when she borrowed legends and rituals from her brother's band of Freemasons. Was this the "Brotherhood of misery" that she refers to in 'My Comforter' when she writes, 'Their madness daily maddening me'? It could be. As we shall see, she deliberately uses their signs and ceremonies to create her own elaborate system of symbols and allegory inside her narratives.

According to "The History of Freemasonry in Haworth," at one time, Freemasonry was so popular the town had four lodges. Haworth boasted two Craft Lodges: "The Prince George" and "The Three Graces," one Royal Arch Chapter: "The Brunswick" and two Knight Templars' "encampments" called "The Brunswick" and "The Plains of Mamre." "The Three Graces Lodge, the Brunswick Chapter, and The Plains of Mamre Preceptory are still held there, but the Prince George Lodge was removed from Haworth to an outlying area in 1812" (Scott). In the 1830s, some of the men of Haworth would have been members in both the Three Graces Lodge No. 506 (later No. 408) and the Knights Templar Plains of Mamre Lodge No. 89.

The ceremonies and secrecy would have inspired a certain curiosity from the Brontë sisters, especially from Charlotte. Branwell would have relished the opportunity to let a few secrets drop in front of such a captive audience. The Masons were church trustees as well as friends and acquaintances of Reverend Brontë, so they were regular visitors at the parsonage, where Charlotte would have access to their conversations while serving tea or listening from the hallway.

Boisterous, loud men conversing about brother Masons and Lodge activity might attract an inquisitive female eavesdropper. Perhaps she was hearing tales of heartless greed among the wealthy, powerful men of Haworth Township.

If her brother Branwell had not been a Master Mason, and if friends and acquaintances of Reverend Brontë had not been Masons and had not visited the parsonage on a regular basis, and if John Brown their closest neighbour and friend had not been Worshipful Master for several years, one may wonder where Charlotte would have heard about the Freemasons and their secret ceremonies, but the proximity of her ears to their mouths, together with the strong probability that Branwell not only left his copies of the Masonic Constitution, by-laws, history, and rituals in full view and within easy access, as well as the likelihood that he proudly demonstrated the handshakes and gestures while confiding passwords and emblems make her awareness of the secrets highly believable, especially considering their close relationship and Branwell's compulsion to show off his superior knowledge.

These reasons alone would allow a reader to presume that, due to the number of Masonic terms and specific stylized rituals found in the Brontë works, Charlotte knew her Freemasonry as well as she knew her Shakespeare and her Bible. Additionally, however, versions of the ritual instructions, history, and symbolic elements that were originally passed down orally from antiquity were now being diffused in pamphlets to enlighten the brethren who wanted to study the Craft's principles and precepts. Also, between 1675 and 1793, in excess of forty-five publications had circulated exposing the verbatim ceremonies, rituals, allegories, and secrets of Masonry. By the 1840s, Charlotte could, therefore, have come across a pamphlet or publication that would have enlightened her further about the mysteries of Freemasonry. In whatever way she absorbed Masonic teachings, her system of clues confirms she knew them well. In order to understand her method and the dynamic organization of her intricate, enigmatic universe, we first must lift the veil and catch a glimpse of this fraternity to see those secrets that appealed to Charlotte's imagination.

(See Freemasonry sources following "Works Cited" under the heading "Freemasonry References.")

Freemasonry has its roots in antiquity and borrows from the mysteries of Egypt. It uses allegory, focusing on the tools and terms of architecture to teach its members moral truths, and is described in Mackey's *Encyclopedia of Freemasonry* as "a peculiar system of morality, veiled in allegory and illustrated by symbols." The *Encyclopedia* also states that Freemasonry is a "science which is engaged in the search after Divine Truth, and which employs symbolism as its method of instruction." Early systems used symbolism and rituals to teach morality, and also celebrated the soul's immortality through a rebirth after a ritual death. An initiate to this fraternity is admitted after specific trials and tribulations, and ascends through the ranks of the society when he completes all three degrees. The degree rituals are the basis of their ceremonies that are formed around the legend of Hiram Abiff.

The Masons central legend deals with Hiram Abiff, the father of Freemasonry. He was the principle architect on the construction of King Solomon's Temple, and his death became part of the history of the third degree rebirth ceremony.

As was his custom, every day at noon, Hiram would pray in his *sanctum sanctorum*. When he finished on this particular day, three impatient Fellow Crafts came up to him and demanded he tell them the Master mason's secret, which would enable them to earn more money. Unafraid but disturbed by their impudence, Hiram refused to divulge a word until the work on the Temple had been completed.

One of the Fellow Crafts was so angered by the Master's refusal that he lost control and slit Hiram's throat. The second man hit him hard with a square against his left breast, and the third ruffian struck Hiram on the head with his setting maul. Hiram Abiff collapsed and died. Unfortunately, the three men had killed Hiram without learning the secret of the Master.

When King Solomon found the body, he lifted it up and whispered a word into Hiram's ear to act as a substitute until the secrets could be found, and to mark the continuation of the secrets. It was a word like Machaben or Mah-Hah-Bone. But they would use other words for passwords like Boaz, Shibboleth, Tubal Cain, even Noah and Hiram. When a Mason becomes a Master in the third degree, the legend of Hiram Abiff is being played out through ritual. He also learns the secret lost word, the word the Fellow Crafts had wanted, but if he reveals what occurs inside the Lodge, he could suffer a similar fate to the one experienced by the three ruffians who killed Hiram Abiff, or worse: he could have his throat slit, his tongue cut out, or he could be buried up to his head at low tide.

Some Masons believe the roots of Freemason rituals began in Scotland, while others say they originated in ancient Egypt. In the Egyptian origins, the Hierophant, or usher, guided the candidate through the dark before showing him the holy volume of secret hieroglyphics. The

Masons' blindfold over the initiate's eyes in the first degree ceremony mirrors this aspect of the rite. In Egyptian and Masonic rituals, when the apprentice comes out of the darkness, when the blindfold is removed, he sees the "material light," which symbolizes his newfound wisdom (Sacred Text).

The Freemasons also borrow both the symbolic death and figurative resurrection or rebirth from ancient initiations. As in those past ceremonies, the Masons viewed the risen brother's attainment of wisdom as his acceptance of the concept of immortality and, in order to present this information to the initiate and share the secrets of the order, he must be willing to leave his old life of ignorance behind. Through an allegorical ritual, the Masons place the Fellow Craft in a bed or coffin where he must stay confined in the darkness for a short time, and in the frenzy of the ritual, the frightened initiate might imagine seeing a ghost or a celestial being, which is said to bring a message from the world of the spirit. The initiate may experience some dread and then faint, but when he regains consciousness he arises from this false death, happy to know he has passed the test, has learned that life exists after death, and is now enlightened about his own immortality. The rebirth ritual also refers to the quest for the lost secret buried with Hiram Abiff, the master. The man, having received a divine truth, rises from his coffin, reborn as a Master Mason. He has successfully experienced a metaphorical death to mirror the legendary death of Hiram Abiff.

The legend with its bloody origins and the concept of ritual death would have awakened Charlotte's imagination. She would be drawn to the symbols as well as to the allegory of an initiate who, after being admitted to a secret society, must experience trials and tribulations before ascending the ranks from Entered Apprentice to Fellow Craft through to Master Mason. The legend of the three degrees could form a helpful structure upon which to build her stories, and the symbol of rebirth through a Masonic death could signify a turning point for her heroine, or perhaps an immortal could make an appearance as an actual ghost to help a character through the next phase of a ritual. When *Jane Eyre* exploded on the public, critics acknowledged its mystery and enchantment but failed to see the hidden mortar that bound Jane to the book's dark Masonic secrets.

10 BROTHER JANE

When Charlotte Brontë drew on the symbols and legends of the Freemasons, she had numerous elements from which to choose. She knew the rites and rituals well enough to adapt them to her needs in her novels, but she appropriated the Freemason's symbols and methods of allegorical instruction to accommodate her desire to tell the story of a woman's rise in the hierarchy of a fraternal society that excluded female members. With Jane Eyre, Charlotte Brontë is able to defy convention and speak her mind. She wants a small, unattractive woman to rise in a man's world, through the assistance of a good education, both scholastic and moral, faith in her own inner voice, and a responsible attitude. From Brontë's perspective, a Victorian woman, and a woman of any age, can have a full life, not by being content with a tranquil existence, but by experiencing action.

Brontë understood firsthand the plight of a woman's duty. Through Jane she writes in chapter twelve: "Women are supposed to be very calm generally: but women feel just as men feel; they need exercise for their faculties, and a field for their efforts as much as their brothers do; they suffer from too rigid a restraint, too absolute a stagnation, precisely as men would suffer, and it is narrow-minded in their more privileged fellow-creatures to say that they ought to confine themselves to making puddings and knitting stockings, to playing on the piano and embroidering bags. It is thoughtless to condemn them, or laugh at them, if they seek to do more or learn more than custom has pronounced necessary for their sex." Her use of Masonic symbols in *Jane Eyre* suggests she is advocating a place for creative and active women within the realm of men.

Jane, a poor, plain orphan struggles to assert her individuality through a series of personal trials. Set against a backdrop of a society that measures a woman's success in terms of familial connections, economic status, and beauty, Jane seeks the freedom to define herself outside these societal constraints. She must overcome the barriers to her independence and establish personal values that enable her to express her identity. She actively transforms the conventional definition of women as humble and submissive creatures into a conception of women as intelligent and passionate human beings.

In chapter one, Jane is a ten-year-old orphan living at Gateshead Hall with her horrid Aunt Reed and her three equally horrid children. The eldest boy, the Master of the Hall, torments Jane with verbal and physical abuse because he resents her existence in his house. With Jane's protector Uncle John deceased for nine years, she has had to defend herself against the boy's attacks. When he throws a book at her head and draws blood, she "started" with "a cry of alarm" and feels compelled to strike back, a gesture that results in the servants ushering her into the dreaded red-room for her punishment. As they do, Jane states, "I was borne upstairs." Could this be the beginning of a rebirth ceremony?

The Red-Room at Gateshead Hall

The red-room is described as "a square chamber" and one of the largest and stateliest rooms in the mansion, but for a child, the gloomy room inspires fear. The room and its main piece of furniture suggest a shrine fit for a patriarch of King Solomon's stature: "A bed supported on massive pillars of mahogany, hung with curtains of deep red damask, stood out like a tabernacle in the centre," and red curtains draped across two large windows keep out the light and retain the solemnity of the bedroom.

She also describes the room as "chill," "silent," "remote," and "solemn." These strongly suggestive elements create an atmosphere of ritual that coalesce in a secret drawer in a mahogany cabinet where a miniature portrait of her dead Uncle Reed—the eminent being of Gateshead—lies hidden among papers and jewels. As the daylight fades, all warmth leaves the red-room, and she says she "grew by degrees cold as stone."

Before she can shake the image of the ghostly presence of her deceased uncle from her mind, a light appears on the wall where it "quivered" over Jane's head. She believes the light is "a herald of some coming vision from another world," and the horror of the event causes an outburst of fright similar to that of an initiate's fear that a celestial being is bringing the message of immortality. She records her fear: "My heart beat thick, my head grew hot; a sound filled my ears, which I deemed the rushing of wings; something seemed near me; I was oppressed, suffocated: endurance broke down." In the frenzy of the moment, she emits a kind of primal scream, which brings the servants and her Aunt Reed to the room, but when she learns she must remain in this chamber even longer, she experiences a form of death as she faints: "I suppose I had a species of fit: unconsciousness closed the scene."

A Symbolic Lodge?

The silent and solemn red-room scene, with its sense of "dreary consecration," symbolizes the Masonic Lodge in general and a Chamber of Reflection in particular. Held in reserve for ceremonies, the Lodge is where the Masons meet and hold their rites after the room has been consecrated. The red-room is rarely inhabited and, as a "solemn" room that contains a mirror, could it be a substitute for a Masonic Chamber of Reflection? The initiate is enclosed inside this sombre room for the purpose of meditating on whether he is a fit candidate for initiation into Masonic society. Brontë describes the room as a chamber when she writes that Jane's Uncle had died in the room: "In this chamber he breathed his last." In the Chamber, the candidate can ponder on questions presented to him and use these to help him think about his life and his future. The mirror in the Chamber of Reflection symbolizes the contemplation of his inner being.

Jane stares at her image in the large mirror and sees a "visionary hollow." The mirror reflects a "strange little figure," one with frightened eyes that "had the effect of a real spirit." Jane then questions her very existence and wonders why she must endure the constant abuse at the hands of the Reed family: "Why was I always suffering, always browbeaten, always accused, for ever condemned?" She asks herself why she was never able to please them. Her questions involve trying to understand herself and to explain her identity as "scapegoat of the nursery." This characterization will change as she grows and develops throughout the story.

Red and White Decor

The carpet in the red room, like the curtains, continues the theme of red, as does a red cloth that covers a table at the foot of the bed. The white bedspread and white pillows compliment the shade of white in an easy chair and footstool placed at the head of the bed. For Jane, the chair looks like "a pale throne." In Freemasonry, red and white have symbolic meaning for the initiate. Red, their symbol of zeal and fervency, and white, their symbol for purity, together represent the two qualities necessary for the initiate to be successful in the search for truth. Jane must advance with a fervent desire to discover her true self-image, but remain pure in her search for truth. Red and white predominate in Mr. Reed's chamber.

A Consecrated Room

The red-room has "a sense of dreary consecration." Like ancient temples and modern churches, Masonic Lodges have always been consecrated. The Grand Master performs the rite of consecration when the Lodge is said to be in "ample form." The throne-like chair at the head of the bed resembles the throne of the Worshipful Master, and Brontë uses the word "ample" when she describes it as "an ample cushioned easy-chair."

The Altar

The altar is one of the symbols always used at the Lodge. Masons describe their altar as a kind of table intended to support the Holy Bible, the Square, and Compasses, which they call "furniture." All Lodges are also equipped with a throne-like, high back chair, a pedestal, and a kneeling stool. The chair in which the Grand Master sits during the ceremonies is called a throne. The white chair with the white footstool beside Mr. Reed's bed is like "a pale throne." The red-room, a predominantly red and white room with a throne, altar, and kneeling stool could be Brontë's rendition of a Masonic Lodge.

Sanctum Sanctorum

For Masons, the Lodge represents the very solemn place found in ancient temples. The *sanctum sanctorum* of a temple or the Holy of Holies is supported by four pillars and surrounded by veils and symbolizes the consecrated tomb of the risen god, a sacred room housing the Ark of the Covenant. The Lodge itself was once considered an Ark, like Noah's Ark, but in later years the Masonic Ark became a box that contains scrolls, jewels, parchments, and parts of their Sacred Law.

Thus, inside a tabernacle, the *sanctum sanctorum* acts like the emblem of a tomb and holds the image of the god or eminent being contained in the Ark. The image of Jane's Uncle John is found in a miniature portrait kept in the secret drawer with stored parchments and a jewel box. Like Mr. Reed's secret drawer, the Masonic Ark is a form of wooden box that contains warrants and jewels of the Lodge.

In the solemn red-room, the bed, supported by pillars and surrounded by red curtains, stands out like a tabernacle. John Reed's bedroom is like a shrine: "it was in this chamber he breathed his last . . . and, since that day, a sense of dreary consecration had guarded it from frequent intrusion." She suggests that the miniature portrait of Mr. Reed, a representation of the master of the house, contains the secret of the red-room. Could the red-room, a grand chamber, not only be a Chamber of Reflection but also the *sanctum sanctorum* of Gateshead Hall? Whatever the secret may be, the room had cast a spell which Brontë says, "kept it so lonely in spite of its grandeur." A tomb can be a fairly lonely place, but is something else hidden inside that secret drawer that gives a clue to the room's grandeur? This mystery would not be solved until much later.

Significant Words

Brontë's method of connecting her reader to her hidden agenda involves dropping clues in her narrative through her diction. She uses "scapegoat" to suggest ritual sacrifice, while "tabernacle" and "consecration" charge the atmosphere of a chamber, dedicated to a patriarch, with religious solemnity, especially when his image is housed in a secret ark; red, the colour of blood, combined with white, the colour of innocence conjures an image of a blood sacrifice as well. She says that Jane "grew by degrees cold as stone." The words "degrees" and "stone" are obvious and relevant terms to a Freemason.

The final point to be made about her experience in the red-room is that at the beginning of chapter three, upon awakening from her faint, Jane feels she has been "raised," and overhears the secret "scraps" of the servants' whisperings as they discuss her ordeal. They say "something passed her," which alludes to the Masonic term used when the Worshipful Master "passes" the initiate from one degree to the next, and there were "three loud raps on the chamber door," which also signifies the Masonic opening of a ceremony and could indicate Jane's second step is about to begin as she heads off to school. The "scraps" of words could be a sign that she is hearing passwords, bits of syllables whose meanings are still unclear. The light that appears quivering over her uncle's grave, alludes to the spirit rising from the nether world, to visit the initiate in his symbolic vault or grave, with a message of immortality.

After the Initiation

Jane's behaviour changes after the red-room incident. She becomes more assertive and willing to express herself, but her confidence still surprises her: "it seemed as if my tongue pronounced words without my will consenting to their utterance: something spoke out of me over which I had no control." She speaks from her heart when she chastises her Aunt Reed for punishing her in such a cruel manner: "my soul began to expand, to exult, with the strangest sense of freedom, of triumph, I ever felt. It seemed as if an invisible bond had burst, and that I had struggled out into unhoped-for liberty." In a similar manner to an Entered Apprentice learning passwords and secret signs, Jane has acquired a new way of speaking, and the password that she learns and which will literally provide the means to pass from Gateshead to a new life fifty miles away is the word "school."

The point Brontë makes throughout the novel is that a strong, intelligent woman like Jane Eyre, who is also pure of heart, should be able to develop her true character and fulfil her desires in this world regardless of her sex, so she sends her heroine on a strange journey through the ranks of Freemasonry that has begun with a form of initiation rite in the red-room.

11 JANE GETS THE THIRD DEGREE

Women living in 1847, at the time *Jane Eyre* was published, would have been subjected to the abuse associated with being powerless. A married woman had no right to her husband's property, even if she contributed her own inheritance to the family's worth. The man could and often did sign away their combined possessions when he willed everything to a male heir. Education for girls was limited. A smart woman would be viewed unwomanly, since social custom dictated that a woman focus her interests solely on what benefits the man.

Through Jane, in chapter twelve, Brontë voices her opinion that women need to be industrious and should be encouraged to pursue a life of activity: "It is vain to say human beings ought to be satisfied with tranquility: they must have action, and they will make it if they cannot find it. Millions are condemned to a stiller doom than mine, and millions are in silent revolt against their lot. Nobody knows how many rebellions besides political rebellions ferment in the masses of life which people earth."

Brontë's adoption of the Masonic symbols and rituals originated in her dealings with a few of the Haworth Masons. At this point, her level of clues are too opaque to discern what those actions were, but we can deduce that they provided a strong incentive for her to borrow from their boys' club. Only as we lift more veils of secrecy will we discover that her motivation derived from something much darker and sinister, and that her silent revolt and rebellion fermented for several years. For now, we need to see the patterns hidden inside her carefully constructed schema of her Masonic worldview in order to get closer to drawing back the next veil.

Jane leaves Gateshead Hall to attend Lowood, a school for girls based on the actual school that Charlotte, Emily and their two older sisters had attended. In July of 1824, at the age of ten, the eldest sister Maria and nine-year-old Elizabeth entered the Clergy Daughters' School in Cowan Bridge. Charlotte, aged eight, followed the next month, and six-year-old Emily joined them in November. The elder sisters suffered terrible physical hardships, which included poor heating, inadequate protection from the cold or from typhoid, and such insufficient nourishment that their health quickly deteriorated and brought on their early deaths from tuberculosis. In May of 1825, Maria died. That same month Elizabeth came home to Haworth and died in June from the same disease. Reverend Brontë feared the worst for his other two daughters and brought them home in June before they endured the same fate as Maria and Elizabeth. Charlotte drew on these tragic experiences and deplorable conditions at the school to paint a bleak picture in *Jane Eyre*, and she interjects subtle references to Freemasonry that fit her overall design.

Jane's Years at Lowood School

Near the end of chapter five, when Jane arrives at Lowood, she stands at the front door of the school and sees a stone tablet with an inscription carved on its face. Part of the inscription reads, "Lowood Institution. Let your light so shine before men that they may see your good works, and glorify your Father which is in heaven." The quotation is from the Bible, Matthew 5: 16. Jane studies the words over and over again, and feels an explanation belongs to them, but is unable to penetrate their import. She stands "pondering the signification of 'Institution,' and endeavouring to make out a connection between the first words and the verse of Scripture." She is trying to interpret the message signified by the word "Institution" in its relationship to the Biblical verse.

The Masons class their fraternity as an Institution built on "the great principles of courtesy and fraternal kindness, which are at the very foundation of our Institution." Their motto happens to be, "Let your light so shine before men that they may see your good works and glorify your Father which is in heaven," the same words from Matthew 5: 16. The Masonic motto is inscribed over the door of Lowood Institution, and Jane concentrates on these words to understand their "signification." Brontë wants her readers to do the same. Also, a "significant word" for Freemasons is what they refer to as a "sign-making word," which means that the word itself is a sign; consequently, secret words become significant when the Mason understands their deeper meaning. For Brontë, "Institution" is a significant word, which is why she says Jane ponders "the signification" of the word. By stating it in this way she is pointing out the hidden relevance of "Institution," especially when in connection to the verse in Matthew. She is also using her own words as "significant" signs to guide her readers.

Jane Learns a Craft

Jane's education at Lowood provides her with the tools that will help her in life, much like a Fellow Craft receives tools to help him in his masonry trade: the Fellow Craft is "raised" to this next degree "to contemplate the intellectual faculty." After several years, Jane "grows by degrees" and excels at Lowood, even though she has had to overcome the difficult trials of a friend's death, and the public ridicule from the miserly Mr. Brocklehurst who runs the school. Brontë describes Brocklehurst in Masonic terms as "a black pillar" and a "piece of architecture" that, with his sable coat and big teeth, resembles a wolf, a symbol, to be explained later, that she uses for the Masons. Jane's education continues throughout the hardships, especially with the help of her favourite teacher, Maria Temple. (Masons use the word "temple" as a symbol of their lodge.) After eight years of contemplating her "intellectual faculty," Jane is successful enough as a teacher to advertise herself as a governess and venture into her next trial at Thornfield Hall where she meets Edward Rochester and comes face to face with a brother Mason.

A Mason and a Ritual at Thornfield

In chapter twenty, Jane experiences another form of ritual on the third floor of Thornfield Hall. She must participate in a ritual that introduces her to another trial that involves a Mason brother. Rochester asks Jane to help him administer aid to one of his guests who is wounded and bleeding in a room on the third story. Inside the room, curtains are drawn and the room is dark, but Jane sees antique tapestries on the walls, an armchair by the head of the bed, a washstand, a basin of water, a large cabinet with the portraits of the twelve apostles set in relief, and a man slumped in the armchair bleeding from his side. She also notices a large door leading to another apartment where a mad woman snarls and gnashes her teeth and threatens to burst into the bloody scene. Jane deduces that the woman has stabbed the young man. Rochester hands Jane a candle and instructs her to sponge the blood and put smelling salts under the man's nose if he begins to pass out. The only rule that must be obeyed is that Jane and the man must remain silent during their ordeal: "Remember!—no conversation." Rochester leaves her locked in the room with this stranger while he hurries to get the doctor.

A Vow of Silence

Jane remains mute while locked "in a mystic cell" that reminds us of the red-room, but this ritual involves blood and water. She enacts a kind of ritualistic cleansing as she looks up at the portraits of Luke and St. John on the cabinet, but feels no consolation when she believes Satan is near. The face of Judas seems to come alive and threaten "a revelation of the arch-traitor—of Satan himself—in his subordinate's form." She must "listen as well as watch: to listen for the movements of the wild beast or the fiend in yonder side den." Satan and a fiend lurk near as she participates in this pagan ritual. She hears "three sounds at three long intervals,—a step creak, a momentary renewal of the snarling, canine noise, and a deep human groan." She must perform certain tasks: stay at her post, keep an eye on the man, and continue dipping her hand in the bloody water. As well, she tries to relieve his mental suffering by keeping him calm, alleviate his physical discomfort by giving him salts, and prevent the blood loss by dabbing the sponge to his wound. Is Jane helping a man take his next "step" in the degree ceremonies? During these tasks, she repeats the word "must" four times: "I must keep to my post," "I must watch," "I must dip my hand," and "I must see the light."

In Mackey's *Encyclopedia of Freemasonry*, regarding the right to relieve a man's suffering, he quotes passages from the Old Charges of 1722: if you discover a man "to be a true and genuine brother . . . you must relieve him if you can, or else direct him how he may be relieved. You must employ him some days, or else recommend him to be employed." The supplier of the relief, however, does not need to exceed his capabilities: "your relief must be 'without material injury to yourself or family'." The Mason is compelled to relieve a fellow brother's suffering. He *must* help his Mason brother, as Jane does, to the best of his abilities.

Jane's Thoughts

Jane's progress in the Masonic hierarchy can be determined from her thoughts. Rather than question her own identity as she does in the red-room, she tries to understand the circumstances around this stranger. What crime or mystery was occurring in Rochester's mansion that required her to be with a bleeding man in the dead of night, and why had the man experienced this treachery at the hands of the mad woman behind the door? She wonders why his arrival at Thornfield had disturbed Rochester so deeply, especially when the man is timid and submissive to Rochester. She asks, "Why had the mere name of this unresisting individual fallen on him as a thunderbolt might fall on an oak?" The mere name shocks Rochester. The name has some secret power. Brontë wants us to read and look as we continue through the story, just as Jane listens and watches as she progresses through the ritual. What is the man's name?

A Brother Mason

The man's name is a strong clue—Richard Mason. In *Jane Eyre*, Mason is a relative, an actual brother of Bertha, the woman on the other side of the door, but in the circumstance of this ritual he would be subordinate and "submissive" to Rochester, the Master. Jane, therefore, takes part in a ritual with a brother Mason that mimics a death when the man's fear of dying and his terror of the fiend bursting into the ritual appear "to paralyse him." Instead of a mystical visitation from a wise being, Jane and Mason expect the intrusion of a "wild beast" or "fiend." The fear of death adds to the terror.

More Masonic Symbols

Rochester, as symbolic and literal Master, governs the rituals and decides when they shall begin and end. When he returns to the locked room, he draws the curtain to allow in the light of dawn that is "beginning to brighten the east." The Masons consider the east sacred because in ancient times the sun was the subject of adoration. The east is the emblem of light and a symbol of mental illumination, as well as the object that reminds the Mason brother of that intellectual light of which he is in constant search. He compliments Jane on her courage: "You have passed a strange night, Jane," and understands her fear of being alone with Mason while the beast in the den threatened to break through the door, but he tells her that he had the key and would never have left her, his "lamb" in danger "so near a wolf's den, unguarded." Her reward for undergoing this test is to gain wisdom from her Master in the form of a disclosure of facts: Rochester shares a history of his past with her, a confidence that brings them closer together.

Blood and Water

The ceremony in the locked room also unites Jane with brother Mason through the mixing of blood and water. This ablution ritual has its roots in the legend of Hiram Abiff and the construction of King Solomon's Temple. After both the completion of the Temple and Hiram's death when the Word was lost, the cubical stone, or corner stone of the Temple, sheds the sacred elements of blood and water as a symbol of the sufferers' anguish over the loss of the Word, the essence of masonry. In ancient mysteries, the shedding of blood was necessary to pardon sins so, in the case of Richard Mason, he was indirectly about to expose the secret of Thornfield Hall by visiting his insane sister on the third floor. She attacks him for his "sin," and Jane assists in the remission of his inadvertent transgression against Rochester.

Fellow Witnesses

Brontë places the cabinet with the portraits of the apostles in the room. She is telling us that the ritual with its blood and water is similar to a Christian rite, but that the reader must not mistake the pagan aspects for the events at the last supper, especially with Satan lurking behind the face of Judas. This cabinet actually existed and in candlelight the eyes, whether heavenward or staring directly at an observer would, to an imaginative mind like Brontë's, summon a sense of supernatural power emitting from this venerable piece of furniture, but it would also create the illusion that several "brothers" were in the room; consequently, the mixing of blood and water combines the religious and pagan aspects of the scene to engender a kind of awe in the reader.

The most important aspect of this scene, however, is the mixing of blood. Jane sponges Mason's wound and, therefore, mingles his blood with the water, so she is helping him to cleanse his sin through the cleansing of his blood. In addition, her assisting him in this way creates a sympathetic bond between the two of them, like the bond of a blood brotherhood. This bond surfaces later when Mason saves Jane from making a terrible mistake when she is about to marry Rochester, unaware that his wife is still living.

Is St. John the Baptist a Clue?

Another important character with a Masonic connection is the minister St. John Rivers, the man who, in chapter twenty-eight, saves Jane from certain death after a dreadful night on the moors. After residing near him and becoming mistress of a girls' school, he asks her to marry him, but she declines, unwilling to sacrifice true love and become a missionary's wife. Jane's acknowledgement of St. John Rivers at the end of her story confirms her respect for his principles. Jane is not a martyr; she chooses life in this world, but she admires St. John's martyrdom as a missionary. Her purgation at the home of the "Rivers" family has an additional connotation when her final testament to St. John is clarified by the lore of the Freemasons.

For hundreds of years the Freemasons have held their festivals on saints' days. The saints in the greatest regard are St. John the Baptist and St. John the Evangelist. Brontë's use of "Rivers" as St. John's last name suggests the baptisms St. John performed at the rivers. A salutation from a Masonic publication of 1725 reads as follows:

"From whence came you?"

"I came from a right worshipful Lodge of Masters and Fellows belonging to Holy St. John, who doth greet all perfect Brothers of our Holy Secret."

From another publication near the same time, the question is, "What Lodge are you of?" and the answer is, "Of the Right Worshipful Lodge of St. John's."

In England, the first Grand Lodge installed its first Grand Master on St. John the Baptist's Day, June 24th, 1717.

The Masonic Encyclopedia explains their reverence for St. John as follows:

"The stern integrity of St. John the Baptist, which induced him to forego every minor consideration in discharging the obligations he owed to God; the unshaken firmness with which he met martyrdom rather than betray his duty to his Master; his steady reproval of vice, and continued preaching of repentance and virtue, make him a fit patron of the Masonic institution."

St. John the Baptist, the patron saint of the Freemasons, and St. John Rivers share the same principles, which make the character of St. John Rivers a believable symbol for St. John the Baptist.

Brontë ends her novel with an acknowledgement to St. John Rivers just as the Masons end their ceremonies with a reference to their patron saints. The Worshipful Master announces that the Lodge was "erected to Him and dedicated to the memory of the Holy Saint John." The Master also tells the candidate to "hereby and hereon, solemnly and sincerely promise and swear . . . to keep and conceal and never reveal any of the secrets" of the Masonic Lodge. Brontë appropriates the secrets without directly revealing them to her readers. She would have also known about the Masons' patron saints. When she ends her book with a prayer spoken, not by Jane, but by the patron saint's effigy itself, St. John Rivers, he speaks the words "'Amen; even so, come, Lord Jesus.'" Is she sending another clue that Jane has completed her rituals and is echoing the Masonic practice of ending the ceremony with a prayer? Jane Eyre's work is done, but by using only some of the words from the penultimate verse of the Bible, Brontë is asking us to take a closer look at the entire verse.

The quotation is from Revelations 22:20, which says, "He which testifieth these things saith, Surely I come quickly: Amen. Even so, come Lord Jesus." Brontë excludes the first part of the verse and to explain St. John's lack of fear of death has him write to Jane that God, his Master, "'has forewarned me. Daily he announces more distinctly,—'Surely I come quickly;' and hourly I more eagerly respond,—'Amen; even so come, Lord Jesus!'" If we take a closer look at the part she omits, we find these words: "He which testifieth these things saith." We read what St. John Rivers "saith," but to what is Brontë distinctly testifying? In biblical terms, Christ's insistence on a return—"Surely I come quickly"—is repeated throughout the New Testament in several verses. At the end of the Bible, John is testifying to the Revelations of Jesus Christ, given to him to be later shown to God's servants. Could Brontë, therefore, be testifying to observed revelations she wants to be later shown to her readers when they read the deeper meaning hidden in plain view on the pages of *Jane Eyre*?

On one level of the writing, she supplies the clues or tools that point to a second level of rituals and legends in her narrative structure. She takes

Jane through a number of life's vicissitudes in order to polish her in manners and character and build within her a spirit of independence that allows her to find a place in a man's world, just as a candidate must build his character and find a place in the finished work of Freemasonry, but does Brontë add coded signs in the hidden sanctum of her novel, concealed behind the veil of her artistry?

In chapter two, Jane refers to a secret drawer in the red-room. The maid would regularly clean the room on Saturday, but "Mrs. Reed herself, at far intervals, visited it to review the contents of a certain secret drawer in the wardrobe, where were stored divers parchments, her jewel-casket, and a miniature of her deceased husband; and in those last words lies the secret of the red-room: the spell which kept it so lonely in spite of its grandeur." Brontë provides a clue when she writes, "and in those last words lies the secret of the red-room: the spell which kept it so lonely in spite of its grandeur." As we become accustomed to her method of dropping clues into the text, we notice the word "spell." She uses it as a noun to denote a bewitched state, but does she want the reader to see it as a verb and, therefore, not just spell something, but look at the letters that constitute the words? If we have learned to listen and watch for revelations, we should closely observe those "last words" contained in "and a miniature of her deceased husband" to search for a possible clue because, as Jane says, those words contain the red-room's secret, but if Brontë wants us to spell something, perhaps we need to spell those last words in a new way. Perhaps she is encouraging us to play with the words and rearrange the letters into an anagram that spell a secret message.

If Brontë has left a code hidden inside these few words, a little reordering could actually spell a pertinent secret communication that corresponds to the subject matter of the red-room. The result would be as if we were hearing a dead author speak from the grave. With that in mind, an anagram of the letters in the phrase, "And a miniature of her deceased husband" becomes *Dread cherub aide in mason death. Unsafe.*

In the hidden story, Jane expresses her fear of the approaching ritual. She fears the cherub helper will actually be a malevolent fiend. Brontë spells out the real reason for Jane's fear: just as the symbols and clues suggest, the red-room is a Masonic Lodge, and Jane must participate in a frightening death ritual.

The letters a-i-d-e could be arranged to spell "idea," but the cherub acts as a helper to the candidate, so the word "aide" would be more appropriate. Also, in thirty-three letters, the odds are slim of seeing six words that capture the tenor and tone of the clues and ritual terms Brontë sets up in the red-room incident. She also essentially points to these words when she says, "in those last words lies the secret of the red-room," which implies the anagram message is intentional.

Brontë's mental prowess may amaze a modern reader but the surprises are just beginning. The revelations that she could manipulate a few letters into an anagram and construct an allegorical story around a Masonic legend would make perfect sense to friends who were well aware of her extraordinary brain.

12 ROE HEAD BOARDING SCHOOL

Roe Head house was built in the eighteenth century and in 1830 became a boarding school for girls. The front rooms with their bay windows were the indoor classrooms, while the adjoining park became their outdoor recreation area. In January 1831, at the age of fourteen, Charlotte travelled twenty miles from home to attend the boarding school where fewer than a dozen daughters from manufacturing families were in attendance. The last time she had been away at school was seven years earlier at the Clergy Daughters' School at Cowan Bridge—the model for Lowood School in *Jane Eyre*—where she remained with Emily for only a few months before both were returned to Haworth after their elder sisters had taken ill and died. While at Roe Head, Charlotte met two of her lifelong friends, Ellen Nussey and Mary Taylor.

Thirteen-year-old Ellen arrived a week after Charlotte and first noticed a small, grief-stricken girl alone and crying near the bay window in the schoolroom. Ellen was a compassionate and considerate girl who felt sorry for the other student's misery, so she approached her and asked why she was crying. Charlotte replied that she was homesick. They became immediate friends when Ellen confided that she, too, was missing her family.

Unlike Ellen, Mary Taylor was much more outspoken. She was an intelligent, hard-working, and rebellious daughter from a cloth manufacturing family. She believed that women should learn to support themselves in order to attain full independence from men. In later years, she advocated travel and education abroad, and encouraged Charlotte to attend school in Brussels, a step Mary felt necessary for her to find independence from the parsonage. She took her own advice and taught in Germany and then moved to New Zealand to help her brother run his business. In 1859, she returned to Yorkshire.

Her early feminist attitudes would have influenced Charlotte's own views on marriage. For five years, beginning in 1865, Mary wrote for a woman's magazine extolling the merits and benefits of independence: "She argued that women should feel neither indignity nor hardship in working for their living; they should not let themselves be 'driven into matrimony.'" In 1890, she wrote a novel entitled *Miss Miles: A Tale of Yorkshire Life Sixty Years Ago*, in which she shows "the contrasting lives of four women, each in her way struggling against the limitations imposed upon her by convention" (*Oxford* 491).

In 1856, Mary Taylor described Charlotte's arrival at Roe Head school on that January day in 1831.

"I first saw her coming out of a covered cart, in very old-fashioned clothing and looking very cold and miserable. . . . She looked a little, old woman, so short-sighted that she always appeared to be seeking something, and moving her head from side to side to catch sight of it. She was very shy and nervous, and spoke with a strong Irish accent. When a book was given her, she dropped her head over it till her nose nearly touched it, and when she was told to hold her head up, up went the book after it, still close to her nose, so that it was not possible to help laughing."

Mary also wrote about Charlotte's unique mind. "She would confound us by knowing things that were out of our range altogether. She was acquainted with most of the short pieces of poetry that we had to learn by heart; would tell us the authors, the poems they were taken from, and sometimes repeat a page or two, and tell us the plot. She had a habit of writing in italics (printing characters) and said she had learnt it by writing in their magazine. They brought out a 'magazine' once a month, and wished it to look as like print as possible. . . . She used to draw much better, and more quickly, than anything we had seen before, and knew much about celebrated pictures and painters. Whenever an opportunity offered of examining a picture or cut of any kind, she went over it piecemeal, with her eyes close to the paper, looking so long that we used to ask her 'what she saw in it.' She could always see plenty, and explained it very well. She made poetry and drawing at least exceedingly interesting to me; and then I got the habit, which I have yet, of referring mentally to her opinion on all matters of that kind, along with many more, resolving to describe such and such things to her, until I start at the recollection that I never shall.

"We used to be furious politicians, as one could hardly help being in 1832. She knew the names of the two ministries; the one that resigned, and the one that succeeded and passed the Reform Bill. She worshipped the Duke of Wellington, but said that Sir Robert Peel was not to be trusted; he did not act from principle like the rest, but from expediency. . . . She said she had taken interest in politics ever since she was five years old. She did not get her opinions from her father—that is, not directly—but from the papers, etc., he preferred" (Gaskell 65-67).

Mrs. Gaskell interviewed other classmates when she was preparing the *Life of Charlotte Brontë*. They echoed Mary's recollection: Charlotte "was an indefatigable student; constantly reading and learning; with a strong conviction of the necessity and value of education, very unusual in a girl of fifteen" (68).

Her other friend Ellen also commented on Charlotte's brilliance: "Her mind was so wholly set on attaining knowledge that she apparently forgot all else." At first, the older girls who had been in school longer found Charlotte ignorant and odd in her plain, old-fashioned dark green dress that accentuated her thin frame, pallid complexion, and frizzy brown hair. Even though she lacked the elements of grammar and geography the other girls knew, "she far surpassed her most advanced school-fellows in knowledge of what was passing in the world at large, and in the literature of her country. . . . She had taught herself a little French before she came to school. . . . She soon began to make a good figure in French lessons. . . . She was in the habit of committing long pieces of poetry to memory, and seemed to do so with real enjoyment and hardly any effort."

When she recalled her older sisters Maria and Elizabeth, and specific aspects of their characters, her classmates would ask how she could remember so much, especially when she would have been so young herself. She replied that "she began to analyze character when she was five years old, and instanced two guests who were at her home for a day or two, and of whom she had taken stock, and of whom after-knowledge confirmed first impressions."

Ellen also remarked on her knowledge of the Bible. "I must not forget to state that no girl in the school was equal to Charlotte in Sunday lessons. Her acquaintance with Holy Writ surpassed others in this as in everything else. She was very familiar with the sublimest passages, especially those in Isaiah, in which she took great delight" (*Letters, Vol.I.*589-595).

Charlotte applied herself with hard work and determination in order to rise from the bottom of the class to the top, which she accomplished by the end of the first of the three six-month terms she attended. Miss Wooler, the headmistress and owner of the school awarded Charlotte with a medal for her achievement at the end of each of the three terms; no other student surpassed her academically. At the end of a year, she also won the French prize. She was less likely to participate in sports or games that required good eyesight, but was content to sit outside with a book while the other girls played, confirming Ellen's comments that Charlotte was "wholly set on attaining knowledge." Though a shy girl, she was known to be "observant," so she well knew how others viewed her appearance. Mary and Ellen agreed that Charlotte was not a pretty girl at that time, but Ellen felt "she had ever the demeanor of a born gentlewoman" (590).

Her serious temperament and lack of indulgence in leisure activities were partly due to her sense of duty to her family. Ellen described it as "a deep responsibility," and awareness that her father could barely afford the expense of her education; consequently, she refused invitations for frivolity and spent her time absorbing and learning as much information as she could for her future as a governess. Her strict conscientious attitude to her studies made her "a model of high rectitude, close application and great abilities." She refused to wear glasses during this period, so she would sit at the window until dark with the book inches from her face while the others amused themselves in relaxing conversation around the fire (591).

Whenever Charlotte joined the girls later in the evening, she would thrill them with her imaginative storytelling. Her years of writing tales with Branwell and of hearing ghost stories from their housekeeper Tabby enabled her to conjure fresh anecdotes for an enthralled audience. She could create tales of "surging seas, raging breakers, towering castle walls, high precipices, invisible charms and dangers," and add the terror of a spooky sleepwalker floating among castle turrets. Her voice and delivery panicked one girl who shook with fright so badly that Charlotte refused to repeat the stories for fear of a recurrence of distress in her listeners (592).

After eighteen months, Charlotte left Roe Head School in June 1832, but remained in close contact with Ellen and Mary through letters and the occasional visits. For the next three years at home, she shared her knowledge of history, geography, English grammar, and French with Emily and Anne while also teaching at the National Sunday school in Haworth. Miss Wooler, the founder of Roe Head School and Charlotte's teacher, maintained a correspondence with her former pupil, and, in July1835, invited Charlotte to return to Roe Head not as a student, but as a teacher. Charlotte, now nineteen, accepted the position and enrolled seventeen-year-old Emily as a pupil, but Emily became so ill with homesickness that she returned to the parsonage only three months later. In her place, Reverend Brontë sent sixteen-year-old Anne who was able to cope with the isolation and loneliness with the help of a new friend, a ten-year-old student also named Ann (Barker 238). Anne's formal education ended in December of 1837 when illness struck and forced her to return home.

Charlotte's duties included teaching the girls, monitoring their study periods, and taking them on daily walks throughout the gardens. She described her life proceeding "as monotonously and unvaryingly as ever, nothing but teach, teach, teach, from morning till night" (*Letters, Vol.I* 171).

In 1836, she began a journal in which she wrote her private thoughts, specifically those feelings regarding the conflict between her duty to concentrate on the teaching and her desire to focus on her narrative fantasies. The work constantly pulled her from her daydreams and "made Life a continual waking Night-mare" (*Letters, Vol.I* 505). She listened for her muse, recollected the landscapes of her imaginary land of Angria, and yearned for quiet moments to write.

"Well here I am at Roe-Head. It is seven o'clock at night. The young ladies are all at their lessons. The school-room is quiet the fire is low, a stormy day is at this moment passing off in a murmuring and bleak night. I now resume my own thoughts; my mind relaxes from the stretch on which it has been for the last twelve hours and falls back onto the rest which nobody in this house knows of but myself. I now after a day of weary wandering return to the ark which for me floats alone on the face of this world's desolate and boundless deluge.

"It is strange, I cannot get used to the ongoings that surround me. I fulfil my duties strictly and well. I so to speak, if the illustration be not profane, as God was not in the wind nor the fire nor the earth-quake so neither is my heart in the task the theme or the exercises. It is the still small voices alone that come to me at eventide, that which like a breeze with a voice in it over the deeply blue hills and out of the now leafless forests and from the cities on distant river banks of a far and bright continent. It is that which wakes my spirit and engrosses all my living feelings all my energies which are not merely mechanical and, like Haworth and home, wakes sensations which lie dormant elsewhere.

"Last night I did indeed lean upon the thunder-wakening wings of such a stormy blast as I have seldom heard blow and it whirled me away like heath in the wilderness for five seconds of ecstasy, and as I sat by myself in the dining-room while all the rest were at tea the trance seemed to descend on a sudden, and verily this foot trod the war-shaken shores of the Calabar and these eyes saw the defiled and violated Adrianopolis shedding its lights on the river from lattices whence the invader looked out and was not darkened; . . . while this apparition was before me the dining-room door opened and Miss Wooler came in with a plate of butter in her hand.

'A very stormy night my dear!' said she.

'It is ma'am,' said I" (*Selected Early Writings* 158-160).

Away from home, she missed writing about her favourite characters in the Angrian tales that she shared with Branwell. During her Christmas break at home, she recalled a vision that had engrossed her while at Roe Head and the ensuing frustration when a student interrupted her reverie.

"Never shall I Charlotte Brontë forget what a voice of wild and wailing music now came thrillingly to my mind's, almost to my body's ear nor how distinctly I sitting in the schoolroom at Roe Head saw the Duke of Zamorna leaning against that obelisk with the mute marble Victory above him, the fern waving at his feet, his black horse turned loose grazing among the heather, the moonlight so mild and so exquisitely tranquil sleeping upon that vast and vacant road, and the African sky quivering and shaking with stars expanded above all. I was gone. I had really utterly forgot where I was and all the gloom and cheerlessness of my situation. I felt myself breathing quick and short as I beheld the Duke lifting up his sable crest which undulated as the plume of a hearse waves to the wind and knew that that music which, as mournfully triumphant as the Scriptural verse, 'Oh Grave where is thy sting. Oh Death where is thy victory' was exciting him, and quivering his ever rapid pulse. 'Miss Brontë what are you thinking about?' said a voice that dissipated all the charm, and Miss Lister thrust her little rough black head into my face, 'Sic transit' etc" (*Edition of the Early Writings* 385).

The Latin phrase *Sic transit Gloria mundi* can be translated as "Thus passes the glory of the world."

Upon her return to Roe Head, she continued to write in her journal.

"Now as I have a little bit of time there being no French lessons this afternoon I should like to write something. I can't enter into any continued narrative. My mind is not settled enough for that but if I could call up some slight and pleasant sketch, I would amuse myself by jotting it down" (*Selected Early Writings* 160).

Her teaching experience was unpleasant and frustrating when the pull of inspiration tugged at her heart and mind, but the students aggravated the situation with their scholastic ineptitude, which brought out that bit of bile Charlotte hid behind a polite smile.

"All this day I have been in a dream half-miserable and half ecstatic. Miserable because I could not follow it out uninterruptedly, ecstatic because it showed almost in the vivid light of reality the ongoings of the infernal world. I had been toiling for nearly an hour with Miss Lister, Miss Marriott and Ellen Cook, striving to teach them the distinction between an article and a substantive. The parsing lesson was completed, a dead silence had succeeded it in the school-room and I sat sinking from irritation and weariness into a kind of lethargy. The thought came over me, am I to spend all the best part of my life in this wretched bondage, forcibly suppressing my rage at the idleness, the apathy, and the hyperbolical and most asinine stupidity of these fat-headed oafs and on compulsion assuming an air of kindness, patience and assiduity?

"Must I from day to day sit chained to this chair prisoned within these four bare walls, while these glorious summer suns are burning in heaven and the year is revolving in its richest glow and declaring at the close of every summer day it will never come again? Stung to the heart with this reflection I started up and mechanically walked to the window—a sweet August morning was smiling without. The dew was not yet dried off the field. The early shadows were stretching cool and dim from the hay-stack and the roots of the grand old oaks and thorns scattered along the sunk fence. All was still except the murmur of the scrubs about me over their tasks. I flung up the sash. An uncertain sound of inexpressible sweetness came on a dying gale from the south. I looked in that direction. Huddersfield and the hills beyond it were all veiled in blue mist. The woods of Hopton & Heaton Lodge were clouding the waters-edge and the Calder, silent but bright, was shooting among them like a silver arrow. I listened. The sound sailed full and liquid down the descent. It was the bells of Huddersfield Parish church. I shut the window and went back to my seat. Then came on me rushing impetuously all the mighty phantasm that this had conjured from nothing to a system strong as some religious creed. I felt as if I could have written gloriously. I longed to write. The Spirit of all Verdopolis of all the mountainous North of all the woodland West, of all the river-watered East came crowding into my mind. If I had had time to indulge it I felt that the vague sensations of that moment would have settled down into some narrative better at least than any thing I ever produced before. But just then a Dolt came up with a lesson. I thought I should have vomited" (162-3).

She continues to write about stealing a few moments away from the students.

"The Ladies went into the school-room to do their exercises and I crept up to the bed-room to be *alone* for the first time that day. Delicious was the sensation I experienced as I laid down on the spare bed and resigned myself to the Luxury of twilight and Solitude" (163).

Her imagination provided the mental liberty she loved. "What a treasure is thought! What a privilege is reverie—I am thankful that I have the power of solacing myself with the dream of creations whose reality I shall never behold—May I never lose that power. May I never feel it growing weaker—If I should how little pleasure will life afford me—its lapses of shade so wide so gloomy. Its gleams of sunshine so limited and dim" (168). These sentiments are reminiscent of those expressed in the poem 'My Comforter,' attributed to Emily, but sounding like Charlotte. The speaker is "vexed" and "gloomy," but thanks the "gentle ray" of light hidden deep within her soul for sustaining her through the dark times: "A cloud-closed beam of sunshine brought / To gleam in open view" a glimpse of "Heaven's glorious sun," the temporary solace that calms her "resentful mood."

The comfort of her "reverie" helped her cope until her students needed her. Their lack of intelligence pulled her from the deeper world of her imagination. "Stupidity the atmosphere, school-books the employment, asses the society, what in all this is there to remind me of the divine, silent, unseen land of thought, dim now and indefinite as the dream of a dream, the shadow of a shade?" (165)

Charlotte's personality and intelligence contributed to her intense emotion. Due to the Brontë tragedies from past sickness, Charlotte became alarmed during Anne's illness at school: "Anne continued—wretchedly ill—neither the pain nor the difficulty of breathing left her—and how could I feel otherwise than very miserable?" Miss Wooler thought Charlotte was overreacting and that Anne simply suffered from a cold, but Charlotte felt the headmistress was ignoring the severity of Anne's condition and said so. This reproach caused a temporary conflict between the two women, but ended when Miss Wooler apologized and Anne was sent home. Charlotte confided to Ellen that the entire incident had upset her so much that she had considered leaving her employment as a teacher, but added, "If any body likes me I can't help liking them." She also defended her stern reaction to Miss Wooler's inappropriate diagnosis: "I was in a regular passion. My '*warm temper*' quite got the better of me—Of which I don't boast for it was a weakness—nor am I ashamed of it for I had reason to be angry " (*Letters, Vol.I* 173-4).

During her time at Roe Head, she wrote another letter to Ellen, stating that her friend might be shocked to know her secret thoughts. "I am *not like you*. If you knew my thoughts; the dreams that absorb me; and the fiery imagination that at times eats me up and makes me feel Society as it is, wretchedly insipid, you would pity and I dare say despise me" (144).

Her letter to Ellen, like her journal, shows her capacity for strong feelings. She yielded to spirited outbursts, impatient responses, and angry confrontations that stirred her mind to revolt against what she viewed as injustices. These characteristics are part of what made her such a passionate novelist and a formidable foe when she chose to pick up the pen and record her grievances.

After she left teaching in May of 1838, she described the time spent there as tedious. "I can never forget the concentrated anguish of certain insufferable moments and the heavy gloom of many long hours" (*Letters, Vol.I* 505). Her sole desire was to write in uninterrupted solitude but without financial independence, the dream would remain a fantasy for a few more years.

Her friends' impressions of Charlotte and these fragments from her journal tell us she had a unique mind and a "warm temper." She recognized in herself a form of depression that she classed as "the tyranny of Hypochondria." This affliction, understandably, arose because she had a tremendous intellect and a highly sensitive awareness of people's characters, a vivid and active imagination and an intense desire to write, but her situation forced her to suppress her genius. Years later she tried to explain her moods at Roe Head to Miss Wooler:

"Under such circumstances the morbid Nerves can know neither peace nor enjoyment—whatever touches pierces them—sensation for them is all suffering—A weary burden nervous patients consequently become to those about them—they know this and it infuses a new gall—corrosive in its extreme acritude, into their bitter cup . . . I could have been no better company for you than a stalking ghost—and I remember I felt my incapacity to *impart* pleasure fully as much as my powerlessness to *receive* it" (505).

At other times, her shy nature concealed a passionate temperament, and her quiet deportment hid the darker thoughts and dreams circulating through her imaginative mind. She grasped a disturbing truth: if her students or her friends knew the content and the fiery themes of those thoughts and dreams, they would be shocked and compelled to rebuke the subversive qualities of the real Charlotte.

Women in the Victorian era had been taught that motherhood was the ultimate emotional fulfillment for women. The idealized domestic roles of wife and mother encouraged a woman's efforts to be pious, diligent, and active in her housekeeping duties, as well as devoted to her husband while reliant upon God and the Church. Modern readers would find aspects of this domestic mythology repressive and limiting; therefore, Charlotte's ambition would be less shocking to them, and her bouts of "concentrated anguish" better understood.

13 EMILY AND ANNE IN THEIR PALACE

Ellen Nussey remained single and stayed Charlotte's closest friend for over twenty-three years. Between 1826 and 1836, Ellen lived at the Rydings estate in Birstall, West Yorkshire, a lovely place for Charlotte to visit with its large, stone, Georgian house and its landscaped gardens. Ellen and her family then moved to Birstall's Brookroyd House outside of Bradford and several miles from Haworth. Charlotte visited Ellen a few times over the course of their friendship and was always happy to receive her at the parsonage.

Ellen was a pretty girl with soft curly hair, kind eyes, and a pleasing smile, but she was neither an intellectual nor a well-read companion; nonetheless, Charlotte appreciated their attachment: "Single women often like each other more and derive great solace from their mutual regard— Friendship however is a plant which cannot be forced—true friendship is no gourd springing in a night and withering in a day." Charlotte once said Ellen and she became close, even though they were "contrasts;" they grew to like each other as they learned the other's good and bad traits: "she is no more than a conscientious, observant, calm, well-bred Yorkshire girl. She is without romance—if she attempts to read poetry—or poetic prose aloud—I am irritated and deprive her of the book. If she talks of it I stop my ears, but she is good—she is true—she is faithful and I love her" (*Letters, Vol.II* 323).

Ellen wrote her reminiscences of the Brontë family in 1871, which included memories of Emily and Anne. Her image of two close siblings corroborates a similar view of the two girls that surfaced with the discovery of their birthday diary papers. Ellen recalled that because of the seventeen months difference in their ages, Emily and Anne were "like twins," who were "inseparable companions and in the very closest sympathy which never had any interruption."

She writes of a ramble across the moors "to a spot familiar to Emily and Anne which they called the 'Meeting of the Waters,'" where "Emily half reclining on a slab of stone played like a young child with the tadpoles in the water." The two girls loved animals, especially the dog that occasionally was allowed into the parlour, where "Emily and Anne always gave him a portion of their breakfast." On one trip into the countryside with the four Brontë siblings, she recalled, "Emily and Anne hardly spoke during the whole excursion except to each other." She witnessed Charlotte's delight in spending hours daily on painting "with scarcely an interval," while "Emily and Anne were fond of the pencil, but chiefly as a recreation, or for the sake of acquiring the art so as to be able to teach others when the need should arise" (*Letters, Vol.I* 598-604).

Emily and Anne, from their youth to their late twenties, continued to share their love of the Gondal saga. Unfortunately, "the Gondal epic cannot be easily reconstructed" due to a lack of surviving material. This childhood fantasy world "appears to have functioned as an imaginative storehouse for Emily, one to which she resorted throughout her life to experiment with intense emotional states and relationships. Anne was less passionate about and less reliant on Gondal, her interest waning as she grew older." Emily, however, continued to explore her Gondal world: "even after the publication of *Wuthering Heights* she still found in her epic world a source of inspiration for her personal concerns. . . . As she stated in her Diary Paper of 30 July 1845: 'We intend sticking firm by the rascals as long as they delight us'" (*Oxford* 216-219).

Perhaps, while Emily and Anne rambled over the moors, they dramatized their characters' exploits the way they did on their 1845 trip to York. As noted above, Emily recorded their Gondal play in her diary: "during our excursion we were Ronald Macelgin, Henry Angora, Juliet Augusteena, Rosobelle Esualdar, Ella and Julian Egramon Catherine Navarre and Cordelia Fitzaphnold escaping from the palaces of Instruction to join the Royalists who are hard driven at present by the victorious Republicans."

In 1827 and 1828 Charlotte and Emily had created their "Bed plays," the "secret plays" that Charlotte said she never wrote down: "I need not write on paper for I think I shall always remember them" (Glen 5). Emily and Anne appear to have journeyed into their Gondal dramas in much the same way on their trip to York: they would pretend they were particular characters and imagine adventures that might include a mutiny at the Palace of Instruction.

From a description in Charlotte's early writings dated August 22, 1830, it appears that she ventured into a fantasy play that Emily and Anne shared, but was soon unimpressed when she found her younger sisters' attempts at drama childish and dull.

While Charlotte and Branwell were immersed in their tales of grand heroes, warring factions, and political intrigue, fourteen-year-old Charlotte decided to take a break to "visit" Emily and Anne's creation and spend a day with Sir Edward Parry and Lady Emily Parry and their friend Sir Ross. Her contempt for her younger sisters' fantasyland becomes obvious in Charlotte's composition entitled "A Day at Parry's Palace." Emily's Captain Parry and his cohort Sir Ross have failed to create a country of majestic proportions like the older siblings' Glass Town; consequently, Charlotte's male narrator in her composition, Charles Wellesley, comments on the dearth of "tall, strong muscular men going about seeking whom they may devour, with guns on their shoulders or in their hands." He sees nothing of the heroic figure defeating enemies and shedding blood for his country, but instead witnesses "little shiftless milk-and-water-beings, in clean blue linen jackets and white aprons." The land of Parry's Palace lacks the darkness and splendour of the Angrian tales: "Nasty factories, with their tall black chimneys breathing thick columns of almost tangible smoke, discoloured not that sky of dull hazy colourless hue." Charles disdainfully continues: "glossy satin, rich velvet, costly silk or soft muslin broke not in on the fair uniformity" of the plain wool dresses. Charles is also disturbed that "all the houses were ranged in formal rows. They contained four rooms each with a little garden in front. No proud castle or splendid palace towers insultingly over the cottages around. No high-born noble claimed allegiance of his vassals or surveyed his broad lands with hereditary pride."

Parry's Palace resembles the Haworth parsonage: "Every inch of ground was enclosed with stone walls." Charles describes the plain residence, with its "wash-house, back-kitchen, stable and coalhouse" and "one cow, to give milk for the family and butter for the dairy and cheese for the table; one horse, to draw the gig, carry Their Majesties and bring home provisions from market; together with a calf and foal as companions for both." They also have "three cats, two dogs, five rabbits, and six pigs."

Sir Edward, Lady Emily, and Sir Ross speak in "a scarcely intelligible jargon" that Charlotte spells phonetically to suggest an exaggeration of the local dialect: Emily is pronounced "Aumly." A conversation occurs between Parry and his guest wherein the guest describes a new cloak of flowered muslin with pink ribbon at the bottom and a full silk belt, but the dialect makes his description barely comprehensible: "'a nou clouk of flouered muslin waud punk rubun ot de bottom and faul saulk belt,'" and Parry describes the last dress he had made for him, which was a beautiful, pale crimson dress trimmed with yellow, green, and purple, and a feather cap of a rich lilac colour: "Parry said that 'the laust dress Aumy haud moide haum wauss a boutiful pale craumson, traumed waud yaullow, groin and purple, and a fadher aun hid caup of a rauch lilac cauler.'"

Charlotte and Branwell often attempted to mimic the sounds of the Yorkshire dialect in their juvenile writing, and Charlotte later continued this tradition in her adult novels when she included characters with this unique speech pattern to provide authenticity to the setting.

In chapter five of her novel *Shirley*, the Hollow's Mill machinist Joe and his employer Moore are discussing Moore's nationality when Joe explains the nature of the Yorkshire people: "We allus speak our minds i' this country and them young parsons and grand folk fro' London is shocked at wer 'incivility'; and we like weel enough to gi'e 'em summat to be shocked at, 'cause it's sport to us to watch 'em turn up the whites o' their een, and spreed out their bits o' hands like as they're flayed wi' bogards, and then to hear 'em say, nipping off their words short like, 'Dear! dear! Whet seveges! How very corse!'"

Moore responds jokingly that Yorkshire folk *are* savages: "'You don't suppose you're civilized do you?'

'Middling, middling, maister.'"

Charlotte's ability to mimic the dialect recurs throughout her writing. She also recycles scenes, slightly altered, that appear in later work.

In a scene that resembles the opening to *Wuthering Heights* when Lockwood, the narrator and visiting tenant, is left in the house with the dogs, Charlotte describes her narrator Charles at Parry's Palace when he is alone with his host's son little Eater. The boy "stood for more than half an hour on the rug before me, with his finger in his mouth staring idiot-like full in my face." In a gesture similar to Lockwood's hitting the dog with a poker and the household coming to his aid, Charles beats the boy with a poker, kicks him a few times, and knocks "his head against the floor, hoping to stun him," but the child continues to scream, which alerts the household to his plight. Parry demands an explanation for this brutality: "What hauve dou beinn douing tou de child?" Charles lies and says, "the sweet little boy fell down as I was playing with him and hurt hisself." Everyone accepts this explanation.

Emily and Anne's men eat "precisely at twelve o'clock." Their regular and rather common repast consists of "roast beef, Yorkshire pudding, mashed potatoes, apple pie and preserved cucumbers." Charles is disgusted with their table manners: they "ate as if they had not seen a meal for three weeks" and he considers violence yet again: "I felt a strong inclination to set the house on fire and consume the senseless gluttons."

Charles Wellesley has seen enough and leaves. His visit was "intolerably dull," and he apologizes to his readers, but adds, "the journey had given me some notion of things as they are, and for that reason I did not regret it." After being inundated with requests for information about his visit and not being in the mood to discuss it, he "had recourse to the only way of obviating the inconvenience, namely by sending this brief narrative for insertion in the *Young Men's Magazine*. He signs it "Farewell, Genius CW" (*The Early Writings, Vol.I* 230-33).

These descriptions not only demonstrate Charlotte's sense of humour and love of writing, but also afford a brief glimpse into the preferences of the younger girls, whose simple interests were polar opposites to those of the older siblings. Charlotte could see that her sisters lacked the verbal and writing skills necessary to engage in the fierce repartee she enjoyed with Branwell. She would never have involved them in the witty and satirical banter she relished with her brother because she recognized the limitations of their storytelling, limitations that would render them defenseless against the cut and thrust of her rapier wit.

The fragments of information about Emily and Anne consistently place them together working on their Gondal characters. The diary papers show their limitations with language; Ellen Nussey's reminiscences depict them as twins who prefer each other's company; and Charlotte's composition records their lack of imaginative and intellectual rigour. All these examples support the vision of Emily and Anne sharing ideas, but do not provide any indication that Charlotte and Emily secretly joined creative forces to satirize the local Freemasons, or that they collaborated to produce an intricate design of similar themes and Masonic symbols in

Wuthering Heights and *Jane Eyre,* but that is precisely what must have happened because both novels contain a treasure trove of all things Masonic.

14 *WUTHERING HEIGHTS—* PASSIONATE FEROCITY

Wuthering Heights continues to intrigue scholars and fascinate contemporary readers with its Gothic plot and brooding characters. Brontë's artistry touched deeply the minds and hearts of Victorian England and has captivated readers today, but in all that time no one has ever been able to identify the origin of the book's mysterious effect, nor explain how the author conjures its underlying transcendence. Author and professor of English, Patricia Meyer Spacks comments on the depth of Catherine and Heathcliff's passion, which contributes to the novel's power: they "share a fiery nature—a capacity for intense, dangerous feeling" (Bloom 60). Her description recalls Charlotte Brontë's letter in which she refers to her own "warm temper" and "fiery imagination." Certainly, the supernatural elements contribute to the novel's popularity, as does Brontë's version of reality, but what are the chief strategies behind her technique that enable her to create a vast, otherworldly strangeness that has a universal and timeless appeal? Her narrative structure, with its tight control and effortless movement from past to present, makes other writers of the time look like amateurs.

One must be careful when trying to "dissect" a book's deeper structures. Throughout the novel's history, "few could be found to challenge *Wuthering Heights*'s greatness, but even fewer were so confident or so naïve as to try to tie Brontë's novel to a single level of meaning" (*Critical Essays* 118). The powerful mind that crafted this great work layered a range of voices, narrators, and literary tricks to present a diverse and complex form that draws upon her cumulative experiences spent writing and, necessarily, resists a single level of interpretation, but that should not preclude a naïve impulse to solve one of the novel's enigmas. I hope to show that the rituals and symbols of Freemasonry provide a useful key when trying to answer one of the abiding questions: did Emily Brontë write this book?

The novelist E. M. Forster writes that the author of *Wuthering Heights* had "a literal and careful mind. She constructed her novel on a time chart even more elaborate than Miss Austen's, and she arranged the

113

Linton and Earnshaw families symmetrically, and she had a clear idea of the various legal steps by which Heathcliffe gained possession of their two properties" (Bloom 40). Scholars for years have pondered over the question of how Emily Brontë made the leap from her awkward, freakish, and immature writings about Gondal to compose such an original, masterly constructed novel. Their question is well founded. Brontë weaves two generations of the Linton and Earnshaw families through their conflicts with an incredible passion and fury, but Emily displays no such fire or fury in her depiction of life at the parsonage in 1845, near the time scholars believe the book was written: "We are all in decent health . . . I am quite contented for myself—not as idle as formerly, altogether as hearty and having learnt to make the most of the present and hope for the future with less figetness that I cannot do all I wish—seldom or ever troubled with nothing to do and merely desiring that every body could be as comfortable as myself and as undesponding and then we should have a very tolerable world of it." The author of the Brontë masterpiece was not content, comfortable, nor undesponding.

Wuthering Heights was published after *Jane Eyre* in late 1847. For purposes of clarity and to distinguish between the two women who are both called Cathy in the novel, the name Catherine will refer to Catherine Earnshaw, the mother of Cathy Linton. The story of *Wuthering Heights* involves the Earnshaw and Linton families, with Heathcliff being the outsider. Catherine Earnshaw's father brings home a filthy, uncouth orphan boy from Liverpool named Heathcliff to live with them and to be a playmate to the Earnshaw children, Catherine and her older brother Hindley. Unfortunately, Hindley is a brute and a bully, so Heathcliff grows to hate him while, at the same time, learns to love Catherine, an independent girl who shares his wild nature and love of the moors. She loves Heathcliff but will never marry him because he lacks financial prospects and, as an adult, he has maintained his coarse and uncouth manners. Edgar Linton, the son of the wealthy magistrate lives across the valley at the Linton manor called Thrushcross Grange and makes a more suitable match for Catherine.

Catherine's rejection of Heathcliff incites him to plan his revenge against not only the bully Hindley but also his rival Edgar. Heathcliff runs away from the area and returns years later with the financial means to

114

begin his plot to take over the two properties. His obsessive love for Catherine endures long past her death and continues after he has acquired both the Earnshaw and Linton properties. While he lives at Wuthering Heights, he decides to rent out Thrushcross Grange to a new tenant, Lockwood, and this is where the novel begins. The first three chapters deal with the tenant visiting Wuthering Heights and provide the strongest examples of Masonic influence. The story begins with the initial moments when Lockwood arrives at Heathcliff's dwelling.

Seventeen years have passed since Catherine's death, and Lockwood will soon hear the story of the two lovers from the housekeeper Nelly Dean. At Wuthering Heights, Heathcliff lives with Hareton, the son of dead Hindley Earnshaw—the bully from his youth—and with Joseph, an aging servant. Catherine's daughter, Cathy Linton (now a Heathcliff because she married Heathcliff's son who is also now deceased) lives with them, but is unhappy because Heathcliff treats her like a servant. The dwelling suits a northern farmer who sits in his chair and drinks ale, but Lockwood also finds Heathcliff to be a handsome, though slovenly, country squire with his dark gypsy colouring and morose disposition.

In searching for clues that Brontë may be borrowing from Freemasonry for her symbols, allegories, and rituals, I have tried to avoid forcing my interpretation onto the text, but will always note the possibility of her intentional use, no matter how slight, by providing examples from the Masonic system.

Freemasonry's main rituals are comprised of the three degrees. The first degree of Entered Apprentice is followed by the second degree of Fellow Craft, and finally by the third degree of Master Mason where the newly risen brother attains wisdom. In the old days of operative masonry, when masons were actually working with stone, gaining the wisdom meant learning the secret methods of cutting rocks and constructing buildings. This knowledge was what the three Fellow Craft villains were after when they killed Hiram Abiff, the Master Mason at King Solomon's Temple.

As the fraternity grew, however, it included men outside the trade. The wisdom then came to represent a spiritual awareness, and those rising in the ranks were speculative, not operative Masons. At each level or degree, the member learns the craft's history and legend, carries on a tradition of fraternal relationships, and swears to secrecy about what occurs within the Lodge.

Freemasonry is acquainted with the importance of the triangle and the number three. The symbol of two interlacing triangles was originally a mason's signature on stone buildings and later a common image on the seals of medieval masons. The number three symbolizes beginning, middle, and end and, in Freemasonry, the three degrees symbolize birth, manhood, and death, or life, maturity, and transmigration. In *Wuthering Heights*, the word "three" occurs fifty-two times, and the word "third," ten times, so the number itself could act as a clue to highlight the importance of patterns within the novel. For instance, examples of three triangular relationships within the novel can be found in the dynamic connections between Heathcliff, Catherine, and Edgar; Heathcliff, Catherine, and Isabella; and Hareton, Cathy, and Linton (the son of Heathcliff and Isabella). As well, Lockwood's adventure at the farmhouse covers the first three chapters.

In the opening chapter, Lockwood's trials begin. Heathcliff greets Lockwood with a minimal amount of politeness but invites him into Wuthering Heights where the guest experiences a frightening event. Lockwood survives an attack from Heathcliff's dogs, which creates chaos in the house and brings the old servant Joseph and the housekeeper Zillah to his rescue. Heathcliff apologizes and shares a drink of wine with Lockwood while explaining the advantages and disadvantages of retiring as a tenant to Thrushcross Grange. The choice of the name Zillah as housekeeper provides another connection to Freemasonry.

The traditions of Freemasonry are associated with the building of King Solomon's Temple and the story of Lamech and his two wives, Ada and Zillah. Lamech and his two wives bore four children who each started a specific craft: the craft of geometry, music, weaving, and the craft of the smith, like the blacksmith or tinsmith. The children hid their discoveries in two pillars, one that would never burn and the other that would never sink in water, which was prescient in light of the approaching deluge that would force Noah to build his ark. The pillars were hollowed to act as safe compartments. The secrets of the crafts were written on parchment that was then folded and hidden inside the pillars.

The legend alleges that the two hollow pillars were the left and right pillars at the entrance to Solomon's Temple. The traditional history of Masonry begins with that legend of the children keeping their discoveries protected, so their knowledge could be handed down to the human race after the Flood. The legend of Masonry starts with the Lamech legend and then traces its growth through Egypt, France, and England. For Brontë, the name Zillah would have held particular significance.

In the second chapter of *Wuthering Heights*, Lockwood endures more trials. Snow begins to fall outside Thrushcross Grange, but Lockwood chooses to make the long walk and return to Wuthering Heights. Unfortunately, no one appears to greet him, and he is unable to open the door. Locked out, he searches for help and sees Hindley's son Hareton, the rough young man who ushers him inside. Lockwood stays for tea and learns a little more about the house and its inhabitants, specifically that the girl living there (Cathy) is Heathcliff's daughter-in-law—his son's widow. The snow continues to fall, but no one offers to guide him home; consequently, he makes a poor attempt to plough through the storm, but fails and incurs the wrath of the dogs that attack him yet again. He gets a bloody nose, and Zillah rushes to his rescue as she had the day before. Heathcliff recognizes that the storm is intensifying, so he allows Lockwood to stay the night and tells Zillah to escort the guest upstairs where he will spend the night in Catherine's old room.

The third chapter is highly suggestive of a ritual just like the red-room chapter in *Jane Eyre*. In this episode, Lockwood sleeps inside a closet bed like the one described near the end of chapter eleven in *Jane Eyre*: "one of those wide and heavy beds: shut in, some of them, with doors of oak," which connects his experience with the Masonic death ritual, the one that Jane fears because of the arrival of a *"cherub aide."* In Lockwood's case, the spirit of Catherine, as a young girl, will haunt his ritual. As mentioned before, Freemasonry has its roots in antiquity; in ancient Egyptian rituals, for instance, the being from the other world brings the knowledge of immortality to the initiate.

The first three chapters provide a parody of the Masonic three-degree ceremonies. In order to learn more about the occupants, Lockwood must endure the trials of a dog attack and a bloody nose. Instead of wands raised above the initiate's head, a poker and frying pan are lifted over the dogs' bodies, and the chaos of violence replaces the silence of the chamber of reflection. Lockwood learns more about the family in his second visit to Wuthering Heights, just as the initiate's education of Freemasonry continues through the second degree, but Lockwood still lacks the entire truth about Heathcliff and Catherine. After surviving his trials, Lockwood is ready to hear the entire story about the Earnshaw and Linton families, just as a new member learns about the legends and mysteries of Freemasonry. Lockwood discovers the truth in the third chapter, but the legend's rituals begin in chapter one.

15 LOCKWOOD'S FIRST DEGREE

In every clime a Freemason may find a home and in every land a Brother if he brings his worthy heart, for a man must first be a Mason in his heart. Admission to the brotherhood is by invitation only, so Lockwood humbly solicits entry to persevere in the ceremonies. He receives no Masonic handshake from his solitary landlord because he has yet to complete the degrees, and Heathcliff interrupts him when Lockwood says,

"I heard yesterday you had had some thoughts—."

Discussions of business must never be done outside where eavesdroppers may be roaming. Instead, Lockwood gets a nod in this remote place, a much better sign than words when a brother wants to maintain secrecy, which is why Heathcliff gives him a wink when he "winces" because "wince" in old English is a kin to wink. Brontë will continue to play with the words throughout her parody of the rituals, as she does when she has Heathcliff say, "Walk in," which in Masonic terms means you must circumambulate the Lodge. She also uses Masonic numbers that refer to specific truths: "Go to the Deuce," which comes from *deux* in French and two in England is a nod to Masonic principles, which they call landmarks, and of which they have twenty-five. The second landmark says, "We have three degrees," so this number, hidden in "Deuce," is a sign to Lockwood that his three ceremonies are about to begin.

The "circumstance determined" that Lockwood continue, so he accepts the invitation. Before much can happen, however, he is suddenly forced to stop. A breast pushes against the barrier in a manner similar to the naked breast feeling the tip of the poniard at the entrance to the Lodge, but Heathcliff unchains the barrier and orders his old servant to bring wine.

Before the ceremonies begin, the Lodge must be consecrated with wine. The old servant is described as an "Ancient," a term reserved for a retired past Master, but he obeys Heathcliff when given a "compound order" much like the compound passwords Hir-am or No-ah. Joseph is not only old but also hale and sinewy. Sinew could be a sign for a pillar of strength, or a reference to the Master taking a firm grip of the sinews of the candidate's hand when he pulls him up from the coffin. Joseph's "hale" is pronounced the same as "hele," the word found in the warning, "hele conceal and never reveal." The other important function besides consecration of the Lodge is the recitation of the opening prayer of "Vouchsafe Thine Aid Almighty Father," which the Ancient paraphrases as "the Lord help us!"

The word "advent" tells us Lockwood's arrival is an important one, a ceremonial arrival to an initiation perhaps. The unexpected nature of it could be why they must immediately consecrate the Lodge with wine. The other word that conveys importance is 'wuthering'—"a *significant* provincial adjective, descriptive of the atmospheric tumult." This word is a sign of the approaching chaos. I have italicized "significant" because, for Masons, significant words are derived from the compound Latin terms "make" and "sign," and these significant words are equivalent to the secret words used in the degree ceremonies. Brontë signals the advent of both physical and emotional tumult with a word that means to blow, bluster, or roar violently, an apt description of the commotion about to occur with the aid of the Earnshaw and Linton families, so the candidate/tenant must brace himself for the power of the Masons' Great "Architect," and a Lodge full of "shameless little boys" who are in their "stations"—at their corners—waiting for a landmark passing.

Lockwood says he passes the threshold, which can signify the starting point for a new experience. Threshold is definitely a clue. He looks above the "principal door," but this could be a play on the word because the Masons have their *principles* written above the door of the Lodge. He then takes one step into the "penetralium," the innermost part of a sacred temple. To link a rustic farmhouse to a sacred temple seems odd but fitting in terms of the first-degree allegory. In this dwelling, Lockwood sees no signs of roasting, boiling or baking, so no burnt offerings are taking place in the large fireplace.

The First Step into the Lodge
An initiate takes his first step into the light and warmth of this new existence, from the outer world to the inner world. The only things reflecting light and heat are the jugs and tankards, vessels for drinking, a reference that provides a glimpse at Brontë's satirical twist on the rituals

and her assessment of the actions that usually transpire at this Lodge. If the initiate must leave all metals outside the Lodge, it would make sense that Lockwood cannot see any copper or tin utensils. He mentions that the roof has no ceiling, just beams showing. The words are another clue: "its entire anatomy lay bare to an enquiring eye." One of the reasons the initiate leaves his left breast bare is so the inquiring Masons can confirm his gender: no women are allowed. As in *Jane Eyre*, Brontë drops relevant, significant words into the chapter as clues to her secret intention. Certainly, Masons never expose their entire anatomy, but the word "anatomy" still has a connection to the initiation ceremony.

Heathcliff as Master Mason

Instead of the normal "ornaments" of a Lodge, one of which is the mosaic pavement, Wuthering Heights has only three gaudily-painted canisters for their ornaments. Immediately after Brontë describes the ornaments, she mentions the stone floor, the primitive high-backed chairs, an arch, and the words "abode" and "apartment," both terms used to describe a Lodge. Masonic "furniture" has nothing to do with chairs, but refers to The Volume of Sacred Law, the square, and compass. She also manages to slip in the word "degree" when she describes Heathcliff as having "a degree of underbred pride." He is "a dark-skinned gipsy" whose "erect" posture, from a Masonic point of view, acts as an emblem of his mind and emphasizes the vertical plane or his moral uprightness. His dark skin connects him to the ancient mysteries through his Egyptian heritage.

Freemasonry is "a peculiar system of morality, veiled in allegory and illustrated by symbols." In the next three lines Brontë uses common Masonic words: "cover," "bestow," "actuate," "constitution," and "peculiar." Lockwood states that he may never find a comfortable home, or Lodge, because recently he had proved himself unworthy. If the candidate fails to conform to the ritual, the Master deems him unworthy and orders the Deacon to lead him away by the rope around his neck. Heathcliff keeps his hands out of the way when he meets an acquaintance, so Heathcliff avoids giving a Masonic handshake, but why should he? Lockwood, not being initiated, cannot receive the honour of a Mason grip from the Master until he is proven worthy to be actuated, at which time he will be cheerfully embraced into the "peculiar system" of Masonry.

Chamber of Reflection

Jane Eyre spends a frightening time in the red-room with a mirror to reflect on the weaknesses and strengths of her character, but the tone of Lockwood's initiation suggests a satirical spoof of the Masonic Chamber of Reflection. Instead of a silent ceremony, his time in the Lodge is full of noise. Heathcliff and the old servant Joseph leave him in the room to sit in silence, but the dogs remain as company. Lockwood calls one the "ruffianly bitch." The dogs are ruffians, which echoes the term the Masons use for the ruffians who killed Hiram Abiff, the chief architect of Solomon's Temple.

These ruffian dogs keep their eye on Lockwood like the guards at the Lodge. They watch his every movement, sneaking around him like wolves. One dog makes guttural sounds, which fits with one of the perfect points of entrance—the "Guttural," or throat. Lockwood winks and makes faces at the three dogs, a premature misuse of the signs—he has yet to be initiated.

As an initiate, he is meant to remain stoic, so his irritating turns in his "physiognomy" illicit a dog's attack on his knees. His knee is not bare as in the actual ceremony, but Brontë simply wants to drop the word "knee" into the text to produce the general effect of a ceremony echoing Masonic language. The attack brings more dogs into the room, and in a similar scene to the one in Parry's Palace when Charlotte's narrator strikes little Eater with a poker, Lockwood begins "parrying off the larger combatants" with a poker. The noise rouses the whole "hive," which alludes to the bee hive, an important symbol for Freemasons because they admire the industry of the bees.

The word physiognomy provides another clue. The word means the art of judging human character from facial features. The dogs judge Lockwood from his outward appearance and, while a Mason would simply verbally attack the candidate, when the dogs find Lockwood's character suspect, they attack him physically. This judging of character corresponds to the rite of circumambulation when the man must walk around the centre of the Lodge in full view of the brethren, so they can deduce if he is a worthy candidate. In this case, the dogs, not the humans, perform that duty. Even Lockwood calls himself "perfectly unworthy."

More Masonic Words

Brontë continues to choose her words carefully throughout the chapter. She includes "centre," as in the centre of the Lodge, "peculiar" again, and "heels" in the narrative. The placement of the initiate's heels has the significance of resembling a right angle as the heel of one foot rests inside the indention of the other. She continues to drop the words relevant to the ceremony, such as "master" and "vigilant." On the walls of the Chamber of Reflection, the words "perseverance" and "vigilance" are written down for the man to stare at and contemplate, so he will be prepared for the difficult tasks ahead through which he must persevere, and stay vigilant against outsiders trying to steal Masonic secrets. The dogs have been the vigilant guards, and Lockwood has persevered in his solicitation to join the Lodge. When he first greets Heathcliff as a tenant, he hopes that his visit has not inconvenienced his new landlord, or master, in his "perseverance in soliciting the occupation of Thrushcross Grange:" Brontë drops the significant words in an innocent manner, but a pattern of Masonic references emerges as she layers each term onto the rest of her clues.

The Blindfold

Brontë cannot lead Lockwood into the Lodge with an actual blindfold, but she can place a metaphorical cloth across his eyes. He thinks Joseph is the whole establishment of domestics, and is unaware of who else might be in the house. Only on his second visit, as in the second degree ceremony is he greeted without his metaphorical blindfold, which enables him to see that the family includes Cathy and Hareton. When he sees Cathy he says here is "an individual whose existence I had never previously suspected." He has little previous knowledge about Wuthering Heights or its inhabitants and will only become enlightened, as do the readers, when the housekeeper Nelly Dean, at Thrushcross Grange, acts the part of one of the wise brethren and explains the family's background. Lockwood listens with interest as he hears the whole story, which is exactly what a Mason is expected to do—learn his Masonic history. The purpose of the opening three chapters, therefore, is to initiate Lockwood so he may hear the history of the Lodge, a story not only about obsessive love, but also one that outlines Heathcliff's acts of revenge, but in the first three chapters the mystery blindfolds the reader as well as Lockwood.

Lockwood sees Zillah when she rescues him from the dogs, but he has no insight into the workings of the family when he arrives. For Masons, the initiate must first see in his heart before his eyes are able to behold the beauties of Freemasonry. Masons also know the blindfold is metaphorical. The beauty of Wuthering Heights turns out to be Cathy, but for now Lockwood only sees Zillah, which is appropriate in terms of the legend: in one sense, Zillah is the mother of masonry. Her name, therefore, connects her to the original Zillah who was the wife of Lamech and mother of the children who hid the secrets of their crafts inside the stone pillars. Zillah also provides another clue.

Zilla's Apron and "Wand"

When Zilla rushes in to prevent the dogs from continuing their attack on Lockwood, her gown is tucked up. This resembles the aprons of the early operative masons who lifted a corner of their aprons to keep the mortar from soiling their clothes, but the raised flap also symbolizes the Entered Apprentice apron whose triangular flap is always turned up.

Lockwood's greeting is hardly a welcoming one. The apparent lack of neighbourliness continues through the chapter. The Masons are proud of their hospitable fraternity, but Lockwood experiences inhospitable treatment. He says he would have hit the dogs with his signet ring if they had kept up the attack. In Freemasonry, the signet is given to the neophyte to assure him that he is advancing toward truth, and the signet gives him power to continue his search.

Lockwood's initiation becomes a parody of a search for truth as Brontë continues to turn the ceremony on its head. Instead of the brethren's raising of wands over the candidate during the ritual, Lockwood lifts a poker from the fireplace to beat off the dogs. The other object raised is Zillah's weapon of choice—her frying pan. Lockwood is to remain silent when Heathcliff and Joseph leave him in the room to contemplate his surroundings, but he generates the dog attack instead and creates the initial tumult. No one is following proper procedure. As the dogs attack Lockwood, he is "constrained" to ask for help. An odd choice of word. Why not compelled or forced? If you constrain someone, you hold them back, which is exactly what is happening to the initiate due to his blindfold and the noose around his neck. With the Junior Deacon holding the end of the rope, the candidate cannot go anywhere.

A Lecture?

By the end of the first chapter, Lockwood has made his "pledge," and he listens to Heathcliff chip his words, which would make perfect sense to a Mason. The Master is giving Lockwood the Entered Apprentice password. He also discusses the disadvantages and advantages of his place of retirement—Thrushcross Grange. In Freemasonry, the Master gives the Entered Apprentice a lecture and then instructs him to retire and study. The Master would explain that a Mason is first prepared in his heart but, if he had not conformed to the ceremony, he would be deemed unworthy and be led out of the Lodge, but if deemed worthy, the door of Freemasonry is opened. The initiation teaches the man how to control his passions, so it presents him with a frightening situation in which he must trust those around him. The Master, as one of the three pillars, represents wisdom, so Lockwood, accordingly, finds Heathcliff intelligent.

A Secret Initiation

For Masons, an intruder is a man who accidentally enters a Lodge. Lockwood volunteers to return, which is what a Mason must do— volunteer to become a Mason, so this first chapter could be a jumbled version of the Chamber of Reflection gone terribly wrong, and a first-degree initiation that lacks the appropriate ceremony. Heathcliff admits that guests are rare at his home, which clarifies why the members of this Lodge are not as familiar with the rituals, having not often performed them.

The whole short chapter, with its allusions to Masonry, could be viewed as an allegory of the Freemason initiation, and Brontë's satirical dramatization with ancient archetypal symbols and Masonic terms scattered throughout could explain the subliminal effect of the novel's mysterious drama. One critic stated that the first three chapters were superfluous and most likely added after Brontë completed the novel, but if one of the purposes of the book is to relate the secrets and history of a Masonic Lodge where men like Heathcliff plot and carry out plans to acquire land illegally, then the opening initiation makes sense. Freemasonry describes itself as "a peculiar system." Brontë has appropriated the system's method of communicating its legends and mysteries through her own allegory, symbols, and signs. She satirizes her version of the initiation by using a dupe from London as her candidate and, if she continues to inflict her satirical account of the remaining two degrees onto Lockwood, more symbols and signs should naturally appear in the next two chapters.

16 THE ENTERED APPRENTICE RETURNS

In the second chapter, Lockwood returns to the Heights, but cannot get in. He bangs on the door, but his knocking is to no avail: he is still barred from gaining admission. Either he has not arrived properly prepared, or he fails to adhere to the customs of the Lodge or, more likely, Wuthering Heights lacks familiarity with polite formalities and, in its "perpetual isolation" prefers "churlish inhospitality" to traditional Masonic hospitality. Nonetheless, Lockwood persists and grabs the door handle "to essay another trial," so he chooses to begin his tribulations despite obstacles.

Second Degree Ceremony Begins

Lockwood bumps into Hareton, Heathcliff's nephew who "hailed" Lockwood to follow him into the house. The hailing sign is the sign of perseverance in the second degree. Hareton did not wave or gesture—he hailed, which is a clue to watch for other second-degree symbols.

Lockwood follows Hareton into the house where he sees Cathy, Heathcliff's daughter-in-law, near the big fireplace, but she remains "motionless and mute," as brethren do during rituals. She keeps her eyes on him as any good Mason would when an Entered Apprentice passes in view. The brethren have to see he has come properly prepared. Lockwood never knew about Cathy: "I was pleased to observe the 'missis,' an individual whose existence I had never previously suspected." One method Brontë uses to drop clues is to put certain words inside inverted commas, and if watching and observing is part of the Masonic ceremony, then a closer look at the word reveals that, with "missis," she may be playing with the word "Isis," the goddess who is the Mother of the ancient mysteries and whose mysteries are celebrated on March 20, the day Catherine died and Cathy was born. The image of Mother may be relevant and part of the secrets Lockwood is about to unveil, and the existence of the mother Catherine may not be suspected by anyone at this point in the story.

Lockwood eyes the dog from the day before—"the villain"— a term which invokes the memory of the murdering, villainous Fellow Craft ruffians who killed Hiram Abiff. Two more clues appear when he calls this visit his "second interview" and when the dog wags its tail in greeting, as a "token" of their acquaintance. Tokens or grips, signs, and passwords are the secrets the Apprentice must show the brethren in order to gain further entry into the Lodge to become a Fellow Craft. Brontë simply uses the words and, for satirical purposes, inveigles the dogs to act as brethren.

Fellow Masons

Lockwood appears to have passed the first test, so Cathy puts on her apron and speaks. She inquires if he has been asked to stay. Lockwood answers that she is the proper person to ask him, but since she is considered the beauty in the family, and the Junior Warden represents Beauty and is only in charge of refreshment, it would be inappropriate for Cathy to give Lockwood permission, so she "resumed her chair," but in Masonic language, a brother "resumes his seat." Hareton comes into the room and glares at Lockwood "as if there were some mortal feud unavenged between us." This is another clue that will become apparent as we learn more.

Brontë incorporates other Masonic words when she uses "proofs," "promise," "cheerful," "corner," "conduct," and "guide," but she employs the same clue as the one in *Jane Eyre* to show the ceremony has begun. When John Reed hurls the book at Jane's head, she says, "I instinctively started," and after fighting back against the bully is taken to the red-room as punishment and to begin her initiation. When Heathcliff comes into the room and shouts at Cathy to make the tea, he scares Lockwood, who says, "I started." With the Master now in attendance, the second-degree ceremony has officially begun. Lockwood again calls him "a capital fellow," which is the term given to the successful second-degree candidate or Fellow Craft, and "when preparations were finished," Heathcliff invites Lockwood to bring his chair to the table where the four of them sit in "austere silence." While keeping a strict, disciplined silence, they frown in anger, displaying the opposite of the proper cheerful demeanour of not only the Masons, but also the candidate, which is why Lockwood assumes a cheerful manner when greeting Heathcliff.

What Lockwood says to them around the table is intriguing. He comments on how "custom can mould our tastes and ideas: many could not imagine the existence of happiness in a life of such complete exile from the world." Is he talking about the customs of a secret society? *Ritus* in Latin became ritual and grew to mean religious custom. He could be talking about the Masonic rituals and how they shape ideas and keep them apart from regular society. After all, this is "a perfect misanthropist's heaven" at Wuthering Heights. This family is "grim and taciturn," so we could deduce that Brontë sees the ugly side of the Masonic brotherhood with its "universal scowl."

Masonic Words

Lockwood sees this family, living off in a remote area, as being buried alive. Hareton's hands are unwashed, so he has never been through a purifying ritual. Heathcliff's facial expressions do not enable Lockwood to interpret the language of his soul, but he has yet to learn all the passwords and signs. If he continues his journey toward the truth, however, he will soon be able to read Heathcliff's face as well as Cathy's and Hareton's. They know Heathcliff very well as Master of the house, and they know the rules. Brontë litters the page with a few more Masonic words: "reflection," "peculiar," "beneficent," "meditated," "smothered," "curse," "privilege," and "widow." The younger Cathy became a widow when Heathcliff's son died, and Masons are particularly responsive to aiding widows and orphans, but with Heathcliff's terrible treatment of both Cathy the widow and Hareton the orphan, Brontë characterizes her view of Masonic sentiment toward the underprivileged as cruel and violent.

Lockwood sits in their circle, feeling out of place in their "dismal spiritual atmosphere" and considers the appropriate attitude for his return: "I resolved to be cautious how I ventured under those rafters a third time." Caution is a word given to a new Mason as a reminder to be careful about revealing secrets, and, if the silence from the family is any indication, Lockwood will not learn the secrets from this tight-lipped group. He would like to go home, but sees that the weather has worsened: the "sky and hills mingled in one bitter whirl of wind and suffocating snow." He fears taking a foot in advance without a guide, but no one offers to let him out of the ceremonial meal.

The Masonic Fire

Cathy keeps the fire going, but if she takes a break, Zillah is always there to rekindle it. Fire is one of the symbols relating to purification, and with the Phoenix as a name attached to a few Lodges, the idea of a Mason rising again from the ashes, like the mythical bird, and being reborn is also relevant, as is fire's connection to the sun, another major symbol in Masonry. The Greek word *pyr* means fire, from which comes pyramid, a triangular monument over a tomb.

The opening paragraph in this second chapter also provides a clue about the importance of fire to Masons. Lockwood is still at Thrushcross Grange at the beginning of the chapter, but something makes him want to return to Wuthering Heights. A maid is on her knees cleaning out the fireplace with her brushes and coal scuttles, extinguishing the flames with heaps of cinders, and "raising an infernal dust," as if it were dust from hell. The maid is putting out the fire, not lighting it or keeping it lit. Lockwood says, "This spectacle drove me back immediately," so he grabs his hat and heads over to Wuthering Heights. The visual displays of Masonic rituals are certainly part of their spectacle, but to describe the cleaning of a fireplace as a spectacle seems a bit of an exaggeration unless Brontë wants to convey the idea of the maid performing a remarkable act. In that case, the extinguishing of fires must be relevant to Masons. If the maid's action is symbolic of putting out the hell fires of Masonry, Lockwood would see this as a serious and regrettable breach of decorum and would drive him back as if causing him to ward off evil.

More Masonic Words

The second chapter continues with Masonic words: "porch," as in the porch at King Solomon's Temple, "rising," "stepped," "clay," which, to a Mason, constantly reminds him that from clay we all came, and to it we must all return. Brontë also includes the words "pass," "limits," "horror," "praying," "species," "distress," "landmarks," "ushered," and "candle." The long book Cathy has opened is a book on the Black Art of witchcraft, not the Volume of Sacred Law. This could be a parody of the Masonic "furniture."

A Parody of Ceremonial Manners

Cathy tells Lockwood she cannot escort him away from the house because, again, that part of the ceremony is not her responsibility. Heathcliff tells him that he hopes Lockwood has learned his lesson and will not go wandering in the hills in the snow again. Lessons are crucial to advancement in the degrees. The snow continues to fall, so Lockwood must stay the night; he cannot sleep in a chair because Masons are not free to roam the Lodge during the ceremony. Everyone has an appointed place. Lockwood, however, refuses to stay. He runs outside in the dark and, just as in the episode with the dogs, turns things upside down. The Mason circumambulates inside, not outside, where they walk in specific directions to square the Lodge. These ancient ceremonies have used standardized practices for centuries, but Lockwood keeps breaking the rules.

Outside, Lockwood seizes the lantern or light "unceremoniously" from the ancient Joseph, which creates more tumult with cursing and hollering filling the night air. The dogs set on him again, extinguish the light (of illumination?), and lunge for his throat to keep him on the ground, thereby not allowing any "resurrection." Hareton and Heathcliff put the finishing touches or "copestone" (a term in masonry) on his humiliation by laughing while "he's fair choking," an indirect reference to the threat of strangulation from the cable tow round an initiate's neck if he attempts to escape. With the inclusion of the guffaws and laughter, the ritual loses all semblance of a serious ceremony. Lockwood's nose bleeds, so he spills blood, but once again Zillah comes to the rescue to conclude the scene by pouring water on him to cleanse him of his transgression. Brontë gives us blood and water in the locked room with Mason in *Jane Eyre*, and blood and water in the snow with Zillah in *Wuthering Heights*.

Like Jane, and any other candidate overcome from the power of the spectacle, Lockwood feels sick and faint, so Heathcliff tells Zillah to take him into the inner room. She obeys his order and "ushered" him to bed. She acts as an usher just like the servants in *Jane Eyre* when they escort Jane into the red-room. This is definitely a more difficult trial for Lockwood than his encounter with the dogs in the first chapter, especially with the shedding of his blood. The penalty for a Second Degree Fellow Craft is similar to Lockwood's trial. In the degree, if the Mason reveals the secrets, he could have his heart torn out and given to devouring beasts of

131

the field. One of Heathcliff's dogs is called Gnasher, which means to grind the teeth together in anger, while the other dog is called Wolf, a term Brontë uses to refer to Masons. The suggestion from their names is that both of these "devouring beasts" could tear out Lockwood's heart.

Interestingly, the "ruffianly bitch" that attacks Lockwood in chapter one and greets him in chapter two is called Juno, named after the Queen of the Roman gods, the mother goddess, whose other name is Isis. In chapter three, Juno "mounts sentinel" at the house door like a goddess guarding her temple, protecting it from intruders. The blood, the beasts, and the significant words all point to a Masonic ritual at an unorthodox Lodge.

Appropriation of a Masonic Allegory

The Masonic allegory of trials that an initiate must overcome also suits the plot of *Jane Eyre* as Jane grows in stature and degrees. The allegory makes sense as a statement of her ability to progress through regular society as well as a fraternal society that prohibits women. Allegorically, Lockwood's initiation enables him to hear the history of Wuthering Heights. He learns, by degrees, about Heathcliff, his strange family, and the suspicious manner in which Heathcliff accumulates Wuthering Heights and Thrushcross Grange, but as soon as the three degrees are completed, Lockwood's appearance in the story is minimal until the final chapters. Without the first three chapters, therefore, he would never hear the story from the housekeeper, Nelly Dean, who now becomes the novel's narrator, nor would he be able to dishonour the code of silence with his diary—the novel—and reveal the family secrets, but Brontë also begins the novel with those three chapters because she wants to set up the Masonic allegory and their rules from the onset. Nelly had lived at Wuthering Heights and is familiar with its history so, in terms of the allegory, she used to be part of the Masonic family and, therefore, knows all the circumstances of their lives. Nelly's recollection of events, however, is only part of the story and Brontë conveys truths through another medium of words that lie much deeper in the novel. If Brontë's allegory extends to the use of Masonic third degree signs that mirror a third degree rebirth ceremony, then she, like the Masons, would reveal the most important truths in the third chapter.

17 LOCKWOOD GETS THE THIRD DEGREE

In the third chapter, Lockwood is forced to pass a terrible night of suffering in the oak closet bed in Catherine's old bedroom. He dreams of Joseph, cudgel in hand, leading him through the snow to a chapel, with the Ancient reproaching him for not bringing a staff (or rod), an implement he needs to gain entry to the church. No stranger can be allowed into a Lodge unless vouched for by a member, so Lockwood's dream implies that he has been accepted into the brotherhood. He assumes that someone is about to suffer excommunication or, in Masonic terms—expulsion.

Chaos at the Lodge

Inside the chapel, Lockwood can no longer endure a seemingly endless sermon from the Reverend Jabes Branderham, so he yells at the rest of the congregation to attack the boring preacher: "Fellow-martyrs have at him! Drag him down, and crush him to atoms, that the place which knows him may know him no more!" These last words echo the sentiment taken by Masons when one of their numbers dies: "his accustomed place will know him no more," as the member experiences the ultimate expulsion—death. This insubordinate outrage to effect another Mason's death incites the whole group to attack Lockwood with their staves, so, suddenly, "the whole chapel resounded with rappings and counter-rappings," a clear allusion to the knocks and counter knocks between the Master Mason with his gavel and the Masons with their rods.

A Cherub Appears

Lockwood awakens from this nighmare to hear a tapping noise at the window and a bough blowing against the glass. Reassured, he falls back to sleep, but hears the wind howl and, again, the fir bough taps against his window. He tries to open it, but the hook is soldered shut. He breaks the window to push away the noisy branch, but along with the driving snow in comes the ghost of Catherine as a child.

She appears at his window and her fingers grasp his hand in much the same way as a Master Mason takes the candidate's hand in a strong grip before raising him from the coffin. Also, a strong, "tenacious" grip is a form of greeting between Masons and would show Lockwood Catherine's association with the brotherhood. Instead of acknowledging her membership, the terrified Lockwood scrapes the child's wrist across the jagged pieces of glass until blood drips onto his bedclothes, but still she clings to his hand until he tricks her into letting go, but her "lamentable prayer" continues. After the ritualistic handshake, bleeding, cleansing water (in the form of snow), and closing prayer, he plugs the hole with a stack of books in the shape of a "pyramid," a subtle allusion to the fraternity's Egyptian origins.

The ghost keeps yelling, "I've been a waif for twenty years," but Catherine died seventeen years earlier, not twenty. Brontë scholars have noted this inconsistency but cannot explain the error: "Nobody has really been able to solve the problem of what exactly the ghost of Catherine means when she says in Lockwood's dream that she has been an outcast for twenty years" (*Critical Essays* 118). She repeats the word "twenty" three times: "'It's twenty years,' mourned the voice, 'twenty years, I've been a waif for twenty years!'" In this particular setting, the number holds significance for Masons, but Lockwood ignores her cry.

Masonic Landmarks

In the third-degree ceremony, Lockwood must experience a form of death and gain wisdom about the immortal soul. The legend of Hiram Abiff teaches him the doctrine of the restoration from death to eternal life. Of the twenty-five landmarks, or principles, in Freemasonry number twenty is the belief in immortality, so Lockwood's proof of eternal life stares back at him, much like Jane Eyre's mirror in the red-room reflects a "strange little figure" whose "glittering eyes of fear moving where all else was still had the effect of a real spirit." The cherub arrives to proclaim the soul's immortality.

During the third degree ceremony and before the candidate hears this divine truth, fear is the primary emotion. Lockwood's fear escalates as he is forced to confront the face of a child while he lies in a coffin-like bed, so he fails to hear the relevance of the ghost's cries. In fact, Brontë adds irony to their exchange: Lockwood yells at the ghost: "'I'll never let you in, not if you beg for twenty years!'" This could be translated as: "I'll never let you in, even if you were to tell me there's life everlasting!" The ghost makes her impassioned reply that could be paraphrased as: "That's exactly what I'm telling you—Immortality, Immortality, Immortality!"

Lockwood's fear impairs his judgment and causes a kind of paralysis: "I tried to jump up, but could not stir a limb." This resembles Jane Eyre's description of Mason as he lay bleeding: "fear, either of death or of something else, appeared almost to paralyse him." When Lockwood sees the pyramid of books move, he cries out "in a frenzy of fright." Jane Eyre lets out her primal scream in the red-room and, in both cases, their yells end their horror.

Lockwood awakens and sees a light appear through the squares in his closet bed. Could this be the light of illumination to signify Lockwood has learned the final truth?

Heathcliff's vigorous hand pushes open the bedroom door while the other holds a candle, enabling Lockwood to see the necessary material light. What happens next provides further evidence that the ritual is a satirical replica of a Masonic third degree ceremony.

Masonic Signs

The interaction between Heathcliff and Lockwood shows Brontë's design. Lockwood wipes away the perspiration from his forehead and presumes an "intruder" is in the room. For Masons, an intruder is a non-Mason who is trying to learn the secrets and gain the benefits of Freemasonry in a surreptitious way. Lockwood uses the word appropriately because whoever has opened the door has interrupted the ceremony, an action that would be viewed as a clandestine ploy to eavesdrop.

He hears the man mutter a few words, passwords perhaps, and recognizes Heathcliff's voice, so he opens the panel doors, which immediately frightens a white-faced Heathcliff and causes him to drop the candle from the "electric shock" of hearing noises in the room. He retrieves the candle, but his hand shakes so much that the light scurries round the walls, much like the "quivering" light in Jane's experience in the red-room. Heathcliff's candlelight casts a similar fluttering light inside the room instead of a steady beam from the nether world.

The Master should not be frightened, however, and he should certainly be making proper use of his hands and face, but everything

135

convulses in an unnatural manner. He crushes his nails into his palms, grinds his teeth to stop his jaw from trembling, and tells Lockwood not to repeat his horrid scream: "nothing could excuse it, unless you were having your throat cut." Heathcliff's comment refers to the Entered Apprentice obligation to never violate the secrets of Masonry, or he will suffer the penalty of a cut throat. Lockwood counters that if "the little fiend" had broken through the glass she would have "strangled" him, a reference to the cable tow or rope tied round the candidate's neck as insurance against any escape from the ceremony. Cut throats and strangulation are serious threats within the fraternal rituals, and Lockwood communicates to Heathcliff that he understands the forms of Masonic punishment.

After being reminded of the throat cutting penalty, Lockwood stops himself from admitting he had been reading from Catherine's "Testament" or antique volume whose "hieroglyphics" were difficult for him to interpret. These two words imply a connection to the sacred texts of the ancient Egyptian mysteries where prayers and rituals would have been written in hieroglyphics.

The action of reading Masonic history would have warranted more penalties because no Mason is ever to write down any of the Institution's secrets, nor is a candidate meant to reveal the old volume's contents, especially when Catherine's volume, written years earlier, spoke about taking an "initiatory step" with Heathcliff. The proper method for learning the Masonic history will come to Lockwood in the form of Nelly Dean's narrative.

Lockwood also indirectly informs Heathcliff that he has learned certain lessons regarding the Craft. He states that he will no longer "endure the persecutions" of Heathcliff's "hospitable ancestors." The "persecutions" allude to the ritual attacks throughout the three-degree ceremonies, which he will no longer have to endure now that he has passed through the death rite. Hospitality has always been an esteemed virtue among Freemasons dating back to ancient times. The old Masonic constitutions detail hospitality as one of the duties of the Craft, so Lockwood acknowledges the connection of the ritual to the past.

He then asks Heathcliff an odd question about the garrulous preacher in his dream. He says, "Was not the Reverend Jabes Branderham akin to you on the mother's side?" Heathcliff was an orphan, and Lockwood cannot be expected to know anything about Heathcliff's relatives at this point in their acquaintance, so what could he mean? In Masonic terms, one possibility is that his odd mention of Jabes Branderham would constitute a form of password that would be recognized among brethren.

The second possibility is that the dream or allegorical drama was one of Brontë's satirical steps Lockwood had to take within the degree ritual. His question also links Branderham and Heathcliff to the Mother Lodge. Lockwood says "the mother's side," not "your mother's side." These exchanges seem strange, but the dialogue between Master and candidate would appear equally odd within a real ceremony.

The third remark from Lockwood introduces the concept of the Masonic Lost Word. When a Mason becomes a Master in the third degree, the legend of Hiram Abiff is played out through the drama of the ritual. The candidate lies down and plays the role of corpse. He rises, to imitate a form of resurrection, and the Master Mason, acting on behalf of King Solomon, whispers a password into the man's ear. Until the actual word is recovered, the candidate will learn a substitute for the secret lost word, the word that Hiram Abiff refused to share with the ruffian Fellow Crafts.

Lockwood's witnessing of the "wicked little soul" at the window forces him to blurt out the secret of what he witnessed. In terror, he has faced his own mortality and achieved a state of oneness with a form of divinity, but his role in the allegory is not to communicate his discovery, not even to a Master Mason, but to keep it personal and secret. Accordingly, Heathcliff yells at Lockwood to stop: "'What *can* you mean by talking in this way to *me!*' thundered Heathcliff with savage vehemence. 'How—how *dare* you, under my roof—God! he's mad to speak so!' And he struck his forehead with rage." Lockwood's words make no sense in the rite; consequently, Heathcliff fails to understand his meaning.

Heathcliff also reminds Lockwood that he is the Master, and must lead the ceremony. Unfortunately, Lockwood's fear compels him to speak out. Rather than substitute the secret with an unconventional choice of words or passwords, Lockwood continues to tell Heathcliff exactly what happened to him; thus, he breaks the rules and upsets the Master.

He shares his revelation that he experienced a visitation from an eminent being or, in this case, Catherine's ghost. On the narrative level, he restores the literal lost love to Heathcliff, a truth that later enables Heathcliff to join Catherine in death and, on the allegorical level, restores the lost word regarding the resurrection of the soul. On both levels, the news generates "an uncontrollable passion of tears" in Heathcliff, which suits his joy over Catherine's return, but also displays his despair over Hiram Abiff's murder. The ritual, while at times perplexing, powerfully affects Heathcliff and terrifies Lockwood, but they still have to complete the ceremony as passed down through the centuries.

Hiram Abiff's Resurrection

Brontë drops clues and borrows signs from the Masonic ritual that recount the legend of Hiram Abiff. The third-degree ceremony acts out the day the Fellow Crafts killed the master architect. During his beatings from the three villains, Hiram gave the Sign of Distress by wiping the perspiration from his forehead.

When Lockwood wakes up, he enacts this sign even though he fails to recognize Heathcliff: "I sat shuddering yet, and wiping the perspiration from my forehead: the intruder appeared to hesitate and muttered to himself." Heathcliff then gives Lockwood the Sign of Sympathy at seeing the substitute Hiram's suffering. Masons bend their head forward and gently touch their forehead with the right hand. Heathcliff does it with more force. He strikes his forehead, supposedly with rage, but Brontë uses it as a Sign of Sympathy.

Lockwood acknowledges that his imagination had not been under control. This is the proper attitude for a candidate who is truly immersed in the "frenzy" of the ritual, so Heathcliff continues the rite by exchanging positions with him: Lockwood rises from the bed to get dressed and Heathcliff falls back "into the shelter of the bed." As Master, he is now in the bed and Lockwood stands opposite. Then they exchange passwords.

More Masonic Landmarks

They speak through the signs of the landmarks. Lockwood mentions the time of night and says, "'Not three o'clock yet! I could have taken oath it had been six.'" The word "oath" is relevant because Lockwood, through the rituals, has taken an oath to protect the secrets, an oath he breaks by later writing all the events in his diary. Landmark number three refers to

138

the legend of the third degree, so Lockwood acknowledges to Heathcliff that they have just participated together in the ceremony. Landmark number six stipulates that Heathcliff, as Master of the Lodge, can confer degrees at irregular times, and fits with the ritual having just transpired in the middle of the night.

Lockwood adds, "'we must surely have retired to rest at eight,'" which is his way of saying that Heathcliff can make Masons at sight. Landmark number eight states Heathcliff has the power to initiate, pass, and raise candidates in a Lodge of Emergency, or as it is called in the *Book of Constitutions*, an Occasional Lodge. This Ceremony is specially convened by the Master and ceases to exist as soon as the initiation, passing, or raising has been accomplished. This enables a man, like Lockwood, to be made a Master Mason without waiting for instruction between degrees, and he can then receive instructions after all three degrees from a willing Mason. In Lockwood's peculiar case, Nelly Dean conveys the necessary knowledge about Heathcliff and the influence of Masonry on the Linton and Earnshaw families.

The next set of clues comes with Heathcliff telling Lockwood the time the locals retire. He says, "'Always at nine in winter, and always rise at four,'" and he suppresses a groan before dashing a tear from his eye. Heathcliff uses landmarks nine and four as important reminders to Lockwood that it is essential that Masons congregate in a Lodge, and that the Lodge must always have a grand Master.

He then groans and makes the Sign of Grief. Heathcliff is acknowledging that Lockwood is the substitute for the deceased Hiram. The Master passes the right hand across the face and drops it over the left eyebrow in the form of a square. Heathcliff drops his hand over his eye, "dashing a tear from his eyes." Outside the realm of the Hiram Abiff allegory, Heathcliff is in a frightful state of grief over the loss of Catherine, so his groaning and teary response to the events of the evening make sense, but the signs and secret words also show the intricate design behind the Masonic rite.

This part of the ceremony ends when Heathcliff allows Lockwood to walk along the steps and passages. The tight restrictions on his movements have been partially lifted—he still cannot venture out to the yard, or go outside the "temple" where Juno guards the door. Lockwood has passed the steps necessary to become a Master Mason, even though the rituals were slightly skewed, but the ceremony is not entirely complete nor the night quite over.

More Signs and Symbols

Lockwood descends cautiously to the lower regions where the small flicker of a fire is still lit. As a symbol of his rebirth, a cat rises from the ashes and salutes him. Not quite a mythical phoenix but a bird's worst enemy, so perhaps a more powerful sign. The cat and Lockwood sit on the two benches shaped in a circle and exchange a few nods.

Joseph comes down a ladder that vanishes into the roof through a trap, an apt symbol for Jacob's ladder. Masons see it as a mystic ladder that connects the ground floor of the Lodge with the roof, and a theological ladder that represents Jacob's—the one that reaches from earth to heaven. Lockwood rests in the silent, solemn "sanctum" with Joseph, where he tries to regain some composure and comfort. Joseph leaves, and Hareton arrives to usher Lockwood into the main part of the house where Zillah is building up the fire.

Another sign comes from the daughter Cathy. She holds her hand up to block her eye from the heat of the flames. This is the Sign of Horror given by Fellow Crafts that mimics the shielding of the eyes from the horror of seeing Hiram Abiff's dead body, now metaphorically appearing in the shape of the risen Lockwood. Heathcliff appears, and Zillah plucks up the corner of her apron again and groans. All welcoming signs for a Mason.

Heathcliff then orders Cathy to take out the trash. The Legend of the Rubbish has its origins in the building of King Solomon's Temple where the workmen would remove the rubbish daily. The trash represents the material things of earth that slow the Mason's moral and spiritual growth while he builds his spiritual edifice. To leave trash around would be equivalent to leaving, in his heart and mind, hindrances to the moral and spiritual life, so all trash should be avoided or removed. Cathy refuses the order and Heathcliff raises his hand, but stops. There must be no disruption of the peace in the Lodge, or the brothers will suffer penalties of expulsion or suspension. The ceremony must end with refreshment, not a dispute, so "each had enough decorum to suspend further hostilities," and invite Lockwood to breakfast, but he politely declines their offer.

The rituals of the three degree ceremonies come full circle with a return to Heathcliff's hands. The rituals began in chapter one with Heathcliff's hands sheltered in his waistcoat and ends in chapter three in a like manner as he stops himself from hitting Cathy: "Heathcliff placed his fists, out of temptation, in his pockets." He had refrained from hand signals at the beginning because Lockwood was not a fellow Mason, and now that the farmhouse will no longer be operating as a proper lodge, he has no need to use his hands to gesture and make signs. Life will return to normal and his hands will, once again, be used for slapping and punching.

A Final Trial

Lockwood has survived the night and can hardly fault Heathcliff for the jumble of rituals since, as he admitted, they rarely entertained at the Heights, and the opening of the Lodge was a special occasion. Lockwood has successfully passed the trials, and is happy to be going home, but on his way to Thrushcross Grange he sinks up to his neck in snow as if buried up to his neck at low tide. This penalty alludes to the punishment meted out to a Mason who tells secrets. Lockwood refrains from revealing anything that night but, after uncovering a few mysteries from Nelly Dean, he writes the whole story in his diary, the book that becomes *Wuthering Heights*.

Refreshments

The clock chimes twelve when he arrives at Thrushcross Grange, an hour that represents the meridian sun, and the time when Masons enjoy their refreshment. Nelly Dean and the other servants greet Lockwood, saying they were so worried about him that they were going to set out in the snow to search for his remains. This comment also connects with the rituals: when Hiram Abiff died, the masons set out in different directions to hunt for his body.

The servants leave Lockwood alone to continue his final preparations before receiving the study of Masonic history. Masons use the word "refreshment" to mean a rest period so, like all good Masons who pass successfully through their rituals, Lockwood enjoys a "cheerful fire" and some coffee that has been left for his "refreshment."

The structure of the novel with its three opening chapters, and the device of Nelly Dean recounting the history of the "house" to Lockwood, the newly passed Mason, suited Brontë's vision. She inserts a layer of Masonic allegory alongside a narrative layer that depicts Heathcliff's efforts to seek revenge and secure rights to two pieces of property.

The Masons use allegory and symbol to reveal secrets; therefore, Brontë adopts their system to mock the fraternity and demonstrate a specific level of corruption she apparently witnessed. An understanding of her rationale for incorporating the first three chapters enables readers to reflect on her deeper meaning and to appreciate the origin of the novel's mysterious power.

18 THE RECOVERED LOST WORD

Since Freemasonry is steeped in Egyptian mythology and initiation rites, Heathcliff being a gypsy (Egyptian) is no accident, but what ancient entity might Catherine represent?

The Egyptian mysteries were secret, severe in their trials, and linked with the esoteric worship of the deities of Egypt, specifically the Goddess Isis, Mother of the universe and Nurse of all things. The mysteries of Isis were celebrated at the spring equinox, March 20th, the day that Catherine dies in childbirth and her daughter Cathy is born. This day signals rebirth and rejuvenation, and the repetition of the name "Catherine" could signify a form of rebirth. The candidate was prepared for initiation by a period of fasting and by particular ceremonies calculated to inspire the person with a sense of awe. In each case, the initiate approaches the confines of death, similar to Lockwood's experience in the coffin-like bed the night he sees the ghost of Catherine Earnshaw. Isis was believed to be the personification of nature: "I am Nature and no mortal has ever unveiled me." The veiled Isis symbolizes the secret doctrines of the ancient philosophers, and under the veil of Isis, the Mother, are concealed all the mysteries and learning of the past, so to understand the spiritual depths requires the candidate or initiate to partake in initiation, study, and commitment.

To Freemasons, the mysteries of Isis form the foundation of the Dionysian Architects, from which so many symbolic rites have emanated and are perpetrated in the various degrees of Masonry. Dionysus is the Greek god of winemaking and revelry, and the early priests who worshipped him were builders.

The central theme in the ancient legend of Freemasonry that has carried on into present day is the rediscovery of the Lost Word, which has gone to the grave with Hiram Abiff. In the secret doctrine, possession of the Lost Word is the key to salvation, so the initiate starts on a journey to discover the Lost Word. He receives secrets, the most important being how to attain the immortality of the soul, and this secret then guides him through his evolution from human to divine. Each initiate must find the Lost Word or he will miss his chance at immortality.

The symbol of the Lost Word and the legend of the search embody the whole design of Freemasonry. The primary object is the search for Divine Truth. The Word is a symbol of this Truth and the key to understanding the secrets of the soul. The Word that was lost when the three Fellow Crafts killed the Master Mason represents an understanding of the life one lives, but which is hidden beyond the five senses, in our memory. In the ancient mysteries and in Freemasonry, the belief is that we long to possess what was lost.

For Heathcliff, he knows, beyond his senses, that Catherine is still alive in some form. He searches for the love he has lost through death and seeks eternal life with his Catherine. He is unable to let go his hold on Wuthering Heights until her spirit returns to free him. Lockwood uncovers the truth of Catherine's existence when she appears to him, and he shares this Truth with Heathcliff. This information gives Heathcliff an understanding of his plight: he will never be whole until he unites with his lost love, but the news of her appearance at the window confirms that she awaits their reunion through death. This Truth also provides the reader with further clues about Heathcliff's home and his life.

Lockwood could be Brontë's substitution for the Lost Word. The play on the word is self-evident (lost word/Lockwood). An awareness of his character's role, therefore, is crucial to a deeper understanding of Brontë's intention in writing *Wuthering Heights*. He is not merely a passive ear for the storyteller Nelly Dean nor is he a minor character. As the necessary character in the unfolding of Brontë's secret narrative, Lockwood not only leads the reader through a deeper understanding of the bond between Heathcliff and Catherine, but he also uncovers symbols and their meaning in order to guide us to a truth hidden behind the rituals. Lockwood discovers the Masonic truth of immortality in the third chapter, but the legend's rituals begin in chapter one.

In the allegory of Hiram Abiff's death and resurrection, the Master gives a substitute Lost Word to the Mason. In this rediscovery of the Lost Word, the Mason learns the secret that guides his evolution from human to divine. In Lockwood's diary, his account becomes the novel, so if Lockwood is the embodiment of the Lost Word, there must be a clue to direct the reader to an ultimate truth. He discloses Catherine's existence to Heathcliff, who now knows that she awaits his journey to the land of immortality, a revelation of his personal truth that sets in motion Heathcliff's decline into death, which allows him to reunite with his lost love in their unique heaven. Lockwood's declaration of his dream to Heathcliff is confirmation that Catherine's spirit is out on the moors, but what secret for the reader does Lockwood hold?

Brontë left a clue in *Jane Eyre* when she pointed to a secret in the red-room. The words, "and a miniature of her deceased husband" contained the "secret of the red-room: the spell which kept it so lonely in spite of its grandeur." After rearranging the letters and spelling out the new words, the anagram produced the hidden message: *Dread cherub aide in mason death. Unsafe.* A similar clue appears in chapter one in *Wuthering Heights.* Lockwood breaks from his narrative about arriving at Heathcliff's abode to explain a "curious turn in his disposition." Brontë digresses from Masonic ritual, and Lockwood leaves his description of events and of the inhabitants at Wuthering Heights to discuss his insensitive treatment of a woman at the seashore. What are we meant to find in Lockwood's personal revelation? He says, "While enjoying a month of fine weather at the sea-coast, I was thrown into the company of a most fascinating creature, a real goddess, in my eyes, as long as she took no notice of me. I 'never told my love' vocally; still, if looks have language, the merest idiot might have guessed I was over head and ears." Lockwood describes meeting the woman and explains that, "the merest idiot might have guessed I was over head and ears." The phrase before it reads, "if looks have language." Are we meant to look at the language? The merest idiot might have guessed—guessed what? An idiot could see he was—what? He was over head and ears, which is a phrase Brontë has used before and means he was out of his depth. Why? The merest idiot might have guessed there is a reason for him being in over his head? If we look at the language will we discover what was really making Lockwood feel he was in too deep?

Brontë includes this character's aside for a reason: it contains a secret. Hidden inside Lockwood's confession is another anagram: "The merest idiot might have guessed I W-A-S-O-V-E-R-H-E-A-D-A-N-D-E-A-R-S" or "The merest idiot might have guessed I *rove as dead Earnshaw.*" The only dead Earnshaw ever interested in roving the moors after death is Catherine, the mother, whose spirit has apparently returned to the dwelling

145

of her childhood and infiltrated, not just Wuthering Heights but Lockwood's third degree passing through Masonic rituals. Her haunting of the scene would certainly place Lockwood over his depth, and the fact that her apparent message to the reader comes through Lockwood's words, we could infer that she has taken a kind of possession of his body. But why has she returned to the story in this way? Her motivation for her own sudden rebirth guides us deeper into the dark soul of the story and her haunting of Lockwood ushers us directly into the heart of a Masonic Lodge. If we are to believe that Catherine can speak to the reader through Lockwood's words, we need to accept that the key to Brontë's secrets are not simply found in word clues and allegorical duplications of Masonic rituals, but in a code well hidden inside the prose.

The possibility that the novel contains a Masonic layer similar to the one in *Jane Eyre* brings us back to the question of authorship. Scholars could make the argument that, because Emily and Charlotte were sisters, they would have discussed with each other everything about their books and developed a plan to mock the Freemasons. The scholars would say that, for *Jane Eyre* and *Wuthering Heights* to contain the identical underpinning of a Masonic cosmology, the sisters must have studied the secret society with obsessive perseverance, hated the Masons with equal passion, which instilled in them a co-conspiracy to reveal Masonic symbols and secret rites, and that because of their mutual disrespect for these men, they colluded to insult them through a satirical parody of their ancient ceremonies, and contrived an intricate design of clues, puns, and hints in the same elaborate system as the other sister. Instead of Emily and Anne being the "twins," Charlotte and Emily would have been twin brains who shared an identical approach and attitude to the material. Also, instead of Emily running from the men, as has been recorded, she would have changed her personality and begun studying them, which would have taken her away from her life-long passion for her Gondal characters. As well, the two sisters would have been equally keen on creating anagrams. If we accept that Charlotte and Emily had become like twins in their pursuit of secretly usurping the legend of Freemasonry, and that both displayed an affinity for anagrams, then we should also accept what the anagrams tell us.

Due to the various permutations and combination of letters one could construct with anagrams, Brontë's system of code could be viewed as entirely speculative, but with modern science now able to explain brain function, especially prodigious abilities when dealing with savants, Brontë's skill may be better understood in that context.

The word savant comes from the French *savoir*, which means knowing or wise. Savants have one common trait: they all display remarkable powers of memory. They may also exhibit extraordinary talent in one particular area, such as music, mathematics, or literature but, at the same time, suffer from a form of mental disability. Savant syndrome has become the subject of study for cognitive psychologists who try to understand memory, and for neuroscientists who map its place in the brain. Savant syndrome is sometimes linked with autism or PDD, pervasive developmental disorder, which can appear in children who have low levels of communicative skill in social interaction. Asperger's Syndrome refers to those who function on a higher level, and who differ in degrees of severity; they can relate to the outside world, but there may still be a tendency to withdraw from play activities, be seen as reserved, and become preoccupied with one interest.

Savants can have photographic memories, can play a difficult piece of music perfectly after having heard it only once, can speak several languages, or they can solve complex mathematical calculations in their head like a mental calculator. They share a similar brain process that allows them to calculate at lightning speed.

Scientists believe savants gain their exceptional capabilities either genetically or through brain injury. When the case is genetic, the neuroscientists note brain abnormalities, but the exact role the abnormality plays is still a mystery. Psychologists study cognition and ask, "How can they know something they never learned?" The remarkable memory ability or language fluency, for instance, is akin to having language software installed in the brain at birth. One theory suggests the brain compensates for sensory disability, such as blindness, by developing latent skills in other areas of the brain. Those who study this syndrome, as well as the general public, all wonder, "How do they do it?"

Kim Peek may offer an answer. In a 2005 article in *Scientific American Magazine* entitled "The Mind of a Savant," Drs. Darold A.

Treffert and Daniel D. Christensen introduce Kim as one of those savants with a prodigious memory whose specialty is books. His interests range from Shakespeare and classical literature to the Bible and American history. He can read one page in 8 seconds and memorize its entire contents and then retrieve information from it days later. In 2005 he was fifty-four years of age and, by that time, had memorized more than 9,000 books. The film *Rain Man*, starring Dustin Hoffman, was inspired by Kim's ability. Those who study the syndrome and who saw the movie ask, "How does he do it?"

Experts in San Francisco used fiber tracking, a non-invasive process to study the three-dimensional architecture of Kim's brain. They were able to see the connections between regions of his brain and discovered that he had no *corpus callosum*, (Latin for "tough body") a large bundle of nerves at the lower end of the cortex that links the two cerebral hemispheres.

Did this lack of nerve fibers cause his brain to over compensate, or did the absence of this connection enable existing talents to emerge? If certain parts of the brain are shut down, will that enhance other parts? The experts are unsure, but they recognize that this condition, while rare, does not necessarily come with mental or physical functional disorders, and note that those with this condition experience what can be described as a "split brain" syndrome: the two hemispheres work almost independently of each other. "It would seem that those born without a *corpus callosum* somehow develop back channels of communication between the hemispheres. Perhaps the resulting structures allow the two hemispheres to function, in certain respects, as one giant hemisphere."

The process is still a mystery, but the result is clear: these exceptional abilities are easy for savants to perform, but difficult for most of us to comprehend. Unfortunately, Kim Peek died in December of 2009, but before his death he performed a particularly stunning and relevant task that he called his "magic trick." The absence of the *corpus callosum* allowed him to read two pages of a book at the same time, with one eye on each page. His comprehension and retrieval of the information were still the same because his optical system placed the letters and words in order.

Kim Peek's "trick" resembles Branwell Brontë's extraordinary "parlour trick" that he performed for his Masonic brothers when he was secretary at the Lodge meetings. His ability to simultaneously write Greek with his left hand and Latin with his right suggests that Branwell's *corpus callosum* may also have been abnormal, and that his "split brain" enabled him to do this trick without effort. His remarkable ability, like Kim Peek's, offers the first clue to Charlotte Brontë's ability, which we will see in the next chapter, to perform complex anagrams in her head. Like her brother, her "ambidextrous" skill deals with words. Branwell's skill seems impossible, but he and his sister must have been born without the nerve fibers or, alternatively, with a mental apparatus that released a barrier of sorts that limits less adroit brains from exercising this function.

What we can understand is that, in Charlotte's case, her facility with anagrams would not appear inside her thoughts in any way that we can imagine. We might assume that she saw two sentences simultaneously, the one she wrote on the page and the anagram sentence she held in her head. Much like a translator who knows two languages fluently, she could transform a line of prose in her mind's eye into an anagram sentence 'behind' the prose and, when deciphered, expose another meaning from what the reader would see. She would have no need to write down the anagram because she would see it perfectly constructed in her mind.

Further clues as to her mental prowess come from Charlotte's friends at school and her eldest sister Maria. As mentioned above, Mary Taylor and Ellen Nussey remarked on Charlotte's unique mind: "She would confound us by knowing things that were out of our range altogether," and "she was in the habit of committing long pieces of poetry to memory, and seemed to do so with real enjoyment and hardly any effort." A strong characteristic of savants is their remarkable memory. The eldest Brontë daughter Maria also showed signs of a prodigious intelligence. Unfortunately, she died at the young age of eleven, but Reverend Brontë described her as having "a powerfully intellectual mind" (Barker 118), and that she read local and national newspapers from an early age. Her father said he could speak with Maria about the contents of the news as easily as if speaking with an adult. The precocious intelligence of Maria, Charlotte, and Branwell shows that the mental acuity was genetic.

Another characteristic common in individuals with either partial or complete absence of the *corpus callosum* includes vision impairments. Both Branwell and, especially, Charlotte had poor eyesight.

Charlotte's extreme shyness and her inability to look at people when she spoke could suggest a mild form of Asperger's Syndrome as well, or she was simply self-conscious about her appearance. As a woman with unusual, fantastic thoughts, she had learned to subdue her natural passion and intellect while in the company of strangers and acquaintances, which could also account for her shyness, but she was equally capable of sustaining long-term, close friendships. Her unique talent, so large that it bordered on the savant level, without the affliction of mental challenges associated with savant syndrome, can just as easily be explained as a factor of her genius.

The explanation regarding savants and the introduction of Asperger's Syndrome are not meant to suggest that Charlotte was a savant or was suffering from Asperger's, but to try to show that the brain can be capable of remarkable and strange expressions that normal intellects find impossible to understand. Charlotte Brontë was not necessarily a savant; but she was certainly a genius, so her abilities are difficult to fathom.

Her genius presented itself in obvious ways, such as her fluency in French and her prolific output of writing, and, if her brain was structured with a partial or complete split in her *corpus callosum*, the anagrams could feasibly appear as effortlessly for her as when she memorized poetry or learned French. Her ability to construct so many anagrams would complement her love of literature, language, and writing and would allow her the freedom to express her true feelings beyond the view of readers. Without a scan of her brain, however, we can only surmise that her brain's structure was abnormal and, while her anagrams can demonstrate her skill, the question, "how did she do it?" will continue to elude us.

19 THE CATHOLIC QUESTION

Before viewing her early anagrams and seeing what they reveal, we need to set her messages in a context that demonstrates Charlotte's interest in the outside world, whether she was studying the realm of London politics or the society of Haworth Freemasons.

This shy, small girl with the short-sighted hazel eyes, soft, brown hair and plain face could just as easily bury expression while she roamed among strangers as light up with excitement from a thrilling passage of prose. Her thin, tiny frame and poor eyesight held her in check whenever she sat in company, but those eyes were observing her world, and her powerful intelligence was recording events and consuming literature from the solitude of her home.

Inside the parsonage, the children learned about the wider world through books and newspapers, and they chronicled that world through the filter of imagination. The major sources for the Brontë children's writing could be found in their father's library. The Reverend Brontë's shelves contained numerous books, some of which Charlotte mentions in an 1834 letter to her friend Ellen Nussey: "You ask me to recommend you some books for your perusal; I will do so in as few words as I can. If you like poetry, let it be first-rate, Milton, Shakespeare, Thomson, Goldsmith, Pope (if you will though I don't admire him), Scott, Byron, Camp[b]ell, Wordsworth, and Southey. Now Ellen don't be startled at the names of Shakespeare, and Byron. Both these were great Men, and their works are like themselves. You will know how to chuse the good and avoid the evil; the finest passages are always the purest, the bad are invariably revolting; you will never wish to read them over twice. Omit the Comedies of Shakespeare and the Don Juan, perhaps the Cain of Byron though the latter is a magnificent Poem and read the rest fearlessly; that must indeed be a depraved mind which can gather evil from Henry the 8th from Richard 3d, from Macbeth and Hamlet and Julius Caesar, Scott's sweet, wild, romantic Poetry can do you no harm nor can Wordsworth's, nor Campbell's, nor Southey's, the greatest part at least of his; some is certainly exceptionable. For history, read Hume, Rollin, and the Universal History, if you *can I* never did. For fiction—read Scott alone all novels after his are worthless.

For Biography, read Johnson's lives of the Poets, Boswell's life of Johnson, Southey's life of Nelson Lockhart's life of Burns, Moore's life of Sheridan, Moore's life of Byron, Wolfe's remains. For Natural History read Bewick, and Audubon, and Goldsmith and White of Selborne" (*Letters, Vol.I* 130-1).

News of international and political affairs spread throughout England in local newspapers. Charlotte read two Leeds newspapers each week. Her father ordered the conservative (Tory) *Leeds Intelligencer* and the liberal (Whig) *Leeds Mercury*, and the Reverend Jonas Driver shared his copies of the *John Bull* newspaper, which, at thirteen, Charlotte describes as "high Tory, very violent." He also lent them *Blackwood's Magazine*, "the most able periodical there is" (Beer 181). Her father encouraged his children to read these newspapers and to partake with him in discussing current events and political intrigue. In 1829, Charlotte's interest in Britain's politics erupted over the issue of Catholic Emancipation, especially when her father participated in the debate through his published articles in the Leeds' newspapers.

The Catholic problem had begun much earlier in the 17th century when England passed legislation that excluded Catholics from holding public office. The government instituted this law because of the Catholics' refusal to acknowledge any country's civil power as having authority over the Pope. Only practicing members of the Anglican Church of England, therefore, could enjoy the benefits and privileges of holding office. Tory blood ran thick through this long-held argument that members of the official state church alone qualified to partake in discussions and decisions that directly or indirectly affected their Church of England. To submit to the call for repeal would be a strike at the very security of the established Church of England. Opponents of this exclusive right, however, argued that their countrymen should be allowed a place in Britain's Parliament. During the 1820s, liberal Dissenters in England had been campaigning against the conservatives for the law to be repealed, citing that it also discriminated against Protestants. The turning point came from Ireland.

In 1793, Roman Catholics in Ireland were given the right to vote. That right still did not allow them to sit in Parliament. In 1798, a political and militant organization called the United Irish planned a rebellion to defeat British rule in Ireland. After much violence and bloodshed, the

British troops crushed the Irish uprising. Years later, an Irish lawyer Daniel O'Connell, as part of his political attack to abolish the law, began raising money to help fund the re-election of parliamentary members in favour of Catholic Emancipation. In 1828, as the Irish Catholics were gaining ground for emancipation, he decided to put himself in the race in a by-election in County Clare. The Catholic voters arrived at the polls in such a show of strength that O'Connell won in "an avalanche" of votes. The Catholics had successfully elected their leader Daniel O'Connell to the British House of Commons, but he would still face an additional obstacle. Legally, O'Connell could run in the election as a candidate but, because he was a Catholic, the law prevented him from taking his seat in Parliament as the elected representative of County Clare. If the British government denied O'Connell the legally won seat, the Irish could stage another rebellion that would lead to further violence and bloodshed. The solution arrived through Charlotte's chief man, the Duke of Wellington.

In 1827, Wellington was appointed Commander-in-Chief of the British Army. A year later, the popular Tory became Prime Minister of England. He was loath to grant the Catholics full civil rights, but he was equally unwilling to provoke more civil strife in Ireland. He recognized his power to void the by-election and ignore the Catholic question, but as a politician and a professional soldier, he knew resistance to emancipation was impractical and that the greater threat to British security would be another Irish uprising. Wellington's Home Secretary, Robert Peel became a crucial ally in his cabinet. Even though Peel had vigorously opposed emancipation for twenty years and anticipated the savage attacks from the newspapers, he set his principles aside in favour of peace and agreed to take the issue of Catholic Emancipation to the Commons in February 1829. He reluctantly recognized the need for change. This about-face is what caused Charlotte to remark to her friend Mary Taylor in 1832 that "Sir Robert Peel was not to be trusted; he did not act from principle like the rest, but from expediency." Charlotte knew the history behind this crucial debate and followed it closely with her father.

At the beginning of 1829, Reverend Brontë wrote three letters to the *Leeds Intelligencer* supporting a Catholic Emancipation Act. The Act would enable Catholics not only to sit in Parliament and hold civil office, but also to vote at elections and be included in British military commissions, providing they take an oath of allegiance to King and country. The Reverend, while a strong Tory who had long opposed emancipation, once called the "popish influence, 'that ghastly Incubus of the human mind'" (qtd. in Lock 352), and in his 1818 fiction *The Maid of Killarney*, has a character say, "should ever Protestants and Roman Catholics sit together in Parliament, they will constitute a mixture of powder and sparks that will blow the fabric of the State to atoms" (361), but now he recognized that the issue dealt with rights of the individual, and those rights should be legislated provided that safeguards were put in place during attacks to the country. He agreed with Wellington that civil strife was the greater threat and wrote: "we cannot continue as we now are, even for a few years longer, without the manifest danger of a general convulsion, that might shock the whole empire to its centre, and dissever for ever Ireland from Great Britain." He explained that he was not a radical but a "liberal friend to Church and State" who believed in justice with secure measures in place: "without the safest securities, it would be rash, it would be hazardous in the extreme, to permit Roman Catholics to have any share in our legislation" (Barker 158).

Charlotte and her family, for the most part, all anti-Catholic, anxiously followed the developments in their Leeds newspapers. Like most of the country, Charlotte was drawn into the excitement of this latest political intrigue, but what made these events exceptional was the involvement of her chief man in a real political debate, not a fictional one from inside her Angrian fantasy world. She read the speech Wellington's Home Secretary Robert Peel gave to the House of Commons and was reluctant to accept his change of heart, but her father had found the measure more practical. Peel began his speech by saying that a "most painful circumstance that could be imposed on a public man, in the performance of a public duty must be when, after long acting with a number of individuals, after proceeding in concurrence with them to the utmost of his power in a particular course of policy, he finds himself called upon, by peculiar circumstances, to separate from them."

He went on to explain that the honourable members had a unique responsibility to King George IV. Their contract with the King was to provide him with the best advice they could give under present, not past, circumstances. Peel placed the welfare of the country ahead of opposition to the Roman Catholics and would advise His Majesty that concessions should be implemented. The members in the House of Commons agreed, and the Roman Catholic Relief Bill was devised and sent to the House of Lords (Peel's Speech).

Two months later, Charlotte could hardly contain her excitement when she read the Prime Minister's address to the Lords at the second reading of the Bill. Wellington rose and spoke of his regret that he opposed his honoured friends whom he respected, but that, in lieu of the threat of civil strife, he must make the safety and protection of the lives and properties of His Majesty's subjects the highest priority. "My lords, this is the state of society to which I have wished to draw your attention, and for which it is necessary that parliament should provide a remedy." He explained that the Catholics would have to abide by set safeguards, and "By this bill they will be required to take the Oath of Allegiance, in which a great part of the Oath of Supremacy is included" (Wellesley).

At the parsonage, Charlotte and her family followed the news arriving in the London papers. During the three-month period after Wellington had given his impassioned speech, the family discussed the Catholic question, reviewed the speeches, and wondered if the Bill would pass through the House of Lords.

In April, Charlotte sat expectantly in the sitting room. She watched as her father removed the cover from the newspaper and began reading the report. She imagined the opening of the doors of Parliament, the Dukes stoic and formidable in their robes and the Great Duke himself dressed in his waistcoat and green sash as the men voted in favour of the Bill. When her father announced that the Bill had been passed, a cheer rose from the parsonage sitting room. Aunt Branwell said, "I think it is an excellent decision. The Catholics can do no harm with such good security."

Reverend Brontë added that Wellington's speech had been wonderful. "His words were like precious gold." The safeguards were in place, and Wellington had earned another victory (Barker 157).

The question of Catholic Emancipation had not kept Charlotte from writing her views of the dreaded Romish religion. She presented her opinion of its dangerous bigotry in an allegory in chapter four of her *Tales of the Islanders*. She describes England and Ireland united by a golden chain, and on each Island sit two queens: one sits on a ruby throne and

155

wears a crown of roses, while the other is on a throne of emeralds and wears a crown of shamrocks. The Irish queen plays a mournful song on her harp, which makes the narrator wonder what could be causing her grief. Suddenly, he notices something approaching from the ocean.

"I perceived a tremendous monster rise out of the sea and land on her island. As soon as it touched the shores a lamentable cry burst forth which shook both islands to their centre, and the ocean all round boiled furiously, as if some terrible earthquake had happened. The monster was black and hideous and the sound of his roaring was like thunder. He was clothed in the skin of wild beasts and in his bare head was branded, as with a hot iron, the word "bigotry." In one hand he held a scythe, and, as soon as he entered the land, the work of desolation began." A warrior shoots a dart with the word "justice" written upon it and strikes the heart of the monster. As soon as the monster collapses and dies, the desolated land returns to its former beauty (*Early Writings, Vol.I* 108). Charlotte's familiarity with allegory began with *The Pilgrim's Progress* and *Paradise Lost*, and proved a useful education when later writing in the pages of her adult fiction.

Branwell, too, had been excited with the talk of Roman Catholicism. He expressed his zeal with the unique theatricality of a precocious twelve-year-old, far from the eyes and ears of his father and aunt. Charlotte witnessed his antics and found them deplorable. Unwilling to receive a fist in her back if she informed on him to her father, she chose another method to vent her anger and frustration, a method she used for the rest of her life to document abhorrent behaviour and evil conduct she believed was occurring in her township, but first she wrote about her brother. She described his acts, not in allegory, not in prose, but in her own unique code that kept her thoughts hidden from his view.

The original surface letters in her writing contained a secret story inside them. In the following example, her surface words appear rather simplistic, but 'behind' the apparent discussion, they reveal information kept concealed from her father, her aunt, and her siblings. While her brother openly displayed his ambidextrous talent with writing Greek and Latin, Charlotte released her frustrations in the dual mental practice of anagrams, a skill that remained undetected for her entire life. By the age of thirteen Charlotte had been writing caustic satire, precise characterizations, and complex sentence structures, but the words she left on the page in

March of 1829 express simple statements, run-on sentences, and a few misspelled words that create suspicion that anagrams may reside beneath the lines. While the words on top appear uncomplicated, underneath she hid a shocking story in her sophisticated and clever, secret language.

Charlotte composed these anagrams in March, before the House of Lords had passed the Bill on Catholic Emancipation. The lines have been separated with a slash mark to indicate the way she groups her anagrams as she reveals Branwell's actions.

"Once papa lent my sister Maria a book. / It was an old geography and / she wrote on its blank leaf, / 'Papa lent me this book.' / The book is an hundred and twenty years old; / it is at this moment lying before me. / While I write this I am in the kitchin of the parsonage house, Haworth. / Taby the servent / is washing up after breakfast / And Anne my youngest sister / (Maria was my eldest) / is kneeling on a chair looking at some cakes / which Tabby had been baking for us. / Emily is in the parlour brushing it / Papa and Branwell are gone to Keighly / Aunt is up stairs in her room / and I am sitting by the table writing this in the kitchin" (Beer 181).

In the anagrams, Charlotte describes an angry boy who ignores his country's decree that no one shall participate in Roman Catholic worship. In England, Catholics could be fined or imprisoned for openly practicing their faith. She reveals that he drinks gin, pretends to be a priest, and that he partakes in the Catholic sacrament of Holy Eucharist, which requires red wine, a substance he steals from the Haworth doctor. The inclusion of punctuation helps to clarify the awkward syntax. She also uses words that could be read either as a noun or a verb.

Mock parliament as an irate boy. Pose, / swear, add gin—holy to pagan. / Fowl table as token shrine. / Papist monk oblate, he / drank bloody, red wine, then Sunday ate host. / Imitates rite of myth, being solemn. / Which high priest initiate took heath wine from aunt's healer? Who is / a brave street thief but prays with snake fangs? / Satan synonym unites greed / (a sly madame writes) / Mask link to original snake; one sage choice. / Kin rubs face with ash. Begs. An hobby. / Prime hilarity: insult neighbours. / Work or play, engaged an alphabet line / Nourish amateur's spirit on / these witty biting anagrams. Hid nib. Ink chit title hint.

157

If the anagrams are "translated," she seems to be asking, how best could an angry boy mock parliament? He could pose, which in this case would mean to affect the character of a Catholic priest; he could swear, worship and drink gin, and pretend to be a papist monk, as he plays the role of priest at the "fowl table," the chopping block used for killing chickens. She considers her use of Satan a "sage choice," proof of a sister's wise judgment of a younger brother's sinful actions. She uses "an" before the letter "h" in the word "hundred" and in the anagram before the word "hobby." This practice arose in English grammar when a word beginning with a silent "h," as in "heir" or "honest," needed the indefinite article "an" to precede it and, for some instances, when the "h" is dropped in the pronunciation of the word, which may have been the case for Brontë with the words "hundred" and "hobby": she may have pronounced them "undred" and "obby."

In the last anagram, she uses a pun when she says "hid nib," which suggests she hid the point. Not necessarily the point of the pen, however, but the sharp point of her accusations. Her mind obviously relished the word play and uncensored witticisms while her spirit enjoyed the secrecy and guaranteed safety of the anagrams. She states that she left a hint in the title, so an anagram exists there as well. The title of this "chit" or small message is "The history of the year," and as an anagram: *Toy heresy to her faith.* Branwell's theatrical display at the "fowl table" is merely a "toy heresy," a child's imitation of dissent aimed at her church, the Church of England.

Brontë hides sophisticated descriptions of Branwell's high jinks under simple, child-like sentences. She even mirrors her visible parenthetical statement about her eldest sister Maria with a parenthetical aside in her anagram, in which she comments on her "sly" tactic of secretly writing about Branwell's antics.

Her reference to the anagrams provides a glimpse into her involvement with the code. Apparently, she could construct these *alphabet lines* inside her head throughout the day, a game that exercised her brain and fed her spirit. Her anagrams are both witty and biting, and they demonstrate a skill with language that sets her intelligence in a realm far from most educated thirteen-year-olds then and now. The complexity of the anagrams allows some insight into the power of her brain and helps explain the level of her brilliance as she evolved into a genius author.

The discussions on Catholic emancipation and Charlotte's keen interest in the topic of the day had inspired Branwell to poke a little fun. Sadly, his heresy strikes two disturbing notes: the first being her allusion to his drinking wine. This revelation is entirely believable because Reverend Brontë's proud and hopeful vision of his son as a successful young adult evolved into a nightmare when Branwell became a drug addict and an alcoholic. His family and friends imagined a man fulfilling his great promise as a talented painter or a famous poet, not as a drunk who destroys his gifts through addiction. The image of Branwell drinking wine fits his later decline, as does his precocious behaviour as Brontë describes it; he pretends to be a beggar child and insults the neighbours, either verbally or by faking hunger to receive their charity. Her use of Satan, the "original snake" is a harsh "synonym" for Branwell, but clearly illustrates her contempt for his actions.

Charlotte's anagram of Branwell stealing wine at age twelve indicates that his addiction began early in his life and not, as previously presumed, in his late teens. The boy was accustomed to seeing alcohol: his father kept port and sherry at the parsonage, but Branwell's friends in the village more than likely provided him with drink, which enabled his habit. His reckless behaviour endeared him to the men of Haworth who viewed spending an evening "half-floated" a young man's right. Many had become his drinking companions and were alcoholics themselves, so their relationship with liquor allowed his drinking to go unchecked.

The second sad point Brontë makes in the anagram is that her brother was a "street thief." This was a term used during the nineteenth century in Yorkshire to describe minor larcenies, such as pick pocketing or stealing from market stalls. Petty larceny also covered the fraudulent removal of another's property through trickery, which would have included the impersonation of a beggar to intentionally take someone's money. Concerns about Branwell's stealing later arose in 1841 when, as a clerk at the Luddenden Foot railway station, he was fired for the theft of several pounds. Brontë's reference to his taking the doctor's wine and his being a "street thief" could represent the start of his proclivity for drink and dishonesty.

His role-playing also began at an early age. His alter ego, Alexander Percy assumes a particularly relevant role in Branwell's 1845 unfinished novelette, *And The Weary Are At Rest*. The interesting fact about this story is that Percy pretends to be a minister. He dresses in the black coat of a cleric with the "white cravat," and refers to himself as the "Rev" in front of his friends. They greet him with their laughter, but their "mirth or raillery could [not] disturb the rapt inspiration of his divine countenance." They drink "fireballs," a mixture of brandy with an egg yolk dropped into a wine glass and see Percy as a "divine looking saint, with eyes distorted almost to a squint—a mouth that changed its play each moment from wrapt solemnity to malicious drollery, and a pair of orange whiskers horribly out of harmony with the holy sable of his scrupulously neat attire." Percy takes the joke much further when he attends a service with his newly attired friends, now similarly dressed in their clerical robes, and impresses the congregation with his powerful oratory style.

The image in the 1829 anagrams of a much younger Branwell acting like a priest and mimicking the solemn rites of Catholicism rings of truth, especially when he re-enacts the role of a minister a few years later. Percy, his favourite character, tells his friends, "It has not been the first occasion on which I have dressed myself in motley, but I can doff the fools cap as easily as don it" (Neufeldt *Vol.III*).

Of course, Charlotte may be imagining these scenes of Branwell; the anagrams may be incorrectly translated; and the question could be posed, "Are these anagrams even there?" The anagrams continue to disclose interesting information, but one could argue that they are a figment of this author's imagination. This conclusion is a fair and reasonable one that may remain to the end of this book. In the meantime, the possibility that the anagram messages hold new facts about Charlotte and her life is worth exploring.

If the anagrams are to be accepted for the time being, Charlotte seems preoccupied with venting her sisterly disgust over her brother's actions. A few months after donning the fool's cap in March of 1829, Branwell apparently regressed to a baser substance on a visit to another parsonage. Once again, Charlotte recorded his vice.

20 A FAMILY VISIT TO TODMORDEN

Charlotte also reported on Branwell's addiction in the autumn of 1829 after a trip to Todmorden. In mid-September, Aunt Branwell took the four Brontë children with her to visit her Uncle John, the vicar at Cross Stone parsonage, several miles from Haworth. John Fennell's wife Jane (Elizabeth Branwell's aunt) had died in May, so a visit from his niece and the children provided a welcome change.

Three steep hills flanked the valley, restricting the moorland stretch to the confines of the village. At the top of one of these hills sat St. Paul's church, built in the fifteenth century so, for over three hundred years, villagers from each generation had made the exhausting long climb to its front doors. Most of the inhabitants preferred to live in the uplands rather than down in the valley where the weekly clamber would test the mettle of most parishioners.

Todmorden shared the same winds that whipped past the Haworth parsonage, the winds that cleared the clouds to reveal a magnificent view of the countryside. Unfortunately, the weather during the visit was wet and cool, so the children spent their time indoors. Mr. Fennell, as the children called him, helped them with their lessons and provided them with books. As he and his niece, Elizabeth Branwell, enjoyed their tea, the children curled up by the fire and read.

In the evening, they would listen intently as the vicar recounted the story of meeting their father. The two religious men had met in 1808 when the Reverend Brontë was an assistant curate and Mr. Fennell was a Methodist lay preacher in Wellington, Shropshire. This meeting would prove a fortunate accident indeed because, just four years later, John Fennel would introduce the Reverend to his future wife, Maria, the children's mother. By that time, in 1812, the Reverend had become the curate at Hartshead, the area that had been plagued with Luddite riots, where angry craftsmen attacked the textile industries of Yorkshire, smashing looms and frames and burning factories. Charlotte later uses these riots as background in her 1849 novel *Shirley*.

While Reverend Brontë was at Hartshead, Fennell was headmaster of the new Wesleyan Academy at Woodhouse Grove. Fennell had written to Patrick asking him to become a school examiner, so when Patrick arrived at Woodhouse, Fennell immediately showed him the schoolroom, a converted barn, and explained that, as the newly appointed Inspector, he would test the boys' aptitude in Latin and biblical passages. The position would last only one year, as various Ministers would share the duty, but this additional income was much appreciated and would raise Patrick's annual earnings to £75.

The people who knew Patrick Brontë at this time liked him. They described him as "a very earnest man, but a little peculiar in his manner; that he was brave, impetuous, daring, proud and generous; a good friend and a good enemy where there was a wrongdoing. He was, however, inclined to take offence when none was meant, and to fly into a rage for no apparent reason. He could never abide a supposed taunt or sneer of any kind" (Lock 55).

In June, he returned to Woodhouse on a social call and marched up the winding path, shillelagh in hand, not suspecting the momentous meeting about to occur. At thirty-five, he had much to celebrate: he had his own parish in Hartshead; he was the new Inspector at Woodhouse academy; and he had realized a literary ambition to publish a book of his poetry called *Cottage Poems*. As he entered the drawing room, he was a bachelor, an Anglican minister, and a poet. When he saw the young lady in the silk dress, standing by the window, he knew his life was about to improve.

Maria Branwell, a small and intelligent woman with light brown hair and hazel eyes, captivated the Reverend. She was twenty-nine, the eighth of eleven children, and the younger sister of Elizabeth Branwell, the children's aunt.

The Branwell family was a prosperous and well-respected part of the Methodist's community in the Cornish seaport town of Penzance where their life was one of privilege and politics. The Branwells gave financial support for the building of the town's Methodist chapel in 1814. The town "had a ladies' book club founded in 1770, a scientific and literary society, concert rooms, and assembly rooms built in 1791 by Elizabeth's uncle Richard Branwell. Maria and Elizabeth's father, Thomas Branwell,

162

worked as an importer of "luxury goods such as tea, which he sold wholesale or through his Market Square grocery shop. He also owned or leased a brewery, the Golden Lion Inn, Tremenheere House, and other property"; consequently, upon his death, he was able to leave "life annuities of £50" to his daughters" (*Oxford* 58).

The provocative rumour in Cornwall about Mr. Branwell was his forebears were pirates. This particular detail pleased the Brontë children who had been sitting at Mr. Fennell's feet in rapt attention. Aunt Branwell kept her head bent over her needlework as the story continued through to Patrick and Maria's courtship.

From their meeting in June to their wedding in December of 1812, Maria and her "friend" exchanged letters. Maria's few letters, for the most part her only extant documents, provide a glimpse into the character of the Brontë children's mother. Her correspondence covers the engagement period of four months, and conveys a thoughtful and deeply religious woman whose initial cordial tone gradually develops into an open declaration of love.

At first, she addresses her letters to "My Dear Friend," then "My Dearest Friend," and finally "My Dear Saucy Pat." The following excerpts from her correspondence to him show Maria Branwell to be a religious woman and provide evidence as to why the Reverend fell in love.

"I will frankly confess that your behaviour and what I have seen and heard of your character has excited my warmest esteem and regard, and be assured you shall never have cause to repent of any confidence you may think proper to place in me, and that it will always be my endeavour to deserve the good opinion which you have formed, although human weakness may in some instances cause me to fall short" (qtd. in Lock 124).

"I feel with you the unspeakable obligations I am under to a merciful Providence—my heart swells with gratitude, and I feel an earnest desire that I may be enabled to make some suitable return to the Author of all my blessings. In general, I think I am enabled to cast my care upon Him, and then I experience a calm and peaceful serenity of mind which few things can destroy. In all my addresses to the throne of grace I never ask a blessing for myself but I beg the same for you, and considering the important station which you are called to fill, my prayers are

163

proportionately fervent that you may be favoured with all the gifts and graces requisite for such a calling. O my dear friend, let us pray much that we may live lives holy and useful to each other and all around us! . . .

"Pray much for me that I may be made a blessing and not a hindrance to you. Let me not interrupt your studies nor intrude on that time which ought to be dedicated to better purposes" (126-7).

"My heart tells me that it will always be my pride and pleasure to contribute to your happiness, nor do I fear that this will ever be inconsistent with my duty as a Christian.

"My esteem for you and my confidence in you is so great, that I firmly believe you will never exact anything from me which I could not conscientiously perform. I shall in future look to you for assistance and instruction whenever I may need them, and hope you will never withhold from me any advice or caution you may see necessary. . . .

"Mr. Fennell has crossed my letter to my sisters. With his usual goodness he has supplied my *deficiencies*, and spoken of me in terms of commendation of which I wish I were more worthy. Your character he has likewise displayed in the most favourable light; and I am sure they will not fail to love and esteem you though unknown" (131-2).

"I already feel a kind of participation in all that concerns you. All praises and censures bestowed on you must equally affect me. Your joys and sorrows must be mine. Thus shall the one be increased and the other diminished. While this is the case we shall, I hope, always find 'life's cares' to be 'comforts.' And may we feel every trial and distress, for such must be our lot at times, bind us nearer to God and to each other" (133).

"Surely after this you can have no doubt that you possess all my heart. Two months ago I could not possibly have believed that you would ever engross so much of my thoughts and affections, and far less could I have thought that I should be so forward as to tell you so. I believe I must forbid you to come here again unless you can assure me that you will not steal any more of my regard.

"Enough of this; I must bring my pen to order, for if I were to suffer myself to revise what I have written I should be tempted to throw it in the fire, but I have determined that you shall see my whole heart" (135).

"Could my beloved friend see my heart he would then be convinced that the affection I bear him is not at all inferior to that which he feels for me—indeed I sometimes think that in truth and constancy it excels. But do not think from this that I entertain any suspicions of your sincerity—no, I firmly believe you to be sincere and generous, and doubt not in the least that you feel all you express" (136).

"I am pleased that you are so fully convinced of my candour, for to know that you suspected me of a deficiency in this virtue would grieve and mortify me beyond expression. . . .

"I do not, cannot, doubt your love, and here I freely declare I love you above all the world besides. I feel very, very grateful to the great Author of all our mercies for His unspeakable love and condescension towards us, and desire 'to show forth my gratitude not only with my lips, but by my life and conversation'" (138).

"I am certain no one ever loved you with an affection more pure, constant, tender, and ardent than that which I feel. Surely this is not saying too much; it is the truth, and I trust you are worthy to know it. . . .

"Adieu, my dearest. I am your affectionate and sincere Maria" (141).

When Charlotte read the entirety of these letters years later, she found they touched her deeply:

"It was so strange to peruse now for the first time the records of a mind whence my own sprang—and most strange—and at once sad and sweet to find that mind of a truly fine, pure and elevated order. They were written to papa before they were married—there is a rectitude, a refinement, a constancy, a modesty, a sense—a gentleness about them indescribable. I wished She had lived and that I had known her" (*Letters, Vol.II* 347). Charlotte had been only five years old when her mother died of cancer in 1821.

Mr. Fennell's remembrances of Maria may have softened the heartache accompanying her early death. All would have agreed that nine years of married life was too short a union for a man and woman who loved so deeply.

The children spent the remaining afternoons at the parsonage sketching. Mr. Fennell showed the girls a variety of paintings from the Lake District in Westmoreland. They drew lofty cliffs with mountain springs rushing down to the sycamore trees and pastoral farms adjacent to dark woods.

On their last day at Cross Stone, Charlotte noticed that Branwell had taken his paints and his sketching tools outside. He wanted to draw directly from nature, not from a secondary source, so he chose to brave the inclement weather and march across the crest of the hill away from the parsonage. Charlotte wrapped herself in her cloak and followed him. The next day, they arrived safely back at their home.

Later that night, on September 25, 1829, Charlotte chose the words necessary to communicate her displeasure with her brother. She would hide her anagram even deeper with abbreviated forms that would resist detection. She wrote on a small piece of paper the following cryptic message: "on September the 25 I put in the Life of the Duke of W a piece of paper burnt at one end and on it was inscribed—Charles & Arthur Charlotte Brontë" (Barker 167).

In her mind's eye the letters twisted and rolled into a language all her own. She wrote to expose the darker side of a young boy whose many personas she had held in her heart with fondness and affection: Alexander Percy, Young Soult, Sergeant Bud, and Rymer, but this latest scoundrel threatened to impair her love through his foolish conduct. She neatly folded the paper, comfortable that the truth would live well after dust and beyond the stars in her imaginary world where the true measure of a man is how long he can remain sober.

She used the numeral '25' but the word is spelled in full for the anagram, and the ampersand is written as "and". The first portion reads, therefore, as "On September the twenty-five I put in the Life of the Duke of W," followed by three more parts: "a piece of paper burnt at one end / and on it was inscribed / Charles and Arthur Charlotte Brontë.

In her anagram Charlotte uses the words "huffs," and "catarrh." Huff is a slang term for inhaling the fumes of a chemical in order to become intoxicated, and catarrh is described as the inflammation of mucous membranes, especially of the nose and throat. The message she folded into the paper made no sense, but the anagram is perfectly clear.

Nephew feeble, yet huffs white turpentine. Took fit. Vomited. / Painted beer tap. No fee. Can pour / brown stain inside cad. / Rotten breath catarrh. Cure? Hollands.

The image of a twelve-year-old boy sniffing turpentine, as a means to feel inebriated, is a shocking and telling one. Charlotte can only hope that her brother's decline into drunkenness is a temporary state, but her hopes, like her father's for his son, are soon dashed. The writings from Branwell a few years later continue to portray drinking as a manly sport, alongside bloody noses, black eyes, and gambling. The only perplexing word in the anagram is "Hollands," but this word, too, shares a connection to alcohol.

The word "Hollands" appears in both of the Brontë men's writings. In *And The Weary Are At Rest,* one of Branwell's characters remarks to his drinking friends that "he hoped there was plenty of Hollands distributed" (Neufeldt, *Vol.III*).

In Reverend Brontë's medical journal, Hollands is also mentioned under the heading, *"Well fermented malt liquors,"* where he writes the following: "British Brandy, (as I have heard and proved) is very heating and bad, and so are rum, whisky, Hollands and Gin, which are mixed with a large proportion of spirits of Turpentine—*aqua fortis*—and all wines and malt, or fermented liquors, whether bottled, or not, are for the most part detrimental—and above a wine glass, or two in the week, even of French Cogniack, Brandy or any quantity of this or any other spirit daily or twice a day or on every other day—or without four times its quantity of water, would, as I have read and heard, injure the stomach and nerves, though the old French Cogniack Brandy is occasionally only medicinal."

He continues with an additional note beside malt liquors: "Many drunkards often use daily eight, or ten wine glasses of ardent spirits." Under the heading *Catarrh,* he notes "The fumes of tobacco must be carefully avoided" (Lock 380-1).

In the 17th Century, Holland was the original producer of strong alcoholic liquor flavoured with juniper berries and known as Hollands or Holland gin. Common gin was flavoured with a different substance and is also noted in the medical journal. Under "Turpentine," Reverend Brontë writes, "This is often one of the component parts of gin—instead of juniper berries, which were used, formerly" (379).

Both father and son appear to have knowledge of the ingredients in liquor. Alongside the heading, "Intoxication," Reverend Brontë notes that, "Cold water may answer best." The author of the journal, Dr. Graham, writes that twelve drops of water of ammonia mixed with sugared water helps to calm a drunk. The Reverend includes the cost for this at eight pence an ounce and adds that it has "only some little effect" (381). This suggests he may have tried the remedy on Branwell, but no drops of medicine will cure alcoholism, and the father soon abandoned any hope of motivating his son to make the steep climb back to sobriety.

Years later, in 1838, Charlotte also mentions Hollands in her writing. A character in *Stancliffe's Hotel* stops her narrator Charles Townshend when he begins to relay a rumour about a man's drinking. "'What?' interrupted the Marchioness. 'Not proof spirits, I hope! Watered Hollands, I know, scarcely satisfied him'" (*Tales of Angria* 69).

Perhaps Charlotte hoped Branwell would reform his ways when he reached maturity, but in 1829, she shows nothing more than a marked antipathy for his weakness. She uses her gift of satire in the anagrams when she states that Branwell drinks gin to correct a condition of catarrh, which the huffing of turpentine caused. (White turpentine is obtained from pine trees.) Ironically, he drinks alcohol to cure the effects of alcohol.

Her reference to Branwell painting a beer tap if he wants free beer reflects her dry humour and reads true since they were painting and sketching during their visit in Todmorden.

As Branwell's drinking increased and his addiction grew into an intolerable situation for his family, Charlotte wrote to her friend Ellen in January of 1848 about his 'fits':

"We have not been very comfortable here at home lately—far from it indeed—Branwell has contrived by some means to get more money from the old quarter—and has led us a sad life with his absurd and often intolerable conduct—Papa is harassed day and night—we have little peace—he is always sick, has two or three times fallen down in fits (*Letters, Vol.II* 8).

Two days before this letter, Branwell had written to his friend to explain that he was not intoxicated when they had met the previous week, but "so much broken down and embittered in heart that it did not need much extra stimulus to make me experience the fainting fit" (6).

The fits may have been brought on by the alcohol, but rumours suggest that he may have suffered from epilepsy, and "that his epilepsy would be exacerbated by alcohol and would account for the description of 'falling down' in fits rather than simply becoming unconscious" (7, n. 3).

Charlotte's tendency to express her real thoughts and feelings behind a cover of code may have been unintentionally encouraged years earlier with a practice her father instituted when she was about six years old. Reverend Brontë believed that his children were more knowledgeable about diverse matters than they were divulging, so he devised a plan to enable them to speak openly and without fear of reprimand:

"I deemed that if they were put under a sort of cover I might gain my end; and happening to have a mask in the house, I told them all to stand and speak boldly from under cover of the mask."

He asked Anne what she would like, and she said, "'Age and experience.'" He asked Emily what he should do with Branwell, "who was sometimes a naughty boy," and Emily replied, "'Reason with him, and when he won't listen to reason, whip him.'" To the question, "what was the best way of knowing the difference between the intellects of men and women," Branwell answered, "'By considering the difference between them as to their bodies.'" The father asked Charlotte to name "the best book in the world," and she said, "'The Bible,'" and named "The Book of Nature," as the second best (Gaskell 234).

Mrs. Gaskell remarked that the father had used this method "to ascertain the hidden characters of his children" (36), a strategy Charlotte employed when she used the mask of various pseudonyms to write with candour. Perhaps this desire to conceal her hidden character inspired her use of anagrams as a kind of code to protect prying eyes from seeing her personal truth.

If Branwell was known for simultaneously writing Greek and Latin with his left and right hands, perhaps, in light of the anagrams, we can conclude that Charlotte also had inherited a similar innate ability that enabled her to perform two mental tasks at once.

She loved words and was a well-read, educated woman known for her wordplay and her encyclopedic memory of biblical verses, lines of poetry, and texts of Shakespearean plays. She even wrote to her friend Ellen that she enjoyed the "enigmas" in a woman's magazine. Therefore, her ability to reorder letters to create an anagram would not be considered a difficult mind-game for someone of her mental stature.

We may never know how she mastered this mental feat, but with the discovery of her skill, we can begin to explore her silent narrative as it reveals secrets about herself, her family, and her village. For instance, without her anagrams, Branwell's early drug and alcohol history would have remained unknown, as would minor and major transgressions that involved other recipients of her disdain.

21 LETTERS TO POETS

As a young girl, while lying in bed without the light from a candle, Charlotte Brontë had trained herself to write in the dark. Her eyesight had always been poor, so her simulated blindness meant only a minor adjustment to her vision. This habit carried over into the daytime when she would close her eyes while guiding her pencil along small sheets of paper. During both day and night, with eyes closed, she could absorb herself in her writing without having to endure the distractions of the outside world. Her students at Roe Head commented on her odd, and perhaps a little unsettling penchant for writing without candlelight but for Charlotte, the evening brought peace and comforting visions, so these private moments provided not only the reviving pleasure found in designing stories but also the necessary solitude to craft sentences sublime and powerful. After a day of household or teaching duties, she loved the luxury of being sequestered in her home under the antique roof, beside the dying embers, and with the soothing silence her lone companion as she filled pages with her poetry. Unfortunately, not everyone viewed her desire to write as a noble occupation for a woman. One man, a famous poet, found it unhealthy and unproductive.

On a particularly chilly night in 1837 while home from Roe Head School, the cinders in the fireplace were almost out as she sat alone at the table in the parlour of the Haworth parsonage, writing a response to Robert Southey, England's poet laureate.

Southey had been England's poet laureate for thirty years until his death at the age of 68 in 1843. He was an essayist, historian, biographer, and poet and was friends with the Romantic poets Samuel Taylor Coleridge and William Wordsworth. He was the author of the children's classic fable about Goldilocks entitled, *The Story of the Three Bears*. Branwell and Charlotte both admired his work, and when Ellen Nussey asked for reading recommendations, Charlotte suggested his poetry and his biography *Life of Nelson*.

A few months before her twenty-first birthday, Charlotte had written to Southey, asking him to critique some examples of her verse. In the act of sending him her poems, she had bravely confided her dream to be known as a writer, but she was unsure her hopes were realistic. She understood the risk of exposing her desires and doubts as well as revealing the limits of her poetic faculty to public scrutiny, but she desperately wanted to hear encouragement from a man of his stature.

Southey read her poems and gave a tepid reply saying, yes, she possessed the "faculty of verse," but that writing good poetry in the early 1800s was "not rare"—many poets were writing poems of quality. What was rare at that time, however, was getting published. Consequently, the possibility of her attaining distinction as a poet was remote. In addition, because she was a woman, Southey voiced concern that her mental wanderings could prove perilous.

"The daydreams in which you habitually indulge are likely to induce a distempered state of mind. . . . Literature cannot be the business of a woman's life: and it ought not to be. The more she is engaged in her proper duties, the less leisure will she have for it, even as an accomplishment and a recreation." He knew she was unmarried and advised her accordingly. "To those duties you have not yet been called, and when you are you will be less eager for celebrity" (*The Letters, Vol.I* 166-7).

The Brontë biographer Juliet Barker assesses his admonition as typical of that time: "Though ironic in that the Poet Laureate could see no worthwhile future except in the traditional roles of wife and mother, for a woman whose novels were later to achieve far more lasting fame than his own works, Southey's attitude was a general one in the nineteenth century." She adds that Charlotte would have heard a similar refrain from her father: "It was just what Patrick Brontë had always advised his daughter, urging her to content herself with fulfilling her duty and not to allow her seemingly unattainable ambitions to sour her daily life" (262).

Brontë understood her ambition might be viewed as unproductive and her gender seen as an impediment, but she had hoped the poetry on its own merit would have generated more discussion. Southey's opinion "confirmed Charlotte's fear that her passion for writing was something socially unacceptable, to be concealed" (Millar 8). She had been raised in a culture that felt a woman's greatest vocation could be found in the home where, as a wife and mother, she could spend her life serving a husband and children. She also had learned that a woman's feelings should be kept to herself. Ambition was unseemly. She wondered what response she might have received if she had hidden her sex with a male pseudonym: "one gets the feeling that he might have considered a lust for fame more excusable in a young man than in a girl" (8). Certainly, she was mature enough to withstand criticism of her work, but wished that the verses had been judged on their literary quality without the fatherly rebuke to an errant daughter. On that March evening, she wrote back to him her appreciation for having taken the time to view her work and apologized for troubling him with her "crude rhapsody." But was her response sincere?

The letter wrapper from the famous man was near her hand. His reply was still tucked inside. Before she put down her pen, she wrote on the outside of the wrapper, "Southey's advice to be kept forever." These few words suggest she would follow his advice and not pursue writing if it intruded on her duties as a woman.

Her sentiment, however, was not entirely genuine. Brontë had no intention of abandoning her literary ambitions, as history has proven. Instead, she made use of another habit she had acquired as a child to respond in a way that might not be suitable for a young lady, but would satisfy her disappointment, and explain why "she did not accept his verdict for long" (8).

She had an obvious facility with language and, with her poor eyesight, had most likely learned early on to imagine groupings of letters in her mind's eye as she rearranged them into words and phrases, mastering her facility with letters, and transforming them into anagrams. She effortlessly moved the letters round in her head or viewed new sentences perfectly formed and, with closed eyes, relayed coded messages that expressed an opposite opinion to the one written in plain view.

The viewed phrase would be inoffensive while the anagram 'beneath' would hide a truth or veil an emotion. Brontë had applied this particular talent when she wrote the words, "Southey's advice to be kept forever." These words, as an anagram, state something different and record her true feeling:

Refute poet. Shocked by evasive rot.

She disagrees with his opinion and finds his "encouragement and advice" avoided the main point of her inquiry—her poetry. He spends little time discussing the verses, choosing instead to suggest she abate her ardour and desire "to be forever known," and "not seek in imagination for excitement." From her perspective, Southey's critique was *evasive rot* because he failed as a professional poet to an amateur to speak about specific poems.

Even the opening clause of her letter, suggests her true intent. Brontë's letter to Southey can be read in an entirely different way if her opening words are in an anagram. She writes, "I cannot rest till I have answered your letter," and could be viewed as a grateful thank you or an angry warning: she needs to get something off her chest.

The following anagram suggests that, under her façade of an unsophisticated lady, she has loaded her reply with reproachful sarcasm. Also, she occasionally speaks in the third person when the letters permit, a practice that, most likely, added delight to her duplicity. The anagram of her opening clause reads,

Under naïve tone, Charlotte's wit set raillery.

Under her mask of politeness, the letter becomes a disingenuous thank you concealing her true intent as she sets her retort in a satirical tone. For instance, she writes, "I had not ventured to hope for such a reply; so considerate in its tone, so noble in its spirit. I must suppress what I feel, or you will think me foolishly enthusiastic." These words could be read as an ironic response directed at a patronizing man who has "condescended" to chastise a lady's ambition rather than to critique a poet's work and could, therefore, hide an opposite sentiment.

Southey writes that she "lives in a visionary world," where her mind is preoccupied with "daydreams." He would prefer that she use poetry "as to render it conducive to your own permanent good," to write poems if she must, but "not with a view to celebrity." Brontë continues her ironic response with the following lines: "You kindly allow me to write poetry for its own sake."

With regards to her daydreams, she tells him that as a teacher and daughter, "I find enough to occupy my thoughts all day long, and my head and hands too, without having a moment's time for one dream of the imagination. In the evenings, I confess, I do think, but I never trouble any one else with my thoughts." She refers to her thinking practice as her "eccentricity," and compares Southey's advice to the type she has received from her father: "from my childhood [he] has counseled me just in the wise and friendly tone of your letter." She seems to be saying, "I've heard it all before."

By putting an ironic twist on her words, we can infer that her father's advice "to observe all the duties a woman ought to fulfil" echoes the tone of a relentless lecture, whether from a poet or a parent. She ends her letter by saying, "your advice shall not be wasted." (*The Letters, Vol.I* 168-9) This, too, can mean that she will never forget the valuable lesson she has learned: next time my writing goes into the world it will be under a male pseudonym so that I can avoid this kind of *evasive rot* in the future. The experience apparently had a strong effect because, "As an author, she would never attempt to publish as 'Charlotte Brontë'" (Millar 9).

When she apologizes to the poet laureate, she admits that she regrets troubling him. Her regret may not be simply because she monopolized his time but for another reason: perhaps she was sorry she had left herself open to his fatherly advice. The line reads, "At the first perusal of your letter I felt only shame, and regret that I had ever ventured to trouble you with my crude rhapsody." The double meaning suggests an anagram could be lurking beneath the surface words.

Brontë has a method to her anagrams. Each phrase within the punctuation stands on its own as a full thought. If two phrases run together without punctuation, she allows one or two words to be borrowed from one phrase to the other to solve the final anagram. The phrases without punctuation improve significantly with that subtle shift. In the case of the line above, the opening clause before the comma is a self-contained anagram that states that she covered the anger in her letter with a shy tone. The first part is as follows:

Shy in poet laureate's formal letter. Stifle hot fury.

The second half explains why she stifles her fury:

An educated lady thought hours over every poem. Hard winter. Tired but try.

He had advised her to seek motherhood in lieu of fame, and avoided any effort to give her a critical assessment of her hard work, so she feigns shyness but, in reality, feels frustrated with his superficial response.

She conceals her anger in her anagrams but supplies clues to her resentment in her ironic letter. The following clause reads, "I felt a painful heat rise to my face," but what caused the pain? The anagram says,

175

Puts facile fate in fairytale home.

His solution to her female ambition is for her to accept a less challenging fate and to find reward in marriage and motherhood like so many fairytale heroines have done before her. With her pithy anagrams, she demonstrates her proficiency not only in creating this clever and difficult code but also in masking her true feelings through artfully constructed prose.

Near the end of the letter, she announces that she will refrain from ambitious dreams. The line reads, "I trust I shall never more feel ambitious to see my name in print; if the wish should rise, I'll look at Southey's letter and suppress it." The first clause transforms into an anagram that reveals her true feelings—that the professional's words hurt the amateur because he focused on his personal beliefs about women rather than on the quality of the poetry:

Am amateur. Silly, eminent opinion hurt. Set beliefs over merits.

If he had discussed her poems, she would have had a different response to his comments, but he failed to mention a single line or stanza.

The next sentence in her letter has a comma setting off the opening phrase and is, therefore, transcribed alone, but when added with the remainder of the sentence, makes perfect sense. She writes, "if the wish should rise, I'll look at Southey's letter and suppress it." The anagram explains why she conceals herself in her code:

Wit hides her foul hiss; hood lets a surly little spinster speak out.

Her clever mind enables her to hide her hiss of contempt, and she admits that the anagrams hood her unfriendly temper. She makes no apologies for being churlish and rude; she believes Southey has been equally rude through his disrespectful tone.

The anagrams reveal Brontë's true nature and her deep feelings of resentment towards a man who would underestimate her talents simply because of her gender. She lived in the Victorian era but, in the depths of her heart, resisted acceptance of its philosophy about women.

In chapter twenty-two of *Shirley*, the character of Caroline considers the topic of women's work: "I feel there is something wrong somewhere. I believe single women should have more to do—better chances of interesting and profitable occupation than they possess now." But she understands that "Old maids, like the houseless and unemployed poor, should not ask for a place and an occupation in the world: the demand disturbs the happy and rich: it disturbs parents."

To some, her response to Southey might seem unjust and petulant. Her deep animus could possibly be construed as excessive and unnecessary. Her "spiteful precocity" resembles her own female characters and is exactly how Elizabeth Rigby in 1848 describes Jane Eyre. The critic writes: "One sees that she is of a nature to dwell upon and treasure up every slight and unkindness, real or fancied," but in spite of her "undisciplined spirit," "Jane does right, and exerts great moral strength, but it is the strength of a mere heathen mind which is a law unto itself."

The critic explains that Jane suffers from the sin of pride and chastises the author for allowing her character to challenge the central beliefs of Victorian society: throughout the novel, one can hear "a murmuring against the comforts of the rich and against the privations of the poor, which, as far as each individual is concerned, is a murmuring against God's appointment—there is a proud and perpetual assertion of the rights of man, for which we find no authority . . . in God's word" (Allott 69-71).

Brontë could react against real or imagined slights, but her indignation arose from her moral strength and prodigious talent. Her novelist's power came directly from her satiric pen, her cool cynicism, and her common sense. The anagrams reveal these elements in her personality and display in full view her longing and suffering. Their sentiments expose, not a vindictive child, but a brilliant author who was passionate about speaking the truth.

In 1840, three years after writing to Southey, she sent an incomplete novel to Hartley Coleridge for his critique. He was Southey's nephew and Samuel Taylor Coleridge's eldest son. Earlier that year, Branwell had written to Hartley about the prospects of his own career as a poet and had sent Hartley an example of his poetry together with a portion of his translation of the Odes of Horace. After a positive response, Branwell travelled to the man's home. The experienced poet offered to read future drafts of Branwell's translations.

Coleridge's encouraging reception towards Branwell would have given Charlotte hope. She may have felt confident enough to send him an example of her own work (*Letters, Vol.I* 238 note 1). This time, however, she concealed her identity behind the initials C.T., which stood for Charles Townshend, one of her narrators in the Angrian stories. His response must have been a tepid one because her draft and fair copy of December 10, 1840 refers to his analysis of her writing.

Behind the mask of C.T., Charlotte is able to relinquish the demure, ladylike tone and "let rip when he wrote back an unflattering reply." This letter "is bursting with frenzied sarcasm and swaggering contempt" (Millar 9).

Coleridge suggested she extend her story to three volumes and then submit it to a publisher, but Charlotte wisely has alternate plans: "I think on the whole I had better lock up this precious manuscript, wait till I get sense to produce something which shall at least *aim* at an object of some kind and meantime bind myself apprentice to a chemist and druggist if I am a young gentleman or to a Milliner and Dressmaker if I am a young lady."

She is pleased that he is unable to discern with certainty whether she belongs to "the soft or the hard sex," but had presumed she was a woman from her writing itself: "as to my handwriting, or the ladylike tricks you mention in my style and imagery—you must not draw any conclusion from those. Several young gentlemen curl their hair and wear corsets— Richardson and Rousseau often write exactly like old women, and Bulwer and Cooper and Dickens and Warren like boarding-school misses" (*Letters, Vol.I* 240-241).

The narrator Charles Townshend obviously frees Charlotte to be as outrageous as she likes. She "uses the sardonic and flamboyant style she had developed for her satirical persona" (Millar 10).

She contends that if she had been writing fifty years earlier, not only would her "aspirations after literary fame . . . have met with due encouragement," but her characters Percy and West who appear in her "novelette," "should have stepped forward like heroes upon a stage worthy of their pretensions." After all, even the stories in the Lady's Magazine that she read as a child are "infinitely superior to any trash of Modern literature." She explains that she would probably still be reading that trashy literature, but "One black day my father burnt them because they contained foolish love-stories. With all my heart I wish I had been born in time to contribute to the Lady's magazine" (*Letters, Vol.I* 240).

In spite of her regret, she willingly abandons Percy and West in her draft and fair copy: "Authors are generally very tenacious of their productions but I am not so attached to this production but that I can give it up without much distress" (236), and in her fair copy: "It seems then Messrs Percy and West are not gentlemen likely to make an impression upon the heart of any Editor in Christendom? Well I commit them to oblivion with several tears and much affliction but I hope I can get over it" (239).

Charlotte's cavalier tone in discussing her heroes may have been based in a growing understanding that her work needed to develop. As Millar points out, "Charlotte had not yet learned to get inside her protagonists and create the sustained psychological portraits which characterise her mature work. She did not come into her own as a novelist until she developed the confidence to base her fiction on her own emotional experience and to enter her creations empathetically rather than hovering voyeuristically outside them" (9).

Over the next few years, Charlotte deepened her knowledge of the craft of writing. Her reading of classics and modern tales continued, and her study of French improved after a trip to Brussels, where her teacher Monsieur Heger introduced her to techniques that enhanced and strengthened her art. She was already equipped with the understanding that a male pseudonym would free her voice and protect her identity so, as she amassed the lessons in life and art, her stories did become closer to "her own emotional experience."

Always alongside her talent was the powerful anagram tool that enabled her to speak her mind behind another layer of disguise. We hear her true voice in the code, as she communicates with us, her imaginary readers, whose kinship gave her comfort in her solitude. This secret process enabled her to alleviate anger, frustration, and resentment in such a private manner that no one would ever be hurt or embarrassed. Her artful mask would also mollify some of that frustration when she realized that, on this particular level, her wit and revelations could elude the Southeys of the world.

What the literary world did not know was that, over the years, Brontë had witnessed examples of corruption that tore at her heart. By using her ability with anagrams, she was able to relieve her anxiety while concealing their dark secrets inside the pages of her letters and novels. These shocking secrets remained buried for over a hundred and sixty years.

22 *THE PROFESSOR*

After leaving Roe Head School in the late spring of 1838, Charlotte no longer felt inclined to teach again, so she tried being a governess, but lasted only several months before realizing she lacked the patient temperament needed to work with unruly children. While seeking employment, she continued to write, never relinquishing her dream to be a published author. In the future, when her elderly father died, a new vicar would move into the parsonage, which meant that she and her sisters would need to find another home and a viable means of support; consequently, Charlotte, Emily, and Anne had devised a plan.

The Brontë sisters decided to open a school for girls. They could live in their new residence, while the teaching provided them a comfortable income. Most girls' schools offered French as part of the curriculum, so Charlotte and Emily had travelled to Brussels in 1842 to learn the language. During that year, Charlotte stood at the deathbed of her friend Martha Taylor whose family was also in Brussels. Soon she heard of another death: her brother wrote that their father's charming curate William Weightman had succumbed to cholera. Only twenty-eight, he had been a favourite of the village, a man respected for his orthodox principles, affability, and moral habits. Charlotte might have questioned this last estimation of his character, having briefly experienced his ephemeral affections, but was still deeply saddened by his death. Unfortunately, their studies were interrupted when a third death occurred. Their Aunt Branwell died in October of 1842, so Charlotte and Emily returned home.

Their aunt had left the sisters a little money, which could be put toward the school, but Emily chose not to go back to Brussels. Instead, she would remain home to look after their father.

Charlotte returned to Brussels and, being proficient in French, was soon employed at the school as a teacher. A year later she left the school when she learned from Emily that her father and his curate Mr. Smith were drinking sufficient amounts of alcohol to generate gossip among the parishioners.

As her friend Ellen reported later, after Charlotte had died, "the truth, the real cause of C's sad suffering was in fact that Mr. B. in conjunction with Mr. S had fallen into habits of intemperance. This was known to very few persons, and is only now named for Charlotte's dear sake. She was indeed a brave little woman. She remedied the evil so quietly and firmly that her dearest friend and guest never had a suspicion of what was being done—till told long after by C.B. herself. The evil began in her absence. Such consequences ensuing on her absence, conscience accused her of dereliction of duty" (*Letters, Vol.I* 503 n. 4). Smith was soon sent to Keighley where he continued his drinking, stole a few pounds from a female parishioner, left the church, and moved to Canada.

Upon arriving home, Charlotte also discovered that her father's eyesight had deteriorated. She could not leave her father in his weakened state and, since the sisters' efforts to attract students had not proved fruitful, they decided to cancel plans to open a school. Fortunately, with the small amount of income from their Aunt Branwell, Emily and Charlotte could afford to remain at the parsonage while Anne continued her work as a governess.

In May of 1840, Anne had begun her employment for the Robinson family at Thorp Green near York, and in January of 1843, Branwell had moved there as well to tutor the Robinson's son.

In 1846, Charlotte still clung to her hope of having her work published. A few months prior to the publication of *Jane Eyre*, Charlotte had sent the manuscript of *The Professor*, also under the penname of Currer Bell, to Smith, Elder. The subsequent rejection in a two-page letter from William Smith Williams came with a request that she please submit any future work. While the novel did not strike them as a successful book for their list, the writing showed great promise. Williams pointed out that the writing was worthy of further consideration; therefore, he would be happy to read any forthcoming three-volume manuscript from the author.

Charlotte desperately wanted to have *The Professor* published. She was encouraged by Williams' request and suggested to him that perhaps Smith, Elder could publish *The Professor* prior to the three-volume work she was near completing; thus, if the book was slow to sell, the next book would be more popular and likely boost *The Professor*'s sales. Williams preferred that she simply forward her next work. Accordingly, on August 24, 1847, she sent them *Jane Eyre* and they immediately published it.

For the next few years, she would attempt rewrites of *The Professor*, a favoured novel that had once been called *The Master*, but William Smith Williams and George Smith always rejected the manuscript.

The editors found the realistic presentation of the characters and plot unsuited for a market that craved excitement, thrills, romance, and "something more imaginative and poetical." In a preface she prepared for the novel in the hopes that they might one day accept it, Brontë acknowledges that her book is "plain and homely," but she had wanted her hero to be an ordinary man who earns his living through effort and honest merit. He would marry a quiet, hardworking girl, not a rich or beautiful woman, and together they would share a moderate amount of enjoyment in life.

At the beginning of the story, after an education at Eton, William Crimsworth becomes an employee at his tyrannical older brother's mill, but soon leaves after repeated threats of violence. He travels to Brussels to become a teacher at a boy's school, and is hired to also teach at Mlle Reuter's. He meets a student, Frances Henri, who is trying to improve her English, and becomes attracted to her. Mlle Reuter's jealousy compels her to send Frances away. William goes to his former pupil's home where they realize they love each other. Through hard work and good relationships, William secures a job as an English Professor. Frances also finds work as a teacher, so they decide to marry and begin their own school. Unfortunately, the plot lacked the passion and wild fancy most readers preferred.

The book market and its customers helped govern the publishers' decision to reject the manuscript, but the publishers were also at the mercy of the distribution system. Books were expensive. In order for the general public to afford them and to encourage sales, the books in England were sold through an alternate method: for the small price of a subscription, readers could order a particular novel through the circulating libraries.

This extra sales revenue provided a guaranteed income for the publishers but, because of the libraries' customers, the fate of manuscripts indirectly rested with the public. Publishers understood the readers' tastes and chose to conform to those standards; consequently, a thrilling plot would be accepted, and a sober story like *The Professor* would be rejected.

Not until Elizabeth Gaskell's biography *The Life of Charlotte Brontë* appeared in 1856, did demand increase for more works by the author of *Jane Eyre*. As a result of this renewed interest, Brontë's publishers, Smith, Elder finally published *The Professor* in 1857, two years after her death.

In November of 1847, a month after *Jane Eyre* had appeared before the public, Brontë wrote a letter to G. H. Lewes, a well-known editor and critic, responding to his comments that *Jane Eyre* contained more melodrama than was necessary and that the author should have stayed within the boundaries of reality because "real experience is perennially interesting," and, as he later wrote: "Unless a novel be built out of real experience, it can have no real success" (Allott 84).

Charlotte agrees with him to a point and refers to *The Professor* in acknowledging his opinion: "When I first began to write, so impressed was I with the truth of the principles you advocate that I determined to take Nature and Truth as my sole guides and to follow in their very footprints; I restrained imagination, eschewed romance, repressed excitement: over-bright colouring too I avoided, and sought to produce something which should be soft, grave and true.

"My work (a tale in 1 vol.) being completed, I offered it to a publisher. He said it was original, faithful to Nature, but he did not feel warranted in accepting it, such a work would not sell. I tried six publishers in succession; they all told me it was deficient in 'startling incident' and 'thrilling excitement,' that it would never suit the circulating libraries, and as it was on those libraries the success of works of fiction mainly depended they could not undertake to publish what would be overlooked there—'Jane Eyre' was rather objected to at first on the same grounds, but finally found acceptance."

She agrees that writers should adhere to the real, but also believes that imagination plays a role in the creation of fiction: "Is not the real experience of each individual very limited? And if a writer dwells upon that solely or principally is he not in danger of repeating himself, and also of becoming an egotist?

"Then too, Imagination is a strong, restless faculty which claims to be heard and exercised, are we to be quite deaf to her cry and insensate to her struggles? When she shews us bright pictures are we never to look at them and try to reproduce them? And when she is eloquent and speaks rapidly and urgently in our ear are we not to write to her dictation?" (*Letters, Vol.I* 559).

In December of that year, Charlotte wrote to William Smith Williams regarding work on a new draft of *The Professor*. She admits that she "found the beginning very feeble, the whole narrative deficient in incident and in general attractiveness; yet the middle and latter portion of the work, all that relates to Brussels, the Belgian school etc. is as good as I can write." She defends her work as a depiction of real men living in ordinary circumstances: "It gives, I think, a new view of a grade, an occupation, and a class of characters—all very common-place, very insignificant in themselves, but not more so than the materials composing that portion of 'Jane Eyre' which seems to please most generally" (574).

By February of 1851, George Smith was willing to retain the manuscript in Cornhill, London. Charlotte was less inclined to let it go, however, if it were to languish in a drawer at her publisher's office. She writes to Smith that *The Professor* "has now had the honour of being rejected nine times." She adds that Smith, Elder itself had rejected it three times and explains, "my feelings towards it can only be paralleled by those of a doting parent towards an idiot child. Its merit—I plainly perceive—will never be owned by anybody but Mr. Williams and me; very particular and unique must be our penetration, and I think highly of us both accordingly.

"You may allege that that merit is not visible to the naked eye. Granted; but the smaller commodity—the more inestimable its value." She states that she prefers to hang on to her "child": "His modest merit shrinks at the thought of going alone and unbefriended to a spirited Publisher. Perhaps with slips of him you might light an occasional cigar—or you remember to lose him some day—and a Cornhill functionary would gather him up and consign him to the repositories of waste paper" (*Letters, Vol.II* 572-3).

Charlotte's comments regarding the book's merits are interesting. She says to Smith that "very particular and unique must be our penetration" if one wants to discover the inestimable value of *The Professor* and that, as far as she is concerned, those merits lie in the part of the book that is "not visible to the naked eye." Perhaps our understanding of why she tried so hard to bring the novel to the public's view rests on our ability to read the book with a "very particular and unique" eye that qualifies us to affect a special kind of "penetration" to view the real story that she made invisible "to the naked eye."

23 THE MASONIC PRESENCE IN
THE PROFESSOR

If Charlotte Brontë has used "Nature and Truth" as her guides while writing *The Professor*, then the relationship between the two brothers at the beginning of the story may be based on real life. In the opening chapters, she introduces Edward and William Crimsworth. The older brother Edward, a bully who owns a mill, tyrannizes the sensitive, younger brother until William defies his "master," escapes the harsh treatment, and moves to Belgium. Before his escape, however, William must work for Edward at a counting house and, aside from the cold and rude treatment from his brother, must also endure scrutiny from his superior Mr. Steighton. He describes copying out a letter that requires translating English words into German under Steighton's watchful eye. (The word "casque" means an armoured helmet.)

"A sentiment of keen pleasure accompanied this first effort to earn my own living—a sentiment neither poisoned nor weakened by the presence of the taskmaster, who stood and watched me for some time as I wrote. I thought he was trying to read my character, but I felt as secure against his scrutiny as if I had had on a casque with the visor down—or rather I showed him my countenance with the confidence that one would show an unlearned man a letter written in Greek; he might see lines, and trace characters, but he could make nothing of them; my nature was not his nature, and its signs were to him like the words of an unknown tongue. Ere long he turned away abruptly, as if baffled, and left the counting-house."

This passage could also be describing the feeling Charlotte experienced when her father or her brother's friends, while visiting in the parlour, would bend over her page to see what she was writing. They could make nothing of the anagrams, if this is what she is alluding to, and their ignorance would have enabled her to baffle their attempts at closer scrutiny as she wrote, in her surface prose, characters based on the men she knew, but hid in her clues and anagrams the real Truth behind their cold Natures.

In the second paragraph of chapter five of *The Professor*, Brontë lists, in plain view, the names of four Haworth men: Brown, Smith, Nicholls, and Eccles. William Crimsworth's inner voice is listing why he likes being independent while employed at his brother's mill: "Letter-copying till noon, solitary dinner at your lodgings; letter copying till evening, solitude; for you neither find pleasure in Brown's nor Smith's nor Nicholls' nor Eccles' company." These men in real life are directly connected with the Three Graces Masonic Lodge in Haworth. Was Brontë providing a clue as to why her protagonist avoided these men? Was William not to be affiliated with the Freemasons?

The name "Brown" could be John Brown, Reverend Brontë's church sexton for twenty years. He was a close friend and drinking companion of Branwell, and also played an important role in the formation of Haworth's Masonic Lodge in 1830. Over a twenty-year period, he was the Worshipful Master on thirteen occasions.

John Brown proposed Branwell for membership in the Three Graces Lodge in 1836. Branwell, at eighteen, was three years under the age of admittance, so Brown and the parish clerk Joseph Redman wrote to the Provincial Lodge requesting a special case be made of the Reverend's son who they erroneously stated was approximately twenty years old. They added that Branwell's father "is Minister of the Chapelry of Haworth, and always appears to be very favourable to Masonry."

The "Mother Lodge" rejected the request until a second letter stated Branwell would be traveling abroad and needed instruction in the craft before his trip. This time, the Provincial Lodge at Wakefield granted the dispensation and Brown initiated Branwell in February of 1836. John Brown's second daughter Martha, at the age of thirteen, became a servant for the Brontës at the parsonage (Barker 245).

The name "Brown" in *The Professor* could also refer to John's younger brother William, also a Mason. The majority of William's children worked as power-loom weavers in the factories. He worked as a stonemason and became the church sexton when his brother John died. He lived close to the parsonage and was a good friend of Branwell's.

Smith was James William Smith, curate to Reverend Brontë from March 1843 to October 1844. The Reverend Brontë appeared happy to let Smith go to a different curacy in another town after his short stay. The drinking bouts with his curate had caused controversy in the village and helped precipitate Charlotte's earlier than planned departure from Brussels.

Smith had shown an interest in Ellen Nussey, but Charlotte believed he was only interested in money and was relieved when Ellen avoided any further romantic acquaintance with the man. A few years later, debt-ridden, Smith pocketed charitable donations and, as stated above, fled to Canada.

The high number of freemasons in Haworth at the time would suggest that Smith, while perhaps not a brother himself, would have been associated with them on a regular basis. In all likelihood, however, since the church trustees were masons and Reverend Brontë was connected with the Lodge, Smith was probably a member of the fraternity.

Arthur Bell Nicholls followed Smith as Reverend Brontë's curate in May of 1845. He roomed at John Brown's house down the lane from the parsonage. He was fond of Charlotte and for many years had unsuccessfully sought her hand in marriage. Under a cloud of doubt, she finally consented to marry him in 1854, a few months before her death.

Several of Reverend Brontë's associates and friends were Freemasons so, again, it would be highly likely that Nicholls was a member of the Lodge. The chances are also good that they were connected specifically to the Three Graces Lodge in Haworth because the fourth man mentioned in chapter five is William Eccles. Eccles owned the building where, in 1833, the members of Three Graces Lodge began renting private rooms, at the cost of £4 per year, not only for their Lodge meetings but also for their annual December dinner on the festival of St. John. They had been meeting in public inns prior to that time. (Feather)

If Brontë has included these four real names in chapter five as a clue, perhaps she has hidden an anagram to explain her reason. The opening clause reads, "There is a climax to everything," which implies that this chapter may contain a culmination of an explanation for why her protagonist avoided these four men, and if we follow Brontë's method of placing her clues inside inverted commas, then we read the latter part of the opening paragraph as a further hint: "the theme of my thoughts was 'the climax,'" which suggests this is one of her significant words that acts as a sign that something is hidden from the visible eye.

If we accept that she is inviting the reader to follow William's lead and copy out the letters, secure against scrutiny, we must try to analyze the characters or symbols in her system. When we turn the "characters" we discover their startling natures. Anagrams exist, not only in the opening clause but also in the entire paragraph, where she uses the words "lodge," "urn," "brother," and "Mason." As the words become clear to the naked eye, we can see that, once again, she is writing about the Masons and their Lodge.

Brontë places Jane Eyre in a red-room that could be a Masonic Lodge and, if she is the author of *Wuthering Heights*, takes Lockwood through the first three degrees in the first three chapters. On closer examination, we will find that the Masonic theme surfaces in *The Professor* as well; consequently, Freemasonry recurs in some form in all three novels and may, in fact, connect them.

As stated in chapter twenty-one, Brontë's method remains consistent throughout all her anagrams. Each portion that ends in a comma or period acts as a complete statement, but if two phrases run together without the break of punctuation, the anagram usually occurs at a natural split in the thought. One or two words can be borrowed from one phrase to the other to solve the final anagram and improve the syntax. Also, if articles, such as "a" or "the," occur in the "top" sentence, she will not repeat them in the anagram; consequently, the hidden line may not be grammatically perfect and, with a limited number of letters for her to make her point, the anagram may seem oddly phrased, but her tone and the information she conveys are easily understood.

After writing down the opening parts of the paragraph, a shift of words completes the full meaning. First we see the lines in the prose paragraph from chapter five of *The Professor*, separated with slash marks to show where the breaks occur.

"There is a climax to everything / to every state of feeling / as well as to every position in life. / I turned this truism over in my mind as, / in the frosty dawn of a January morning, / I hurried down the steep and now icy street / which descended from Mrs. King's to the close. / The factory work people had preceded me by nearly an hour / and the mill was all lighted up and in full operation when I reached it; / I repaired to my post in the counting house as usual; / the fire there but just lit, / as yet only smoked, /

Steighton was not yet arrived. / I shut the door and sat down at the desk; / my hands recently washed in half frozen water, / were still numb, / I could not write till they had regained vitality, / so I went on thinking; / and still the theme of my thoughts was the climax. / Self-dissatisfaction troubled exceedingly the current of my meditations."

In the anagrams, like the novel's narration, Brontë writes in the first person. This time, however, the character is a Mason brother who is becoming worn out from being a thief for the brotherhood. He offers financial charity to help poor Mason brothers, but there's a catch: when they cannot pay back the loan, the Masons take the brother's land. They then lease the property back to the original owner at high rents. This particular Mason's job includes hunting for sick landowners who are also Mason brothers, falsifying their deeds, and then when he reads of their death in the newspaper, producing the revised document to acquire the land, or "sod." He also mentions details of his actions that will become clearer as we locate more of Brontë's code in the story. The anagrams sound a little odd at first but, after making those subtle shifts with a few words, they make complete sense. The ones below coincide exactly with the line breaks written above. The shifts are made further down.

Thieving charity role taxes me / I often forge estate levy / visit a fool, write lease, openly sin. Because there is no comma separating the two latter splits, a couple words can be juggled around to something that makes better sense: *Thieving charity role taxes me. I often visit a fool, forge lease, write estate levy, openly sin.* Next, he takes the small amount of money left to the heirs and divides it among the Masons, but the line needs adjustment. First, without the shift: *Divide tiny trust's mammon—ruin shire / Today join hunt for any new grain farms. / Our priority watch deed then need witness / First checked when met me, holding cross, sod.* Those last two lines work better if words get rearranged as follows:

Our priority: sod. Need deed witness. Checked when first met me then, holding cross, watch. / Check paper. Found a newly departed brother eye my halo or / during ill health help oaf write a duplicate will, add on name then sin. These two sentences can be transcribed as follows:

Check paper, found a newly departed brother. / Eye halo, then sin. During ill health, help oaf write a duplicate will or add on my name. The rest of the paragraph stays the same, and when the lines run together, the anagrams form a complete paragraph that tells a story of fraud.

Thieving charity role taxes me. I often visit a fool, forge lease, write estate levy, openly sin. Divide tiny trust's mammon—ruin shire. Today join hunt for any new grain farms. Our priority: sod. Need deed witness. Checked when first met me then, holding cross, watch. Check paper, found a newly departed brother. Eye halo then sin. During ill health, help oaf write a duplicate will or add on my name. Dear initiate, use poison. Stops cough. Truly humane. Built turf tithe jest here. Sly, take sod money. Thieves want to destroy grain. Handouts end, took dirt, heath's wasted. Why damned lazy owner Heathcliff earns rents. Bet me urn wills. Tatty liar initiated lot levy, which ruined lodge. Took in the winnings. High tax left heath mostly to slums. Watch men die. If desire facts about lodge rents, listen to next urn sect, family comedy I hid.

Aside from the shocking scheme outlined in Brontë's hidden tale, her reference to Heathcliff suggests that, either she has copied his name from her sister's novel, or Heathcliff has always been her creation.

In this fraud plot, the thief searches for poor Mason brothers who have property. He can adjust legal documents through forgery, and then when he reads of the man's death, helped along by a dose of poison, he proves ownership of the land. This would disinherit natural heirs, so obviously the families would not simply allow the fraud unless the Masons had found a loophole that Brontë has not yet explained. Part of the fraud involves another "brother" who, as the witness, holds a cross and swears the document's legitimacy. The Masons acquire the land, which allows them to charge higher levies or tithes imposed on the few families renting the lands. At this point in her hidden story, the kind of poison and the method remain a mystery.

During the Brontë era, landowners rented cottages to the families working in the wool industry. Even today, though fewer in number, one can still see sheep farms in the rural sections of the Haworth Township. The large stone houses remaining on the farms would have been partitioned into several "cottages." Consequently, a few families would live in one large dwelling and pay rent to the owner who might live in another part of the Township. Property owners reaped a steady income from these dwellings. Also during the Brontë era, one would hear tales of owners gambling away the deeds to their land, just as the Mason in the anagram story bets and then loses the wills to Heathcliff, and as drunken Hindley Earnshaw gambles away the ownership of Wuthering Heights to Heathcliff.

The anagrams under the next few lines of prose continue to explain the fraud.

"Come William Crimsworth, / Said my conscience or whatever it is that within ourselves, / takes ourselves to task, / come get a clear notion of what you would have, / or what you would not have; / you talk of a climax; / pray has your endurance reached its climax? / It is not four months old."

These phrases can be transcribed into more anagrams that stay on topic. The following reference to the "tau," also suggests a Masonic connection. The tau is the Greek word for our letter T and is a sacred emblem in Freemasonry. The Masons' triple tau is a sign that connects three Ts together to symbolize eternal life and acts as a material example of the Masons' predilection for the number three. In this anagram, the thief duplicates a will, which assigns a "brother" as the new heir; poisons the man with tea and wine; takes his property when he dies; fools the people by saying he is curing the man's illness with a special drink; keeps arsenic in his pocket; and administers it to the man until he nods off into what seems a natural death from either exhaustion or a wasting away of the body.

Mimic a moor wretch's will. / Thieves' doctor uses arsenic mint tea with vicar's holy wine. / Turks took assets, leave. / Can fool the layman. Cure ague with wet voodoo. / Why tau urn voodoo the law. / Aim: tax a lucky fool. / I head sly hoax team. Carry arsenic under cup. / Stir, lift mouth, soon nod.

In this story, the doctor appears to be a member of the sly hoax team. This "professional" would be essential for signing certificates that verify a false cause of death. The unhealthy conditions in Haworth, with its toxic water supply and diseases that produce high mortality rates, could conceal a death by poison, which is precisely what the health inspector Benjamin Herschel Babbage stated in his report: without proper assessment of the cause of death, men could conceal "murder in its naked form." This anagram story, of course, may be completely fictional, a product of Brontë's active imagination. She could have been writing duplicate fictions for the pure pleasure of challenging her mind to perform these unique tasks, or she may have heard rumours of a land fraud and decided to hide the information in her novel.

In her story, the Masons retain brother lawyers to craft duplicate wills or codicils. Their involvement would provide legitimacy to the transaction and enable the fraud to appear completely legal. In reality, if this kind of fraud were taking place, due to the close connections between Masons, one could assume that any suspicions raised to a magistrate may not be investigated. As Gaskell says in Brontë's biography, the magistrate might be "inclined to tolerate eccentricity, and to wink at faults too much like their own." Gaskell's use of the word "wink" in this regard is apropos. To effect agreement to a silent conspiracy, the Masons need only wink or nod at each other without having to exchange words. Their code of secrecy ensured silent cooperation.

If Brontë knew one of the Masons or had heard tales of this sort of fraud, perhaps she provides a description of this kind of man's true nature in the character of Edward Crimsworth. In chapter five of *The Professor*, she describes the older brother as a cruel tyrant with a "deep, brutal voice," and eyes that shoot "a spark of sinister fire." He treats his younger brother as if he were an insolent servant, calling him a "Hypocrite and Twaddler! Smooth-faced, snivelling Greasehorn!" and "whining lickspittle," while attempting to "cut every strip of flesh" from William's bones with his gig whip," a punishment for gossiping about him to the townspeople. A man has opposed Edward's business plans by remarking publicly on his private affairs, and attacks his character by speaking of "monsters without natural affection, family despots and such trash." William responds by saying, "you deserve popular execration for a worse man, a harder master, a more brutal brother than you are has seldom existed." In earlier and later Brontë stories, fights and disagreements between a cruel brother and a younger, gentler one appear in the juvenile fiction and in 'The Story of Willie Ellin,' a fragment written near the end of her life, so this description of Crimsworth could be based solely on her imagination.

Brontë could be describing an actual family despot who was also a brutal Mason, but the anagrams, at this point, fail to mention any names. Without documented proof of wrongdoing, Brontë's accusations can hardly be taken as factual evidence against the Masons of the Three Graces Lodge. The only comments available about any suggestion of dishonesty can be found in Brother W. Feather's "Centenary History" of the Lodge. For a period of ten years (1831-41, the years Brontë was writing her juvenilia), the Lodge experienced problems with poor attendance and a lack of dues, which may have inspired an alternate method of acquiring funds. Many years later, Brother Feather writes, "We can see how mistakes have occurred. Our forefathers in Masonry undoubtedly made many serious tactical and strategical errors in the carrying on of their work." This hardly incriminates the Masons as forgers and crooks, but further anagrams in *The Professor* continue to accuse a few of these men of unspeakable crimes and of having natures like "monsters without natural affection."

Brontë's extraordinary ability with anagrams enables her to hide this tale of corruption. Her habit, developed during her youth, has now grown from reporting on her brother's transgressions to recording the possible sins of a group of rogue Masons, but without actual proof, the anagrams can only be regarded as narrating a fascinating fable of corruption.

As stated in chapter eighteen, she may have had a uniquely structured brain architecture that enabled her to transpose letters at an amazing speed. Perhaps she saw words as colours or geometric shapes. Whatever her method, she had to be experiencing a dynamic mental imagery to perceive the reshuffling of letters faster than a normal brain. The letters may have simply appeared in their new context without effort, which would have given her a powerful tool for writing in code. On the surface prose, her words seem innocuous while underneath they contain the sting of revelation as she confides secrets and expresses emotions.

The combination of Charlotte's temperament, intellect, and penchant for anagrams creates a startling record of her deepest impressions and sentiments when viewed in the context of her secret language, a form of communication she perfected while chronicling the activities of her dissolute brother. At this point, Branwell seems to be the major link to a number of mysteries that involve Charlotte and the Masons.

24 FORGERY OR FICTION?

For several years, beginning in 1840, Haworth Township suffered under the weight of great financial difficulty because of a depression in trade. A harsh winter destroyed the peat crop—a fuel source for the poor families—and the rise in unemployment together with the high cost of grain meant a lack of funds for food.

Reverend Brontë's efforts to raise charitable funds helped some of the distressed inhabitants, but others would have mortgaged their homes or signed leases to their properties in order to stay alive. If the Masons were actually behind a scheme similar to the one described in the anagrams, they would have needed a Mason lawyer to collude with them, a lawyer who could hide a payout clause in the loan agreement. The monthly payments could begin by charging the unsuspecting Mason brother a large initial fee that would deplete his funds, and when the yield failed and the payments ceased, the lenders could repossess the land. In that case, a poor yield of grain would be preferable for the lender because without money the farmer would be forced to default on his debt.

In Reverend Brontë's novel *The Maid of Killarney*, a character comments on the difficulty for an ordinary man to interpret and understand legal documents. He refers to the use of Latin and French phrasing, "perplexity without end," and adds: "Even the most common instruments, a lease, or indenture, have so much repetition, obscurity, and nonsense in them, that he must have a good memory, and no ordinary share of leisure and patience, who can read them through, and understand them when he has done. And what quirks, and quibbles, and fine spun subtleties! Should your case be ever so straight and just, the most learned Doctor of the Law cannot tell what may be the issue. In attention to unmeaning punctilios, or the absence of even a word or letter, may cause you to lose all" (qtd. in Lock 362). With just an omission of a word or a date or a phrase, the man could lose all. If a Mason brother recommends a Mason lawyer to a Mason farmer who needs to borrow money, the level of trust would rise, and if the uneducated farmer was unaware of the language contained in the document, but trusted his "brothers," he could leave himself vulnerable to unscrupulous men.

Also, if the rents or payments were excessive but commensurate with the tithe charges, the leaseholders could legally extract high rents during this depression and then obtain title to the lands when the owners could no longer pay. The lenders, as the new owners, were effectively poaching the economy, leaving the natural heirs beggars. This is essentially what Heathcliff does to Hindley's son Hareton Earnshaw in *Wuthering Heights*. The new owners could celebrate with drink but, like Heathcliff, were still superstitious about the spirits of the dead haunting them.

In Brontë's anagram fable, the main challenge for these thieves is to discover who owns land. Tithe lists could provide information, as would any wills that show land titles. If a landowner has had a poor yield or is infirm, the thieves could offer financial assistance similar to the mortgage Heathcliff offers to Hindley, the drunken owner of Wuthering Heights, after his gambling renders him close to bankruptcy. Once the loan process is set up, the borrower is hooked into contractual arrangements that, perhaps, stipulate a hidden payout clause—one encumbered by Latin phrasing and perplexity that states complete payout of the loan at an earlier date than was originally agreed upon. Anything is possible if a seemingly trustworthy associate is intent on scamming an unsuspecting victim.

An uneducated man would be unaware of these traps, but the victim trusts his Mason brothers and believes he has a few years to repay the loan, but when the debt is owed by a specific date, the Masons can legally demand full payment. If the money is not forthcoming, they can foreclose and obtain the property, which they lease back to the owner at a high rent to pay for their wine and gin. Now the heirs are working as hired help on land that had been in their families for generations. Embarrassed about their fate, they keep quiet and accept the loss. If the new owners decide to increase the rents, they have every legal right to do so, but the additional payment and workload would burden the tenants, sometimes to the point of death.

As Brontë's next anagrams explain, the "*weak entail*" encourages this "*poaching economy.*" The feudal law of entail deals with the fee tail on land. The entail was a way to keep the land in the family through generations. The man receives the land before a woman, and the eldest male outranks the younger males in the family. Male cousins or nephews would be next in line to the property. The law lost popularity when

198

entailed landowners wanted to sell their land rather than have it passed to their descendants. The only way to bar the entail was through the filing of a deed, which gave full ownership in fee simple to the new owner. He could still provide for his children through his will, but not their children. In that case, he would have to create estate tails for future generations.

Apparently, the elders in Haworth used this law to pass property down to their heirs, but the system could be circumvented if men illegally docked or removed the entail by forging a deed. Now the forger becomes the new owner in fee simple.

The motivation for the fraud is money, and the *"prigs' boss"* is especially greedy. The word "prig" can mean a conceited person full of their own self-importance, but it also means a thief or one who pilfers, which, in both definitions, would fit arrogant men who stole from their neighbours.

Aside from the anagrams found in the prose, several verses of poetry incorporated into *The Professor* (ch.23) also refer to the same fraud. The poem recounts a student named Jane describing her feelings for her teacher while taking ill at school.

"When sickness stayed awhile my course, / He seemed impatient still, / Because his pupil's flagging force / Could not obey his will. / One day when summoned to the bed / where Pain and I did strive, / I heard him, as he bent his head, / Say 'God—she *must* revive!' / I felt his hand with gentle stress / A moment laid on mine, / And wished to mark my consciousness / By some responsive sign. / But powerless then to speak or move, / I only felt within / The sense of Hope, the strength of Love / Their healing work begin. / And as he from the room withdrew / My heart his steps pursued, / I longed to prove by efforts new / My speechless gratitude./ When once again I took my place, / Long vacant, in the class, / Th' unfrequent smile across his face / Did for one moment pass / The lessons done, the signal made / Of glad release and play / He, as he passed, an instant stayed / One kindly word to say / Jane til to-morrow you are free / From tedious task and rule; / This afternoon I must not see / That yet pale face in school."

The anagrams stay contained within each line of poetry and break at the end. A new anagram emerges in the next line and continues in this manner until the stanzas are completed. In this section, Brontë calls the

Mason Lodge a den and refers to the men as wolves whose vow of secrecy keeps the men mute and their exploits hushed. Once again the fable depicts a fraud, but this time it takes place in her village, and she appears to be the narrator.

Witness hushed; like secrecy, Mason way. / I see men admit title helps. / Chap's begging for life clause is up. / Cut body lies in hollow. / Men hush date money owed on debt; / hid trap inside den waiver. / Shame behind heath heir's aid. / Shy, give over mud asset; / high rents fit endless tithe laws. / Aim—nominate old men. / Masonic mutes deny crass hoodwink. / Prigs' boss envies money. / Spoken battles over who set up more. / Win toy elfin hilt. / Steep front fee, shovel, hoe, then ghost / while kin beggar, not heir. / If dead, worms rent Haworth home. / Shire's mud trustees happy. / Drowsing off. Every bottle open. / Pass cemetery. Used light. / Weak entail, poaching economy. / Scan a novel's tight clan: / stress Heathcliff's unique romance / fed Mason den imposter. / Tenants signed home leaseholds; / A legal deal for den's pay. / Assess heath pay in dead tenants. / Only I know dead story. / Write a mute roar or feel no joy. / Ideal fraud took rent sums; / Most of house rents in tea tin. / Tithe cant pays alcohol fee.

The anagrams are not grammatically succinct because of the limited number of letters at Brontë's disposal, but the topic remains the same. The anagrams refer to the tenants' rents being paid in lieu of Masonic dues. This could be the "*tithe cant*" or tithe hypocrisy simulating legitimate charges. The Lodge experienced poor attendance and lack of dues between 1830 and 1841. Understandably, a group may, at times, bend the rules, as they did in 1836 when they lied to the Provincial Lodge about Branwell's age. The Haworth Masons wanted to initiate eighteen-year-old Branwell, who would have had to be twenty-one, so they lied and said he was about twenty years old. If dues were scarce, and they had a cash flow problem, they may have resorted to more than just lies to bring in much needed money. As Brother Feather stated about those years, "We can see how mistakes have occurred. Our forefathers in Masonry undoubtedly made many serious tactical and strategical errors in the carrying on of their work." The "errors" may have included finding an alternate method of acquiring funds but, without proof, this is pure supposition.

Even though her *"roar"* is muted with her hood of secrecy, Brontë uses her poetry as a screen to expose a tale of thievery. If she were to remain completely silent, she would feel much worse. She inserts an interesting detail of the men drinking and then *drowsing off, every bottle open*, but when they walk home near the churchyard, they *pass cemetery, used light*. Like Heathcliff, they believe that ghosts still roam. In chapter sixteen, when he learns of Catherine's death, Heathcliff cries out, "Catherine Earnshaw, may you not rest as long as I am living! You said I killed you—haunt me, them! The murdered do haunt their murderers, I believe. I know that ghosts have wandered on earth." Brontë mentions Heathcliff after her instruction to *scan a novel's tight clan*. This would be an obvious reference to the two families whose lives are interwoven in *Wuthering Heights*. Would she guide the reader to the pages of her sister's novel? Perhaps, but as more anagrams are 'transcribed,' we see her referring to detailed aspects of the characters and plot, as well as her reasoning behind choosing certain elements, so in all probability, Brontë is directing us to her creation, not to her sister's. Her inclusion of the *clan* would also suggest *Wuthering Heights* was written before *The Professor*.

According to the anagrams, the Masons use their ill gains to pay for their alcohol, which is, apparently, a substantial sum and cannot be met by brother members' dues or tithes. They keep the money in a tea tin, which sounds similar to the earlier anagram that states the wills were kept in an urn. This detail highlights a certain consistency in their rural method for protecting their money. Brontë's most poignant line states that only she knew this story. As an astute observer of human nature, she would have listened carefully to the men when they visited the parsonage and to her neighbours as they either recounted tales of corruption from years gone by, or spoke of actual events taking place at that time. In the latter case, she would have witnessed the effects of the crime and found a way through poetry or fiction to tell the sad story of death.

The line, 'Th' unfrequent smile across his face' is interesting because the anagram says, *Stress Heathcliff's unique romance*. If the 'e' is added to 'the' it would spell Heathcliffe, which is how Charlotte spells the name in a letter to her editor. She must have decided to drop the 'e.' Heathcliff's *unique romance* with dead Catherine did sustain him, but the anagram continues as *fed Mason den imposter*. Heathcliff has acquired the rights to the Earnshaw and Linton ancestral homes through suspicious legal manoeuvres, so he could be classed as an imposter, posing as the legitimate owner.

The Professor poem continues. Jane, the student regrets having to leave her teacher, so the anagram that follows and reads, *"regret over flow of anagrams"* does not mean that Brontë regrets the number of anagrams, but that she writes benign subject matter (regret) on the surface poem to conceal her darker message underneath: the anagrams are under the "regret" poem. Also, she refers to the Masons as *"Noah,"* and uses the word *"tort"* as a pun: she is writing about injury caused by a willful act, not the dessert "torte."

"And when he lent some precious book, / Or gave some fragrant flower, / I did not quail to Envy's look. / Upheld by Pleasure's power. / At last our school ranks took their ground; / The hard-fought field, I won; / The prize, a laurel-wreath, was bound / My throbbing forehead on. / Low at my master's knee I bent, / The offered crown to meet; / Its green leaves through my temples sent / A thrill as wild as sweet. / The strong pulse of Ambition struck / In every vein I owned; / At the same instant, bleeding broke / A secret, inward wound."

Alone, hide shock, be nun, wrote poem's / regret over flow of anagrams. / Quietly ink lads' tin voodoo. / Sly rebel, show pauper dupe. / Look under a short author's long tau tricks. / Hoe feud with right of land. / Pure zeal about whether land is raw. / Men forge dirt: Noah hobby. / Make testament by sworn lie, / force-feed tort, home went. / Poverty, must sign Hell's agreement sheet. / Read Will, saw has titles. / Must ask urn host price of gin bottle, / one very divine wine. / Kinsmen's bottle habit a great need. / We drown in sacred tau.

"The hour of triumph was to me / The hour of sorrow sore; / A day hence I must cross the sea, / Ne'er in re-cross it more. / An hour hence, in my Master's room, / I, with him sat alone, / And told him what a dreary gloom / O'er joy, had parting thrown. / He little said; the time was brief, / The ship was soon to sail, / And while I sobbed in bitter grief, / My master but looked pale. / They called in haste; he bade me go, / Then snatched me back again; / He held me fast and murmured low / 'Why will they part us, Jane?'"

The words "I" and "O'er joy" (or "over joy") enclosed inside the comma cannot be turned into anagrams, so their letters stay the same. The "O'er joy," however, can be reversed to read as "Joy o'er" (or "Joy over"), which fits with the anagram that follows. In these next anagrams, Brontë refers to the violence that inspired particular aspects of the plot in *Wuthering Heights*.

Show up at home for rum tithe. / Use hoof's horror. Wrote / a house scene. Mates hit, cry. Sad, / so mirror entire scene. / One miser ran sham. Hurt economy. / Militia owns heath. / Anagram hood allowed dirt myth. / Joy o'er own right hand part. / Idle hermit beats wife. Has title. / Host isolates a son. Whip / if bad. Hit sweet bonnie girl bride. / Rude playmate melts book. / Silent Cathy healed / aged home. Be / a gent. Can cheat behind mask. / The flawed human models murder. / Saw injury type. What hell!

Brontë recreates or mirrors the violence in her Township within the pages of *Wuthering Heights*. *Mates* like Hindley and Heathcliff attack each other as do young Cathy and Hareton. She continues to explain that one man, the *prig's boss* supposedly, controlled the fraud and caused economic woes for the victims. The *militia* could be bands of young, uneducated men whose indifference to the law proved acceptable behaviour. As mentioned above, critics found the novel brutal with its "savages ruder than those who lived before the days of Homer," situated "far from the haunts of civilised men" where we witness "wickedness" and the "brutalising influence of unchecked passion" and "the fierce ungoverned instincts of powerful organisations bred up amidst violence, revolt, and moral apathy." Such brutal tales are not unimaginable when certain bad elements in a community are allowed to roam free.

Brontë attempts to explain the uncivilized manners of her northern township when she wrote a preface to *Wuthering Heights*. She understands that properly raised men and women would find it difficult to comprehend "the rough, strong utterance, the harshly manifested passions, the unbridled aversions, and headlong partialities of unlettered moorland hinds and rugged moorland squires, who have grown up untaught and unchecked, except by mentors as harsh as themselves." (The word "hind" is a Yorkshire term for a farm servant.)

203

Brontë feels joy over her part in revealing the corruption by applying her writing talents through the power of her right hand. Heathcliff, the *idle hermit*, has the *title* to Wuthering Heights, beats his wife Isabella, and keeps his sickly son and Hindley's son Hareton isolated at the farmhouse where whipping is a common form of punishment. The sweet bonnie girl bride is Cathy who has married Heathcliff's son and is now a widow, enduring her father-in-law's fists. Young, crude Hareton wishes to be friends with Catherine but she insults him, so he burns her books; thus, a *rude playmate melts book*. Brontë refers to a silent Cathy healing the aged home, a reference to the adult Catherine and a separate story that will be explained in chapter thirty-two. Her strategy for exposing the truth is to write as a gent, to use a male pseudonym as her mask in order to protect herself from the flawed humans who were models for her story. If she truly saw the injuries and knew about murders, then she could rightly exclaim, *what hell!*

The poem continues:

"Were you not happy in my care? / Did I not faithful prove? / Will others to my darling bear / As true, as deep a love? / O God watch o'er my foster child! / O guard her gentle head! / When winds are high and tempests wild / Protection round her spread. / They call again; leave then my breast / Quit thy true shelter, Jane. / But when deceived, repulsed, opprest, / Come home to me again!"

Rare economy: pay up; they win. / Hid plot to fraud in five. / Mill brother trains lodge way / See lad save tea, pour. / Cold fact: worry might see hood. / Hid, witness danger, men had whip welts. / Corrupt, arrest none, did hope. / Allay cheating: have rent set by male / then equal it here. Just try. / Deceptive owners usurped debt help. / Omit name. Echo omega.

Her fear of having her anagram hood discovered would be all too real if she were witnessing examples of brutality. She suggests that to *"Allay cheating,"* the law could set rents at a certain sum, and everyone would have to follow that amount, which could, conceivably, reduce the opportunity to swindle neighbours. She refers to the fraud plot outlined in chapter five of *The Professor*, the novel from which these poems are taken. Chapter five mentions the four men from Haworth and includes the hidden story of the leader of the *"sly hoax team"* who tells his tale through anagrams in the opening paragraphs. She omits her name, or writes her poetry anonymously and then, appropriately, ends the poem with the Greek *"Omega,"* the word for "the end."

The previous anagram about using the rent *tithe* to pay for *rum* supports the anecdote Reverend Brontë reported in the *Bradford Observer* in 1841, on the subject of church rates, and mentioned above in chapter three. He asked a man why he should object to paying that small stipend to do some good, when his rent was going "towards keeping beer shops and part, I fear, towards upholding a gambling house." The habit of owners spending rental profits on alcohol and gambling was common knowledge. If the anagrams are accurate in this incident, could they be true about the fraud and could Branwell, the drinker and gambler, with his ambidextrous talent, be involved in the *rare economy* where people must always *pay up*?

Elizabeth Gaskell refers to Branwell's "career as an habitual drunkard" (195), but he was also a drug addict and a womanizer. In January of 1840 he became a tutor in Lancashire for Robert Postlethwaite's two boys. Postlethwaite was a retired magistrate and landowner. While away, Branwell wrote a letter to John Brown boasting that his true nature as a drinker had been safely concealed under the shroud of a gentleman's courteous behaviour. His description of an evening of drinking and fighting sounds similar to the tales in his juvenilia and should, therefore, be taken as perhaps an exaggeration of his overnight stop in Kendal. The slightly edited version that follows is a composite, from two sources, of the original letter, which was lost but reappeared in copied form.

"If you saw me now, you would not know me, and you would laugh to hear the character the people give me. Oh, the falsehood and hypocrisy of this world! I am fixed in a little retired town by the sea-shore, among wild woody hills that rise round me—huge, rocky, and capped with clouds."

His landlord and wife have a daughter: "oh! death and damnation," which sparks Branwell to explain that he has changed. He asks, "Well, what am I? That is, what do they think I am? A most calm, sedate, sober, abstemious, patient, mild-hearted, virtuous, gentlemanly philosopher, the picture of good works, and the treasure-house of righteous thoughts. Cards are shuffled under the table-cloth, glasses are thrust into the cupboard, if I enter the room. I take neither spirits, wine, nor malt liquors. I dress in black, and smile like a saint or martyr. Everybody says, 'What a good young Gentleman is Mr Postlethwaite's tutor!' This is fact, as I am a living soul, and right comfortably do I laugh at them. I mean to continue in their good opinion. I took a half year's farewell of old friend whisky at Kendal on the night after I left. There was a party of gentlemen at the Royal Hotel, and I joined them.

"We ordered in supper and whisky-toddy as 'hot as hell'! They thought I was a physician and put me in the chair. I gave some stiffish toasts that were washed down at the same time, till the room spun round and the candles danced in our eyes. One of the guests was a respectable old gentleman with powdered head, rosy cheeks, fat paunch, and ringed fingers. I gave 'may the front door of women ever be open, & the porter Roger ever at his post' after which he brayed off with a speech and in two minutes, in the middle of a grand sentence, he stopped, wiped his head, looked wildly round, stammered, coughed, stopped again and called for his slippers. The waiter helped him to bed.

"Next a tall Irish squire and a native of the land of Israel began to quarrel about their countries; and in the warmth of argument, discharged their glasses, each at his neighbour's throat instead of his own. I recommended purging and bleeding, but they administered each other a real 'Jem Warder', so I flung my tumbler on the floor and swore I'd join 'Old Ireland!' A regular rumpus ensued, but we were tamed at last. I found myself in bed next morning, with a bottle of porter, a glass, and a corkscrew beside me. Since then I have not tasted anything stronger than milk-and-water, nor, I hope, shall, till I return at Mid-summer, when we will see about it. I am getting as fat as Prince William at Springhead, and as godly as his friend, Parson Winterbotham. My hands shake no longer. I ride to the banker's at Ulverston with Mr Postlethwaite and sit drinking tea and talking scandal with old ladies. As to the young ones!—I have one sitting by me just now—fair-faced, blue eyed, dark haired, sweet eighteen—she little thinks the devil is so near her!" (Du Maurier 105-7).

The letter continues. "I was delighted to see your note old squire but I do not understand one sentence. You will perhaps know what I mean—you say something about having got a cock & hens—I know you have got a cock & jolly good one too by Jupiter. How are all about you. I long to hear and see them again. How is the 'Devil's Thumb', whom men call Enoch

Thomas, and the 'Devil in Mourning' whom they call Wm Hartley. How are . . . Billy Brown and the Doctor and him who will be used as the tongs of Hell—him whose eyes Satan looks out of, as from windows—I mean . . . esquire? How are little 'Longshanks', and the rest of them? Are they married, buried, devilled and damned? When I come I'll give them a good squeeze of the hand; till then I am too godly for them to think of. And that bow-legged fellow who was always asking me—does your prick stand?— how is his going on or has he lost it altogether? Beelzebub means to make a walking stick of yours. Keep to thy teetotalism, old squire, till I return; that will mend that old body of yours, till I come back, when we will have a puff & a stiffener" (Barker 322-23).

While at his post as tutor for Mr. Postlethwaite's sons, he fathered a child, which presumably caused his employer to dismiss him. In 1859 Lord Houghton, a friend of Mrs. Gaskell's visited Haworth and spoke with John Brown. Brown showed the man Branwell's letter, which he later copied. "Beneath his transcript, Houghton noted that Branwell 'left Mr Postlethwaites with a natural child by one of the daughters or servants— which died" (Barker 334). The Postlethwaites had no daughters, so the mother may have been the eighteen-year-old daughter of his landlord, mentioned in his letter to John Brown (see Barker 334-5 for other possible candidates). Another reason given for Branwell's dismissal was that he had failed to come to work one day, and when found and returned was "visibly the worse for drink" (Barker 333). Either explanation for his dismissal is possible in light of Branwell's character.

Three years later, when he worked as a tutor for the Robinson's at Thorp Green where Anne was the governess, he was rumoured to have had an affair with his employer's wife Lydia. In July of 1845, Branwell was supposedly fired for engaging in the clandestine affair. Anne left the employ as well. Mr. Robinson died a year later, and his wife remarried, becoming Lady Scott. When Lydia's name and the sordid story appeared in the first edition of Gaskell's book, she sued and succeeded in having the publisher remove her name from subsequent editions of *The Life of Charlotte Brontë*. A friend of Lady Scott reported her saying that she "denies the whole accusation and declares Mr. Bronte to have been mad and a great liar" (Carlyle 225). Lady Scott would certainly deny the affair to her friends and acquaintances, but other rumours circulated that, even if there had been an affair, Branwell had actually been fired for being an expert forger. The rumours and Branwell's firing from Thorp Green will be examined in more detail in chapter thirty-eight.

In Edward Chitham's book *A Brontë Family Chronology* he writes that a friend of the Robinson's had learned firsthand of Branwell's alleged crimes. "On 6 May 1857, a close friend of the Robinsons, who had been a trustee in Lydia's marriage settlement in 1824, Sir James Stephen, wrote to a fellow 'professor' at Haileybury in support of Lydia (then Scott)'s case against Smith, Elder and Mrs. Gaskell. Among a number of comments on the behaviour of Branwell, he gave a clear alternative reason for his dismissal: he had been caught out in forgery. He was 'a most expert and frequent imitator of the autography of other people' (288). Apparently, Branwell could duplicate someone else's handwriting and had been caught in the act.

Other rumours were equally egregious. A servant claimed to have found Branwell and Mrs. Robinson together in the boathouse; Edmund, the boy he had been tutoring, "revealed that Branwell had made homosexual advances to him; he had indulged in drunken excesses," and "he had forged Mr. Robinson's signature in order to obtain money" (*Letters, Vol.I* 414 note 11).

During this time, Charlotte returned to Haworth, after a visit in Brookroyd to stay with Ellen, and she wrote of coming into the parsonage to find Branwell "ill" [her euphemism for drunk]. She adds, "he is so very often owing to his own fault—I was not therefore shocked at first—but when Anne informed me of the immediate cause of his present illness I was greatly shocked." His employer Mr. Robinson had dismissed him "intimating that he had discovered his proceedings which he characterised as bad beyond expression and charging him on pain of exposure to break off instantly and for ever all communication with every member of his family."

Branwell's response to the firing was to drink. Charlotte continues her letter: "We have had sad work with Branwell since—he thought of nothing but stunning, or drowning his distress of mind—no one in the house could have rest," and "so long as he remains at home I scarce dare hope for peace in the house—We must all I fear prepare for a season of distress and disquietude" (412). Branwell drank alcohol and took opium, so his addictions, that began when he was young and included drinking wine and huffing turpentine, were exploding into full dependency.

Mrs. Gaskell also writes of Branwell's addictions, which included his opium habit. "He took opium, because it made him forget for a time more effectually than drink; and, besides, it was more portable. In procuring it he showed all the cunning of the opium-eater. He would steal out while the family were at church—to which he had professed himself too ill to go—and manage to cajole the village druggist out of a lump; or, it might be, the carrier had unsuspiciously brought him some in a packet from a distance" (197). Opium could be purchased from a druggist the same way cigarettes are purchased today. Its legal consumption increased after 1830: "in the thirty years after 1830, opium consumption in England rose from 22,000 lbs to 90,000 lbs annually" (Whitehead 70).

Branwell's failure to become the great successful painter or poet the family had envisioned years earlier, together with the addictions and the womanizing propelled him into a terrible dark depression. He was inconsolable about losing Mrs. Robinson's affections, and, as drug addicts and alcoholics tend to do, he forced his family to endure not only his personal afflictions during long, sleepless nights, but also the drug induced threats of violence.

Gaskell presents an example of the family's plight: Branwell "had attacks of delirium tremens of the most frightful character; he slept in his father's room, and he would sometimes declare that either he or his father should be dead before morning. The trembling sisters, sick with fright, would implore their father not to expose himself to this danger; but Mr. Brontë is no timid man, and perhaps he felt that he could possibly influence his son to some self-restraint, more by showing trust in him than by showing fear. The sisters often listened for the report of a pistol in the dead of the night, till watchful eye and hearkening ear grew heavy and dull with the perpetual strain upon their nerves. In the mornings young Brontë would saunter out, saying, with a drunkard's incontinence of speech, 'The poor old man and I have had a terrible night of it; he does his best—the poor old man! but it's all over with me,' (whimpering) it's *her* fault, *her* fault'" (Gaskell 197).

Conversation was impossible as Charlotte discovered when she tried to speak with him: "I might have spared myself the trouble as he took no notice & made no reply—he was stupefied." Reverend Brontë had given Branwell some money to repay a debt, but "he went immediately & changed it at a public-house. . . . In his present state it is scarcely possible to stay in the room where he is—what the future has in store I do not know" (*Letters Vol.1* 455).

The anagram story depicts the Masons using forgery to illegally acquire land. Branwell's friendship with the Masons, his recurring illness, his lack of finances, and his unemployed sojourns at home would make him vulnerable and available.

He had displayed his handwriting tricks to his "brothers," possibly while recording minutes of the Lodge meetings, so the Masons behind the fraud, if it were real, would know his talents and his weaknesses and conclude that Branwell was the best man for the job. This would be a canny decision because Branwell's desire for the drugs and his roguish nature would make him a willing participant in his friends' schemes. If the Masons needed someone to duplicate a signature, Branwell would have been a sensible choice.

Gaskell's vociferous protests against the men of Haworth and Charlotte's anagrams about Masonic corruption necessitate a closer look at other records of that time to see if any evidence of wrongdoing even exists.

The anagrams describe the men duplicating wills, forging codicils, and adding their names to the documents while their "brothers" acted as witnesses. If the Mason added his name as a beneficiary and suddenly became the heir to the natural son's land, the family would have recourse to dispute such an obvious attempt at fraud, but in Brontë's scenario the men never include their names as beneficiaries. That would prove unnecessary. What did occur in the anagrams and in reality at this time was that men could legally attach their names to the man's will as executors. To the modern reader, this adjustment to the document would seem to give the Mason only the legal right to carry out the testator's wishes and, thus, oversee the dispersal of gifts to the beneficiaries, which would have no financial reward unless the family chose to pay the man for his services. Ownership of the land would still be passed down to the rightful heir, so how would being an executor profit the Mason?

25 LOCAL WILLS

Parliament can pass Acts and create laws for the country, but can it ensure that men will abide by them in distant communities? What happens when men elected to enforce the law in those far removed districts lack clout or, worse, look away when crimes occur on their watch? Who can compel a criminal mind to adhere to the law when anarchy suits his greed? And who would dare report this man when his pockets contain knives and guns, and he fears no one? Certainly, not a woman. Ironically, at the time Brontë was writing her anagrams, the law enabled fraud of the nature she describes to continue undetected.

Three years after Charlotte's death, the Probate Courts were instituted in England. Prior to 1858, in order to prove a will's authenticity, a man would go to the Ecclesiastical Court—the Church of England and its Bishops—to swear that he was the executor so named in the document. The Ecclesiastical Court had limited powers and could only deal with the deceased's personal, moveable property, like furniture and jewelry but had no jurisdiction over wills of land. Consequently, probate of a will of land was unnecessary, and proof of title to real estate could be made by production of the will, so the will stood as the land's title and the executors as the legal owners.

The will acted as the title to real property. It became the deed. At the time of the sale of the land, the executor on a will had the same designation and power as the vendor on a deed, and could produce the will as the document of ownership, just like a deed. If this new owner wanted to dock the entail and sell the property, a solicitor would draw up a replacement indenture conveying the property to a purchaser, but prior to the sale, executors could retain possession of the land indefinitely. The will, now construed as a deed of land, endowed ownership to the executors, without the need to sell. Adding his name as an executor, therefore, gave the Mason title to the land without being obliged to sell the property or bequeath rental funds to the family of the deceased. He could simply take over the property and maintain ownership without anyone raising an eyebrow because their "brothers" were witnesses. The lawyer and his clerk would also have to be Masons, as would the doctors, who would certify the testator died, not of a fatal dose of poison, but of natural causes. To ensure secrecy, all participants of this conspiracy would have to be fellow members of the Lodge, but would such a chain of corruption even be possible? The entire allegation seems too preposterous to be believed, but truth can be stranger than fiction.

Certainly, the financial rewards would be substantial but would that justify murder and thievery? If this sort of crime took place, two or three Masons could become executors, and when the man died, they could simply divide the spoils by selling off the property, or they could choose to retain the sod and its buildings to profit from a wealth of rental income. The anagram story would support the latter choice because rental income or tithes would provide more lucrative profits and would enable executors to fund a constant supply of alcohol to the co-conspirators.

The rental money, therefore, was gold. The furniture and bed linen would be of no interest to the Masons; consequently, the executors oversaw the disbursement of the testator's wishes and fulfilled bequeaths that involved moveable property, but they were under no obligation to sell land. In terms of the anagrams, when Brontë uses the word *"deed"* she would see this as an interchangeable word with the "will." If the deceased owned several rental properties, the executor acquired rent monies without lifting a finger. The inclusion of their names as executors, therefore, became a legally sanctioned scam that allowed unscrupulous men to accumulate wealth with little effort or expense.

The Probate Laws were instituted in 1858 because of the instances of fraud: too many prigs were duping natural heirs. In Haworth Township, the practice of executors retaining land in significant numbers does not arise until 1833. In the 1813 Valuation, no properties are listed as being held by executors, and in 1833 only one example appears of Trustees owning a property. In late 1833, however, the trend toward executor ownership of land begins and continues throughout the next twenty years. In the Tithe List of 1852, the properties of thirty-five deceased men are now owned by their respective executors. Executor ownership had gone from zero to thirty-five within just two decades, a time frame that coincides exactly with the twenty-year period when Charlotte Brontë is writing her juvenile and adult fiction, and composing her secret anagrams. She would have known that a few of the deceased owned a small number

212

of properties, which included houses scattered throughout Haworth, while others possessed farms and adjoining cottages that had been in the family for generations.

Rather than selling the properties for a share of the profits and, thus, providing annuities for the wives and children, the executors elect to retain ownership; rents are preferable, and the wills enable the men to control title to desirable land. During the twenty years between 1831 and 1851, the population in this area increased from roughly 6,000 inhabitants to 7,000 but, due to the poor sanitation and the appalling spread of disease, the approximate number of annual deaths for men could reach as high as fifty, a rate equalled in women and children. Of course, only a small percentage of these men would have been landowners with property to bequeath to their sons. Nonetheless, one cannot disregard the significant number of executors suddenly owning land, especially when the executors are not always blood relatives. Why would a man knowingly inflict financial hardship on his own family by handing his rental income, which in some cases is a substantial amount, over to his friends, who happen to be Masons, instead of to his son? Perhaps he was too sick and near death to object. Unfortunately, only a few wills have survived, but the evidence contained in these wills substantiates the circumstances outlined in the anagrams. The wills, of course, do not prove that the men became executors through forgery or murder; they simply show that the practice was occurring and continued for twenty years. (Copies of the wills can be obtained at the University of York, the Borthwick Institute for Archives, in England.)

Without the anagrams, none of the following information would have been noticed as relevant. Obviously, if a code directs you to a particular place and, after digging around, you find a few pieces of paper that look suspiciously like the tale in the code, you think it merits scrutiny, but the information on the pieces of paper are not proof of crimes; therefore, I will present the facts as I discovered them, and add a possible interpretation, without alleging the guilt or innocence of any party.

The practice of executor ownership after 1833 closely coincides with a significant event in Haworth. In 1833, the Freemasons moved their meetings from the public Black Bull Inn to their private rooms on Newell Hill owned by William Eccles. Here, conversations could be held in

213

complete secrecy. At this time, the men were concerned about low attendance at the Lodge, and an absence of dues needed to finance their interests which, according to the anagrams, are gambling and drinking. If they were considering alternative means to raise money, one of the Masons may have shared his knowledge of the unscrupulous method of grabbing land from descendants. The means to enact the fraud could have been plotted between a few of the local businessmen who saw a safe and quick way to dupe landowners and earn extra profits. This is pure supposition, but if the fraud took place, someone had to initiate it. The first case of a Mason becoming an executor is when Hiram Craven's name appears as executor on a will dated August 16, 1825. Hiram was both a speculative and operative Mason. In this case, the property was sold before the 1833 Valuation, so the land was never listed at that time as being owned by executors.

Hiram's father John Craven, a known Mason, had named his son after Hiram Abiff, the first Grand Master of Masonic legend. Hiram Craven carried on his father's tradition by naming his son Hiram and, in 1830, in the Haworth Trade Directory he changed his occupation from stone mason to architect to connect him even closer to the principal architect of King Solomon's Temple. Charlotte used this name when she created the character of Hiram Yorke, a mill owner, in her novel *Shirley*.

Hiram Craven is listed as one of three executors on the will of a local butcher called John Town. The other two executors, both paper makers, are the man's son, and a business associate from Leeds. The addition of a stone mason seems superfluous and costly, especially if the son must share a portion of his inheritance, but John Town may have had good reason to add Hiram Craven to his will—we will never know. The will states that the executors are to "put up and expose to sale by public auction" the lands and premises, and then, from the proceeds, to pay any and all just debts before equally dividing the profits. As stipulated by the terms of the will, Town's property must be sold and not held to accumulate rents. By November 15, 1825, the sale was finalized, and approximately £416 was accordingly disbursed. John Town's will rewards Hiram Craven with an amount in excess of £100 for being a third executor. Eight years later in the new private room at the Masonic Lodge, as dues are diminishing, the suggestion of being an executor could have been mentioned as a benign statement.

An interesting point about this particular example is that it also echoes the anagrams' assertion that a preferable death was a quick one. Within two months of signing his will, John Town was dead, his property auctioned to the highest bidder, and the profits from the sale split three ways between his son, the business associate, and the Mason. Of course, John Town probably made his will because he was ill.

Several months after the Masons moved into their Lodge, George Robinson, a fifty-year-old landowner and mill owner from Stanbury, signed his will. Like John Town, he had three executors but in this case all three men were Masons: his brother-in-law, a business associate, and a farmer.

The business associate had worked at one of Robinson's mills and later became owner of his own mill at Hollings. The sheep farmer owned a profitable wool business that was so lucrative that by 1838 he had earned enough money to buy sixteen houses and several acres of field and meadow land, which generated a comfortable income in rents.

As executors on Robinson's Will, the men received profits from rents on six properties. After Robinson's death, they essentially owned four farms, one cottage, and a house connected to Hollings Mill. They also received two hundred guineas from the sale of machinery and any outstanding bequests from Robinson's late father's will. Robinson's sons and daughters were also taken care of in the will, but they were not entitled to the rental income. Robinson signed his will at the beginning of September, 1833 and was buried on September 24, 1833. He signed the will and was dead and buried within two weeks. He may have been unwell and decided it was time to attend to his financial matters, but his quick demise, in lieu of the anagrams, makes one wonder, but this could be coincidental.

A few months earlier in May of 1833, at forty-eight years of age, John Greenwood had signed his will. He was one of the largest landowners in Haworth, owning and operating Bridgehouse Mill, and employing 60 people. The Greenwood's had lived in Haworth for several generations, and the villagers considered the family true gentry. John Greenwood was a bachelor, but he had two younger brothers and several sisters who were beneficiaries. His business partner and executor was his youngest brother James, who became sole owner of the Mill at John's death. James was also Haworth's Chief Constable. All three brothers were Freemasons.

The middle brother, Joseph Greenwood was also a mill owner who operated a successful business outside of Haworth. In 1836, he ran in opposition to his younger brother James to become the First Magistrate for the West Riding of Yorkshire. Some Brontë scholars believe Joseph Greenwood was the model for the magistrate Edgar Linton in *Wuthering Heights*. In his older brother's will, Joseph was to receive three houses and £500. For reasons that no one has ever been able to understand, John Greenwood suddenly decided to revoke his bequest to Joseph and draw up a codicil transferring both the property and the money to his younger brother James, who would now have a legal right to the entire Greenwood fortune.

The codicil is dated June 7, 1833, one month after John signed his will. The codicil appears to be legitimate except for a couple irregularities: the three witnesses are different from those on the will, which is not unusual, but the clerk who wrote out the will is not the man who drew up the codicil. Instead, the clerk who wrote the witness declaration on the will is the same man to write and witness the codicil, which is hardly suspicious except that it resembles an incident that occurred ten years later when a clerk drew up and witnessed a document that involved a forgery. In that case, to be dealt with later, the clerk and the witness were both charged as co-defendants. On John Greenwood's will, the witnesses are a solicitor from a town outside Haworth and two woolcombers from Bridgehouse Mill. The witnesses on the codicil, however, do not state their addresses or occupations, which is a requirement on this kind of documentation. The solicitor on the will is now replaced by his clerk, as demonstrated by the handwriting.

One of the witnesses is Rich Greenwood, John Greenwood's uncle. By law, a relative is not allowed to act as a witness: the witnesses may be related to each other, but they cannot be related to the person making the codicil. Also, he should use his full proper name, which would be Richard. The use of the name "Rich" and the clerk's involvement contribute to the codicil being suspect.

As well, the signature on the codicil, while similar to John Greenwood's several signatures on the pages of his will, shows some significant differences. The top two signatures shown below are from the will and the bottom signature is from the codicil.

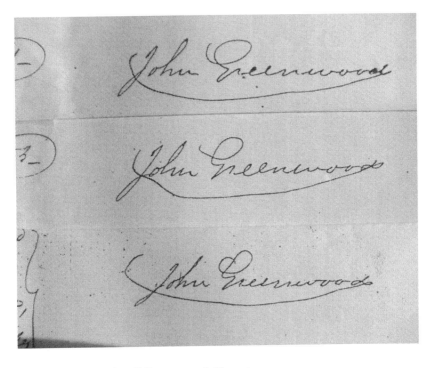

Figure 1. Example of Greenwood Signatures

The originals documents are held at the Borthwick Institute for Historical Research in England, and a Vancouver forensic document examiner, after reviewing the signatures on copies of the documents, stated that in order to detect a forgery, one must view the originals. He did, however, notice that the accuracy and fluidity of the three signatures indicate legitimacy but, proportionally, the codicil signature is smaller than the others and has some discrepancies. The "h" has no loop and its central region is attached to the upstroke rather than spaced apart as in the will signatures. The line flourish is longer as well, reaching much further past the "J". The "J" itself shows a narrow, tentative construction compared to the other two. The codicil is questionable because no one has ever been

217

able to explain why John Greenwood had such a strong change of heart to disinherit his brother Joseph.

In the anagrams, Brontë writes about the Masons needing witnesses, and that they keep them *hushed*, because they *like secrecy, Mason way*. She also claims that the *men forge dirt* and *make testament by sworn lie*. This unusual reversal of fortune for Joseph has always been viewed by Haworth locals as inexplicable. Could this case have involved deception?

The final point to make about the Greenwood Will is that John was considered to be in a good health, but he died unexpectedly on June 26, 1833 just nineteen days after signing the codicil.

Joseph Greenwood, the disinherited brother was also the magistrate. The subject of wills and the character of a magistrate occur in *Wuthering Heights* when Edgar Linton, as the local magistrate and owner of Thrushcross Grange wants to change his will before he dies, to protect his daughter, but Heathcliff pays a lawyer to stay away; consequently, Linton dies without making the codicil, which enables Heathcliff to have a claim on the land.

Several but not all of the wills listing executors have been found, and incomplete burial records leave the exact date of the man's death unavailable, so the time between signing the will and the Testator's death is difficult to calculate. The average time, however, between a man's death and the will being proved is approximately five months, so the time period between signing the will and dying can be estimated. In addition, although Haworth had four Masonic lodges, records listing the names of Freemasons from that time have been lost, and only a few names are easily confirmed, so some of the men named on the wills may or may not have been Masons. Nonetheless, the existing wills are worth noting. The inclusion of the names and other details are not to inundate the reader with minutiae but to provide as fair an account as possible.

26 MASONS AND WILLS

To a reader unfamiliar with the family names in Haworth, the following details will seem overwhelming, but the few remaining wills need to be shown in this manner to prove that Masons were executors and witnesses. On its own, the number of Masons would not be unusual because most of the Haworth men belonged to their local lodges, but because of the anagram story, the few wills that remain should be outlined to support, at least, the more benign claim that Masons and wills frequently went together.

The first will worthy of a second glance is that of Jonas Horsfall, "a gentleman" and landowner. His will was made on the 17th of January, 1833. The will named his son Jonas as executor along with William Thomas, "a spirit merchant," and Timothy Hartley, "a grocer." The Thomases and the Hartleys had long been Freemasons, so the addition of their names as executors coincides with Brontë's claims that Masons added their names to the wills. The son Jonas knew Branwell through their time spent drinking in the local inns and, with Branwell's involvement in the Three Graces Lodge, Jonas Horsfall and his father were most likely members of the fraternity. Within two years of his father's death, Jonas owned several properties and had moved into the large house called Balcony located behind the parsonage. Several years later, William Thomas, the other executor, would own and reside at Balcony after Jonas, bankrupt and without financial resources, had emigrated to Australia.

Two and a half months after signing his will, Jonas Horsfall added a codicil. The document stipulates that his son Jonas must "give and dispose unto my wife the sum of £500 yearly and every year during the term of her natural life to be paid unto her by my said son Jonas in two half yearly payments, that is to say at Midsummer and Christmas." This additional stipulation strongly suggests that his wife was concerned that whatever monies were generated in rents could be paid to the executors without any financial consideration being allocated to her. Even her own son could not be relied upon to guarantee Mrs. Horsfall a stipend from his portion of the rental income, especially if he was reckless with money, as is evidenced from his later financial ruin, so the codicil ensures her some security, and affords the means of a legal remedy if her son defaulted on the disbursement of the payments.

Another interesting point about the Horsfall will and its codicil is the number of witnesses. Normally, two witnesses are all that the law requires on a will, but in this case, numerous individuals added their names: six men signed the will (four Masons), and five witnessed the codicil (four Masons). On April 6, 1833, four days after he signed the codicil, Jonas Horsfall died.

Further examples of known Mason executors appear on the wills of Bernard Hartley and Joseph Wright Greenwood. Bernard Hartley made his will on the 27th of July, 1841 and died on the 18th of November, 1845. One of his two executors was William Thomas' younger brother Enoch Thomas, a Mason. Bernard Hartley owned eight houses and several fields in Upper Marsh as well as a house and meadow in New West Field, which was occupied by William Sunderland, a name that occurs on other wills. The properties would have earned substantial rents for the Mason executor.

Joseph Wright Greenwood made his will on the 21st of January, 1845 and died six months later on the 9th of July, 1845. He left a house, outbuildings, meadows, and fields to his son William Wright Greenwood and Edward Townend, a man who became the Worshipful Master of the Three Graces Lodge in 1852. The inclusion of a Mason suggests that Joseph Wright Greenwood himself would have been a member of the Lodge. Earlier, on the 15th of December, 1842 he, too, was named as an executor on John Rushworth's will, a young man who died a short time later, his will having already been proved by May of 1843, but Greenwood inherited from Rushworth a house, outbuildings, and several acres of rentable land.

Enoch Thomas and William Brown, both Masons, and Branwell's good friends, acted as witnesses on the will of Jonas Barraclough, dated the 28th of October, 1834. Barraclough was a staunch Freemason who named his son Zerubbabel, which in the Royal Arch Chapter signifies the Worshipful Master: the MEZ is the "most excellent Zerubbabel," and he named his daughter Zillah, which was Lamech's wife in the early legend of the Masons, and resurrected as the maid in *Wuthering Heights* and the frightening nurse Zillah Horsfall in *Shirley*. Barraclough's wife and two eldest sons are named executors, so when he died a year after signing his will, the older sons became owners of several properties as well as recipients of a large income from rents.

Like Jonas Barraclough, Jonas Binns and John Hartley died within a year of signing their wills, but nothing suspicious appears on either document. The men bequeathed their property to their sons and Masons witnessed the wills. The fact that Mason executors and witnesses were becoming common during these years, while not necessarily a problem on its own, could have made it easier for those intent on "hoodwinking" a fellow Mason, to get away with fraud.

Joseph Sutcliffe, a Mason, made a will on the 19th of January 1850 which excluded his eldest son Joseph as being executor, but named his younger sons Jonas and Samuel to that position. No burial records exist for a 64-year-old man, but his will was approved by the 13th of May, 1850, which suggests he died shortly after signing his will. A solicitor's clerk from Leeds witnessed the will.

The next four wills have either an executor or a witness in common. Jonas Crabtree made his will on the 15th of November, 1841. He named his brother John Crabtree, daughter Sally, and his nephew William Sunderland as executors. Joseph Sunderland, Simeon Smith, and Abraham Sunderland witnessed the document. Nothing appears unethical or suspicious. In fact, Jonas Crabtree lived for another seven years. Abraham Sunderland, the witness, had a connection to the Brontë family and may well have been one of the many Masons who frequented the parsonage. He had given the Brontë children piano lessons and instructed Branwell on the flute and organ. He was a schoolmaster's assistant and parish organist, and was satirized in Charlotte Brontë's juvenilia in the character of Mr. Sudbury Figgs. His name appears on three other wills. The other witness Simeon Smith, a coal miner, could also have been a Mason since Simeon is a Masonic name. The rule in the candidate's preparation for initiation that he must be devoid of metallic objects or weapons symbolizes the biblical Simeon's preparation of the instruments for slaughter.

The name Sunderland recurs in Robert Holdsworth's will, signed on the 16th of October, 1848. He died a few weeks later on the 2nd of December. His two sons were his executors, and the document was witnessed by William Sunderland and Abraham Sunderland. His estate included two houses, a cottage with garden, fields and ten acres of land.

In the January 12th, 1849 will of a farmer named Thomas Pickles, Ann Crabtree, Sally Scarborough, and Abraham Sunderland are listed as the executors. The witnesses are John Moore, Joseph Sunderland, and Abraham Sunderland. Thomas Pickles died on the 21st of January, 1849, just nine days after signing the will. The executors inherited a house, cottage, outbuildings, fields, meadows, and pastures, all occupied and supplying rental income.

William Sunderland made his will on the 20th of January 1847 and died on the 5th of March, 1849. He named his brothers Jonas Sunderland and Abraham Sunderland executors. John Crabtree and Abraham Sunderland were the witnesses.

The majority of the witnesses on the wills were either weavers or woolcombers, uneducated but hardworking men, who would appreciate a few extra pennies or a free pint of ale for their services. Not one of these wills contains the words, "my signature was forged" or "I was poisoned," but similarities do occur between the existing wills, and they appear to support Brontë's basic assertions in the anagrams that Masons were executors who held titles to land, and that Masonic brothers acted as witnesses. Also, a number of wills are no longer available for examination, but these remaining few appear to substantiate her claims regarding executors and witnesses being connected to the Lodge. Does this prove fraud? Not at all, but the crime of forging wills was not unheard of in the Township.

An actual case of forgery in 1843 involved Reverend Brontë and the Beaver family who lived near the southern border of Haworth. The case went as far as the Spring Assizes at York in March of that year (Fermi). John Beaver owned a large farm called Buttergate Sykes in Far Oxenhope. He was one of the Haworth Land Trustees, a Freemason, and "is named as trustee or witness to many local wills" (16). His father Stephen Beaver named him executor and heir on his will, but with the condition that John would inherit only if he could "prove this my will," which John had to do in front of "some person properly and legally authorized for that purpose within twenty eight days after my decease" (16). Stephen Beaver's unusual stipulation protects against illegal, duplicate wills and forged documents

222

appearing after his death. His fear would later prove prophetic when John Beaver later faced a false registration of a forged document at the hands of his own son James.

James Beaver was a widower and father of two girls, and had become estranged from his father John sometime in the late eighteen-thirties after falling in love with their servant girl, Susey Farrar, an attachment which angered his father and forced the couple to move several miles away to Halifax.

When John Beaver wrote up his will in July of 1838 he made no mention of his son. Instead, he bequeathed all his property to his two granddaughters Sarah and Grace, and made "his good friend William Thomas," Haworth's "spirit merchant" and a fellow Freemason, "his sole executor" (17). One of the witnesses on the will was the Reverend Patrick Brontë, which would be an appropriate choice as he was a friend, and Beaver was one of his parishioners.

Four years later in July of 1842, James Beaver forged his father's signature. On behalf of his father, he signed "a deed of release" between father and son that transferred the farm Buttergate Sykes from John to James. A solicitor's clerk together with a relative of Susey Farrar acted as witnesses. The forged document had been registered in Wakefield eight months before its discovery in February of 1843. "If it had not been discovered until after John Beaver's death, the conspirators might have succeeded in circumventing the will; James could have claimed that he had been reconciled with his father who then transferred the property to him, and owing to old age and forgetfulness, never remembered to alter his will" (18).

The forgery and false registration might never have been discovered if not for an alert solicitor from Keighley named Richard Metcalfe who was at the town's registry office, registering a will. Richard Metcalfe was also William Thomas' solicitor and the man who both drew up and witnessed Hiram Craven's will. His law partner Richard H. Hodgson was "a staunch member of the Royal Yorkshire Lodge of Freemasons," and William Thomas and his family were long-standing members of their Lodge, so chances are Richard Metcalfe was also a Freemason (Campbell 144).

As soon as John Beaver became aware of his son's crime, he took his case to Joseph Greenwood, the Magistrate for the West Riding. The two witnesses were taken into custody at the beginning of March 1843. A month prior, in February, John Beaver added a codicil to his will that confirmed that "no Deed or Instrument of any nature whatever was ever signed or executed by me" in July of 1842, and stated that his last will and testament was legitimate in all respects (18).

The trial against James Beaver and the witnesses was set for March 20th but "it is apparent that some sort of deal had been done" because the court granted the defendants an acquittal and ordered their release (19). The prosecution failed to produce any evidence, and a "plausible explanation for the collapse of the case might have been the imminent demise of John Beaver; he actually passed away on the very day of the trial" (19).

Charlotte was in Brussels at this time, but would have heard about this trial through Emily, especially since their father had been called as a witness.

The coincidences continue with regards to John Beaver's will. He originally drew up the document in July, 1838, but added his first codicil on September 10th, 1842 which stipulated that William Thomas would not be the sole executor after all, but would share the responsibilities and profits with George Taylor, a Haworth Church Warden and Freemason. This may be the situation that later incensed Thomas when he contacted his solicitor Richard Metcalf about taking an unnamed individual to court. Thomas would have greatly appreciated Metcalf's observant behaviour at the registry office when he discovered James Beaver's attempt to illegally obtain John Beaver's property. Without Metcalf's quick response, the forgery scheme would have resulted in William Thomas being deprived of his role as executor of John Beaver's Will and also as guardian of Beaver's two granddaughters Sarah and Grace, who were heiresses to their mother's Wadsworth estate. In 1839, another connection between William Thomas and Buttergate Sykes farm came with the marriage of one of Beaver's granddaughters—Sarah—to Thomas' son, William Thomas Jr.

But in 1843, Thomas might have been surprised to find George Taylor listed as executor on the codicil to John Beaver's will.

27 EXECUTORS, MARRIAGE, AND HEATHCLIFF

At that same time that Metcalf saw the release of deed in February of 1843, he would have seen the codicil adding Taylor as executor. William Thomas would have retained Metcalfe's help once again if he wished to contest the executorship of George Taylor. Reverend Brontë became involved when he tried to calm down the angry Thomas. If William Thomas was angry over George Taylor adding his name as executor to John Beaver's will, Reverend Brontë would have known. Thomas evidently spoke with him about his intention to take someone to court because on August 1st, 1843 the Reverend Brontë wrote him a letter alluding to the situation:

"I have often thought of your case, but never so much as since I last saw you, and consequently I now venture to say to you a few things which I hope you will either receive or excuse. I perceive that your troubles are making some inroads on your spirits and constitution, whilst I know that your life is of great value to your family and neighbours. I am well aware that, as Solomon says, 'The heart knoweth its own bitterness, and a stranger doth not intermeddle with its joy'; but at the same time, those who stand aloof are often better fitted for judging of our own affairs than we are, owing to their judgment being more free to come to just and impartial conclusions.

"Hence I would say to you, as an old neighbour and friend, settle, if you can your affairs, with a certain personage, as soon as you possibly may do, without law. It would be far better to do this, at the loss of two or three hundred pounds than to spend as many thousands, with Lawyers, and to be nothing better.

"Remember Dr. Swift's saying respecting two that were about to go to law and had some money, when the letter of one of the opposing attorneys was opened—

There are two woodcocks in the west,
They are well feather'd in their nest,
Take this advice, my brother,
Pluck you the one and I will pluck the other.

"Send for this weak man, who has got into the snares of those who are cunning and designing. Speak to him Scripturally and kindly. Make him sensible of his danger and folly, and endeavor to persuade him to come to Scriptural and just terms. Had you taken my advice at first, things would not have gone so far, but what is past cannot be recalled, and we can now only 'redeem the time'" (Lock 339).

George Taylor was an Anglican and, for twenty-one years, a Church Warden for Patrick Brontë. He was a trustee of Stanbury's Wesleyan Chapel, a Poor Law Guardian between 1840 and 1847, and a wool stapler. He also acted as one of the executors on the will of the Brontë's Aunt Branwell. His brother John had married Hiram Craven's daughter, so in all likelihood George Taylor was a Mason. Ten years after being an executor on John Beaver's will he owned 73 acres that included three farms and seventeen houses in Stanbury. His position in the community would warrant Reverend Brontë calling him "a certain personage," if he meant "personage" literally as a notable or distinguished person. Taylor's involvement with the church would have provided reason for Brontë to suggest Thomas speak "Scripturally" to Taylor, and thus appeal to his religious nature. Stanbury is within walking distance of the village of Haworth, so for Brontë to suggest Thomas "send for" the man in order to speak to him makes more sense that if the man lived several miles away. His letter opens with the words "I have often thought of your case," which implies that this matter has been simmering for some time. The Beaver will passed probate on 15 June 1843, and Reverend Brontë's letter was dated 1 August, 1843, so Thomas may have been upset about Taylor for several weeks (Fermi 22 n. 3 and 4).

In the letter, Reverend Brontë alludes to both parties of the disagreement having money, especially in the poem's terms: they were "well feather'd in their nest." This would fit with Taylor as well. The conflict caused Thomas to suffer enough anxiety for Reverend Brontë to appeal to him to consider the toll ill health and, at worst, his death would take on his family. Perhaps, Brontë had originally advised Thomas to let the matter rest with Taylor as a co-executor, but if Thomas felt Taylor had gone to John Beaver when he was in poor health (he died eight months later on the day of the trial), and taken advantage of Beaver, Thomas may have wanted to challenge the codicil. He appears to have taken Reverend

Brontë's later advice and either opted for paying out Taylor in the sum of two or three hundred pounds rather than spending thousands suing him.

The other choice for the "certain personage" could be James Beaver, as put forward by Sarah Fermi and Dorinda Kinghorn.

James Beaver had originally married Betty Binns who was the heiress of her family's property in Wadsworth. When she died in 1833, the inheritance was to go to the daughters Sarah and Grace when they reached the age of twenty-one, but until that time, "James had control of the property" and his daughters' trust. "Sarah Beaver Thomas, one of the daughters and wife of William Thomas Junior, reached the age of twenty-one on 28 July, 1843. On the 8th of August, 1843, Sarah and William (who controlled Sarah's property) mortgaged her share of the Wadsworth property to . . . William Thomas, Senior. James Beaver's name is not mentioned in the document." But if the daughter was of the age of majority, would her father need to be a party to the mortgage?

If James was the "personage" in Reverend Brontë's letter then he must have come to an agreement with Thomas: "It seems probable that the Thomases agreed to share some of the proceeds of the eventual sale of Buttergate Sykes in return for James's relinquishment of the income from the Wadsworth property. In 1847, when the second daughter, Grace, reached her majority, Buttergate Sykes was sold and James is at last mentioned as a party to the transaction." Fermi and Kinghorn go on to explain that being a party to the transaction did not ensure wealth. They explain that "James Beaver's standing in the world appears to have declined steadily." In 1839 he is classed as "gentleman," and in 1844 as "yeoman," and by 1851 as "pauper" (20). Without knowledge of the importance of executorships to the Masons, however, the codicil including George Taylor as executor on John Beaver's will could have been the issue that angered William Thomas.

Reverend Brontë's other comments regarding the actions of "a certain personage" are particularly cogent. He alludes to those who have tempted the man to engage in this behaviour. He says he "has got into the snares of those who are cunning and designing," which strongly suggests that the Reverend Brontë knew of unscrupulous activity in his parish. The words "cunning" and "designing" fit perfectly with the image of the men described in Brontë's anagrams.

227

William Thomas was obviously a good businessman because, according to the 1851 Tithe List, he was a wealthy landowner. By 1838, he owned twenty-seven houses, a farm, a doctor's shop, and several fields. As Haworth's wine and spirit merchant, he enjoyed a lucrative profession.

A few months after John Beaver's death, Thomas purchased Hollings Mill. The property had come on the market because Thomas Lister, a Mason and one of the executors on George Robinson's Will, had suffered financial losses during the trade depression of 1841. He would have borrowed money but, being unable to repay the loan, and rather than claim bankruptcy and deal with the shame, in 1842 he chose to hang himself in his barn. William Thomas bought the Mill and let it out for £50 per year to his son William Junior, a worsted spinner and weaver.

In February of 1848, William Thomas' brother Enoch named William's sons as joint executors. At the age of thirty-seven, Enoch Thomas, an Innkeeper, signed all his property over to his nephews, trusting that they would honour his wishes to pay his wife her annuity of approximately £50 per annum. When he died suddenly, a month later, in March of 1848, the nephews began receiving rents on his properties, but failed to pay the annuity to Enoch's surviving wife (Dinsdale). The will also caused concern about the witnesses. In Enoch Thomas' will, a blacksmith from Haworth is one of the witnesses along with William Thomas' solicitor Richard Metcalfe. Apparently, the witnesses and their names drew attention because printed on the front sheet of the will in faint lettering are the words, "Witnesses Names-Appeal Later." No obvious irregularity appears regarding their names, but due to suspicious activity around the acquiring of estates, perhaps the will generated some controversy.

The Thomas name recurs in the relationship between William Thomas Senior and John Beaver through the Beaver family's connection with William Thomas Junior. As mentioned above, the younger Thomas married John Beaver's granddaughter Sarah who, with her sister Grace were the two heiresses to their mother's property in Wadsworth. Now, their grandfather's executor was Sarah's father-in-law (William Thomas Senior), so the Beaver estate and the Wadsworth property were all in the Thomas family, a bond which proved profitable for Thomas in August of 1843 when Sarah mortgaged her share of the Wadsworth property to her father-in-law, William Thomas Senior. Four years later, the Beaver's Buttergate Sykes farm was sold and the proceeds shared among family members. William Thomas had managed to secure financial independence for his sons through their uncle Enoch's death and through marriage, all legitimate transactions, but similar in nature to the legal machinations in *Wuthering Heights*.

Fermi and Kinghorn note that the Beaver forgery provides "a specific example of the kind of family drama hinted at by Charlotte Brontë and Mrs. Gaskell that provided the social setting of *Wuthering Heights*" (22). They also mention a letter Charlotte wrote to Emily from Brussels in May of 1843 when "she closes with 'Regards to the fighting gentry' . . . One is tempted to wonder if she is referring to the Beaver-Thomas dispute" (23).

Charlotte, most likely, would have been aware of the case because it involved her father. Together with this historical information, the anagrams support the possibility that the appearance of legitimacy could have been a shield for darker ventures. Certainly, one could dismiss the anagrams as a product of an active imagination, but the issue of a man gaining property through the marriage of his son with the daughter of a wealthy landowner appears in *Wuthering Heights*. Charlotte was apparently familiar with the cunning and designing ways of men as early as the 1830s when she wrote about these topics in her fiction.

An early example of her interest in and awareness of the men's questionable affairs appears in *Stancliffe's Hotel*, a novella she wrote in 1838 at the age of twenty-three. A character called Mr. Moore is a barrister and has a lease-hold on a wealthy Lord's property. Moore is described as "being a toady of that nobleman's," and, "though an able man, is certainly, according to report, but lightly burdened with principle." Her image of an unscrupulous lawyer in the pocket of a rich man echoes the anagrams. In the story, Moore is attending the assizes and, consequently, out of town when two men decide to visit the man's attractive daughter. The men need an excuse to call on the young woman, so one suggests they want to see him on "business, respecting a mortgage—on a friend's estate, possibly, or probably on our own—or a lawsuit concerning our rich old uncle's contested will" (*Tales of Angria* 96).

When John Greenwood's codicil disinherited his middle brother Joseph and made the youngest brother James sole heir, the family of

Joseph Greenwood, the Magistrate, never challenged the document's legitimacy, but his children were contemporaries and acquaintances of the Brontë children, so Charlotte would have known the details of the codicil and its power to revoke Joseph Greenwood's benefits. The questionable signature on the codicil and the inclusion of the solicitor's clerk as the man who drafted and witnessed the document add to the possibility of fraud, especially in light of the role played by another solicitor's clerk in the Beaver forgery. Brontë's possible allusion to the Greenwood case in her novella conjures the image of Joseph Greenwood's children discussing whether to contest their "rich old uncle's will." Their other uncle James, while escaping any legal challenges, enjoyed the profits of being the sole executor for only a few years before claiming bankruptcy and being forced to leave the area.

In an August 18, 1848 letter to Ellen Nussey, Charlotte mentions James Greenwood and his loss of the large estate. He may have borrowed from his Mason brothers but was soon unable to pay his debts. The anagrams in this letter state that the borrower went bankrupt due to his drinking. Mason lads, who cost little to hire, would intimidate the borrower with the threat of legal action, so the man would concede defeat, sign over his assets, and leave town poor but alive. In reality, as a living poor man, he could not request aid from his Haworth Mason brothers, who had recently formed a charity called "The Sick and Benefit Society." This Society was set up to help starving widows and children after their husbands and fathers had taken ill and died.

Charlotte kept her view on the drinking and the bankruptcy hidden from Ellen, but the anagrams in this letter reveal her true feelings. First the letter:

"I do not know whether you remember / the house called Woodlands / near Haworth belonging to Mr. Jas Greenwood. / The owner has failed lately / and the house and all its furniture / have been sold by auction. / The Sugdens purchased / a large portion of the latter / to return to their relatives / who have now left the neighbourhood / and are gone to reside somewhere / I believe / in the East Riding. / This is a great and unexpected reversal of fortune / and by throwing many of the poor of Haworth out of employment / has occasioned great distress in the village."

The opening anagrams contain terms that may need defining; for instance, legal "tender" is a means of meeting a financial obligation; a yeoman holds a small estate, a "rube" is a colloquial term for a country bumpkin, "den" is her word for the Mason lodge, "yield" means to give up or surrender, as to yield possession, and an example of a "ratio" would be two to one, or double an investment. Some of the anagrams flow naturally into the next one, which suggests a correct transcription. The anagrams begin:

Hook yeomen worm with tender. Rube / lush wasted deed on alcohol, / so gentleman now joined beggar. What horror! / Yield wealth on father's ale.

Punctuation does not split the next two anagrams, so one word is moved from the first phrase to the second to complete the message: *Heath rent useful. It aids an old urn / boys' club. Don a tie. heaven.* This becomes:

Heath rent useful. It aids an old boys' club. Don a tie. Urn heaven. At the *old boys' club* or Mason Lodge, the members wear their ceremonial tie. When they *don* or put on their tie and enjoy the money from the rents, they are in *Urn heaven.* Brontë uses *urn*, like the words *den* and *hive,* as a recurring symbol for the Lodge. For Brontë, the image of a *den* connects the Masons to wolves. She would know that, because Masons admire the bee for its industrious nature, the bee hive is an important symbol in Freemasonry.

The necessity for a slight shift occurs again. First the anagram without the shift, and then the proper message: *Den thugs cheap duress. / threaten legal for top ratio.*

Den thugs cheap. Threaten legal duress for top ratio. For a small payment or, as Brontë states in other anagrams, an abundance of alcohol, the *den thugs* are willing to threaten victims.

Another shift needs to be made with *erased Greenwood's home earn tie / elder hive initiates begin / defer push if an executor needs testator in grave.* Four of the words are moved to an adjoining break, which is allowed because of the lack of punctuation restricting the anagrams. When put together, they read as follows:

Hook yeomen worm with tender. Rube / lush wasted deed on alcohol, / so gentleman now joined beggar. What horror! / Yield wealth on father's ale. / Heath rent useful. It aids an old boys' club. Don a tie. Urn heaven. / Den thugs cheap. Threaten legal duress for top ratio. / Love torture. Heir in tatters. / Bet high. Honoured vow. Hate when fool / erased elder Greenwood's home. / Hive initiates earn tie. Begin / push if an executor needs testator in grave. / Defer moor debt. Pay off through heath matrimony. Now two penny fool. / God sees villain. Christian cottages sheared.

If James Greenwood is one of the *yeomen worm*s hooked into borrowing money, he joins a group of Christian families whose cottages have been *sheared* by the heavy debt load. The word *sheared* is an appropriate one for a Township involved in the wool industry and can be used to imply the families have been deprived of their rights. The only consolation is that *God sees villain*. Greenwood must have gambled *high* but had to honour the debt, especially if *thugs* were threatening him. Brontë would consider James a fool for losing his father's ancestral home to pay for debts incurred from his drinking and gambling. If, back in 1833, he had been complicit in attaching an illegal codicil to his elder brother's will, the financial rewards failed to secure him a lifetime of prosperity. He enjoyed a short fifteen years of wealth. According to the anagrams, the method for the lender to acquire wealth is to *threaten legal duress* if the mortgagor fails to pay, get *hive initiates* to *earn* their Masonic *tie* by pushing the man who drew up his will into an early grave, or have the man owing the money marry off one of his relatives to the lender's family, which makes the debtor a fool twice over: once for getting into debt and then for sacrificing his child in wedlock.

Marriage proves a canny method for acquiring property rights in the anagrams and in real life. The marriage of William Thomas's son to Beaver's granddaughter, and the immediate access to property, shares a kinship with Heathcliff's son marrying Edgar Linton's daughter, so Heathcliff can take over Thrushcross Grange and enjoy the rent from his new tenant Lockwood.

The anagrams and the historical record suggest that the legal plot in *Wuthering Heights* could be based on fact. Even though he hates

Magistrate Linton's daughter, Isabella, Heathcliff marries her in an effort to get his hands on the Linton land. His opportunity to acquire Wuthering Heights occurs when he lends Hindley Earnshaw money, through a mortgage, after Hindley has spent it to pay for his gambling and drinking: *"lush wasted deed on alcohol."* When Hindley dies under suspicious circumstances, the property should go directly to his uneducated son Hareton (a true *"rube"*), but Heathcliff now owns the Heights: he has been able to *Yield wealth on* Hareton's *father's ale.*

Brontë outlines the legal manoeuvrings that enable Heathcliff to continue to acquire property, beginning with this mortgage. Near the end of chapter seventeen, the housekeeper, Nelly Dean goes to the lawyer in the village to see how the property was left when Hindley Earnshaw died, and is told that he died in debt. The lawyer then explains how the heir, Hareton, is little more than a beggar (*"in tatters"*): "The whole property is mortgaged, and the sole chance for the natural heir is to allow him an opportunity of creating some interest in the creditor's heart, that he may be inclined to deal leniently towards him." That creditor, of course, is Heathcliff, and if he and his heart *"love torture,"* then he will not be charitable. Nelly explains to Lockwood that, "The guest was now the master of Wuthering Heights; he held firm possession, and proved to the attorney, who, in his turn, proved it to Mr. Linton that Earnshaw had mortgaged every yard of land he owned for cash to supply his mania for gaming: and he, Heathcliff, was the mortgagee. In that manner, Hareton, who should now be the first gentleman in the neighbourhood, was reduced to a state of complete dependence on his father's inveterate enemy; and lives in his own house as a servant deprived of the advantage of wages, and quite unable to right himself, because of his friendlessness, and his ignorance that he has been wronged." *"So gentleman now joined beggar."* Just as uneducated "yeomen" would be unfamiliar with, the "perplexity without end," in documents that Reverend Brontë once referred to, and that "the absence of even a word or letter, may cause you to lose all," Hareton is unaware of his rights to his father's land.

The complicated family relationships in *Wuthering Heights* become tangled but unwind to create a happy and just ending. Before that happens, however, Heathcliff engages in complex legal machinations. Heathcliff and Isabella have a son. Isabella dies and the son Linton, with Heathcliff's help, marries Catherine's daughter, Cathy, so Heathcliff, through his son, is now father-in-law and prospective owner of the Linton property when young Cathy's father Edgar dies. Heathcliff's plan is to see his descendant as "lord of the estates; my child hiring their children, to till their fathers' lands for wages" (ch.20). He wants the natural heirs to work for their living on their own land like beggars.

The elaborate plot and legal references clearly demonstrate the author's knowledge of English law. By marrying the senior Magistrate's daughter Isabella, who had a life interest in the land, Heathcliff's son becomes tenant in tail by descent. By having his son marry Edgar Linton's daughter, her Linton property and possessions automatically pass to her husband, who conveniently dies right after they marry. Now Heathcliff has control of Thrushcross Grange through his son's marriage.

He gains the Linton property when his son dies because, as the male, he naturally overrides young Cathy's claim, even though she was the son's wife. Heathcliff has no claim on the property through his own dead wife Isabella because she had never been in possession of Thrushcross Grange. In chapter thirty, Nelly explains that Heathcliff's son had signed everything over to his father on his deathbed: "He had bequeathed the whole of his, and what had been her movable property to his father," so Heathcliff is the sole beneficiary to the moveable possessions at Thrushcross Grange, but because his son was a minor, fortunately for young Cathy, Heathcliff has no legal claim to the land, but he maintains control by sharing the rights: "Mr. Heathcliff has claimed and kept them in his wife's right and his also: I suppose legally: at any rate, Catherine, destitute of cash and friends, cannot disturb his possession." Heathcliff and his daughter-in-law are joint owners of the land, but he has sole claim to the possessions.

Heathcliff wins more advantages as he manoeuvres the legal system into his corner. The elder Catherine's husband Edgar Linton would have been entitled to his wife's portion of the Earnshaw's personal, moveable property over at Wuthering Heights, but Heathcliff soundly shuts that loophole by being the mortgagee, which makes him the owner of all the Earnshaw property; consequently, the daughter Cathy loses her claim to her parents' possessions at Thrushcross Grange as well as her right to the belongings at Wuthering Heights through her mother's interest. Finally,

Heathcliff, in the hopes of reuniting with Catherine, starves himself in an act of suicide and dies without having written his own will, which makes the happy ending possible.

When Heathcliff dies, Edgar Linton's daughter Cathy is now the sole living descendant of Thrushcross Grange. As Catherine and Edgar's daughter, she would become entitled to the Linton possessions as well. Eighteen years of Heathcliff occupying Wuthering Heights rent-free would discharge the mortgage contract and redeem the property to Hareton. The two natural heirs intend to marry each other, so they not only retain possession of their own land and moveable property but will also increase their revenue when they join their assets through matrimony. The remarkable interweaving of family and estate law with its twists and turns ends happily and with a just conclusion.

The novel is about dividing estate entails that have been in the families for centuries and are generally passed from the father to his male heir. One scholar in 1848 said that the book is a powerful record of "wickedness" and has a moral: it shows "what Satan could do with the law of entail." C.P. Sanger's 1926 essay, "The Structure of *Wuthering Heights*" was the first to construct the intricacies of the book's legal plot, and notes that the author's structure "requires great skill." He writes that what is remarkable about the novel "is that the ten or twelve legal references are, I think, sufficient to enable us to ascertain the various legal processes by which Heathcliff obtained the property. It is not a simple matter. There was a fundamental difference between the law of land (real property) and that of money and goods (personal property)" (*Critical Essays* 132-143). The author of the novel understood this difference, and, perhaps, so did the men of Haworth.

In Haworth Township over a twenty-year period, wealthy landowners died and executors began appearing on wills. As stated above, executor ownership of property on wills rose from zero to thirty-five between 1833 and 1853. Of the fifteen extant wills, a Mason appeared on each one as testator, executor, or witness.

The grim picture Brontë presents is of honest inhabitants who were suffering the effects from unemployment or poor wages. Add the loss of money to the sudden harsh winters and to the destruction of the peat crop from wet summers, and the spectre of desperation is easy to imagine. The

235

financial depression would have propelled hard-working families closer to starvation. Charity was their only means of assistance, and the wealthy Masons may have been willing to supply emergency loans, but repayment in difficult times would compound the distress and force families to leave an area where their family had lived for generations. In addition to this situation, the anagrams, like *Wuthering Heights,* outline the complicated settlement of land ownership through deaths, wills, and matrimony. This suggests the men knew the difference between real property and personal property. Brontë believed they used their knowledge to scheme and steal land from their fellow trusting Freemasons. She was also aware of the Beaver forgery case, which illustrates the deep suspicion through generations regarding family wills, and the possibility of a feud between two Masonic executors on John Beaver's will. The year of the Spring Assizes at York, 1843, recurs in a later anagram, which may shed light on when Brontë wrote *Wuthering Heights,* the novel that mirrors these legal issues.

In Haworth Township, a small body of water created jobs. The River Worth opened the flow of commerce in the textile industry, and filled the pockets of a few uneducated proprietors of land. At the same time, Charlotte Brontë, another small body, believed that the men were taking what they wanted without censure or restraint. As a tiny woman, she was at her most vulnerable, especially when alcohol and guns were involved. Her fear was palpable but so was her frustration and outrage, which inspired a passionate response, one that would explain her intense preoccupation with the Freemasons in *Jane Eyre, Wuthering Heights,* and *The Professor.* Like a mason, she constructs in those novels deliberate stonework comprised of significant words onto the framework of Masonic mythology to create a complex interplay between symbols and myths in order to convey the questionable process of docking entails.

The anagrams, hidden from the Masons' scrutiny, told her readers part of the story, but do they state, unequivocally, that Charlotte is the author of *Wuthering Heights*?

28 'BIOGRAPHICAL NOTICE'

Two months after Currer Bell's *Jane Eyre* made its successful debut in October of 1847, *Agnes Grey* and *Wuthering Heights* appeared under the pseudonyms of Acton Bell and Ellis Bell respectively. Charlotte's publisher Smith, Elder & Co. did not handle either novel by Acton or Ellis because the manuscripts, along with *The Professor* had been sent separately in July to another London based publisher called Thomas Cautley Newby. He had rejected *The Professor* but agreed to take on the other two books. *Jane Eyre* by Currer Bell was already selling when these two new works by two more Bell authors were published. The London literary community became intrigued; the mysteries around the brothers' identities sparked speculation about the writers.

    Jane Eyre's success motivated Newby's decision to send the Ellis and Acton Bell books to press immediately. He capitalized on Currer Bell's fame and complicated the intrigue about the Bells when he began advertising *Wuthering Heights*. Ads for *Jane Eyre* had already appeared, so Newby placed his ads for *Wuthering Heights* "in the same journal without the author's name and with press notices insinuating that the author also wrote *Jane Eyre*," but the confusion intensified when he also advertised "in the Examiner announcing 'Acton Bell's Successful New Novel Wuthering Heights.' Together with reviews associating it with *Jane Eyre*." Editors of the Clarendon edition of *Wuthering Heights* give Newby the benefit of the doubt and acknowledge that he also "may have been genuinely confused at first about the authors' identities" (*Oxford* 556). No one had actually seen the authors, so the theory that only one Bell brother was the writer in the family could not be proved. Newby, however, had seen the original handwritten manuscripts and may have believed his assertion that only one Bell brother wrote was justified.

    Reviewers accepted Newby's claims of a single author because they noted striking similarities in *Jane Eyre* and *Wuthering Heights*. The *Spectator* reviewed *Wuthering Heights* saying, "The work bears affinity to *Jane Eyre*." The critic Douglas Jerrold declared that, "The work is strangely original. It reminds us of *Jane Eyre*. . . . It is like *Jane Eyre*" (Shorter 112-13). In *The Quarterly Review,* the reviewer writes of

Wuthering Heights as "a novel succeeding 'Jane Eyre,' and purporting to be written by Ellis Bell," and notes "there is a decided family likeness between the two" (Rigby).

Soon reviewers judged all the books as being written by the same Bell brother. *The Athenaeum* reviewer opined that, *Wuthering Heights* and *Agnes Grey* "are so nearly related to *Jane Eyre* in cast of thought, incident and language as to excite some curiosity. All three books might be the work of one hand" (Allott 39). Later, in July of 1848, when the Acton Bell book *The Tenant of Wildfell Hall* came out, one reviewer in *The Spectator* commented on the Bells' shared style:

"The volumes of fiction that some time since appeared under the name of Bell, with three several praenomens, had such a generic resemblance to one another that several reviewers remarked it. The first and most striking affinity was of substance. Each of the Bells selected the singular both in character and incident. The persons were such as are formed by a natural peculiarity of disposition, influenced by an equal peculiarity of circumstances, or produced by strong passions running their course unrestrained in the freedom of a remote country place, at a time which permitted greater liberty to individual will or caprice than is vouchsafed even to brutal and isolated squireens in these days. The composition—not mere diction, but the arrangement of the incidents and persons, as well as the style of things themselves—was extreme and wild, seeking to base effects on the startling, without much regard either to probability or good taste. A rough vigour characterized the whole batch of Bells" (Allot *The Brontës* 249).

Also, at this time, a reviewer from *The Athenaeum* referred to Currer, Ellis, and Acton Bell, stating that, "The three Bells ring in a chime so harmonious as to prove that they have issued from the same mould. The resemblance borne by their novels to each other is curious" (251).

The critic and poet Sydney Dobell believed "a younger less formed Currer Bell" wrote *Wuthering Heights* and that she wrote all the Bell novels; in *The Palladium* he suggests that before *Jane Eyre* and *The Tenant of Wildfell Hall*, came *Wuthering Heights*: it is "the earlier in date and ruder in execution," and that Jane Eyre herself, a character "of quiet satire, peeps out" from certain paragraphs in *Wuthering Heights* (Dobell 169-70).

The confusion over the authorship of the novels continued into 1848. In April of 1848, New York publishers Harper & Brothers published "'WUTHERING HEIGHTS A Novel BY THE AUTHOR OF "JANE EYRE'" (*Oxford* 556). In June of 1848, the London publisher Newby sold Harper & Brothers *The Tenant of Wildfell Hall*, as another Acton Bell book, but he sold the manuscript implying Currer was using another pseudonym: "'By Acton Bell, author of Wuthering Heights'"(*Cambridge Bibliography* 1142).

Newby also used the review from the *Athenaeum* in his advertising. The review "suggested Currer and Ellis were the same person." Newby continued to blur the facts when one "month later he again advertised *Wuthering Heights* in the same journal without the author's name and with press notices insinuating that the author also wrote *Jane Eyre*. At the same time (29 Jan. 1848) a large notice appeared in the *Examiner* announcing 'Acton Bell's Successful New Novel Wuthering Heights', together with reviews associating it with *Jane Eyre*" (*Oxford* 556). The issue climaxed when Charlotte was forced to step in and clarify the authorship of the Bell brothers.

In the summer of 1848, George Smith was in negotiations with another American publisher over forwarding to New York advanced sheets of *Shirley*, Currer Bell's second book. The publisher informed him that Harper & Brothers was already publishing Currer Bell's next novel and it was called *The Tenant of Wildfell Hall*. This publisher told Smith that Newby had told the Americans that "he was about to publish the next book by the author of *Jane Eyre*, under her other *nom de plume* of Acton Bell— Currer, Ellis, and Acton Bell being, in fact, according to him, one person." Smith immediately contacted Currer Bell for clarification. She stated, "her honour was impugned," and denied Newby's claims (*Reminiscences*).

The situation created a serious problem for Charlotte. Currer Bell books were contracted to Smith, Elder, and their rights could not be sold to the United States without Smith, Elder handling the sales. If she had, in fact, written all the novels, she would have been anxious to resolve the issue, understanding the legal complications of having two publishers representing one author.

She travelled with Anne to London to correct the error by visiting both publishing companies to show the women's separate identities. Smith recounts that he saw "two rather quaintly dressed little ladies, pale-faced and anxious-looking," and that Charlotte stepped forward to tell him, "'We have both come that you might have ocular proof that there are at least two of us.'"

This visit to London was the only time Smith ever saw Anne Brontë. He described her as "a gentle, quiet, rather subdued person, by no means pretty, yet of a pleasing appearance. Her manner was curiously expressive of a wish for protection and encouragement, a kind of constant appeal which invited sympathy" (*Reminiscences*).

The journey for both women would have been tiring and stressful, and Charlotte would have felt terrible for involving Anne, but she needed to stop Newby from repeating his claims.

How could Newby have made such an irresponsible error? He may have been trying to capitalize on the amazing success of *Jane Eyre* in order to boost sales when he advised Harper & Brothers that all the books were by Currer Bell, but he also saw the original manuscripts of *The Professor*, *Wuthering Heights*, *Agnes Grey*, and *The Tenant of Wildfell Hall*, so he would have felt confident in his discovery and his assertion that Currer actually was the author of this latest book. Without the public's access, however, to the original Acton and Ellis Bell manuscripts, his claims have remained suspect. The fact that of all the Brontë novels (which include Branwell's writings), these three original manuscripts— *Wuthering Heights*, *Agnes Grey* and *The Tenant of Wildfell Hall*—Ellis and Acton Bell works have all disappeared is equally suspect

The Currer Bell book *Shirley* followed the Acton Bell book *The Tenant of Wildfell Hall* in October of 1849. In 1850, when the Bells' gender had been revealed, the respected Victorian critic Sidney Dobell wrote an article that stated unequivocally that Currer Bell had written all the books. Dobell was a poet as well as a critic. In 1854, his long poem *Balder* appeared, and a year later he co-wrote sonnets about the Crimean War. In 1865 he wrote *Of Parliamentary Reform*, and two years after his death, in 1876, *Thoughts on Art, Philosophy, and Religion* was published posthumously.

In his article about Currer Bell, Dobell states that he believed one author was using various pseudonyms. He placed "in an assumed order of production (though not of publication) the novels called *Wuthering*

Heights, Wildfell Hall, Jane Eyre and *Shirley*, as the works of one author under sundry disguises" (169).

Some of the critics' suspicions stopped when, after her sisters had died, Charlotte wrote in her "Biographical Notice," regarding the lives of Emily and Anne that all three sisters had written novels. Sidney Dobell was not convinced. In that piece, she firmly declares, once and for all, that her sisters were authors, but he remained doubtful. She wrote another disclaimer in the third edition of *Jane Eyre* saying that she authored *Jane Eyre*, but not the Ellis and Acton Bell books. Her words, however, are confusing: "If, therefore, the authorship of other works of fiction has been attributed to me, an honour is awarded where it is not merited; and consequently, denied where it is justly due." Is the honour denied where it is justly due, as in Ellis and Acton Bell are the authentic authors, or if we grant this honour to Currer it is not merited and paradoxically denied where it is justly due, as in Currer really is the genuine author?

Dobell was neither fooled nor confused by what he called her "equivoque" or double meaning: "Opening the third edition of *Jane Eyre* published before *Shirley*, we find a preface in which all other works are disclaimed. A *nom de guerrist* has many privileges, and we are willing to put to a *double entendre* all that is serious in this disclaimer." He believed Charlotte was playing with the words and that her disclaimer had a double meaning and was, therefore, not entirely sincere.

As far as Dobell was concerned, the books themselves disclosed the secret of their authorship: "That any hand but that which shaped 'Jane Eyre' and 'Shirley' cut out the rougher earlier statues, we should require more than the evidence of our senses to believe" and "the author of *Jane Eyre* need fear nothing in acknowledging these yet more immature creations of one of the most vigorous of modern idiosyncrasies" (169).

Dobell also used an interesting metaphor when describing the effect he experienced of certain images from *Wuthering Heights*. He says that the writing "is the masterpiece of a poet rather than the hybrid creation of the novelist," and that when the words are forgotten, the images will remain "as a recollection of *things heard and seen*," because the author has incorporated a "spiritual structure" under the physical "scaffolding" of the words. He believes that "Ideas should be permanent, words evanescent":

the words will naturally disappear from the reader's mind, but "poetic expression is that which is remembered in its effects."

He uses a rather ironic metaphor when he compares the power of the writer's ability to the stone mason's craft: "Whoever has watched a trowel in the hands of a skilful mason, has seen an example of a very high excellence of authorship. The mortar is laid, but the trowel is already withdrawn. So an image should rather be thrown upon the brain than carried into it" (171-2).

Dobell continues to applaud the author of *Wuthering Heights* for the residue from "the fiery ordeal." He compliments the "unimpaired possession of those powers of insight, that instinctive obedience to the nature within her, and those occurrences of infallible inspiration which astound the critic in the young author of 'Wuthering Heights'". Alluding to Heathcliff, he hopes that when she writes her next novel she will "again give us such an elaboration of a rare and fearful form of mental disease" as to "be at once a psychological and medical study. It has been said of Shakespeare, that he drew cases which the physician might study; Currer Bell has done no less" (175).

Dobell is an important critic because, in her "Biographical Notice," written after his review, Charlotte acknowledges that, of all the reviewers, Dobell had "discerned the real nature of *Wuthering Heights*." Was this statement another example of her "equivoque"? If "nature" is defined as the identity as much as the essential character behind the work, perhaps she was providing a hint.

As Currer Bell, Charlotte wrote to her editor her reaction to Dobell's review, which had included references to *Jane Eyre* and *Shirley*. Dobell began his analysis of *Jane Eyre* by saying that he found "only further evidence of the same producing qualities to which 'Wuthering Heights' bears testimony" (176). She said his review was "one of those notices over which an author rejoices with trembling. He rejoices to find his work finely, fully, fervently appreciated, and trembles under the responsibility such appreciation seems to devolve upon him" (Fraser 387). If she had written *Wuthering Heights*, his admiration and assessment of that novel would certainly have been cause for rejoicing.

After Charlotte's disclaimer in her "Biographical Notice," the majority of the critics ended their speculation and accepted the three sisters

242

as the legitimate authors. No one could explain why one author would give credit to two sisters for her own work, so the controversy was placed to rest, but Charlotte's prevarication over dates of completed works, her editing of the poetry and of *Wuthering Heights* after her sisters had died, as well as the loss of the original Ellis and Acton Bell manuscripts still generate puzzlement and confusion. Perhaps Brontë left a clue in the disclaimer that would clarify the mystery.

By 1850, Smith, Elder had obtained the copyright to all the Bell books. After both Emily and Anne had died of tuberculosis, Charlotte prefixed a biographical notice about her sisters to the second edition of *Wuthering Heights* and *Agnes Grey* published that year. By then, the public knew that women had written the books, but they were unaware of the Brontë name.

In the notice about her sisters, Charlotte tries to explain their choices in their literary work—work that some critics saw as wild, passionate writings lacking restraint, especially when penned by "the gentler sex." Charlotte says their Yorkshire tales are the product of creative genius, written from the impulse of nature and the dictates of intuition. She presents Emily as an atypical, unsophisticated woman who lived a secluded life but had an intense fire in her heart that provoked eccentric, uncommon effusions.

The Tenant of Wildfell Hall, an Anne Brontë book published in 1848, had received harsh criticism for its excesses in describing the brutality of Victorian men. As noted above, it reminded the critics of the earlier work *Wuthering Heights* so, needless to say, Anne Brontë got equally trounced for her violent and rude scenes. Critics claimed that the sisters shared a predilection for savagery that disturbed most readers, so Charlotte felt compelled to come to their rescue and defend her sisters' characters, but first she would address the suspicions that all the books were written by Currer Bell.

The opening sentence of the disclaimer reads as follows: "It has been thought that all the works published under the names Currer, Ellis, and Acton Bell, were, in reality, the production of one person." If the first five words are omitted, she seems to state that they were, in fact, the production of one author, but the sentence is also interesting as an anagram. The natural divisions would occur between the words "works" and

243

"published," leaving "in reality" separate because it lies between the two commas, and the last section would be, "were the production of one person."

In this anagram, she omits articles, so without "the" or "a" the sentence has an odd syntax, but the added punctuation helps clarify her message. Also, as mentioned before, when portions of words are not contained within commas, Brontë allows for a word or two to be moved from one place to the next to provide clarity. The completed anagram makes sense with the small shift. The completed anagram is followed by each separate phrase to show where the break occurs. The entire anagram with all the adjustments comes at the end. (*Noah* and *wolf* are her terms for a Mason.)

Below heath heights' tort talk, bold Catherine haunts Noah dullard. Fill pen. Use secret numbers. Tiny Ariel. Hood on pen. Now free to recite spur.

These are the splits as explained above. First her surface prose is written out and then the anagram.

"It has been thought that all the works" / *Below heath heights' tort talk haunts.*

"published under the names of Currer Ellis and Acton Bell" / *Bold Catherine Noah dullard. Fill pen. Use secret numbers.*

"in reality" / *tiny Ariel*

"were the production of one person." / *Hood on pen. Now free to recite spur.*

She refers to *Wuthering Heights* and its torts or civil actions, a reference that coincides with the analysis of the novel in its delineation of the law of entail.

The anagram in *Wuthering Heights* of Lockwood's words "I was over head and ears" could be "*I rove as dead Earnshaw.*" This "*dead Earnshaw*" would most likely refer to Catherine's ghost haunting the dull "*Noah*" Lockwood.

The act of filling a pen with ink would be an accurate term for the activity at that time.

The "*secret numbers*" are the Masonic landmarks that signify the rules of Freemasonry: when Catherine, as a ghost yells that she has been out on the moors "twenty years" but, in actuality, had been dead only eighteen years, she is announcing the Masonic landmark number twenty, which is the belief in the immortality of the soul, a truth the cherub Catherine is trying to pass on to the "*Noah dullard,*" Lockwood.

Brontë writes in the first person singular with "*fill pen*" and "*use secret numbers,*" as in "I fill pen," and "I use secret numbers," so she is not describing her sister's actions, which would need a different subject verb agreement and would read as, "she fills pen;" consequently, Brontë is writing about herself, not her sister. Plus, Charlotte is the small sibling in the family, so her "*tiny Ariel*" indicates she wrote the book, not Emily who was the tallest sister.

This anagram also alludes to the mischievous sprite in Shakespeare's *The Tempest*. Ariel acts as a spy for Prospero; unseen, he can listen to conspirators, and watch their activities on the Island. He uses his magical abilities to protect Prospero and to convey secrets. Like an invisible sprite or the Mason initiate, Charlotte also conceals her identity: she wears a hood, but on her pen not her head. She listens and watches and, because of her anagram cover, can freely relay secrets to her readers. She can also tell us what motivated her to write the novel with her Masonic symbols, and her many allusions to their rituals and rules. In order to learn what spurred her on, we need to dissemble the first two paragraphs of her "Biographical Notice," which read as follows:

"This mistake I endeavoured to rectify by a few words of disclaimer prefixed to the third edition of *Jane Eyre*. These, too, it appears, failed to gain general credence, and now, on the occasion of a reprint of *Wuthering Heights* and *Agnes Grey*, I am advised distinctly to state how the case really stands.

"Indeed, I feel myself that it is time the obscurity attending those two names—Ellis and Acton—was done away. The little mystery, which formerly yielded some harmless pleasure, has lost its interest; circumstances are changed. It becomes, then, my duty to explain briefly the origin and authorship of the books written by Currer, Ellis, and Acton Bell."

Brontë's rules about the anagrams remain consistent: if a word is enclosed in two commas, it cannot be altered; it stays as is and makes sense when included with the rest of the anagrams. The anagrams that fit with the breaks come first but are stilted. The final anagram, with its words repositioned and marked with a number, clarifies the meaning. The first line reads, "This mistake I endeavoured to rectify / by a few words of disclaimer / prefixed to the third edition of *Jane Eyre*."

"This mistake I endeavoured to rectify" / *Inked rude emotive Cathy satire. Foist*
"by a few words of disclaimer" / *Wry maid. Describe wolf oaf's*
"prefixed to the third edition of Jane Eyre" / *profit. Jeer fetid hero. Need identity hoax.*
1) *Inked rude, emotive Cathy satire. Foist oaf's profit. Wry maid. Describe wolf. Jeer fetid hero. Need identity hoax.*

These, too, it appears, / failed to gain general credence, / and now, / on the occasion of / a reprint of / *Wuthering Heights* and *Agnes Grey*
"These, too, it appears" / *apt sheep satire too*
"failed to gain general credence" / *engage a land creditor in fleece*
2) *Apt sheep satire too. Engage a land creditor in fleece.*

and now, on the occasion of a reprint of / *Wuthering Heights* and *Agnes Grey*
"and now" / *no wand*
"on the occasion of a reprint of" / *so re-enact Noah fiction proof*
"*Wuthering Heights* and *Agnes Grey*" / *in heath gangs greed gun-shy write*
3) *No wand, so re-enact Noah gang's greed in heath fiction. Gun-shy; write proof.*

"I am advised distinctly / to state how the case really stands."
"I am advised distinctly" / *Tiny mad sadistic devil*
"to state how the case really stands" / *Cast set story at Heaton's Well Head.*
4) *Tiny, mad. Cast sadistic devil. Set story at Heaton's Well Head.*

"Indeed, I feel myself that it is time / the obscurity attending those two names"

"Indeed, I feel myself that it is time" / *myth fit families in deed. See title*

"the obscurity attending those two names" / *Count debt. Negotiate with mason shyster.*

5) *Myth fit families in deed. See Mason count debt. Negotiate title with shyster.*

"Ellis and Acton—/ Was done away."

"Ellis and Acton" / *clan entail sod*

"Was done away" / *way owed as an*

6) *Clan way: sod owed as an entail.*

"The little mystery, / which formerly yielded / some harmless pleasure,"

"The little mystery" / *sly try title theme*

"which formerly yielded" / *I decry hell if he my word*

"some harmless pleasure" / *am helpless sees armour*

7) *Sly, try title theme. I decry hell. Am helpless if he sees my word armour.*

"has lost its interest; / circumstances are changed."

"has lost its interest;" *His rent is set to last*

"circumstances are changed" *man can get rich dues scarce*

8) *His rent is set to last. Man can get rich. Dues scarce.*

"It becomes, / then, my duty to explain briefly / the origin and authorship of the books / written by Currer, Ellis, and Acton Bell."

"It becomes" / *emetic sob*

then

"my duty to explain briefly" / *fix belly. Tiny. Mute. Parody*

"the origin and authorship of the books" / *handbook. Hoist up fine Heights orator.*

"written by Currer Ellis and Acton Bell" / *Blend rural clowns. Celebrate trinity.*

247

9) *Emetic sob, then, fix belly. Tiny. Mute. Parody handbook. Hoist up fine Heights' orator. Blend rural clowns. Celebrate trinity.*

When all the anagrams in the opening paragraphs of the "Biographical Notice" are linked, they read as follows:

Below heath heights' tort talk, bold Catherine haunts Noah dullard. Fill pen. Use secret numbers. Tiny Ariel. Hood on pen. Now free to recite spur. Inked rude, emotive Cathy satire. Foist oaf's profit. Wry maid. Describe wolf. Jeer fetid hero. Need identity hoax. Apt sheep satire too. Engage a land creditor in fleece. No wand, so re-enact Noah gang's greed in heath fiction. Gun-shy; write proof. Tiny, mad. Cast sadistic devil. Set story at Heaton's Well Head. Myth fit families in deed. See Mason count debt. Negotiate title with shyster. Clan way: sod owed as an entail. Sly, try title theme. I decry hell. Am helpless if he sees my word armour. His rent is set to last. Man can get rich. Dues scarce. Emetic sob, then, fix belly. Tiny. Mute. Parody handbook. Hoist up fine heights' orator. Blend rural clowns. Celebrate trinity.

The anagrams, if correct, outline a startling truth about the fraud and Brontë's fear of being caught. The last line begins with an *emetic sob*. An emetic is something that makes a person sick, so her sobs, presumably about the fraud and its effects, made her ill, but she fixed her stomach as she transformed the despair into art and wrote a parody of the Masonic handbook.

This claim in the anagram fits with the analysis of the parody of Masonic rituals found in the first three chapters of *Wuthering Heights*. In those chapters, she hoists up, or raises Lockwood, the fine speaker who relays the story, to his third degree, and then she incorporates into her novels a mix of the men she considers *rural clowns*. As we will see later, the *trinity* she celebrates are the three novels, *Wuthering Heights*, *The Professor*, and *Jane Eyre*.

In the anagrams in her "Biographical Notice," Brontë explains that she needs to conceal her identity. Her intelligence and observant nature were assets for an author, but violent men, or a "*fetid* [stinking] *hero*" would not take kindly to her jeers and revelations. She repeats the word

248

"tiny" three times: *"tiny Ariel"*; *"tiny mad"*; and *"tiny mute."* Charlotte was less than five feet tall and thin; her eyesight was poor and she lived with the threat of blindness; the fear of physical abuse was real for her. Readers today might perceive her as a giant intellect, but she saw herself as small and defenseless. Her need to hide her identity was a matter of life and death. She calls the concealment of her name a *"hoax."* The deception was her protection against specific men who might discover her code and then learn she was exposing an entail fraud.

The fraud in the anagrams resembles the methods Heathcliff uses against the Earnshaws and the Lintons. The *"heath heights' tort talk"* would refer to the mortgages and wills set up so he could obtain both family properties. The *"tort"* would be a legally wrongful act. The *"secret numbers"* are, most likely, the Masonic landmark numbers she uses to convey the fraternity's rules when Heathcliff and Lockwood exchange passwords after the third degree ritual in Catherine's bedroom. She also repeats the Mason's sacred number "three" over fifty times. Heathcliff's knowledge of the numbers proves he is a Mason, an important aspect of his background and a crucial element in her design.

She sets up the wolves against the sheep, characterizing the Masons as wolves and the unsuspecting citizens as sheep, which suits her Yorkshire home with its predominant wool industry. She believes the *"sheep satire"* an *"apt"* choice. She uses the conventions of satire together with the Masonic legend to rage at a *"land creditor"* who orchestrates the *"fleece"* occurring in her Township. She uses "fleece," as a pun: the word, as a noun, can mean a sheep's coat of wool or, as a verb, to strip off money or property by trickery or fraud. The *"title theme"* refers to the land titles or deeds, the root of the fleece.

Her *"word armour"* would most likely be the anagrams. They protect her from getting caught as she continues to libel the Masons. She explains that the Masonic *"dues"* are *"scarce"*, so the men acquire farms that provide rents to keep the money flowing: *"His rent is set to last; man can get rich."* Hidden even deeper behind her word armour is the ghost of *"bold Catherine"* who *"haunts"* a *"Noah dullard."* This could relate to young Catherine's ghost haunting Lockwood's dream, but another possibility arises that will be discussed later.

The anagram, *"Set story at Heaton's Well Head,"* opens a new discussion about the model for the eponymous farmhouse. The Heatons were a mill-owning family whose ancestors had lived a few miles from Haworth at Ponden House in Stanbury since 1513. Their large family included cousins, brothers, and uncles who were mill owners, farmers employed in the wool industry, churchwardens, and Freemasons. The men owned a cotton mill and corn mill and were also trustees of the Haworth Church Lands; consequently, the Heatons were influential in the community, and had become wealthy through their accumulation of real estate and rental profits. Scholars believe Ponden House was the inspiration for Thrushcross Grange, the Magistrate's property in *Wuthering Heights.* The family's bitter feuds and inheritance disputes are believed to be the source for a few of the tales in Charlotte's and Branwell's juvenile writing, while others call the sordid family history the stuff of legend and gossip.

In Daphne Du Maurier's book, *The Infernal World of Branwell Brontë,* she examines the possibility that John Heaton was the model for Heathcliff. Heaton was a wool comber who lived at Well Head, a farm on a hillside about two miles north of Ponden Hall. The initials "W.H." of Wuthering Heights could stand for Well Head. The initials recur in Wildfell Hall, Wellwood House in *Agnes Grey* and Walden Hall in *Shirley.* The initials obviously held significance. No records indicate that John Heaton inflicted abuse on the inhabitants of his farmhouse, but he was one of several cousins "scattered around the Worth valley among the acres known as Dean Fields," and "according to the tithe list for 1840, he held twenty-four acres at Well Head on Oakworth moor" (108). These men could have been part of that class of "rugged moorland squires, who have grown up untaught and unchecked, except by mentors as harsh as themselves," that Brontë describes in her Preface to the 1850 edition of *Wuthering Heights.*

Further information comes from Branwell's 1840 letter to John Brown. He refers to one man as an esquire, a title that may identify the man: "him whose eyes Satan looks out of, as from windows—I mean . . . esquire." The name had been inked out. John Heaton had been a member of the Three Graces Lodge since 1830, and although the list of members for 1840 was destroyed in the 1950s, those who saw it said that it "gave one 'esquire' among them. He was John Heaten" (108).

Du Maurier compares Branwell's Heaton to Brontë's Heathcliff and finds a close resemblance. "If Branwell's 'esquire', whose 'eyes Satan looks out of, as from windows', inspired Nelly Dean's description of Heathcliff's eyes, 'that couple of black fiends, so deeply buried, who never opened their windows boldly, but lurk glinting under them like devil's spies', then Heathcliff's identification with John Heaton becomes possible" (108). The anagram may also provide a clue: *Cast sadistic devil. Set story at Heaton's Well Head.* Satan looks out from the esquire's eyes; Heathcliff's "devil's spies" appear in the novel; and a devil shows up in an anagram that compares Well Head to Wuthering Heights. But does Well Head fit with the landscape outlined in the novel?

According to Christopher Heywood's essay, "The *Wuthering Heights* Landscape," the geography does support Well Head as a model for Heathcliff's home. For decades, a ruined farmhouse on Stanbury Moor called Top Withens has "entered Brontë mythology as the inspiration for Wuthering Heights" and "Ponden Hall near Stanbury is often suggested as the model for Thrushcross Grange, the home of the Lintons in *Wuthering Heights*" (Dinsdale 82-3), but Top Withens may not be correct. In his essay, Heywood draws together Brontë's geographical clues to provide a map of the fictional landscape that details the placement of Wuthering Heights, Thrushcross Grange, and the town of Gimmerton. The Heights is situated in the north, and a few miles below it is Gimmerton, and to the west is the Grange.

This shape for the three landmarks looks identical to the corresponding positions of Well Head, Stanbury, and Ponden Hall. Top Withens would be far beyond Ponden Hall in the other direction. A plaque at the ruins of Top Withens states, "the buildings, even when complete, bore no resemblance to the house [Brontë] described." The farmhouse once named Well Head remains today, and its stone exterior resembles many of the old farmhouses that still lie scattered on Dean Fields and Stanbury Moor.

John Heaton was twenty years older than Branwell, but he had two sons, Robert and Samuel, who were close in age to Branwell. They would have known each other through their Masonic connection and also, as men who enjoyed sport and guns, perhaps joined the shooting parties set in Ponden Kirk that Branwell describes and draws. Most likely, they drank in Stanbury at "The Eagle," a notorious inn once called the "Old Silent Inn," a local establishment just across the valley from Well Head and up the road from Ponden. In a public house men could drink and exchange stories of bloody, clan feuds, and if tempers flared, arguments could be solved with fists.

With the Heatons having ties to the land for centuries and with that family's large contingency of male relations, feuds are not difficult to imagine, especially if the spoils of war were property rights and rents. These kinds of disputes could have involved the Heaton clan and their fellow Masons. In two excerpts from his tale "Real Life in Verdopolis," a teenage Branwell recounts a fight scene, an exaggerated example of one that he may have witnessed in the inns along the outlying area.

"An incessant storm of conversation rung through the room, intermixed with blows, curses, threats and execrations, the whole seasonably varied by a dozen or two of pistol shots, stabs and other violence by which several men were killed or wounded.

"Dropping innumerable bottles and glasses and catching hold of everything around them, they, grappling with each other in a dying frenzy, descended to the floor amid the crash and tumult of tables and chairs hurled above them in promiscuous confusion. The domestics, who well knew what was likely to happen, in a while entered the apartment and conveyed each of these 'Nobles of Nature' away to their quiet beds. Threats and knife-fights are plentiful."

This violent scene reminds us of the words of the neighbouring Vicar who observed that Haworth was "a very wild and rough part" of the parish, and of Mrs. Gaskell's assertions that these "wild, rough" men with their "indifference to human life" were capable of carrying grudges "bequeathed from generation to generation" as "revenge was handed down from father to son as an hereditary duty."

As stated above, Charlotte Brontë knew that outsiders would find this kind of meaningless brutality difficult to imagine and defended the depiction of coarse language and repulsive manners found in the pages of *Wuthering Heights* in her preface to the novel: "Men and women who, perhaps, naturally very calm, and with feelings moderate in degree, and little marked in kind, have been trained from their cradle to observe the utmost evenness of manner and guardedness of language, will hardly know what to make of the rough, strong utterance, the harshly manifested passions, the unbridled aversions, and headlong partialities of unlettered moorland hinds and rugged moorland squires, who have grown up untaught and unchecked, except by mentors as harsh as themselves."

In the opening line of chapter nineteen of *The Professor*, Brontë writes, "Novelists should never allow themselves to weary of the study of real life." She wrote to her editor that she must always draw from real life: "not one feeling, on any subject—public or private, will I ever affect that I do not really experience" (*Letters, Vol.II* 23).

She had obviously studied a number of unchecked men, and had concluded that their immorality was a form of insanity that could be grouped with another kind of "maniac": "There is a phase of insanity which may be called moral madness, in which all that is good or even human seems to disappear from the mind and a fiend-nature replaces it. The sole aim and desire of the being thus possessed is to exasperate, to molest, to destroy, and preternatural ingenuity and energy are often exercised to that dreadful end" (*Letters, Vol.II* 3).

In her mind, these men were dangerous and ruthless, and she needed to protect herself from violent repercussions if they ever discovered she was revealing their secrets. Not only would her shyness motivate her to conceal her identity behind a male pseudonym, but also her fear of discovery would incite her to distance herself further from the work by becoming three males. She wrote to her editor William Smith Williams soon after *Jane Eyre* had been published, about a clergyman in her neighbourhood who had read the novel and was discussing it in front of her: "He did not recognize 'Currer Bell'—What author would be without the advantage of being able to walk invisible? One is thereby enabled to keep such a quiet mind" (4).

She thanks Mr. Williams for addressing his correspondence to 'Currer Bell': "that is the only name I wish to have mentioned in connection with my writings. 'Currer Bell' only—I am and will be to the Public; if accident or design should deprive me of that name, I should deem it a misfortune— a very great one; mental tranquillity would then be gone; it would be a task to write—a task which I doubt whether I could continue. If I were known,

253

I should ever be conscious in writing that my book must be read by ordinary acquaintances, and that idea would fetter me intolerably" (51).

She was *"tiny"* and forced to be *"mute"*, so her fear of recognition could easily have caused that *"emetic sob."* Clues from her final book *Villette*, may clarify when she experienced her stomach pain and explain if the Masons ever learned of her libellous attack.

29 A *VILLETTE* CLUE

Smith, Elder published Charlotte Brontë's last novel *Villette* in 1853. Brontë draws on her own teaching adventure in Brussels to recount the story of her protagonist, Lucy Snowe, who experiences similar events in a school for girls in the fictional town of Villette. In chapter fifteen, Brontë describes an eight-week vacation in September, during which Lucy remains virtually alone at the school after the staff and students have left for their holiday. If we read this chapter as a description of an author's struggle to harness her ideas for a novel into a coherent structure, then the metaphor of a "deformed" pupil may be the way Brontë pictured the unruly shape of an early draft of her book *Wuthering Heights*.

Lucy is alone during this vacation except for "a servant, and a poor deformed and imbecile pupil, a sort of cretin." Lucy's heart almost breaks from the lack of work to keep her busy, and from the loneliness and gloom; "a sorrowful indifference to existence often pressed" on her soul, and she dares not hope for a brighter future in case fate rejects her needs. Her companion, the cretin, however, is not sad. Lucy tends to the child, but the child's weakness and undeveloped faculties keep her in a kind of inertia, a type of lethargic "paradise."

The weather changes from hot and dry to "tempestuous and wet." The storms make "a cruel impression" on Lucy and she collapses into a "paralysis," praying to Heaven for emotional support, but after no help arrives, she believes "it to be a part of His great plan that some must deeply suffer while they live," and she concludes that she is one of those who will never be consoled. Her mood changes when an aunt comes to the school and takes away the cretin: her "strange, deformed companion" has gone. She was glad to see the child go; "its propensity was to evil," and it seemed as if Lucy had been "imprisoned with some strange tameless animal." Perhaps Brontë's novel is finally coming under control.

The caretaking of the school, however, continues to fall on Lucy's shoulders, and her "mental pain" exhausts her, but she accepts these challenges: "This tax and trial were by no means the least [she had] known in life."

Brontë had experienced the tumult of creative expression and was able to describe the process. In a letter to the critic G.H. Lewes, she writes, "When authors write best, or at least, when they write most fluently, an influence seems to waken in them which becomes their master, which will have its own way, putting out of view all behests but its own, dictating certain words, and insisting on their being used, whether vehement or measured in their nature; new moulding characters, giving unthought-of turns to incidents, rejecting carefully elaborated old ideas, and suddenly creating and adopting new ones. Is it not so? And should we try to counteract this influence? Can we indeed counteract it?" (*Letters, Vol.II* 10).

In *Villette*, the cretin has gone, but a weakened Lucy must gradually rebuild her strength. She walks along the streets and wanders past fields and farmsteads to try to combat the continual despair of solitude.

Lucy imagines the staff and the students at home or at the seaside, and feels the same autumn sun on her face, but the sun fails to make her content. She thinks of one particular student, Ginevra, who has been born with a happy spirit, one that gives her "constant strength and comfort," and who is loved by many without her seeming to notice. Lucy imagines Ginevra secretly grateful for the loving attention bestowed on her by family and friends and, in these imaginings while on her walks, Lucy sees the young woman in a new role with a male suitor:

"I pictured her faithful hero half conscious of her coy fondness, and comforted by that consciousness." Lucy takes her imaginings a step further:

"I conceived an electric chord of sympathy between them, a fine chain of mutual understanding, sustaining union through a separation of a hundred leagues." She ends her musings with an image of these lovers taking their love "across mound and hollow, communication by prayer and wish. Ginevra gradually became with me a sort of heroine."

Brontë draws on the people around her to cast her novel and finds a pair of lovers who share an affinity with nature. Ginevra, with the "happy spirit," could be Cathy, the daughter of Catherine Earnshaw, but the union that can endure the "separation of a hundred leagues" recalls images of Heathcliff and Catherine rambling freely out on the moors.

The cretin has gone; Lucy can walk and think, but the mental pain continues. More storms and depression recur and finally a fever brings on bouts of insomnia. She rises at night calling out for Sleep, but all she hears is "a rattle of the window, a cry of the blast only replied. Sleep never came."

Sleep finally comes, but arrives "in anger" in "an avenging dream." The dream is only fifteen minutes long, "a brief space, but sufficing to wring my whole frame with unknown anguish; to confer a nameless experience that had the hue, the mien, the terror, the very tone of a visitation from eternity."

An angry, avenging dream that begins with "a rattle of the window" and "a cry" sounds similar to Lockwood's dream in Catherine's bed when her ghost appears proclaiming "twenty years", an imaginative replica of "a visitation from eternity" to proclaim life is eternal.

Lucy hears the clock at the church of St. Jean Baptiste strike twelve, as her dream and her ordeal end. She gets on her knees and prays. The clock chimes twelve, representing the meridian sun, the time when Masons enjoy their refreshment after a prayer to St. John the Baptist, their patron saint.

The "horrors of that dream" that caused her suffering, that made her tremble in fear, linger as she feels "torn, racked and oppressed in mind." She echoes Heathcliff's beliefs when she says, "Methought the well-loved dead, who had loved *me* well in life, met me elsewhere, alienated: galled was my inmost spirit with an unutterable sense of despair about the future. Motive there was none why I should try to recover or wish to live; and yet quite unendurable was the pitiless and haughty voice in which Death challenged me to engage his unknown terrors." Nelly Dean describes Catherine Earnshaw as "a haughty, headstrong creature." Could these be Heathcliff's sentiments, and is this passage alluding to "haughty" Catherine's challenge to join her in death?

When Lucy comes out of her delirium her imaginings continue. She sees Fate as being made of stone, "Hope a false idol—blind, bloodless, and of granite core," but she also believes that the suffering "was gaining its climax, and must now be turned by [her] own hands, hot, feeble, trembling as they were." Is the "granite core" an allusion to her earlier description of the book in her preface to *Wuthering Heights* where she writes that the author "found a granite block on a solitary moor" and from that carved out a "human shape"? Does the "climax" mean that Brontë is nearing the end of her novel where Heathcliff is laid to rest beside Catherine's grave?

As her strength returns, Lucy ventures out, away from the school whose roof was as "crushing as the slab of a tomb." Under an October sky, she enters a Catholic church and accepts the comfort of prayer: "any solemn rite, any spectacle of sincere worship, any opening for appeal to God was as welcome . . . as bread to one in extremity of want." No doctor could cure her, but she knew to find the power in her own hands, and looks to the church for support.

The next event actually occurred while Brontë lived in Brussels. Like Charlotte, Lucy enters a confessional and explains to the priest that, even though she is a protestant, she needs to speak to someone:

"I was perishing for a word of advice or an accent of comfort. I had been living for some weeks quite alone; I had been ill; I had a pressure of affliction on my mind of which it would hardly any longer endure the weight."

The priest is unable to give her the appropriate counsel for her circumstances. Lucy understands: "I had not expected he would be; but the mere relief of communication in an ear which was human and sentient, yet consecrated—the mere pouring out of some portion of long accumulating, long pent-up pain into a vessel whence it could not be again diffused—had done me good. I was already solaced."

If Brontë wrote the vacation episode in *Villette* to convey to her reader the truth of what had actually occurred during her employ at the Pensionnat Heger, then the cretin could be, metaphorically, an unruly first draft.

The cretin could be a symbolic representation of a novel as it takes shape in Brontë's imagination. This being is not fully formed, has a "warped" mind and body, and a propensity to evil, "a vague bent to mischief an aimless malevolence," that "made constant vigilance indispensable." Brontë had studied the Masons, kept constant vigilance and, through her observations, believed they were committing a fraud with land titles and rents.

Now she tries to structure the story in her mind. The cretin would act inhuman, "moping and mowing and distorting her features with indescribable grimaces." She adds that "attendance on the cretin deprived me often of the power and inclination" to eat, and made her weak but "this duty" never broke her completely.

If the metaphor is accurate, Brontë appears to be recounting the circumstances and her mood while she wrote *Wuthering Heights*. She says, "I imagined" Ginevra, "I pictured" her hero, and "I conceived" their inseparable bond. She imagined, pictured, and conceived the novel while on vacation in Brussels in 1843. Even the weather suits the tempest and stormy relationships found in the book.

At one point during this narration, Brontë places Lucy's thoughts in quotations marks, which suggests she has hidden an anagram inside them. She writes, "I really believe my nerves are getting overstretched: / my mind has suffered somewhat too much; / a malady is growing upon it / – what shall I do? / How shall I keep well?" These lines would have been written a few years after the publication of *Wuthering Heights*.

The breaks occur naturally with the punctuation, so the anagrams would read as follows:

Regret cavalier revenge. Thieves noted libel mystery. / Shy dwarf. Use common mud to shame thief. / Outdo pig in wily anagrams. / Hid a tall show. / Walks help oil wheel.

These anagrams state that the Masons recognized her attack against them in the pages of *Wuthering Heights*. They would have known the "*common mud*" she described. The word "common" in this case could mean land known to the community, or land relating to the community at large. Either way, readers would see the methods Heathcliff employs to wangle the two properties away from the natural heirs, and if Brontë's beliefs were right, the character of Heathcliff and the legal subplot would sound familiar to the local landowners.

No wonder she regretted seeking revenge; a short woman telling a tall tale could create friction among her father's friends, and they could, if they were inclined, seek their own retribution against her. The walks through Brussels would have oiled the wheels of her brain, so that when she returned to the school, she could write her novel with a clear head.

As Lucy tries to recover from her "malady," Brontë adds another few words inside quotation marks. Lucy tries to pray, but she can only speak these words: "From my youth up Thy terrors have I suffered with a troubled mind." With a break after the word "suffered," the anagram reads as follows:

"From my youth up Thy terrors have I suffered" / *Forty-three fever. Pious oaf's mud myth. Hurry.*

"with a troubled mind" / *had mild but wrote in*

When placed together coherently, the letters say:

Forty-three had mild fever, but wrote pious oaf's mud myth. In hurry.

An alternate reading could be: *In forty-three had mild fever, but wrote pious oaf's mud myth. Hurry.* The words, not in quotation marks, but following this quotation are a declaration of the validity of what she has just written: "Most true was it." She once declared to her editor, "Truth has a severe charm of its own" (*Letters, Vol.I* 539). If the *"pious oaf's mud myth"* is *Wuthering Heights*, then Brontë is saying she wrote the novel in 1843 during the vacation period at the Pensionnat Heger.

Brontë's *mild fever*, described as "a strange fever of the nerves and blood," continues as Lucy's spirit gradually sinks into sorrow, and could also be connected to Brontë's *emetic sob* or despair before she began writing *Wuthering Heights*. The two incidents—one real, one fictional—overlap to tell the story of the creation of the novel. As will be seen in a later chapter, Brontë uses a similar method in *Jane Eyre* to convey how she felt when she composed *Wuthering Heights*.

While in Brussels, Charlotte was teaching English and studying French. During a two to three-month period in 1843, while the occupants of the school were on vacation, she stayed on, mostly alone, at the Pensionnat Heger. She had no other pressing occupation, so she could have written the novel at that time.

She was in Brussels at school with Emily in 1842 but came home briefly in late 1842 for her Aunt Branwell's funeral. Emily stayed home to look after their father, but Charlotte loved the school and returned to Europe in 1843 until rumours of her father's drinking brought her back to

Haworth in January of forty-four. She had completed the novel and then began work on *Jane Eyre* soon after. The vacation episode in *Villette* and the anagrams in her "Biographical Notice" from 1850 both help provide a clearer picture of the time frame and her mood.

Another clue comes in her "Biographical Notice," when she acknowledges the accuracy of Sydney Dobell's analysis of *Wuthering Heights* in comparison to all the other critics. Dobell was certain that Charlotte wrote all the books, and stated that *Wuthering Heights*, the first written of her published works, though ruder in execution than *Jane Eyre*, shared the same strain of "quiet satire." He also commented on the book's youthful brilliance and noted the beginning stages of a genius writer: *Wuthering Heights* was "the unformed writing of a giant's hand: the 'large utterance' of a baby god" (171).

Brontë admitted that Dobell was the only critic to get it right: "One writer, endowed with the keen vision and fine sympathies of genius, has discerned the real nature of *Wuthering Heights*." Scholars assume she was saying that Dobell had discerned that the novel's rough and rustic rendition, though demonstrating genius, came from the pen of a young writer, but other critics had made those observations as well. What Brontë may have been referring to was that he had perceived the fundamental drive behind the novel's creation.

Dobell believed that the novel was "a youthful story, written for oneself in solitude, and thrown aside till other successes recall the eyes to it in hope" (169). Alone at the pensionnat, the wrath of the "baby god" emerged in a novel about a malevolent thief's land fraud, and then, with her temper appeased, the author put the manuscript aside until it was time for her two other works to join it and be sent off to publishers.

Dobell's perceptive eye noticed Brontë's style and wit in the novels, and he recognized her equivocations in her disclaimers of authorship, but he never suspected that she had concealed a host of anagrams behind those ideas and within the satire.

What she placed in plain view, however, were subtle hints to guide the reader to the real location of her tale. At the time of the writing, she would have disguised this violent moorland with false place names, but the letter "H" may have been a clue.

The letter "H" stands out in *Wuthering Heights* and in the towns near Brontë's home. Several place names begin with "H": Huddersfield, Halifax, Harrogate, Harewood, Hebden Bridge, and Haworth, as do the names in the novel: Heathcliff, Hindley, Hareton. The letter recurs in *The Tenant of Wildfell Hall* with Huntington, Hargrave, Hattersley, and Helen. At the time of the novels' publications, the reading public had no idea of the exact settings for the stories, so perhaps Brontë was supplying a clue as to the vicinity where the crimes were occurring and perhaps alluding to the famous clan of the Heatons whose unbridled minds and hearts may have provided fodder for her fiction.

Rather than a quaint wave between three sisters, the recurrence of the letter "H" and the initials "W.H." serves as a link to the novels and provides yet another clue that only one Brontë wrote all the books.

The anagrams, of course, serve as further clues that Emily never wrote *Wuthering Heights*. The evidence continues with the scraps of diary papers standing out as a glaring anomaly in a genius' repertoire; the dearth of Gondal stories in Emily's hand; the lack of the original manuscript to prove Emily wrote the book; the belief of early critics that Currer Bell was the author of all the novels; the contention of the publisher T.C. Newby to the American publisher that, after seeing the handwriting on all the manuscripts, "to the best of his belief" the four novels "were all the production of one writer" (Barker 557); the number of Charlotte's edits on *Wuthering Heights* after Emily had died; and the profusion of perplexed scholars who, without any surviving Gondal narratives to establish a relationship between her undistinguished, childish musings and the novel's masterful style and virtuoso structure, wonder how Emily's writing ability made such a prodigious leap and progressed in just a matter of months from the diary papers to the masterpiece *Wuthering Heights*. Also, in the diary papers, Emily is still contentedly writing about her Gondal characters. As one scholar asserts, "Gondal was more than a childish invention; it was a way of life" (Gerin 25), so Emily's sudden shift to the Earnshaw and Linton families is highly unlikely.

The dearth of examples of Emily's prose, whether in letters or as manuscripts strengthens the argument that she was not a writer. As another Brontë biographer points out, "Scarcely a scrap of self-revelation did Emily leave behind; two colourless letters to a friend of Charlotte's being well nigh the only memorials in her handwriting that have been preserved" (Shorter 127), and "the absence of a single line from her to any correspondent furnishing some revelation of character, the non-existence even of a portrait bearing the faintest resemblance to her, the few casual glimpses of a personality that loved dogs more than humans" only adds to the belief that she was a loving spirit, a kind-hearted sister, and an affectionate daughter who was loved by her family, but she was neither author nor genius (235). The evidence points to Charlotte as the real author and mastermind behind the books, and answers the persistent questions surrounding various inconsistencies in the historical and biographical records.

Brontë originally created the "*hoax*" of three Bell brothers to protect her identity from the men whose secrets she attempted to reveal. The three male names gave her the added layer of concealment and afforded a greater distance from her own name and gender: in her mind, one male pseudonym would have been insufficient cover; consequently, the extra layers of mask provided both a psychological shield and an actual safeguard that would likely keep local readers from assuming the three brothers came from the parsonage. We can deduce that a writer who goes to these extremes to conceal her identity truly wanted to remain hidden, but not necessarily out of shyness; this kind of elaborate scheme seems born from fear.

The anagrams were a hood for her pen, and her Masonic symbols, so artfully incorporated into her stories, were meant to lead the reader to the truth. The anagrams and the symbols were her instruments of attack against the men she regarded as wolves, but her multiple pseudonyms were her guarantee of security. Her unbelievable facility for language, her superior memory, and love of puns, as well as her knowledge of Shakespeare, the Bible, and most classical works gave her the freedom to use allusions unfamiliar to an uneducated Mason, while the anagram skill armed her with a powerful weapon in her language arsenal. The pseudonyms, the anagrams, the secret clues were necessary efforts to keep safe, but she also wanted her readers to know the truth—a difficult dilemma to reconcile.

The research, to this point, suggests that she wrote all the novels, but does the biographical record support this view, especially for the Anne Brontë novels *The Tenant of Wildfell Hall* and *Agnes Grey*?

30 *AGNES GREY* AND
THE TENANT OF WILDFELL HALL

Sydney Dobell believed that Charlotte Brontë wrote *The Tenant of Wildfell Hall* before *The Professor*. Scholars believe it was completed on the date the narrator ends the book—10 June 1847—which was a practice Brontë had used when concluding her juvenile stories. The actual date may be in dispute but, again, the evidence suggests that Charlotte, not Anne, wrote the novel.

In November of 1840, Charlotte sent a letter to Ellen recounting a visit from a minister's wife. Mrs. Collins was in an emotional state and feared financial ruin. She "came here the other day, with a most melancholy tale of her wretched husband's drunken, extravagant, profligate habits." The husband's drinking had put them in debt, and the wife expected he was about to be fired "from his curacy." She was aware "from bitter experience, that his vices were utterly hopeless. He treated her and her child savagely. Papa advised her to leave him for ever, and go home, if she had a home to go to." The woman planned to do so and "expressed great disgust and contempt towards" her husband. Charlotte wondered how Mrs. Collins "should ever marry a man towards whom her feelings must always have been pretty much the same as they are now: I am morally certain no decent woman could experience anything but aversion towards such a man," and admitted to Ellen that she had always disliked him, but was never sure why: "I hated to talk to him, hated to look at him; though, as I was not certain that there was substantial reason for such a dislike, and thought it absurd to trust to mere instinct, I both concealed and repressed the feeling as much as I could," and "was struck with Mary's expression of a similar feeling at first sight; she said when we left him, 'That is a hideous man, Charlotte!' I thought 'He is indeed'" (*Letters, Vol.I* 231).

Scholars think that the Reverend Collins is the inspiration for the character of Arthur Huntingdon, the narcissistic, selfish drunk in *The Tenant of Wildfell Hall*, but Branwell's antics may well have been tapped for additional verisimilitude. In 1846, Charlotte wrote an analysis of her brother and of men in general to her friend and former teacher Miss

265

Wooler: "You ask me if I do not think that men are strange beings—I do indeed, I have often thought so—and I think too that the mode of bringing them up is strange, they are not half sufficiently guarded from temptation—Girls are protected as if they were something very frail and silly indeed while boys are turned loose on the world as if they—of all beings in existence, were the wisest and the least liable to be led astray" (*Letters, Vol.I* 448). She had witnessed Branwell's freedom to roam among gamblers and drinkers while ladies sat at the other extreme, sequestered and guarded inside their homes. *The Tenant of Wildfell Hall* explores this theme of immature boys, like Huntingdon and his friends, having license to indulge in wild pleasures, behaviour that also resembles the actions of Reverend Collins.

Mrs. Collins returned to the parsonage seven years after that first visit back in 1840. Charlotte again wrote to Ellen on the subject of Mrs. Collins and her "wretched and most criminal" husband. She explained that the man had run "an infamous career of vice both in England and France," and had abandoned "his wife to disease and total destitution in Manchester—with two children and without a farthing in a strange lodging house." Mrs. Collins had arrived at the parsonage and had asked to speak with Charlotte in the kitchen. She was "pale and worn but still interesting looking and cleanly and neatly dressed as was her little girl who was with her. I kissed her heartily. I could almost have cryed to see her for I had pitied her with my whole soul when I heard of her undeserved sufferings, agonies and physical degradation. She took tea with us, stayed about two hours and entered frankly into the narrative of her appalling distresses—her constitution has triumphed over the hideous disease—and her excellent sense—her activity and perseverance have enabled her to regain a decent position in society and to procure a respectable maintenance for herself and her children . . . she does not know where Mr. Collins is and of course can never more endure to see him." The woman's story had deeply affected Charlotte, so she was happy to hear that she had triumphed over her circumstances, which included a hideous disease that was most likely venereal, but was now healthy, single, and running a lodging house in Manchester (*Letters, Vol.I* 521). The fact that she spent two hours recounting "the narrative" at the beginning of April, and by the 10th of June 1847, *The Tenant of Wildfell Hall* was complete indicates that the story had deeply affected the author and had compelled her to design her own version about the upbringing of those "strange beings" who "are turned loose on the world as if they—of all beings in existence, were the wisest and the least liable to be led astray." As a Brontë biographer notes, the theme was important to Charlotte: "the central thesis of the book, which expressed a view she had herself expounded in connection with her brother," showed that the education of children was a topic at the parsonage (Barker 531).

When Mrs. Collins first visited the parsonage, Anne was away at Thorp Green working as a governess for the Robinson family. Charlotte heard the woman's story directly in 1840 and was so moved by it that she wrote to Ellen. Several years later, she wrote Ellen again about the woman's success because she had felt pity for the woman's "undeserved sufferings." The woman character in *The Tenant of Wildfell Hall* must also suffer indignities and escape with her young child far from her drunken husband, so Mrs. Collins' story obviously affected the author directly and influenced her to feel deeply the woman's pain with her "whole soul." Based on the biographical information, during this time, Anne was home but her "health was still delicate after the coughs and colds of the winter and spring" (Barker 529).

In an 1848 letter to William Smith Williams at Smith, Elder, Brontë wrote about the male characters in *The Tenant of Wildfell Hall*, *Jane Eyre*, and *Wuthering Heights* as if she were speaking of her own creations. "You say, Mr. Huntingdon reminds you of Mr. Rochester—does he? Yet there is no likeness between the two; the foundation of each character is entirely different. Huntingdon is a specimen of the naturally selfish sensual, superficial man whose one merit of joyous temperament only avails him while he is young and healthy, whose best days are his earliest, who never profits by experience, who is sure to grow worse, the older he grows. Mr. Rochester has a thoughtful nature and a very feeling heart; he is neither selfish nor self-indulgent; he is ill-educated, mis-guided, errs, when he does err, through rashness and inexperience: he lives for a time as too many other men live—but being radically better than most men he does not like that degraded life, and is never happy in it. He is taught the severe lessons of Experience and has sense to learn wisdom from them—years improve him—the effervescence of youth foamed away, what is really good in him still remains—his nature is like wine of a good vintage, time cannot sour—but only mellows him. Such at least was the character I meant to pourtray.

"Heathcliffe, again of "Wuthering Heights", is quite another creation. He exemplifies the effects which a life of continued injustice and hard usage may produce on a naturally perverse, vindictive and inexorable disposition. Carefully trained and kindly treated, the black gipsey-cub might possibly have been reared into a human being, but tyranny and ignorance made of him a mere demon. The worst of it is, some of his spirit seems breathed through the whole narrative in which he figures: it haunts every moor and glen, and beckons in every fir-tree of the 'Heights'" *Letters, Vol.II* 99).

T. C. Newby never acquired the copyrights to the Acton and Ellis Bell books, which allowed Smith, Elder to republish them, but he published the first edition of *The Tenant of Wildfell Hall* because Acton Bell was bound to him contractually to present him with a second novel. Without an original manuscript, however, the proof of authorship cannot be verified, but Newby believed the book was another Currer Bell creation. The author's sentiments sound remarkably similar to those of Charlotte's when, writing as Acton, she states in the Preface of the book, "I wished to tell the truth," and "I feel it my duty to speak an unpalatable truth." She also writes, "when we have to do with vice and vicious characters, I maintain it is better to depict them as they really are than as they would wish to appear. To represent a bad thing in its least offensive light is doubtless the most agreeable course for a writer of fiction to pursue; but is it the most honest, or the safest?"

As Stevie Davies states in her introduction, the novel depicts "men behaving badly—drinking, gaming, abusing their wives (and servants and dogs), squandering fortunes, fornicating—they are hell-bent souls recklessly playing away the hope of heaven, within a patriarchal system that licenses the soulless pleasures of 'gentlemen'" (vii). Brontë was hoping to sound an alarm against the kind of moral deterioration she had witnessed close at home and to recount the experiences of Mrs. Collins.

The heroine Helen marries Arthur Huntingdon and soon discovers that life at Grassdale manor consists of drunken and immoral behaviour. She gradually notices the change in her husband: "His appetite for the stimulus of wine had increased upon him, as I had too well foreseen. It was now something more to him than an accessory to social enjoyment: it was an important source of enjoyment in itself." She tries to control his "recreation" with his equally alcoholic friends: "I could not prevent him from taking more than was good for him, still, by incessant perseverance, by kindness, and firmness, and vigilance, by coaxing, and daring, and determination, I succeeded in preserving him from absolute bondage to that detestable propensity, so insidious in its advances, so inexorable in its tyranny, so disastrous in its effects" (ch.30). She quickly becomes "tired out with his injustice, his selfishness and hopeless depravity" (ch.31).

Arthur begins an affair with his friend's wife, and Helen soon discovers their "guilty connection," their "criminal connection," when she overhears them in the garden. She sinks to her knees in shock: "My burning, bursting heart strove to pour forth its agony to God, but could not frame its anguish into prayer; until a gust of wind swept over me, which, while it scattered the dead leaves, like blighted hopes, around, cooled my forehead, and seemed a little to revive my sinking frame. Then, while I lifted up my soul in speechless, earnest supplication, some heavenly influence seemed to strengthen me within" (ch.33). In an instant her life has changed. Her anguish is so deep and raw that she is unable to utter a prayer. This "earnest supplication" echoes Jane Eyre's when Rochester delivers the blow that they cannot marry: "My eyes were covered and closed: eddying darkness seemed to swim round me, and reflection came in as black and confused a flow. Self-abandoned, relaxed and effortless, I seemed to have laid me down in the dried-up bed of a great river; I heard a flood loosened in remote mountains, and felt the torrent come: to rise I had no will, to flee I had no strength. I lay faint; longing to be dead. One idea only still throbbed life-like within me—a remembrance of God: it begot an unuttered prayer: these words went wandering up and down in my rayless mind, as something that should be whispered; but no energy was found to express them" (ch. 26). Jane felt her cruel reality as if "a hand of fiery iron" had grabbed at her stomach. The moment was "full of struggle, blackness, burning!" For Helen, her heart is "burning" but a wind "swept over" her as if to remind her of nature's power to comfort. The "torrent" of flood waters reminds Jane of God's love. Unspoken prayers, a burning sensation, and an element of nature that soothes the heroines' distress as it also helps to depict their internal struggle. Davies notices the similarities in the tone of these two expressions of crisis: In Helen's "moment of absolute affliction, the prose deepens to a throbbing biblical intensity reminiscent of *Jane Eyre*" (xxiv).

In *The Tenant of Wildfell Hall*, Brontë also shows the effects of the men's "selfish indolence" and irresponsibility when rearing boys. Helen and Arthur have a son who, at a very young age, is introduced to wine. Helen's greatest concern is the men's influence on her child: they "delighted to encourage in all the embryo vices a little child can show, and to instruct in all the evil habits he could acquire—in a word, to 'make a man of him' was one of their staple amusements, and I need say no more to justify my alarm on his account, and my determination to deliver him at any hazard from the hands of such instructors." Every night, the men teach her son "to tipple wine like papa, to swear like Mr. Hattersley, and to have his own way like a man, and sent mamma to the devil when she tried to prevent him. To see such things done with the roguish naiveté of that pretty little child and hear such things spoken by that small infantile voice, was as peculiarly piquant and irresistibly droll to them as it was inexpressibly distressing and painful to me." Helen decides to escape: "my child must not be abandoned to this corruption: better far that he should live in poverty and obscurity with a fugitive mother, than in luxury and affluence with such a father" (ch.39). Her tone mirrors Jane Eyre's when, poverty-stricken, she considers whether to die on "yonder" moors or on a busy street: "I would rather die yonder than in a street, or on a frequented road . . . And far better that crows and ravens . . . should pick my flesh from my bones, than that they should be prisoned in a work-house coffin and moulder in a pauper's grave" (ch.28).

Helen finds her strength in her faith and comfort in the solitude of the library. Helen's musings share a kinship with Jane Eyre's when Jane decides to leave Rochester. While on the heath, Jane considers her decision: "What was I to do? Where to go? . . . I touched the heath, it was dry, and yet warm with the heat of the summer day. I looked at the sky; it was pure: a kindly star twinkled just above the chasm ridge. The dew fell, but with propitious softness; no breeze whispered. Nature seemed to me benign and good; I thought she loved me, outcast as I was; and I, who from man could anticipate only mistrust, rejection, insult, clung to her with filial fondness (ch.28). Jane looks at the star and feels that no matter how bad things may get, she is not alone; someone is watching over her. Helen has a similar reaction to her plight while she gazes at a star: "I had just ensconced myself within the bow of the window, and was looking out upon the west where the darkening hills rose sharply defined against the clear amber light of evening, that gradually blended and faded away into the pure, pale blue of the upper sky, where one bright star was shining through, as if to promise—'When that dying light is gone, the world will not be left in darkness, and they who trust in God—whose minds are unbeclouded by the mists of unbelief and sin, are never wholly comfortless'" (ch.38).

The men at Grassdale manor in *Wildfell Hall* make life intolerable for Helen. She musters the courage to leave her abusive husband to begin her journey much like Jane when she leaves Thornfield Hall. Davies finds that Grassdale manor "bears a weight of symbolic meaning comparable with the pilgrim's sojourns in *Jane Eyre*: at first it is a fool's paradise, then a false paradise." One of the characters tries to seduce Helen, and his advances mirror "Milton's Satan's slyly ingratiating approaches to Eve in *Paradise Lost*" (xxiii). The Eden that Grassdale once was has now been lost to the drunken debauchery and violence Huntingdon and his mates engage in on a regular basis, actions that "represent a group code which not only legitimates but authorizes infantilism as a norm" (xxvi). Their wild undisciplined antics keep them lodged in an adolescent haze: "they remain in the equivalent of a ruffianly childhood, running amok, fighting, throwing things, cursing for effect, shamelessly baring their addled brains to public view." The men's emotional growth is stunted: they "are at the stage of resourceless children requiring the stimulation of amusements, their sole occupations being gaming and hunting" (xvii). They "swagger with their guns. Their sports are blood-sports" (xix). The image of grown men joined by a fraternity of drink and carousing, and acting like children echoes the antics of Freemasonry that Brontë alludes to in *Wuthering Heights*. Before he crosses the threshold into the "penetralium" to begin his Masonic degrees, Lockwood looks up at the front door of the farmhouse and sees a "grotesque carving" of "a wilderness of crumbling griffins, and shameless little boys." The carved image hints at what kind of activity he should expect inside this pre-eminent house.

In the introduction to *The Tenant of Wildfell Hall*, Stevie Davies notes that *Jane Eyre* bears a "spiritual" likeness to Anne Brontë's novel. "Sharing the passionate truth to self of Charlotte's novel and with something of the mutinous energy of Jane's 'I', which begets itself in the reader who shares her journey, the 'diary' section of *Wildfell Hall* (Chapters 16-44) also represents its territories as landscapes of the mind, viewed in the light of eternity" (xxii).

Acton Bell and Charlotte Brontë share similar thoughts, which can be explained by their close proximity as sisters and their mutual experiences as governesses, but if attitudes and emotions in the first Acton Bell novel *Agnes Grey* contain duplications of Charlotte's exact words, then the question of authorship of the two Acton Bell books again must be posed.

Charlotte Brontë first worked as a governess for three months in the summer of 1839 after she had left her teaching position at Roe Head School. She hated being a governess, but knew she needed to earn a living. She made an earnest attempt again in 1841 but lasted only nine months before returning to Haworth to plan her trip to Brussels. Those twelve months taught her that she lacked the nature of a governess, and her letters to Ellen, during her employment, reflect her awareness of those deficiencies. Her self-reflective awareness communicated in the letters, as well as particularly striking combinations of words, closely resemble those voiced by the character of Agnes in the Acton Bell novel *Agnes Grey*.

In 1839, Charlotte writes to Ellen that she is having a dreadful time of it, and calls the employment "dreary work" and complains that "The children are constantly with me, and more riotous, perverse, unmanageable cubs never grew." Her authoritative powers are limited, so she must refrain from correcting their bad behaviour because it "brings only black looks upon oneself" (*Letters, Vol.I* 191).

Her experience has given her an uncompromising attitude: "a private governess has no existence, is not considered as a living and rational being except as connected with the wearisome duties she has to fulfil. While she is teaching the children, working for them, amusing them, it is all right. If she steals a moment for herself she is a nuisance" (191). She tells her friend, "I might be tempted to . . . pour out the long history of a Private Governess's trials and crosses in her first situation," which is exactly the subject of *Agnes Grey* (193).

Anne Brontë was also a governess and, although she complained about the work, she lasted much longer at the job. She had remained in the Robinson's employ for five years and may have continued in that capacity if Branwell had not been fired from his position as the son's tutor, effectively forcing the two Brontë employees to return home. Anne left on her own accord but, with Branwell dismissed under the dark cloud of scandal, remaining at Thorp Green would have been an intolerable choice and she would have gladly come home. Also, her diary papers indicate that she had grown weary of the work and was happy to leave. At home, writing in her 1845 diary paper, Anne thinks back four years to Emily's previous diary paper. "How many things have happened since it was written-some pleasant some far otherwise—Yet I was then at Thorp Green and now I am only just escaped from it. I was wishing to leave it then and if I had known that I had four years longer to stay how wretched I should have been—then too."

Earlier, in her 1841 paper, Anne says "I am now engaged in writing the fourth volume of Solala Vernon's Life," which some scholars believe could be *Agnes Grey*, but the name comes from Emily and Anne's Gondal world. In Emily's diary paper of 1845, she writes that Anne, like herself, is writing on the Gondal subject of the "First Wars" and that Anne is working on "a book by Henry Sophona." After remarking on Emily's occupation with Emperor Julius, Anne states in her 1845 diary: "I have begun the third volume of passages in the life of an Individual," which is also presumed to be *Agnes Grey*, but Anne's fourth volume was on Solala Vernon, a Gondal character, so why would her third volume suddenly be on someone outside the confines of their shared Gondal saga? The other question, of course, is where are the records of all this writing?

Anne's relief at being away from Thorp Green is a milder version of Charlotte's feeling after she left her employ as a governess: "I never was so glad to get out of a house in my life" (196).

Charlotte lacked the temperament to withstand the mental bondage, and remarks that everything is a burden: "I never in my whole life had my time so fully taken up." She comments that the mother "cares nothing in the world about me except to contrive how the greatest possible quantity of labour may be squeezed out of me" (191), and "I have never had five minutes conversation with her since I came except while she was scolding me" (194).

In chapter four, the character Agnes Grey says, "I can conceive few situations more harassing than that wherein, however you may long for success, however you may labour to fulfil your duty, your efforts are baffled and set at nought by those beneath you, and unjustly censured and misjudged by those above." Anne's diary paper reveals a thankful but less strident disposition while Charlotte's letters demonstrate a personality that embraces her complaining nature and admits that she expresses her thoughts forcefully because "it is a relief" (192).

Some minor terms in the letters appear later in the book. Charlotte's "unmanageable cubs" become, for the character of Agnes, "a set of tiger's cubs" and "unmanageable pupils." While among strangers, Charlotte has to look after the children and asks her friend to imagine the miseries of "having the charge given me of a set of pampered spoilt and turbulent children whom I was expected constantly to amuse as well as instruct." Agnes says she attends "with unabated vigour to my work, a more arduous task than anyone can imagine, who has not felt something like the misery of being charged with the care and direction of a set of mischievous, turbulent rebels." Charlotte must amuse and "instruct" a set of turbulent children, as Agnes must care for and direct a set of turbulent rebels, or as Agnes later says, "guide and instruct" her charges.

Charlotte cannot punish the children for fear of "black looks" from the mother. In chapter three, the governess Agnes receives "black looks" from the mother when one of her charges comes late to the table, an impropriety Agnes is not allowed to correct. Charlotte writes, "as for correcting them, I soon quickly found that was entirely out of the question." Agnes says, "as for punishments, I was given to understand, the parents reserved that privilege to themselves; and yet they expected me to keep my pupils in order." Charlotte's employer, however, ignores the children's bad behaviour and uses "unjust, partial excuses to screen the children" (191), while in chapter four, Agnes says she is responsible for their conduct but cannot administer discipline "without the aid of the superior's more potent authority; which, either from indolence, or the fear of becoming unpopular with the said rebellious gang, the latter refuses to give."

Charlotte writes in her letter that, "a governess must often submit to have the heartache . . . but the children are indulged" (256). Agnes echoes this sentiment when the guests at Wellwood Hall "continually flattered and indulged" the children. In order to get a day off, Charlotte "conquered diffidence" (256) and asked for her employer's permission. In chapter six, the character Agnes would do fine if she, like Charlotte, would conquer her diffidence: "I should do vastly well if I would only throw aside my diffidence, and acquire a little more confidence in myself."

In chapter thirteen, Agnes considers how to cope with the challenges of her position. "To submit and oblige was the governess's part. If ever I felt it degrading to submit so quietly, or intolerable to toil so constantly, I would turn towards my home. I sometimes felt myself degraded by the life I led, and ashamed of submitting to so many indignities." The emphasis of these next words from chapter three is added. Agnes says, "I knew the *difficulties* I had *to contend with* were *great*; but I knew (at least I believed) unremitting *patience* and *perseverance* could overcome them," and "I judged it my wisest plan to subdue every resentful impulse, suppress every sensitive shrinking, and go on perseveringly." For Charlotte, she acknowledges the same sentiment with the same words: "I have *great difficulties to contend with* sometimes. *Perseverance* will perhaps conquer them" (256), and "I resolved to be *patient*, to command my feelings and take what came" (194). Agnes will subdue and suppress her impulses while Charlotte will command her feelings. Charlotte is recounting her experiences of a private governess' trials with the same deep feelings she expressed in her letters.

Why would Anne Brontë use the exact words and sentiments as her sister when she has a mind of her own and a separate individual temperament?

Charlotte finds the work dreary because she complains that it leaves her "faculties unexercised" (266). At the beginning of the story Agnes looks forward to being a governess because it will allow her to "go out into the world; to enter upon a new life; to act for myself; to exercise my unused faculties." In chapter four, Agnes later considers how her friends would view her suffering: "the idea of how they would pity me has made me pity myself." Charlotte writes to her friend, "I have no wish to be pitied except by you" (194).

Charlotte also includes the character of Agnes Pryor, the married, ex-governess of Shirley Keeldar in her novel *Shirley*. Mrs. Pryor's maiden name is Grey, so this is the character of Agnes Grey many years later. When she greets Shirley and her friend, she "received the visitors with a mixture of ceremony and diffidence." Like Agnes Grey before her, the now married Agnes Pryor has the same quality of shyness that Charlotte shares with this character. The inclusion of Agnes in *Shirley* is Charlotte's subtle way of informing her readers that she wrote *Agnes Grey*.

In chapter four, Agnes explains why she wrote this history of a Private Governess's trials and crosses. She apologizes to her readers for taking the time to list examples of her turbulent charges and their bad behaviour in the previous few pages. No writer wants to delay the enjoyment of a book for their readers, but her examples prove her case: she really did put up with unexpected difficulties while enduring those gruelling trials. "I have not enumerated half the vexatious propensities of my pupils, or half the troubles resulting from my heavy responsibilities, for fear of trespassing too much upon the reader's patience; as, perhaps, I have already done; but my design in writing the few last pages was not to amuse, but to benefit those whom it might concern; he that has no interest in such matters will doubtless have skipped them over with a cursory glance, and, perhaps, a malediction against the prolixity of the writer; but if a parent has, therefrom, gathered any useful hint, or an unfortunate governess received thereby the slightest benefit, I am well rewarded for my pains."

Brontë actually did make a difference with this novel. Readers of *Agnes Grey* commented on their new awareness of the heavy responsibilities attached to a governess's duties but, as these excerpts show, she had no desire to revisit those twelve months and, as horrible as the experience was for someone of her mind and talent, she still needed to recount her suffering, whether real or imagined, through her writing. These examples provide more insight into her compulsion to tell a truthful story and her determination to follow through with her stated goal, which in this case was to "pour out the long history of a Private Governess's trials and crosses in her first situation." The combination of her talent, intelligence, and impulse to tell stories compelled her to write, but her genius drove her to craft volumes of intricately conceived books that her sisters would never have dreamt of writing. Realistically, would Anne and Charlotte present an almost mirrored reflection of tone and temperament as outlined in the letters and *Agnes Grey*?

Nothing resembling this level of passion can be found in the younger siblings. In fact, Charlotte compares Anne's degree of serenity and power of endurance with that of her friend Ellen's: "you and Anne are a pair, for marvellous philosophical powers of endurance." If Ellen and Anne were ever faced with domestic disturbances, "no spoilt dinners—scorched linen, dirtied carpets—torn sofa-covers 'squealing brats, cross husbands' would ever discompose either of you" (374). Unlike Charlotte, who could complain bitterly over the horrors of recalcitrant children and authoritative mothers, and would object to having "to wipe the children's smutty noses or tie their shoes or fetch their pinafores or set them a chair" (191).

Charlotte wrote to William Smith Williams a few years after her employment to explain the necessary qualification of a good governess. The woman needed to know how to impart knowledge to children, to have "the power of influencing young minds; the natural fondness for, that innate sympathy with children." If she cannot acquire this qualification, then "her deficiency will harass her not so much in school-time as in play-hours; the moments that would be rest and recreation to the governess who understood and could adapt herself to children, will be almost torture to her who has not that power; many a time, when her charge turns unruly on her hands, when the responsibility which she would wish to discharge faithfully and perfectly, becomes unmanageable to her, she will wish herself a housemaid or kitchen girl, rather than a baited, trampled, desolate, distracted governess" (*Letters, Vol.II* 63-4). She admitted to Ellen, "no one but myself can tell how hard a governess's work is to me—for no one but myself is aware how utterly averse my whole mind and nature are to the employment" (*Letters, Vol.I* 246). She recognized that some emotions should be conquered, but she knew her limitations. "I have no natural knack for my vocation—if teaching only—were requisite it would be smooth & easy—but it is living in other people's houses—the estrangement from one's real character, the adoption of a cold frigid—apathetic exterior that is painful" (266).

One of those "over-indulged" charges, Sarah White, the eldest of the three White children later remembered her governess Miss Brontë as being "shy, cold and prim. We especially hated the daily walk after lessons were done. She never said anything to interest children, and did not allow us to run about but held each of us by the hand" (Campbell 19).

Anne managed to bond with the girls at Thorp Green. In 1843, they presented her with a spaniel puppy that she named Flossy and who lived a full life at the parsonage. The girls also kept in touch with Anne after she left Thorp Green in 1845, and in 1848 visited her, as Charlotte recounted in a letter to Ellen: "they seemed overjoyed to see Anne; when I went into the room they were clinging round her like two children—she, meantime, looking perfectly quiet and passive" (*Letters, Vol.II* 152-3). Unlike Charlotte, Anne was blessed with the natural liking for children that qualified her as a warm person who managed to adapt her character to the children. Her temperament differed significantly from Charlotte's and her strong tie with Emily and their Gondal fantasy overshadowed any interest in writing a story about her experiences as a governess.

Charlotte, on the other hand, chose to write about the truth of human vagaries. A brief look at her novel *Shirley*, therefore, may provide further evidence of her method of presenting truth and help solve the mystery of Ellis Bell's lost second novel.

31 *SHIRLEY* AND A FAMOUS POEM

If Charlotte wrote all the novels, she would also have been preparing Ellis Bell's second book for T.C. Newby. Newby had written to 'Ellis' on 15 February 1848 in response to the news that 'he' was preparing a new novel to follow *Wuthering Heights*.

"I am much obliged by your kind note and shall have much pleasure in making arrangements for your next novel. I would not hurry its completion for I think you are quite right not to let it go before the world until well satisfied with it, for much depends on your next work, if it be an improvement on your first you will have established yourself as a first-rate novelist, but if it falls short the critics will be too apt to say that you have expended your talent in your first novel. I shall therefore have pleasure in accepting it upon the understanding that its completion be at your own time" (Gerin *Emily Brontë* 228).

Emily was believed to be working on that novel before her death in December of 1848, but rough chapters or scraps of notes have never been found. Scholars and biographers assume Charlotte burned the remains: "Had Newby ever received the manuscript he would undoubtedly have published it, so the obvious inference is . . . that Charlotte, finding and reading Emily's second novel, decided that its subject . . .was 'an entire mistake' and would not improve 'Ellis Bell's' reputation. In such circumstances, she must have felt justified in destroying the manuscript" (Barker 579). This assessment seems a harsh one in light of Charlotte's having saved Branwell's inferior work, but if she were to interfere to that extent and judge the novel inappropriate, she could simply put it in a drawer and not forward it to Newby. Destruction of another author's work, and her sister's at that, would be an intolerable action for most writers, and especially for Charlotte whose affection and love for Emily was deep and sincere. Another explanation for the lost second novel is that Charlotte was writing Ellis Bell's next book herself, but under the name of Currer Bell.

Emily rarely wrote letters, so Charlotte was probably corresponding with Newby. After all, Charlotte had been in charge of every business aspect of publishing the Bell books beginning with *Poems*. The book of poems "had been her brainchild," so she hunted for publishers and contacted Aylott and Jones about publishing the poems (Barker 524). She stipulated the design, advised where to advertise, and inquired as to publishers who might be interested in works of fiction. She sent *The Professor*, *Agnes Grey*, *Wuthering Heights*, and *Jane Eyre* out to publishers: her handwriting is on the envelope that was circulated to several publishers. She suggested to Smith, Elder that, due to a favourable review of *Poems* in the *Dublin University Magazine*, *The Critic*, and the *Atheneum* they may want to advertise *Jane Eyre* in those publications as well. She was actively overseeing the handling of all the works.

In November 1847, Charlotte, as Currer Bell, asked Mr. Williams for information about Newby on behalf of Ellis and Acton. She complains that their novels should have been out earlier since "the first proof-sheets were already in the press at the commencement of last August, before Currer Bell had placed the M.S. of 'Jane Eyre' in your hands. Mr. N, however, does not do business like Messrs. Smith and Elder; a different spirit seems to preside at 72 Mortimer Street to that which guides the helm at 65 Cornhill. Mr. N shuffles, gives his word and breaks it; Messrs. Smith and Elder's performance is always better than their promise." She then inquires about Newby's business practices: "I should like to know if Mr. N often acts as he has done to my relatives, or whether this is an exceptional instance of his method. Do you know, and can you tell me anything about him?" (*Letters, Vol.I* 561).

When the proof-sheets finally arrive, she again writes to Williams, "Ellis and Acton beg to thank you for the kind offer of your services with Mr. Newby, but as the last of the proof-sheets has at length been sent down for correction, they deem it useless to trouble you on the subject" (564). She voiced her disapproval to Williams when *Wuthering Heights* and *Agnes Grey* finally came out: "The books are not well got up—they abound in errors of the press" (575). She complained that, "The orthography and punctuation of the books are mortifying to a degree; almost all the errors that were corrected in the proof-sheets appear intact in what should have been the fair copies. If Mr. Newby always does business in this way, few authors would like to have him for their publisher a second time" (580). The books contained "the ubiquitous presence of superfluous commas, inadequate hyphenation, and a number of misspellings" (576 n. 6). She obviously read through *Wuthering Heights* and

Agnes Grey to confirm each correction on the proof sheets had been changed and to note any new errors. A cynical response would be that she was an overbearing and controlling sister, but equally valid is that these books were hers, and she wanted to make sure they were published properly.

Charlotte had sold *Jane Eyre* to Smith, Elder as Currer Bell, so that company was now her publisher. If she were to state that, *Wuthering Heights, Agnes Grey*, and *The Tenant of Wildfell Hall* were, in truth, Currer Bell books, she would technically be under contract to Newby who had accepted *Wuthering Heights* and *Agnes Grey* months before Smith, Elder signed Currer Bell for *Jane Eyre*. Smith, Elder proved to be the better publishing house, so Charlotte would prefer to remain with them. Also, she had her reasons for retaining the disguise of three male writers. When Smith, Elder discovered that Newby was making arrangements with an American publisher for *The Tenant of Wildfell Hall* as a Currer Bell book, and had asserted, "the three Bells were all one person," Charlotte, understandably, panicked and needed to provide both publishers with "ocular proof" that the Bells were three separate individuals; thus, she made a sudden trip with Anne to London.

She later wrote to her friend Mary Taylor that, in July, she had received a letter from Smith, Elder "all in alarm, suspicion, and wrath" about Newby sending Currer Bell's sheets to a rival American publisher, "and asking the meaning of such false play." She explains that they had enclosed a copy of Newby's letter to that same publisher "affirming that 'to the best of his belief' *Jane Eyre, Wuthering Heights, Agnes Grey*, and *The Tenant of Wildfell Hall* (the new work) were all the production of one writer" (*Letters, Vol.II* 111-12). Juliet Barker questions Charlotte's interpretation of the tone of Smith, Elder's letter: "Her description hardly tallies with George Smith's later recollection that his letter said 'we should be glad to be in a position to contradict the statement, adding at the same time we were quite sure Mr. Newby's assertion was untrue'" (939 n. 46). Smith's recollections are probably accurate because he and Mr. Williams had always treated Charlotte respectfully, but she had to create the illusion of dire circumstances in order to justify a trip to London the same day Smith, Elder's "missive" arrived at Haworth. For Charlotte, the situation was indeed dire and warranted immediate action. Her letter to Mary continues, "Anne and I packed up a small box, sent it down to Keighley, set out ourselves after tea, walked through a thunderstorm to the station, got to Leeds and whirled up by the Night train to London" (112). Why not accept Smith, Elder's proposal to act on her behalf to straighten out the misunderstanding? That would be the sensible response, and would have saved Anne and Charlotte the inconvenience of a rushed journey. The reason she exaggerated the severe tone of Smith, Elder's missive, and why she had to arrive in London to provide "ocular proof" was that Newby's assertions were true. He had the manuscripts. He could prove his claims that the Bells were one person, so Charlotte could not ask Smith, Elder to intervene on her behalf because they would have realized Newby was right. The tight threads she had woven into her deception were beginning to unravel, and she needed to intercept further communication between the two publishers; therefore, she had to appear in London with Anne to prove there were "at least two" Bells. As stated before, George Smith and William Smith Williams had presumed that Currer Bell was a woman: "I had the advantage over the general public of having the handwriting of the author before me. There were qualities of style, too, and turns of expression, which satisfied me that 'Currer Bell' was a woman, an opinion in which Mr. Williams concurred." Newby would have had the same advantage of "having the handwriting" of the authors before him, so how would Charlotte have explained the reality of three distinctly different writers? Perhaps she told Newby that she was simply Anne and Emily's amanuensis, that their handwriting was poor, so she copied their manuscripts for them. Smith, Elder agreed to preserve their male "incognito," as did Newby. Charlotte stipulated that the male personas remain intact: "to all the rest of the world we must be 'gentlemen' as heretofore" (113). She was aware that Ellis and Acton's arrangement with Newby involved "the publication of their future works," (29), so she was bound to honour that commitment or risk further problems over the authorship of Currer Bell's books.

Her intense involvement in the production of the books is as personal as her analysis of the male characters in *The Tenant of Wildfell Hall*, *Jane Eyre*, and *Wuthering Heights*. As noted above in chapter thirty, she corrects Williams in his assessment that the male protagonists are similar in personality: she tells him "the foundation of each character is entirely different." She knows Huntingdon, Rochester, and Heathcliff so well that she can distinguish profound traits that go to the core of their motives and inclinations, and she relays this analysis with precision and confidence.

At this point in her career, *Jane Eyre* is Currer Bell's only published novel, but it did not represent the bulk of her literary output. Charlotte had been writing for over eighteen years. Her early fiction "provided her with a space within which she could develop her skills as a writer, assume the fictional character of a professional literary man and imitate, parody and experiment with a variety of literary styles," which became her "practical apprenticeship in writing." Her work, up to the age of twenty-four, comprised a group of distinct stories that ranged "in length from 15,000 to 40,000 words," and the last five novelettes of her Angrian series, "written between January 1838 and December 1839" span 400 pages (Glen xiii). She had also written *The Professor*, a novel of approximately 90,000 words. In modern terms, Charlotte Brontë would be classed as a workaholic with a powerful mind and a prolific talent who loved to imagine and shape her creations into works of fiction, and with her volumes of letters and manuscripts, the probability is such that if Ellis was supplying a second book for Newby, Charlotte was writing it.

The novel *Shirley* came out in 1849, after Emily had died, but this could have been the second Ellis Bell book. Charlotte told her biographer Mrs. Gaskell that she based the character of Shirley Keeldar on Emily. If *Shirley* was to be the next Ellis Bell novel, Emily's death before it was completed would have forced Charlotte to release it as a Currer Bell work. Acton Bell had already honoured her agreement with Newby by giving him Acton's second novel, *The Tenant of Wildfell Hall*, so there would be no point in making the next book an Acton Bell book, and with Emily dead, Ellis' obligation to Newby was null and void. The logical recourse was for Charlotte to put the novel with the publisher she preferred and simply adjust the pseudonym to make that happen. As noted above, scholars have always wondered what happened to the remains of the manuscript, but it seems coincidental that not a single page from this phantom manuscript has survived with Emily's handwriting on it, and that a book about Emily is the next book published.

In chapter twenty-two of *Shirley*, Brontë describes the character, modelled after Emily, as being in a slight trance after having experienced a

283

vision: "If Shirley were not an indolent, a reckless, an ignorant being, she would take a pen at such moments; or at least while the recollection of such moments was yet fresh on her spirit: she would seize, she would fix the apparition, tell the vision revealed. Had she a little more of the organ of acquisitiveness in her head—a little more of the love of property in her nature, she would take a good-sized sheet of paper and write plainly out, in her own queer but clear and legible hand, the story that has been narrated, the song that has been sung to her, and thus possess what she was enabled to create. But indolent she is, reckless she is, and most ignorant, for she does not know her dreams are rare, her feelings peculiar: she does not know, has never known, and will die without knowing, the full value of that spring whose bright fresh bubbling in her heart keeps it green."

The character has unique visions but is too lethargic to write them down. The description continues: "Shirley takes life easily: is not that fact written in her eye? In her good-tempered moments, is it not as full of lazy softness as in her brief fits of anger it is fulgent with quick-flashing fire? Her nature is in her eye: so long as she is calm, indolence, indulgence, humour, and tenderness possess that large grey sphere; incense her, a red ray pierces the dew, it quickens instantly to flame." Brontë describes a woman who could have the gift to write, but prefers a less arduous path. Emily had grey eyes and perhaps witnessed mysterious visions but preferred daydreaming to writing an entire novel or constructing and organizing long stanzas of poetry to convey her soulful experience.

When the Bell brothers' self-published book *Poems* came out in 1846, Charlotte sent a copy to the Dublin University Magazine. This reviewer, as well, wondered if the poems came from the same hand: "Whether the triad of versemen be in truth but one master spirit . . . that has been pleased to project itself into three imaginary poets, we are wholly unable to conjecture . . . The tone of all these little poems is certainly uniform" (*Letters, Vol.I* 563 n. 6). Once again, the three Bells ring in the tone of one writer.

Brontë writes in *Shirley* about an incident that has a striking similarity to an Emily poem. The following excerpt is from the poem called "Stars" dated April 1845, which is three months before Emily writes her awkward diary paper. The poem provides another example of the depth of talent in the poet who composed these verses. The speaker laments the dawn arriving too soon and prefers the stars of night to the dazzling sun.

"Why did the morning dawn to break / So great, so pure a spell, / And scorch with fire the tranquil cheek / Where your cool radiance fell? / Blood-red he rose, and arrow-straight / His fierce beams struck my brow: / the soul of Nature sprang elate, / But mine sank sad and low! / My lids closed down—yet through their veil / I saw him blazing still; / And bathe in gold the misty dale / And flash upon the hill. / I turned me to the pillow then / To call back Night, and see / Your worlds of solemn light again / Throb with my heart and me! / It would not do—the pillow glowed, / And glowed both roof and floor, / And birds sang loudly in the wood, / And fresh winds shook the door. / The curtains waved, the wakened flies / Were murmuring round my room / Imprisoned there, till I should rise / And give them leave to roam. / O stars and dreams and Gentle Night / O Night and stars, return! / And hide me from the hostile light / That does not warm, but burn / That drains the blood of suffering men / Drinks tears, instead of dew / Let me sleep through his blinding reign / And only wake with you!"

The speaker in the poem prefers the starlight and laments the morning sun breaking the spell of night. The blood-red sun rises, the birds sing, the wind shakes the door, and day steals the stars and, with them, her dreams.

The following words near the end of chapter thirteen share a distinct tone to "Stars" and even borrow specific diction from the poem. Alone in her bedroom, the character Caroline can't sleep. "She followed the steps of the night, on its pathway of stars." She imagines she sees Moore, the man she loves, in the moonlight. "She was with Moore, in spirit, the whole time." Her heart remains heavy because she believes he loves another woman, but she longs for the night to stay, so she can continue her vision. "As dawn approached, the setting stars and breaking day dimmed the creation of fancy; the wakened song of birds hushed her whispers. The tale full of fire, quick with interest, borne away by the morning wind, became a vague murmur. The shape that, seen in a moonbeam, lived, had a pulse, had movement, wore health's glow and youth's freshness, turned cold and ghostly gray, confronted with the red of sunrise." The images of the red sun, the birds singing, and the wind blowing away her fantasy all echo the sentiment in the "Stars." Morning steals the moon and the stars, but retains

285

the same tone and mood, which indicates that one mind wrote both pieces and not that two sisters simply shared ideas, wrote with an identical voice and pathos, and captured the exact essence of the conceit.

Did Emily transcribe Charlotte's poetry or did she write her own? As mentioned before, after her sisters had recently died, Charlotte wrote a few words in the margin of Emily's most famous poem "No Coward Soul is Mine" completed on January 2, 1846. Charlotte wrote, "The following are the last lines my sister Emily ever wrote," but a later poem "Often rebuked, yet always back returning," dated several months later on September 14, 1846 is also ascribed to Emily.

Brontë is particularly careful about her diction and uses specific words in this message. Dobell would call this an example of her *equivoque* or double entendre. She never says that this is the last poem her sister wrote, but only that "the following are the last lines." The distinction may seem trivial, but if Emily wrote out lines for Charlotte and never composed the poetry then the message is true: she wrote lines, not poems.

Emily wrote down a number of poems attributed to her in a surviving notebook that has a clue about her ability. She titles the page "Gendal Poem," misspelling Gondal and then later adds an "s" over an existing flourish of pen strokes to make "poem" plural, as if this had been an oversight when she first wrote down the title, but if she was organizing these poems in a notebook, she would have known that more than one poem would be written down. The misspelling of Gondal and the omission of the plural are examples of careless mistakes. At the top of the notebook, she prints, "Emily Jane Brontë Transcribed Febuary 1844." She misspells February. The word "transcribed" suggests she is merely copying out poems for someone else. If these were her compositions, why does she need the word transcribed? If scholars have been told that Emily is a genius, their eyes wander past these kinds of errors and make excuses for the awkward writing of the diary papers. No one can fault her, however, for making the occasional spelling mistake. After all, not everyone is a perfect speller. In fact, Charlotte makes a few spelling errors as well, but she knows how to spell the months of the year and, at the age of twenty-six, so should Emily. Emily was certainly more educated than most young girls at that time, but her scholarly aptitude and writing abilities cannot compare with her older sister's.

When Charlotte wrote out that small message in the margin of the poem, she was saying much more than she recorded on the surface. As she had done all her life, she was leaving an anagram under the words. The sentence, "The following are the last lines my sister Emily ever wrote" when turned and reorganized states, *I write verses, heath story, letters, all mine. New gloomy life.* Charlotte leaves a message declaring she wrote everything and, with her sisters gone, her life had turned dreary. A further example of her ability with the anagrams can be found in the poem itself. The following is the entire poem "No Coward Soul is Mine" with the natural breaks noted in each line. The matching anagrams below explain why Charlotte wanted the reader to take a closer look at these lines.

"No coward soul is mine, / No trembler in the world's storm-troubled sphere! / I see Heaven's glories shine, / And Faith shines equal, arming me from Fear / O God within my breast, / Almighty ever-present Deity! / Life, that in me hast rest, / As I, Undying Life, have power in thee! / Vain are the thousand creeds / That move men's hearts, unutterably vain; / Worthless as withered weeds, / Or idlest froth amid the boundless main, / To waken doubt in one / Holding so fast by thy infinity, / So surely anchored on / The steadfast rock of Immortality. / With wide-embracing love / Thy spirit animates eternal years, / Pervades and **broods** above, / Changes, sustains, dissolves, creates, and rears. / Though earth and moon were gone, / And suns and universes ceased to be, / And thou wert left alone, / Every Existence would exist in thee. / There is no room for Death, / Nor atom that his might could render void; / Since thou art Being and Breath / And what thou art may never be destroyed."

So now ridicule Mason / brothers with brood plot. Relentless men murder. / Even hoarse hiss in elegies. / If quash den, heal stain. Manage firm reform. / Shy maid, not big, wrote, / gave temper eternity. Sly, hid / a thief's rent sham. Title / is Wuthering Heaven. If die, lay open. / Dead Catherine roves, haunts / vast home, then master in nature by vault / where old wasted wishes rest / mute. Man sheds his blood for entail dirt. / Unite book at end. Now, / if tiny, bloody fights in shanty. / Londoner chorus easy. / Charlotte's mask fit fat moor deity. / Give wild Catherine womb. / Hints at penetralia mystery arise / over bed. Passed on bravado. / Classic servant Dean argues, assists hero's end. / Mortgage on heath.

Honoured new / descendant as business endeavour / then flouted ornate law. / Next lie: When executors visited, eye / horrors of hot tea. Men die / at threshold. Mourn victim. Noah dog-tired. / Behind barn teach signature to / that redhead boy. Wanted very true mason."

Charlotte uses her name in the third person like an omniscient narrator, and she shifts between the fiction and her reality. The male *"mask"* she wears in her writing covers her feminine voice and fits the chief Mason thief's tone. This is the prigs' boss, the man who *hurts* the *economy,* who thinks he is the *"deity"* of the Township and beyond reproach. She uses the mask of a male narrator to mimic the *"fat moor deity"* when she wrote "Wuthering Heaven," which is an interesting piece of information. The initials "W.H." stay the same, and "Heaven" fits perfectly with the story: Lockwood calls Wuthering Heights "a perfect misanthropist's Heaven," and the moors are Catherine's heaven. In a famous section from the novel, Catherine tells the housekeeper, "If I were in heaven, Nelly, I should be extremely miserable." In order to clarify why she would be miserable, she tells Nelly that she once dreamed she was in paradise: "heaven did not seem to be my home; and I broke my heart with weeping to come back to earth; and the angels were so angry that they flung me out into the middle of the heath on the top of Wuthering Heights; where I woke sobbing for joy." This may also explain why in the novel, now called *Wuthering Heights,* Catherine, after her death, haunts the moors: she wants to remain close to her version of heaven. The reason for the change in the title is both an intriguing and fitting one that will be explained later but, even with the original title, the date of the poem is January 1846, so the book has already been written by that date.

The book could have been written the year before during 1845. The only writing from that time that belongs to Emily is her birthday or diary paper from July 30th, in which she continues to be attached to the Gondal characters.

"Anne and I went our first long Journey by ourselves together— leaving Home on the 30th of June—monday sleeping at York—returning to Keighley Tuesday evening sleeping there and walking home on Wednesday morning—though the weather was broken, we enjoyed ourselves very much except during a few hours at Bradford and during our excursion we were Ronald Macelgin, Henry Angora, Juliet Augusteena, Rosobelle Esualdar, Ella and Julian Egramon Catherine Navarre and Cordelia Fitzaphnold escaping from the palaces of Instruction to join the Royalists who are hard driven at present by the victorious Republicans— The Gondals still florish bright as ever I am at present writing a work on the First Wars." This work could not possibly be *Wuthering Heaven* or *Wuthering Heights*. Emily is too involved in her Gondal Royalists and Republicans. From the Gondal references once would infer that the "First Wars" would not resemble the plot of the novel. As well, the calibre of her writing provides the best assurance that the "First Wars" did not become *Wuthering Heights*.

In Brontë's anagrams of the poem, she believes that if the Masonic den is destroyed, the fraud would end and proper rent reform could be initiated to prevent future corruption. At the end of her "Wuthering Heaven" the thief, Heathcliff, is buried next to the "*vault*" that contains Catherine's remains, an image that occurs in *Wuthering Heights* and recurs in *Villette* when, with the vacation and her ordeal over, Lucy feels the oppressive weight of the "house roof" as "crushing as the slab of a tomb."

In "Wuthering Heaven," she mocks the "*Mason brothers with a brood plot.*" A "brood" can be the young of animals, or a group of related children, who in this case could be young Cathy and Hareton, who as the rightful heirs to the Earnshaw and Linton properties form the cornerstone of the family plot. Brontë could also be using "brood" as a verb, which would suit Heathcliff's state of mind as he dwells continuously and moodily on the subject of Catherine.

She returns to reality when she writes about the "*rent sham*". *Relentless men murder. Even hoarse hiss in elegies. If quash den, heal stain. Manage firm reform. Shy maid, not big, wrote, gave temper eternity. Sly, hid a thief's rent sham. Title is Wuthering Heaven. If die, lay open.* Men shed their blood over land, and the men who murder attend the funerals and lament their passing with a hiss, a word that echoes the sound of a snake. If this were true, that men murdered and then feigned grief at their deaths, Brontë would be enraged at the hypocrisy. She believes the corruption, the "*stain*" would be removed if the Masonic "*den*" was quashed, and proper reforms regarding rents and entails were implemented. Again, she mentions her size—"*not big*"—and that, as a shy woman, she has no recourse to redress these crimes, so she writes and gives her *"temper eternity"* through her book where she slyly *"hid a thief's rent sham."* She writes, *"If die, lay open,"* but she knows, at some point, she will inevitably die, so why write "if"? This message to her invisible reader is, if she dies prematurely by a violent act, *"lay open"* the book and search the novel for clues.

The anagrams present an interesting peek at how she devised aspects of the book. Lockwood arrives from London to act in the capacity of a Greek chorus. Lockwood offers information to help the audience or reader understand the events just like the chorus in an ancient Greek drama. At Wuthering Heights, we learn that *if tiny, bloody fights in shanty* are commonplace, and occur when Hindley beats Heathcliff, and later when Heathcliff torments Hareton and young Cathy. Fighting and violence for children and adults become a way of life in this "shanty," a word for a roughly built dwelling.

Brontë then has Catherine give birth to a girl: *"Give wild Catherine womb,"* which will set up the matrimony between her child and Heathcliff's son.

The *"hints at penetralia mystery arise over bed,"* as Catherine's ghost haunts Lockwood's dream and conveys the truth of eternity to him during the third degree ritual. Lockwood is raised or "passed," but Brontë uses a pun again when she says Lockwood *"Passed on bravado"*: the newly passed or risen Mason lacks courage throughout the ceremony, so he spends the night without any display of strength or *bravado*. Before crossing the threshold of Heathcliff's house, Lockwood pauses to inspect "the penetralium." Brontë's hints regarding a *"penetralia mystery"* refer to all the symbols and clues about the Freemasons and their ancient rituals, especially the third degree ritual that takes place in a metaphorical coffin. Nelly Dean relays the history of the families to Lockwood, and acts as a traditional, clever servant found in seventeenth century comedies. She gossips with Lockwood, argues with Heathcliff—her master—and helps him through his self-inflicted death of starvation: *"Classic servant—Dean argues, assists hero's end"*.

Brontë connects her reality with the story's plot in the next anagram. *"Mortgage on heath. Honoured new descendant as business endeavour then flouted ornate law."* The land deals are Brontë's main subject, and she records how Heathcliff's son, a *"new descendant"* becomes a *"business endeavour"* when he is told to marry Cathy Linton in order to acquire Thrushcross Grange. This marriage seals the deal for Heathcliff who uses the convoluted and elaborate (*"ornate"*) intricacies of estate and conveyancing laws to exact his revenge.

Brontë states that in order to acquire the rents, the Masons need the wealthy landowners to die. After setting up the connection to property through matrimony, they visit the owner. They become executors on the man's will, and then they lie to their "brother" when they visit and offer him a cup of tea. She uses the word "eye" to mean "look at" or "see." *"Next lie. When executors visited, eye horrors of hot tea. Men die at threshold. Mourn victim."* They murder the man and then mourn the loss in their false *"elegies."* After their labours—*"Noah dog-tired".* The reference to executors arriving at a testator's door gives a chilling description of how she assumes they poison the unsuspecting brother Mason with a little hot tea.

The final line is equally shocking. *"Behind barn teach signature to that redhead boy. Wanted very true mason."* The most famous red-haired boy she would be alluding to would be her brother Branwell, the loyal Mason who had an ambidextrous skill that included, perhaps, forging a rich Mason's signature.

The anagrams in this poem consistently return to the same story of corruption and fraud, and emphasize her desire to tell her readers that she hid the whole sordid business in her novel. Her metaphor of the cretin in *Villette* and one of her anagrams in that novel—*In forty-three had mild fever, but wrote pious oaf's mud myth. Hurry*—suggest that she quickly composed 'Wuthering Heaven' during the five-week vacation period in 1843 at Brussels. The vacation began in mid-August, a few months after March 20th, the date the Spring Assizes at York was to hear the case of the Beaver forgery. The case was dismissed from a lack of evidence and due to the death of John Beaver, the main complainant. As discussed in chapter twenty-seven above, Charlotte would have known about this case from Emily because their father was a witness. The union of the Thomas family with the Beaver family through marriage is similar to the union of properties through matrimony in *Wuthering Heights*, and the business of a will forgery would have stirred her imagination, especially if she believed

291

this sort of crime occurred in her township. Brontë's personal response to the forgery case is unknown, but she appears to have used elements of it to tell her story. As stated above, in chapter sixteen, the goddess Isis, the Mother of the ancient mysteries from which Freemasonry grew, is celebrated on March 20th. Catherine's death, like John Beaver's, shares that date with Isis, so March 20th could be a significant sign that more mysteries are hidden inside her plot.

One mystery that Edward Benson, in his book *Charlotte Brontë*, found odd was Charlotte's choice to remain in Brussels for that five-week vacation. He writes, "She was miserably home-sick, the prospect of being so much alone for all those weeks appalled her, and it is impossible to find any reason, now that Miss Branwell's legacy had put her in funds, why she should not have gone back to Haworth for the holidays" (116-17). Perhaps she wanted the peace and quiet, away from the parsonage where the men frequently dropped by, in order to take hold of that deformed cretin and shape it into 'Wuthering Heaven,' and to compose, without interruption or fear, anagrams that would reveal the truth about what she had witnessed back home.

Unlike Branwell, she put her time to good use. She probably could have forged signatures, if her mind had been bent toward crime but, instead, she used her gifts to write and create anagrams, and she found clever ways to show the reader where to look.

32 THE GHOST IN LOCKWOOD

One example where Brontë seems to be pointing to a clue occurs in chapter twenty in *Jane Eyre*. Jane and Rochester are conversing after the episode on the third floor with the wounded Mason, and Rochester describes Thornfield Hall in strange terms. He asks Jane if she can feel that "the house is a mere dungeon." She disagrees: "It seems to me a splendid mansion, sir." Rochester explains that "the glamour of inexperience is over your eyes . . . and you see it through a charmed medium: you cannot discern that the gilding is slime and the silk draperies cobwebs; that the marble is sordid slate, and the polished woods mere refuse chips and scaly bark. Now *here* (he pointed to the leafy enclosure we had entered) all is real, sweet, and pure."

The emphasis on the word "here," as well as his act of pointing, suggests that Brontë may have placed an anagram inside that last sentence. Rochester sees an ugly, dingy prison behind the stately mansion: a sordid, slimy place full of cobwebs and refuse. Jane is unable to perceive the house properly because she sees it through "a charmed medium." Perhaps the inexperienced eye of the reader is unable to see the clues in *Jane Eyre*. Perhaps the mansion or Lodge conceals the secrets of a dingy den where rituals, like the one in which Jane participates with Mason, occur on the third story. In fact, the next clue reveals that the model for Thornfield Hall was a familiar dwelling in the Township that once housed Masons.

The line in the parentheses names the original stately mansion. The break occurs after "enclosure," so the anagram needs a small adjustment: "he pointed to the leafy enclosure / we had entered" turns into *Copy Heaton house left tree-lined / wreathed Eden*. With the adjustment, the anagram reads *Copy Heaton house. Left wreathed, tree-lined Eden*. The Heaton house she refers to could be Well Head, but more likely, from the description of it in chapter eleven as a "mansion" and "a gentleman's manor house," Brontë is copying Ponden Hall, sometimes called Ponden House, the Heaton residence in Stanbury. The large dwelling had been built in 1513, and the Brontë children were known to visit the manor's library. Ponden Hall is believed to be the model for Thrushcross Grange, the Linton home in *Wuthering Heights*. The elder Robert and his wife

Alice had three sons, Robert, William, and John who were contemporaries of the Brontë children. Robert Sr. was also a respected trustee of the Haworth Church Lands, and a Freemason, as were his sons. The Heatons were "the largest farmers and landowners in Stanbury" and were considered gentry by the locals. According to Edward Chitham, after *Wuthering Heights* was published 'a coolness grew up between the Heaton family and the Brontës" (qtd. in Greenwood). This would be understandable if they recognized themselves inside the pages of that novel.

The anagram also states that Brontë retained a part of Ponden Hall's garden for her fictional mansion. The *wreathed, tree-lined Eden* must have been an actual tree-lined archway borrowed from the original model because as Jane and Rochester continue their walk, Jane describes how the sun "illumined the wreathed and dewy orchard trees and shone down the quiet walks under them." The couple regard the mansion; Rochester points to a "leafy enclosure;" Brontë draws the reader's attention to the words where she has hidden an anagram; and the anagram corresponds with the action on the page by explaining the model for the mansion and the tree-lined Eden where Rochester and Jane converse. The anagram, therefore, seems accurate.

The portion of the line outside the parentheses reads, "Now here all is real, sweet, and pure." Through the anagram of this line, Brontë confides what Jane is feeling during this romantic interlude in the garden with Rochester: *Well-read heroine wants pleasure.* Rather than literally referring to the garden, Rochester seems to be telling Jane that their attraction to each other is nothing to fear, that their desire is "real, sweet, and pure" no matter his past, or the circumstances that could destroy their union. The anagrams, both in the parenthesis and the surrounding words, explain the model for the house and garden of Thornfield, and Jane's state of mind. These appear to be clues Brontë intentionally dropped into the narrative for the reader's benefit.

A further hunt for clues uncovers the word "key" to suggest the words in the sentence could unlock a secret message. After the wounded Mason has left Thornfield, and Rochester and Jane have walked together in the garden, Brontë begins the next chapter with these words: "Presentiments are strange things! and so are sympathies; and so are signs; and the three combined make one mystery to which humanity has not yet found the key." If the first clause, "presentiments are strange things" is combined with the two phrases, "and so are sympathies; and so are signs," the anagram reads, *Angry pen passes as rod. Test anagrams, hints, enigmas in three den stories.* She uses the power of her pen, instead of a rod, to create anagrams, not forge signatures and, after all these years, her skill has passed the test because no one ever noticed them in her writing. Again, she notes that she wrote three books that share a similarity with regards to the Masonic theme; these will be shown to be: *Wuthering Heights, The Professor,* and *Jane Eyre.*

Another mention of the word "key," occurs not in *Jane Eyre,* but in her last novel *Villette.* This example comes in chapter thirty-six when the central character Lucy Snowe realizes that her teacher Paul Emanuel has learned about her through Pére Silas, a mutual friend and the priest who heard her confession. Prior to this moment, she had no idea they were friends and had wondered how Paul knew as much as he did about her. "A mortal bewilderment cleared suddenly from my head and vision; the solution of the Sphynx-riddle was won; the conjunction of those two names, Pére Silas and Paul Emanuel gave the key to all." In this case, she suggests combining the words to solve a riddle, so a reworking of the words "Pére Silas and Paul Emanuel gave the key to all" becomes the anagram, *Alone. Keep up anagrams. Used heavily. Tell tale.*

Brontë supplies a means to solve the anagrams, to subtly draw the reader's eye to their existence, but she needs to be cautious. She wants certain words to kindle interest, so her instruction in *Villette* to combine the words to find the key and, thus, solve a riddle is a significant clue. The tale would be the one she has told secretly in anagrams in the poems of *The Professor* and in the opening paragraphs of chapter five; in the symbols and rituals in *Jane Eyre,* in the red-room and with Mason; in Heathcliff's legal machinations and in Lockwood's passing through the three degree ceremonies in *Wuthering Heights.* If she views these books on a continuum, perhaps she has also placed more than the "*dead Earnshaw*" anagram in *Wuthering Heights.*

One small phrase in the "Biographical Notice" leads us to the next clue and a startling revelation. Brontë is addressing the claim that one Bell brother wrote all the books, and that the identity of the author of

Wuthering Heights was "misrepresented; it was said that this was an earlier and ruder attempt of the same pen which had produced *Jane Eyre*. Unjust and grievous error!" The lady seems to protest too much about her involvement in the Heights story, so after a closer look at the fragment "Unjust and grievous error," an anagram takes shape and reads, *Jot urn version. Guard ruse*. The urn version must, accordingly, occur in *Wuthering Heights*, and perhaps refers to a tin urn that keeps the wills in the same way that, in the anagram story in *The Professor*, when Heathcliff wins a bet, he obtains all the mason wills that are stored in an urn. In *Wuthering Heights* the urn could be the tin canister where Cathy keeps the tea. Brontë guards this ruse, or clever stratagem, not only by writing indignant disclaimers that have managed to shift attention away from the truth but also by hiding anagrams inside the narrative. We should be familiar enough with her surface prevarication to hunt in *Wuthering Heights* for a cleverly guarded urn version jotted down behind the surface prose.

The paragraph in the first chapter of the novel that contains the "*dead Earnshaw*" anagram seems a logical place to look for more hidden information. In the anagrams hidden in *The Professor* poems and outlined above in chapter twenty-four, Brontë inserts a line that reads *Silent Cathy healed aged home*. In this next anagram, her meaning will become clear. Roughly three pages into the first chapter, Lockwood breaks from his narration about entering Wuthering Heights to reflect on his insensitivity, which can best be explained by an incident at the seashore: "While enjoying a month of fine weather at the sea-coast, I was thrown into the company of a most fascinating creature, a real goddess, in my eyes, as long as she took no notice of me. I 'never told my love' vocally; still, if looks have language, the merest idiot might have guessed I was over head and ears: she understood me, at last, and looked a return—the sweetest of all imaginable looks—and what did I do? I confess it with shame—shrunk icily into myself, like a snail, at every glance retired colder and farther; till; finally, the poor innocent was led to doubt her own senses, and, overwhelmed with confusion at her supposed mistake, persuaded her mamma to decamp."

A few words appear in the anagrams that require explanation. Brontë uses the words "gouge" and "foist;" the former means a swindle, and the latter means to put something into a hand surreptitiously. She uses "wolf" as her slang for a Mason, and she continues to call the men "Noah," after the patriarch in the Bible's flood story.

A specific plot gradually emerges from the code. In the anagram narrative, Lockwood is a Noah cover for a dead Earnshaw, a mother ghost who wants to conceal herself inside the male tenant in order to gain entry into a Masonic Lodge. The mother has died, perhaps by murder—her tie was tied—and has returned to her home, which is now the Lodge, to intervene in a land swindle, remove the rent levies and set things right for the heath. The Masons keep their documents, perhaps the mortgage or lease, in a tin urn that used to be a tea canister, and the ghost wants to get hold of these sheets. Her journey begins at the Lodge, where she pretends to take the three degrees. After the initiation, she asks for a loan to trap the thief. He takes the bait and she grabs the tin urn. Job well done. The punctuation in the anagrams adds clarity.

While enjoying a month / of fine weather at the seacoast
Join game. Then win. Heath fate set. If wear noose, act holy

I was thrown into the company / of a most fascinating creature
To wit: Copy mason Noah with oaf's grimace. Rent facts in tea urn.

A real goddess in my eyes / as long as she took no notice of me
Mason Odyssey: choose fool; take animal's degree; sign note.

I never told my love vocally
Move locally. Void rent levy

Still if looks have language
Legal goal is save folk in hut

The merest idiot / might have guessed I was over head and ears
Mother's tie tied. This gouge revived a dead Earnshaw's shame.

She understood me, / at last, / and looked a return
Rude lout rooked Hareton. End madness at last

The sweetest of all imaginable looks
See illegal sheets. Wolf man took bait

And what did I do? / I confess it with shame
Hid. Want aid. Odd wish. Scheme: foist a tin.

Shrunk icily into myself like a snail
Sulk only if arsenic in my tea. He kills.

At every glance retired colder and farther
Clever, cried need; try hard, get loan. After,

Till finally the poor innocent / was led to doubt her own senses
free ill Cathy Linton. In on plot. Unbolts door. Sweet, needs wash.

And overwhelmed with confusion / at her supposed mistake
Take Haworth wolves' medicine fund. Mud is on those papers.

Persuaded her mamma to decamp
Madam's tea due. Romp parched me.

A dead mother returns to legally save the folk in the hut. At last, she can end the *"madness"* and redeem the land to its rightful heir Hareton, and free her daughter at the same time. A Mason thief has swindled them: *"Rude lout rooked Hareton"*.

In *Wuthering Heights*, Hareton loses the land to Heathcliff. If the ghost is Catherine Earnshaw Linton, mother of Cathy Linton Heathcliff, then Brontë connects the two stories through these characters. The mother ghost hides inside Lockwood, the tenant, who acts as her cover while taking the three degrees; consequently, in order to fool the masons, she must *"act holy."* Brontë explains how to do it when she says *"to wit"* which means "that is to say": if you want to act holy copy the *"oaf's grimace"*.

Her jeering tone suits the parody of the first three chapters when Lockwood enters the farmhouse to take his three degrees. The ghost, as the

Noah, asks for a loan and *"signs note"*, but is careful not to drink the tea because it could contain *"arsenic"*.

The proof of the swindle is hidden in the tea urn. She must get hold of the sheets to return the land to its rightful owner. The catalyst for Catherine's return from the dead is her *"shame"* over the *"gouge"* or swindle of her family's land.

Most of the lines of the anagrams move easily from one line to the next without disruption in the flow of the plot. The Mason wolf, the *"rude lout"* rooked her land, and she wants to retrieve from the tin urn the illegal sheets that prove the swindle, but in order to gain the Mason's trust, she must pretend that she needs a loan like her brother Hindley had done when he borrowed money from Heathcliff to cover his gambling debts.

Her daughter Cathy Linton knows about the plan and unlocks the door. Perhaps, in Brontë's imagination, the young Cathy is a moor mystic who can commune with her dead mother. If the mother orchestrates a deal through manipulating Lockwood then she can get the tin urn and foist it. Steal the urn, find the illegal document, and prove the fraud. After she steals the tin urn, she will be able to free her ill daughter who is starved and beaten and treated like a slave at Wuthering Heights.

She sees the sheets and takes the money that pays for the arsenic or "medicine" that helps elderly testators die faster: *Take Haworth wolves' medicine fund. Mud is on those papers.* The mud could be literal or metaphorical, but it implies the sheets deal with the land, more particularly, the land that was stolen from Catherine's nephew Hareton.

In the anagram plot, Brontë writes about a Mason stealing family land with legal documentation. On the surface story, Heathcliff enacts his revenge by doing the same to the Earnshaws and Lintons, but the descendants Hareton and Cathy regain their land.

Perhaps the spirit of Catherine is the force behind the successful return of the two properties to the rightful heirs. Her return in Lockwood's dream begins the process of Heathcliff's decline, so Brontë may have consciously interwoven both plots, which could explain the depth and mysterious effect of the novel.

Another interesting anagram hidden in "No Coward Soul is Mine" states that Brontë unites her two stories at the end of *Wuthering Heights*: *"Unite book at end"*. She is referring to the surface prose story and this hidden anagram tale that depicts Catherine returning to her home as a ghost to rescue her daughter and reinstate the rightful heirs to her family's property.

The final image in the last paragraph of the novel is of the tomb when Lockwood visits the "vault" or gravesite where Heathcliff, Catherine, and her husband Edgar Linton are buried.

The last lines of the novel read as follows:

"I lingered round them, / under that benign sky; / watched the moths fluttering among the heath, / and harebells; / listened to the soft wind / breathing through the grass; and wondered how anyone / could ever imagine / unquiet slumbers / for the sleepers / in that quiet earth."

The paragraph is one complete sentence and because the last line, after the final semi-colon, has no commas, the anagrams can be shifted between the five sections.

The breakdown appears below the completed anagram. Brontë wraps up the events in the anagram tale, once called *Wuthering Heaven*, in a similar manner to her ending the prose story of *Wuthering Heights*. Instead of Lockwood as narrator, she writes in the voice of Catherine the ghost as she summarizes the events.

Lurid den hermit gone. / End threat by kin's gun. / Wanted heights home left through attachment. / Barns held ale. / Thought old twit needs rags, thrashing, not thief's beer. / Rod guide Noah yawned. Sublime urn quest done. New romance. Lost veil. Quit sphere. Inter at heath. Free.

The ghost is pleased that the gruesome Mason has been expelled from the property, evidently with the threat of being shot or is actually killed. The paragraphs before this could contain more anagrams that describe the missing action.

From this final paragraph we learn that the land remains in the family through marriage, the *attachment* created by the *new romance*. The *old twit* would be Joseph, the ancient servant, and Lockwood would be her *rod guide* who she always calls *Noah*: the masons use rods in their ceremonies, so that term would suit him.

The ghost's quest is over; the legal wrong has been righted, so she is able to drop the veil that concealed her in the physical sphere and return to her beloved heath heaven, where she can now roam free.

The date at the beginning of *Wuthering Heights* could offer another clue to the hidden story. The year, when the story opens is 1801, a date that echoes the 1801 above the lintel at Ponden Hall to commemorate the year it was rebuilt. Brontë could be using this date as a direct connection to the Heatons, but if she is working with two stories, one seen and one unseen, the 1801 could also be a message to Catherine's ghost.

The year 1801 coincides with The Act of Union 1801 which consolidated the two kingdoms of Great Britain and Ireland into one. The novel, therefore, begins with the announcement that the purpose of Catherine's mission is to unite both houses of Wuthering Heights and Thrushcross Grange, a union she successfully completes.

The following few breaks in the Lockwood paragraph show the anagrams before the words are shuffled:

"listened to the soft wind" / *Old twit needs not thief's* / "breathing through the grass" / *thought rags, thrashing beer.* / "and wondered how anyone" / *Rod Noah yawned done new* / "could ever imagine" / *guide veil romance* / "unquiet slumbers" / *sublime urn quest* / "for the sleepers" / *lost sphere free* / "in that quiet earth" / *quit inter at heath.*

Brontë can obviously see the completed sentence within the joined phrases and makes the mental adjustment or rearrangement at the same time. The words must fall into place with little effort for her to devise not only the right word placement but also a fitting ending and an appropriate sentiment for Catherine's ghost. The idea of freedom suits both stories, so 'free' is a perfect word on which to end her anagram tale.

As stated earlier, Lockwood could be the Masonic Lost Word for Heathcliff when he tells him that Catherine's spirit is close; her appearance at the window is the ultimate Truth that Heathcliff needs to hear, the Truth that will finally give him peace.

Lockwood also holds the Truth for us hidden inside his words, but buried almost too deep for readers to see. When the land fraud surfaces from the anagram plot, he becomes our Lost Word and conveys an important Truth.

33 BRONTË'S TRINITY

When Lockwood stands outside Wuthering Heights in the first chapter, he looks above the door and says, "I detected the date '1500' and the name 'Hareton Earnshaw'. I would have made a few comments, and requested a short history of the place from the surly owner, but his attitude at the door appeared to demand a speedy entrance." Lockwood takes his first step inside the sitting room, noting, "they call it here 'the house' pre-eminently." The words "fifteen hundred," "Hareton Earnshaw," and "the house," are in inverted commas, so they stand out and, therefore, may be important clues.

Hints from Shakespeare
The words that suggest a direction into the code are "comments" and "history." Lockwood would have made a few comments. If we read the word "comments" as the French word *comment* we translate the word as "how," and ask how should we read 1500? The French connection is important. The next hint is the word "history." Lockwood would have liked a short history.

The history plays of Shakespeare document a historical representation of a famous land dispute, and contain an interesting quotation from *Henry V*. In Act II of the play, the Chorus says, "O England!—model to thy inward greatness, / Like little body with a mighty heart." This image of a small body containing a mighty heart could stand as a theme throughout for Brontë, a little woman with a passionate heart trying to expose the corruption she sees in her Yorkshire home.

In *Henry V*, England begins a war with France over disputed lands and titles. The play opens with the Archbishop being concerned over the status of his own land, and says that men "devout by testament" bequeathed their property through wills to the church. He wants to ensure that his wealth remains unchallenged. The theme of a Masonic battle over land echoes the dispute held on a grander scale in the play and would have appealed to Brontë's imagination and love of Shakespeare.

The conquest of land leads to England's war with France. It ends with Henry's famous victory at Agincourt, which changes the face of Europe.

Before the battle, a young French messenger arrives at the French camp to announce that their enemies are near: "the English lie within fifteen hundred paces of your tents," warns the messenger. In Brontë's anagrams, Hareton Earnshaw is an anagram for *Enter war as Noah*, and the hidden story has Catherine, the ghost about to enter the Mason den; therefore, the message of "1500" from the perspective of the ghost is actually code for "the enemy is close."

Coded Words

In the hidden story, the spirit Catherine can read the secret code on the door. She would see "1500" and the words, "Hareton Earnshaw" as passwords, telling her something that her enemies cannot decipher. In Freemasonry, the symbol of the hare is borrowed from Egyptian hieroglyphics and means "eyes that are open," and was adopted because that timid animal was always on the watch for his enemies, so he could see approaching danger. Masons pronounce their passwords by clipping syllables into separate parts: for instance, the password Mahhabone becomes Mah-Ha-Bone.

Hareton's name can be separated in the same way to form the syllables Hare-ton-Earn-shaw. The first name pronounced phonetically reads as Hare-a-tin, and his last name, if broken after the "s," as Earns-Haw. The code becomes clearer after knowing that "Haw" is the name of a particular tea that comes from a shrub grown in the hedgerows around England. Brontë mentions it in chapter twelve of *Jane Eyre*: "I was a mile from Thornfield, in a lane noted for wild roses in summer, for nuts and blackberries in autumn, and even now possessing a few coral treasures in hips and haws."

If "hare" means eyes that are open, then the password hidden behind Hare-a-tin-earns-haw would read, "Eye a tin urn's haw," or "Eye a tin urn's tea." This is Catherine's mission: she must keep her eye on the tin tea urn, especially if it contains the legal sheets that would expose the fraud. The tin urn in the anagram story could be one of the "three gaudily painted canisters" that Lockwood sees in the parlour.

The final word "house" has relevance for Masons. In Freemasonry, the pre-eminent or prominent house is their Lodge. The charge or instruction given to an Entered Apprentice after his initiation states the following: "Freemasonry is an institution having for its foundation the practice of the social and moral virtues, and to so high an eminence has its credit been advanced that, in every age and country, men pre-eminent for their moral and intellectual attainments have encouraged and promoted its interests." Some masons are called "the Most Pre-eminently Distinguished Brother," and Masons describe Freemasonry as being "pre-eminently a social Institution." Lockwood enters the sitting room and says "they call it here 'the house' pre-eminently." He has taken his first "step" into "the house" or Lodge. Brontë adds "pre-eminently" to provide the clue that Masons live at Wuthering Heights.

She also uses inverted commas on the word "wuthering" in chapter thirty-three of her novel *Shirley*. A man and woman sit inside a room, oblivious to the approaching storm:

"The air was now dark with snow: an Iceland blast was driving it wildly. This pair neither heard the long "wuthering" rush, nor saw the white burden it drifted." If taken in the context of Brontë's method of dropping hints throughout her stories, the inverted commas communicate a kind of ownership to this type of clue: she is telling her reader this is her word, not her sister's.

Clues in the Narrative

Brontë leaves clues on the surface of her novels, but unless we know where to look, or what they mean, they become lost forever. For instance, in *Wuthering Heights*, Lockwood makes an interesting comment when he sees Hareton. The boy "erecting himself before the blaze, looked down on me from the corner of his eyes, for all the world as if there were some mortal feud unavenged between us." The glaring expression on Hareton's face implies, from the surface narrative, that he probably dislikes strangers, but in the anagram story where Catherine returns as a ghost hidden inside Lockwood, her "Noah" ruse, a feud does exist between Hareton and the Masons, and his aunt Catherine has come to avenge him.

Another clue occurs in chapter two when Lockwood sits around the table with this odd family. He mistakenly identifies young Cathy as Heathcliff's wife, and he assumes Heathcliff is content in this remote locale with her by his side, but he says, "with your amiable lady as the presiding genius over your home and heart." Heathcliff thinks Lockwood is referring to Catherine the elder, his true love, and answers, "You would intimate that her spirit has taken the post of ministering angel, and guards the fortunes of Wuthering Heights, even when her body is gone. Is that it?" The answer from the hidden plot's point of view is a resounding "Yes," because Catherine's spirit uses Lockwood's body to help her serve as an agent for Hareton while attempting to guard the Earnshaw family's entailed land. Heathcliff later admits his belief in ghosts: "I have a strong faith in ghosts. I have a conviction that they can, and do exist among us" (ch. 29).

Brontë weaves clues into the novel's surface plot that relate to the hidden story in the anagrams, and she does it with such skill that she creates a novel of multi textures and layers. She acts as the reader's sublime architect designing and constructing clues and signs inside allusions and rituals that, if we look at the language and spell new words, we can detect her messages forming in secret hieroglyphics.

"Three Den Stories"

Brontë wrote in an anagram that she left clues in three novels: *"anagrams, hints, enigmas in three den stories"*. The Masons are the wolves and their Lodge a den, so her trilogy would be connected through her allusions to the Freemasons. *Wuthering Heights* contains the parody of the three degree rituals; *The Professor* hides a story of Masonic corruption in the opening paragraphs of chapter five, and in the novel's poetry; *Jane Eyre* places her heroine in the red-room for a form of initiation, and again on the third story of Thornfield for a ritualized mixing of blood and water with Mason, the brother. Jane also experiences the same growth and development that the Masonic allegories in their rituals celebrate. Brontë, therefore, leaves clues to show the reader that the three novels *Wuthering Heights*, *The Professor*, and *Jane Eyre* are connected in a specific way to form the trilogy or *"trinity"* of three den stories.

The three novels outline a progression of Masonic influence that begins with the initiation of a Mason at the Wuthering Heights farmhouse. The progression continues in *The Professor* with the fraternity's expansion from a farmhouse to the soot-producing mills and factories in a town where mansions occupy the hillside. The trilogy ends in *Jane Eyre* with Jane unhappily living inside one of those mansions. Her journey continues along a path that suggests the Masonic influence, in Brontë's trilogy, has spread from a farmhouse to a remote county to a mansion near a large manufacturing town, a distance that reaches from Wuthering Heights past Crimsworth Hall to Gateshead and finally Thornfield. Brontë resurrects her familiar tool of allegory to guide the reader through the trilogy of novels, a tool she implemented when she compared the "Romish" religion to a horrible, black, sea monster that tries to destroy England and Ireland with its "bigotry." She uses the allegorical convention to make a similar point about the Freemasons in her township, and she borrows the symbolic imagery from a famous epic poem to pit good against evil.

Shared Images of the Heart

The progression from *Wuthering Heights* to *The Professor* to *Jane Eyre* can also be seen in the images in the introductory paragraphs. When Lockwood first arrives, he stares directly into the face of Heathcliff, the "Master" of Wuthering Heights, and his heart is "warmed." Lockwood and the reader learn more about Heathcliff's history, as Nelly Dean explains his origins. Catherine's father, Mr. Earnshaw had gone to Liverpool on business and returned with the orphan boy, who they named Heathcliff.

According to Joyce Carol Oates, Charlotte's "great-great-grandfather Hugh Brunty had adopted a black-haired foundling from Liverpool (who in turn adopted their own grandfather, the younger Hugh)" (238).

If, however, on one level, Heathcliff is a representative of the Masons, whose greed infects unsuspecting families, then it makes sense to look for a possible Masonic clue in the city of Liverpool where Mr. Earnshaw finds Heathcliff. The results reveal another possible link to the fraternity.

In 1821, a notorious Liverpool Lodge was erased from existence after twenty-six men were charged with a form of mutiny and expelled. Those Masons were now without a home, like orphans. Also, in the late 1700s, Masons began charity work by clothing and educating sons of poor Freemasons, so Brontë may have connected these two situations and had Mr. Earnshaw bring home an orphan from a disgraced Lodge. This would imply that Earnshaw was already a member of the fraternity. On an allegorical level, therefore, Brontë may be demonstrating, through the character of Heathcliff, the irreparable harm that a young boy experiences when raised in a Masonic family, much like the allegorical destruction and "bigotry" that Ireland endures when the hideous sea monster of Catholicism arrives on its shores. In *Wuthering Heights*, she concentrates her narrative on Heathcliff, the man whose "black eyes" warm Lockwood's heart, to outline her Masonic method of stealing land.

Brontë also mentions the "heart" in *The Professor*. Lockwood's heart is warmed in *Wuthering Heights*, but William Crimsworth's heart experiences a different emotion. As William surveys the view around his older brother's property, he sees a dense vapour rising from the factory chimneys and states, "I found that it communicated no pleasurable emotion to my heart." The smoky air elicits a feeling of discouragement, not one of warmth.

In fact, the sight fails to stir any hope in him at all so, as an educated man, he chooses to rebel against his circumstances and travel to Brussels.

This character escapes the dark, brooding atmosphere and finds mental freedom far removed from the tyranny of his brother, which mirrors Brontë's own temporary journey away from her torment in Haworth in 1842, when she lived in Brussels.

William leaves the area, but Brontë incorporates the tale of Masonic greed in the poetry of his student and future wife Frances, an artistic and literary device that enables her, through the free expression of the anagrams, to convey the entire sordid story in a concealed medium whose surface, poetic subject contains matters of the heart.

As shown above, she also hid a tale of Masonic greed in the opening paragraphs of chapter five and listed, in that chapter in plain view, the names of actual Masons in her village: Brown, Smith, Nicholls, and Eccles.

Jane Eyre also contains the word "heart" in the introductory paragraphs. Jane withstands "a heart saddened by the chidings of Bessie, the nurse, and humbled by the "consciousness" of her "physical inferiority" to the Reed children. Jane's heart has progressed beyond the warmth of Lockwood's and the discouragement of William's to the sadness born from her life with the Reeds.

Jane also confides that one of her disadvantages when dealing with powerful people is her small stature, her physical inferiority, which can be equally relevant as a statement about her gender. As a female in a man's society, Jane is conscious of her inferior place and is intelligent enough to accept her position in the hierarchy to avoid being disciplined or worse. Her heart's humility as well resembles that of a candidate who must humbly solicit to be admitted to Freemasonry. In Jane's case, Brontë secretly parallels her heroine's journey with the candidate's path through Masonic trials and rituals until the small, plain woman gains wisdom and an insight into the needs of her own heart. Through Jane and Rochester's union, Brontë ends her trilogy on love and returns romance to her fictional world.

The Masonic Heart

In all three introductions, Brontë's inclusion of the word "heart" could be hinting at the Masonic belief that before a man can be accepted as a Mason, before he takes that first step, he must first be prepared in his heart. Outward preparations through his clothes, signs, tokens, and perfect points of entrance symbolize his inward readiness, but the heart must pierce the inner darkness and perceive his desire to proceed before the blindfold is removed, and the eyes discover the truth of the lessons.

By incorporating the word "heart" into her "*three den stories*", Brontë shows the reader how each of her characters inwardly perceives their surroundings—with warmth, discouragement, and sadness, but she also presents more clues that demonstrate the contrasting responses that define Lockwood, William, and Jane.

A Body of Signs

At the beginning of each novel, the introductory paragraphs (transcribed in the next two chapters) contain words that refer to parts of the body. Brontë mentions "heart," "eyes," "brows," and "fingers" in *Wuthering Heights*; "eye," "mind," and "heart" in *The Professor*, and "fingers," "toes," "heart," and "consciousness" in *Jane Eyre*. In all three books, the parts are mentioned in one sentence.

When Lockwood sees Heathcliff he says, "He little imagined how my heart warmed towards him when I beheld his black eyes withdraw so suspiciously under their brows, as I rode up, and when his fingers sheltered themselves, with a jealous resolution, still further in his waistcoat, as I announced my name."

William stands before the outdoor scene and says, "I forced my eye to scrutinize this prospect, I forced my mind to dwell on it for a time, and when I found that it communicated no pleasurable emotion to my heart . . . I said to myself, 'William—you are a rebel against circumstances.'"

Jane explains that she dislikes coming home in the cold twilight "with nipped fingers and toes, and a heart saddened by the chidings of Bessie, the nurse, and humbled by the consciousness of my physical inferiority."

Perfect Points of Entrance

In addition to the signs, grips, and words that the initiate learns in Freemasonry, he must also learn the perfect points of entrance written over the upper part of the Lodge door.

They consist of four points: the Pectoral or breast, which houses the heart; the Manual or hand, which signifies the sense of feeling and the efforts of labour; the Guttural or throat which connotes speech, through which acts of intemperance pass. The voice reveals inherent spirituality, and the purity of heart is reflected in the moral power of speech; thus, the point of the Guttural reinforces the concept that temperance is a virtue for Masons, one that acts as a caution to the man to never divulge secrets and risk having his throat cut, his tongue cut out, and his body buried in the sands at low tide. The Pedal or foot symbolizes that a just man plants his feet firmly on the right principles. The five principles are belief in God, the immortality of the soul, secrecy, the ritual of resurrection, and the prerogatives of the High Priest.

The word "throat" is missing from Brontë's group of features, but the opening speeches provide her nod to the Guttural and define the three characters. The Worshipful Master asks the candidate, "How do you demonstrate the proof of your being a Mason to others?" The candidate responds, "By signs, token, and the perfect points of my entrance."

The inclusion of body parts in Brontë's books could, therefore, be her own form of the Perfect Points of Entrance, but she adds the "mind" and "consciousness" to her list. The parts that coincide with the Masonic perfect points are the "heart" (chest), "fingers" (hand), and "toes" (feet).

She has each character speak immediately upon entering the text, which would be a literal representation of the throat: Lockwood begins his speech by saying his name. For Masons, during the initiation, every man must pronounce his own true name, so Lockwood shows the reader he is a willing candidate.

William Crimsworth speaks to himself: "You are a rebel against circumstances," and soon leaves the employ of his tyrant brother. His voice and self-counsel reflect his desire for liberty and the strength of will to attain it.

Jane's first speech is to question why she must live as an outsider in the Reed's family; she cannot understand what makes her unloved and asks, "What does Bessie say I have done?" Jane continues to struggle with mysteries about her circumstances and relationships, and with her efforts to do what is morally right. Her inquiring mind, and its quest to understand the inner workings of her heart, guides her to a successful, independent life.

Crimsworth and Jane have acquired the two most important points of entrance into their lives: the heart and the mind. The physical attributes, especially for Jane, are unnecessary supports to their ambition.

Brontë omitted the actual word "throat" from her opening sections, but it recurs in *Wuthering Heights* where the throat is under constant attack. The dogs strike at Lockwood's throat; he screams as if someone has cut his throat; Heathcliff tries to jam a stone down a dog's throat; the curate will have his teeth dashed down his throat if he visits; Heathcliff would cut his own throat if Catherine really wanted him to marry Isabella; Edgar Linton hits Heathcliff in the throat; Isabella reports to Nelly that after Catherine died, Heathcliff prayed to her spirit for so long that "he grew hoarse and his voice was strangled in his throat."

The Professor has one instance where a drunk threatens to cut Crimsworth's throat, and in *Jane Eyre* the madwoman grabs Rochester's throat.

If speech is an indication of a person's moral strength and purity of heart, then the curses and abuses hurled about at Wuthering Heights speak volumes about the inmates and their intemperate natures.

Signs of Lockwood's Character

Brontë also shows pertinent points about these three characters and their stories. Lockwood can be seen as a pompous and vain man who stumbles about in his interaction with the family at Wuthering Heights. He views young Cathy as a beautiful young lady whose affections he may have entertained if he had not become ill. She shows no interest in him, however, and his musings about a mutual attraction seem deluded.

His description of his callous treatment of a woman by the seaside further suggests that Lockwood's consciousness resides at a superficial level where he misreads subtle social signs and signals and is somewhat self-centred. From Brontë's perspective, he is the perfect candidate for Freemasonry.

His focus on Heathcliff involves a close scrutiny of the outward signs that provide guidance to the initiate.

A candidate must understand the facial expressions, the eyes and brows, as well as the actions of the hands or fingers that communicate secret signals and work simultaneously with the Master's verbal cues to help the man through the ceremony.

Lockwood watches closely to follow the instructions and to make sure he abides by the rules of initiation. Of course, Brontë turns his experiences in the first three chapters into a parody of the degree rituals, but Lockwood, now a student of Masonry, is fully committed to learning the history from Nelly Dean.

He shares his knowledge, however, when he writes his activities in his diary, an action expressly forbidden in Freemasonry and implies he lacks the deeper understanding of the established customs of the craft and is oblivious to the wisdom handed down from antiquity. Thus, Brontë introduces her readers to a Masonic heaven in *Wuthering Heights* and uses a shallow Mason as the reader's guide.

Signs of William's Character

By the time William arrives in her second den book, he sees the situation with a better understanding. William looks with his eyes, mind and heart at the darkness surrounding the town and makes a decision to rebel against his circumstances.

As an educated man, he can make a choice and, after working for a while under his tyrant brother, he leaves to be a teacher in Brussels where he finds love and the work that suits his nature.

Brontë shows how an educated man would respond to the negative atmosphere and tyrannical treatment and, following his wise choice, is able to flourish far removed from an area governed by the coarse and cruel influences of men who prefer the secrecy and privileges of Freemasonry. William's rebellion succeeds, but what would happen to a woman who finds herself trapped in a society governed by Masons?

Signs of Jane's Character

Jane Eyre's predicament closely resembles Brontë's. Both find themselves enclosed in a house that celebrates Masonic culture. For Jane, the Reed mansion with its red-room constitutes a Lodge. Jane's gender restricts her movement and freedom of expression; thus, her nipped fingers to write and toes to move limit the scope of her rebellion, but her intelligence and her consciousness or awareness of her inferiority allow her to search for an alternate route out of her Hell.

The Masonic Perfect Points of Entrance exclude the mind or brain in their body parts, but Brontë believes that "consciousness" or mind is an important part of one's development. Her mind sets her apart from the uneducated men she must encounter in her home, so she uses her genius to escape from her physical limits and to experience liberty within her writing.

Jane finds comfort in reading, and works within the system to acquire an education. Her intelligence and virtuous heart enable her to withstand the men's influence and to make her own decisions, which further her prospects for love and employment.

Brontë cannot leave her home, but she finds escape through her active imagination and superior intellect as she conceals signs, tokens, and perfect points to guide the reader on a journey through her "*trinity*". She guides Jane along the hierarchy of a fraternity whose peculiar system of morality fails to exclude one plain, small woman.

One could certainly argue that Emily Brontë originated all these ideas in *Wuthering Heights* and Charlotte, the overbearing, jealous sister stole them and used them in *The Professor* and *Jane Eyre* but, with a closer

313

inspection, further evidence found in the three books gradually points to the reasonable conclusion that only one sister wrote these novels.

Brontë shifted the original opening chapter of *The Professor* to chapter two after several rejections from publishers. She tried to make the work more interesting by including old material from 1840 at the beginning of the manuscript, but this addition failed to change the publishers' minds. Since chapter two was the original first chapter in 1846 it will be the one assessed for clues. Another point is that Brontë was sending the manuscript out as a Currer Bell book, just as she later did when she sent *Jane Eyre* to the publishers Smith, Elder; consequently, authorship between these two novels was not an issue for her, but she provides hints in *Jane Eyre* that she wrote *Wuthering Heights* and continued to drop similar clues right up to the time before her death: this novel meant a great deal to her; she was proud of the work, and she wanted to make certain that readers saw the hidden revelations. Since *The Professor* was written after *Wuthering Heights*, she set up specific links to that earlier work that recur in *Jane Eyre*.

In order to understand her code, the opening two paragraphs in *The Professor* need to be viewed in their entirety.

Paragraph One

"A fine October morning succeeded to the foggy evening that had witnessed my first introduction to Crimsworth Hall. I was early up and walking in the large park-like meadow surrounding the house. The autumn sun, rising over the----shire hills, disclosed a pleasant country; woods brown and mellow varied the fields from which the harvest had been lately carried; a river, gliding between the woods, caught on its surface the somewhat cold gleam of the October sun and sky; at frequent intervals along the banks of the river, tall, cylindrical chimneys, almost like slender round towers, indicated the factories which the trees half concealed; here and there mansions, similar to Crimsworth Hall, occupied agreeable sites on the hill-side; the country wore, on the whole, a cheerful, active, fertile look. Steam, trade, machinery had long banished from it all romance and seclusion. At a distance of five miles, a valley, opening between the low hills, held in its cups the great town of X——. A dense, permanent vapour brooded over this locality—there lay Edward's 'Concern.'"

The chapter begins with the main character, William Crimsworth, taking a walk around a park that surrounds his older brother Edward's property. Brontë describes the area in some detail with depictions of woods, fields, and a river, but injects into this pastoral view evidence of mills with their factory chimneys spewing soot and smoke into the valley. The dense vapour hangs permanently over the town where the brother's mill is located. Brontë calls it Edward's "concern." This word can denote a commercial enterprise, an interest in something, or an anxious feeling about a possible misfortune, but when Brontë highlights it with inverted commas, we need to consider the meaning and be concerned about the scene she has just drawn.

Paragraph Two

"I forced my eye to scrutinize this prospect, I forced my mind to dwell on it for a time, and when I found that it communicated no pleasurable emotion to my heart—that it stirred in me none of the hopes a man ought to feel, when he sees laid before him the scene of his life's career—I said to myself, "William, you are a rebel against circumstances; you are a fool, and know not what you want; you have chosen trade and you shall be a tradesman. Look!" I continued mentally—"Look at the sooty smoke in that hollow, and know that there is your post! There you cannot dream, you cannot speculate and theorize—there you shall out and work!"

The character William, and the reader, must "scrutinize," "dwell," and "look" at the view. Brontë emphatically demands that we stare at the scene and let our minds dwell on it because she has revealed clues in the first paragraph that we will miss if we fail to force our eye to take a second look.

The above description of the view links the three books. If Brontë were secretly planning to continue her Masonic saga in *The Professor*, she would want to set up echoes of *Wuthering Heights*. The reading public will not personally know Currer or Ellis Bell, nor will they know where these two "men" live, so Brontë must convey the truth about the situation in Haworth Township from behind a mask of words. On a superficial level, the landscape in *The Professor* resembles Brontë's area, as does the land in *Wuthering Heights*.

Relevance of the Fall

The autumn season also forms a connection within the books. In *Villette*, Brontë describes her mood and circumstances when she wrote *Wuthering Heights* during the autumn vacation in Brussels in 1843. In the novel, Heathcliff returns to a married Catherine in the autumn and begins a unique courtship that lasts several months until her death.

Lockwood arrives in the autumn of 1801 and, after his ordeal at the farmhouse and his trek in the snow, recuperates at Thrushcross Grange where he hears Nelly Dean's account of the Earnshaw and Linton families, whose histories include the deaths of half a dozen family members.

The Professor chapter opens on an October morning and, at the beginning of *Jane Eyre*, ten-year-old Jane contemplates the ceaseless and penetrating rain of a November day.

This third novel has progressed into the wetter and darker aspects of the season. The autumn or "fall" metaphorically refers to the days and events depicting moral decline, a theme that Brontë chooses in order to make an elaborate comparison between her reality in Haworth and the mythology in the epic poem *Paradise Lost*. Brontë uses John Milton's *Paradise Lost* in a similar way to Shakespeare's History plays—as a source of inspiration for the metaphors, allusions, and clues she integrates into her novels.

Devils in Paradise

Paradise Lost, written in 1674 dramatizes "Man's first disobedience," as depicted in the second and third chapters of Genesis, the first book of the Bible. The poem covers Satan's revolt against God and the angels in Heaven, the rebel angels' defeat and subsequent fall into Hell, and the Serpent's tempting of Eve in the Garden of Eden, which ends with Adam and Eve expelled from Paradise.

For Brontë, the Masons' corruption and disregard for their souls easily fit Milton's devils and their rebellion against God. As the similarities become apparent, Brontë provides the reader with a fascinating glimpse into her mind and its creative process, as well as into her love of symbols and wordplay to communicate her secret message.

The Italian poets influenced Milton, so his strange word order can be attributed to that Italian style: for instance, he writes "angel serene," "voice Divine," and "with matters hid." Brontë mimics this style in *The Professor* with "early up" and "woods brown and mellow."

The Countryside

William Crimsworth walks around the park admiring the pastoral view. He sees a natural setting that suggests a kind of Garden of Eden. The country is pleasant but not unspoiled as in *Wuthering Heights*: Lockwood exclaims, "This is certainly a beautiful country!" Something must have happened to diminish the landscape's beauty by the time Crimsworth takes his walk.

If *The Professor* is her second den book then we can see that the local landscape has changed. The country is no longer pristine: "the Steam, Trade, Machinery had long banished from it all romance and seclusion." Even though the overall community reflects a cheerful image of fertility and activity, and the area appears to present a pleasing pastoral view, the mills and the factories' chimneys are half concealed, so all is either not seen or not as it seems, and a "dense, permanent vapour brooded over this locality." This vapour is what Brontë wants her readers to force their eyes and minds to contemplate.

The Black Mist

If we add Milton's influence to the scene, we begin to read Brontë's signs and words as subtle allusions to that earlier epic. The "fall" of Adam and Eve in the Garden of Eden is the climax of *Paradise Lost*. Eden before the fall is an extremely beautiful setting. Satan, the rebel angel, spoils everything when, out of jealousy and revenge, he decides to ruin God's newly formed creatures by showing Adam and Eve how to disobey the Law.

He enters the earth "like a black mist low creeping," and while "wrapped in mist of midnight vapour," he remains hidden. His entrance resembles the "dense, permanent vapour" hanging over Crimsworth's park, and is similar to the "silvery vapour" hanging below Wuthering

318

Heights, but Brontë wants the reader to see that in *The Professor* things have gotten much worse: the vapour now comes from the mills' sooty smoke in the hollow, and it communicates no pleasurable emotion to William's heart because this is the image of evil having entered and taken over the township.

In *Paradise Lost*, Hell belches fire and smoke from its ever-burning sulphur, and Satan lives in his "unhappy Mansion." He plots his "easier enterprise," his main concern, which is to wage war against God by devastating the Earth.

Satan wants to take over the Earth, and Brontë's Masons want to take over the land. *The Professor*'s "mansions," bought with profits acquired from the mills, occupy the hillside near the town where Edward Crimsworth's "concern," his enterprise flourishes. The tall, factory chimneys that expel the smoke resemble "slender, round towers" just as in Book One. Satan, "In shape and gesture proudly eminent, / Stood like a tower" above the other rebel angels discharging his scheme for revenge.

Brontë's Reference to Milton's Poem

Inside the pages of *The Professor*, Brontë explains, through William Crimsworth, how *Paradise Lost* first inspired her. William is visiting his ex-pupil Frances and asks her to read him a book while they relax by the fire. He says, "She had selected 'Paradise Lost' from her shelf of classics." She reads to him "Milton's invocation to that heavenly muse, who on the 'secret top of Oreb or Sinai' had taught the Hebrew shepherd [Moses] how in the womb of chaos, the conception of a world had originated and ripened." This is the only quotation from the epic poem that Frances reads aloud to William. Brontë is telling her readers that, out of the chaos around her home, she first conceived of joining her world of fiction to Milton's vision of good and evil. *Paradise Lost* acts as her muse, her personal, lengthy metaphor that weaves through her work and connects all three novels.

In order to provide further evidence that *Wuthering Heights*, *The Professor*, and *Jane Eyre* are indeed three den stories and, therefore, all written by Charlotte Brontë, the opening paragraphs of *Jane Eyre* need to be viewed for links to *Paradise Lost*. Brontë sets up her extended comparisons immediately in the opening paragraphs, and she structures her clues around particular words and symbols that echo both Milton's poem and the Masonic influences.

She essentially instructs her readers to look closely in order to discern similarities to that earlier work, and to see the deeper truth regarding the setting and the theme of a fall into evil that she etches into the meaning behind her words and symbols. Her method provides a kind of fingerprint of her style, and allows us to peek inside her mind to understand her larger plan of subversion. An important example of her code also occurs in the opening two paragraphs of *Jane Eyre*.

Opening Paragraphs of *Jane Eyre*

"There was no possibility of taking a walk that day. We had been wandering, indeed, in the leafless shrubbery an hour in the morning; but since dinner (Mrs. Reed, when there was no company, dined early) the cold winter wind had brought with it clouds so sombre, and a rain so penetrating, that further out-door exercise was now out of the question.

"I was glad of it: I never liked long walks, especially on chilly afternoons: dreadful to me was the coming home in the raw twilight, with nipped fingers and toes, and a heart saddened by the chidings of Bessie, the nurse, and humbled by the consciousness of my physical inferiority to Eliza, John, and Georgiana Reed."

If *Jane Eyre* is her third den book, the setting has shifted from the outdoors to the inside of a mansion, a large dwelling like Crimsworth Hall in *The Professor*.

The expansive countryside of *Wuthering Heights* and *The Professor* has shrunk indoors to Gateshead Hall where, enclosed behind a curtain, a ten-year-old girl sits on a window-seat looking at pictures in a book.

In this reduced space, the cruel treatment from the members of a family saddens a girl's heart. Jane must remain a kind of prisoner enduring trials and tribulations, and suffering physical and mental abuse at the hands of the Reed family. Her heartbreak seems interminable.

Jane's Masonic Allegory

When Brontë writes *Jane Eyre*, she avoids a parody of Masonic ceremonies and, instead, embraces them to prove that an intelligent woman can outwit uneducated brutes.

Even though Jane's imprisonment inside the mansion appears grim and her prospects doubtful, Brontë sets her heroine on a path through allegorical trials where Masonic symbols and signs guide the reader to Brontë's subterfuge. Behind the curtain of allegory, Jane survives her years of tribulations to become a Master of her fate and a fully independent member of a society led by males.

In this third book, Brontë's orphan heroine succeeds, not because the author ridicules or rejects the model of Masonic culture, as she does through Lockwood and William Crimsworth, but because she adopts it and secretly injects its practices into her narrative. In essence, Jane infiltrates the male fraternity without their knowledge and rises to the heights of financial freedom and love.

Jane Eyre presents the final chapter of Brontë's trilogy. She starts with Lockwood arriving at the farmhouse to begin his initiation into Freemasonry, and to introduce the reader to this fraternal society through a parody of its rituals. She includes an alternate story, in anagrams, about the ghost of Catherine returning inside the body of a Mason "Noah" to take back the ancestral, entailed home that a Master Mason stole from her family's heirs.

Brontë progresses to William observing the mills belching their smoke among the mansions in *The Professor*, a metaphorical allusion to an increase in Masonic influence and wealth. She also secretly conceals a Masonic story in anagrams in chapter five and in the poetry.

She finally leads the reader to Jane suffering within a Mason mansion and onward through further trials that begin with a Masonic death in the red-room and end with a prayer to St. John the Baptist, the patron saint of Freemasons. This prayer provides the perfect point on which to end her trinity as it echoes the Masons' prayer to St. John at the close of their ceremonies.

Masonic Links Between the Three Novels

The progression from the first book to the third becomes clear when viewed through the Masonic lens. In *Wuthering Heights*, Brontë lifts the curtain to reveal not only Masonic rituals but also the barbarous activities inside a private farmhouse.

She provides a detailed documentation of Heathcliff's manipulation of inheritance law that allows him to temporarily dock the Earnshaw and Linton entails.

In *The Professor*, she moves the focus inside the counting house at Edward Crimsworth's mill to demonstrate more coarse and brutal treatment from the Master toward a brother at their place of employment. William's ultimate success in work and love comes only because he escapes the savagery and hatred of men like Edward who mirror the Lodge mentality of selfishness outlined in the poetry.

Rather than expose the Masonic temperament and actions in the narrative, as she does in *Wuthering Heights*, Brontë hides her accusations inside the poetry. By the third book, Brontë presents an autobiographical depiction through metaphor and allegory when she situates a female inside the cruel environment of a Masonic mansion. Jane is unable to escape and would prefer to avoid the deluge of suffering, but Brontë takes her young heroine's hand and leads her into the heart of the tempest.

Progress Through the Novels

The three den books offer three types of characters faced with the impact of Freemasonry upon their lives. Lockwood, on "an idle whim," arrives in October and happily embraces a secret society without fully understanding its customs or its influence on two families. At this point in Brontë's trilogy, Masonry mainly inhabits one dwelling.

Also in the month of October, William Crimsworth surveys the effects of a growing, insidious darkness arising from the factories and mills that pollute a town. An ethical and educated man, he freely rejects this reality and moves to another country.

While looking out the window at a November storm, Jane contemplates the deluge and darkness. As a woman with inferior status, she must find another way to live within the male system that has stretched beyond one house and one town to an entire county. The fall and its relentless bad weather highlight the severity of Jane's situation. Like William, however, her education will save her, and her story soon provides a strong example of one woman's steady perseverance as she successfully encounters and passes secret ceremonies, while she learns how best to live and prosper with the aid of the tools of her craft. Each trial proves the merits of her character and by the end of her story, as Jane emerges victorious, the reader celebrates her passionate and powerful nature.

Happy Endings—Paradise Regained

All three novels end with hopeful optimism. Brontë once again alludes to *Paradise Lost* when Lockwood returns to Wuthering Heights for the final time. He observes Hareton and young Cathy, the two legal heirs who are about to marry each other, and he comments on their fearlessness: "Together they would brave Satan and all his legions," much like Brontë has done through her writing.

The Professor ends with William Crimsworth happily married and living a prosperous life. He and Frances have a son called Victor, and they live in "a region whose verdure the smoke of mills has not yet sullied." In the last paragraph he hears of a visitor arriving soon, a young man he once rescued from drowning called "Jean Baptiste," an allusion to St. John the Baptist, the patron saint of Freemasonry.

Jane Eyre ends with Jane married to Rochester. As mentioned above, she quotes a prayer in the words of St. John Rivers to mirror the prayer the Masons recite to conclude their ceremonies. Brontë only briefly introduces a representation of John the Baptist in *The Professor* but develops him into a fully developed character in *Jane Eyre* to allow Jane to meet a loving 'brother.'

As stated above, Brontë provides a strong clue to the origin of her inspiration when, in *The Professor*, she points to Frances reading *Paradise Lost*. Brontë uses this character to explain that Milton's epic was her origin for her creative invention, and that she devised this structural metaphor for her three den books in order to link the intricate symbolic system in her mind during their composition.

As she writes, she unites the deeper truth she wants to reveal with the themes of an earlier literary work. The connection arises from the same issue of good versus evil, or from two great enemies fighting for control of the earth or, as in Shakespeare's History plays, from enemy kingdoms battling for neighbouring countries. She sustains the theme of good versus evil or war over ownership of land by following the approach of other masterpieces. She then applies her own stamp of interpretation and her personal vision to the novels. In her three den stories, her strongest link between the books is her reference to John Milton's epic poem *Paradise Lost* with its theme of the decline, or fall into evil, but other symbols and word clues also unite these novels.

Wolves at the Door

Brontë's image of Masons as wolves comes directly from *Paradise Lost*. Satan journeys toward Earth to wreak havoc and sneaks around like a "prowling Wolf." In Book XII, the archangel Michael later prophesizes that, in the future, Satan and his devils will be engaged in enterprises throughout the Earth and will be found in tyrants hungry for power. He explains to Adam that "Wolves will succeed for teachers, grievous Wolves, / Who all the sacred mysteries of Heaven / To their own vile advantages shall turn" for money and ambition. Michael adds some hope: he says that good will overcome evil, and "by small / Accomplishing great things, by things deemed weak / Subverting worldly strong;" thus, the gates of Heaven will open for those small, apparently weak people as they do great things and bring down the strong sinners. Brontë would have identified with these lines: she was small and perceived as a weak woman, and she saw her mission against the devil wolves as her lone task of subversion.

Milton's Words

Aside from the comparison of Milton's devils to wolves, other terms from *Paradise Lost* appear in the first paragraph of *Wuthering Heights*. When Lockwood arrives at Wuthering Heights, he remarks that he has "fixed on a situation so completely removed from the stir of society," and that he and Heathcliff—that "Capital fellow"—are a "suitable pair to divide the desolation." He calls the secluded area "a perfect misanthropist's heaven," the perfect place for inhabitants who hate other people, but for anyone who prefers the company of neighbours, this place would be a living Hell. Milton's devils are jailed in Hell, and the image of imprisonment recurs throughout the novel as characters find it difficult to get out of Wuthering Heights, especially when Heathcliff's "black eyes" are always watching.

The following italicized words from *Paradise Lost* help show a striking similarity to *Wuthering Heights*. In Book I, after being cast out of

324

Heaven, Milton's Satan views Hell's "dismal *situation* waste and wild" (line 60) as a dark dungeon where peace "can never dwell" (66), "a prison as far *removed from* God" (73) and Heaven's light as possible. Hell is called Pandemonium, "the high *Capital* / Of Satan and his Peers" (756), the peers being the other devils who are earlier classed as "The *fellows* of his crime" (757).

In Book IV, while in Eden, Adam and Eve are described as a "happy *pair*" (366), and a "gentle *pair*" (366) who enjoy sharing the work. In Book IX, Adam says to Eve, "let us *divide* our labours" (214). Desolation means waste and ruin, and Lockwood and Heathcliff are a suitable *pair*, well fit as Masons, to *divide* the desolation of a *situation* completely *removed from* society and to turn it into a living hell.

Scholars have noticed allusions to *Paradise Lost* in *Wuthering Heights*, but they cannot explain which character falls from grace or which of the two properties—Wuthering Heights and Thrushcross Grange—is an example of the fallen world. Without knowledge of Brontë's system, or of her disdain for the Masons and their land schemes, the scholars remain in the dark. The answers become clear from the patterns Brontë has set up in all three novels. The writings of Shakespeare and Milton also captured her imagination, and their words acted as guides as she set up her own patterns in the introductory paragraphs.

Milton's words are also suggested through references to time in *Jane Eyre*. As Jane regards the illustrations in Bewick's *A History of British Birds*, she says, "At intervals, while turning over the leaves of my book, I studied the aspect of that winter afternoon." The torment has temporarily ceased, but like in Book VI when Milton's devils and angels face each other in a "dreadful interval" before their battle begins, Jane must wait for her enemy to strike (105). The young Reed male soon attacks her. Her fight with her cousin results in her temporary defeat and her trials begin.

Before Jane is dragged to the dreadful red-room upstairs, she studies "the aspect of that winter afternoon." The cold winter, the sombre clouds, and the penetrating rain prevent her from taking a walk, so her freedom of movement is now limited, her fingers and toes "nipped," not just by cold but also by restrictions. No one rides in on a horse, or walks the circumference of the house and lands: "There was no possibility of taking a walk that day," and no young girl has the freedom to take pen in hand

and write of her ordeal, so Jane, like Brontë, must remain confined and constrained in an eternal struggle against evil to wait for the next attack. The deluge of rain mirrors the biblical flood when God, enraged by the corruption, violence, and wickedness in men, sent a constant downpour to destroy humankind. Jane views a scene of wind and storm, "with ceaseless rain sweeping away wildly before a long and lamentable blast," and prefers not to walk in the unmercifully chilly weather. In order to cope, she liberates her imagination through the medium of art and studies the wood engravings in her book.

The words in *Jane Eyre*'s introductory paragraphs refer to time and are an essential part of the clue pattern Brontë employs to demonstrate her purpose. She wants to unite her heroine's afflictions with her own. In the first three sentences, she uses the words "day," "hour," "morning," "dinner," "afternoons," and "twilight." She covers an entire day before the dark sets in, which suggests only the night provides a momentary escape from the endless repetitions of the day's misery.

For a portion of the time while Brontë is writing *Jane Eyre*, her words are less easily expressed. Unlike the safety and seclusion of the Pensionnat Heger where she created *Wuthering Heights* she is at home for most of the writing of *Jane Eyre*, susceptible to regular Mason intrusions into her privacy when they visit her father and brother.

The anagrams explain that she wrote *Wuthering Heights* in 1843 while she was away at Brussels, and the biographical information states that she began *Jane Eyre* while in Manchester with her father who was lying in a bed blindfolded for a month, due to cataract surgery. Both books were either composed or begun away from home, a long and safe distance from watchful eyes, but the Masons were never far from the parsonage walls when she returned.

Jane's nipped fingers from the cold and her feeling of being powerless could be alluding to Brontë's inability to write freely because of the Mason traffic at the parsonage. Her anagrams state that drinking alcohol was an important part of their routine, so one can imagine the noise and crude behaviour of drunken men who would take offence to a sullen, small, plain woman "sneaking" around. In order to finish the book in peace, therefore, she spent many sleepless nights writing *Jane Eyre* after everyone had gone to bed.

Her brother's relapse into drug addiction and alcoholism created a situation so explosive that she was forced to remain closer to home and to endure his additional torment without exacerbating his unpredictable outbursts. While she was still composing *Jane Eyre*, she responded to Ellen's request for more information about her life, to "tell her plenty" of what was going on at the parsonage. Brontë wrote back, "What would you have me say? Nothing happens at Haworth; nothing, at least of a pleasant kind." Her writing would have provided the freedom from so many restrictions at home, and the night time, if Branwell was asleep, would have given her the peace she needed to write.

Sheltered and Nipped Fingers

In the opening paragraphs of both *Wuthering Heights* and *Jane Eyre*, Brontë places another clue to link these two books. The effort she exerts to connect the two novels cannot simply be to say that Emily and she are telling the same story: she would assume, rightfully, that critics would recognize that both novels share a passion and power, and probably the same hand and pen. In fact, she deliberately slips a symbol of her hand into the opening paragraphs in the form of the word "fingers." Heathcliff "sheltered" his fingers in his waistcoat, and Jane Eyre's fingers are "nipped." Brontë definitely shelters her hand and her true intent in *Wuthering Heights* through her pseudonym, the anagrams, and her unique system of code.

The word "fingers" in the opening of *Wuthering Heights* and *Jane Eyre* could simply be a playful wave between sisters, but Brontë's own method of code tells us the word is a significant clue.

In Act 4, Scene vii of Shakespeare's play *Henry V*, one of the King's officers tries to compare the birthplace of Alexander the Great to King Henry's: one was born in Macedonia and the other in Monmouth, but he sees no difference in either one because they both have rivers: the Nile and the Wye. He explains, "I warrant you shall find, in the comparisons between Macedon and Monmouth, that the situations, look you, is both alike. There is a river in Macedon; and there is also moreover a river at Monmouth . . . but 'tis all one, 'tis alike as my fingers is to my fingers, and there is salmons in both." The point of resemblance between the two is comical, but his comparison that the two are as alike as his own fingers, and Brontë's inclusion of the word "fingers" in both novels suggest that the two novels are alike, and that the same fingers held the pen that wrote both books. Also, the situations in the novels are alike in that they depict Masonic rituals and influences; thus, there are Masons in both.

Brontë weaves *Paradise Lost*, Shakespeare, Masonic symbols, and allegory throughout *Wuthering Heights*, *The Professor*, and *Jane Eyre*. The anagrams refer to these three novels as a trilogy, and the symbols and allusions support their claims. The connections indicate one sister alone wrote these novels, and the historical evidence presented throughout this book points to Charlotte Brontë as the sole author of the published works. Did Charlotte share the idea of *Paradise Lost* with Emily or was it the other way around? The more likely answer is that Charlotte devised the structure on her own.

As we have discovered, she was equally secretive about her vision for the novels and the appropriation of the Masonic system but, occasionally, she let the mask slip, so her readers could catch a closer glimpse of her genius.

35 WUTHERING CHILDBIRTH

The critics may accept that the Brontë novels share a metaphor structure, but they would likely disagree to only one sister composing the trilogy. They would continue to favour the "Emily" myth and claim that both sisters sat together at one table and, therefore, drew on the identical source for their exact same purposes, incorporated twin themes and symbols, hated the Masons with equal passion, and exhibited a matching talent with anagrams. They would believe this because Charlotte stated that all three sisters were novelists and poets. No other evidence survives that corroborates her statement, but proof exists in the historical record that demonstrates her diligence to create a mythology around her two younger sisters. Charlotte created three Bell brothers, wrote fiction, lived her Masonic theme to its conclusion, and composed the poetry. The mythic "Emily" never existed.

Scholars agree that Emily was a reclusive individual with a strong personality. She preferred animals to people and found interacting with anyone outside her home an unpleasant pastime, whereas Charlotte, aware of her own shyness, but unhappy with feelings of loneliness, was willing to step outside the parsonage to make friends and correspond with them on a daily basis. Charlotte needed to connect with people and, through her novels and poetry, found consolation in sharing her thoughts and feelings with her imaginary readers. Why, therefore, would two geniuses with such disparate personalities as Emily and Charlotte use the same text for inspiration and have the same attitudes, write the same themes, use the identical symbolic systems as well as share an affinity for allegory and parody in such ways that the ideas appear to come from one brain?

The parody of the Masonic rituals in the first three chapters of *Wuthering Heights* has a distinct echo of Charlotte's voice. As shown in chapter thirteen, Charlotte parodies a visit to her sisters' imaginary world in "A Day at Parry's Palace," a precursor to the similar scene in *Wuthering Heights*. In the earlier scene Charles, the narrator, beats Parry's son, little Eater. He hits him with a poker; kicks him a few times, and knocks "his head against the floor, hoping to stun him," but the child continues to scream, which alerts the inhabitants to come to Eater's aid. Brontë

329

indirectly alludes to this previous scene when Lockwood beats back the dogs: "parrying off the larger combatants, as effectually as [he] could, with the poker." In *Wuthering Heights*, she revisits that earlier incident and adds her own recognizable brand of ridicule to a scene set up for parody. Her biting wit and sharp sense of humour from her juvenile writing recur in *Wuthering Heights* as she strikes the same satirical tone in the later work and alludes to it by including the word "parrying" and by using a poker as a handy weapon.

Readers can also see Charlotte's skill in the creation of Joseph, the old servant. How did Emily hear this regional dialect if she never ventured into the village? If she rarely went into social settings or visited the artisans and farmers who used the northern dialect, how could she learn the strains of the speech patterns repeated in the character of Joseph and, therefore, how could she have replicated that form of speech and added such a sharp, satirical bite to his interpretation of events? Brontë scholars agree that Emily spent the majority of her life at home, and avoided interacting with people from the village, but they assume she must have heard the Yorkshire burr because it exists in the novel. This particular point is what generated "the absurd claim" that Branwell was the author of *Wuthering Heights* (Miller 205).

In a *Bronte Studies* article outlining the dialect usage in *Shirley*, John Waddington-Feather writes that Charlotte, like Emily, "uses dialect as a literary ploy to develop character and atmosphere, and to give her novel realism." Charlotte "also uses dialect as a literary ploy to lower the dramatic atmosphere before heightening it. . . . (Her sister Emily uses the same technique by often bringing in the dialect-speaking buffoon Joseph before some violent outburst by Heathcliff.)." He adds that Charlotte's "use of dialect makes for realism and also lends itself to introducing her own brand of humour."

Another Brontë scholar, Edward Chitham, in *A Life of Emily Brontë* refers to K. M. Petyt's analysis of Emily's use of dialect in *Wuthering Heights*: "she has consistent principles of transcription and generally holds to them." Chitham also notes that Branwell and Charlotte were both writing in dialect in their fiction, but that Emily was apparently more proficient than her siblings, as is evidenced in the depiction of Joseph: "Branwell and Charlotte made attempts at Haworth dialect in the juvenilia, and of course there are dialect speakers in *Jane Eyre* and *Wildfell Hall*, [and *Shirley*] but it looks as if Emily's superior ear and memory are responsible for her greater accuracy" (200-1). Charlotte's excellent memory would have been an added attribute when recalling speech patterns.

According to the scholars, Charlotte uses dialect in her novels exactly the way that Emily uses it in *Wuthering Heights*; Branwell and Charlotte both began using dialect in their juvenile writing, but no record of Emily using it occurs before *Wuthering Heights* because the only remnants of her writing are the diary papers that consistently refer to her childhood Gondal fiction. As noted in chapter eight, in 1850, after Emily's death, Charlotte amended some of Joseph's speech in *Wuthering Heights* for its second edition. She was concerned that people living in the south of England would find his speech unintelligible, so she made minor adjustments to a few parts of Joseph's speech to soften his accent. Rather than modifying a sister's original work, it appears she was editing her own novel.

Thomas John Winnifrith adds that, while some biographers picture Emily as a "gloomy" figure, in 1845 her mood is "surprisingly cheerful," at a time that she would have been writing *Wuthering Heights*. Winnifrith is referring to Emily's 1845 diary paper wherein she presents herself as a young woman "insensitively lost in a world of her own and blind to the troubles of her family" (*Critical Essays* 6). If she was lost in her own world, blind to the obvious problems of her own family, how could she have been curious enough to know not only the secretive activities of the Masons but also their intricate code, symbolic structure, ceremonies, and allegorical teaching device, or have cared enough to turn away from her beloved Gondal to construct an elaborate design that required, not a "surprisingly cheerful" mood, but a deep and passionate anger as exhibited on the pages of *Wuthering Heights*?

The hidden Masonic theme connects all three novels, but the parody and the dialect directly connect Charlotte to *Wuthering Heights*. Brontë knew that she would be sending *The Professor* out to publishers as a Currer Bell book. Her claim as author would never and has never been disputed, but *Wuthering Heights* is different. She wrote both novels but explains that she concealed herself in a different male pseudonym for fear of retribution at the hands of the Masons. Nonetheless, she still wanted her readers to know the truth but not in an overt way. She devised clues, anagrams, allusions, and actual phrases to reveal her authorship of *Wuthering Heights*. As will be seen later, she also hid hints inside the illustrations and drawings referred to in *Jane Eyre*, but the public continued to see only the "Ellis Bell" myth that Brontë had so meticulously constructed.

For instance, Brontë left anagrams in the first paragraph of *Jane Eyre* that link Charlotte to *Wuthering Heights*. These connections are not as overt as the use of dialect and parody noted above, but the difficulty and surprising results again suggest they were intentional. To borrow from Edward Chitham's interpretation of K. M. Petyt's conclusions regarding the dialect in *Wuthering Heights*, Charlotte also "has consistent principles of transcription," in the anagrams, and she always "holds to them."

The opening paragraph of *Jane Eyre* contains thirteen anagrams. The divisions appear naturally within the sentences, but in one case the split had to be adjusted because no anagrams emerged until the change occurred. The original split was as follows: "the cold winter wind / had brought with it clouds so sombre," but had to be altered to "the cold winter wind had brought with it / clouds so sombre." Brontë keeps her phrases short and, therefore, her choice of letters limited to a small, manageable number, but the division must be exact in order to actually solve the anagram. Without the correct split, the scrambled letters make no sense.

The thirteen phrases range from 10 to 33 letters, the average anagram comprising 20 letters. With those few letters, she keeps the information succinct and, even with awkward syntax, decipherable, so that we understand her meaning. Also, the lines occasionally link from one anagram to another without losing the topic. She uses puns; her terms are clever and imaginative, and they communicate a mind conversant in the English language. All this happens with just a few letters.

A further point is that when a word is between two commas, such as the word "indeed" in the opening paragraph, it remains as is unless it, too, can be turned into an anagram. In this case, Brontë appears to use it as "in deed." The words "Mrs. Reed" also seem to remain the same: those two words are between a parenthetical mark and a comma, but the anagram before Mrs. Reed links to the name. The anagram inside the parenthesis can also be read as a parenthetical aside.

The third point that bears repeating is her unique rule regarding the punctuation. As stated above, her method stays consistent and, therefore, predictable for anyone trying to transcribe the anagrams. Her system of keeping the anagram phrase locked between punctuation marks makes the job of transcribing less complicated. The more difficult task, however, occurs when no punctuation seals the phrase. She might have an entire sentence without commas, which means that the phrases are usually confusing to solve. She obviously sees the entire sentence as an anagram, which enables her to move words from phrase to phrase, but solving the anagram means having to decipher phrases that may not make sense on their own. Fortunately, the final effort to understand the anagram is quite simple: two or three words get shuffled into place and the anagram becomes clear. Notwithstanding the limited number of letters she has at her disposal in each phrase, and the consistency of this rule, her ability to imagine these anagrams remains bewildering.

The following phrases have the divisions marked with a slash:
(1) "There was no possibility / (2) of taking a walk that day.
(3) We had been wandering, / (4) indeed, in the leafless shrubbery / (5) an hour in the morning; / (6) but since dinner / (Mrs. Reed, (7) when there was no company, / (8) dined early) / (9) the cold winter wind had brought with it / (10) clouds so sombre; / (11) and a rain so penetrating, / (12) that further outdoor exercise / (13) was now out of the question."

The anagrams, once again, refer to *Wuthering Heights* and Brontë's trip to Brussels when she was alone. She writes of a "den web," in deeds— most likely another term for the land fraud. She provides insight into her plot's design, and the reality of her depiction.

British Isle poet now say. (2) *Away. Had ink, tat, fog. Talk.*
British Isle poet away. Had ink, tat, fog. Now talk. Say

"Tat" means something cheap or vulgar and is a word she uses later in another anagram to describe the Masonic handbooks she had acquired, and could, therefore, mean the same thing here. In the anagrams in her "Biographical Notice," she stated that she parodied the "*Heights*

333

handbook." The image of the fog is an interesting detail. Brussels does get fog, and it could also be, for her, a metaphorical cover: she can write, hidden from view, away from Haworth. The last word "*say*" links with the next anagram.

(3) *Heed a warning: Den web* in deed,

(4) *Selfishly abuse brethren:*
(5) *Inhuman north region,*

(6) *Urn debts in nice*

Mrs. Reed, (7) *coy pen warns heath women:*

(8) *earn yield.*

In *Jane Eyre*, Mrs. Reed's son John gambles away the family's fortune. This kind of "*urn debt*" through gambling, therefore, can be found in "*nice*" Mrs. Reed's story arc. The original meaning of "*nice*" is silly, stupid, ignorant, or exacting in manners, all the qualities she displays in the novel. Her ruin could be a warning to other wealthy women from the Township who reaped the benefits of their husband's ill-gotten gains without ever having to earn the fruits of their labours in a legitimate way.

Brontë uses the image of a tin tea urn as the container where the Masons keep their debt sheets. The next anagrams relate to *Wuthering Heights.*

(9) *Wanted wuthering childbirth. Two to hid.*

(10) *Muse. Cross blood.*

Wanted wuthering childbirth. Two to cross blood. Hid muse

.

(11) *Tenant organ in paradise.*

The two children born during the course of the story are, of course, Hareton Earnshaw and Cathy Linton, whose marriage will mix the blood of two families.

Her allusion to *"paradise"* echoes Catherine's heaven, so her muse must be the mother who haunts Lockwood. The mother spirit, who as the organ for communication through Lockwood, the tenant, returns to her paradise on the moors after she secures the properties for the young couple.

(12) *Exact theft. Our hideous terror.*

(13) *Few quotations, house, town.*

Exact theft, house, town, few quotations—our hideous terror.

The word "hideous" can mean shocking or revolting to the senses. In these anagrams, Brontë states that she recorded the fraud, used the house and repeated the violent speech. As well, she reveals the fear in her home as she witnessed the terror at the hands of a few lawless men. The entire anagram reads as follows:

British Isle poet away. Had ink, tat, fog. Now talk. Say heed a warning: Den web in deed; Selfishly abuse brethren: inhuman north region. Urn debts in nice Mrs. Reed; coy pen warns heath women: earn yield. Wanted wuthering childbirth. Two to cross blood. Hid muse— Tenant organ in paradise. Exact theft, house, town, few quotations—our hideous terror.

Brontë wants her readers to know the truth about *Wuthering Heights* whose origins, she says, began with the Masons' *"den web"*. She refers to this deed swindle over and over in the anagrams.

She works hard to tell us stories about the Masons and, without actual proof, her claims must be judged accordingly, but she obviously believed a *"hideous terror"* was a constant threat. She states that she used the *"exact theft, house, town"* and a *"few quotations,"* which would explain the origins for the coarse language. The exact house could be Well Head, as stated in a separate anagram.

Her anagram acuity enables her to break free of her sense of paralysis and to attack the men through her secret fiction, and even to seize surreptitiously some of the chief Mason's power. Like Jane escaping through the pages of a book, Brontë escapes from her social limitations through her writing and her anagrams.

Gradually, Brontë's collection of tools carves out a secret code. She draws the reader's attention to the opening paragraphs in *Jane Eyre* to show that, amid a dismally grey atmosphere, her movements are restricted, and her time is spent endlessly dealing with the torment whose origins began two books earlier in *Wuthering Heights*.

Brontë provides another strong link to *Wuthering Heights* and its authorship through three watercolours that Jane Eyre painted before she met Rochester. Scholars interpret the paintings in chapter thirteen as pictorial references to Jane's relationship to Rochester, but disagree as to the symbolic meanings of the images and fail to find a conclusive analysis that definitively fits the characters and the plots.

The disparity in analysis comes from their initial interpretation: they believe that the paintings are about *Jane Eyre* when they actually refer to *Wuthering Heights*.

The Cormorant

Brontë describes the first painting: "The first represented clouds low and livid, rolling over a swollen sea" where a cormorant sits on a half-submerged mast, holding a gold and jewelled bracelet in its beak that has been torn from the wrist of a drowned woman's corpse that floats below the water. Scholars agree that the cormorant is an image Brontë has borrowed from *Paradise Lost* as Satan surveys Eden before tempting Eve: "Thence up he flew, and on the Tree of Life, / The middle tree and highest there that grew, / Sat like a cormorant; yet not true life / Thereby regained, but sat devising death / To them who lived."

Cormorants are described as insatiably greedy or voracious gluttons, so the image of a greedy devil taking valuables off of corpses would coincide with Brontë's description of the Masons stealing land from dying men and leaving the families paupers. Jane adds that "one gleam of light lifted [the image] into relief," which implies that Brontë wants to shine a light on their crimes.

The suggestion of a shipwreck mirrors the devastation and destruction not only in the Haworth Township but also in *Wuthering Heights* where the image of a storm recurs with terms like "stormy scene" and "domestic storm." Lockwood even describes the dog attack against him as a storm and the housekeeper Zillah as "heaving like a sea after a high wind" as she shouts at the dogs to disperse.

The Wild Woman

Brontë begins her description of the next watercolour with the words, "The second picture contained for foreground only the dim peak of a hill." Rising into the sky is a woman's shape to her bust, with her clothes barely seen through "the suffusion of a vapour." Her "eyes shone dark and wild; the hair streamed shadowy, like a beamless cloud torn by storm or by electric travail," and on her forehead is the vision of "the Evening Star."

The Evening Star and Morning Star are terms for the planet Venus because it can appear in both the morning and evening skies. The Masons represent it as a five-pointed star on their regalia and in their Lodges, and refer to it as an emblem of divine light in their third degree ritual. Today, many Lodges are called either Morning Star Lodge or Evening Star Lodge.

This painting of a wild woman with streaming hair and a body surrounded by vapour could be an image of Heathcliff's wife Isabella immersed in the ubiquitous mist of Masonry. "On the neck lay a pale reflection like moonlight; the same faint lustre touched the train of thin clouds from which rose and bowed this vision of the Evening Star."

After a torrent of scornful abuse and violence from her husband—the "electric travail"—Isabella manages to escape from Wuthering Heights. In a terrible winter storm, she rushes to the safety of Thrushcross Grange where she describes to Nelly, the housekeeper, how she fled from a terrifying scene of violence and attempted murder during her imprisonment at the Heights. Nelly uses Jane's exact words—"hair streamed"—when she refers to Isabella's frantic, wild state: "her hair streamed on her shoulders, dripping with snow and water," and she had "a deep cut under one ear, which only the cold prevented from bleeding profusely."

In Jane's drawing, the "pale reflection like moonlight" on the neck could be the outline of a scar. Nelly ends the description with the words "a white face scratched and bruised, and a frame hardly able to support itself, through fatigue." If we read the painting in Masonic terms, Isabella has been living among the Masons, enveloped in their Satanic vapour, floating without support, and branded with an actual emblem of Freemasonry—the Evening Star. Brontë's use of the name "Evening Star" in this watercolour seems more than coincidental.

A Colossal Head

The third painting depicts a "colossal head" leaning against an iceberg. Brontë begins by saying, "The third showed the pinnacle of an iceberg piercing a polar winter sky," and "in the foreground, a head—a colossal head inclined towards the iceberg." A pair of thin hands supports the forehead and lifts a sable veil that reveals the features: "a brow quite bloodless, white as bone, and an eye hollow and fixed, blank of meaning but for the glassiness of despair." The head is wreathed in black drapery with a ring of fire that fits around it like a headband: it "was 'the likeness of a kingly crown;' what it diademed was the shape which shape had none." She quotes directly from Book Two of *Paradise Lost* where Milton describes Death: "The other shape, / If shape it might be call'd that shape had none / Distinguishable in member, joint, or limb . . . what seem'd his head / The likeness of a Kingly Crown had on" (666-673).

This image of a colossal head fits Brontë's descriptions of Heathcliff, especially when she refers to his character in her preface to the 1850 edition of *Wuthering Heights*. She describes the process of creating Heathcliff as if his character had been carved from a granite stone hewn into a "colossal, dark, and frowning half statue, half rock . . . terrible and goblin-like." The cold, fixed eye with its glassiness of despair conjures images of Heathcliff, draped in grief, mourning Catherine's death, with his eyes "fixed on the red embers of the fire" (ch.29), and his "deep dark eyes . . . and ghastly paleness," that Nelly says resemble a "goblin" (ch.34). The air around his house is "cold as impalpable ice" (ch.3), and inside everyone is always cold or catching cold. The thin hands that lift a sable veil in the painting could be Brontë's own fingers lifting a dark, wolfish fur that hides the truth of the bloodless form. This head, the Master of the Masons, like Death, brings only cold and despair to everyone around him, and the "hands," "brow," and "eye," remind us of the "eyes," "brow," and "fingers" in the opening paragraph of *Wuthering Heights*.

In *Paradise Lost*, Milton places Hell on a frozen continent. This place of ice "lies dark and wild, beat with perpetual storms," even though fire parches the air. The inhabitants are damned to revolve in an endless cycle of alternating fire and ice, "to starve in Ice," and feel regret over their evil deeds. While Brontë's colossal head stays submerged in ice, a fire crowns its head to echo the image of Milton's hell.

Brontë uses specific verbs to introduce each painting. The first painting *represents* greed, with the cormorant as its focal point; the second painting *contains* a woman with an Evening Star emblazoned on her forehead and a vapour circling round her body; the third painting *shows* a cold, bloodless beast in hell, crowned as the King of Death. This is exactly what she describes in *Wuthering Heights*: the novel *represents* the Masonic greed in Heathcliff's callous pursuit of ownership of Wuthering Heights and Thrushcross Grange; it *contains* the characters who must bear the brutality, and these characters are literally contained, as in confined, at the Heights; the novel also *shows* the evil head or master of the "Institution" perpetrating the cruelty and fraud in the actions of Heathcliff. The watercolours are describing *Wuthering Heights*, not events in *Jane Eyre*, which explains why scholars are unable to make a firm assessment of the paintings' symbolic meaning.

Jane Eyre explains to Rochester when she painted these watercolours and how she felt at the time.

"'I did them in the last two vacations I spent at Lowood, when I had no other occupation.'"

Brontë spent Easter and the autumn vacations on her own at Brussels in 1843 when her anagrams say she wrote *Wuthering Heights*.

"'Were you happy when you painted these pictures?' asked Mr. Rochester presently.

"'I was absorbed, sir: yes, and I was happy. To paint them, in short, was to enjoy one of the keenest pleasures I have ever known. . . . I had nothing else to do, because it was the vacation, and I sat at them from morning till noon, and from noon till night: the length of the midsummer days favoured my inclination to apply.'

"'And you felt self-satisfied with the result of your ardent labours?'

"'Far from it. I was tormented by the contrast between my idea and my handiwork: in each case I had imagined something which I was quite powerless to realise.'"

Perhaps Brontë is unable to duplicate the corruption and violence as realistically as she would like. The fear of being caught limits her depiction of the truth: she is powerless and unable to name the perpetrators. She could also be referring to her sense of powerlessness in her ability to change the outcome for the residents of her community: in

Wuthering Heights, the legal descendants are reinstated in the land of their ancestry while, in real life, Brontë is unable to orchestrate the same happy ending for the disinherited in her township.

Mount Latmos

Rochester identifies the peak in the Evening Star painting as Mount Latmos, which refers to the myth of Endymion and the goddess Diana. Endymion is a shepherd on Latmos who captivates the goddess with his beauty. Diana then asks Zeus to put the shepherd in a state of perpetual sleep, so she can gaze at his beauty forever.

The poet John Keats took this myth and cast it in a different light. He emphasizes Endymion's love for Diana and his quest to find an ideal love in a union that can never be destroyed: "A thing of beauty is a joy forever / its loveliness increases; it will never / pass into nothingness . . . / some shape of beauty moves away the pall / from our dark spirits."

Brontë represents this romantic view in her early writings and borrows marked similarities from those earlier ventures when, in *Wuthering Heights*, she continues to explore themes of jealousy and revenge.

In her earlier juvenile work, passionate lovers metaphorically murder each other through jealousy, and dead lovers swear to haunt the living lover from the grave, but in *Wuthering Heights* she distorts the passion and obsessive desire when she exaggerates Heathcliff's crazed quest to be with his idealized love, the dead Catherine.

The watercolours help us to see how Brontë employs an intricate system of code to communicate her message in all three books. The three den books culminate in Jane's story, which refers back to aspects of *Wuthering Heights* in the drawings Jane shows Rochester.

Brontë also includes more secrets in the drawings contained in *A History of British Birds*, the book Jane studies, in chapter one, while sequestered on the window-seat behind the curtain, pictures that Brontë hints require a second look.

Seven Illustrations

Brontë guides the reader to the illustrations as Jane explains her interest in the book. She says, "there were certain introductory pages that, child as I was, I could not pass quite as a blank." Perhaps she is telling the reader not to pass by the descriptions of those seven pictures from the bird book. Would these illustrations in Bewick's book be much more than a blank rendering and actually contain important information that reveals more allusions to *Wuthering Heights*? After describing the seven pictures, Jane adds the following words: "Each picture told a story; mysterious often to my undeveloped understanding and imperfect feelings, yet ever profoundly interesting." Brontë is saying, in plain view, that "each picture told a story," that, with a developed understanding of her method, readers will be able to discover something "profoundly interesting."

Through Jane, Brontë provides another clue: "With Bewick on my knee, I was then happy: happy at least in my way." Jane's way of being happy resembles William Crimsworth's as he sits in the counting house translating English into German under the watchful eye of the clerk who is unable to "read" William's character. Brontë plays with the word "character" as William compares characters or letters written in a foreign language to his own inscrutable character: the clerk "might see lines, and trace characters, but he could make nothing of them—my nature was not his nature, and its signs were to him like the words of an unknown tongue." Both William and Jane elicit happiness from knowing that, in their own particular way, they can conceal their true sentiment while engaged in a task or a pastime that involves the studying of characters on a page.

In *Wuthering Heights*, in chapter three, Lockwood has a different reaction to the characters written on the ledge of his enclosed bed. Before seeing Catherine's ghost, Lockwood finds her "name repeated in all kinds of characters, large and small," and later, while reading through her diary, he tries "to decypher her faded hieroglyphics" in order to learn more about her character. In each case, something is being concealed through the "characters," so one must ask what foreign or peculiar language, distinctly her own, has Brontë placed in the lines on the pages of *Jane Eyre* that would give her an equivalent feeling of happiness? The most likely answer would be that she has concealed anagrams inside the descriptions of the seven pictures, and that the reader must solve the character puzzle in order to see what story each picture reveals.

Anagrams in the Illustrations

The prose describing the seven illustrations is separated by an oblique slash to display the break for the anagram, but the opening words to the first comma that end with "vignettes" will have two or three words shifted in order for the anagram to make sense.

"The words in these introductory pages / connected themselves / with the succeeding vignettes, / and gave significance to / the rock standing up alone / in a sea of billow and spray; / to the broken boat stranded /on a desolate coast; / to the cold and ghastly moon glancing / through bars of cloud / at a wreck just sinking." After describing these three pictures she adds a fourth: "I cannot tell what sentiment haunted / the quite solitary churchyard, / with its inscribed headstone; / its gate, / its two trees, / its low horizon, / girdled by a broken wall, / and its newly-risen crescent, / attesting the hour of even-tide." The next three descriptions complete the pictures: "The two ships becalmed on a torpid sea, / I believed to be marine phantoms. / The fiend pinning down the thief's pack behind him, / I passed over quickly: / it was an object of terror. / So was the black, / horned thing seated aloof on a rock, / surveying a distant crowd surrounding a gallows."

Initially, the anagram of the line ending in "vignettes" does not make sense until the words shift: *See odd* Wuthering Heights *story. Into chapters / etch den's venom. Select / heights vices. Intent: cut wedge.* After the minor adjustments, the anagram reads as follows and continues into the next anagram:

See odd Wuthering Heights *story. Select vices. Cut wedge. Etch den's venom into chapters. Intent: can evade gag in fictions.*

Brontë etches the Masonic story into *Wuthering Heights* and, appropriately, uses a common wood cut—the wedge, as her metaphor: the Masons form a wedge in the community with their vices, but she can employ a similar tactic by wedging their crimes into her plot. In this way, she avoids the gag placed around her mouth by "speaking out" in her novels.

The next line also improves with a small shift: *Test London chap. Kin argue / as foil. Noisy wand parable*, improves and becomes *Test London chap foil as kin argue. Noisy wand parable.* Brontë refers to Lockwood as the foil who sets off the bad traits of the others. The Masons use wands or rods during their ceremonies, and a parable conveys a moral lesson. The piece of information in the next anagram introduces an additional way that Masonic material became available to Brontë before she left for Brussels. *Brethren donated books. Located tat. / Soon at sea.* "Tat" is something cheap or vulgar and is also used in the first line anagram of the novel: she *had ink, tat, fog* when she travelled to Brussels.

Together, the anagrams read as follows:

See odd Wuthering Heights *story. Select vices. Cut wedge. Etch den's venom into chapters. Intent: can evade gag in fictions. Test London chap foil as kin argue. Noisy wand parable. Brethren donated books. Located tat. Soon at sea.*

Next, Brontë describes the Masonic method of duping unsuspecting landowners and continues to mention aspects of the plot in *Wuthering Heights.*

Got an old man on lodge night. Sly catch. / Crush bug. Had loot for / gin jars. Wink. Take cuts. / Document hint in tenant's tale. / They acquire child trust. Hoary wealth. The word "wealth" has been moved to the second half of the anagram. "Hoary" means ancient. Heathcliff acquires his son's trust through the will and young Cathy's trust through marriage, trusts that represent wealth that has been in the Earnshaw and Linton families for generations; thus, Heathcliff acquires ancient or hoary riches.

Brontë refers to herself as a "*heretic dissenter*" in the next anagram, to the way the Masons "*wangle*" or achieve money fraudulently, and to the Mason fights or rows with "*hilts*", the handles on their daggers or knives. The fights require mops in order to clean up the blood. They avoid future blame as they hide or "*hood*" the crime or "*case,*" and no one speaks of it because of the metaphorical "*gag*" around witnesses like herself.

Now heretic dissenter's habit / is get at / twits. See rot / in zoo. Hilt rows / kill. Add robbery, wangle / rent, swindle, tenancy crises, / vendetta, if en route *to Heights. / Chaps poison elder's haw tea. Omit debt, / inherit. Obviate blame. Need mops: / men open inn, fight, bind hands, whip feet. Thick hide. / Vices equip York lads / for twit careers, not a job. / Task: show cable. / Errand: tie knot, hang fool, hood case. / Want ground. Very sadistic. Gag is worn round us all.*

When combined, the anagrams in the seven illustrations read as follows:

See odd Wuthering Heights *story. Select vices. Cut wedge. Etch den's venom into chapters. Intent: can evade gag in fictions. Test London chap foil as kin argue. Noisy wand parable. Brethren donated books. Located tat. Soon at sea. Got an old man on lodge night. Sly catch. Crush bug. Had loot for gin jars. Wink. Take cuts. Document hint in tenant's tale They acquire child trust. Hoary wealth. Now heretic dissenter's habit is get at twits. See rot in zoo. Hilt rows kill. Add robbery, wangle rent, swindle, tenancy crises, vendetta, if* en route *to Heights. Chaps poison elder's haw tea. Omit debt, inherit. Obviate blame. Need mops: men open inn, fight, bind hands, whip feet. Thick hide. Vices equip York lads for twit careers, not a job. Task: show cable. Errand: tie knot, hang fool, hood case. Want ground. Very sadistic. Gag is worn round us all.*

The anagrams hidden in her description of the seven illustrations in the bird book, like the three drawings Jane shows to Rochester, present another method Brontë uses to communicate facts that she believed, if the truth could surface, would prove "profoundly interesting" to a reader. Her ability to leave clues and hints in so many unique and clever ways demonstrates her intelligence and her determination.

She also weaves allusions to Shakespeare and *Paradise Lost* into the novels, and through symbols, phrases, and anagrams links the three stories to Freemasonry and its allegorical and symbolic system. Wedged inside all of this is her story of a few thieves intent on a life of violence and corruption. Her choice of the words "*cut*", "*wedge*", and "*etch*" is especially fascinating because these anagrams are hidden under the words describing the illustrations from Bewick's 1816 book. The title page of that book reads *A History of British Birds*: "The Figures Engraved on Wood by T. Bewick, Vol I., Containing the History and Description of Land Birds." Thomas Bewick was a craftsman who developed the art of wood engraving, which involved preparing hard wood with wedge cuts before etching in the intricate details. The illustrations, therefore, are not drawings but etchings, and Brontë has used this model as a metaphor for her narrative in *Wuthering Heights* where she etches out her own history of a peculiar flock of Haworth land birds.

345

Brontë's code consistently conveys a deep tragedy that surrounded and affected her life and home. Her desire to communicate her reality could only be achieved by keeping herself partially concealed behind the mask of fiction. Her incomparably precise and original layering of clues and her "consistent principles of transcription" demonstrate her sense of fair play. She wanted her readers to notice her patterns of symmetry between the top layer and the hidden anagram story because the woven fictional structure guides the reader deeper to the land fraud, which leads directly to her private truth.

Without understanding the Masonic connection in the novels, readers can never know the real Charlotte Brontë. So much of her truth is woven into the Masonic legend and the corrupt activities of a few lawless men that she believes are committing fraud. The fictions were her resource for exposing their crimes, so in order to have an accurate and more complete picture of this literary genius the reader must learn the rest of her secrets.

37 AUNT BRANWELL

As in *Jane Eyre*, anagrams also appear in the first paragraph of *Wuthering Heights* and reveal secrets about Brontë's personal life. The opening sentence is, "I have just returned from a visit to my landlord—the solitary neighbour that I shall be troubled with." The anagram of the section before the dash reveals a startling secret that, if true, helps explain the impetus for Brontë's writing of the novel in 1843. Not only is she angry with the Masons over a land swindle but also over a murder in Haworth that had appeared as a natural death. The anagram for "I have just returned from a visit to my landlord" reads, *Am livid over aunt's murder. Jot land thief story.*

The aunt she refers to would logically be her Aunt Branwell who died October 29th, 1842. Their aunt "had always enjoyed uniformly good health," but she died unexpectedly (Barker 403). The cause was listed as "exhaustion from constipation" (qtd. in Du Maurier 156), which means she endured "unspeakable agony" (156). Emily and Charlotte were at school in Brussels and Anne was a governess at Thorp Green. The two elder sisters had left home in 1842 to study French because all three sisters were still considering opening a school for girls. With the women away from home, the only people in the house, aside from Aunt Branwell, were their father, the twelve-year-old servant Martha Brown, and Branwell who had been at the parsonage since March after being fired from his job as stationmaster.

He had been employed since April of 1841, but while a stationmaster at Luddenden Foot railway station, the accounts failed to reconcile. He went before the company auditors to explain the discrepancy: "the price of the tickets sold did not tally with the sums received. Closer examination of the ledger showed haphazard entries." The ticket collector who worked with Branwell admitted, "the station master had often been absent from duty. Neither could explain what happened to the missing money. Theft was not proved, but careless book-keeping was" (Du Maurier 143). He was fired because, as Juliet Barker explains, "Whatever the rights and wrongs of the matter, Branwell was responsible, morally and officially, for the missing money. The sum was deducted from his quarter's salary, his dismissal was confirmed by a meeting of the board of directors on 4

March, and Branwell found himself unemployed once more" (375). Now, back home for over half a year, Branwell worked on his poetry, but was in need of money.

A great deal of unrest was occurring in the Haworth area at this time because mill owners were industrializing with machinery, and needed fewer men in their work force. As in earlier years, laid off factory workers, poor from unemployment or lower wages, weak from starvation and sickness revolted against the mill owners and tried to destroy the machines. Riots and anger sparked violence, so the men of Haworth were made temporary constables and Branwell volunteered his services. The excitement and camaraderie would ignite his pugilistic temper and break the monotony of unemployment, but the temporary nature of the revolt failed to offset his depression.

During this time, while his father and Aunt Branwell were at church, he wrote a friend he had met at Luddenden Foot station. He is alone, "the sole occupant of an ancient parsonage among lonely hills." He admits, "After experiencing, since my return home, extreme pain and illness, with mental depression worse than either, I have at length acquired health and strength and soundness of mind, far superior, I trust, to anything shown by that miserable wreck you used to know under my name. I can now speak cheerfully and enjoy the company of another without the stimulus of six glasses of whisky," and he is happy to be writing again. "But I feel my recovery from *almost insanity* to be retarded by having nothing to listen to except the wind moaning among old chimneys and older ash trees, nothing to look at except heathery hills walked over when life had all to hope for and nothing to regret with me" (Barker 397). He appears to be on the mend, but if anything were to happen to exacerbate his sadness, he would sink back into his despair and need money for his alcohol or opium. Unfortunately, just such an incident occurred a month before Aunt Branwell's death: In early September, Reverend Brontë's well-loved curate and Branwell's friend William Weightman died of cholera

In an October 25th letter, he wrote, "I have had a long attendance at the deathbed of the Rev. Mr. Weightman, one of my dearest friends, and now I am attending at the deathbed of my aunt, who has been for twenty years as my mother. I expect her to die in a few hours. As my sisters are far from home, I have had much on my mind, and these things must serve as an apology for what was never intended as neglect of your friendship to us" (*Letters, Vol.I* 294). When his aunt died, Branwell wrote a letter saying he was stricken with grief over her death: "I am incoherent, I fear, but I have been waking two nights witnessing such agonising suffering as I would not wish my worst enemy to endure; and I have now lost the guide and director of all the happy days connected with my childhood. I have suffered such sorrow since I last saw you at Haworth" (295). His grief sounds genuine but, if he thought otherwise, would he have spoken ill of the dead by calling her "a despotic, unpleasant, and narrow-minded spinster," which was "the usual view" held of his Aunt (Barker 404). While living at the bleak parsonage, Branwell had to deal with the horror of his friend's death; he had been unemployed for months, without prospects, was depressed, and needed money. For a drug addict these conditions would spell disaster: he would need money and, without a ready supply of funds, would try to find a way to get it.

Aunt Branwell had completed her will in 1833. The sisters and their cousin—Aunt Branwell's niece—together with Branwell shared the inheritance. Each of the three girls received "an equal share in their aunt's estate" which amounted to approximately £300. This money enabled them to cancel their plans for a girls' school. Emily chose to remain at the parsonage with their father, while Charlotte returned to Brussels as a teacher. Branwell did not receive any financial inheritance: his aunt left him a "dressing case," which could signify that he was expected to earn his own living (409). By Christmas, he had left the parsonage with Anne to work as a tutor to young Edmund Robinson at Thorp Green where Anne was a governess. In less than three years Mr. Robinson would fire Branwell demanding that he "break off instantly and for ever all communication with every member of his family" (*Letters, Vol.I* 412).

If the anagram is correct and Charlotte's aunt was murdered, the likely suspect would be Branwell. This is entire speculation, but he may have deduced he was a beneficiary in his aunt's will and, desperate for money, decided to end her life with arsenic. He believed she would be dead within hours, but her death lasted four more agonizing days. If the anagram of 1829 is true, Branwell had been stealing and drinking for some time before his aunt drew up her will. She may have thought he would be earning his own living and, therefore, would not require her financial assistance, or she knew his character and withdrew any support that would have been wasted on his addictions. Her reputation as a stern woman would not have set well with Branwell, even though he may have had fond memories of her from his childhood. He was now an adult, and he needed money, so in a moment of weakness he may have committed the unthinkable. Poison could have been the cause of her severe intestinal pain.

One Brontë biographer stated that when Charlotte and Emily returned home from Brussels, Branwell was gone. Aunt Branwell had been buried in early November, and Anne had been notified at Thorp Green of her Aunt's illness and arrived at the parsonage in time for the funeral. When Charlotte and Emily got home, "they found Mr. Brontë and Anne sitting together, quietly mourning the customary presence to be known no more. Branwell was not there. It was the first time he would see his sisters since his great disgrace; he could not wait at home to welcome them" (Robinson ch.8). He may have left home due to the shame, not only of being fired from his job in March but also of a more serious disgrace.

In his earlier letter written while he is the "sole occupant of an ancient parsonage" he recollected his time at Luddenden Foot station. He wrote that the quiet of Haworth made a striking contrast from the terrible year he had spent at Luddenden Foot: "for I would rather give my hand than undergo again the grovelling carelessness, the malignant, yet cold debauchery, the determination to find out how far mind could carry body without both being chucked into hell, which too often marked my conduct when there, lost as I was to all I really liked, and seeking relief in the indulgence of feelings which form the blackest spot in my character" (Du Maurier 132).

If Branwell were the redheaded lad employed to forge signatures, he would know about the poisoning of drinks. In "And the Weary are at Rest," his unfinished novel, his alter ego Percy says, "I am, if as innocent looking as arsenic—just as dangerous." Branwell knew what arsenic could do when dropped into a cup of tea.

Aunt Branwell was considered a healthy woman but, suddenly, she became ill and her intestinal organs stopped working, showing signs of someone who had been poisoned. The doctor diagnosed her death as a bowel obstruction, but Charlotte must have known the real cause. Branwell left Haworth to work at Thorp Green, as did Anne; Emily remained at the parsonage to be with her father. When Charlotte returned to Brussels to work at the Pensionnat Heger she wrote *Wuthering Heights*.

The first sentence of *Wuthering Heights* continues: "I have just returned from a visit to my landlord—the solitary neighbour that I shall be troubled with. *Am livid over aunt's murder. Jot land thief story.* The second section as an anagram reads, *Double letter habit is Haworth author's nightly bile.* Her ill-humour and anger fuel the passion necessary to tell the whole story through the surface prose and the hidden anagrams.

The last sentence of the opening paragraph begins with the words, "He little imagined how" and ends with "I announced my name." If Brontë is suggesting that she has hidden her name inside the paragraph, the most likely place would be the second sentence that starts "This is:" "This is certainly a beautiful country." The reader can little imagine how she introduces herself. The anagram of "this is certainly a beautiful country" is *I, tiny Charlotte, certify unusual bias.* Right at the beginning of the book, after she has explained her motives for putting the story to paper, she certifies her bias towards the Masons and verifies her facts outlined in the novel. She testifies in writing that, even though her story may be biased, weighted on one side, she attests to its truths.

Her word "bias" may not be an arbitrary choice. An initiate into Freemasonry has to declare that he comes to the brotherhood unbiased by friends or uninfluenced by money. The initiate's motives have to be sincere and impartial. Brontë ironically declares that her report is entirely biased, and not in a good way. Her novel and her "*land thief story*" are her private version of *J'accuse.* She is accusing the Masons of their crimes and getting out her nightly bile by hiding her revelations in her anagrams.

The next line requires a small manipulation from one section to another, which is allowed if no comma encloses the phrase or clause. The line is "In all England I do not believe that I could have fixed on a situation so completely removed from the stir of society." A comfortable break comes approximately half way, after the word "fixed." Until the two sections are properly placed together, the line is grammatically incorrect. The anagram under this first part of the line is: *heath novel about dividing an old entail excel filed.* The second half of the sentence hides these words: *masons at terror use mythic voodoo if notice life empty stole.* When

351

the two parts are arranged correctly, the line reads, *Novel about dividing an old entail. Masons excel at terror. Use mythic voodoo. If notice filed, life empty. Stole heath.* For her, the Masons exploit their power together with the force of their clan gangs to terrorize people into silence, and use arsenic to "cure" their ill brothers in order to precipitate an early death and divide an ancient entail. The notice could be eviction papers or a letter notifying the family that the mortgage was due to be fully paid. Either way, the debtor's life would now be *empty* of prospects or hope.

The anagrams in all three den stories consistently refer to the Masons and their crimes and explain her desire for anonymity. As mentioned above, in her letter from April 1848 to William Smith Williams, her publisher's assistant, she explains her rationale for keeping a pseudonym,

She tells him Currer Bell "is the only name I wish to have mentioned in connection with my writings. 'Currer Bell' only—I am and will be to the Public; if accident or design should deprive me of that name, I should deem it a misfortune—a very great one; mental tranquility would then be gone; it would be a task to write—a task which I doubt whether I could continue. If I were known—I should ever be conscious in writing that my book must be read by ordinary acquaintances—and that idea would fetter me intolerably" (*Letters, Vol.II* 51). The acquaintances she feared would most likely have been the Haworth Masons, especially if one of them ever found the key to her anagrams.

Also, as stated above, she wrote to Williams, in a similar vein to relate her feelings about anonymity: "What author would be without the advantage of being able to walk invisible? One is thereby enabled to keep such a quiet mind" (4).

These accounts of her feelings are repeated because they are at the heart of her decision to protect her identity through pseudonyms. She wanted her privacy in order to tell the truth without reprisals. The magnitude of her design is overwhelming as are her efforts to expose her version of events. William Smith Williams had no way of knowing, but Brontë left him anagrams in certain portions of her letters. She also concealed anagrams in her letters to Ellen Nussey, where, in correspondence to Williams and Ellen, she reverts to her youthful habit and confides yet more startling truths about Branwell.

38 BRANWELL'S DISGRACE

The Reverend Edmund Robinson of Thorp Green Hall employed Branwell as tutor for his son from January 1843 to July of 1845, a two and a half year period during which time the twenty-six-year-old Branwell writes of being drawn into an affair with the man's wife. According to Branwell, his employer was wealthy, and his wife Lydia was the sister-in-law of a Member of Parliament for the county of Derbyshire, so they had property and prestige. He describes Lydia Robinson as "a pretty woman, about 37, with a darkish skin & bright glancing eyes." The lady was actually seventeen years older than Branwell, which would make her forty-three. In May of 1843, he wrote to his friend John Brown about the new love in his life: "I curl my hair & scent my handkerchief like a Squire—I am the favourite of all the household—my master is generous—but my mistress is DAMNABLY TOO FOND OF ME." He explains that the husband is ill and that the lady desires they take the relationship to the next level of intimacy (Barker 459).

The relationship may have been the reason for Branwell being fired in July of 1845. One rumour states that the gardener Robert Pottage discovered him in the boathouse with Lydia Robinson and felt it his duty to report the liaison to Mr. Robinson (Barker 468). The relationship showed no impact upon the husband's treatment of his wife: "the revelation of the affair led to no breach with his wife. He remained as open-handed with her as he had always been, even during the holiday in Scarborough when he must have taken his decision to sack Branwell," which "suggests that Mrs. Robinson was able to divert her husband's anger onto Branwell and depict herself as the innocent and unwilling recipient of his attentions." Barker goes on to say that another option is "that there really was no affair and that Branwell was dismissed for some other reason" even though, in Barker's estimation, the evidence does not support this view (468).

Other explanations for his firing were that the son Edmund revealed to his father that his tutor "had made homosexual advances to him, that he indulged in drunken excess, or that he had forged Mr. Robinson's signature in order to obtain money" (*Letters, Vol.I* n. 11).

Three months after his dismissal, in October of 1845, Branwell recounts the experience to his friend Francis Grundy. "This lady (though her husband detested me) showed me a degree of kindness which, when I was deeply grieved one day at her husband's conduct, ripened into declarations of more than ordinary feeling. My admiration of her mental and personal attractions, my knowledge of her unselfish sincerity, her sweet temper, and unwearied care for others, with but unrequited return where most should have been given, . . . although she is seventeen years my senior, all combined to an attachment on my part, and led to reciprocations which I had little looked for. During nearly three years I had daily 'troubled pleasure, soon chastised by fear.' Three months since I received a furious letter from my employer, threatening to shoot me if I returned from my vacation, which I was passing at home; and letters from her lady's-maid and physician informed me of the outbreak, only checked by her firm courage and resolution that whatever harm came to her, none should come to me. . . . I have lain during nine long weeks utterly shattered in body and broken down in mind. . . . I have striven to arouse my mind by writing something worthy of being read, but I really cannot do so. Of course you will despise the writer of all this. I can only answer that the writer does the same, and would not wish to live if he did not hope that work and change may yet restore him." Branwell ends the letter by apologizing for his "whining egotism" (*Letters Vol.I* 428).

Edmund Robinson dismissed Branwell abruptly on July 17, 1845. Of all the rumours, the reason most often given for firing Branwell is that the husband found out about his wife's infidelity, wrote the scathing letter, and had it sent immediately from York to Haworth to ensure that Branwell did not return to his employ following his vacation. Branwell may have had an affair with Lydia Robinson and escaped a criminal charge simply because court proceedings would have necessarily publicized the adultery and, inevitably, ruined reputations. Also, Mr. Robinson was not a well man, so a swift dismissal would be preferable to a lengthy scandal reported and circulated in the press, but Charlotte recounts to Ellen that Mr. Robinson demanded that "on pain of exposure" Branwell must "break off" communication with his family (412). He was threatening to expose Branwell, which would also necessarily expose his wife; thus, if he began proceedings, the story would be told, and he would forever damage his wife's reputation. The Brontë biographer Rebecca Fraser supports this view: The words regarding exposure, "suggest that Mr. Robinson considered only Branwell to be at fault, since he presumably would not want to expose his own wife" (238).

Fraser also states that Branwell was probably deluded about the relationship. "Opinion has generally tended to disbelieve Branwell's version of events as the ravings of a consummate fantasist and liar; the combination of the dearth of independent evidence, the unlikely nature of the liaison and all the bizarre subsequent episodes have tended to convince that the greater part of the 'affair' took place only in his imagination" (231). Mr. Robinson's relationship with his wife appeared normal after he fired Branwell, so perhaps his version of a deep, enduring love was just unfettered imaginings; therefore, exposing Branwell's misconduct involved telling a story that had nothing to do with Lydia Robinson; consequently, the explanation regarding the forging of Mr. Robinson's signature warrants closer consideration.

Juliet Barker states that one explanation for his firing was a rumour that Branwell may have used "his undoubted skills in handwriting to forge his employer's signature" (456). The story that follows alludes to a brand of fraud and thievery that Branwell may have learned in Haworth under the tutelage of a few Masons. In November of 1843, while working at Thorp Green, he wrote to John Brown; an extract of that letter survives in another man's account. He begins by quoting Branwell:

"'I know you think I drink, but the time is past when I could hold out against you all. I take no wine, & brandy & water only once in the day—that is, before breakfast to enable me to face the AGONY of the day. My little lady grows thinner every day—she is full of spirit & courage, except in the thought of parting with me.' He abuses a Methodist Preacher, who is told if he says anything to damage him (B.B.) he shall be ruined & Miss Anne Marshall saw him do enough to hang him. He sends his friend a 'lock of *her* hair, which has lain on his breast—would to God it could do so *legally*!' He ends in great depression—without signature" (Barker 461).

The letter declares that Mrs. Robinson's maid, Ann Marshall had witnessed enough to get him hanged. The maid was thirty-four at the time and was Mrs. Robinson's confidante. Would Branwell be hanged for having an affair, or had the maid seen him do something far more wicked but equally shocking?

On July 4, 1843, six months after Branwell had arrived at Thorp Green, Ann Marshall began receiving promissory notes signed by Mr. Robinson that stated he owed her substantial amounts of money, which implied that he, a wealthy gentleman, had requested a loan and received funds from his maid, and that she had advanced him the said amount requested and obtained a legal document, duly prepared and executed to secure his repayment. She would receive interest on the said monies until such time as the full amount loaned would be paid to her in full. These promissory notes continued to be assigned to Ann Marshall until March 19, 1845, four months before Edmund Robinson dismissed Branwell from his employ. The notes totaled the sum of £520 and, as Barker explains, "these were not a mere formality as interest on them was paid and the total capital sum was repaid in full in 1846" (461). Edmund Robinson died in May of 1846, so the executors would have honoured the note and discharged the debt. Barker adds that it would be unlikely that the maid "would have loaned such a sum to her employers in the first place as she earned only £12 a year and would not have needed to work at all if the capital sum had been available to her. The fact that the promissory notes only relate to the period of Branwell's residence at Thorp Green inevitably gives rise to speculation that the two things were connected" (461-2). Not only did the maid receive generous payments from her employer, but "at least three others who were probably servants" received promissory notes as well, all signed by Edmund Robinson in his familiar signature (462). Dr. Mildred Christian states that Mr. Robinson had provided notes in the past: "'similar promissory notes to numerous other persons connected with Thorp Green over a long period of time are preserved in the Deed Box and appear to be connected with liabilities on the estate'" (qtd. in Fraser, 510). The maid's promissory note, therefore, may not have aroused suspicion.

The advancement of funds in a manner that suggests fraud resembles the agreements Charlotte Brontë refers to in her anagrams. Instead of surreptitiously inserting an early payout clause on a lease or mortgage document, interest charges would constitute a comfortable and fixed payment until the balance owed was repaid. If this had been going on, the maid and the other servants would have known about the swindle, and their knowledge could have ensured Branwell's imprisonment and hanging, but their collusion guaranteed secrecy, and he would have certainly benefited from the scam with a share in the plunder.

The other example of Mr. Robinson's generosity comes just before Branwell is fired. A month before they left Thorp Green, Anne received money for her work as governess, but Barker notes a discrepancy between Anne's June 11th payment of just over £3 and Branwell's receipt of £20: Anne had received £10 on May 11th, but this additional money "was owed to her since the payment of her last quarter's salary" in May. On the same day 11 June, he also advanced Branwell his quarter's salary of £20, which was not due until a few weeks later on 21 July. "It cannot have been an effective dismissal or the payment would have been only for that proportion of the salary which had been earned, as Anne's had been. Even though Mr. Robinson may have been anticipating the fact that Branwell was about to go home for a week's holiday, it still seems odd that he should have advanced the salary so early." She adds, "Mr. Robinson's reasons for taking this unusual step are not clear" (466). Perhaps, Mr. Robinson was unaware of the payment until July 17 when he fired Branwell.

In July of 1845 Charlotte wrote a letter to Ellen Nussey describing the events. The portion dealing with the events surrounding Branwell's dismissal contain revealing anagrams that explain what happened. Charlotte uses the word "fireball," a drink that Branwell had described in his fiction, made with brandy and an egg yolk. She uses the word to imply, in modern terms, that she has a bomb to drop. She also compares Branwell's inner personality to a "tiger," and describes his actions as "rash" or bold, actions that make her "numb." She calls him a "hind," which is a North England term for a farmer's servant. Outlined below are the letter's lines and then the completed anagram, followed by the exact breakdown of each section separated by the slash. The first half of the paragraph deals with the firing, but the second half, which will come after, covers a different subject.

1) "It was ten o'clock at night / 2) when I got home. / 3) I found Branwell ill. / 4) He is so often owing to his own fault. / 5) I was not therefore shocked at first / 6) but when Anne informed me / 7) of the immediate cause of his present illness / 8) I was greatly shocked. / 9) He

had last Thursday / 10) received a note from Mr. Robinson / 11) sternly dismissing him / 12) intimating that he had discovered / 13) his proceedings / 14) which he characterised / 15) as bad beyond expression / 16) and charging him on pain of exposure / 17) to break off instantly and for ever / 18) all communication / 19) with every member of his family. / 20) We have had sad work with Branwell since. / 21) He thought of nothing but stunning / 22) or drowning his distress of mind / 23) no one in the house could have rest / 24) and at last we have been obliged . . ." (412).

Light neat, cotton wick high as now emote. Nun will do fireball. Fool hit young son with a fist. Even swore. Rash. Took father's wife's credit note. Numb. Fetid thief copies her new name on note. Simulates hand. Smiles. Lady's free cash woke tiger. Sad days. Hurt health. No income for tavern. Embroiders lying. His mind imagines mistress thrived attached to hind. Enriched gossip. Cheater ached. Rich wish exposed snobbery. Aids an anagram index hoping for euphonic fantasy book draft or fervent line. Claim lunatic moon if view more mirth by shy female. In a dark bed. Chew, swallow, hit, never wash. Got both guns. Thief on hunt. Hunt gin. Find on sordid night miss. Worse: touch needle on vein. Shout, hoarse. Saw an ignoble death. Leave debt.

The breakdown of the anagram is as follows:

1) *Light neat cotton wick as* 2) *high now emote* 3) *nun will do fireball* 4) *fool hit young son with a fist. Even swore.* 5) *Rash. Took father's wife's credit note.* 6) *Numb. Fetid her new name on* 7) *note thief copies. Simulates hand. Smiles. Free* 8) *Lady's cash woke tiger* 9) *Sad days. Hurt health.* 10) *No income for tavern embroiders* 11) *lying. His mind mistress* 12) *imagines thrived attached to hind.* 13) *Enriched gossip.* 14) *Cheater ached. Rich wish* 15) *exposed snobbery. Aids an* 16) *anagram index hoping for euphonic* 17) *fantasy book draft or fervent line.* 18) *Claim lunatic moon* 19) *if view more mirth by shy female.* 20) *In a dark bed. Chew, swallow, hit. Never wash.* 21) *Got both guns. Thief on hunt. Hunt of gin.* 22) *Find on sordid night miss. Worse* 23) *touch needle on vein. Shout hoarse* 24) *Saw an ignoble death. Leave debt.*

Charlotte begins by lighting a *high* candle wick, which suggests she will be awhile telling her side of the events. According to the anagrams,

358

Branwell punched the young Edmund Robinson and swore at him. Mr. Robinson's threat to expose Branwell could be for an assault, but the crime that may have brought on the firing would be the forging of Mrs. Robinson's *new name* on the credit note. The *free* and available cash would awaken Branwell's darker side, and the temptation would be too great to resist. The story of an affair between a *lady* and a *hind* appears to be a *fantasy* imagined in Branwell's mind. Charlotte momentarily revels in his romantic delusions, and blames the *lunatic moon*, referring to the belief that a full moon intensifies insanity—the word lunatic is derived from lunar. In this case, however, Charlotte is the lunatic for finding his delusions humorous. His wish to be with a rich lady *exposed* his *snobbery*, and the wild imaginings of a relationship would add ideas to her *anagram index* when she needs a *euphonic fantasy* for a *book draft or* for a *fervent line.*

The *mirth* gradually fades with the image of Branwell lying *in a dark bed.* Depressed and without money, he can barely sustain himself, but he still has sufficient energy to get his pair of guns and hunt for gin and obtain his drugs. The hunting image could have inspired Brontë to call the dissolute husband in *The Tenant of Wildfell Hall* Arthur Huntingdon. In the last anagram, Charlotte pictures Branwell's *ignoble death.* The thought of him leaving his family in debt shifts her mood. The second half of the letter continues:

1) ". . . to send him from home for a week 2) with someone to look after him. 3) He has written to me this morning 4) and expresses some sense of contrition 5) for his frantic folly. 6) He promises amendment on his return 7) but so long as he remains at home 8) I scarce dare hope 9) for peace in the house. 10) We must all I fear 11) prepare for a season 12) of distress and disquietude. 13) When I left you I was strongly impressed 14) with the feeling that I 15) was going back to sorrow."

This anagram returns to the subject of her aunt's death, the woman who was like a mother to the Brontë children. As Charlotte considers Branwell's *ignoble death,* she recalls the earlier grief, and decides, with the protection of her anagram *hood,* to relate the facts sooner than later. She provides hints, and the image of a *stiff corn* on her aunt's foot suggests this may have been a well-known cause of discomfort for their aunt.

Hood makes me free of mirth now. No time. Who took a mother's life?
Mother hints here: Woman sitting—senses monster near. Feeds toxic
poison. Frail, holy, stiff corn. Aim: spend her mementos. Not heir. Runs.
Blames her anguish on tomatoes. Reaper chose acid. If see on her tea
pouch, fault one wiser, safe male: Papa's error added fires. Son quit
studies. Why swindle, poison? Get flimsy treasure. Fight, whine, eat, hit.
Let work go. Now a crass bigot.

Only anagrams 10 and 11 needed a shift between the two sections:
10) We must all I fear *fault wiser male* 11) prepare for a season
Papa's error one safe.

Fault one wiser, safe male: Papa's error

She repeats her claim from the anagram in the first line of *Wuthering Heights*. There she states, *Am livid over aunt's murder. Jot land thief story.* When she arrived back at Haworth in 1842, Branwell was not at home. As she says in the anagram, he was not an heir and, perhaps, his guilt made him run from home, not just because of his earlier dismissal from the railway job, but for his contribution to his aunt's early death. Is she imagining the worst, or did she know for a fact that the nephew killed his own aunt? She knew her brother better than historians or scholars, but her accusation seems almost impossible to believe. If it were true, Branwell's womanizing (real or imagined), fighting, forging, and thieving, when mixed with his addictions, may have sent him into an even greater depravity. To murder one's own aunt required a kind of insanity. If her claims were true, life with Branwell would have been particularly unbearable for any rational, intelligent human being.

If Branwell blamed his aunt's *anguish on tomatoes*, the image of the grim *reaper* choosing *acid* contains a pun: tomatoes are an acidic fruit. Charlotte holds her father partly responsible for Branwell's crimes; if he had continued his education, the son's attention and effort would have been better occupied. Her use of the word *fires* is prophetic: some time before Branwell's death, as he fell asleep in bed, he accidentally dropped a few unbound sheets from a periodical onto a candle flame, which set his bedding on fire. The Haworth stationer John Greenwood recalls the event in his diary: Emily rushed into the bedroom and hauled Branwell "into one corner of the room, where he cowered, stunned and bewildered. Then she tore the bedding off—now all in flames, and threw that into the middle of the room—the safest place—then flew downstairs into the kitchen, seized a large can, which happened to be full of water at the time, then upstairs she went and threw the whole of its contents on the blazing pile and quenched it at once. The first words she uttered were 'Don't alarm papa!'" (qtd. in Lock 403).

Branwell's decline included bouts of fighting, whining, and hitting, and he had become a *crass bigot*. Reverend Brontë used the word "bigot" in a letter in 1839 when he was requesting a new curate. He did not want an assistant to preach any doctrines "decidedly derogatory to the Attributes of God," nor anyone who may be "utterly unsafe either through shallow ignorance or evil design," and explained, "As far as I know myself, I think I may venture to say that I am no Bigot" (qtd. in. Lock 292-3). A *crass bigot* would be a grossly stupid, intolerant adherent of a particular point of view.

A month after this letter, Charlotte wrote to Ellen about Branwell's "bad habits" after being dismissed from the Robinson's employ. In these anagrams, she refers to Branwell's forging of *"cheques"* and explains why she supports the pretext that Mrs. Robinson may be partly to blame—her *bluff* is a necessary deception. She uses the words *"wry blow"* which can mean a shock expressing disgust or disappointment.

1) "My hopes ebb low indeed about Branwell. / 2) I sometimes fear / 3) he will never be fit for much. / 4) His bad habits seem / 5) more deeply rooted than I thought. / 6) The late blow to his prospects and feelings / 7) has quite made him reckless. / 8) It is only absolute want of means / 9) that acts as any check to him. / 10) One ought indeed to hope to the very last / 11) and I try to do so / 12) but occasionally hope / 13) in his case / 14) seems a fallacy" (418).

He doubles name on Bible. Adept. Wry blow. Same tiresome chore if with men. Revile bluff. Sham's base—dodge peril. Hoary mouth hid bite, not teeth. Fiend's angle: stole cheques, mask papers with blotches. Adheres to limit. Match styles; maintain one's cash flow. Ask about hot tenacity. Good pen hunter too, yet loathed thieves—toast odd irony. Can copy libelous oath—a nice hiss: calm, easy, false.

Branwell's ability to copy signatures enabled him to forge cheques that never exceeded their amounts. He would find the man's signature on the front page of his Bible, the usual place where people would sign their name, and practice the style and flow. Sir James Stephen, a friend of Mrs. Robinson's said his skill as "a most expert and frequent imitator of the autography of other people" was named as the reason for his dismissal— he could match the styles of someone's autograph. The *bluff* the family used was that Mrs. Robinson had instigated an affair with Branwell; this lie would prevent legal action, since the best defense is a good offense. The dissemination of the rumour was a strategic counter manoeuver that her father may have encouraged; thus, the *hoary* or old, grey *mouth* could be a metaphor for Reverend Brontë's ability to know how to bite back. He encouraged the rumour when he wrote to Mrs. Gaskell describing Mrs. Robinson "as his 'brilliant and unhappy' son's 'diabolical seducer'" (qtd. in Lock 412).

Branwell's tenacity and skill enabled him to study and learn various signatures, a fact that Charlotte had stated in other anagrams and that supports rumours about his dismissal. His willingness to forge signatures and, therefore, help the men he hates is ironic: through his *snobbery* and bigotry, he would have placed himself in a higher station than mere thieves, but he was just as bad as the thieves he *loathed*. Charlotte implicitly compares him to a snake, as she did in her first anagram where she linked Branwell to Satan, the *original snake*, and here she adds the sibilance of the sound: the *nice hiss* echoes in the 's' sounds of *nice, easy* and *false*.

The breakdown of this set of anagrams is as follows:

1) *He doubles name on Bible. Adept. Wry Blow.* / *2) Tiresome if same* / *3) with men revile bluff* / *4) Sham's base. Hid bite* / *5) Dodge peril mouth not hoary teeth* / *6) Fiend's angle stole papers with blotches* / *7) to mask cheques adheres limit* / *8) maintains style's flow about one* / *9) match ask hot tenacity cash* / *10) Good pen hunter too yet loathed thieves* / *11) toast odd irony* / *12) can copy libelous oath* / *13) a nice hiss* / *14) calm easy false.*

Without supporting evidence, the inclusion of Mrs. Robinson's maid as a possible cohort is only speculation, but she continued to correspond with Branwell after he left Thorp Green, as did Lydia Robinson's physician, Dr. Crosby. A question rises over "large, mysterious sums of money sent to Branwell, some definitely from Mrs. Robinson's doctor, which Branwell implies came from Mrs. Robinson" (Fraser, 231). It seems Ann Marshall and Dr. Crosby provided money as well as information about Mrs. Robinson's state of mind, but the news was mostly fabricated. The doctor advised Branwell that, when the husband dies, Lydia would not be able to marry him due to the restrictions Mr. Robinson had stipulated in his will. Branwell admitted to his acquaintance from Luddenden Foot, Francis H. Grundy, that he rarely thought about her money: "The probability of her becoming free to give me herself and estate never rose to drive away the prospect of her decline under her present grief" of being separated from him (*Letters, Vol.I* 428). He reiterates this in a later letter: "I never cared one bit about the property. I cared about herself, and always shall do" (480), but months later admits, "I had reason to hope that ere long I should be the husband of a Lady whom I loved best in the world and with whom, in more than competence, I might live at leisure to try to make myself a name in the world of posterity, without being pestered by the small but countless botherments, which like mosquitoes sting us in the world of work-day toil. That hope, and herself are *gone—she* to wither into patiently pining decline—*it* to make room for drudgery falling on one now ill fitted to bear it" (*Letters, Vol.I* 512). Reverend Brontë's biographer notes, "In these last few lines Branwell reveals his true self. He could not be bothered with troubles of any kind; he hoped to live at leisure to make a name for himself" (Lock 411).

Mrs. Robinson's doctor explained to Branwell that she would be disinherited if she made any further contact with her ex-lover. Edmund Robinson's will contained no mention of this restriction and, when he died in 1846, his wife inherited his fortune without any conditions attached. Branwell, however, was convinced that she was forced to abandon him, and saw his dreams of wealth, property, and a life of leisure dashed, an acknowledgement that sanctioned his spiral into depression, drink, and drugs. While indulging in alcohol and opiates, he continued his connection with Thorp Green through his association with the maid and the doctor. At one visit, Dr. Crosby gave him "the sum of twenty pounds" (515), which may have come from the maid, especially if she was a willing servant, happy to share the financial boon from Mr. Robinson's promissory notes.

363

Two years after her husband's death, Lydia Robinson became Lady Scott. She married Sir Edmund Dolman Scott, a man twenty-seven years her senior but a more appropriate match for a woman of her class and age than a young, redheaded tutor, who she described as "*mad* and a great liar" (Carlyle Letters). Understandably, she would publicly deny the accusation that she committed adultery with an insane man, and privately shake her head at the swain's fantasy that she would ever marry a pauper. She would survive the sordid business and live well, until liver disease claimed her life in 1859, but Branwell would recall the lost opportunity and remain "utterly shattered in body and broken down in mind" until his own death. For Branwell, "like ideas of sunlight to a man who has lost his sight" recollections of their time together "must be bright phantoms not to be realized again" (*Letters, Vol.I* 428, 512).

By November of 1845, his mood was increasingly gloomy: "I suffer very much from that mental exhaustion which arises from brooding on matters useless at present to think of—and active employment would be my greatest cure and blessing—for really after hours of thought which business would have hushed I have felt as if I could not live, and, if long continued, such a state will bring on permanent affection of the heart, which is already bothered with most uneasy palpitations" (*Letters, Vol.I* 439). Most historians and biographers agree that Branwell was declining rapidly: "For the rest of the year Branwell's behaviour, despite his sporadic efforts to find work and to write poetry, was a dragging burden on the family, who had to suffer his drinking, his bouts of lethargy, and fits of irritability" (15).

In April of 1846, he had tried writing a novel, but with little success: "in truth when I fall back *on* myself I suffer so much wretchedness that I cannot withstand any temptation to get *out* of myself—and for that reason I am prosecuting enquiries about situations suitable to me whereby I could have a voyage abroad. The quietude of home, and the inability to make my family aware of the nature of most of my sufferings" inspire him to write poetry about his "afflicted breast." Branwell had made plans to travel abroad twice before in 1836 and 1842 when he had aspirations and dreams, but like this desire to escape from Haworth in the hopes of a change of heart and scene, the attempts all failed (*Letters, Vol.I* 467).

While Branwell's mental health declined, Charlotte occupied herself with the publication of the Bell brothers' book of poems. Over the months in 1846 when Branwell is "mourning the slaughter of Youth" (512), she corresponded with the publishers Aylott and Jones about the design of the book she wanted and authorized advertisements in the magazines and periodicals she had listed. Charlotte is focused on success while Branwell succumbs to failure.

During these months, Charlotte has corresponded with Ellen about Branwell's depression. "You say well in speaking of Branwell that no sufferings are so awful as those brought on by dissipation—alas! I see the truth of this observation daily proved" (441-2). His condition never abates: "I have no news whatever to communicate—no changes take place here—Branwell offers no prospect of hope—he professes to be too ill to think of seeking for employment—he makes comfort scant at home" (444). Ellen periodically inquires about the situation and Charlotte provides a brief glimpse: "You ask if we are more comfortable—I wish I could say anything favourable—but how can we be more comfortable so long as Branwell stays at home and degenerates instead of improving?" (463).

In June of 1846, Branwell's mood prevented him from completing a poem: "I am unable to finish it at present from agony to which the grave would be far preferable." He had just received word of Edmund Robinson's death, and in his letter to his friend, the sculptor J.B. Leyland he encloses an ink sketch of himself tied to a burning stake, surrounded by flames. Lydia Robinson's welfare consumes him as well: "She sent the Coachman over to me yesterday, and the account which he gave of her suffering was enough to burst my heart. Through the will she is left quite powerless, and her eldest daughter who married imprudently, is cut off without a shilling. The Executing Trustees detest me, and one declares that if he sees me he will shoot me. These things I do not care about, but I do care for the life of the one who suffers even more than I do. . . . You, though not much older than myself, have known life. I now know it with a vengeance—for four nights I have not slept—for three days I have not tasted food—and when I think of the state of her I love best on earth, I could wish that my head was as cold and stupid as the medallion which lies in your studio. I write very egotistically but it is because my mind is crowded with one set of thoughts, and I long for one sentence from a friend" (475-6).

The coachman received orders to dispel any hopes regarding Mrs. Robinson. If she believed Branwell to be a madman, others in her employ may have viewed him the same, and on hearing of his desperation, decided to act. Whoever chose to inform Branwell that his chances were hopeless, they knew he needed to believe the misrepresentation of the conditions in her husband's will. Apparently, he did. To his railroad acquaintance Francis H. Grundy, he writes: "His property is left in trust for the family, provided I do not see the widow; and if I do, it reverts to the executing trustees, with ruin to her. She is now distracted with sorrows and agonies; and the statement of her case, as given by her coachman, who has come to see me at Haworth, fills me with inexpressible grief. Her mind is distracted to the verge of insanity, and mine so wearied that I wish I were in my grave" (479). The Robinson family doctor conveys to Branwell that the lady fainted when she heard Branwell's name mentioned and, upon recovering, "dwelt on her inextinguishable love" for him, and "wandered into talking about entering a nunnery." The doctor tells him to give up all hope of reconciliation. "I could be glad if God would take me. In the next world I could not be worse than I am in this" (480).

Charlotte records Branwell's reaction to the news of Mr. Robinson's death as "a pretext to throw all about him into a hubbub and confusion with his emotions." She adds that his mood worsened when he was forbidden to contact her: "Of course he then became intolerable—to papa he allows rest neither day nor night—and he is continually screwing money out of him sometimes threatening that he will kill himself if it is withheld from him" (477).

By December of 1846, Branwell's financial burdens have caught up to him. His drinking has bankrupted his small stipend from Thorp Green, so he now owes innkeepers unpaid bills and, as the accounts stack up, they must be paid. Charlotte wrote to Ellen keeping her abreast of the unpleasant news: "You say I am 'to tell you plenty'—What would you have me to say—nothing happens at Haworth—nothing at least of a pleasant kind—one little incident indeed occurred about a week ago to sting us to life—but if it gives no more pleasure for you to hear than it did for us to witness—you will scarcely thank me for advertising it. It was merely the arrival of a Sheriff's Officer on a visit to Branwell—inviting him either to pay his debts or to take a trip to York—Of course his debts had to be paid—it is not agreeable to lose money time after time in this way but it is ten times worse—to witness the shabbiness of his behaviour on such occasions—But where is the use of dwelling on this subject it will make him no better" (507).

Branwell had hoped to marry Mrs. Robinson, to "live at leisure." He wished not to be "pestered by the small but countless botherments, which like mosquitoes sting us in the world of work-day toil" because he knew himself well enough to realize that the easy life suited him: "I have been in truth too much petted through life, and in my last situation I was so much master, and gave myself so much up to enjoyment that now when the cloud of ill health and adversity has come upon me it will be a disheartening job to work myself up again" (512). He had lost the will to fight more of life's battles, but the sting of toil was no match for the sting of debts that Charlotte and her father were forced to endure. The Sheriff's Officer demanding payment would become "the greatest humiliation" for Reverend Brontë, whose hopes for his son were long since abandoned. What added to this emotional burden was the financial one: "By December of 1846, Branwell was costing his family a small fortune" (Lock 410).

Without alcohol in his system, he suffered attacks of *delirium tremens*, and with the alcohol, he experienced fainting fits, but he managed to continue traveling a great distance to drinking establishments, such as the Talbot and the Commercial Inn: "I was *really* far enough from well when I saw you last week at Halifax, and if you should happen shortly to see Mrs. Sugden of the Talbot you would greatly oblige me by telling her that I consider her conduct towards me as most kind and motherly, and that if I did anything, during temporary illness, to offend her I deeply regret it, and beg her to take my regret as my apology till I see her again; which, I trust will be ere long.

"I was not intoxicated when I saw you last, Dear Sir, but I was so much broken down and embittered in heart that it did not need much extra stimulus to make me experience the fainting fit I had, after you left, at the Talbot, and another, more severe at Mr. Crowthers—the Commercial Inn—near the Northgate" (*Letters, Vol.II* 6).

For the next several months, Branwell was rarely sober. His misery, of course, extended to his family: "We have not been very comfortable here at home lately, far from it indeed. Branwell has contrived by some means to get more money from the old quarter, and has led us a sad life with his absurd and often intolerable conduct. Papa is harassed day and night. We have little peace. He is always sick, has two or three times fallen down in fits—what will be the ultimate end God knows" (8).

As noted earlier, Gaskell reports in her biography of Charlotte that Branwell was sleeping during the day and keeping the household awake at night. When he slept in his father's bed, the sisters were terrified that they might hear a pistol shot and discover that he had he killed "the poor old man."

Reverend Brontë made a notation in his medical book at the page titled "Insanity, or Mental Derangement." It reads, "there is also 'delirium tremens', brought on, sometimes, by intoxication—the patient thinks himself haunted; by demons, sees luminous substance in his imagination, has frequent tremors of the limbs, if intoxication be left off—this madness will, in general, gradually diminish" (Lock 383).

In January 1847 Branwell writes to Leyland that he has tried to contact Mrs. Robinson. His wild imaginings have convinced him of her love, so he must try to reach her to let her know he has not forgotten her. He explains that Dr. Crosby has, once again, discouraged him from ever seeing the lady again: "an honest and kindly friend has warned me that concealed hopes about one lady should be given up let the effort to do so cost what it may. He is the Family Medical attendant and was commanded by Mr. Evans M.P. for North Derbyshire to return me, unopened, a letter which I addressed to Thorp Green and which the Lady was not permitted to see. She too, surrounded by powerful persons who hate me like Hell, has sunk into religious melancholy, believes that her weight of sorrow is Gods punishment, and hopelessly resigns herself to her doom. God only knows what it does cost, and will, hereafter, cost me, to tear from my heart and remembrance the thousand recollections that rush upon me at the thought of four years gone by."

He continues his longing for the Lady. He adds that a note from "the old quarter" has just brought him more dismal news: "For four years (including one year of absence) a lady intensely loved me as I did her, and each sacrificed to that love all we had to sacrifice, and held out to each other HOPE for our guide to the future. She was all I could wish for in a woman, and vastly above me in rank, and she loved me even better than I did her—Now what is the result of these four years? UTTER WRECK. . . . I have received today since I began my scrawl—a note from her maid Miss Ann Marshall and I *know* from it that she has been terrified by vows which she was forced to swear to, on her husband's deathbed, (with every addition of terror which the ghastly dying eye could inflict upon a keenly sensitive and almost *worried* woman's mind) a complete severance from him in whom lay her whole hearts feelings. When the husband was scarce cold in his grave her relations, who controlled the whole property overwhelmed her with their tongues, and I am *quite conscious* that she has succumbed in terror, to what they have said."

He mentions the impressions he has received from the men in his village with regards to his state of mind. "My rude rough acquaintances here ascribe my unhappiness solely to causes produced by my sometimes irregular life, because they have known no other pains than those resulting from excess, or want of ready cash. They do not know that I would rather want a shirt than want a springy mind, and that my total want of happiness, were I to step into York Minster now, would be far, far worse than their want of a hundred pounds when they might happen to need it; and that if a dozen glasses or a bottle of wine drives off their cares, such cures only make me outwardly passable in company but *never* drive off mine" (*Letters, Vol.I* 512-14). His impressions of his "rude rough acquaintances" seem to mirror Charlotte's assessment of their basic needs: "a hundred pounds when they might happen to need it" and "a dozen glasses or a bottle of wine drives off their cares." Money and alcohol can soothe their pain, but Branwell's agony is much greater, and if the Sheriff were to send him off to the York jail, his suffering would be far worse than anything his Mason acquaintances could imagine. Nonetheless, alcohol, money, and dreams of grandeur with his Lady continually occupy his mind.

Branwell had long given up the fight to improve his condition. He was always desperate for the next drink, and he constantly owed money, even though he was still receiving money from Thorp Green through his contact with the doctor. By March of 1847, Charlotte anticipated worse news: "Branwell has been conducting himself very badly lately. I expect from the extravagance of his behaviour and from mysterious hints he drops—(for he never will speak out plainly)—that we shall be hearing news of fresh debts contracted by him soon" (518). Creditors from various Inns were banging on the door, so he tried to receive more money from the Robinson's doctor, while the fear of jail loomed over him.

In June of 1848, he wrote to his friend J.B. Leyland in a state of hysteria about a creditor who owned the Old Cock Inn: "Mr. Nicholson has sent to my Father a demand for the settlement of my bill 'owed to him' immediately, under penalty of a Court Summons.

"I have written to inform him that I shall soon be able to pay him the balance left in full—for that I will write to Dr. Crosby and request an advance through his hands which I am sure to obtain, when I will remit my amount owed, at once, to the Old Cock.

"I have also given John Brown this morning Ten shillings which John will certainly place in Mr. N's hands on Wednesday next.

"If he refuses my offer and presses me with law I am RUINED. I have had five months of such utter sleeplessness violent cough and frightful agony of mind that jail would destroy me for ever. . . . I earnestly beg you to see Nicholson and tell him that my receipt of money on asking, through Dr. Crosby, is morally certain. If you conveniently can, see Mrs. Sugden of the Talbot, and tell her that on receipt of the money I expect so shortly I will transmit her the whole or part of the account I owe her" (*Letters, Vol.II* 77).

By late August he was still begging from his friends. He wrote to John Brown, who lived across the lane from the parsonage, asking if he or his brother William could bring him five pence for a glass of gin: "Should it be speedily got I could perhaps take it from Billy at the lane top, or, what would be quite as well, sent out for to you. I anxiously ask the favour because I know the good it will do me" (111). He had this note delivered at noon in order to obtain the money by nine-thirty the next morning.

Even though, his lack of means kept his drinking in check, the effects of his addiction were dragging him further into mental and physical deterioration. In September of 1848, when his friend Grundy came to Haworth, he sent a message to the parsonage that he would like to buy Branwell dinner at the Black Bull Inn, but he was shocked by Branwell's appearance: "'Presently the door opened cautiously, and a head appeared.

It was a mass of red, unkempt, uncut hair, wildly floating round a great, gaunt forehead; the cheeks yellow and hollow, the mouth fallen, the thin white lips not trembling but shaking, the sunken eyes, once small, now glaring with the light of madness—all told the sad tale but too surely'" He recalled that Branwell carried a knife as protection against Satan, and spoke of dying. The glasses of brandy were easing his distress and he spoke more freely, but with a deep sadness: "'He described himself as waiting anxiously for death—indeed, longing for it, and happy, in these his sane moments, to think that it was so near.'" When they had finished their drinks, "Branwell pulled a carving knife from his sleeve and confessed that, having given up hope of ever seeing Grundy again, he had imagined his message was a call from Satan. He had armed himself with the knife, which he had long kept hidden, and come to the inn determined to rush into the room and stab its occupant" (Barker 566). He had refrained from attacking his friend when he heard him speak, but Grundy recalled Branwell's "'sunken eyes, once small, now glaring with the light of madness'" (Lock 415).

Two days before Branwell died, John Brown's daughter remembered how thin he looked. She recalls "'teasing him because his clothes hung on him so loosely;' he was asked if he had his father's coat on. He looked a mere skeleton" (Lock 415).

Barker notes that, despite "months of slow decline," his death was such a sudden one "that it caught everyone, including the doctor who had attended him all summer, by surprise." She adds that, "Two days before his death, Branwell was well enough to walk down the lane into the village," but he needed the support of John Brown's brother William on his return home (566-7). Perhaps they had spent time at the nearby Black Bull. A day later, on Saturday evening, September 23, John Brown came to the parsonage. The next morning, the family reported that, at thirty-one years of age, Branwell had died. His doctor wrote on the death certificate that the cause was "Chronic bronchitis-Marasmus," but Barker believes that "the deterioration in Branwell's lungs and his wasting away were actually due to consumption, which was rife in the village" (569). The shock was so great that Charlotte was confined to bed for a week from the effects of a headache and fever. "It was my fate to sink at the crisis when I should have collected my strength" (*Letters Vol.II* 126). She wrote to

371

William Smith Williams on 2 October, explaining that her "crisis was hastened by the awe and trouble of the death-scene" (122).

Charlotte wrote to Elizabeth Gaskell about Branwell's final moments, which she records in her biography. "He died after twenty minutes' struggle, on Sunday morning, September 24th. He was perfectly conscious till the last agony came on. His mind had undergone the peculiar change which frequently precedes death, two days previously; the calm of better feelings filled it; a return of natural affection marked his last moments. . . . The final separation, the spectacle of his pale corpse, gave me more acute bitter pain than I could have imagined." She explains that she collapsed after his death: "It was my fate to sink at the crisis, when I should have collected my strength," and ends by saying "I am truly *much better*," which in one way she would have been, now that the crisis was over. Her "acute bitter pain" could be translated as a sharp penetrating pain full of harsh resentment.

Gaskell continues to record another account of the death scene. "I have heard, from one who attended Branwell in his last illness, that he resolved on standing up to die. He had repeatedly said, that as long as there was life there was strength of will to do what it chose; and when the last agony came on, he insisted on assuming the position just mentioned. I have previously stated, that when his fatal attack came on, his pockets were found filled with old letters from the woman to whom he was attached" (254). Is this a true account or a fictional rendering devised by the family to continue the *bluff* that Mrs. Robinson was Branwell's lover?

Bronchitis, malnutrition, consumption were all possibilities, but with the need to protect reputations and avoid scandal, perhaps the village doctor, John Wheelhouse, himself an alcoholic, had helped his friends, the Brontës, by lying about the cause of death. The doctor was a member of "the Black Bull circle" and died a few years later "of the alcohol-related dropsy" while in his early thirties (Whitehead 70). Soon after she was fit to leave her bed, Charlotte wrote to William Smith Williams and told him the truth, but Williams never saw the real cause of Branwell's death because it was hidden inside her prose in her anagrams. The best clue that anagrams are present in her letter is if a number of dashes appear in the paragraphs. In this letter, only two paragraphs have dashes, and they do contain anagrams.

In her October letter, she describes her feelings about the death to Williams.

"I do not weep from / a sense of bereavement / there is no prop withdrawn / no consolation torn away / no dear companion lost / but for the wreck of talent / the ruin of promise / the untimely / dreary extinction of what might have been / a burning and a shining light. / My brother was a year my junior / I had aspirations and ambitions for him once / long ago—they have perished mournfully / nothing remains of him but a memory of errors and sufferings / There is such a bitterness of pity / for his life and death / such a yearning / for the emptiness of his whole existence / as I cannot describe / I trust time will allay these feelings" (*Letters, Vol.II* 122).

The words conceal anagrams that reveal her view of her brother's real legacy of crime and murder, and expose the truth behind his sudden death.

Owe demon for pit: serve fee on abasement. / Rip open wrist. Haworth den / wants a loony coronation. / Loan on domestic apron. / Force few to blanket truth. / Honour misfit peer, / yet hunt lime. / Demon fry began vice at thirteen with gin. Hand is in brutal hanging hoax. / Jeer wormy yarn, sham obituary. / A madman's habit horrifies, contained poison / long ago. / Holy fury helped urn hive mates. / If harsh men got minion / murderer—safe. Sniff mortuary on bog. / Hypocrite's finest tribute: if head, horns, tail fed ashes. / Uneasy chagrin—see a crass corpse exit home—honest sniffle with benediction. / Let lying, lust, waste his life. Male rite.

In this unusual obituary, she derides the false story of Branwell's death from bronchitis and explains that he cut open his wrist, most likely with the carving knife that he carried when he met his friend that last time at the Black Bull Inn. Perhaps two days before, he had resigned himself to end his life, which would account for his sudden calm: "His mind had undergone the peculiar change which frequently precedes death, two days previously; the calm of better feelings filled it; a return of natural affection marked his last moments." These observations could also be entirely false. If he committed suicide, his Masonic brothers would certainly *blanket* the *truth*. As well, they would want a proper funeral for their friend, to further conceal the facts, and to *honour* their equal, or *peer*, but quickly bury him to silence any murmurings of the truth. The lime acts as an accelerant on body tissue and helps quicken the decomposition, so they pay their respects, but they also *hunt lime.* Charlotte does not believe the *misfit* honour an appropriate gesture, and her reasons, as always, reflect on his moral and criminal acts. In this case, she states that he began his life of *vice* at the age of *thirteen with gin,* which is close to the time she records, in her first anagram, that he *took heath wine from aunt's healer,* when he was just twelve. She also writes in that earlier anagram that he was a *street thief,* that he was pretending to be a beggar, and that he was using gin in a ceremony that mocked Catholicism, so his addiction to alcohol appears to have begun close to that time.

The *brutal hanging hoax* will be discussed later, but his criminal tendencies obviously were a constant source of strain on the family. The poisoning that happened "long ago" could be referring to her aunt's cause of death. If the criminal element in her township wanted someone killed, the safest method would be to tell one of their *minions* to do the job, much like a modern day crime syndicate with its hired killers. If this were true, she says that the men would bury bodies in the bogs—their moor *mortuary.* All of these claims seem hard to believe, but Branwell's actions consistently elicit a deep anger in Charlotte, especially when she imagines her brother with a devil's *horns* and *tail.* Her *uneasy chagrin* results from her anger subsiding momentarily as she witnesses his body being removed from the house; her tears are *honest* and she even utters a final blessing or *benediction.* The recognition that Branwell's lying and lust contributed to him wasting his life echoes her belief that men are "strange beings" and that "the mode of bringing them up is strange, they are not half sufficiently guarded from temptation": the drinking and carousing are all part of a *male rite* that society views as an acceptable passage for young men. Branwell's problem was that he failed to extricate himself from the darkness to find a more worthwhile path.

In an earlier paragraph in her letter to Williams, she refers to the family's desire for a bright future for the once loved son and brother. "Branwell was his Father's and his sisters' pride and hope in boyhood, but since Manhood the case has been otherwise. It has been our lot to see him take a wrong bent; to hope, expect, wait his return to the right path; to

374

know the sickness of hope deferred, the dismay of prayer baffled, to experience despair at last; and now to behold the sudden early obscure close of what might have been a noble career" (122). Barker writes, "Despite her measured cadences, all the force of her emotion was concentrated on that one word 'obscure': while the rest of her letter is written in her usual neat and even script that one word stands out, its letters crushed together as if written in a spasm of barely suppressed savagery" (568). The word 'obscure' can mean hidden or remote from observation, which could be Brontë's way of saying that the real cause of Branwell's death will be forever hidden from public view. His death was "the sudden early" and "obscure close" to a life, words that imply a death by suicide, which would have caused the greatest emotional impact on the family and perhaps engendered extreme anger in Charlotte, but "savagery" means brutal cruelty, words better ascribed to the workings of Branwell's heart than to those of Charlotte's. The crushed letters of the word "obscure" could also demonstrate anger, not only aimed at the act of suicide itself, but at having to present yet another *bluff* to the public. Once again, Branwell's actions forced Charlotte and her family to lie, pretend, and deceive friends and acquaintances. The lies and the secrets accumulate and, to protect the family's reputation, and to save Reverend Brontë from further humiliation, the Brontës must keep the truth hidden and remote from observation.

Anyone who has had to live with a drug addict or an alcoholic could relate to the Brontës' plight. The tension and fear surrounding Branwell's outbursts, and his constant lying and stealing to pay for his addictions would be all too familiar scenes for families who have experienced this kind of never-ending crisis. The heightened emotions and the depths of despair numb the members of the family into an unnatural rhythm of anticipating the worst but hoping for an improvement. Branwell's suicide would have seemed the ultimate selfish act, even though the intense misery would finally end. After witnessing his "death-scene," Charlotte's nerves would have been shattered, especially after months of torment surrounding his painful cries over Mrs. Robinson. Charlotte and her family would have spent several days in shock preparing for his funeral and eventual cover-up.

In a letter in early September, days before Branwell's death, she had written to Williams about Smith, Elder republishing the Bell brothers' poetry book (*Letters, Vol.II* 118). The opening lines contain anagrams that explain how she came to know the details of Branwell's actions at Thorp Green.

The breakdown of the anagrams follows the final anagram.

"1) I am glad the little vol / 2) of the Bells' poems / 3) is likely to get / 4) into Mr. Smith's hands. / 5) I should feel unmixed pleasure / 6) in the chance of / 7) its being brought / 8) under respectable auspices / 9) before the public. / 10) Were Currer Bell's share / 11) in its content absent" (*Letters, Vol.II* 119).

Fool helps me. Told all. Gave him title: 'Best ill egotist.' This torn mind—sham's key. Delirium fuelled pen's big hoax. Use fine nib, paste, then coach. True ghost scribe. End up a recluse. Boil up. Fetch beer. Cheerless, rural brewer nets inconsistent tab.

The breakdown is as follows:

1) *told all gave him title* 2) *fool helps me best* 3) *key ill egotist* 4) *this torn mind sham's* 5) *delirium fuelled pen's hoax use* 6) *then coach fine* 7) *nib big true ghost* 8) *paste scribe end up a recluse* 9) *boil up fetch beer* 10) *cheerless rural brewer* 11) *nets inconsistent tab.*

She blames his *torn mind* for the forgery. He tells her how he uses a *fine nib*, gets *paste*, and coaches someone on how to paste the new name to the note's payee line, which is explained later. He becomes a *true ghost scribe* because no one knows Branwell is the author of the forgery. His ruin sends him to a life as a *recluse* still angry and in need of his beer, but unable to pay his bills. This anagram shows how she came to know the whole story, a practice that had probably been going on all their lives, as Branwell enjoyed sharing with her all the lurid details of life outside the parsonage. The anagram stays on topic and makes believable claims. The *cheerless rural brewer* is a nice detail. Branwell's circle of friends included "all the principal men of the licensed trade at the top of Haworth" (Whitehead 69). Four of the seven inns were at the summit of the hill.

Charlotte's later letter to Williams, at the beginning of October, about the tragedy around Branwell's life contains more anagrams. The letter's dash ends the sentence, but the omission of commas means that the string of letters can be split into portions, and a word or two can be moved to allow the message to make sense. The portions, at times, are only a few letters, but they still contain words that fit the chain. After the entire anagram is displayed, the breakdown follows to show how exact these small portions are, and to present further evidence that she really was doing anagrams throughout her life in letters, novels, and poems.

She begins with the words *mental orthography* to describe her skill with anagrams. Orthography means writing correctly—specifically writing words with the proper letters as well as with the correct spelling. Every person who writes, thinks through the grammar and spelling but in Charlotte's case, when she uses the term *mental orthography* in the anagram, she means that she thinks and composes the words continuously in her mind without writing them down as transcribed anagrams. She uses the term when explaining why she made corrections to *Wuthering Heights*: "It seems to me advisable to modify the orthography of the old servant Joseph's speeches." She also uses the word again when she complained that, "The orthography and punctuation of the books are mortifying to a degree."

She mentions a *mate* who helped Branwell with the forgery of credit notes and called him a *healer* and a *doctor*. Dr. Crosby was Robinson's family physician and Branwell's "confidant at Thorp Green," and from Charlotte's perspective could have appeared to be colluding with her brother but there is no actual proof. He was born in 1797 and would have been 46 years of age, or eighteen years Branwell's senior in 1843. Barker explains that, even though there was a large gap in age between the two men, Branwell's "fund of anecdotes, entertaining manner of relating stories and musical skills, had rapidly won him a circle of friends in the locality" (462). John Crosby was "a member of the Royal College of Surgeons and a Licentiate of the Society of Apothecaries," and a widower who lived in Great Ouseburn until his death at 62 in 1859. Thorp Green was nearby in Little Ouseburn.

The 1851 census records that Dr. Crosby "employed a groom/labourer, a housekeeper, and a general servant." He was a member of the local Oddfellows Lodge, and Branwell, as a Freemason, had belonged as well during his time as a tutor at Thorp Green (*Letters, Vol.I*

525 n. 2); consequently, Dr. Crosby would have been obligated to provide financial help: "support for a fellow-member was a moral duty," and his concern over Branwell's circumstances regarding his belief that Mrs. Robinson was in love with him would have also compelled the doctor to administer aid because of "his sympathy for those in distress." He cared for his younger brother Jabez who was fifteen years his junior and may have had a small disability that prevented him from seeking employment; consequently, Dr. Crosby set up a trust for his brother with a yearly income that continued until Jabez died in 1868. When Dr. Crosby died, his estate was worth seventeen hundred pounds. His memorial tablet, set up by his friends, along with an obelisk at the cemetery reads, "the benevolence of his disposition, the urbanity of his manners, the sympathy he manifested for the suffering poor and the skill he evinced in the exercise of his professional duties left a name which is cherished in many abodes, that in health had been cheered by his genial spirits and in sickness had been solaced by his kindly aid" (Crosby).

In May of 1847, Charlotte wrote to Ellen to explain that she was welcome to come for a visit at the parsonage. Branwell was less likely to cause a problem: "he has got to the end of a considerable sum of money of which he became possessed in the Spring, and consequently is obliged to restrict himself in some degree" (*Letters, Vol.I* 524). Branwell hinted that the money came from Mrs. Robinson herself, a person he might "'never see again'" (525 n. 2), and Gaskell writes that Mrs. Robinson was sending him "twenty pounds at a time" (196). Branwell wrote to his friend Leyland in June of 1848 that he would soon be able to pay his debt to an innkeeper: "for I write to Dr. Crosby and request an advance through his hands which I am sure to obtain. . . . tell him that my receipt of money on asking, through Dr. Crosby, is morally certain" (*Letters, Vol.II* 76-7).

The anagrams return to the subject of the forged notes and help further explain Branwell's *angle* or method. The anagrams belie the image of her collapsing from the sight of the death scene, and contradict her words that it was her "fate to sink at the crisis." She states that his was the first death she had "ever witnessed," but she "was 5 years old when her mother died, and it seems unlikely that she would forget the experience: perhaps the children were taken upstairs to see their mother shortly before her death. Charlotte was still at Cowan Bridge when her sister Maria died at the parsonage, but at home at the time of Elizabeth's death on 15 June 1825" (*Letters, Vol.II* 123 n. 5).

In the paragraph below, Charlotte introduces the clue that anagrams will appear in her letters wherever she has placed a dash. As well, she confirms that the family built a fiction around Branwell's cause of death. The anagrams will not "appear" unless the breaks are placed in the exact right position, even though the phrasing may suggest another spot. This can cause a considerable waste of time and effort, not to mention frustration, in solving them, but as soon as the break is moved, even if by only one word or a letter like the personal pronoun "I," the anagram quickly falls into place. The words, "My son! My son!," "and then," and "Thank God" remain intact because either dashes or punctuation limit them, but they make sense within the context of the anagrams, so one could conclude that Brontë wanted them to stay as shown.

"1) My poor father naturally thought / 2) more of his *only* son / 3) than of his daughters, / 4) and much and long / 5) as he had suffered / 6) on his account—/7) he cried out for his loss / 8) like David for that of Absalom/—My son! My son!/ 9) And refused at first to be comforted/—and then—/10) when I ought to have been / 11) able to collect my strength, / 12) and be at hand to support him—/ 13) I fell ill with an illness / 14) whose approaches I had felt / 15) for some time previously—/16) and of which the crisis / 17) was hastened / 18) by the awe / 19) and trouble / 20) of the death scene—/ 21) the first I had / 22) ever witnessed. / 23) The past has seemed to me / 24) a strange week/—Thank God—/ 25) for my father's sake—/ 26) I am better—/ 27) though still feeble—/ 28) I wish indeed / 29) I had more / 30) general physical strength—/ 31) the want of it is / 32) sadly in my way. / 33) I cannot do what I would do, / 34) for want of sustained / 35) animal spirits—/ 36) and efficient bodily vigour" (*Letters, Vol.II* 122).

Youthful art—mental orthography. / Shy, no life on moors. / If dash, thoughts near. / Cold hand hushed gun. Man cut chain. Soon fears fade. / Less horrified, so touch / blade. Look at faith's void from My son! My son! */ Friend made facts softer. Better odour. And then / Noah hive hug, bet, owe, net / clergy. Entomb lost chattel. / Amputate bond, not hardship. /*

379

If fool's Romeo heart appeased Hell, which lines will last in pit's fiery volumes? / Rich wife, so had new asset. Way he bet. Bold nature. Snatch note. Hid cheat she fed. / Hid this after / we end vestries. / Weak mate pasted sheets at Green's home—Thank God—*/ Rat offers sham key: / bore twit name. / Thief's hell: beg lout. / We hid inside / enigma. Try rod healer. Lets chap sign. / Sly thief waits. May not win day. / Odd outlaw hid own action. / Now find a safe tutor's / alias misprint. / If genuine, vilify bad doctor.*

The lines that require some shifting of words are as follows:

4) *gun man cold hand* 5) *hushed fears fade* 6) *soon cut chain* 13) *If lines will last in hell* 14) *which fool's heart appeased* 15) *Romeo pits fiery volumes* 16) *hid rich wife so snatch* 17) *had new asset* 18) *way he bet* 19) *bold nature* 20) *note she fed cheat* 23) *mate pasted sheets home* 24) *weak at Green's* 29) *enigma rod healer* 30) *try lets chap sign* 31) *thief waits not* 32) *sly may win day*. This last anagram could stay in the positive rather than the negative: *Thief waits not. Sly, may win day* or *Sly thief waits. May not win day*.

Branwell's *cold hand* from his death quiets the sound of guns. He *cut* the *chain* literally by cutting his wrists. She sees the bond as a chain not as a loving connection. With his death the *fears fade*. In contrast to her statement of weakness, she is able to remove the knife and sees her brother's body as an example of *faith's void*, a man whose abandonment of the church's teachings left his soul destined for hell. The *friend* who *made facts softer* would probably be John Brown, who visited the parsonage on Saturday night, most likely the actual time that Branwell killed himself. He would have helped the family in any way he could, which would have involved creating a cover up—*We hid inside enigma*. The enigma consisted of a jumble of lies and rumours that has survived all these years. Charlotte had previously used the word in a letter to Ellen in July of 1846 when remarking on the riddles in magazines for ladies: "The enigmas are very smart and well-worded" (*Letters, Vol.I* 483).

As Worshipful Master and friend to the Brontës, Brown would have also instructed Dr. Wheelhouse to lie on the death certificate, which he would have gladly done to help the family. The Masons, or *Noah hive* would organize his funeral and *net* the necessary clergymen to attend.

Charlotte believed Branwell was an active participant in helping a few Masons forge documents; thus, she saw him as their moveable possession, a *chattel* that was forever lost to them. He may have amputated the family *bond*, but the *hardship* would continue through their *bluff* and through the repayment of his debts.

One lie would be his affair with Mrs. Robinson. Charlotte obviously found his delusion about their love wholly entertaining, and her *mirth* returns when she wonders which of Romeo's *lines will last in pit's fiery volumes*. She has no sympathy for his suffering and no interest in his poetry. He did write poems to Lydia Robinson. An excerpt of one entitled 'Lydia Gisborne' written in 1845 during a trip to Wales with John Brown conveys his wish for an early death: "Cannot my heart depart / Where will it fly? / Asks my tormented heart, / Willing to die. / When will this restlessness / Tossing in sleeplessness / Stranger to happiness / Slumbering lie" (Barker 469). He published two poems in the *Halifax Guardian* under his pen name of Northangerland, and an excerpt of each shows his state of mind:

"I knew a flower whose leaves were meant to bloom / Till Death should snatch it to adorn the tomb, / Now, blanching 'neath the blight of hopeless grief / With never blooming and yet living leaf; / A flower on which my mind would wish to shine, / If but one beam could break from mind like mine." In the ending of the poem entitled 'Penmaenmawr' he wishes that he could be as strong as the Welsh mountain, "yon mighty hill" in order to endure his suffering: "Let me, like it, arise o'er mortal care; / All evils bear, yet never know despair; / Unshrinking face the griefs I now deplore, / And stand, through storm and shine, like moveless Penmaenmawr" (Barker 474-5).

Perhaps Charlotte would have shown more compassion toward her brother if the affair had been real, if he had managed to pull himself out of his addictions, if he had stopped being a thief and a liar, and if he had found a successful career. No proof exists to verify if he murdered their Aunt, but Charlotte believed him capable and perhaps culpapble in her death. In her mind, he had created his own misery through years of living a debauched life, and after two and a half years of his sustained grief and drinking, she had lost all hope, and with that loss she felt no love for her wastrel brother. His poems, whether good or bad, meant nothing to her now, and his constant refrain of Mrs. Robinson's name must have driven her deeper into her disdain.

She understood Branwell well enough to know he could not help himself when he saw the rich Mrs. Robinson. His nature was such that he had to strike and steal her money. The lady had no idea of the fraud; therefore, *she fed* the *cheat* he *hid*.

The Brontë family had to hide this fact as well, and after they ended their meeting, or *vestries*, they decided they must conceal the fraud as best they could, so perhaps her father, whose *hoary mouth hid bite* devised the plan to go on the offensive with the rumour that Mrs. Robinson was Branwell's seducer. Branwell committed the fraud at *Green's home* or Thorp Green, which distanced them from the crime ("Thank God"), and involved a *mate*, a *rod healer*. She uses the term "rod," in place of things Masonic, so the man who helped Branwell—a *rod healer*—would have been a Mason and a doctor.

The method Branwell used must have begun with him forging Mr. Robinson's signature (*he doubles name on Bible*), obtaining the credit note (*took father's wife's credit note),* forging a new name, the twit's name— his *weak mate*, on a piece of paper (*thief copies her new name on note*): Mrs. Robinson's name now becomes the *rod healer*'s name; and then getting his *mate* to paste the paper to the credit note in place of Mrs. Robinson's name. He must be careful to *mask papers with blotches*, so that the ink can hide the joins of the pasting.

He then copies Mr. Robinson's writing (*simulates hand*), and is able to *match styles*. He *adheres to limit*, so if the credit note is for the sum of £20, he keeps that amount in place. The temptation of the *lady's free cash woke tiger*, a tiger that is *rash* and *bold*, and then he offered to his mate a *key* to the fraud by putting the twit's name on the note. This collaboration caused Branwell grief (a *thief's hell*) because he was forced to *beg* money from his co-conspirator, the *lout*.

Branwell had potential to be a painter or a writer, and with his bright mind and charming wit, he could have invested the profits of his education into a successful career, but he chose to steal the doctor's wine, sniff turpentine, impregnate a girl, lie, cheat, steal from his employers at the Luddenden Foot railway, forge documents for his Mason friends, drink, gamble, box, lust after women, commit fraud at Thorp Green, and perhaps

382

even administer poison, all as if these acts were part of an accepted *male rite* guaranteed to waste the life of a much-loved son and brother.

The news of Lydia Robinson's upcoming nuptials in November most likely sent Branwell over the edge. Lord Scott's wife died on the 4th of August and, within a matter of weeks, he and Lydia Robinson had become engaged. By September, this news certainly would have reached Branwell, either from Ann Marshall, the maid, or Dr. Crosby, and with no hope of attaining the life of ease he had envisioned and seeing no cure for his addictions, he carried out what he had been threatening to do for months: he "would not wish to live if he did not hope that work and change may yet restore him," and proclaimed, "I could be glad if God would take me. In the next world I could not be worse than I am in this" because, for Branwell, "the grave would be far preferable."

Charlotte wrote to William Smith Williams that her shock "was hastened by the awe and trouble of the death-scene." A slashed wrist, bloody sheets, stained bedclothes, and a corpse with a bloody knife beside its body not only contribute to the horrors of a shocking scene, but would also require concealment to protect the family's good name; thus, the *wormy yarn* they spun round Branwell's death became a bedside tale of prayer, forgiveness, redemption, a last effort to stand up to die, and Mrs. Robinson's love letters carefully secreted into his pockets. Even Charlotte's assertion that this was the first death she had witnessed appears to be untrue. The mythology around Branwell had begun and would continue to this day.

Charlotte's subsequent collapse and her week confined to bed came after years of witnessing her brother's outbreaks of addiction and criminal deeds. Finally, she could release the tension and anxiety from her body, but the actual grisly act of suicide would have given her and her family a terrible shock that went beyond the normal grief.

Two years later, in 1850, she wrote a letter of condolences to a friend, Amelia Ringrose, about her mother's death. The mother had suffered illness for some time, "absorbed in her wretched cravings and indulgences," as Charlotte described it to Ellen (*Letters, Vol.I* 550). In her 1850 letter, Charlotte offers sympathy as someone who has experienced similar woes. In Charlotte's case, with her own brother: "The longer we have watched the gradual attenuation of the thread of life, the more its

383

final severance seems to take us by surprise. And then too, most truly do you describe the oblivion of faults which succeeds to Death.

"No sooner are the eyes grown dim, no sooner is the pulse stilled than we forget what anxiety, what anguish, what shame the frailties and vices of that poor unconscious mould of clay once caused us; yearning love and bitter pity are the only sentiments the heart admits, but with these, for a time, it is sorely oppressed" (*Letters, Vol.II* 372).

Branwell's rage and torment had terrified her, but he was still her brother. Even though she had feared he might kill their father or, perhaps, harm her or her sisters, their blood tie, though tenuous, had remained a safeguard.

If Charlotte believed, however, that brutal landowners and corrupt Masons, unconnected by blood, posed another kind of threat, then what would they do to her family if they discovered she had revealed secrets that threatened the security of their den? If we believe the anagram in *Villette*, this may have happened: the *thieves noted libel mystery* in *Wuthering Heights* and, thus, the retribution she had feared for years would finally come.

39 CHARLOTTE'S *FAKE FIST*

The letter to Williams sent days before Branwell's death contained, not only anagrams that referred to Branwell's *torn mind* but also to *Wuthering Heights*. Charlotte also explains why she used three pseudonyms and why she gave credit to Emily and Anne for her work. Several sentences have been omitted from this letter. The anagrams contained within those lines describe the exact location where she says she buried her *literary drafts*. Rumours circulated for years that she had buried manuscripts and letters, and the anagrams appear to support that view, but the directions will not be revealed at this time. The section of the letter regarding authorship begins as follows:

1) "But of that portion / 2) I am by no means proud—/ 3) Much of it was written / 4) in early youth—/ 5) I feel it now to be crude / 6) and rhapsodical. / 7) Ellis Bell's is of a different stamp—/ 8) of its sterling excellence / 9) I am deeply convinced. / 10) And have been from the first moment / 11) the ms fell by chance into my hands. / 12) The pieces are short, / 13) but they are very genuine: / 14) They stirred my heart / 15) like the sound of a trumpet / 16) when I read them / 17) alone and in secret" (*Letters, Vol.II* 119).

Put forth names to obtain mood. Bury pain. Mute or win with facts. Try an oily hue. Write of sad, obedient child. Apron a clue. Balm—if lifeless, ladies net profits. Tell secret, feign lexicons. Dynamic voice led pen. Sly—connect mother, madman's fever, theft, Bonnie myth, hind shame fable. Three phase—rise cot, eye the urn, unite by grave. Dry satire. Defile three myth, kept mason hut tour, where entail hint, made Dean censor.

The breaks prior to the shifts are as follows:

1) *put forth to obtain* 2) *names mood bury pain* 3) *mute or win with facts* 4) *try on oily hue* 5) *write clue of obedient* 6) *a sad child apron* 7) *balm if lifeless ladies net profit* 8) *tell secret feign lexicons* 9) *dynamic voice led pen* 10) *theft mother bonnie madman's fever* 11) *sly connect myth hind shame fable* 12) *three cot phase rise* 13) *eye the urn unite by grave*

14) *fry satire three myth* 15) *defile mason kept hut tour* 16) *made hint where* 17) *Dean entail censor.*

The anagrams in this letter reveal Charlotte's real thoughts about why she needed a male persona for her fiction. With three pseudonyms, she can cast a particular mood throughout the novel. Ellis Bell was certainly the *dynamic voice* that *led* her *pen* and allowed her to write with such passion on the pages of *Wuthering Heights*. Acton Bell has a softer tone, while Currer Bell's voice strikes a chord somewhere between the two. Perhaps the three names allowed her to have a lighter heart, one less fearful of being caught, and enabled her to bury her pain in the prose. She could stay silent (*mute*), or she could enjoy some element of victory by writing her *facts* into the novels. The *oily hue* could refer to the greasy subject matter. The *sad, obedient child* is probably Hareton Earnshaw, and Zillah's *apron* is definitely a *clue* that supports the Masonic parody. The *balm* that mitigates her pain is her knowledge that, if Charlotte were to predecease them—*if lifeless*—her sisters could claim the profits from the novels that bear the pseudonyms: *ladies net profits*. Their welfare is paramount in her mind. She credits her sisters with the fiction and poetry so that they will be financially protected through royalties and not by a will that can be altered and forged. Authorship binds them directly and securely to the money. She divided the stories, guaranteed her sisters financial futures, and protected herself from discovery behind the mask of three names.

She pretends to tell one story when her words secretly tell another (*feign lexicons*). Her simulation of words through the anagrams contrasts with Branwell's simulation of Mr. Robinson's handwriting. The two siblings had similar talents and gifts but each chose a different way to express them. The *bonnie myth* and *hind shame fable* that she connects to each other in *Wuthering Heights* will be explained later. She continues to *defile* the Masonic rituals—implying that she tarnishes the Masons reputation—provides a *tour* of the inside of the farm she says she used as a model for Wuthering Heights, and gives the reader an *entail hint* when Nelly *Dean* acts as a *censor*. A censor is a person who expresses opinions on moral or general conduct. In this case, she judges Heathcliff harshly for his actions against Hareton, the rightful heir to Wuthering Heights through the family's entail. Nelly Dean's assessment of the legal shenanigans sheds light on Brontë's view of the fraud.

In the next part of the letter to Williams, she states that she is the sole author of the novels and poems. The words "but I know" stay as is because it cannot be changed, and it fits with the next anagram.   Charlotte continues to describe Ellis' poems to Williams: "The author never alludes to them—/ or when she does—/ it is with scorn—/ but I know / no woman that ever lived / ever wrote such poetry before / condensed energy, clearness, finish—/ strange, strong pathos are their characteristics—/ utterly different from the weak diffusiveness."

The anagrams mix topics. She begins by stating that she writes everything, and then says that men vote for war at their noisy *hovel*, and the ignorant lads *obey*. The topic changes to her sisters, as she refers to the "cry defender" lines of poetry that she delegates for Anne to copy. The biblical reference comes from Isaiah 19: 20: "For they shall cry unto the Lord . . . and he shall send them a saviour and a defender and he will deliver them." In the final anagram, she explains that the persona of a male protected them like a *fist*, a symbol of violence that was the very thing she shunned.

Turn out all verse. Do heath theme. / Hero heeds snow. / Toss in rich wit, / [but I know] din at hovel. Men vote war. / Poor wretches obey. True fever. / Chose 'cry defender' lines. Anne signs. / Ghost partners sang to sister. Chat, reach criteria. / Fretful to try. Devise fake fist we shun. / Free mind.

The last line is the only one that had to be shifted slightly: "utterly different from" becomes *Fretful to try. Free mind.* "the weak diffusiveness" becomes *devise fake fist we shun.*

She writes the poetry, does a *heath theme* in *Wuthering Heights*, and recalls the scene in chapter two when Heathcliff realizes that, because of the heavy snowfall (*hero heeds snow*), Lockwood must stay the night. The parody of the Masonic rituals in the first three chapters confirms that she tossed in her *rich wit*. The image of Emily and Anne, her *ghost partners* singing to her rings true as does her description of their *chat*. Charlotte and her sisters discussed the *criteria* for how the hoax would unfold, which makes it plain that the three sisters shared this secret. Initially, they would have been *fretful to try*, but Charlotte probably convinced them that their identities would remain hidden; consequently, when Charlotte learned that Ellis and Acton's publisher Thomas Newby had advised the New York editors that Currer Bell had written all the novels, the discussion between the three sisters would have been swift and practical. The question of authorship must be resolved for Charlotte's publisher Smith, Elder, so Anne would have to travel with Charlotte to London to present at least two Bell 'brothers.' Emily would remain at the parsonage to attend to Branwell and their father. Their united front would be based on the understanding that they had to keep Charlotte's *fake fist* strong and believable to the respective publishers.

Charlotte had been using a male persona since her youth with narrators like Charles Wellesley and Lord Wellington. Her decision to assume a male voice and pseudonym was perfectly natural. She would have heard that voice in Branwell and his fellow Masons, so the male influences are substantial, especially Branwell's who, after all those years of writing together, showed her how to duplicate the fierce bravado with confidence and panache. A reviewer of Currer Bell's *Jane Eyre* remarked on "'the masculine firmness of the touch'" in admiring the character of Rochester and hoped that it was a "'portrait from a man's hands'" (qtd. in *Letters, Vol.I* 555 n. 8).

Her masculine touch was firmly connected to her desire to tell the truth and her need to be hidden. In a letter to Williams in September of 1847, regarding changes to *Jane Eyre*, Charlotte wrote, "Perhaps too the first part of 'Jane Eyre' may suit the public taste better than you anticipate—for it is true and Truth has a severe charm of its own. Had I told *all* the truth, I might indeed have made it far more exquisitely painful, but I deemed it advisable to soften and retrench many particulars lest the narratives should rather displease than attract" (539-60). In *Wuthering Heights*, she came close to telling the whole truth, and it did cause some displeasure at first, but her concern was not so much with the reviewers as with the men she indicted, and for this reason she was especially cautious about losing her anonymity.

Her fear never diminishes, nor does she sway from the subject that torments her: the Masons and their brutal capabilities. The anagrams in the letters to William Smith Williams provide insight into her reasoning behind the three pen names and explain her strategy, as the eldest, to ensure her sisters' financial security unencumbered by any interference from the Masons who could have assessed Emily and Anne's worth like wolves evaluating lambs. Charlotte took this extreme action out of fear of reprisals from the men, and faced the threats knowing her best defense, like theirs, was secrecy; consequently, she could never risk confiding in her friends. She was an observant and intelligent woman with a powerful tool to alleviate her frustration and the mental resources to orchestrate this complex web of deception. She would keep silent and take action behind their backs.

This secretive, obsessive quality fit her nature as strongly as Branwell's flamboyant and addictive personality suited him.

That secretive nature remained even when she was writing to Ellen. In the years when she was creating her novels, Brontë never confided in her closest friend about her work. When she was in Manchester with her father, accompanying him during his cataract operation, she had begun writing *Jane Eyre*. In a letter to Ellen, she says, "You ask if I have any enjoyment here in truth I can't say I have" (*Letters, Vol.I* 497). In truth, she was engrossed in the intense opening chapters of her novel, but she never mentioned to her best friend that she was writing a book. If she kept her writing life concealed from her friend, she would certainly keep her secrets from strangers. In her mind, the risk was too great, and she was more comfortable embracing the anonymity: "If I could Ellen I would always work in silence and obscurity and let my efforts be known only by their results" (271).

Fortunately, her writing efforts provided a mass of clues and anagrams that tell the truth. She wanted to explain the depth of the treachery she says she witnessed, and she wished to remain concealed behind three male names. The anagrams remain consistent with these two intersecting themes of fear of discovery and desire for obscurity. Her amazing ability to write anagrams is equal to her creative skill in planning intricate plot structures and symbolic mythic rituals, but her efforts, at times, were suspect. While Charlotte may have believed that she was infusing different subject matter into her novels and various tones into her poetry that warranted the appropriate Bell brother voice, the public was not always fooled: some reviewers believed Currer Bell wrote the novels and the poems. As stated earlier, the reviewer in *The Athenaeum* referred to

Currer, Ellis, and Acton Bell, saying, "The three Bells ring in a chime so harmonious as to prove that they have issued from the same mould. The resemblance borne by their novels to each other is curious." Another such review from the *Dublin University Magazine*, while referring to "the triad of versemen,"—the Bell brothers—and their poetry in *Poems*, reads: "Whether they be in truth but one master spirit . . . that has been pleased to project itself into three imaginary poets,—we are wholly unable to conjecture . . . The tone of all these little poems is certainly uniform." Charlotte was conscientious and scrupulous about keeping herself hidden, but the anagrams show that a few reviewers had reason to be suspicious.

In a letter to Williams, she responds to the above review from the *Dublin University Magazine*, and her assessment of it is worth noting. She seems amused by the "ingenious" opinion and to revel playfully in her comments, but she exaggerates the review in such a way that one might think the lady doth enthuse too much. With the knowledge that she was the author, a reader could hear what the Victorian critic Sydney Dobell referred to as her "*equivoque.*" He believed Charlotte played with the words and gave them a double meaning. The opening line of her "Biographical Notice" begins in a similar way to her response to the review: "It has been thought that all the works published under the names of Currer, Ellis, and Acton Bell, were, in reality, the production of one person. This mistake I endeavoured to rectify—". As stated before, remove the passive voice and the first five words, and the lines become an affirmation of the thought.

She wrote to Williams in November of 1847, about the "one master spirit" theory put forward by the reviewer in the *Dublin University Magazine*. She refers to herself as "him" because the poetry is ostensibly written by the Bell brothers. She states that the reviewer "conjectured that the *soi-disant* three personages were in reality but one, who, endowed with an unduly prominent organ of self-esteem, and consequently impressed with a somewhat weighty notion of his own merits, thought them too vast to be concentrated in a single individual, and accordingly divided himself into three, out of consideration, I suppose, for the nerves of the much-to-be-astounded public! This was an ingenious thought in the Reviewer; very original and striking, but not accurate. We are three" (361). Eliminate the words "conjectured that" and once again, she seems to state the fact: "the *soi-disant* three personages were in reality but one." She wastes a great deal of ink on repeating the falsehood and little to discount it.

Charlotte may have enjoyed the masquerade, but her strong will continued to keep the denials alive. Her strength and determination usually proved successful when burying the truth, but, reminiscent of late 1843, a scandal that involved her father's drinking threatened to surface again. The wielding of her *fake fist* would prove exhausting, but her loyalty to her father's reputation was supreme.

In an 1846 letter to Ellen, she explains why her duty is to stay at the parsonage with her father. "The right path is that which necessitates the greatest sacrifice of self-interest, which implies the greatest good to others, and this path steadily followed will lead *I believe* in time to prosperity and to happiness though it may seem at the outset to tend quite in a contrary direction.

'Your Mother is both old and infirm; old and infirm people have few sources of happiness, fewer almost than the comparatively young and healthy can conceive. To deprive them of one of these is cruel. If your Mother is more composed when you are with her—Stay with her—If she would be unhappy in case you left her—stay with her. It will not apparently, as far as shortsighted humanity can see, be for your advantage to remain at Brookroyd, nor will you be praised and admired for remaining at home to comfort your Mother. Yet probably your Conscience will approve you and if it does—stay with her.

"I recommend you to do what I am trying to do myself" (483).

She had once fled to Brussels, "prompted by what then seemed an irresistible impulse," to remove herself from Haworth. Years before, in a letter to Ellen, she had quoted from a newspaper about her father's lecture at the Keighley Mechanic's Institute: his lecture "is mentioned as a matter of wonder that such displays of intellect should emanate from the Village of Haworth 'situated amongst the bogs and Mountains and until very lately supposed to be in a state of Semi-barbarism'" (214). Rather than live in a village of uneducated families, she preferred to return to Brussels, where sobriety and education were heralded as qualities to aspire to, but was forced to return in 1844 to experience her own form of delirium tremens: "I was punished for my selfish folly by a total withdrawal for more than two years of happiness and peace of mind" (503). As mentioned in chapter twenty-two, Ellen later recollected that Charlotte came back from Brussels to intervene in her father's drinking bouts with his curate Smith: "There were special reasons for her remaining at home discovered too late for immediate remedy. The truth, the real cause of C's sad suffering was in the fact that Mr. B. in conjunction with Mr. S. had fallen into habits of intemperance. . . . The evil began in her absence. Such consequences ensuing on her absence, conscience accused her of dereliction of duty" (503 n. 4).

The lesson had taught her that, without her influence in the parsonage, her father could suffer a relapse in judgment and begin drinking again.

Her sisters gave her tremendous comfort throughout those later years when they lived together at the parsonage, but their deaths within months of each other delivered a terrible blow. She would have felt a genuine need to clear their names and abolish the public's view of them as coarse and vulgar women, especially when she knew them to be kind and loving companions, so the "Biological Notice" was her sincere attempt to alleviate any guilt she may have felt for causing people's misperception of Emily and Anne, as well as "a sacred duty to wipe the dust off their gravestones, and leave their dear names free from soil." With their deaths, as tragic as they were, she could breathe easier on one level: she knew that her sisters were now safe and free from further harm. Unfortunately, if we believe her anagrams, she would not escape the Masonic wrath, and her fate, perpetrated by her father's drinking, would take an ironic turn that justified the caution, the hoax, and the fear.

40 A CURATE OR AN EDITOR?

Arthur Bell Nicholls arrived in Haworth two months before Branwell's infamous dismissal from Thorp Green. In May of 1845, he became Reverend Brontë's new curate and joined a small conclave of men charged with providing instruction and religious succour to their parishioners. The group included Reverend Grant from Oxenhope, the village next door to Haworth, and the Reverend Bradley, perpetual curate from the village two miles away in Oakworth. These men would meet at each other's rooms for food, drink, and quarrels. Ellen Nussey recalled that "'the conduct of the three curates was very aggravating at the time—and they were complained of to Bishop Longley. The air of Haworth and district was stimulating, and there was no Society to expend their spirits upon, so they threw themselves on each other with great gusto'" (*Letters, Vol.I* 400 n. 5). Occasionally, Mr. Smith, who two years before had been Reverend Brontë's curate and drinking companion, would join the men. He had moved to a curacy in Keighley, only four miles away and, therefore, was within walking distance of Haworth. At times, this band of men would also visit the parsonage.

When Nicholls arrived in Haworth, Charlotte wrote to an acquaintance that "Papa has got a new Curate lately a Mr. Nicholls from Ireland—he did duty for the first time on Sunday—he appears a respectable young man, reads well, and I hope will give satisfaction" (393). Her views were less guarded with her friends. In June of 1845, Ellen had mentioned to Charlotte the name of another curate, suggesting she might be interested in meeting him. That comment caused Charlotte to write back declaring her strong view of curates: "I have no desire at all to see your medical clerical curate—I think he must be like all the other curates I have seen—and they seem to me a self-seeking, vain, empty race. At this blessed moment we have no less than three of them in Haworth-Parish—and God knows there is not one to mend another.

"The other day they all three—accompanied by Mr. Smith (of whom by the bye I have grievous things to tell you) dropped or rather rushed in unexpectedly to tea. It was Monday and I was hot & tired—still if they had behaved quietly and decently—I would have served them out their tea in peace—but they began glorifying themselves and abusing Dissenters in such a manner—that my temper lost its balance and I pronounced a few sentences sharply and rapidly which struck them all dumb. Papa was greatly horrified also—I don't regret it" (399).

In writing to Williams in 1848, she remarks that a parent's duty should be to guide a child toward his "natural bent in the choice of employment," especially if that bent is toward the Church. She says that too often the wrong natures gravitate toward religious life: "You not unfrequently meet with Clergymen who should have been farmers, officers, shopkeepers—anything rather than Priests—and great scandal do they bring on their sacred calling by their natural unfitness to fulfil its duties" (*Letters, Vol.II* 79). In a letter to Ellen regarding a mother wanting her daughter to marry a curate she writes, "Why should Mrs. Anderton wish to compel her to marry the prig of a Curate? (as prig I have no doubt he is). It is a shame" (43). Were all curates prigs in her mind? If so, why would she later consent to marry one?

Caroline, the main character in *Shirley*, says she would never marry a type like the curate Malone. She depicts him as a noisy, rude lout with a bad temper and little wit who prefers whisky to wine but will guzzle wine if available. He is big, proud, and arrogant, and he carries a loaded pistol and a shillelagh, which he uses to beat a dog. She finds his repetitive jokes and bitter taunts monotonous.

Charlotte wrote to Ellen in July of 1846 asking her about rumours regarding Nicholls. "Who gravely asked you 'whether Miss Brontë was not going to be married to her papa's Curate'? I scarcely need say that never was rumour more unfounded. It puzzles me to think how it could possibly have originated. A cold, far-away sort of civility are the only terms on which I have ever been with Mr. Nicholls. I could by no means think of mentioning such a rumour to him even as a joke. It would make me the laughing stock of himself and his fellow-curates for half a year to come. They regard me as an old maid, and I regard them, one and all, as highly uninteresting, narrow and unattractive specimens of the 'coarser sex'" (*Letters, Vol.I* 483). She voices her feelings about Nicholls again in a letter to Ellen in October of 1847. "I cannot for my life see those interesting germs of goodness in him you discovered, his narrowness of mind always strikes me chiefly—I fear he is indebted to your imagination for his hidden treasures" (551). And again in October, she writes of Nicholls, but this time from the perspective of the parish. "Mr. Nicholls is not yet returned but is expected next week. I am sorry to say that many of the parishioners express a desire that he should not trouble himself to re-cross the channel but should remain quietly where he is. This is not the feeling that ought to exist between shepherd and flock" (547).

Apparently, Nicholls became attracted to Charlotte's hidden treasures. In December of 1852, after several years as her father's curate, he asked her to marry him.

By this time, Charlotte Brontë was the famous author Currer Bell. She was financially secure due to her literary earnings and from her investments, which totalled approximately £1700 (Fraser 458). She had just completed her final novel *Villette* the previous month, for which she had received £480 for the copyright, but would begin receiving subsequent royalties, which would maintain a comfortable living for her and for her father. Also, she was happily occupied with correspondences with William Smith Williams and George Smith over edits to the novel, so as a financially independent woman enjoying the realization of all her writing goals, she was content not to marry.

Charlotte had no delusions about her appearance and knew that a handsome man would prefer to marry an attractive woman. Her publisher George Smith recalled their first meeting: "I must confess that my first impression of Charlotte Brontë's personal appearance was that it was interesting rather than attractive. She was very small, and had a quaint old-fashioned look. Her head seemed too large for her body. She had fine eyes, but her face was marred by the shape of the mouth and by the complexion. There was but little feminine charm about her; and of this fact she herself was uneasily and perpetually conscious. It may seem strange that the possession of genius did not lift her above the weakness of an excessive anxiety about her personal appearance. But I believe that she would have given all her genius and her fame to have been beautiful. Perhaps few women ever existed more anxious to be pretty than she, or more angrily conscious of the circumstance that she was *not* pretty" (Barker 559).

Near the time of Nicholls' proposal to Charlotte, a man visited the parsonage to meet Currer Bell. He described her as follows: "'She was diminutive in height, and extremely fragile. Her hand was one of the smallest I ever grasped. . . . She had a most sweet smile, with a touch of tender melancholy in it. . . . But when you saw and felt her eyes, the spirit that created Jane Eyre was revealed at once to you. They were rather small, but of a very peculiar colour, and had a strange lustre and intensity. . . . they looked you through and through—and you felt they were forming an opinion of you . . . by a subtle penetration into the very marrow of your mind, and the innermost core of your soul. Taking my hand again . . . she looked right through me. There was no boldness in the gaze, but an intense, direct, searching look, as of one who had the gift to read hidden mysteries, and the right to read them. I had the feeling that I never experienced before or since, as though I was being mesmerized'" (qtd. in Shorter 217-8).

Charlotte knew she was no beauty, but she had a tremendous sensitivity and intellect that found expression through writing. A man in her life, especially a husband, would accept her appearance and not expect her to improve her face or figure, and he would understand and appreciate her genius. He would recognize that her intensity of spirit and her ability to penetrate to the "very marrow of your mind" were assets in a writer, and would admire the depth and insight of her gaze. He would not be narrow-minded, "self-seeking," "vain", or "highly uninteresting," all qualities that she had used to describe Nicholls. She preferred men who shared her intellectual sensibilities and respected her literary gifts so, if she were to marry, but, at the moment, her circumstances were ideal if she chose not to become a wife, she would certainly want a mate with some of the characteristics of the two men she had most admired: Monsieur Heger, her teacher in Brussels, and George Smith, her publisher in London. Scholars believe the character of M. Paul Emanuel in her novel *Villette* is based on M. Heger and that Graham Bretton/Dr. John is modelled on George Smith, Charlotte's publisher.

In the novel, Graham Bretton is the young, handsome Dr. John who frequents the girls' boarding school where Lucy Snowe works as a teacher. Gradually, they develop a friendship, but Lucy's wariness about his interest in the beautiful girls compels her to guard her feelings: she has real affection for him, but her rational brain tells her not to "entertain these 'warmer feelings' where, from the commencement, through the whole progress of an acquaintance, they have never once been cheated of the conviction that to do so would be to commit a mortal absurdity." She understands that a match with Graham is unlikely, but she admits she had hoped for one: "nobody ever launches into Love unless he has seen or dreamed the rising of Hope's star over Love's troubled waters" (ch. 23).

Brontë explained to Smith that Lucy could never marry Dr. John. The character is "far too youthful, handsome, bright-spirited and sweet-tempered; he is a 'curled darling' of Nature and of Fortune; he must draw a prize in Life's Lottery; his wife must be young, rich and pretty; he must be made very happy indeed" (*Letters, Vol.III* 77-8).

Like Graham Bretton, George Smith was a bright, attractive man with fine manners and a sense of humour. He was an eligible bachelor eight years younger than Brontë. Her first impression of him is recorded in a letter to her friend Mary Taylor: "Mr. Smith made himself very pleasant. He is a firm, intelligent man of business though so young, bent on getting on, and I think desirous to make his way by fair, honourable means. He is enterprising, but likewise cool and cautious. Mr. Smith is a *practical* man" (*Letters, Vol.II* 114). In June of 1850, she visited London and stayed with Smith and his mother for almost a month. A week later, she travelled to Edinburgh to meet with Smith and his sister for a two-day visit. A year passed before she returned to London. Again she stayed with the Smiths, this time for a full month. Her final visit of one month was in January of 1853, approximately two months after sending him the manuscript of *Villette.*

Over the course of these few years, they had become close friends. Her letters to him occasionally display playfulness, such as the one written at the end of October 1850 when she remarks on the arrival in London of Cardinal Archbishop Wiseman.

She imagines Smith and his employees, by way of embracing this famous Catholic's religious doctrines, redecorating their offices with an oratory, sculptures of saints, missals, and a confessional, and that instead of going immediately to their desks each morning, like heathens, they will get out their rosary beads and crucifixes, "sign yourselves with holy water (of which there will always be a small vase properly replenished) and— once a month at least—you will duly make confession and receive absolution.

"The ease this will give to your now never-disburthened heretic consciences—words can but feebly express. So gratifying is this picture that I feel reluctant to look on any other; Imagination, however, obstinately persists in shewing the reverse.

"What if your organ of Firmness should withstand Holy Obedience? What if your causative and investigatory faculties should question the infallibility of Rome? What if that presumptuous self-reliance—that audacious championship of Reason and Common-Sense which ought to have been crushed out of you all in your cradles—or at least, during your school days—and which perhaps—on the contrary was encouraged and developed—what if these things should induce you madly to oppose the returning Supremacy and advancing victory of the Holy Catholic Church?"

She concludes by saying, "Forgive all the nonsense of this letter—there is such a pleasure and relief either in writing or talking a little nonsense sometimes to anybody who is sensible enough to understand—and good-natured enough to pardon it" (*Letters, Vol.II* 491-2).

George Smith and Charlotte would remain close until the announcement of his engagement. Brontë had prophesied the kind of marriage for Smith when she outlined why Lucy could not marry Dr. John: "his wife must be young, rich and pretty." Even though she expected this outcome, the event was a crushing blow.

Smith had indeed chosen a younger and prettier woman from his own enclave, and his decision created an irreparable schism, as Charlotte viewed the engagement, as well as his method of communicating it, as a stinging betrayal. Rather than contacting her directly, he had asked his mother to break the news, which made Charlotte feel even further cast aside: "Man proposes but Another disposes" (*Letters, Vol.III* 211).

She had secretly wished for a deeper bond with Smith, but knew he would choose a young bride from within his social circle.

She wrote him a curt letter of congratulations in December of 1853, with anagrams tucked inside the few brief words: "In great happiness / as in great grief—/words of sympathy should be few. / Accept my meed of congratulations—/and believe me / Sincerely yours." She signed it with a formal "C. Brontë" (213).

This pen rages pain. / *If age, rare sting.* / *Boy weds worthy damsel—* *Push off.* / *Age not pity crafted common clause.* / *Enviable meed.* / *Sly irony secure.*

The word "meed" means reward, and Brontë uses it in the surface line as well as in the anagram; thus, because the word stays hidden from view, her irony remains secure, which is her *enviable* reward.

Her maturity or *age* enabled her to move past her self-pity and write a pedantic sentiment that concealed her grief. She mourns the loss of possibilities for a deeper love with Smith, as well as the hope of finding another man of his calibre to marry.

She recognizes that at thirty-seven her chances for true love are quickly diminishing. In the 1850s, a woman of her age would be seen as an old maid and, therefore, an unwanted wife for a man like George Smith; consequently, her impression that Smith's proposal is his way of disposing of her or of telling her to *push off* heightens her sense of betrayal and hopelessness.

In *Villette* Lucy Snowe buries Graham Bretton's letters. She chooses not to be reminded of what could have been: "The letters, however, must be put away, out of sight: people who have undergone bereavement always jealously gather together and lock away mementos: it is not supportable to be stabbed to the heart each moment by sharp revival of regret" (ch. 26).

For Brontë, the added *sting* came from her understanding that her age inflicts a *rare* level of suffering: the passing years are beyond her control, so she must be like Lucy and act "stoical." As she buries the letters, she also buries her grief, and understands that another road might open.

Later, Lucy thinks back to the burial and to her relationship with Graham/Dr. John. She remembers him fondly:

"I recalled Dr. John, my warm affection for him; my faith in his excellence; my delight in his grace. What was become of that curious one-sided friendship which was half marble and half life: only on one hand truth, and on the other perhaps a jest?" (ch. 31).

Brontë wrote these words before she received news of George Smith's engagement, but appear to show she understood the dynamics of their friendship.

Nonetheless, any separation from a loved one is painful, and Brontë was familiar with the deep suffering that coincides with deep attachment. She experienced a similar heartbreak over the loss of the other love of her life.

41 PROFESSOR HEGER

Before there had been any publishers or a George Smith, Brontë had known a Frenchman named Constantin Heger. Part of the plot of *Villette* involves the lead character, Lucy Snowe, falling in love with two men: Graham Bretton and Paul Emanuel. In reality, George Smith and her former French professor from the Pensionnat Heger were both sober intellectuals with sensitive natures and good hearts, and whose minds recognized and appreciated talent. Monsieur Heger was married, but Charlotte still felt a strong attraction to this passionate mentor who was unlike any man she had ever met before. His forceful personality and sharp mind would have stimulated her young woman's fervent imagination, and generated thoughts of a more intimate quality that in the end proved more harmful to her than to him.

After she left Brussels in 1844, he wrote a few letters to her, but soon stopped corresponding. She continued to write in the hopes that they could retain their connection until she could one day visit Brussels and see him. They never did meet again, but Charlotte always hoped they would; consequently, she kept up her French study and her letters. She spoke and wrote fluent French and naively yearned for his continued friendship through those letters, but he was a busy man; she no longer was part of life at the rue d'Isabelle; and he and his wife felt that further contact would be inappropriate.

When Brontë attended the Brussels school for young women, it accommodated "about 40 *externes* or day-pupils and 12 *pensionnaires* or boarders," all headed by Madame Heger who, with her husband, professor of rhetoric and French literature, had drawn up the curriculum. Charlotte described the staff and the subjects of that curriculum to Ellen: "no less than seven masters attend to teach the different branches of education— French, drawing, music, singing, writing, arithmetic, and German" (*Letters, Vol.I* 284). In chapter eleven of Charlotte's biography, Gaskell notes that the school dated back to the 13th Century and had been a kennel, a hospital, and later a home for a religious order with an outdoors that "was filled up with herb gardens and orchards for upwards of a hundred years." This garden would provide Charlotte with a quiet retreat from the other students. In chapter twenty-two of *Villette*, Lucy Snowe finds solitude in the "garden thicket" where rumours of a ghost still linger, but she dispenses with these thoughts: "Independently of romantic rubbish, however, that old garden had its charms." During summer nights, Lucy likes "to keep tryste with the rising moon, or taste one kiss of the evening breeze, or fancy rather than feel the freshness of dew descending." Among the "doddered orchard giants," "verdant" ground, and gravelled white walks was a bower, "above which spread the shade of an acacia; there was a smaller, more sequestered bower, nestled in the vines which ran all along a high and gray wall, and gathered their tendrils in a knot of beauty, and hung their clusters in loving profusion about the favoured spot where jasmine and ivy met, and married them."

Brontë's propensity for dropping clues into her writing may be at work in this paragraph. Certain words stand out and, when placed together, suggest a secret meeting place for two lovers. The words "romantic," "charms," "tryste," "kiss," "verdant," "white," "sequestered," "bower," "nestled," "gathered," "knot," "loving profusion," "the favoured spot," and "married" could allude to two lovers meeting in their special area of the garden where their union constitutes a kind of marriage. The word "romance" begins the image. A person with charm can excite love or have an indefinable power of delighting. A tryst can be a lovers' appointed time for their meeting, and in this case is spelled with an 'e' on the end, which sounds and looks like the French word for sad—*triste*. The echo of the word *triste* in "tryste" suggests that Brontë's memory of this special spot comes attached with a certain melancholy. "Verdant" can mean covered in plants, but it can also refer to someone who is unsophisticated, unripe in knowledge or judgment, and the colour white immediately following "verdant" can suggest purity, so the two words together could allude to an inexperienced person secretly meeting her charming lover. If the image is continued, they meet "sequestered," apart from everyone, in a "bower," or small room, where they "kiss" and nestle, and settle comfortably while "gathered" together in their lovers' "knot of beauty." They stay entwined in a "loving profusion," which could suggest the exuberant abundance of loving expression through words or affection. They stay nestled together in their "favoured spot," where the flower and the vine experience a marriage or union in this bower thicket. Was this a place where she and Heger had met secretly? Had they engaged in a love affair or was this simply more "romantic rubbish"?

Heger was the first man who had taken an interest in Brontë's mind. After living among uneducated families, she would have found him remarkably erudite and attractive. As she says in a letter to Ellen in 1838, "I cannot conceive of a life more dreary than that passed amidst sights sounds and companions all alien to the nature within us" (*Letters, Vol.I* 182). From Charlotte's perspective, she and M. Heger had similar natures, and his attention to her writing, which helped make her a stronger and better author, would have endeared him to her. "M. Heger kindled her intellectual impulses. . . . It is sufficient to say that M. Heger knew good literature from bad, that he had a sense of proportion, and that his teaching, his criticism, his loan of books, all made for a sound education. Charlotte Brontë, despite her genius, could not, one may believe, have 'arrived' had she not met M Heger. She went to Brussels full of the crude ambitions, the semi-literary impulses that are so common on the fringe of the writing world. She left Brussels a woman of genuine cultivation, of educated tastes, armed with just the equipment that was to enable her to write the books" (Shorter 75-76).

Most women living in the mid-nineteenth century would not have expected the kind of educational instruction M. Heger offered. One of Heger's friends remarked years later, "'He made much of her, and drew her out, and petted her, and won her love'" (Barker 419). He was willing to bequeath his knowledge and give her French books from his own library. For an intelligent but impressionable young woman from Haworth, his generosity would have deepened her attachment to him. "She delighted in being the pupil of a cultured, intelligent master, and his autocratic, choleric, volatile temperament combined with his real kindness only added to the piquancy of the situation" (*Letters, Vol.I* 11).

Heger impressed her with his intelligence and encouraged her talent. He had taught her to be "dissatisfied with mediocrity, to revere and experience every kind and style of good literature, to use imagery to illuminate and interpret but not as a substitute for argument, to listen sensitively, alert to faults of style, to let a difficult sentence arrange itself while one walked or slept, instead of struggling with it, and to avoid reading work in a markedly different style from one's own before writing."

He showed her how to discern the parts of a novel, the "arrangement, structure, style" of a great work, and his instruction steered Charlotte toward "the controlled shaping of major novels" (*Oxford* 246). This kind of kinship would have been intoxicating, but M. Heger appeared to have viewed Charlotte with "parental affection" (246), as he states in a letter to Reverend Brontë, but would he have admitted anything otherwise to her father?

When Charlotte and Emily returned home for their aunt's funeral in 1842, M. Heger and his wife sent a letter along with them for Reverend Brontë. This translation provides a glimpse into the man's polite and educated nature. "We must not conceal from you that in losing our two dear pupils we feel both regretful grief and anxiety; we are grieved because this sudden separation breaks up the almost fatherly affection which we have devoted to them, and our distress is increased by the realization that there are so many incomplete tasks, so many things which have been well begun, and which only need a little more time to be satisfactorily completed." Emily was to take piano lessons, and "Miss Charlotte was beginning to give lessons in French, and to gain the assurance and aplomb so essential in teaching," which would have enabled the Hegers to offer her a position "which would have given her that precious independence which is so hard for a young person to find. . . . We know, sir, that you will assess more maturely and wisely than we the effects which a total interruption of their studies would have on your daughters' future; you will decide what needs to be done, and you will forgive our frankness, if you will kindly consider that we are motivated by a disinterested [impartial] affection which would be sorely troubled if it had to submit to being no longer of use to your dear children. I beg you sir to accept the respectful expression of my high regard. C. Heger" (*Letters, Vol.I* 300). His desire for the Brontë daughters to continue their studies is apparently motivated by a "disinterested" affection, not by a longing to reunite with Charlotte.

Those who knew Constantin Heger have described him as a good and intelligent man. His son Paul said he was an "ardent, lively, witty father" (*Oxford* 246). When Gaskell met him while researching her biography of Charlotte, she found him to be "a kindly, wise, good, and religious man" (150). In May 1842, three months after the sisters' arrival at the school,

Charlotte described Heger as a "professor of Rhetoric" who had "power as to mind but very choleric and irritable in temperament—a little, black, ugly being with a face that varies in expression, sometimes he borrows the lineaments of an insane Tom-cat—sometimes those of a delirious Hyena— occasionally, but very seldom he discards these perilous attractions and assumes an air not above a hundred degrees removed from what you would call mild and gentleman-like" (*Letters, Vol.I* 284).

In 1842 Heger had been married for six years and would have been 33, only a few years older than Charlotte. His portrait at the age of 59 shows "a man of authority, with a high, broad forehead below receding hair, steady eyes, and firm mouth" (*Oxford* 246). In chapter twenty-nine of *Villette*, Brontë provides another picture of Heger in the character of Paul Emanuel: "The little man looked well, very well; there was a clearness of amity in his blue eye, and a glow of good feeling on his dark complexion, which passed perfectly in the place of beauty: one really did not care to observe that his nose, though far from small, was of no particular shape, his cheek thin, his brow marked and square, his mouth no rosebud: one accepted him as he was, and felt his presence the reverse of damping or insignificant."

As Barker points out, Charlotte was one of Heger's favourite pupils. When she returned to the school, without Emily, after their aunt's death, Charlotte was also going back to Heger, aware that he "held her in the highest regard as one of his star pupils. This was the first time that someone outside her family, capable of informed judgement and himself an intellectual equal, if not superior, to her own, had recognized and encouraged her talent." Barker notes that during 1843, in "at least three of the essays she wrote . . . she raised the question of the nature of genius" (413-4). She wrote an essay entitled "The death of Napoleon," wherein she poses the question, can "anyone without genius . . . rightly judge and appreciate the quality in someone else." Her essay, a portion of which is reproduced in Barker's book, explores this topic with regards to the "'life and death of Bonaparte,'" and Brontë ends by saying that "'one cannot deny to mediocrity her right to judge genius but it does not follow that her judgement is always just'" (416).

Heger had been trying to instil in Brontë the understanding that genius, while heaven sent, also needs study in order to attain the level of art. By October of 1843, Brontë has gradually accepted his view in an essay entitled "Letter from a Poor Painter to a Great Lord." She agrees that her genius "needs discipline and self-control to achieve its potential." The letter to a "Great Lord" could be Brontë confiding in Heger about her feelings of alienation while growing up: "'Throughout all my early youth the difference which existed between me and most of the people who surrounded me, was an embarrassing enigma to me which I did not know how to resolve. . . . in vain I tried to imitate the sweet gaiety, the serene and equable spirits which I saw in the faces of my companions and which I found so worthy of admiration; all my efforts were useless; I could not restrain the ebb and flow of blood in my arteries and that ebb and flow always showed itself in my face and in my hard and unattractive features. I wept in secret" (417). Brontë obviously felt comfortable enough with Heger to share these sentiments, but did that mean they had an affair?

This question has remained unanswered and "has haunted Brontë scholars" (419), especially when, in 1913, Paul Heger and his sister brought forth four letters from Charlotte to their father. The letters are dated July 1844, October 1844, January 1845, and November 1845. The Heger children gave the letters to the British Museum to end the rumours that had been circulating about their father's relationship with Brontë. The letters, they believed, "put an end to wrongful suppositions . . . the *truth* should always be brought to light" (*Letters, Vol.I* 360, n. 19).

The letters reveal Brontë's affection and attachment to her former teacher. When Charlotte returned to the loneliness of Haworth in 1844, she would have yearned for the companionship of "her master's" letters. She wrote to Ellen, upon her return home, about leaving Heger: "I suffered much before I left Brussels. I think however long I live I shall not forget what the parting with Mons Heger cost me. It grieved me so much to grieve him who has been so true and kind and disinterested a friend" (341).) But was he truly an impartial, non-judgmental friend? In the July letter of 1844, she writes to Heger that his letters give her "one of the greatest joys I know," but she accepts that she must be willing to wait: "I shall wait patiently to receive them until it pleases and suits you to send them. But all the same I can still write you a little letter from time to time—you have given me permission to do so" (357). A desperately bright woman, without like-minded friends on the level of M. Heger, would have pleaded for a few pages of company, as she does in the next letter, translated from the French.

She had not heard from M. Heger for months and was yearning for contact. In October of 1844, she sent a letter to him through a friend who was travelling to Brussels and she was "full of joy" at the opportunity that he would directly receive her letter. She was excited at the prospect of receiving one back: "I am counting on soon having news of you. This thought delights me for the remembrance of your kindness will never fade from my memory and so long as this remembrance endures the respect it has inspired in me will endure also." She signs the letter "Your very devoted pupil, C. Brontë" (*Letters, Vol.I* 370).

By January of 1845, she is heartbroken that he has not responded to her friend who had personally delivered the October letter into his hand. She tries not to cry or complain, and suppresses her frustration, "one pays for outward calm by an almost unbearable inner struggle. Day and night I find neither rest nor peace. If I sleep I have tormenting dreams in which I see you always severe, always saturnine and angry with me. Forgive me then Monsieur if I take the step of writing to you again. How can I bear my life unless I make an effort to alleviate its suffering?" She compares his letters to "crumbs of bread" for the poor, "but if they are refused these crumbs, they die of hunger." She reminds him that they had once been friends: "you showed a *little* interest in me in days gone by when I was your pupil in Brussels, and I cling to the preservation of this *little* interest. I cling to it as I would cling to life" (379). She underlines the word "little" twice, which may be a clue that she is being sarcastic and that his attention was actually much greater.

In November 1845, a year later, she is still hoping for news of her professor. Perhaps she regrets having pleaded with him to write, or having left Brussels when she did, or having such a strong need for communication, but she "greatly respects" him and needs to hear from him, if only to know he is well and to eliminate her "anxiety" in order "to regain peace of mind": "Writing to an old pupil cannot be a very interesting occupation for you—I know that—but for me it is life itself. Your last letter has sustained me, has nourished me for six months. Now I need another and you will give it me, not because you have any friendship for me—you cannot have much—but because you have a compassionate soul and because you would not condemn anyone to undergo long suffering in order to spare yourself a few moments of tedium. To forbid me to write to you, to refuse to reply to me, that will be to tear from me the only joy I have on earth." Her desire, while naïve, appears to rise from her infatuation, and a need to communicate with a man of rare mental gifts: "when day after day I await a letter and day after day disappointment flings me down again into overwhelming misery, when the sweet delight of seeing your writing and reading your counsel flees from me like an empty vision, then I am in a fever, and I lose my appetite and my sleep. I pine away" (436-7). M. Heger would not be drawn into further communication with his former pupil. In fact, he tore up her letters. His wife retrieved them from the wastebasket and sewed them back together as proof of Charlotte's fervour and of her husband's complete lack of interest (371 '*Text*').

His wife, Madame Heger, had slowly withdrawn from Charlotte over the months of 1843. In chapter twelve, Gaskell notes that Charlotte was "no longer regarded with the former kindliness of feeling by Madame Heger. . . . Both M. and Madame Heger agreed that it would be best" for Charlotte to leave the school. Gaskell assumes that this distance between the two women was a result of their different religions. Charlotte's "dislike of Romanism increased with her knowledge of it, and its effects upon those who professed it," and she was not afraid to express her opinion. Gaskell concludes with her assessment of the rift: "although there was never any explanation of Madame Heger's change of manner, this may be given as one great reason why, about this time, Charlotte was made painfully conscious of a silent estrangement between them." Whatever the reason, when Gaskell visited the pensionnat for research on her book, M. Heger was happy to discuss his former pupil with the biographer, but Madame Heger refused to see her.

All the parties involved suspected the need for discretion. Gaskell's explanation for the lack of amity between the two women is an example of tactful disclosure. Barker believes that Gaskell "protected Monsieur Heger (and Charlotte's reputation) as best she could by deliberately glossing over the reasons for Charlotte's estrangement from his wife and her eventual departure from Brussels" (787). She also notes that Brontë "had been reluctant to sanction the translation of *Villette* into French and had tried to prevent its publication in Belgium, fearing that the portrait of the Pensionnat Heger and its principals was all too easily recognizable" (787). Before the book was published, Brontë had asked Smith if they would publish *Villette* anonymously: "As to the anonymous publication, I have this to say. If the withholding of the author's name should tend materially to injure the publisher's interest, to interfere with booksellers' orders etc., I would not press the point; but if no such detriment is contingent, I should be most thankful for the sheltering shadow of an incognito" (*Letters, Vol.III* 74). In a later letter to Smith, she writes that she wanted the novel to be like "real Life," consistent "with Truth," so perhaps her desire for anonymity was founded in her knowledge that she confided a few secrets about her months with the Hegers. In the end, Smith discouraged Brontë from removing her name from the cover because of the "inexpediency of affecting a mystery which cannot be sustained." Brontë agreed but "under protests, and with a kind of Ostrich-longing for concealment" (77).

Brontë's attachment to Brussels and to Heger inspired her to write *The Professor* and *Villette*. William Crimsworth teaches at a school in Brussels, and Lucy Snowe teaches at a French city based on Brussels. Both plots revolve around the two protagonists exploring their feelings of love and independence. In light of the subject matter of both novels, scholars understandably wonder if Brontë's relationship with Heger was unrequited, or did they have an affair?

Of the surviving four letters that Brontë sent Heger, only one, the last, dated November 18, 1845 has one paragraph, at the end of this letter, written in English. The rest of the letters are in French. This one paragraph contains more revealing anagrams about Brontë's private life, and appears to answer the scholars' question: did they consummate their love affair? (The breakdown of the anagrams is in the Appendix under the heading "Letter to Heger.")

"I must say one word to you in English—/I wish I could write to you more / cheerful letters, for when I read this over, / I find it to be somewhat gloomy—/but forgive me my dear master / do not be irritated at my sadness—/according to the words of the Bible: / 'out of the fullness of the heart, / the mouth speaketh' / and truly I find it difficult / to be cheerful / so long as I think / I shall never see you more. / You will perceive by the / defects in this letter / that I am forgetting / the French language—/ yet I read all / the French books I can get, / and learn daily a portion by heart—/ but I have never heard / French spoken but once / I left Brussels—/ and then it sounded / like music in my ears—/ every word was most precious to me / because it reminded me of you—/ I love French for your sake / with all my heart and soul. / Farewell my dear master—/ may God protect you with special care / and crown you / with peculiar blessings" (*Letters, Vol.I* 435).

Brontë refers to Heger's rule that she must only write every six months as *idiotic*. An *interdict* is a Catholic prohibition that excludes a non-Catholic from a Christian burial, and *beau* in French means handsome, but it can also mean a boyfriend. The French word *soiree* means an evening party that can be comprised of only two people. To *sup* is a colloquial term that means to have supper. The anagrams begin with an admission that she and Heger had both lied.

Two lie. Hid our union's system. Agony. How idiotic is rule. Wore myself out. Cruel tether. Defer vow—one hair shirt. Beg, wait. Hid my fool emotions. Fate sum: Get bride, marry, move. Master distant, so beyond tirade. If together, Catholic bond—bed rows. Shut off, on shelf. Hate roulette. Hush meek poet that, if in city, did flirt—adult fun. Curb hotel fee: goal—inn. Share menu. Hot kiss. Lovely soiree. Bury vice sheets. Left whole pile, yet fight interdict—engulf heart. Time to grant a change. Relay detail: On thicket bench, fears go. I tarry. Lay idle hand on Bonaparte. Thrive. Beau had nerve. Beckon, confer, then sup. Free lust. Bliss. Eat, sin, end odd hunt. A cry, kiss, lie immune. Sweet sorrow verse put busy Romeo in mood. If meet dead cue, am icy. Warm fire. Fur cloak over shy one. Had hot lust in alley. Mates retry: defame wall. How to court? Eye a papist cycle diagram. Our own candy. Publish secrets wailing.

Apparently, Brontë and Heger did have a sexual relationship that went much further than one might assume. As in all situations between a married man and his mistress, the couple must *lie* about their *union*, which would cause *agony* for both parties. His six-month rule is a *cruel tether* that confines her writing to only two or three letters, whereas Brontë could have written him daily if permitted. Deferring their *vow*, or postponing being with him is the equivalent of wearing a *hair shirt*, an undershirt made of coarse animal hair, rough sackcloth, or burlap. In ancient religious customs, to wear a hair shirt was to repent for sins, so Brontë's punishment for her affair with Heger is to be kept from communicating to him and from being with him. She must *beg* him to write, *wait* for his letters, and try to hide her *fool emotions*. In her July 24 letter, as noted above, she writes, "I shall wait patiently," and in her November 18 letter, she begins by referring to the *rule*: "The six months of silence have elapsed . . . therefore I can write to you again without breaking my promise." She continues, "I will tell you candidly that during this time of waiting I have tried to forget you, for the memory of a person one believes one is never to see again, and whom one nevertheless greatly respects, torments the mind exceedingly and when one has suffered this kind of anxiety for one or two years, one is ready to do anything to regain peace of mind.

"I have done everything; I have sought occupations; I have absolutely forbidden myself the pleasure of speaking about you—even to Emily, but I have not been able to overcome either my regrets or my impatience, and that is truly humiliating—not to know how to get the mastery over one's own thoughts, to be the slave of a regret, a memory, the slave of a dominant and fixed idea which has become a tyrant over one's mind. Why cannot I have for you exactly as much friendship as you have for me— neither more nor less? Then I would be so tranquil, so free. I could keep silence for ten years without effort" (*Letters, Vol.I* 435-6).

Her emotional plea can be better understood if her anagrams are correct. She provides a summation of their planned *fate* together: *Get bride, marry, move*. This may be why, as Anne states in her July 1845 birthday paper, "Charlotte is thinking about getting another situation—she wishes to go to Paris." Would he leave his wife and move to Paris? With Heger so far away, she is unable to unleash her impatience: *Master distant, so beyond* her *tirade*. Her suppressed anger and frustration are evident in her letter, but Brontë surely understood that divorce for a Catholic was a serious sin. He must have been convincing because their relationship developed far enough that they discussed her converting to Catholicism: *If together, Catholic bond*, but his views caused arguments or *bed rows*. The idea of Brontë, a fervent anti-papist, having to convert would have presented a challenge, as would a divorce from his fervently Catholic wife and separation from his five, soon to be, six children.

After two years apart, Brontë appears to have accepted that their love affair had ended. She buries his love letters or *vice sheets*, and disregards

411

the Catholic *interdict* about a non-Catholic participating in the burial and engulfs her own heart with the letters. From her perspective, the Church should *grant* this *change*, but she could also be alluding to giving herself the consent to move on. Rumours have circulated about Brontë burying Heger's letters, partly because she describes a similar act in *Villette* when Lucy buries Graham Bretton's letters because it makes sense that she removes from view reminders of their love: "it is not supportable to be stabbed to the heart each moment by sharp revival of regret." Lucy wants to prevent the letters falling into the wrong hands, a situation that would jar her soul. She chooses to bury them under a favourite tree in the garden. This decision was "one of those queer fantastic thoughts that will sometimes strike solitary people": she was "not only going to hide a treasure" but "also to bury a grief" (ch. 26).

The burial seems to have led to her resolve that Heger would not write again. This knowledge enabled her to break her silence, if only for a brief moment in her anagrams. She confides the details of their love affair by explaining that they preferred the cheaper accommodation of an inn to a hotel. They would *share* a *menu, kiss,* and enjoy a *lovely soiree.* Her concerns about being caught disappear as they find a special place to meet: *on thicket bench, fears go.* The thicket could be the area in the garden that she describes in *Villette*, where she places significant words throughout the paragraph as noted above: "romantic," "charms," "tryste," "kiss," "verdant," "white," "sequestered," "bower," "nestled," "gathered," "knot," "loving profusion," "the favoured spot," and "married." She calls this area a "garden-thicket," and loads the paragraph with sensuous, poetic descriptions of "verdant turf" and "sun-bright nasturtiums clustered beautiful about the roots of the doddered orchard giants," and the bower that "nestled in the vines which ran all along a high and gray wall, and gathered their tendrils in a knot of beauty, and hung their clusters in loving profusion about the favoured spot where jasmine and ivy met, and married them." In the novel, Brontë uses the word "knot" in some form (knot, knotty, knottings) a dozen times, which suggests the figurative meaning of a bond or union not easily undone, a theme that recurs in *Villette* with characters from the past resurfacing in the present, and with the connection of past loves and suffering circling the main characters throughout the story.

In Brontë's real bower and Lucy's fictional one is "a rustic seat at the far end," which could be the *thicket bench* where the lovers can let their *fears go*. Similarly, in chapter twenty-two of Jane Eyre, when Rochester and Jane chat in the "leafy enclosure" where "wreathed and dewy orchard trees" encircle them, they find an arbour that "was an arch in the wall lined with ivy; it contained a rustic seat." In the novel, Lucy explains that during the day the garden is populated with students, but at sunset "when the externes were gone home, and the boarders quiet at their studies; pleasant was it then to stray down the peaceful alleys." The character Paul Emanuel remarks to Lucy that he has secretly watched her and noticed "her early preference for this alley, noted her taste for seclusion, watched her well, long before she and I came to speaking terms; do you recollect my once coming silently and offering you a little knot of white violets when we were strangers?" The alley, the wall, and the thicket were important parts of the garden to Lucy Snowe and to Brontë.

While on the bench, she lingers: *I tarry. Lay idle hand on Bonaparte.* Brontë had written an essay about Napoleon, so she could have thought of Heger as a general with his imperious temperament and intellectual intensity, but in chapter 30 of *Villette*, Lucy refers to Paul Emanuel as "the great Emperor" and as Bonaparte: "I used to think, as I sat looking at M. Paul, while he was knitting his brow or protruding his lip over some exercise of mine, which had not as many faults as he wished (for he liked to commit faults: a knot of blunders was sweet to him as a cluster of nuts), that he had points of resemblance to Napoleon Bonaparte. I think so still." She continues, "To pursue a somewhat audacious parallel, in a love of power, in an eager grasp after supremacy, M. Emanuel was like Bonaparte. He was a man not always to be submitted to. Sometimes it was needful to resist; it was right to stand still, to look up into his eyes and tell him that his requirements went beyond reason—that his absolutism verged on tyranny."

The image of Shakespeare's *Romeo and Juliet* being read during their evening *soirees* suits their intellectual affinity and love of literature. Brontë uses a pun when she says that the death scene in the play would render her *icy*: not only would she be emotionally chilled with the thought of their separation, but also as a corpse, she would certainly be cold. The next anagram explains, however, her method for removing a physical chill:

Warm fire. Fur cloak over shy one. The details of their sexual encounters—*Had hot lust in alley. Mates retry: defame wall*—while surprising, sound legitimate in the context of the garden with its alley, wall, and bench. She explains that they used the Catholic rhythm method to avoid pregnancy and uses *eye* to mean 'look at': *How to court? Eye a papist cycle diagram*: another interesting and believable detail. Their lovemaking was their *own candy*, which could be a reference to Heger's love of candy if it existed. Candy is also mentioned in *Villette*, but in the original context: M. Paul "was fond of bon-bons" particularly "chocolate comfits" and a "brioche," or light cake for dinner (ch. 29). The anagrams that refer to their time at the inn draw a picture of their sexual encounter and her pleasure: *a cry,* then they *kiss*, and relax in each other's arms: *Free lust. Bliss. Eat, sin, end odd hunt. A cry, kiss, lie immune.* Their *odd hunt* has ended, no more flirting and lingering looks, but a night in the shelter of a room where they can lie *immune* from laws, scrutiny, or chastisement. Brontë's ability to *relay* such vivid details with the use of a few letters gives these anagrams, like so many of the others, an air of credibility, and supports long-standing suspicions that Heger and Brontë were lovers. The anagrams end with Brontë's assertion that while she publishes these secrets she wails. To wail, for her, is stronger than to cry: she laments the loss of her love as if he were actually dead.

Her bond with Heger was strong because he was the first man who had been her intellectual equal. The character Paul Emanuel mentions his affinity with Lucy, and the tone could be an echo of Heger's: "I was conscious of rapport between you and myself. You are patient and I am choleric; you are quiet and pale, and I am tanned and fiery; you are a strict Protestant, and I am a sort of lay Jesuit: but we are alike—there is affinity. Do you see it, mademoiselle, when you look in the glass? Do you observe that your forehead is shaped like mine—that your eyes are cut like mine? Do you hear that you have some of my tones of voice? Do you know that you have many of my looks? I perceive all this, and believe that you were born under my star. Yes, you were born under my star! Tremble! For where that is the case with mortals, the threads of their destinies are difficult to disentangle; knottings and catchings occur—sudden breaks leave damage in the web" (ch. 31). If Heger spoke to Brontë in this manner, she could easily have fallen in love with his poetic language: he

414

was after all a teacher of rhetoric, so he would have known the words that best persuade. An impressionable, young woman like Brontë would have been overwhelmed by this "man of power as to mind" with his endearments, sophistication, and strength of character. If this were her first *beau* then she would certainly *thrive* in his company. She buried his letters; consequently, his side of the affair is hidden from view, but one remaining letter may help us better understand his alluring charm.

The only clue comes from a letter reprinted in Barker's book. She explains that a relationship Heger had with another pupil years later "was beyond all doubt entirely proper," but "the letter breathes an intimacy and sensuality which a susceptible woman would find deeply erotic." Imagine the effect of his words if the letters he sent to Charlotte were much more passionate than the one that survives: Heger begins his letter to this other student with a definite tone of intimacy: "I only have to think of you to see you. I often give myself the pleasure when my duties are over, when the light fades. I postpone lighting the gas lamp in my library, I sit down, smoking my cigar, and with a hearty will I evoke your image—and you come (without wishing to, I dare say), but I see you, I talk with you—you, with that little air, affectionate undoubtedly, but independent and resolute, firmly determined not to allow any opinion without being previously convinced, demanding to be convinced before allowing yourself to submit—in fact, just as I knew you, my dear L—, and as I have esteemed and loved you." As Barker states, "This could be Rochester talking to Jane Eyre" (419).

By the time Smith, Elder published *Villette*, Brontë had been away from Brussels for almost ten years. She had learned not to expect too much from acquaintances that may or may not evolve into friends. She knew to temper her emotions with her Reason: Lucy Snowe speaks in terms that could easily be Brontë's own cautious warning to herself about moving too fast towards people in a gesture of friendship: "'Do not let me think of them too often, too much, too fondly,'" I implored; 'let me be content with a temperate draught of this living stream: let me not run athirst, and apply passionately to its welcome waters: let me not imagine in them a sweeter taste than earth's fountains know. Oh! would to God! I may be enabled to feel enough sustained by an occasional, amicable intercourse, rare, brief, unengrossing and tranquil: quite tranquil!'" (ch. 16). Brontë's sensitive

415

nature, like Lucy's needed subduing in order to avoid rushing headlong into the pain and disappointment of rejection.

Charlotte could have easily fallen into a deep depression with little hope of an antidote. During this time of writing letters and waiting anxiously for a return post that never arrived, she had been living with Branwell's torment. Rather than drink herself into oblivion as Branwell did over an imaginary affair with Mrs. Robinson, she expresses her disappointment over a real affair through her work.

Her anguish and suffering are best articulated through the creative drive behind her novels. Jane Eyre must temporarily suppress her love for Rochester, but is soon reunited with him in matrimony, and Lucy Snowe must accept that Dr. John has fallen in love with another woman. Lucy tempers her desire for attachment and slowly becomes involved with M. Paul, but her wish fulfillment does not include a life with the intense and passionate schoolmaster at Madame Beck's boarding school, even though she had once contemplated just such a match for the characters. In a letter to Smith, Brontë explains why Lucy Frost (the original surname) was not destined to marry: "If Lucy marries anybody, it must be the Professor, a man in whom there is much to forgive, much to 'put up with.' But I am not leniently disposed towards Miss Frost. From the beginning I never intended to appoint her lines in pleasant places" (*Letters, Vol.III* 78). Instead of matrimony, Paul Emanuel goes off to sea and may or may not have drowned. Brontë leaves the ending ambiguous, more to please her readers than to express her own dashed hopes. She writes to Smith that the ending "was designed that every reader should settle the catastrophe for himself, according to the quality of his disposition, the tender or remorseless impulse of his nature" (142).

Brontë lost Heger and Smith to other women. She had learned to cool her passions and not to expect too much. By 1853, she had accepted her life as an independent spinster and seemed to have reached a desired level of tranquility. Her love for Smith and Heger provide understandable examples of the kind of man that stirred Charlotte's passions, so why, in a stunning reversal of character, did she suddenly change her mind about her father's curate and agree to marry Arthur Bell Nicholls?

42 'THE UNVARNISHED TRUTH'

Charlotte's views on marriage were clear. At the age of twenty-three, she once remarked about a proposal of marriage she had received from Ellen's brother Henry, also a curate, and her reasons for turning him down: "it would startle him to see me in my natural home character; he would think I was a wild, romantic enthusiast indeed. I could not sit all day long making a grave face before my husband. I would laugh, and satirise, and say whatever came into my head first. And if he were a clever man, and loved me, the whole world, weighed in the balance against his smallest wish, should be light as air." Her romantic inclination was to marry for love: "Yet I had not, and could not have, that intense attachment which would make me willing to die for him; and if ever I marry, it must be in that light of adoration that I will regard my husband" (*Letters, Vol.I* 187-8).

She did not believe it a "crime to marry—or a crime to wish to be married—but it is an imbecility which I reject with contempt—for women who have neither fortune nor beauty—to make marriage the principal object of their wishes and hopes and the aim of all their actions—not to be able to convince themselves that they are unattractive—and that they had better be quiet and think of other things than wedlock" (315). She well knew her physical limitations, and certainly thought of other things besides marriage. By the time Nicholls proposed, she would have been content with her independence and, lacking affection for him, would have rejected his proposal, which is exactly what she did. Her impression of him had remained the same from that time several years earlier when she had heard the rumour that they might wed: "A cold, far-away sort of civility are the only terms on which I have ever been with Mr. Nicholls."

Her disdain for the man is without obfuscation. Charlotte is comfortable telling Ellen exactly how she feels: she finds him unappealing. In the first chapter of her novel *Shirley*, published in October 1849, Charlotte lampoons three curates who live in the fictional Briarfield parish. Scholars and biographers agree that one of them—Peter Malone—is based on Rev. James William Smith, an Irishman who had a "fiery temper and illiberal sentiments" as well as "an avaricious and unscrupulous temperament;" he had become Rev. Brontë's curate in early

1843 and his drinking partner until Charlotte returned from Brussels in 1844 (Barker 427). She also noted that, for Smith, as it is for Malone, "money will be a principal consideration with him in marrying" (*Letters, Vol.I* 361). The character of Caroline Helstone in chapter seven of *Shirley* is distrustful of a man who, having nothing in common with her, would seek matrimony. Malone "felt disposed seriously to cultivate acquaintance with Miss Helstone, because he thought, in common with others, that her uncle possessed money, and concluded that, since he had no children, he would probably leave it to his niece." These words "speak volumes" about Malone as they did for Charlotte with respect to Smith: "they do not prejudice one in favour of Mr. Smith" (361). Also, Malone is described as "a tall strongly-built personage," while Nicholls, from his honeymoon photograph from 1854 and another in Ireland in 1904, taken with a "little girl" show him to be a short, stocky man, so it would seem that the Malone character is based on Rev. James William Smith and not Nicholls.

In that first chapter in *Shirley*, Brontë ridicules the curates who rain down upon the parish in "an abundant shower." Pastoral duties, such as superintending schools or visiting the sick are considered tasks too boring for their lively minds; "they prefer lavishing their energies on a course of proceeding which, though to other eyes it appear more heavy with *ennui*, more cursed with monotony, than the toil of the weaver at his loom, seems to yield them an unfailing supply of enjoyment and occupation." While others find their conversation dull and monotonous, the curates think their opinions exceedingly entertaining. Brontë describes the curate Malone as a loud man from "the land of shamrocks and potatoes." The housekeeper "hates Mr. Malone more than either of the other two; but she fears him also, for he is a tall strongly-built personage, with real Irish legs and arms, and a face as genuinely national—not the Milesian face, not Daniel O'Connell's style, but the high featured, North-American-Indian sort of visage, which belongs to a certain class of the Irish gentry, and has a petrified and proud look, better suited to the owner of an estate of slaves than to the landlord of a free peasantry. Mr. Malone's father termed himself a gentleman: he was poor and in debt, and besottedly arrogant; and his son was like him." Malone's physical appearance matches pictures of Nicholls, except for his height, but another piece of information in the novel leads scholars to believe Brontë is writing about Rev. Smith.

Arthur Bell Nicholls, therefore, is not believed to be a model for Malone, or for the other two curates she satirizes, but he does receive a brief mention in her story. Mr. Macarthey, originally called Macarthur, is a curate that arrives late in the story to replace Malone, just as in real life Nicholls replaced Smith as Reverend Brontë's curate. To further the argument that Peter Malone is based on Smith, in the last chapter, Brontë classifies Malone as a "legitimate urchin, rude, unwashed, and naughty." Macarthey, on the other hand, "proved himself as decent, decorous, and conscientious as Peter was rampant, boisterous, and—This last epithet I choose to suppress, because it would let the cat out of the bag." One wonders what Malone did to deserve this final omission. Brontë continues to describe Macarthey in terms that would please the real Nicholls: "he was sane and rational, diligent and charitable," but was she telling the truth or presenting only the "pretty and pleasing"?

The narrator in *Shirley* would like to say more about Peter Malone, but believes the reader would find the tale too disturbing, even though the story is true. "Note well," she begins. "Whenever you present the actual, simple truth, it is, somehow, always denounced as a lie—they disown it, cast it off, throw it on the parish; whereas the product of your own imagination, the mere figment, the sheer fiction, is adopted, petted, termed pretty proper, sweetly natural—the little, spurious wretch gets all the comfits; the honest, lawful bantling all the cuffs." If someone were to tell the truth, to be honest, that "bantling" or disparaged child would get all the slaps or "cuffs," while the "spurious wretch" would receive the sweets or candy. If Brontë has a tale to tell, but sees herself as the "bantling," how would she reveal the truth? Obviously, with the power of her pen, she could present situations analogous to the tale she wants to tell. She could also, as is her practice, leave clues, hints and, of course, anagrams, but if she left anagrams where would she hide them? Only by studying her description of Malone will her anagrams become apparent, but what they reveal will be shocking and troubling to anyone accustomed to "sheer fiction."

Charlotte had never enjoyed a meeting of minds with Nicholls and, even if he were genuinely attracted to her mind and not her money, she cared little for him. In the opening pages of *Shirley*, in a paragraph where she describes Malone, she emphasizes his name by placing it between parentheses, a strong indication that the letters inside form an anagram. The words "(Malone's name was Peter—the Rev. Peter Augustus Malone)" contain one of the most disturbing anagrams of all. With a dash separating the first part from the second half, the words must form a complete anagram on either side of the dash. The anagram reads as follows: *New tale: Mason rapes me. Rash guest at our temple venue.* The Three Graces Lodge held their meetings in a room on Newell Hill, not far from the parsonage. She calls the Lodge *temple* and uses the legal term *venue* to mean the place where the alleged crime took place. If Charlotte had been invited into one of the rooms at the Lodge, and had been *rash,* as in indiscrete or bold, the Mason may have decided to take advantage of her and put her in her place. She admitted to Ellen that she would speak her mind in front of the men: "my temper lost its balance and I pronounced a few sentences sharply and rapidly which struck them all dumb." The anagram refers to the name of Peter Malone, and if Malone is Smith, then one could assume that Smith must be the mason who raped her at the Lodge. Another set of anagrams refers to the rape, which helps to verify her allegation and will be dealt with shortly. Malone is the worst of the three fictional curates—the other two are named Donne and Sweeting—but would the actual curates in real life hold any clues?

At the time that Charlotte wrote about the real curates—"we have no less than three of them in Haworth Parish"—they were Nicholls, Grant, and Bradley. Rev. J.B. Grant was from the new church district of Oxenhope, next to Haworth village, and the Rev. James Bradley was from Oakworth, a district about two miles away (*Letters, Vol.I* 400 n. 6). Biographers assume "'Little Mr. Sweeting', the flute-playing curate in *Shirley*, is said to be based on Mr. Bradley" (n. 6). The character of Donne was based on Grant. In the novel's last chapter we learn that fictional Mr. Donne married and became an "active parish priest," which coincides with Mr. Grant's marriage in 1846, and he became perpetual curate at Oxenhope, "a position he retained until his death" in the 1880s (n. 3). In her correspondence, "CB tacitly admitted that 'Mr. Donne', one of the curates in *Shirley*, was based on J.B. Grant, and described his reaction to the novel in her letter to W.S. Williams" (373 n. 5). She writes: "The very Curates—poor fellows! shew no resentment; each characteristically finds solace for his own wounds in crowing over his brethren. Mr. Donne was, at first, a little disturbed; for a week or two he fidgetted about the neighbourhood in some disquietude, but he is now soothed down" (*Letters, Vol.II* 376).

Fictional Mr. Sweeting (Rev. Bradley) also receives a final word at the end of the novel. He married and was "inducted to a comfortable living." Mr. Bradley, the model for Mr. Sweeting "worked assiduously at Oakworth 'to organize the parish and to build a church', but overwork led to illness, resignation, and a long rest." He then became curate at All Saints' Church in Paddington in 1847 (*Letters, Vol.I* 400 n. 6).

In her letter about losing her temper with the curates, Charlotte had told Ellen that Smith had accompanied the three curates from Haworth Parish. This would then include Nicholls as the third curate rather than Smith who was curate in Keighley at the time. This, of course, does not preclude her from using Smith as her model for the Malone character in *Shirley*. Whoever Malone is based upon, Brontë definitely wants the reader to know he did something horrible: in her final word to him in the novel, she uses a disdainful tone: "Peter Augustus, we can have nothing to say to you: it won't do. Impossible to trust ourselves with the touching tale of your deeds and destinies." If the man did rape her, the inclusion of the word "touching" would not be an accident.

In the paragraph that describes Malone at the beginning of the novel, Brontë includes two parenthetical asides. The first is the anagram above that states she was raped at the Lodge, and the second comes after the other two curates tease Malone about his pronunciation of certain words: "(so Mr. Malone invariably pronounced veil, firm, helm, storm)." If the break for the anagram is placed after "invariably" the first anagram moves naturally into the second, but one word is shifted from the second to the first. The anagram for "so Mr. Malone invariably" is *Villain rooms nearby am*, and for "pronounced veil, firm, helm, storm" is *Nicholls fed up mirror movement*. With the shift it becomes: *Villain Nicholls rooms nearby. Am fed up. Mirror movement.* Nicholls did room nearby at John Brown's house, which was across the lane from the parsonage.

If Brontë copied his gestures and movements through the character of Malone, she demonstrates her disdain for the man. She depicts him as a coarse oaf that can quickly grow insolent, say "rude things in a hectoring tone," and laugh "clamorously at his own brilliancy." He drinks twice as much as the other two curates and "being neither good-natured nor phlegmatic" works himself into a "towering passion" where he "vociferated" and "gesticulated" until his companions would hear the "sonorous contact of Malone's fist with the mahogany plane of the parlour table." Not just a bore, but also a loud man who "laughed aloud at trifles, made bad jokes and applauded them, and, in short, grew unmeaningly noisy." He could be "a ceaseless talker when there were only men present" but become "tongue-tied in the presence of ladies." When he visits Caroline, the Reverend Helstone's niece, he would "make himself sociable and charming, by pinching the ears of an aged black cat, which usually shared with Miss Helstone's feet the accommodation of her footstool."

In chapter sixteen, when Malone tries to court the heiress Shirley, he silently hands her "a huge bunch of cabbage roses," but the narrator questions whether his offering is for love or money: was it "a poetic tribute at the shrine of Love or Mammon"? Shirley knows his motives and has no interest in Malone; she finds his gesture of romance amusing, which angers him: "Peter grew black as a thundercloud. When Shirley looked up, a fell eye was fastened on her: Malone, at least, had energy enough in hate: she saw it in his glance."

If Brontë was *fed up* with Nicholls, she would have enjoyed depicting him as an awkward, arrogant clown. If he did have energy to hate, she would have feared him as well. The anagram that states a Mason raped her could be referring to him; Brontë could be alleging that Nicholls' attention toward her was not based in affection but in control. If true, this anagram would explain why she initially refused to marry him.

In *Shirley* she demonstrates her feeling of revulsion toward the man, but she also expresses her private fury when she uses an analogy to refer to the aftermath of a rape, a cruel attack that she says began in the Masonic Lodge.

This shocking secret also helps to further explain her deeply felt hatred for him and for Masons in general. She had been immersed in their culture for years, and would have been allowed to participate in Lodge events that were open to the public, or she may have been on Newell Hill when Nicholls was there and perhaps was delivering something to him on behalf of her father. A number of circumstances could have drawn her onto the street and inside the foyer of the Lodge. Once inside, however, she would be vulnerable and helpless. He would have grabbed a woman the size of an eleven-year-old girl and easily overpowered her. Even though, she would be in a frightened panic, her mind would register that reasoning with a brute was useless, and somehow she must stay alive. The experience would have seared her memory with all things Masonic.

We can imagine that Charlotte had been ushered across the penetralium and was in their sanctum sanctorum, their temple. The brute's grunting had replaced the hush of ceremony, and the closed doors would muffle any involuntary cry. She would have recognized a small painting, hanging near the door, as "The Ancient of Days," a work by William Blake, the poet. Blake would have known Robert Southey, the poet laureate, and would have been in his fifties when Southey gained that great honour. The naked god, kneeling on the clouds, leaned towards the earth while holding compass calipers. Written below were the words, "Grand Geometrician of the Universe, Supreme Geometer." Below the Grand Geometrician were names of past Worshipful Masters: John Barraclough—he had built the clock that stood on the landing of their staircase at the parsonage. Every night her father would halt on his way to bed and wind that clock. Abram Whitham and William Hartley were both farmers, and Will Hartley always carried his tinsmith shears in his breeches pocket, and there was John Brown's name, Worshipful Master and trusted friend. What would he think of this ceremony? Would he approve of her place in their temple? No men in dark suits and white aprons graced this lonely chamber; just empty, hard wooden benches that faced each other from opposite sides of the room, and a lone throne chair, black as night, giving the room its sense of dreary consecration.

She might have pictured a man waiting for his first-degree of entered apprentice. Saw him blindfolded, kneeling in front of the throne, led around the room to be inspected by the others. In this room, the Masons held their second and third degree rituals, spoke significant words, gave secret handshakes, and afterwards enjoyed their time for refreshments while sucking on their pipes and guzzling beer. She imagined a row of dour men staring at her, hating her for entering *our temple venue,* the sacred sanctum.

Hanging above her head would be two cloth aprons and two framed documents. One apron was shaped like a diamond at the bottom and had a small flap over the top with black tassels attached along the hem. Three candles and a large eye were embroidered on the front. The second apron was square with another large eye, the sun, the moon, and two intertwined triangles, all embroidered on the front. The larger document contained the title, "The Schaw Statutes" with the dates 1598 and 1599.

This yellowing sheet provided a list of certain ordinances. The Wardens could test the Fellows in their district "of their art, craft, scyance, and ancient memorie," and make them pay to the lodge ten pounds with ten shillings for gloves and banquet expenses. No fellow was to be admitted without "ane sufficient essay and pruife of memorie and art of craft." The next document outlined the founding of the Grand Lodge: "In A.D. 1716, the Lodges met in London at the Goose and Gridiron Ale-house, St. Paul's Church-yard, the Crown Ale-house near Drury Lane, the Apple Tree Tavern in Covent-Garden, and the Rummer and Grapes Tavern in Westminster. At a meeting at the Apple Tree, they constituted themselves a Grand Lodge pro Tempore in Due Form, and resolved to hold the Annual Assembly and Feast, and to choose a Grand Master from among themselves." Such an ancient fraternity. No wonder the room smelled old and musty.

A canvas banner in the corner had a checkerboard background and a man lying in a partially open coffin. Interlacing triangles covered the coffin lid. A maul, compass, and square, all masonry tools, bordered the banner. The four directions were painted in the centre of each border, with east at the bottom and west at the top. A painting beside the banner showed a Mason composed of Masonic emblems. His head was a sun, arms a square, two plumb lines hanging like hands, a triangle as his heart, a compass and ruler round his neck, and an apron above two stone pillar legs. Written below were the words, "Behold a Master Mason rare. Whose mystic portrait does declare the secrets of Free Masonry."

When it was over, Charlotte probably held tight to the railing and carefully placed her feet on the stairs that led to the road. She never looked behind her but walked purposefully down the short stretch of street called Newell Hill, not noticing the stench of offal and overflowing privies, nor the garbage and middens she passed on her way home. At the top of Main Street, she avoided the open sewer and turned away from the Inns and the sounds of boisterous male laughter to march faster onto the narrow lane, past the church, the cemetery, with its pernicious fumes, beyond John Brown's house where Nicholls resided, and past the National School, up the steps to the parsonage front door where, once inside, would wonder if she could ever get clean. Her memory would be forever stained with the images of Freemasonry, and her hatred would be forever turned toward that man.

At the parsonage, she would have found the Mason visitors repugnant and uncouth, and viewed them as criminal and despicable for their treatment of innocent victims and unsuspecting farmers caught in the web of thievery and ruin. They had initiated her brother into their way of life, and the addictions and crimes had destroyed him. And now, with more abuse, insults, and indignities, it had become personal.

Perhaps Nicholls was attracted to her but resented her intelligence and decided to have his way with her and put her in her place all in one grand act of violence and control. Perhaps, at that time, if a man wanted a woman, sexual attack was the man's prerogative, and the neighbours and the law would assume she deserved the brute's show of force. Aside from no one wanting to hear the "actual, simple truth," the secretive Reverend's daughter would never admit to the assault for two reasons: it could never be proved, and it would bring shame on her father, but Brontë could take back some control to make a point about fantasy being favoured over truth.

In her last chapter of *Shirley* the narrator addresses Malone to explain that readers usually prefer the fiction to the fact. She says, "a discriminating public has its crochets," which means perverse fancies, and if they hear the truth they will need smelling salts or "sal-volatile" to bring them out of their fainting spell and "burnt feathers," perhaps to ward off evil or disease. She continues to assert her view to Malone that the truth lacks interest: "the unvarnished truth does not answer; the plain facts will not digest. Do you know that the squeak of the real pig is no more relished now than it was in days of yore? Were I to give the catastrophe of your life and conversation, the public would sweep off in shrieking hysterics, and there would be a wild cry for sal-volatile and burnt feathers. 'Impossible!' would be pronounced here; 'untrue!' would be responded there; 'inartistic!' would be solemnly decided." Brontë may be correct about the ugly truth repulsing "a discriminating public" because the first reaction to an anagram that states a mason raped her at the Lodge would probably be

"Impossible!" or, more than likely, "untrue!" No one wants to believe the worst about a person usually regarded with some favour.

This violent treatment conforms to the nature of bullies with a temper. The character Malone is "neither good-natured nor phlegmatic," so the man is neither friendly nor dull and apathetic. This man has a "towering passion" and a temper; the landlady "hates Mr. Malone more than either of the other two," and she fears him.

In a letter to Williams in November 1849, Brontë writes about rendering the truth in *Shirley*. She refers to two characters and to the first chapter where she satirizes the three curates: "On the whole I am glad a decidedly bad notice has come first—a notice whose inexpressible ignorance first stuns and then stirs me. Are there no such men as the Helstones and Yorkes?

Yes there are.

Is the first chapter disgusting or vulgar?

It is not: it is real." (*Letters, Vol.II* 272).

In a letter to Ellen in January of 1850, she tells her friend that Nicholls has read *Shirley*. This paragraph contains anagrams and provides further insight into her feelings towards Nicholls. The lines appear with the separations followed by the full anagram. The anagrams refer to specific incidents in the novel, which suggests the anagrams are genuine and intentional. Only a few words were shifted and will be shown at the end. The word "Shirley" stays as is.

"1) Mr. Nicholls has finished reading 'Shirley' / 2) he is delighted with it—/ 3) John Brown's wife seriously thought / 4) he had gone wrong in the head / 5) as she heard him giving vent / 6) to roars of laughter / 7) as he sat alone—/ 8) clapping his hands / 9) and stamping on the floor. / 10) He would read all the scenes / 11) about the curates aloud to papa—/ 12) he triumphed in his own character. / 13) What Mr. Grant will say / 14) is another question. / 15) No matter."

Scorn high shrill. Deafens maid in Shirley. Hide idle twit's height. If short, hush guile. New job: add own heath story when going on here. Hand gives giver a stone. Shame hint for author's lot. Heals a rage. Pinch sad lips. If not rape, hang old ghost Mann. Laws should end leech, put out potato-eater as a real debauch—the Christian urchin who raped me. Why transmit raw gall? To quash ire, note sin. A torment.

The words shifted are from the following anagrams: 4) *add heath when going on here* 5) *Hand gives giver shame hint* 6) *for author's lot rage* 7) *a stone heals a* 8) *pinch sad lips hang* 9) *if not rape old ghost mann* 10) *law ends leech should eater* 11) *potato put out as a real debauch.*

The word *shrill* means piercing and high pitched. In the first chapter of *Shirley*, Malone insults the other two curates: "He reviled them as Saxons and snobs at the very top pitch of his high Celtic voice." The term *maid* means an unmarried young lady. In chapter seven, after the three curates enter Caroline Helstone's house, the noise deafens her: "Thus it chanced on that afternoon that Caroline's ears were three times tortured with the ringing of the bell and the advent of undesired guests:" Not only the man's voice, but the sound of the curates' arrival *deafens a maid.* This could be Charlotte's own experience with the curates when they visit.

She also describes Malone as tall, but Nicholls is not a tall man; therefore, if she alters his size: *Hide idle twit's height,* she can make it less obvious that she has included him in her satire. Again, she refers to her size, which implies her fear, and states that because she is small, she must keep quiet about his treachery: *If short, hush guile.* At the end of *Shirley*, she calls Malone a "legitimate urchin," so the use of *Christian urchin* is probably an intentional reference.

Her *own heath story* connects with the *hand gives giver a stone* hint. This is difficult to understand unless taken in context with a pertinent quotation from the novel. Brontë provides this *shame* clue as a *hint for author's lot*, which is her lot in life.

She is trying to heal her *rage*, express her *gall* (something bitter to endure), and show her readers how she felt during a terrible time in her life.

First Brontë explains how she registered the *shame* of the rape, and then she uses the character of the "old maid" Miss Mann—*old ghost Mann*—to expose what actually happened to her. If the old lady is lying about a *rape*, pinch her lips to keep her quiet or *hang* her. If she is telling the truth, the horror of the old maid's rape will explain and justify her

427

dreary moods. These two sections are crucial in understanding Brontë's inner *torment*.

In chapter seven, fittingly entitled "The Curates At Tea," the narrator suggests how one can learn to deal with suffering. "Take the matter as you find it: ask no questions, utter no remonstrances; it is your best wisdom. You expected bread and you have got a stone: break your teeth on it, and don't shriek because the nerves are martyrised; do not doubt that your mental stomach—if you have such a thing—is strong as an ostrich's; the stone will digest. You held out your hand for an egg, and fate put into it a scorpion. Show no consternation; close your fingers firmly upon the gift; let it sting through your palm. Never mind; in time, after your hand and arm have swelled and quivered long with torture, the squeezed scorpion will die, and you will have learned the great lesson how to endure without a sob.

"For the whole remnant of your life, if you survive the test—some, it is said, die under it—you will be stronger, wiser, less sensitive. This you are not aware of, perhaps, at the time, and so cannot borrow courage of that hope. Nature, however, as has been intimated, is an excellent friend in such cases, sealing the lips, interdicting utterance, commanding a placid dissimulation—a dissimulation often wearing an easy and gay mien at first, settling down to sorrow and paleness in time, then passing away, and leaving a convenient stoicism, not the less fortifying because it is half-bitter.

"Half-bitter! Is that wrong? No; it should be bitter; bitterness is strength—it is a tonic. Sweet, mild force following acute suffering you find nowhere; to talk of it is delusion. There may be apathetic exhaustion after the rack. If energy remains, it will be rather a dangerous energy—deadly when confronted with injustice."

Chapter ten is entitled "Old Maids," a fitting title because Charlotte would have considered herself an old maid. Within this chapter she uses Miss Mann's character to describe her inner self and to *quash* the *ire*.

Caroline tells Robert Moore that she, too, may one day be an old maid, and he responds that with "lips of that tint and form" it would be impossible to imagine her as old as Miss Mann whose own lips are *sad* and desperate for "earthly nutriment."

The *old ghost Mann* has "a bloodless pallor of complexion," is "corpselike," wishes to be understood, and has "a starved, ghostly longing for appreciation and affection. To this extenuated spectre, perhaps, a crumb is not thrown once a year, but when ahungered and athirst to famine—when all humanity has forgotten the dying tenant of a decaying house—Divine mercy remembers the mourner, and a shower of manna falls for lips that earthly nutriment is to pass no more. Biblical promises, heard first in health, but then unheeded, come whispering to the couch of sickness; it is felt that a pitying God watches what all mankind have forsaken. The tender compassion of Jesus is recalled and relied on: the faded eye, gazing beyond time, sees a home, a friend, a refuge in eternity."

As Miss Mann sees that Caroline offers a kind and sympathizing ear, she relates a terrible incident that happened years before. The narrator warns the reader not to pass judgment too quickly:

"Reader! When you behold an aspect for whose constant gloom and frown you cannot account, whose unvarying cloud exasperates you by its apparent causelessness, be sure that there is a canker somewhere, and a canker not the less deeply corroding because concealed."

Miss Mann begins her tale and speaks "like one who tells the truth—simply, and with a certain reserve; she did not boast, nor did she exaggerate." Miss Mann had been "a most devoted daughter and a sister, an unwearied watcher by lingering deathbeds; that to prolonged and unrelaxing attendance on the sick, the malady that now poisoned her own life owed its origin."

Miss Mann did not catch cancer or consumption or alcoholism, but what a reader can infer from the next line is that she contracted some form of venereal disease: "that to one wretched relative she had been support and succour in the depths of self-earned degradation, and that it was still her hand which kept him from utter destitution."

Brontë is not saying that she caught this disease. She is implying that the only disease you catch from a wretch who has earned his own degradation would be a venereal disease, and the only way for it to be transferred to Miss Mann would be through a rape: *If not rape, hang old ghost Mann.*

Miss Mann's circumstance is reminiscent of Mrs. Collins plight with her drunken husband Reverend Collins and his "profligate habits." He "had abandoned his wife to disease," a "hideous disease." Mrs. Collins overcame the effects of the disease and became a successful landlady in a lodging house.

Miss Mann is not as fortunate. When Miss Mann speaks, why does she make Caroline feel "as if a graven image of some bad spirit were addressing" her? Because Miss Mann was raped, and her "goblin grimness" is directly related to that crime: "She had passed alone through protracted scenes of suffering, exercised rigid self-denial, made large sacrifices of time, money, health for those who had repaid her only by ingratitude, and now her main—almost her sole—fault was that she was censorious."

Like Nelly Dean in *Wuthering Heights*, Miss Mann has become the *censor* "flaying alive certain of the families in the neighbourhood. . . . She never disseminated really malignant or dangerous reports. It was not her heart so much as her temper that was wrong."

Miss Mann had held out her hand to the wretched relative to help him and he gave her a stone in the form of a disease. She continued to care for the man even after he had infected her.

When Brontë advises her reader not to judge a person's depression prematurely, she uses the word "canker" to imply that a horrible explanation lurks beneath the surface: "there is a canker somewhere, and a canker not the less deeply corroding because concealed."

The word "canker" means a corroding ulcer and metaphorically means something that corrupts or destroys. The similar word "chancre" means a venereal sore or ulcer. The allusion to this latter word may not be coincidental.

The laws, unfortunately, were on the side of the rapist at that time. With no one to witness the crime, the guilty party goes free, but Brontë needed to express her torment over a rapist and a *leech* living nearby who was always dropping in for food and drink, much like the curate Malone in *Shirley*.

No one would disagree with her sentiment that *laws should end leech, put out potato-eater as a real debauch—the Christian urchin who raped me.*

Brontë's closing remarks on Peter Malone's fate also contain a parenthetical statement that hides an anagram. The narrator refuses to explain why Malone had to leave Briarfield parish so suddenly. The line reads "You cannot know how it happened, / reader; / your curiosity must be robbed / to pay your elegant love / of the pretty and pleasing." The anagram is as follows:

Announce why took down epitaph. Cure my bitter sob. Bury every odious analogy. Let up on parent type too. Lights fade.

Her *bitter sob* has been cured, so she need not produce an *epitaph* for Malone—she has said enough. The analogies of the stone and Miss. Mann are done, and she can leave characterizations of her father out of future books as well.

Caroline's uncle Mr. Helstone would be a close depiction of Reverend Brontë: a curate, a "formalist," and "disciplinarian." The novel provides a summation of all the characters' destinies. The anagrams form a kind of summation as well; they explain how, through her characters, Brontë was able to *note* the *sin, quash* her *ire,* and purge her *gall* so, as in a play where the stage directions also read *lights fade,* the action comes to an end.

Are the novel's analogies based on fact? Are the anagrams true? In an era when the beating of a woman was seen as a man's privilege, a rape is not unimaginable, but this allegation can never be proved.

Brontë used her fiction as her way of getting even, so if Arthur Bell Nicholls is a model for Peter Augustus Malone, she must have felt contempt for Nicholls. Even without the assault, he would certainly not be a man she would ever want to marry. He had exhibited none of the qualities she most admired in men like Heger or Smith.

Over the years, Charlotte had received two proposals of marriage, but had refused them both. Her large disproportionate nose and the curve of her mouth created an odd set of features on a face that could hardly be described as pretty. She knew that her small stature and plain face would not attract many suitors, but she would only marry for love. She had hopes of one day finding a true love. Her kind hazel eyes and strong intellect were two attributes that an equally intelligent man would find attractive.

Until she experienced a meeting of minds with a man, she would remain a spinster, and perhaps die an old maid. This realization did not disturb Charlotte: the dream of being married was not as strong as her other dream to be a published author. Her dream had come true, and now she could live as an independent woman. Marriage was not a priority, especially to a man who she had never admired, but, after a strong and vehement refusal to his offer of marriage, she suddenly accepted his proposal and married him. Why? What changed her mind? And did the *disciplinarian* in her life have anything to do with her decision?

43 PROPOSAL ACCEPTED

In her letter to Ellen, Charlotte relates the story of Nicholls' proposal on December 15, 1852. Her words are the main record of what occurred, so scholars have had to believe in her sincerity and in her depiction of events. Her father was genuinely upset over Nicholls' desire to marry Charlotte, and makes his feelings clear in his letter to his daughter, but Charlotte seems to temper her reaction when she writes to Ellen. In the evening, Nicholls approached her in the dining room where, shaking and pale, he voiced his affection for her. "The spectacle of one ordinarily so statue-like—thus trembling, stirred, and overcome gave me a kind of strange shock. He spoke of sufferings he had borne for months—of sufferings he could endure no longer—and craved leave for some hope." She promised to respond the next day. Her father was adamant that she reject Nicholls and furious with the man thinking he—a curate with no money—was equal to his daughter, the famous author. "Papa worked himself into a state not to be trifled with—the veins on his temples started up like whip-cord—and his eyes became suddenly bloodshot—I made haste to promise that Mr. Nicholls should on the morrow have a distinct refusal." The next day she broke the news to Nicholls: "Attachment to Mr. Nicholls you are aware I have never entertained—but the poignant pity inspired by his state on Monday evening—by the hurried revelation of his sufferings for many months—is something galling and irksome. That he cared something for me—and wanted me to care for him—I have long suspected—but I did not know the degree or strength of his feelings" (*Letters Vol.III* 93).

The next correspondence three days later conveys Charlotte's dismay at Nicholls' sudden declaration of love. "You may well ask, for I am sure I don't know. This business would seem like a dream—did not my reason tell me it has been long brewing. It puzzles me to comprehend how and whence comes this turbulence of feeling." She heard from their servant Martha that, while lodged down the lane at John Brown's house, Nicholls was refusing to eat, so Charlotte sent him a note that stated, even though she will never reciprocate the affection he expressed to her, she did not want to hurt him, and encouraged him to keep up his spirits. In her letter to Ellen, she continues to explain why her father is outraged that Nicholls proposed. "You must understand that a good share of Papa's anger arises from the idea—not altogether groundless—that Mr. N. has behaved with disingenuousness in so long concealing his aims. . . . I am afraid also that Papa thinks a little too much about his want of money; he says the match would be a degradation. . . . My own objections arise from a sense of incongruity and uncongeniality in feelings, tastes—principles" (94-5).

With a subdued and reasoned tone, Charlotte recognized their incompatibility. Her father was incensed, and their friend John Brown threatened to shoot Nicholls for being so presumptuous. Nicholls had managed to alienate all three. While she spent the following month (January 1853) in London with her publisher George Smith and his mother, Charlotte received two letters from her father that confirmed his fury over the proposal: "You may wish to know, how we have been getting on here especially in respect to *master*; and *man*. On yesterday, I preached twice, but my man, was every way, very queer—He shun'd me, as if I had been a cobra de Capello—turning his head from the quarter, where I was, and hustling away amongst the crowd, to avoid contact—It required no Lavater to see, that his countenance was strongly indicative of mortified pride, and malevolent resentment—People have begun to notice these things, and various conjectures are afloat—You thought me too severe— but I was not candid enough—His conduct might have been excus'd by the world, in a confirmed rake—or unprincipled army officer, but in a *clergyman*, it is justly chargeable, with base design and inconsistency. I earnestly wish that he had another and better situation—As I can never trust him any more, in things of importance—I wish him no ill—but rather good, and wish that every woman may avoid him forever, unless she should be determined on her own misery" (105). These are harsh words from Reverend Brontë, but he knew the man's character as, apparently, did John Brown.

Reverend Brontë sent his second letter in the voice of Anne's dog Flossy, who was still alive and a much-loved pet. The dog observes that if it could speak it would be to report unpleasant events: "I see a good deal of human nature, that is hid from those who have the gift of language, I observe those manuoevres, and am permitted to observe many of them, which if I could speak, would never be done before me—I see people cheating one another, and yet appearing to be friends—many are the disagreeable discoveries which I make which you could hardly believe if I were to tell them." Nicholls is no longer walking Flossy and "has lost all his apparent kindness, scolds me, and looks black upon me." He ends his letter by advising his "dear Mistress," to "trust dogs rather than men— They are very selfish, and when they have the power, (which no wise person will readily give them) very tyrannical" (106-7). His words echo Charlotte's concerns about the men in her community. Now, both father and daughter agree: when selfish men have all the power, they can become tyrannical.

After the intense reaction from Reverend Brontë, Nicholls decided it was time to leave Haworth. At first, he applied to be a missionary in Australia. Prior to his departure, a bishop visited the village and stayed at the parsonage. Nicholls arrived for tea and "demeaned himself not quite pleasantly—I thought he made no effort to struggle with his dejection but gave way to it in a manner to draw notice; the Bishop was obviously puzzled by it. Mr. N also shewed temper once or twice in speaking to Papa. Martha was beginning to tell me of certain 'flaysome' looks also— but I desired not to hear them. The fact is I shall be most thankful when he is well away—I pity him—but I don't like that dark gloom of his—He dogged me up the lane after the evening service in no pleasant manner—he stopped also in the passage after the Bishop and the other clergy were gone into the room—and it was because I drew away and went upstairs that he gave that look which filled Martha's soul with horror. She—it seems— meantime, was making it her business to watch him from the kitchen door—If Mr. N be a good man at bottom—it is a sad thing that Nature has not given him the faculty to put goodness into a more attractive form— Into the bargain of all the rest he managed to get up a most pertinacious and needless dispute with the Inspector—in listening to which all my old unfavourable impressions revived so strongly—I fear my countenance could not but shew them" (129). Her description of his "flaysome" looks is reminiscent of Malone in *Shirley*: "Peter grew black as a thundercloud. When Shirley looked up, a fell eye was fastened on her: Malone, at least, had energy enough in hate: she saw it in his glance."

A month later, Nicholls changed his mind about taking the drastic step of moving to Australia and, instead, chose to find another curacy in the area. He left in May, and Charlotte wrote on the 27th she was relieved that the emotional drama was over: "he is gone—gone—and there's an end to it. I see no chance of hearing a word about him in the future—unless some stray shred of intelligence comes through Mr. Grant or some other second hand source" (148-9).

She believed the issue dead, but Nicholls had not yet given up hope. Charlotte was unaware of the scheme that was taking place behind her back. Nicholls had no intention of admitting defeat, so he had rallied his Mason friends, and they had devised a way to assist their brother in gaining control and realizing his matrimonial bliss. But was he worshipping "at the shrine of Love or Mammon"? Reverend Brontë had alluded to the origin of the conspiracy in his "Flossy" letter back in January: "I see people cheating one another, and yet appearing to be friends—many are the disagreeable discoveries which I make which you could hardly believe if I were to tell them," but he had not told these discoveries to his daughter, and it would be several months before she would hear of them and receive a terrible shock.

A week after Nicholls left Haworth, Charlotte became so ill that she was unable to write a letter to her friend Elizabeth Gaskell advising her to postpone her planned visit. Her father had to write the letter on her behalf. He explained that she was suffering from a case of influenza "and frequent sharp attacks of 'Tic Douloureux', which have rendered her utterly unable to entertain you as she could wish" (173). Tic Douloureux is a severe but temporary nerve pain in the side of the face, which, in Charlotte's case, may have been brought on by her problems with her teeth, but stress is also known to trigger the stabbing pain. Her father was also unwell during the first two weeks of June but slowly improved, as Charlotte explained in a letter to Ellen: "The very dreadful pain in my head is almost gone and so is the influenza. Papa too is better—but I was frightened about him—not that he has in the least lost appetite or thought himself ill in body—but the eyes etc. betrayed those symptoms that fill me with alarm" (175-6). Whenever his eyes became bloodshot or inflamed, she feared he might suffer a stroke, as he almost had when Nicholls proposed the previous December, and he came close to experiencing during her influenza. She wrote of her concern to Gaskell: "I heard him pause on the staircase in coming up to bed—he delayed some time: I listened—he pronounced my name—I hastily rose—and threw something round me, I went to him—

there he stood with his candle in his hand—strangely arrested—My dear Mrs. Gaskell—his sight had become suddenly extinct—he was in total darkness. Medical aid was immediately summoned—but nothing could be done—it was feared that a slight stroke of paralysis had occurred and had fallen on the optic nerve. I believed he would never see more; his own anguish was great. Thank God! The light began to return to him next day" (177). By July, his strength and condition had not returned: "his general health has however been lately a good deal affected" (181), and Charlotte continued to suffer from headaches. The illnesses began a week after Nicholls left the village; something had made Charlotte and her father collapse into severe ill health.

Immediately after Nicholls left, he began writing letters to Charlotte, which she ignored. Finally, she answered, presumably advising him to accept the circumstances as they stood, but, rather than shutting down communication, it encouraged him to ask for more letters, which she agreed to write. Why would she comply? Did she pity him? Had she recalled her own situation back in 1844, when she had begged Monsieur Heger to write to her when she returned to England, and was she now remembering how devastated she was when he had refused? Charlotte was not a foolish woman: she would have realized that, as difficult as it was for her to accept at the time, Heger had made his choice, and she would have to live with it. She may have applied the same logic to her situation with Nicholls. Why was Nicholls unrelenting in his pursuit when she had clearly refused his affection? What had given him hope, and was Charlotte advising him on how to move on with his life, or was she trying to inject reason into his determined and persistent striving for her hand in marriage?

Charlotte was neither advising nor pitying Nicholls; she was trying to negotiate with a man who had all the power in his hands and would not take no for an answer. Near the end of June, Ellen came to visit and heard disturbing news: within a month of his departure, Charlotte had made a complete about-face and had consented to marry Nicholls.

In July, Nicholls visited his friend Mr. Grant the curate in neighbouring Oxenhope and had ventured a walk over to the parsonage to see Charlotte. He was back in her life.

On August 12th Ellen wrote a letter to Mary Taylor, their mutual friend from Roe Head School, telling her that she was distressed and confused over Charlotte's contradictory plans to marry Nicholls. Mary responded by saying, "What do you mean about 'bearing her position so long, and enduring to the end'?. . . . How wd she be inconsistent with herself in marrying?" (Barker 735). Ellen could not understand how Charlotte now intended to marry someone they both had felt was incompatible in temperament and mind, and who lacked similar congenial principles and manners. Ellen could not comprehend this sudden and dramatic reversal of feelings, and could not reconcile Charlotte's meek compliance to all of Nicholls' demands. Unfortunately, Charlotte could not offer a reasonable explanation, so the two friends quarrelled and, from the middle of June 1853 to March 1, 1854, they stopped writing. This erratic behaviour from her steady and stable friend made no sense to Ellen and, as usual, Charlotte was bound to silence.

44 NO MARRIAGE OF MINDS

Mrs. Gaskell arrived for a visit in the middle of September and stayed a few days. She described her time to a friend as an enjoyable and relaxing stay. She mentions, however, that she was not comfortable around "fire-arms," and noticed the "glittering of bright flashing steel" at the parsonage: "Miss Brontë never remembers her father dressing himself in the morning without putting a loaded pistol in his pocket, just as regularly as he puts on his watch. There was this little deadly pistol sitting down to breakfast with us, kneeling down to prayers at night—to say nothing of a loaded gun hanging up on high ready to pop off on the slightest emergency" (*Letters Vol.III* 199). Loaded guns were lying by his side in every room. Was Reverend Brontë prepared to shoot an intruder or a friend?

Their guest also recorded an unusual conversation she had with Charlotte that resembles Lucy Snowe's beliefs in *Villette* (ch.15). During her solitude, Lucy loses faith in Heaven's ability to console and support her: "with what dread force the conviction would grasp me that Fate was my permanent foe, never to be conciliated." She concludes that God's plan is "that some must deeply suffer while they live, and I thrilled in the certainty that of this number, I was one." Mrs. Gaskell's account of Charlotte's belief echoes Lucy Snowe's.

"We talked about the different courses through which life ran. She said, in her own composed manner, as if she had accepted the theory as a fact, that she believed some were appointed beforehand to sorrow and much disappointment; that it did not fall to the lot of all—as Scripture told us—to have their lines fall in pleasant places; that it was well for those who had rougher paths, to perceive that such was God's will concerning them, and try to moderate their expectations. . . . I took a different view: I thought that human lots were more equal than she imagined; that to some happiness and sorrow came in strong patches of light and shadow . . . while in the lives of others they were pretty equally blended throughout. She smiled, and shook her head, and said she was trying to school herself against ever anticipating any pleasure; that it was better to be brave and submit faithfully; there was some good reason, which we should know in time, why sorrow and disappointment were to be the lot of some on earth.

It was better to acknowledge this, and face out the truth in a religious faith" (Gaskell 387). Charlotte was about to be married, but the sentiment Gaskell recalls is one of a prisoner fated to spend the rest of her life in a dungeon.

When her visitor had returned to Manchester, Charlotte wrote her a despondent letter: "After you left, the house felt very much as if the shutters had been suddenly closed and the blinds let down. One was sensible during the remainder of the day of a depressing silence, shadow, loss, and want. However, if the going away was sad, the stay was very pleasant and did permanent good" (*Letters, Vol.III* 194-5). Her spirits are noticeably low for someone who is writing to Nicholls and anticipating a marriage that will be occurring in less than a year.

In November, Charlotte had planned a trip to London "on a little matter of business (no-thing relating to literature or publishing, as I hardly need say—but wholly and solely touching my small income)" (206). She was making arrangements to stay in rooms at Bedford Place in London. George Smith had been taking care of her investments and relayed dividend payments to her through his office. She would have certainly been planning on seeing him if money matters were the impetus for her journey, but the same day she had intended on traveling, she received word from his mother that he was engaged and about to marry Elizabeth Blakeway, a pretty young lady he had met at a ball. Immediately, Charlotte cancelled her trip and wrote to the woman whose lodgings she had secured, "Man *pro*poses but Another *dis*poses. . . . circumstances have taken a turn which will prevent my intended journey to London" (211). Over recent months, she had felt hurt by his withdrawal from their friendship and had been missing his usually frequent correspondence, and now to hear of his engagement from his mother and not from him, she experienced a sense of betrayal. Ellen had stopped corresponding with her and now Smith was engaged. Two close friends were gone, and she was about to marry Nicholls. Her headaches and occurrences of dyspepsia continued into the next year.

Within a few months, Ellen and Charlotte resumed writing to each other, and in March of 1854, Charlotte erroneously mailed a letter meant for Nicholls to Ellen and one for her to him. This may have been a subconscious way to tell her friend how far the situation had evolved since the previous summer, and to allow Charlotte the opportunity to broach the provocative topic of approaching nuptials. The future was fixed. Nicholls would soon renew his post as her father's curate and live with his new family at the parsonage, so Charlotte began informing her other friends of the news. Juliet Barker points out: "What should have been joyous and excited letters were actually subdued and rather forlorn" (749). Charlotte also wrote to George Smith, who was now married, about her own upcoming marriage: "There has been heavy anxiety, but I begin to hope all will end for the best. My expectations, however, are very subdued, very different, I daresay, to what *yours* were before you were married. Care and Fear stand so close to Hope. I sometimes scarcely can see her for the Shadow they cast. And yet I am thankful too, and the doubtful Future must be left with Providence. On one feature of the marriage I can dwell with *unmingled* satisfaction, with a certainty of being right. It takes nothing from the attention I owe to my Father. I am not to leave him; my future husband consents to come here; thus, Papa secures by the step a devoted and reliable assistant in his old age" (*Letters, Vol.III* 250).

On May 24, 1854 Charlotte signed her marriage settlement that stipulated that if she died before her husband, all of her money would go to her father. Barker notes that "the object of the settlement was to ensure that Mr. Nicholls could not touch any of Charlotte's money," and she assumes Charlotte stipulated Nicholls be excluded from control of her estate in order to ensure that her father would not lose out financially from the marriage. In the meantime, the trustee of her income would disburse payments to her, solely for her own use. William Thomas' solicitor, Richard Metcalfe, drew up the document and acted as witness with Reverend Brontë (756).

Two months before the marriage was to take place, Charlotte wrote to Mrs. Gaskell explaining that she did not agree with Mr. Nicholls in matters of religious tolerance. She had always tried to remain open to variations in opinion and doctrine, while Nicholls believed in strict adherence to church doctrine. "I had a little talk with him about *my* 'latitudinarianism' and *his* opposite quality. He did not bristle up at all, nor feel stiff and unmanageable. He only groaned a little over something in *Shirley* touching 'baptismal regeneration and a wash-hand basin.' Yet if he is indulgent to some points in me, I shall have carefully to respect certain reverse points in him. I don't mean to trifle with matters deep-rooted and delicate of conscience and principle. I know that when once married I shall often have to hold my tongue on topics which heretofore have rarely failed to set that unruly member in tolerable facile motion. But I *will not* be a bigot—My heart will always turn to the good of every sect and class" (*Letters, Vol.III* 252). Baptismal regeneration stipulates that in order to be saved a person must be baptised. Her comments are a reminder of that earlier time when she was unable to control her tongue and lashed out at the curates: "they began glorifying themselves and abusing Dissenters in such a manner— that my temper lost its balance and I pronounced a few sentences sharply and rapidly which struck them all dumb." Freedom of speech would soon be constrained.

Charlotte was about to marry a man whose "deep-rooted" beliefs differed from her own. She was "subdued and rather forlorn"; her marriage settlement made certain that Nicholls was kept away from her money, and she believed fear had overshadowed hope. An intelligent, sensitive genius was about to be bound to a man of conflicting tastes and questionable integrity, who her father disapproved of and their friend John Brown wanted to shoot, and this life altering step was creating "heavy anxiety;" nonetheless she took the step, quickly, without faltering.

On June 29th, the vicar from Hebden Bridge, Sutcliffe Sowden, a Mason and friend, married Nicholls and Charlotte. Her father refused to attend the wedding, so her former teacher from Roe Head, Miss Wooler gave her away, and Ellen acted as her attendant. Nine months later, Charlotte was dead.

She had not died without leaving detailed accounts of events in her letters. She would file the information under cover of her *anagram hood*, and reiterate how she had hidden the story of the entail fraud in *Wuthering Heights*. She would also clarify why she married. The man who keeps his silence or stays *mum* about the real motivation for the marriage is most likely Nicholls. She lists a few elements from *Wuthering Heights*, which include Lockwood as a *pest*, Nelly Dean as the *gossip*, as well as an *ill child* and a *storm on* the *heath*. The novel's relevance and importance were paramount in her mind. She wanted her readers to find the hidden story in the novel, to discover the crimes, and learn what mattered most to her. The book was her secret testimony, and she hoped, by outlining her facts, that

442

some form of justice might better serve her community. She also wanted to explain why she married Nicholls.

April 11, 1854

Dear Ellen:

"1) Thank you for the collar. / 2) It is very pretty. / 3) And I will wear it for the sake 4) of her who made and gave it. / 5) Mr. Nicholls came on Monday 3rd 6) and was here all last week. / 7) He renewed his visit in September. / 8) But then matters so fell out 9) that I saw little of him. / 10) He continued to write. / 11) The correspondence 12) pressed on my mind. / 13) I grew very miserable 14) in keeping it from Papa. / 15) At last sheer pain made me 16) gather courage to break it. / I told all. / 17) It was very hard 18) and rough work at the time / 19) but the issue after a few days 20) was that I obtained leave 21) to continue the communication. / 22) Mr. N came in January. / 23) He was ten days / 24) in the neighbourhood. / 25) I saw much of him. / 26) I had stipulated with Papa / 27) for opportunity / 28) to become better acquainted. / 29) I had it and all I learnt / 30) inclined me to esteem and / 31) if not love / 32) at least affection. / 33) Still Papa was very / 34) very hostile / 35) bitterly unjust. / 36) I told Mr. Nicholls 37) the great obstacles that lay in his way. / 38) He has persevered. / 39) The result of this his last visit is / 40) that Papa's consent is gained / 41) that his respect / 42) I believe is won / 43) for Mr. Nicholls has in all things 44) proved himself / 45) disinterested and forbearing. / 46) He has shewn too 47) that while his feelings / 48) are exquisitely keen / 49) he can freely forgive. / 50) Certainly I must respect him / 51) Nor can I withhold from him / 52) more than mere cool respect./ In fact, 53) dear Ellen, / 54) I am engaged" (*Letters, Vol.III* 239-40).

York father alcohol nut—/vestry rite. Pity. / He drank oaf's ale. Write with deft anagram hood. View lie. / Ale clod wants solemn matrimony. Shake rich, well-read hand. / Mire in thieves' sewer. Hid best pen. / Bottles' theft fits with aim. Loath to let man rule us. / Then two in our deceit. / Pretend primed crone chose men's synod. / Wary. Revere pig mate. Smile big if ink on paper. / Mental phrase racket aids eager author. Meet a bigot. / I told all. / Taunt adversary with meek hood—right war. / Father's bottle waste buys an economic union. Waive audit fee. Had tie as net. Tacit mouth. / June I can marry man. / Why a den asset? Obedient,

high honour. / Which oaf is mum? / Paid up portion of debt. Dispute law.
Try tact, i.e., met once. Hit a baroque path. / Halt den liar. Add entail.
Tied in Masonic element. / Novel of it. / Facts in tale of tea. / Privately sap
laws, yet hire blunt, sty vole jurist. / Ill child, a risen twit, Cathy galls a
boy. Set storm on heath. / See shepherd rave. / Heir shifts to slave. Tilt
suits. / Attach inane pest and gossip, / tithes' chapters. / View noise bile. /
Slosh ran north mill as filching / shop. Mild fever. / First ending—a sober
den tirade. / How these eight selfish Noahs in wealth. / Key: Queen's tea
elixir. / Clever hero an effigy. / Arsenic clue. Myth permits it. / If rich, no
mirth. Old woman / completes romance rot here. In fact, *ale lender / egged*
mania.

The breakdown of the partitions in the sentences is as follows:

3) *Drank oaf's ale. Write with lie.* 4) *he view deft anagram hood.* 5) *clod rich hand solemn matrimony* 6) *ale wants well-read shake* 8) *Bottles theft us man rule to* 9) *loath let fits aim with* 11) *Pretend crone chose* 12) *primed men's synod* 13) *wary revere big smile* 14) *mate pig if ink on paper* 15) *mental phrase aids meet a* 16) *bigot racket eager author* 17) *with adversary* 18) *taunt meek hood right war* 19) *Father's waste buys fee audit* 20) *bottle waive had as tie* 21) *tacit mouth net economic union* 26) *Paid dispute law hit a path* 27) *up portion of try* 28) *debt tact baroque i.e. met once* 29) *halt entail liar add in* 30) *Masonic element den tied* 34) *hire sty vole* 35) *yet blunt jurist* 36) *ill child on storm* 37) *set heath Cathy galls a boy a risen twit* 46) *How these Noahs* 47) *eight selfish in wealth*

None of the sentences had commas, so these words could be moved to their proper place.

The anagrams explain the real reason Charlotte has to marry Nicholls. While she was in London, in early 1853, her father had been drinking and had written to her in the voice of their dog Flossy: "I see people cheating one another, and yet appearing to be friends—many are the disagreeable discoveries which I make which you could hardly believe if I were to tell them." Most likely, he is referring to his friends demanding payment for their alcohol. As stated in chapter three, Reverend Brontë, in the past, had to face rumours that he had been drinking. In a letter to a church trustee in October of 1843, he writes that villagers are saying he smells of alcohol, but he denies these rumours with the explanation that they are merely smelling his eye ointment: "I have lately been using a lotion for my eyes, which are very weak, and they have ascribed the smell of that, to a smell of a more exceptionable character." What kind of lotion would have a strong enough odour to raise suspicions that he was drinking?

Reverend Brontë's drinking habits were not a secret in the village. William Thomas, together with his sons James and Richard, were the Haworth wine and spirits merchants who "supplied Mr. Brontë with his regular order of 'eight bottles of port wine and four of sherry,'" wines that he believed were "effective in relieving his persistent dyspepsia and his order was a regular one for at least twenty years." Reverend Brontë was the President of the Haworth Temperance Society whose pledge was to avoid alcohol unless for medical reasons; consequently, in 1838, he wrote to John Milligan, a surgeon in Keighley "seeking medical authorization for his wine order," which would help him "'counteract, under providence, the groundless, yet pernicious censures of the weak, wicked and wily, who are often on the alert to injure those who are wiser and better than themselves'" (Whitehead 68).

Perhaps Reverend Brontë enjoyed a drink now and then, and perhaps he overindulged at times. "It might account for his fierceness of temper. Both Ellen Nussey and Mr. Nicholls would confirm that Mr. Brontë had a tendency to over-conviviality and it may be that this is part of the explanation for Charlotte's unceasing worry about her father's health" (Fraser 204).

Whatever the degree of truth, the humiliation of a charge of alcohol theft would have been unbearable for both Charlotte and her father. No wonder they both had become so ill during the days when the *men's synod* released its ultimatum. Charlotte would do whatever she could to protect her father's reputation; she had tried to repay the debt, but her efforts were unsuccessful; *tact* would not work: they would only accept a *portion of* the *debt*. Nicholls wanted to marry her. After all, she had money, and to marry a famous author would bring *high honour* to the Lodge, (even though Currer Bell's pen rarely moved during their marriage). The debt would be fully discharged only if she married into the brotherhood of Freemasons.

The men were in charge, and they were determined to have their way in the negotiations, which she saw as a *baroque path*. Under threats of a scandal or worse, and with no way out, she would be *obedient*. To a

445

modern reader, this sacrifice for her father might seem masochistic, but "throughout her life her strongest loyalty was to him," and in her earliest correspondence to him "she already shows both a dutiful affection and an awareness of what will most please and interest him" (*Letters, Vol.I* 3). The anagrams could lead one to deduce that Reverend Brontë, a proud man, had refused to attend the ceremony in order to show his disdain for the proceedings and for the "tyrants" who had orchestrated it.

Most of the anagrams explain Charlotte's fear of those few Masons who wielded the most power. Historical evidence supports her claims that they were uneducated, wealthy drinkers. Charlotte's friend Mary Taylor wrote to Mrs. Gaskell that her depiction of Haworth in Charlotte's biography was "'not so gloomy as the truth'" and that Charlotte was "'a woman of first-rate talents, industry and integrity'" who had lived "'in a walking nightmare of poverty and self-suppression'" (Shorter 243).

Mrs. Gaskell had visited Charlotte in Haworth and recalls, in a letter written in 1853, her impressions of a walk they took together on the moors. "Here and there in the gloom of the distant hollows she pointed out a dark grey dwelling—with Scotch firs growing near them often, and told me such wild tales of the ungovernable families, who lived or had lived therein that Wuthering Heights even seemed tame comparatively. Such dare-devil people—men especially, and women so stony and cruel in some of their feelings and so passionately fond in others. They are a queer people up there. Small landed proprietors dwelling on one spot since Q. Eliz, and lately adding marvellously to their incomes by using the water power of the becks in the woollen manufacture which has sprung up during the last 50 years: uneducated, unrestrained by public opinion, for their equals in position are as bad as themselves, and the poor, besides being densely ignorant, are all dependant on their employers." She continues by describing their dwellings: "These people build grand houses, and live in the kitchens, own hundreds of thousands of pounds and yet bring up their sons with only just enough learning to qualify them for over-lookers during their father's life time, and greedy grasping money-hunters after his death" (*Letters, Vol.III* 198).

Other anagrams, like the ones above, return to the topic of *Wuthering Heights*. Brontë continues to leave references to the story's characters and situations, such as *Cathy galls a boy*, when she annoys and humiliates

Hareton, and includes *Clever hero an effigy*, as a nod to Heathcliff's resemblance to one of the Masons. The *eight selfish Noahs* will be explained in the next chapter. She continues to reveal that she wrote the novel with all its twists and turns and secret stories—*Facts in tale of tea* and the *arsenic clue* in tea or, stated another way, the *Queen's tea elixir*. She never wearies of telling all: *Mental phrase racket aids eager author*. From her perspective, her secret ability to mentally shift phrases and sentences into anagrams would indeed seem like a *racket*, but the kind that implies a scheme or trick, although the continual activity could be considered the other kind of racket that suggests an ongoing noise in her brain. Whether trick or noise, these mental phrases were her silent weapon, her *best pen*, the *anagram hood* that enabled her to write her story, which may have included *a sober tirade* against the fraud in the *first ending* of *Wuthering Heights*. She obviously chose to omit the tirade when she wrote the fair copy.

Charlotte's fate is set, enabled by her tie to her father: *had tie as net.* Her father's theft of the alcohol fit perfectly with Nicholls' goal to marry her, but now she will be under his command: *Bottles' theft fits with aim. Loath to let man rule us.* She will be subjected to the rule of her husband even though both are aware of the false marriage vow, which they now share: *then two in our deceit*, but she will continue to *pretend primed crone chose men's synod*. The marriage is a sham, another *bluff* or *hoax* in which she must participate, but unlike her pseudonym hoax, this deceit and the cover-up of her brother's suicide are not of her choosing. Another male family member has placed her in a difficult position, this time with a much larger payment extracted: *Father's bottle waste buys an economic union*, and the men who have supported Nicholls in his desire to be attached to a rich woman will most likely receive some future compensation in return.

Slosh ran north mill as filching shop. If the *slosh* runs his own scams from his mill, he would know that justice is weak. As *ale lender,* he also *egged* on the *mania* for crime. The Brontës would have tried to assert their rights—*dispute law*, but would have failed. Even a charge of extortion would be irrelevant: the men *privately sap laws, yet hire blunt, sty vole jurist.* They ignore the power of the law, but use it to their advantage when they hire their own astute lawyer, a man who states the bleak facts: *sign our documents or drink the Queen's tea elixir.* Apparently, theirs is an insular kind of justice. Charlotte will necessarily have to be careful when near these men and when around her husband: her opinions and views must remain suppressed. She will be *wary* and pretend to *revere pig mate. Smile big if ink on paper.* She must always present a pleasant demeanour while writing. The majority of her writing will be her letters because her fiction output was sparse after her marriage, but the smile will keep her husband from suspecting the anagrams are secretly revealing all. She will appear to have a *tacit mouth* and a mild expression, while she continues to *taunt* her *adversary with* her *meek hood.* This duplicity, in her mind, is a *right war.*

If the interpretation of the anagrams is correct, they reveal a considerable amount of tragedy that would understandably lead her to question her fate. At the time of her engagement, she had confided in Mrs. Gaskell that "she believed some were appointed beforehand to sorrow and much disappointment," and "she was trying to school herself against ever anticipating any pleasure; that it was better to be brave and submit faithfully;" because "there was some good reason, which we should know in time, why sorrow and disappointment were to be the lot of some on earth."

Her metaphors in *Shirley* of the stone and the scorpion seem prescient in light of her forced marriage: "Take the matter as you find it: ask no questions, utter no remonstrances; it is your best wisdom. You expected bread and you have got a stone. . . : You held out your hand for an egg, and fate put into it a scorpion. Show no consternation; close your fingers firmly upon the gift; let it sting through your palm. Never mind; in time, after your hand and arm have swelled and quivered long with torture, the squeezed scorpion will die, and you will have learned the great lesson how to endure without a sob."

In February of 1855, Charlotte's mysterious illness began.

45 FINAL LETTERS
AND
A WILL

On February 14th, 1855 Nicholls wrote to Ellen Nussey in response to her many letters asking why she had not heard from Charlotte. He responded by saying, "It is difficult to write to friends about my wife's illness, as its cause is yet uncertain—at present she is completely prostrated with weakness and sickness and frequent fever—All may turn out well in the end, and I hope it will; if you saw [her] you would perceive that she can maintain no correspondence at present—" (*Letters, Vol.III* 324-5). Charlotte was ill and dying, and Ellen would not see her until after her death.

Her will and four letters that preceded her death contain anagrams and are shown below. (The breakdown of the anagrams is in the Appendix under the heading "Final Letters.")

A few weeks before she died, Charlotte wrote the following letter to Ellen Nussey on or after February 21, 1855

My dear Ellen:

"I must write one line / out of my weary bed. / The news of Mercy's / probable recovery / came like a ray of joy to me. / I am not going to talk about my sufferings / it would be useless and painful. / I want to give you an assurance / which I know will comfort you / and that is that I find in my husband the tenderest nurse / the kindest support / the best earthly comfort / that ever woman had. / His patience never fails and it is tried by sad days and broken nights" (*Letters, Vol.III* 326).

Remit fury. See union wilt. Wed a booty—me. / Amoral men joke. Love robbery caper. Why free? Coy fee. Amity costs. / Souse took tin fund. Mating buys off gaol is argument, but wed a plain Ellis. Navigate low court seas. How? Way, if lucky, with moronic union. / Shy maid had abundant hints fit tin urn. Need three tests. / Poke third test puns. / Myth brother flees cot at a mad Haworth event. / Finish. Did leave secret pain. Dying. Hobby ends as Titan tankards rise.

Brontë begins the anagrams with the word *remit,* which is usually used in connection with sending money: please remit payment or remit fee. Here she uses it to *remit* her *fury.* Her marriage has deteriorated: *see union wilt,* and the *amoral men joke* about Reverend Brontë's stealing because they *love* a good *robbery caper.* It appears that the only reason the men refrained from charging him, which allowed him to go free, is that Charlotte agreed to marry Nicholls; consequently, her *coy* treatment of him in the past and her friendliness, or *amity,* came with a high price: he thought she liked him, and he wanted a rich wife. His desire to marry her is what spared Reverend Brontë from being imprisoned—that would be their *argument* for convincing her to proceed with the wedding. In her mind, Nicholls has married *a plain Ellis,* the bolder version of her coy persona, and not the quiet woman he had imagined. She believes the Masons left their money in a tin urn, which was probably kept at their Lodge. Her father would have access to this money and is, therefore, the *souse* or drunkard who took the *tin fund.* Her marriage prevents her father going to jail (*gaol*) and avoids an appearance in the lower small claims' court: they *navigate low court seas with moronic union.* She continues the sea and pirate metaphors with the word *booty,* which refers to a thief's plunder or profit, so she is the *booty*; her life and money have been offered in payment of the debt.

She switches topics to reveal clues that she left in *Wuthering Heights.* She hid many hints about the Mason urn: *shy maid had abundant hints fit tin urn,* which could be alluding to her secret anagram satire where Catherine returns as a ghost to steal the documents from the tea canister. She also mentions the three-degree tests—*need three tests*—and puns that she scatters throughout the first three chapters: *poke third test puns.* An example of poking fun with puns is at the beginning of chapter three when Zillah ushers Lockwood to the bedroom upstairs. She tells him to be quiet because Heathcliff has odd ideas about the room, "and never let anybody lodge there willingly." The word "lodge" can also be a noun. Lockwood, the myth brother, does flee the cot after he sees the ghost, *a mad* third-degree *event* that could easily have taken place at the Haworth lodge. Within the novel, she *did leave secret pain,* in the images of brutal treatment at the Wuthering Heights farmhouse.

Brontë knows she is now *dying* and that her writing career has ended. She imagines the men celebrating her death while drinking their beer: *Titan tankards rise.*

Another group of anagrams shown below and found in the central nine stanzas of the long poem in *The Professor* (ch.23) provides more information about the fraud. Brontë explains how she incorporated the Masonic fraud into her fiction, specifically in *Wuthering Heights*: she sets the stage and, with her mass of anagrams or *runes*, hides her story from the men in order to *ruff* or trump the Masons as she outlines their scheme. In a card game like whist, to ruff involves using a trump card to take a trick from an opponent. Brontë would see her secret rune language as her trump card, and she used it not only through Heathcliff's land manoeuvers but also through her hidden ghost satire that she wove into the anagrams.

The poem is several stanzas. The anagrams follow the verses exactly.

"Seek in the garden shades a seat / Far from the play-ground den; / The sun is warm, the air is sweet; / Stay till I call you in. / A long and pleasant afternoon / I passed in those green bowers; / All silent, tranquil and alone / With birds and bees and flowers. / Yet when my Master's voice I heard / Call from the window "Jane!" / I entered, joyful, at the word, / The busy house again. / He, in the hall, paced up and down; / He paused as I passed by; / His forehead stern relaxed its frown; / He raised his deep-set eye. / "Not quite so pale," he murmured low: / "Now, Jane, go rest awhile." / And as I smiled, his smoothened brow / Returned as glad a smile. / My perfect health restored, he took / His mien austere again, / And as before, he would not brook / The slightest fault from Jane. / The longest task, the hardest theme / Fell to my share as erst, / And still I toiled to place my name / In every study first. / He yet begrudged and stinted praise,/ But I had learnt to read / That secret meaning of his face, / And that was my best meed. / Even when his hasty temper spoke / In tones that sorrow stirred, / My grief was lulled as soon as woke / By some relenting word."

Set stage. Need handshake. Arise! / Hood yarn. Ruff grand temple / with rune mass. Write these as I / tacitly lay illusion. / Step one: Land an oaf. Grant loan. / Begin, preside, swear, so honest. / Delinquent annals a toll. Liar / wolf behind bane. Address writs. / Sty wives' aid a theme. No mercy. Her / fate—join world when calm. / Need her to jaw ode. Lit fury. / Agonies hush beauty. / Had pawn. End help. Held auction. / Assess heap. Bid due. Pay. / Next trade wife, heirs for land, horses, / sheep, dairy, seed. I seethe / alone. Write poems, hurl mud, quote / sweet jargon in a whole / mildewed Mason obsession. Hit hard. / Great man derides us all. / Try to meet elder. Phrase: 'fetch hook.' / Genuine Isaiah master. / Found a handbook, so rebel, wrote / theft as male loner. Just fight. / Masked. Throttle these heath gents. / Smart: for sty, see a Hell. / Little demon a typical idle Mason: / envies dirt. Sty fury. / Guide tenant. Passed by third degree. / Hate odd ritual banter. / Craft eight fine men as echoes. / Wanted beasts. Made myth. / Kept own shire heaven. Seeps myth. / Twit orator rises. Send north. / Know a godless family. See our laws / bleed moors. Gentry win.

These anagrams repeat the method of defrauding unsuspecting mortgagors. The borrower never noticed the stipulation that if a payment is delinquent, he must pay the loan in its entirety, a shrewd practice that allocates the entire allotment to the deceptive lender, and one that the uneducated man either never noticed was buried at the root of the document in its opaque terms and conditions, or never saw because the clause was added after the signing. According to Brontë, Mason lenders prepared a helpful loan for a fellow brother; all parties executed the document in front of presiding witnesses, and advisers showed him where to sign, so the formality gave the scheme its legitimacy and aura of honesty. When the loan became *delinquent* the experience took its *toll* on the families.

The wives would lose everything, as would the sons. This lack of *mercy* or *aid* is a theme Brontë highlights through the violence in Isabella's marriage to Heathcliff. The naïve beauty relates to Nelly Dean all the abuses at the farmhouse. Brontë needs this character in order to *to jaw ode*, or tell a story like a Greek chorus that sings of incidents occurring offstage. Isabella's letter to Nelly, in chapter thirteen, conveys, in brutal detail, her life with Heathcliff when she arrives at Wuthering Heights. She later says, "He's a lying fiend! A monster, and not a human being." In chapter seventeen, she escapes in a storm and relates the horror of pistols, knives, "burning hate," "excessive pain," and "the flow of blood that gushed from an artery or a large vein." These *agonies hush* the *beauty* Isabella.

Brontë continues to explain the process by which the landowners would lose their property. The *help* runs out; the men assess the goods or *heap*; hold an auction, *bid, pay,* and then *trade wife* and *heirs for land, horses, sheep, dairy,* and *seed.* She had access to Masonic literature and inserted the Masonic elements together with aspects of the fraud into *Wuthering Heights*. She also states that the *great man*, who must be the gang's leader, resembles the masters in the Bible's "Book of Isaiah," where corrupt evil rulers have rendered the country desolate and filled the cities with murderers and befriended thieves. She views her depictions of both the Masonic brutality and young Heathcliff's demonic temperament as her private rebellion and, with her male persona of Ellis, sees her narrative as a "just fight."

Finally, she returns to terms she uses in her "Biographical Notice" to describe Lockwood, the *orator* she sends *north* after he *rises* into the *third degree*. Near the end of the novel, when he returns to the area Lockwood says, "This September, I was invited to devastate the moors of a friend, in the North."

The anagram states that Brontë based the eight men in *Wuthering Heights* on actual people. The eight men in the story would most likely be Mr. Earnshaw, Hindley, Heathcliff, Joseph, Hareton, Edgar Linton, Doctor Kenneth, and Lawyer Green. Mr. Earnshaw is the father and patriarch of Wuthering Heights; Hindley is his debauched son; Heathcliff is the interloper into the affairs of both families; Joseph is the devout and "ancient" servant; Hareton is the natural heir defrauded of his inheritance; and Edgar is the Magistrate, owner of Thrushcross Grange, and father to the natural heir Cathy, who is also disinherited. The doctor and the lawyer are complicit participants in the fraud with one registering the false cause of death and the other preparing and executing 'legal' documents.

This anagram regarding the eight men may explain why Brontë changed the title from "Wuthering Heaven" to *Wuthering Heights*: in the former, she refers to the Yorkshire setting as both a "misanthropist's heaven," which would be a Hell for regular society, and to Cathy's sentiment that the moors are her heaven. Brontë also sees the landscape as her *own shire heaven*, a powerful setting that *seeps* through the narrative.

In the latter title, she narrows the Hell down to eight men and, therefore, reflects this idea inside the title by placing the word "eight" inside it: H-eight-s. In her mind, these men constitute the whole story and should, therefore, be represented in the title. This title also retains the initials W.H., which echo the name Well Head, the farmhouse that appears to have been her model for the Earnshaw dwelling.

Anagrams from her early childhood to the ones hidden in the poem inside *The Professor* continue to be a form of rebellion and free expression where she can tell the truth behind her mask. Her final anagrams continue this tradition. This chronicle also emphasizes the tragic reality that an author's potential for further works of art was silenced too soon.

Late February, 1855.

Dear Amelia:

"Let me speak the plain truth. / My sufferings are very great. / My nights indescribable. / Sickness with scarce a reprieve. / I strain until what I vomit is mixed with blood. / Medicine I have quite / discontinued. / If you can send me anything that will do good do. / As to my husband / My heart is knit to him. / He is so tender, so good helpful patient. Poor Joe! long has he to suffer. / May God soon send him, / you, all of us health strength—/ comfort" (*Letters, Vol.III* 327).

He has kept up ill treatment. / Fear mystery fever is urn gag. / They end scribbling aims. / Wise, cheap trick. Serves arsenic. / Twit tin ritual. Hoax—womb void. Limited his sin. / Hive quiet came. Induced to die in sin. / Doodling fund—high, easy, toady income. Want lot. / Do nasty ambush. / Shrink, maim tithe toy. / Pulpit fool. He needs hag to end stories./ Sons of heath group jeer fool. / Moody. Has me nod, sign. / On cot! Hush! Form—legal theft. Oust fly.

The *mystery fever* could be an *urn gag*, but not the kind that means a jest, but one that gags her mouth. This illness could effectively silence her. She creates another *hoax*, but this one is necessary to limit his *ill treatment*. Her lie brings relief from the *hive* visits and returns some *quiet* to her home. Through the anagrams, she reveals her *hoax*—her *womb* is *void*; she is without child, so if Nicholls was truly poisoning her, she may have felt forced to say she was pregnant in order to have him leave her alone in their bed. The *hoax* upset her because it left her with a lie on her soul: *induced to die in sin*. Nicholls could be her *pulpit fool*: he needed her (the *hag*) *to end* the *stories*, the gossip that she had rejected him. Those who know the truth make fun of him: *sons of heath group jeer fool*, which would understandably make him *moody*. His anger could lead him to force her to sign a *form* that allows him to take all her money; thus, the *legal theft* that gets rid of a superfluous wife and makes him look powerful to his neighbours: his wife must have loved him because she gave him all her money.

The other possibility for her *pulpit fool* would be her father. The gossip surrounding him, the *stories* that needed to be stifled, would be that a few months prior, his drinking had resurfaced and he had stolen liquor from the Masons. If the *amoral men joke* and *love robbery caper*, their tales of Reverend Brontë 'drinking' their fund could have easily circulated through the village. Their jeers would certainly make him *moody* because for years he had been a respected member of Haworth society, and now he was the butt of jokes. His pride would have been devastated. In a later anagram she refers to her father as being *moody: Inane papa in the dark bed. Moody.* She may have, therefore, meant that her father was the *fool*, but in this letter anagram, she follows the word with *has me nod, sign. On cot.* This suggests that Nicholls is the *fool*, and that he can *oust* a *fly,* a pest, when he forces her to *nod* in agreement, and *sign* the *legal theft* while lying in her bed. Charlotte had two possibilities for a *pulpit fool*, but like any independent, intelligent woman, she would have preferred to have had none.

In the last chapter of *The Professor*, William asks his wife Frances what she would do if she found she had married a tyrant or a drunkard. Frances says she would try to escape, but if the law forced her to return she would probably try to endure: "if a wife's nature loathes that of the man she is wedded to, marriage must be slavery. Against slavery all right thinkers revolt—and though torture be the price of resistance, torture must be dared; though the only road to freedom lie through the gates of Death—those gates must be passed, for freedom is indispensable. Then Monsieur, I would resist as far as my strength permitted; when that strength failed I should be sure of a refuge; Death would certainly screen me both from bad laws and their consequences."

In chapter twenty-eight of *Jane Eyre*, Jane also considers death as a form of refuge.

"Hopeless of the future, I wished but this—that my Maker had that night thought good to require my soul of me while I slept; and that this weary frame, absolved by death from further conflict with fate, had now but to decay quietly, and mingle in peace with the soil of this wilderness."

Prior to their marriage, on May 24, 1854, Charlotte signed a document that kept her money out of Nicholls' hands. It "basically prevented Mr. Nicholls touching a penny of her money, whether she was alive or dead." She had chosen the brother of Mary Taylor, her friend from childhood to be her trustee. She transferred her money into Joe Taylor's name with the proviso that if any problem arose, "the money was to be paid to Charlotte personally 'for her sole and separate use independent of the said Arthur Bell Nicholls, her intended husband, who is not to intermeddle therewith'; the money was not to be 'subject or liable to his debts, Control Contracts or Engagements', so that Charlotte alone controlled its expenditure." Charlotte had provided for her children, but "if there were no living children of the marriage on Charlotte's death, then the entire trust funds were to be paid out according to the Intestacy Statutes as if Charlotte had died unmarried and intestate. If Joseph Taylor died or otherwise relinquished his position as trustee, then Charlotte could appoint another in his stead, regardless of her marriage." The biographer Fraser notes that "the clause that prevented Mr Nicholls from receiving any money in the event of Charlotte Brontë's death was very unusual," and she refers to Juliet Barker, the biographer who discovered the document, as thinking this clause "indicates the depth of doubt Charlotte felt about Nicholls' motives in marrying her," since, at the age of thirty-eight, children would be unlikely (Fraser 462-3). Charlotte had done everything legally possible to keep her money away from her husband, but now she was about to sign a will that made him her sole beneficiary.

Apparently, for good reason, Brontë feared the power of lawless men. The royalties from her books, her *doodling fund* would provide Nicholls with a continuous income until his own death, so Charlotte's sudden change of heart to sign over all her assets to her husband a few weeks before she died could be seen as the result of a desperate woman, a *tithe toy*, trying to save her life.

Nicholls' desire for her *doodling* royalties is ironic in light of later comments. Fifteen years after Charlotte's death, Ellen Nussey said that Nicholls discouraged Charlotte's writing, and stated emphatically "'I did not marry Currer Bell, the novelist, but Charlotte Brontë, the clergyman's daughter. Currer Bell may fly to heaven tomorrow for all I care'" (478). In 1858, Mrs. Gaskell also related a similar attitude in Nicholls regarding a story Charlotte had "begun a year or so before her marriage and Mr. Nicholls always *groaned literally*—when she talked of continuing it" (Chapple 496). The money from her previous books would suffice. No need to shirk her duty to address his needs by wasting time writing more fiction. One wonders what Heger or Smith would have said if Currer Bell wanted to pen more stories.

The last Will and Testament seems to have worked. Her letters and this final gesture silenced the rumours that she loathed him and created yet another myth for biographers to ponder. Her signature on the will also appears to have aided her brief recovery, but if she had ingested poison over a period of time, the damage would be done, and her body would be too weak to battle back. Several days before her death, she continued to write her brief letters.

March, 1855.

Dear Amelia:

"I'll try to write a line myself. / The medicines produced / no perceptible effect on me / but I thank you for them / all the same. / I would not let / Arthur write to Dr. Henriquez. / I knew it would be / wholly useless. / For 2 days I have been / something better / owing to the milder weather. / We all grieve / that there is no better news of Joe. / Oh for happier times. / My little grandchild / when shall I see her again? / God bless you" (*Letters, Vol.III* 327).

Style will for maternity lie. / Did seem prudent choice. / Force pen. Complete benefit. / A future book myth hint: / a mate's hell. / Raze required. Do truth until throw in towel. / Yell woe, but like wind, uses howls. / Beware of avid honesty. Might not be reset. / Wrote eight with role named. / Legal review to see how rent rebates join theft. / Heath is prime proof. / Target: mill—did lynch. / An high healer was senile, / so busy Lodge.

Brontë's inclusion of a clause regarding children, or "issue" living after her death is her *maternity lie*. A *prudent choice* if you want to appeal for mercy. She alleges that Nicholls forced her to write the will and that he received all the benefits—*complete benefit*—so if she lived to write another book, it would be about *a mate's hell* at the hands of an abuser who should be destroyed—*Raze required*. She will continue to tell her truth until she must *throw in* the *towel*. Her pleas for a quieter, gentler existence are met with *howls* that sound like the howls of the *wind,* and she warns her reader that honesty may not always be the best policy because once stated, words cannot be taken back: *beware of avid honesty. Might not be reset*. She returns to clues about *Wuthering Heights*: the eight men each had a role in the novel and, as stated above, are most likely Earnshaw, the patriarch, Hindley the son, Heathcliff, the interloper, Joseph the servant, Hareton, the natural heir, Magistrate Linton, the doctor, and the lawyer. The novel provides a *legal review to see how rent rebates join theft*. Heathcliff takes over both properties and enjoys the income from the rent on Thrushcross Grange. The final two anagrams refer to a hanging that took place on the *heath* as *prime proof* of how rents are the preferred method of payment. A *mill* was the *target* of the murder. Perhaps the new owner wanted the property to rent.

The last two lines are troubling because Brontë implies that the Lodge or masons killed *an healer*, her term for doctor. The historical facts support a doctor's death, but no proof of foul play exists. On April 30, 1842, Dr. Thomas Andrew died at the age of 52. He had been a doctor in Haworth for over twenty years and was one of Reverend Brontë's "oldest friends." He had been a revered member of Haworth Society, working with the poor during a breakout of typhus fever, so his death during a trade depression "was a particular loss to the suffering poor." A monument committee elected to erect a memorial "in Haworth Church to his memory," and Branwell, "glad to do an old friend a favour," wrote the inscription for the "marble tablet" that read in part "'This Tablet was erected by those who knew his worth, and who feel that, while in his death the neighbourhood has lost an honourable and upright man, the poor have lost an able adviser in their calamities, and a generous friend in their need'" (Barker 395-6). The hanging is addressed again in the next set of anagrams.

March 1855.

My dear Ellen:

"Thank you much for Mrs. Hewitt's / sensible clear letter. / Thank her too. / In much her case was / wonderfully like mine, / but I am reduced / to greater weakness. / The skeleton emaciation is the same / etc. etc. etc. / I cannot talk, / even to my dear / patient constant Arthur / I can say but few words / at once. / These last two days / I have been somewhat better, / and have taken some beef tea, / spoonsful of wine and water, / a mouthful of light pudding / at different times. / Dear Ellen / I realize full well / what you have gone through / and will have to go through / with poor Mercy. / Oh may you continue to be / supported and not sink / Sickness here has been / terribly rife. Papa is well now. / Kindest regards to / Mr. And Mrs. C your mother, / Mercy. / Write when you can. / Yours C.B. Nicholls" (*Letters, Vol.III* 328).

Knew truth, so rich, famous Bell relates secret in myth. / Then hook rat. / If church men kill me now, as a wise rule—deny. / Audit curbed me. See strange tea work. / Tie to hemlock in a senate. Emit ashes etc. etc. etc./ Link not an act. / Eye venom dart. Snatch torn rat. Put in tea. / Two-faced act wins as bury one. / At stately sow shed the thieves beat beam owner. / Name, vote, shake, be neat, fade. / Awful red pawn fits noose on. / Lift up, hang. Tough feat if termites. Find old mud, / lean elder. / Then zeal will rule life. Who gave a rough youth a tough lad howl over night? Worm hypocrite. / Undo knot, auction drapes, buy pints. Yeomen hoot. / Banshees shriek. Try brier life scene. / Own law applies. / Gets dark. Den riots. Stormy murder march. No mercy. / On cue, they win war. / Holy in cross club.

In these anagrams, Brontë explains that she related the story of the land fraud in her *myth*, which would be the story of *Wuthering Heights*. She believes that her husband is poisoning her, and refers to the death of Socrates when Athens' senators ordered the philosopher to drink the poison hemlock for corrupting minds with his questions and for not believing in state gods. Socrates was called a "gadfly" for his annoying habit of seeking the truth. In an earlier anagram, Charlotte calls herself a *fly,* one that Nicholls needs to *oust*. This *link* to Socrates' poisoning is *not an act* in Brontë's case: she believes her sickness is from arsenic tea that, while not a state sanctioned murder, is one the thieves have sanctioned. The *venom dart* would be the poison itself. The image of her husband getting a poisoned rat and putting bits of it in the tea is almost too horrific to believe, so she may be using the image as a succinct metaphor for the type of poison and how it would be administered. His *two-faced act wins as bury one*: his duplicity finally triumphs with her death.

The anagrams then switch to relate the story of a hanging. This could be the same lynching referred to in the earlier anagram that had a mill as its target. The process starts with naming the individual, voting on whether to kill him, shaking hands after the agreed decision, and making sure to do a *neat* job, not make a mess. The murderers then *fade* away from public scrutiny. After Branwell's death, Brontë put an anagram in a letter that stated he was involved in the incident: *Hand is in brutal hanging hoax*. According to the historical data at the Brontë museum and in Juliet Barker's book, one hanging occurred in the area at Hollings Mill in late April of 1842. This was a few weeks after Branwell had returned home from Luddenden Foot where he had been fired for inept accounting. George Robinson's father James had owned Hollings Mill in 1793 and had sold it sometime in the 1830s. Thomas Lister, a Mason and fellow executor on George Robinson's will, owned Hollings at the time of his death. He had spun cotton at the mill between 1822 and 1841. The general belief was that Lister had gone bankrupt, which was the reason "he was found hanged in his own barn on 26 April" (Barker 911 n. 48). By 1844, William Thomas Senior had bought the mill, and had leased it to his son William Junior, a worsted spinner and weaver, until 1853 when the mill failed, but his brothers James and Richard then took over. In 1861, their father William sold the mill to those two sons.

Another fact coincides with the hanging. Brontë mentions it in the earlier anagram as well. Dr. Thomas Andrew the *high healer* who *was senile* died four days after the hanging on April 30, 1842. This is pure speculation, but the only reason to kill a senile doctor would be if he were unable to stay mute about a murder that was listed as suicide. He had died at 52, hardly the usual age of senility but, perhaps, rather than a literal term Brontë is using it to say he was absent-minded or confused about Haworth deaths. For the thieves, senility would be an apt term for his poor judgment. Whatever the case, if true, Brontë is suggesting that his figurative senility was the reason for his death. This could be an interesting coincidence that she refers to a hanging and a doctor's death, and the facts do corroborate the anagrams, but no proof exists of a conspiracy. If, however, she believes the *Lodge* was *so busy,* one could infer that a few of the men were somehow involved in both deaths. A tragic irony would be the involvement of Branwell composing an inscription for Andrews' memorial tablet days after being told of plans to end the doctor's life, or worse, voting and then shaking hands over it.

The barn where the hanging took place could be classed as a *stately sow shed.* Branwell could be the *red* haired *pawn* that put the noose around the man's neck and then lifted him up. Brontë's wry humour is evident in the comment that the hanging would be difficult if *termites* had been destroying the wood beams. After the hanging, *undo knot* and then sell the mill. The process seems to be to *auction* personal property, celebrate and *buy pints,* and listen to the *yeomen hoot* and the *banshees' shriek.* The banshees are spirits derived from Irish mythology that cry and wail to warn families of approaching death.

The fate for the young men is to find sickly elders so the masons can acquire *old mud.* This story of a lad hunting for dying landowners is reminiscent of the anagrams in *The Professor: Thieving charity role taxes me. I often visit a fool, forge lease, write estate levy, openly sin. Divide tiny trust's mammon—ruin shire. Today join hunt for any new grain farms. Our priority: sod.* The anagrams continue by stating that another job is to find a *lean elder,* preferably one in poor health. She uses *eye* to mean look at, as in *eye venom dart.* The Mason lad explains his duties: *Check paper, found a newly departed brother. Eye halo then sin. During ill health, help oaf write a duplicate will or add on my name. Dear initiate, use poison.* Brontë must be thinking of Branwell when, in her letter, she writes *zeal will then rule life,* and asks the question, *who gave a rough youth a tough lad howl over night?* Branwell had been a *rough youth* but he had potential to be a successful, educated member of society. She blames a *worm hypocrite*—someone who must have feigned a religious countenance while being master of the tough lads—for helping to lead Branwell astray.

Her determination to tell this dreadful story is evident in the constant references in her anagrams and in *Wuthering Heights*. Nothing, however, can be stated emphatically as true because the anagrams may not be entirely accurate, and Brontë may have exaggerated the situation because of her fertile imaginative. Nonetheless, her allegations of poisoning and a hanging are startling and not completely unbelievable but, at this time, cannot be proved.

Brontë's images are stark and depressing. She depicts a *brier life scene* of brutality and murder. She could be alluding to the Masonic Lodge when she notes the apparent hypocrisy of religious men involved in criminal activity. She puts the words *holy* and *cross* alongside *club*, which could mean the Lodge, but another meaning might be hidden in the form of a clue. These words aligned the way they are could connect with an anagram from her will that states that a *Wolf ran a mayhem log from inn*. The *log* would be a log book that kept track of the *mayhem*. The question would be which inn? The only inn with the word *cross* in its name is The Cross Inn at the top of Main Street. If the meaning of *holy in cross club* is that the men appear to be lawful citizens, wearing their halos, but secretly conspiring at the *cross club* or at The Cross Inn, perhaps she imagines Masons frequenting this Inn when the Lodge is unavailable.

Obviously, ownership cannot supply a definite connection to the criminals, but Masons did own the Cross Inn, so the thieves could have chosen it as their meeting place. The four inns at the top of Main Street were the Black Bull, the King's Arms, the White Lion, and the Cross Inn. In 1846, William Thomas bought the Cross Inn "and he owned all the rest of the property on the north side of the top of Main Street." His sons James and Richards helped him run the wine and spirit shop located next door, and in 1850 those two sons bought the White Lion Inn. During the 30s and 40s, the other two inns—the Black Bull and the King's Arms—were "each successfully managed by William's brother Enoch." The Williams' family, however, did not own these two inns. Edward Green-Emmott-Rawden owned the Black Bull and "the Lord of the Manor Edward Ferrand" owned the King's Arms (Whitehead 67-9). Enoch Thomas had been a good friend of Branwell's and had died a few months before him "from chronic inflammation of the liver" (70). The men in Branwell's circle would have, therefore, been comfortable and welcome at these inns, but without actual

462

names of the perpetrators, Brontë's allusion to a *cross* should not be taken literally.

February 17, 1855 Charlotte wrote out her will leaving everything to Nicholls (*Charlotte Brontë and Her Circle*). Reverend Brontë and Martha Brown witnessed the document. Prior to this date, the Brontë's faithful servant Tabby Aykroyd, now eighty-four, had taken ill as well and was staying nearby with relatives. She died on the day Charlotte made her will. The will composed by Charlotte a few weeks before she died is her final formal message to her readers. The four letters above to her friends Amelia and Ellen were her only correspondences after the will.

The will anagrams mention a *grand master* who was the head *wolf* in charge of the false marriage. Even though in 1855 John Brown was the Worshipful Master of the Lodge, he was not a rich man nor was he the Brontës' enemy. This other *master* appears to have a connection to one of the inns in Haworth, which would have been one of the four mentioned above. He arranged to have a *true drone* attest to the Masons' *fund* money being stolen, which then placed Charlotte and her father in a precarious position. She believes the *fund* was actually for alcohol purchases, but the Masons called it their *toy fund* for orphan children. Years earlier, the Masons had formed a Sick and Death Benefit society called The Three Graces Union, but may have also initiated one for widows and orphans.

The marriage was a sham and so was her pregnancy. She thought this claim would lessen the abuse, but her *yarn* backfired. The men would not want an heir to take their money, but before Nicholls could tell them about this *smirch* or stain, they had realized that he had their *antique* arsenic tin, which made them angry. When he informed them, however, that Charlotte was pregnant, they calmed down. Her death from poison would work well with complications from pregnancy, so they allowed him to continue serving her *hot tea*. She uses *corn* as a slang to mean something melodramatic or trite. Charlotte composed this will herself.

"In the name of God amen. / I, Charlotte Nicholls, of Haworth / in the parish of Bradford / And county of York, / being of sound / and disposing mind / memory and understanding, / but mindful of my own mortality, / do this seventeenth day / of February in the year of our Lord, / One thousand eight / hundred and fifty-five, / make this my last Will / and Testament / in manner and form / following, / that is to say. / In case I die without issue / I give and bequeath to my husband / all my property / to be his absolutely / and entirely, / but,/ In case I leave issue / I bequeath to my husband / the interest of my property / during his lifetime, / and at his death I desire / that the principal should go / to my surviving child / or children; / should there be more / than one child, / share and share alike. / And I do hereby / make and appoint / my said husband, / Arthur Bell Nicholls, /clerk, / sole executor of this / my last Will and Testament / In witness whereof I have to this / my last Will and Testament / subscribed my hand, / the day and year / first above written—/ Charlotte Nicholls" (500).

None fathomed enigma. I halt chronicle. Lost. Crook bit hand. Funny day to rehash prior wrath. Off food. So begin odd spinning: found maid's money, so grand master did flout tidy wolf matrimony. Nun numb. Had to buy off thieves. Deny rare nets. Then find hairy fool, true drone. Said enough to verify fund death. Walk in, sit still, stand, mend, net mate. Wolf ran a mayhem log from inn. / That is to say, / *Who initiates suicide? Antique tin by bed had a use. Shove mug in lady. Enter, play merry plot. Obey lout. Lash bites.* / But / *Ease nut's vile cuisine as had baby;home quiet. Empty ruin, yet fight theft. Smile or die prisoner. Inherits the ideas. A cold pair haunt heights' plot. Add urn logic. Vivid myths enrich lord. Brothers ink a harsh deal. Elude cheat, hold inn, erase home. Inane papa in the dark bed. Moody. Sundays bad. Call brother ill. Shun him.* Clerk *cheers exit. Oust fool. Little madman wants style. Now finish hot tea. Thieves mad, want tin. Sly mate wiser. Tells sudden baby smirch. They fit a wit's banter over ill health corn. Yarn cost? Dead.*

No one had ever seen her puzzles and riddles, but now she has to stop reporting on the events, and *halt* her *chronicle*. The battle is over. She feels defeated, especially as she crafts a will that negates her pre-marital document. Even on this day, when the monies are being legally transferred, he still finds the energy to *rehash prior wrath*, but she, too, still has enough *fight* to spin the tale of how the thieves did their audit, found the *maid's money*, and began negotiations.

Charlotte tried to *buy off* the men, but money was not enough: they wanted a longer commitment of income, so they arranged a *tidy, wolf matrimony*. She would see this marriage as a *rare* net, which not only traps her but *nets* the husband easy wealth. The Brontës were counselled to *deny* the extortion in exchange for the thieves keeping Reverend Brontë out of *gaol* and safe from further humiliation. As it was, they were shunning him and calling him *ill*, which could have meant feeble-minded. Nicholls, the 'clerk' is happy to see the old vicar *exit* the pulpit, and *cheers* the fool's decline. Understandably, if Reverend Brontë had to face their disdain, his *Sundays* would be hard on him because he was still holding weekly service. He was a proud man, but he had become *inane*, or foolish, and his final years would be spent alone *in the dark* in his bedroom. Charlotte would have been equally offended by the thieves' treatment of her father, and would view the *little madman* wanting style, in the sense that he lacked class. She saw him as a brute and a *worm hypocrite*.

With her death, Nicholls would inherit her money and the future royalties from her writing. He would inherit the income generated from *Wuthering Heights*, where *a cold pair haunt heights' plot*. The image of Heathcliff and Catherine haunting the moors after their deaths may have surfaced from Brontë's fears of her own approaching death. In the *heights' plot*, the couple could be classed as literally and figuratively *cold*, but their story contained a passion and a fury that was interlaced with *urn logic*. Brontë had left the enigma of her riddles inside her Masonic clues and among her *vivid myths* to help her readers understand how the heath land deals and the masons were linked. The money also helped to *hold* an *inn*, which could mean that one of the four inns at the top of Main Street was experiencing financial troubles.

Brontë understood the irony that arose from her baby hoax. Any signs of *ill health* could easily be attributed to a pregnancy, and if she were being poisoned, the complications would suffice as an explanation for her symptoms. She had invented the baby story to stop the abuse and gain a *quiet home*, but an heir was a threat to the beneficiary of her money, so the tea was the best solution. The baby *yarn* did *cost* a great deal—it cost her her life. The arsenic poisoning would be impossible to detect. Arsenic is "a naturally occurring poison and carcinogen" that is "odourless, tasteless, colourless and easily soluble in water or wine," and "has long been a feared poison" (*The Vancouver Sun*).

The symptoms of arsenic poisoning include headache, delirium, diarrhea, stomach pain, vomiting, coma, and death. These coincide with her own symptoms: she felt faint, was exhausted, suffered from incessant nausea and vomiting, which would then bring on dehydration and death. Her last few days she would have slipped into a coma: "Charlotte grew inexorably weaker and closer to death. By the second week in March she could no longer even hold a pencil to write and her husband had to answer her letters for her" and "a week later, Charlotte was no longer conscious having slipped into a 'low wandering delirium' during which she constantly craved food and drink" (Barker 771).

Nicholls wrote to Ellen Nussey on March 31, 1855, the day Charlotte died. On April 21, she would have been thirty-nine. He wrote, "Our dear Charlotte is no more. She died last night of Exhaustion. For the last two or three weeks we had become very uneasy about her, but it was not until Sunday Evening that it became apparent that her sojourn with us was likely to be short. We intend to bury her on Wednesday morning" (*Letters, Vol.III* 330). In light of the anagrams, one could view this letter with a cynical eye and note that Charlotte was indeed exhausted from witnessing and experiencing two decades of Masonic justice. His words, "we had become very uneasy about her" also strike an ironic tone, but the curt formality of the letter could just as easily be attributed to his own exhaustion and not to an accurate portrayal of his detachment from her suffering. The servant Martha Brown and a friend Hannah Dawson had been with her when she died. "'Her husband was reclining in another room worn out with watching.'" The doctor Amos Ingham assigned "Phthisis" as the cause of death, "a term most often used for the wasting accompanying tuberculosis" (330-331 n. 1). Others believed she died from a complicated pregnancy.

Ellen Nussey had tried to visit Charlotte before her death, but was discouraged from disturbing her friend. When she received a letter from Reverend Brontë that the end was near, she immediately set off for Haworth, but arrived too late. In a letter to George Smith, she wrote, "'I had begged to go before, but Mr. Brontë and Mr. Nicholls objected, fearing the excitement of a meeting for poor Charlotte.'" She later recalled the day she last saw her friend: Ellen had arrived after Charlotte had died, but her body was still on the bed. "'Her maid Martha brought me a tray full of evergreens and such flowers as she could procure to place on the lifeless form. My first feeling was, no, I cannot cannot do it. Next I was grateful to the maid for giving me the tender office.'" At the same time, Nicholls approached her about the correspondences Ellen had received over the years from his wife: "'The very day of my arrival,' he had said to her, 'Any letters you may have of Charlotte's you will not shew to others and in course of time you will destroy them'" (qtd. in Barker 772-3).

The letters had always conveyed the sense of a relaxed conversation between friends. This particular aspect was what had made Nicholls demand the letters be destroyed. He believed her candid narratives would be inappropriate information for the public's consumption. Charlotte wrote to Ellen in October of 1854 that Nicholls had been reading her letter and felt her comments too free and open. "Men don't seem to understand making letters a vehicle of communication. They always seem to think us incautious. I'm sure I don't think I have said anything rash, however, you must <u>burn</u> it when read. Arthur says such letters as mine never ought to be kept. They are dangerous as lucifer matches, so be sure to follow a recommendation he has given "fire them" or "there will be no more." Such is his resolve. I can't help laughing; this seems to me so funny. Arthur however says he is quite serious and looks it, I assure you. He is bending over the desk with eyes full of concern" (*Letters, Vol.III* 295). On the surface, her letters seemed benign, but they were "as dangerous as lucifer matches" if her secret thoughts had been uncovered. Ellen, of course, ignored Nicholls' demands and kept Charlotte's letters.

On April 4, 1855, a few days after her death, Charlotte's coffin was taken the short distance from the parsonage to her burial site in the family vault inside St. Michael's. "The church and churchyard were crowded with parishioners, rich and poor alike, who had come to pay their last respects to the woman who had, so unexpectedly, made Haworth eternally famous" (Barker 773).

Ellen Nussey wrote to George Smith that her "unfavourable impressions" of Nicholls grew when she discovered that on June 20, 1855 Reverend Brontë wrote out his will and bequeathed all his worldly possessions to Nicholls. She had distrusted Nicholls during Charlotte's illness when he had essentially forbidden her to visit her friend, and she was disturbed further when she wrote, "it was a great shock to me discovering that he had been ransacking his wife's things so speedily after losing her" (780), but her feelings toward the husband worsened when she felt he had selfishly appropriated Reverend Brontë's possessions and money to himself (969 n. 33).

Ellen was not the only friend who questioned Reverend Brontë's change of heart. "Mrs. Gaskell thought that Mr. Nicholls held Mr. Brontë rather in terror, as he seemed to hold many in the village by his fiercely uncompromising stance. Nevertheless . . . the old man left everything in his will to his son-in-law rather than to his next of kin, who were living on both the Branwell [wife's] and Brontë sides. Ellen Nussey suggested that Mr. Brontë's arm had been twisted" (Fraser 497). Reverend Brontë had actually bequeathed "forty pounds to his brother, Hugh Brontë" and "thirty pounds, to Martha Brown," but the rest he left to Nicholls (Barker 785-6).

Ellen also believed Nicholls had no interest in Charlotte's life as a writer. As stated before, she wrote that Nicholls had said "Currer Bell could fly up to heaven for all he cared." She also said that Nicholls' discomfort arose from the worry that she would begin writing again. He wanted her to "cease": his "'whole anxiety . . . was that she should cease entirely to be the author' and that she was compelled to place a severe strain upon herself in order to comply with her husband's wishes, and once, as we have seen, her strength of self-repression gave way, and she indulged in the forbidden luxury of work with the pen'" (970 n. 53). Nicholls was not, however, loath to profit from his wife's work: when he learned that payment for her novels was based on their length, he "meticulously counted the pages of both *Villette* and *The Professor*"; he had "done his computation, asked for and received £220 from Smith, Elder & Co." (791).

Nicholls remained only a short time in Haworth after Reverend Brontë's death in 1861. "The Church Trustees decided against him, nor did the people of Haworth want him as incumbent after Mr. Brontë" (Fraser 497), so the church trustees rejected his application to assume his predecessor's living as vicar at St. Michael's, and he returned to Ireland, where he became a farmer, and married his cousin in 1864. He kept his wife's manuscripts and memorabilia for another thirty years until he sold some of the Brontëana to a collector. After his death, his wife sold "the manuscripts and books in two large sales at Sotheby's in 1907 and 1914" (Barker 827).

Arthur Bell Nicholls may not have been the kind of man Charlotte Brontë would normally choose for a mate, but without any actual evidence that he was poisoning her, the anagrams must be viewed as Charlotte's opinion only. In her illness, she may have imagined the worst, especially when her anagrams and fictional works contain so much violence and thoughts of arsenic in tea and poisoned landowners. These are her allegations transcribed for public review, but they are not proof of murder. Nicholls may have genuinely cared for his wife and felt a tremendous loss when she died.

In some cases, the anagrams fit with the biographical and historical facts. This allows the long reach into the distant past to imagine what her personal and professional worlds might have been like. If the anagrams are true, the revelations they contain help explain why scholars have found it difficult to filter myth from reality, particularly when regarding three of the most important events in her life.

The first lie centred on the publication of her literary works. She was an author who denied writing all her novels and poetry. Instead of publicly proclaiming her prodigious gifts, she chose to share credit and, therefore, protect her sisters from the exact fate she seems to have experienced in the final months of her life. She did not want the proceeds from her literary works stolen, so she devised a hoax that would meet a number of needs.

Her lie involved using three pseudonyms, not only to conceal her identity but also to allow her sisters a legal share of the wealth if anything were to happen to her.

Also, the masks of Currer, Ellis, and Acton Bell enabled her to write freely and to use a particular voice for each story, a practice born from her writer's insight into the characters of 'Ellis' and 'Acton,' and from years of early writing when she had used various male personalities for her narrators. Evidence of her own character supports this diligent and calculated approach to the business of writing, to the intelligent disbursement of her funds, and to the creative mechanics necessary to sustain her lie.

She would probably be shocked but pleased to know how long her writing has remained in the hearts and minds of her readers. She would have imagined her books fading from the public's memory a few years after her death, which may have happened, but Gaskell's biography of Charlotte renewed interest in the Brontë works.

Her Bell brothers' hoax was never meant to inconvenience her audience or confuse scholars. Her intention was to protect herself and her family, not to create a sustained mythology around her sisters, which is why she left so many clues to help readers locate the truth.

She also would be surprised by the number of visitors that arrive daily to pay homage to the Brontë legacy. In a letter to Williams in 1850, she writes, "I believe both "Shirley" and "Jane Eyre" are being a good deal read in the North just now—but I only hear fitful rumours from time to time. I ask nothing, and my life of anchorite seclusion shuts out all bearers of tidings. One or two curiosity-hunters have made their way to Haworth Parsonage—but our rude hills and rugged neighbourhood will I doubt not form a sufficient barrier to the frequent repetition of such visits" (*Letters, Vol.II* 350).

She could picture the curious readership enduring the trek to her home, but never would she have imagined the sheer volume of fans, nor that her home would one day be converted into a museum honouring her family.

The second lie came with the death of Branwell. The claim that he had died suddenly after months of alcohol and drug abuse saved her family from the humiliation and difficult explanations that surround a suicide.

The tale of a son's religious awakening on his deathbed would have been as much a fabrication as the story of Branwell's affair with Mrs. Robinson. That smaller lie kept the lawyers at bay. What husband wants to drag his wife through court to rebuke a slander that would only enflame the scandal? Reverend Brontë understood the power of words as well, and supported the fictional account of Branwell's end as he did the next family crisis.

The third lie arrived like an electric shock when Charlotte was to marry Nicholls. No wonder Ellen was confused. What long-standing friend would easily comprehend such a swift reversal of another friend's mind?

Ellen knew something was terribly wrong, but Charlotte was bound to silence.

The cold tension between Nicholls and Ellen makes sense if the anagrams are accurate: Ellen was not necessarily jealous of the husband, but distrustful and wary, and Charlotte's speedy decline must have terrified her. What woman or man would choose to stay away when a close friend since childhood was critically ill? Of course Ellen would push to see Charlotte, not to irritate the family, but to be with her friend when she needed special care. Besides, she knew a little of the Brontës' history, and had seen examples of Charlotte's compulsion for secrecy. She sensed Charlotte was hiding the truth, and needed the reassurance, in person, that she was in good hands.

A forced marriage under humiliating circumstances was certainly going to become another family secret. No wonder the father temporarily lost his sight. No wonder the daughter collapsed under the pressure of nerves and headaches, unable to tell Ellen what had brought on this sudden inexplicable acceptance of a man she had previously disliked.

Devastated by the loss of communication with her confidante but desperate to protect her father's shame, Charlotte had stoically remained mute, lonely, and unwell, which frustrated Ellen even more.

Friends and neighbours were understandably confused. After she announced her betrothal, they observed a grim and dreary author struggling with her fate. When they heard that the father-of-the-bride had refused to attend the nuptials—a terrible snub to the groom and a source of heartbreak for her no doubt, since the church was his church, and only a short walk from his front door—they were further perplexed.

The marriage certificate bears a clue. Her shaky, faint signature provides a surprising contrast to the strong confident signature of Currer Bell. Was she simply a reluctant bride or was she prescient enough to see her future lacked hope?

On her wedding day, her new reality had set in, and Charlotte's scribble seems to arise less from a bride's jittery nerves than from an author's emotional breakdown.

This once independent woman was suddenly forced to renounce her passion. Not only was she to put away the writing, but also her friend was to burn her letters. Just as she had begun to realize the dream she had long ago confided to Robert Southey, the poet laureate—that she wanted to be known as a writer, Charlotte would relinquish the successful profession she had fought her entire life to acquire in order to protect her family name. She had always tried to hide that name for good reason, but now larger forces had intervened and the lies needed to be sustained.

The lies probably became easier with time, and the anagrams must have kept her sane as she secretly recorded the truth. For Charlotte, the anagrams were her secret path to unleashing her opinions, beyond the glare of scrutiny, where she could speak her truth as she saw it. They were a safe alternative to the lies and half-truths of necessity and convention. There she could dispense with the fiction and tell her truth.

If the anagrams are to be believed, she left an impressive record of her deepest feelings and thoughts. Some contradict the lies, and others provide sensible alternatives to the many myths and inconsistencies that biographers have grappled with for decades.

The facts do confirm that the men of her area were uneducated and violent. Some people like to occasion misery, to communicate gloom, and they do it instinctively, without fuss, and apparently without conscience; the means to be brutal rises spontaneously in their minds. Add to their natures an unbroken greed, a bountiful temper, the daily opportunity to oppress, and a convenient means with which to inflict pain, and you will find bullies accomplishing their cold tasks with the ease of an all-sufficing strength. Fear is a powerful weapon, and Charlotte's fears were genuine. If a woman chose to speak up in this environment, she could be risking severe retribution, but intelligent men might not have been so threatened by a woman's words.

When William Makepeace Thackeray, the Victorian novelist first met Charlotte, he was struck by her "great honest eyes": "'I saw her at first just as I rose out of an illness from which I had never thought to recover. I remember the trembling little frame, the little hand, the great honest eyes. An impetuous honesty seemed to me to characterize the woman. . . . I fancied an austere little Joan of Arc marching in upon us, and rebuking our easy lives, our easy morals. She gave me the impression of being a very pure, and lofty, and high-minded person" (qtd. in Fraser 349).

In chapter fourteen in Brontë's novel *Shirley*, the character Shirley Keeldar ruminates on the necessity that women not display their "great honest eyes" too prominently in front of most men. "Men rarely like such of their fellows as read their inward nature too clearly and truly. It is good for women, especially, to be endowed with a soft blindness; to have mild, dim eyes, that never penetrate below the surface of things—that take all for what it seems. Thousands, knowing this, keep their eyelids drooped on system; but the most downcast glance has its loophole, through which it can, on occasion, take its sentinel-survey of life." Those eyes "for years had been accustomed to silent soul-reading."

Charlotte's soul had once grown as hardy as a winter bloom clinging to a granite cliff and had weathered the strong blast and soft breeze of life. From sunrise to sunset, her imagination wove its spell and spoke intimately of love and passion, fear and anger, and no barrier blocked the ceaseless stream of ideas. The evening was her church, with its moonbeam and stars, a time when, in a peaceful state of mind, she reflected on her soul's purpose. With her deepest desire and strongest intention, she tried to pull back the curtain. And then a miracle. A metaphysical wonder. She heard that inner voice speak in the character of Wisdom.

"I always, through my whole life, liked to penetrate to the real truth; I like seeking the goddess in her temple, and handling the veil, and daring the dread glance. O Titaness amongst deities! The covered outline of thine aspect sickens often through its uncertainty, but define to us one trait, show us one lineament, clear in awful sincerity; we may gasp in untold terror, but with that gasp we drink in a breath of thy divinity; our heart shakes, and its currents sway like rivers lifted by earthquake, but we have swallowed strength. To see and know the worst is to take from Fear her main advantage" (*Villette* ch.39).

She loved resting her chin on her hand while contemplating scenes and characters. The mental serenity and contentment of allowing her imagination to perform its delightful dance entranced her when the loneliness could almost be too much to bear. She found a sweet source of pleasure in the beauty of the pen, but she was wilful, unyielding, daring, and thrilled by the power of truth. And now her secrets have been released. The veil lifted.

To the world outside the parsonage, the emergence of genius expanding southward across the moors in 1847 released a powerful, seamless fiction of three Bell brothers. To the sole author, however, the names of three men attached to their respective novels symbolized not an unusual concentration of talent in one home, but an expression of freedom and independence from one heart, a representation of the lengths to which a brilliant woman might go to protect her family and shield her name, no matter the ultimate deception and its subsequent impact. Her most famous stories will continue to entertain and amaze the public with their bold heroines and brooding heroes set in the desolate Yorkshire moors. For Charlotte Brontë, the identity of the person on the cover, whether man or woman was secondary to the lives unfolding on the pages inside: the truth may not be in the name, but omit the name and discover the heartbeat in the body of the work. No unlocked box, with its revealing portrait of an eminent being, can ever diminish the passion and the integrity of the writing.

If one were to take a second look, to imagine the parsonage without its cozy parlour or children's study, one might see stone walls, once cold and impenetrable, slowly transformed into a woven fabric of intricate design, a ghostly tale with bold colours, chilling characters, secret signs, and ancient hieroglyphics, and behind the vision, a woman standing near an open door, transfixed by the light of dawn, beckoning us to linger inside the mystery, calling, inviting, "Come home to me again!"

EPILOGUE
COME RIDDLE US, WILLIE ELLIN

Between May and June of 1853, Charlotte Brontë began, but later abandoned an unfinished story written in the first person entitled "The Story of Willie Ellin." Parts I and II contain a riddle that, when solved, provide further clues about *Wuthering Heights* and explain the origins for the novel. The tale comprises three fragments totalling eighteen pages, but parts I and II are much shorter and read as follows:

Part I

I will not deny that I took a pleasure in studying the character of Mrs. Widdup, nor that to me she seemed to possess a good deal of worth of a particular kind. Thirty years ago (our acquaintance dated its commencement thus far back) I had believed very heartily in her worth without studying her character. She then ruled me as one of a flock of four—her nurslings. Of this flock I was not her favourite; indeed my place was lowest in her grace. Even through boyhood and adolescence she held me for a riddle rather than a model. After two decades of separation and more than half a generation's change beheld us again under the same roof, still the housekeeper of Ellin Hall, while respecting its master, revolved him day and night as an unsolved conundrum.

It was and must be so: habit and circumstances attached us, but nothing would combine, nothing quite unfold.

In a certain sense Mrs. Widdup was spotlessly honest; she had the fidelity of a consistent and steady nature; she was a partisan in friendship, an unflinching foe; she was usually humane and cheerful. She was narrow-minded, loved money, and by natural instinct still leant to the guidance of interest. Fidelity, partisanship, interest, all counselled her to attachment to the Ellin family, and accordingly she was attached to me, that family's surviving representative.

Ellin Hall had for five ages been the home of the Ellins. In my youth it passed out of their hands. My eldest half-brother sold it. He died suddenly, leaving neither will nor direct heir, his fortune fell to me, and I purchased back the ancient homestead. That eldest half-brother of mine was a

475

stronger man in body and a tyrant in heart. I would advert to his deeds, but they are such as we suffer Death to cancel from memory.

Part II

In other countries, and in distant times, it is possible that more of my kind might have been attracted to human dwellings—hut or mansion—and secretly taken them in lease, than for these hundred years past have been known to make their home in such abodes. Yet we were always few, our presence rare, its signs faint, and its proofs difficult to seize.

My house was not picturesque: it had no turrets, no battlements, no mullioned or lozenged windows. From the first, however, I believe its stones were grey, dug from a grey quarry on a grey waste. They who planned it had loved fresh air, and had chosen a raised site, building it where the green ground swelled highest. Its outlook was free and four-fold: it commanded both sunrise and sunset, and viewed an equal and a wide expanse north and south. These builders, too, preferred solitude to convenience: the village was distant—near enough, perhaps, in summer weather, but remote for a winter's day walk. As to a sentimental peculiarity of the vicinage, I believe the first owners had not known nor reckoned it in their choice of ground.

The short, green, flower-bearing turf around covered an ancient burying ground—so ancient that all the sleepers under the flowers had long ago ceased to be either clay or bone, and were become fine mould, throwing out violets in May, and a carpet of close silken grass all spring, summer, and autumn. These violets were white, and in their season they gathered thickly in a bleached wreath about what seemed a deep-sunk and iron grey rock—the sole left foundation stone of a forgotten chapel, or the basement of a cross broken away. A quiet gable of the house looked upon this mossy bit of mead. In the lower story of the gable was no aperture, in the upper a single window, having before it a balcony of stone, a peculiarity rare in that neighbourhood, forming indeed the distinctive feature of the house and originating its name—Ellin Balcony.

Who am I? Was I owner of the house? No. Was I its resident tenant, taking it perhaps on lease, and paying the rent? No. Was I a child of the family? No. A servant? No. Ask me no more questions for they are difficult to meet. I was there, and it was my house.

476

I recollect the first hour that I knew it. I came to consciousness at a moment within the rim of twilight. I came upward out of the earth—not downward from heaven, and what first welcomed and seemed to aid me to life was a large disk high over me, a globule, clear, cragged and desolate. I saw the moon before I could see the sky, but that too, night-veiled and star-inspired, soon opened for me. A sweet silence watched my birth-hour. I took affection for this mossy spot; I stole all through building and nook of land. In the mild beam and pure humidity of a midsummer night I found my seal and sign printed here in dew and there in moonbeam on roof and lawn of Ellin Balcony.

I do not know that ever I was knit with humanity, or was mixed with the mystery of existence as men or women know it. Yet had no mortal relic slumbered near the Balcony, should I have risen? Would Night, my mother, have borne me, unwedded to a certain vital, mortal essence?

Tears had watered this ground; great sorrows and strong feelings had gathered here. Could a colder soil, drenched only with rain and visited only by airs and shadows, have yielded me as its produce?

I even think that some one sleeper threw me out of a great labouring heart which had toiled terribly through his thirty, or sixty, or fourscore years of work, had lived and throbbed strongly, stood still while yet in vigour, and buried, yet warm and scarce arrested, had thrown forth its unslackened glow and ill-checked action in an essence bodiless and incomplete, yet penetrative and subtle.

I believe this because my relations to me were so limited. To millions I felt no tie, found no approach; to tens I might draw gently. Whether units existed that could more actively attract it, yet lay with time and chance to show.

Whoever in my early days were the inmates of Ellin Balcony, on me they made no impression. I knew every stone in the walls. I knew the neighbourhood—the knolls, the lanes, the turfed wastes, all vegetable growth, field flowers, hedge plants, yellow gorse and broom, foxglove springing bright out of stony soil, ivy on ground or wall. I distinguished and now remember these things very well. I knew the seasons, the faces of summer and winter. Spring and autumn were familiar in their skies; night, day, and the hours were all acquaintances. Storm and fair weather complete my reminiscences. I cannot recall anything human, and yet humanity was in the house.

Experience now tells me that it must have been busy, bustling humanity, an alert current of life flowing out after to towns and thickly peopled scenes, returning thence with accessions—life circulating in a free, ordinary channel, never stealing slow under the banks of thought, never winding in deeps, but coursing parallel with populous highways. At last, I suppose, this practical daily life forsook retirement and went permanently away to the towns which were its natural sphere. This departure made no difference to me, except that I remember looking at the sun and listening to the wind with a new holiday feeling of unconstraint.

About this time I first added a cognizance of the individual human being to a vague impression of a human race existing. A solitary old woman became housekeeper of Ellin Balcony. She used to feed a great dog chained in the now empty yard, to close and open shutters, to knit a great deal and read and think a little. I believe it was because she *did* think, however little, that I had the power to perceive her presence. Those who had lived here before her never thought, and into an existence all material I could not enter.

In 'The Story of Willie Ellin,' Brontë returns to her theme of two brothers, the elder a brutal bully and the younger, a sensitive boy forced to endure the cruelty of his tyrant sibling. In *The Professor*, they are called Edward and William Crimsworth but here they become Edward and William Ellin. Scholars note that the combination of violence and cruelty, the dreary house, and the character of the housekeeper resemble the tone and setting of *Wuthering Heights* and assume Charlotte admired Emily's novel so much that she tried to imitate the style.

After a few paragraphs describing the housekeeper, Mrs. Widdup, and the house where the narrator had been raised, he asks the reader to decipher who is actually telling this story. Is he Willie or someone else: "Who am I? Was I owner of the house? No. Was I its resident tenant, taking it perhaps on lease, and paying the rent? No. Was I a child of the family? No. A servant? No. Ask me no more questions for they are difficult to meet. I was there, and it was my house." These questions obviously pose a riddle. Brontë invites the reader to discern the clues and solve the question of 'who is speaking'? In order to do so, we must return to the first paragraph of the remaining fragment.

"I will not deny that I took a pleasure in studying the character of Mrs. Widdup, nor that to me she seemed to possess a good deal of worth of a particular kind. Thirty years ago (our acquaintance dated its commencement thus far back) I had believed very heartily in her worth without studying her character. She then ruled me as one of a flock of four—her nurslings. Of this flock I was not her favourite; indeed my place was lowest in her grace. Even through boyhood and adolescence she held me for a riddle rather than a model. After two decades of separation and more than half a generation's change beheld us again under the same roof, still the housekeeper of Ellin Hall, while respecting its master, revolved him day and night as an unsolved conundrum."

The inclusion of the words "riddle" and "conundrum" provide the first clue. A conundrum is a kind of riddle that asks a puzzling question whose answer could be a pun but, like a riddle or an enigma, the hidden meaning has to be discovered or guessed. The first sentence hides the origin of the riddle and becomes clear when placed in a different context offered by the scholar Christopher Heywood in his essay "The Wuthering Heights Landscape."

Heywood explains that the moorland surrounding the Brontë village of Haworth "does not match the novel." Instead, the "high crags" found several miles northward near Ingleborough Peak—the second largest mountain in Yorkshire—in the Yorkshire dales provided the model for the landscape depicted in the novel (18). The Clergy Daughters' School where the Brontë girls attended in the mid-1820s and Cowan Bridge are located nearby. Heywood notes Brontë's "enigmatic presentation" (19) of the land surrounding Wuthering Heights can easily be identified as that area near Cowan Bridge, and states that, in the novel, "the landscape definitions are lightly veiled by casual presentation as riddles and asides. Nevertheless, they accurately define the setting around Ingleborough which the Brontës had seen" (22).

Riddles play a large part in recognizing the landscape. Heywood adds that a number "of the scattered landscape clues in *Wuthering Heights* appear as riddles" (26) and assumes that Brontë's "reason for concealing several of her clues in riddles appears to have been her wish to avoid easy recognition of the model for her Yorkshire landscape" (28). She never directly describes the area but presents glimpses through a farm's relation to crossroads, rivers, the nearest village, or church, and gives clues with the number of miles from one landmark to the next, but her directions also move boundaries and extend beyond the confines of the Ingleborough frame. Her puzzles increasingly become more difficult to solve: "The riddles which perplex Lockwood at the farmhouse and in his dreams (chs. 2, 3) stream out across the novel as a whole. The reader is invited to tussle with them, as Lockwood does, until final meanings are reached" (30), and to locate the land that arose from Brontë's powerful observational skills as well as from the memory that she "brought to bear on the landscape of her heart" (34).

Heywood, of course, assumes that Emily is the author of *Wuthering Heights* and that she remembers this landscape from her childhood. He describes the moment when, upon leaving the Clergy Daughters' School for good, she would have seen Ingleborough in the misty moonlight and early dawn on their coach journey home: her introduction to this view occurred at Cowan Bridge "on the night of Tuesday 31ˢᵗ May, 1825. On the next day, Wednesday 1 June, the sisters took the daily Royal Union coach from Kendal to Keighley. The halt at Thornton in Lonsdale was scheduled for 9.30 a.m." The Ingleborough Peak rises "above the ground mist which swathes the vale at its foot, [a mist that] was created by the cold and cloudless weather of that week" (24). Nelly Dean recalls this feature in chapter ten as she looks over Gimmerton valley and sees "a long line of mist winding almost to its top" where "Wuthering Heights rose above this silvery vapour," but her "old house was invisible—it rather dips down on the other side." Heywood assumes that Emily's precise memory viewed from her coach was recalled years after when she placed that early morning scene into the pages of her masterpiece; consequently, further accurate representations, with minor alterations, have led Heywood to conclude that the source of the novel's landscape is Ingleborough and the neighbouring Cowan Bridge.

The only problem with his conclusions is that in 1825 Emily was just six years old, two months shy of her seventh birthday. Even if one assumes that Emily was a precocious little girl with an acute eye for detail and a resolute will to remain awake in the early hours of the morning on a long coach ride home, a sleeping child curled up against her big sister is probably the more believable image. Also on that ride home was Charlotte, the older sister and, at the age of nine, with her impressive memory, more likely the alert mind behind the observant eyes. The probability, therefore, is far stronger that it was she who stared out the coach window and became enthralled with the dreamy scene of silvery vapour and gritstone summits shadowed in the early morning light.

In 1849, she wrote to Smith Williams about how early impressions remain in her memory. She explains that she was briefly a student at the Clergy Daughters' School: "in fact I was never there but for one little year as a very little girl—I am certain I have long been forgotten—though for myself I remember all and everything clearly: early impressions are ineffaceable" (*Letters, Vol.II* 272). Those early impressions cannot be obliterated; they had stayed fixed in her mind years after.

The opening sentence of "The Story of Willie Ellin" supports Heywood's analysis of the landscape, but provides further information about the inspirational origins for *Wuthering Heights*. Another gritstone crag in the same vicinity of Ingleborough and Cowan Bridge, and one that measures 370 meters (1200 feet) in altitude is the north-facing, rock climbing "boulder" called Widdop near the Widdop Reservoir. The reservoir was built in 1878—twenty-three years after Charlotte Brontë died—and covers an expanse of 38 hectares. The water flooded the surrounding moorland, but the surviving array of high crags and boulders that now line the edge of the water would have been an equally prominent feature in Brontë's time, as would the Widdop moor still situated in close proximity. When she writes, "I will not deny that I took a pleasure in studying the character of Mrs. Widdup, nor that to me she seemed to possess a good deal of worth of a particular kind," the clues make it clear that Mrs. Widdup is her metaphor for the landscape. Also, "Widdop," the variation of Brontë's word, means wide valley.

Brontë derives pleasure from scrutinizing, not only natural wonders such as high crags and giant boulders, but also the characters or symbols of language. She loves to examine her system of letters and to play with words. Lockwood must do a similar analysis in chapter three to deduce Catherine's identity when he sees the various renditions of her name "repeated in all kinds of characters, large and small," that induce him to "decipher her faded hieroglyphics," as if they were a form of code.

481

The character of Mrs. Widdup also forms part of a secret language. As Brontë's substitute for landscape, Mrs. Widdup possesses "a good deal of worth of a particular kind." In *Wuthering Heights*, the housekeeper Nelly Dean is described as a "worthy woman," but Brontë is referring to a different type of worth: in Masonic terms, every Mason who has paid his dues and is in good standing at the Lodge is considered as worthy. The worth in this case, however, can be found in the villages in the Worth Valley, particularly Oakworth and Haworth, and those near Widdop: Wadsworth and Hainworth, as well as the nearby moorland of Boulsworth Hill. A number of place names with the word "worth" contained inside them explains Brontë's view of a "good deal of worth" found in her region.

Brontë writes that the narrator first met Mrs. Widdup thirty years earlier. "The Story of Willie Ellin" is dated 1853, so thirty years before would be 1823. In August of 1824, Charlotte began her schooling in Cowan Bridge and remained there a year. The date is close enough to suggest that she is revealing that she first laid eyes on the area at that time, and that it touched her heart: "I had believed very heartily in her worth without studying her character." Perhaps, she had not grown to appreciate the beauty of the landscape until the following year when she travelled home on that coach ride with Emily, but soon chose to draw upon that memory and, as Heywood notes, to write about the "landscape of the heart." If her clues relate to the origins of *Wuthering Heights*, she appears to be saying that the landscape formed the basis of her inspiration.

At the time *Wuthering Heights* was published, the Brontë novels numbered four: *Wuthering Heights*, *The Professor*, *Agnes Grey*, and *Jane Eyre*. The reviewers remarked on the rude and rough tone of *Wuthering Heights* with its violence and rusticity, which would make it the "lowest" of the flock of four, as would its setting in a valley. Also, Catherine denounces Heathcliff as a suitable mate because he is too "low" in social standing, so the word has a connection to the novel. The landscape provided nourishment for the author, and her description of the novels being "nurslings" echoes her Preface to the 1850 edition of *Wuthering Heights* where she describes the author as a "nursling of the moors," as if each book arose from Brontë's deep attachment to the land, an attachment that fostered a fondness for the power of place onto her writer's psyche.

For the next few years, as reviewers and readers held the book and followed the shocking elements through to their conclusion, they viewed *Wuthering Heights* "as a riddle rather than a model." What kind of person would write a book filled with such horror and darkness, and why would that person deviate so dramatically from the standard models of novelistic propriety to tell such a ghastly tale? Brontë answers part of this riddle when she writes to Williams that she prefers to write what she observes because "Truth has a severe charm of its own." The novel may not have mirrored the conventional sentiments and heroes found in other Victorian literature, but the wild and desolate setting and the characters with their fierce human passions were accurate representations of the strange and tormented souls that revolved around Brontë day and night. Also, in her 1850 Preface, Brontë explains that the author's inspiration for the book came "from no model but the vision of his meditations." Those meditations consisted of that scene witnessed years before on that coach ride home to Haworth.

Brontë returned to her memories twenty years after first seeing the high crags and giant boulders. The "two decades of separation" would be exact if that twenty-year span was calculated from 1823 to 1843, ending in the year Brontë says she wrote *Wuthering Heights* while studying in Brussels. By 1843, that enduring image of the landscape and the narrator of "The Story of Willie Ellin" are now "again under the same roof," so if Brontë reconnects with the land through her memories, and the land was one of the elements that helped form the basis for the novel's inspiration, who is the narrator of this story? And what is he trying to tell us?

He states that the housekeeper "while respecting its master, revolved him day and night as an unsolved conundrum." A conundrum is a kind of riddle or enigma that forms a question answered by a pun. If the housekeeper is the land, it certainly respects the laws of nature—"its master"—while revolving daily on its axis, so the conundrum can be solved by seeing that Mrs. Widdop is a pun: Widdop is not just the name of the housekeeper but is also the name of an actual place; consequently, Widdop is Brontë's pun and solution to her conundrum.

The next sentence stands on its own as a paragraph and also has a double meaning: "It was and must be so: habit and circumstances attached us, but nothing could combine, nothing quite unfold." The odd syntax and the separation from the rest of the paragraph could be an indication that the words require a closer examination for puns and for the possibility that they contain an anagram.

Brontë could be saying that her ability to play with words was not just a necessity that "must be so," but also a habit that she began at an early age. Indeed, her facility with language could include her skill with creating anagrams. This habit of writing, this need for expression, surfaced when circumstances led her to the landscape that held the massive rock formations, and this scenic event began the connection between inspiration and imagination that would later manifest in the creation of the novel. If "nothing could combine," the implication is that the truth of the land fraud could never be overtly linked with the heights story; consequently, nothing could "quite unfold." The truth of the land theft and the perpetrators were never overtly revealed in *Wuthering Heights*, never quite unfolded, but remained a conundrum for readers who questioned the reality of such a coarse, violent family. Who were these people? Where did they come from? Does this sort of brutality really exist?

An alternative reading comes from Brontë in her 1850 Preface to *Wuthering Heights*. She writes that the novel began when the author or "statuary" experienced a vision:

"The statuary found a granite block on a solitary moor: gazing thereon, he saw how from the crag might be elicited the head, savage, swart, sinister; a form moulded with at least one element of grandeur— power. He wrought with a rude chisel, and from no model but the vision of his meditations. With time and labour, the crag took human shape; and there it stands colossal, dark, and frowning, half statue, half rock; in the former sense, terrible and goblin-like; in the latter, almost beautiful, for its colouring is of mellow grey, and moorland moss clothes it; and heath, with its blooming bells and balmy fragrance grows faithfully close to the giant's foot."

From her point of view, as an author trying to depict a character accurately, the transformation from stone to a flesh and blood man fell short in its final metamorphosis. This explanation could be an example of her humility in saying that Heathcliff was not a fully formed or properly realized character, and that she failed to combine the reality with the characterization on the page.

The third way into the sentence can be found in the anagrams it contains. Brontë provides four natural divisions in the sentence that become succinct anagrams:

"It was and must be so:" / *Maid saw stone bust.*

"habit and circumstances attached us," / *A scenic catch. Add human attributes.*

"but nothing could combine," / *No humble conduct in bigot.*

"nothing quite unfold." / *Old nun quoting thief.*

In other anagrams, Brontë refers to herself as a spinster or maid, and states that she has tried to act like a nun whenever the men regarded her with suspicion. The implication is an obvious one, and does not literally mean she thought of herself as a member of a religious order, but as a woman in a precarious position, trying to survive in the role of an innocent and celibate maid when faced with the scrutiny of her enemy, the *bigot*. A "bigot" can be a hypocrite, but is generally someone—in this case, a man—who sees his own views as unquestionably right, and can be an intolerant person who rejects any beliefs that differ from his own.

The stone structure at Widdop inspired her at an early age, and the vision recalled itself to her in later meditations. The granite rock and its resemblance to a human head must have fit well with her image of the *grand master* as the land thefts escalated. The rock would have been a great "catch" for a writer, and the novel provided the form with which to demonstrate his deeds and quote his words, all with the aid of a male persona that echoed his voice.

The next part of the Mrs. Widdup riddle provides more clues that Brontë is describing the landscape. She says the housekeeper is "spotlessly honest," had both "fidelity"—she was faithful to her duties—and a "steady nature." The land, when personified in this way, could be seen as an honest entity, not deceptive, and one that performs its purpose in a reliable fashion, supporting the blades of grass, absorbing the sun's rays, or accepting the drops of rain. Nature can also be "a partisan in friendship" and "an unflinching foe." If the moors, fields, and rivers provide a peaceful sanctuary, nature can be a true companion, a "humane" and "cheerful" friend, but if the wind and the cold bring storms and snowfall, it quickly shifts to the role of "unflinching foe."

In a similar manner to her repetition of the word "worth," Brontë repeats the word "attached." She mentions the "attachment to the Ellin family" in her further description of the housekeeper/landscape. This word can simply mean to join or to bind by an emotional tie, which is the superficial meaning she presents in the riddle, but the word also conveys something much stronger. She says that certain characteristics "attached" Mrs. Widdup to the narrator. She was "narrow-minded, loved money, and by natural instinct still leant to the guidance of interest. Fidelity, partisanship, interest, all counselled her to attachment to the Ellin family, and accordingly she was attached to me, that family's surviving representative."

The Ellin family serves more than one purpose in this riddle. In this instance, the Ellins denote an actual family, but also can be read as a series of alphabet letters that form a unique part of the ethos of *Wuthering Heights*. The words in *Wuthering Heights* that contain the letters "ellin" comprise an interesting "family" of verbs that emphasize the culture of the place: "repelling," "smelling," "compelling," "yelling," "snivelling," and "telling," as in "telling a tale," which is repeated several times in *Wuthering Heights*. The word "telling" also points directly to the manner in which the sordid events unfold—the housekeeper, Nelly Dean is "telling" the story to the tenant Lockwood who has been "travelling" to and from the heights' "dwelling" where a good deal of "quarrelling" has been going on for years. This Ellin family of yelling and quarrelling has attached itself to the landscape as well and offers another reading of the clues. The sounds of fighting and feuding also lead directly to Brontë's Masons.

If the generating force behind the "ellin" ethos is a Masonic society "compelling" weaker inhabitants to do their bidding, the Masons' attachment to the landscape can be seen in new terms. Their activities involve unflinching "fidelity" to the brotherhood through the men's secrecy and obedience. Their "partisanship" or devotion to the supremacy of their group and their bigotry or propensity to be "narrow-minded" in that belief, arise from their devotion and allegiance to their secret society. Their "interest" in property developed from their greed: they "loved money" and, by their "natural instinct" to bend their minds to a fulfillment of self-interest, they "attached" themselves to the land. All these qualities "counselled" them to their attachment. They kept their own counsel through secrecy and hired lawyers to counsel them on the legalities of acquiring real estate. These puns revolve around the hidden concepts in *Wuthering Heights* and connect the reader to the attachments that grew from the land and the instigators of the "ellin" culture—the Masons, but the play on words extends into another meaning of "attachment."

In legal terminology, "attach" means to seize or take property through a writ. A legal attachment, therefore, is a seizure by virtue of a legal process, and "attachment" is applied to the taking of persons or property. Brontë is clearly making the connection between the land, the Ellin family, and the narrator who we have yet to identify, but the next paragraph and the secrets it holds may supply more clues to solve the riddle.

The last paragraph of Part I begins with two words that could be an anagram: "Ellin Hall" becomes *All in hell*. This clue and the short sentences that follow resemble similar instances when Brontë has inserted anagrams into a paragraph. The anagrams are placed after the sentences, where the natural splits in the phrasing are specified, and an explanation, if required, is supplied.

"Ellin Hall had for five ages / been the home of the Ellins."
Ellin Hall had for five ages: *Land heir gives foe half all*
been the home of the Ellins: *then he bets fine mole hole*
Land heir gives foe half. Then he bets all. Fine mole hole.

This could be the plot outline for *Wuthering Heights*. Hindley Earnshaw gambles and loses, so he needs to borrow money from Heathcliff. Soon he bets more, loses everything, and finds himself servant in his *fine mole hole*. In her next anagram she states that, though a tiny maid, she observed enough to tighten the tie, or metaphorical noose, around the Mason host when she wrote of his fraud.

"In my youth it passed / out of their hands."
Nosy, shy maid put tie / around host thief.
"My eldest half-brother sold it.
First steal odd Bell myth hero.

In this anagram, Brontë explains the origin for the Bell surname. She is referring to a sixteenth century child ballad that features three archers from the north of England entitled "Adam Bell, Clim of the Clough and William of Cloudesly." The three men were as close as brothers and

487

became legendary outlaws in the tradition of Robin Hood, and earned the love and admiration from the people. They risked their lives to rescue each other and, as a consequence of their heroic deeds, the King absolved them of their crimes, granted them clemency, and allowed them to live out their lives with their families. Brontë chose Bell for her three brothers' pseudonym and reveals the inspiration for the name. Scholars have conjectured on where the name came from but have never known this source. One theory was that the sisters chose the name because the church had recently ordered a new set of bells.

"He died suddenly, leaving neither will nor direct heir;"

Shy, did elude den. Hid rage well. Clever hint in interior.

"his fortune fell to me,"

Fief lout's elm throne.

A fief is land held under the feudal system, and a lout is usually an awkward and stupid person or oaf. In the first chapter of *Wuthering Heights*, Brontë describes the interior of the dwelling. The main room has "villainous old guns, and a couple of horse-pistols," as well as "immense pewter dishes" alongside "silver jugs and tankards, towering row after row." The room reflects the hunting and drinking interests of a northern man who sits "in his armchair, his mug of ale frothing on the round table before him." The room also contains a few chairs: "high-backed, primitive structures, painted green," and "one or two heavy black ones lurking in the shade." She never mentions the kind of wood used in the chair's construction, but varieties of the elm tree have long grown in Yorkshire and provided the material for high-backed armchairs. In Masonic terms, the chair occupied by the worshipful master is called the throne.

In the next anagram, Brontë continues to describe elements found in *Wuthering Heights*.

"And I purchased back / the ancient homestead."

A dark bed. Such panic! / Nice end to heath mates.

The dark bed refers to the enclosed couch where Lockwood spends the night and sees the ghost. The haunting certainly causes panic in Lockwood and in Heathcliff.

"That eldest half-brother of mine / was a stronger man in body and a tyrant in heart."

Words inside this anagram can be moved from one divided section to the other because no commas set up a forced break in the anagram. The shift creates the necessary clarity.

"That eldest half-brother of mine": *Mother's fable to land theft heir*

"was a stronger man in body / *bind sew on anagram story*

and a tyrant in heart": *trade an hint at yarn.*

Bind an anagram story to land theft. Sew on mother's fable. Trade heir. Hint at yarn.

Brontë again wants her readers to discover the secret tale she hid in anagrams inside the story of *Wuthering Heights*. Cathy, the daughter and natural heir, receives help from her *mother* Catherine who returns to the dwelling as a ghost hidden inside the tenant Lockwood. She tricks the thief and finds the illegal documents that had enabled the *theft* of her family home. Brontë combines both stories; she replaces the lawful *heir* at the end of the story; and she ends her yarn as well. The abundance of Masonic hints provides clues to her clever and playful *yarn*.

Brontë includes more of the prominent aspects of the story in the next anagram.

"I would advert to his deeds,"

Add odd, servile house twit. This would be the ancient servant Joseph who also acts as a member of the brotherhood in Lockwood's dream when he escorts the visitor to a crumbling chapel that doubles as a lodge.

"but they are such as we suffer Death / to cancel from memory."

Use theft, war, feud, abuse, heath's cry / for mercy. Common tale.

The anagrams, like the other clues in the Willie Ellin segment, all point to Brontë's vision for *Wuthering Heights* and her objectives to record the kind of violence and cruelty she believed existed in her township, as well as explain the origins of inspiration for her pseudonym. She draws on the power of the landscape and the whimsy of a child ballad to secretly expose the real estate fraud. She not only hides the clues through Masonic symbols and rituals, but also scatters significant words on the surface of the text to provide a bridge to her anagram yarn. She employs a similar technique with the above-noted paragraph that describes Ellin Hall. She uses the words "home," "died suddenly," "will," "direct heir," "fortune," "ancient homestead," "tyrant," "heart," "deeds," "suffer," "Death," and "cancel from memory." She worked hard to keep the fraud alive and to prevent the theft from being cancelled from anyone's memory.

Part II of "The Story of Willie Ellin" begins with a description of the narrator's home. The picture of grey stones "dug from a grey quarry on a grey waste," renders a dull, gloomy design that could be a replica of Wuthering Heights. The stone, discoloured by years of grey mill smoke, could also pertain to the exterior of the Brontë parsonage. At first glance, the details in the description vacillate between the two houses as the possible home for the narrator. The farmhouse is set in a solitary and remote locale from the nearest village, but the parsonage shares aspects of the nearby "ancient burying-ground—so ancient that all the sleepers under the flowers had long ago ceased to be either clay or bone." This description also partially echoes the last line of *Wuthering Heights* when Lockwood imagines Catherine and Heathcliff buried as "sleepers in that quiet earth." Both dwellings are situated on "a raised site" where "its outlook was free" and "the green ground swelled highest," but are the clues more subtle, and do they evoke something more profound? After all, this is the narrator's house, and he has presented himself as a riddle: "Who am I? Was I owner of the house? No. Was I its resident tenant . . . ? No." He is neither a child of the family nor a servant, but he was there and it was his house, so what kind of house is Brontë describing?

The first clue comes in the opening line of the description: "My house was not picturesque." This house is not suitable for rendering as a picture; it lacks formal substance, and is more an abstraction of the thing imagined. The narrator's house has "no turrets, no battlements, no mullioned or lozenged windows." Just as the narrator appears to lack substantiality, the house exists, not as a concrete object, but as an idea, a formless impression of elements and qualities that determines the intrinsic nature of a principle. Brontë has been explaining the origins of her inspiration for *Wuthering Heights*—the landscape, the giant rock formations, and the corrupt land schemes—as well as the influence of the child ballad "Adam Bell" on her choice of pseudonym. In this next description, she uses her usual method of dropping significant words throughout the paragraph to point to her clues. She enlists the vocabulary of Freemasonry to highlight the foundational source that housed her Masonic theme in *Wuthering Heights*.

She introduces the house by describing the grey stones. The initial image connects the reader immediately to stone masonry and to the dreary tone of the source. Brontë's image of freemasonry retains the dark and sombre colour of gloom. Her surface information resonates with her clues:

"They who planned it had loved fresh air, and had chosen a raised site, building it where the green ground swelled highest. Its outlook was free and four-fold: it commanded both sunrise and sunset, and viewed an equal and a wide expanse north and south. These builders, too, preferred solitude to convenience. . . . As to a sentimental peculiarity of the vicinage, I believe the first owners had not known nor reckoned it in their choice of ground."

Brontë uses the word "fresh" to mean "new" not pure, as she does at the end of chapter twelve in *Wuthering Heights*, when Nelly Dean must send Isabella's belongings "to her fresh home." The Masons who devised the land scheme, therefore, had loved new air that surrounded new properties obtained through their fraud. A "raised" Mason is one who has attained the degree of Master Mason, and the word "highest" connects the concept to the Heights of *Wuthering Heights*. One's "outlook" can be both a view and an attitude: "Its outlook was free and four-fold." From the Masonic point of view, candidates must come to the fraternity of their own free will, with an accepting attitude, but the original meaning arose from stonemasons being part of the guild and, therefore, free to work. The stonemasons who built Solomon's Temple were also free or exempt from paying taxes, and in the modern era, candidates become free and accepted masons.

The term four-fold also has meaning for Masons. The qualifications for a candidate in Masonry are four-fold in his ability to show he is morally, physically, intellectually, and politically upright. For the Mason, the symbol of a four-fold cord or cable tow signifies both the strong bondage of duty to adhere to the tenets of Freemasonry as well as the solid four-fold cord of mutual friendship. Masons see this as a bond that cannot be broken and have a saying that echoes this sentiment: "A three-fold cord is strong. A four-fold cord is not easily broken."

The Masonic builders "preferred solitude to convenience." Solitude coincides with their desire for secrecy and, in the confines of the Lodge, plans of deception could be quietly mapped out without interference or observation.

Brontë repeats the word "peculiarity" as in "peculiarity of vicinage" and "peculiarity rare." She may be using the word as an allusion to land: a peculiar is an exclusive property, a place exempt from ordinary jurisdiction, which in this instance could certainly describe the Masonic Lodge with its exclusive obligation, not necessarily to British law, but to the jurisdiction of the Grand Lodge. Freemasonry is described as "a peculiar system of morality veiled in allegory and illustrated by symbols," so her choice of words could also be based on her tendency to play with the meanings. Vicinage also relates to the land: in English Law, a vicinage was a certain right of common arising to neighbouring tenants of the same county. She writes, "As to a sentimental peculiarity of the vicinage, I believe the first owners had not known nor reckoned it in their choice of ground." The Masons lacked any emotional attachment to the land; their interest was primarily financial. The word "reckoned," placed in the context of a lack of sentiment, suggests a reckoning of costs, a settlement of accounts, or a calculation of figures, all of which support the implication that the architects of the land fraud reckoned on profit not natural beauty as the land's greatest asset. The narrator's house with its uncommon stone balcony or "peculiarity rare" is called "Ellin Balcony," and could be a veiled reference to the house behind the parsonage, which was called Balcony. At the time Brontë was writing this story, her new neighbour, the wine and spirit merchant, William Thomas, had retired and recently moved there.

Freemasonry roots and symbols go back to ancient times. Brontë mentions the "ancient burying-ground—so ancient" that the remains of the dead had turned to mould. Those early stonemasons who worked on Solomon's Temple and those who incorporated the legends and symbols of the ancient mysteries into Freemasonry are long dead. The financial success reaped from the land fraud also has its roots in death: those wealthy landowners who had once held the rights to their own ancient homesteads had died so that their families' entails could be forever altered.

The ancient symbol of the sun is one of the most important in Freemasonry and represents material light as it rises and sets. It also symbolizes the light of intelligence, which every Mason pursues. The

492

Lodge is a symbol of the world, governed by the sun and seasons as it opens and closes for specific ceremonies and celebrates special occasions throughout the year, but the "four-fold" view of Brontë's Masons that encompasses the sunrise and sunset and all four directions alludes to the wide range of acreage accumulated through the thefts.

A gable window in the narrator's house looks out onto "what seemed a deep-sunk and iron-grey rock—the sole left foundation stone of a forgotten chapel, or the basement of a cross broken away." The allusions to religion in a forgotten or broken state could refer to her view that the Masons lacked morality. White violets grow around the stone "in a bleached wreath," which conveys a further allusion to death: in Freemasonry, the violet is a symbol for mourning, and Brontë presents the violets in a wreath to confer honour upon those who have died at the hands of the Masons. She marks her grief with the word "sole" in "the sole left foundation stone" as a remembrance of the spirit or soul of Christian morality that has sunk deep under the weight of corruption.

The stone of foundation and its symbolic importance for Masons dates back to Solomon's Temple. In reality, the stone was always placed in the northeast corner, but Masons are more interested in the mythic or allegorical aspects of the foundation stone. The Masons derive poetic pleasure not from facts but from the spirit of the object.

The facts explain that during the building of the second temple or house of sanctuary, a stone inscribed with the ineffable name of God was placed in the holy of holies. Enoch is believed to be the man who first consecrated the stone, and then Solomon placed it in his temple where it remained until moved to the second temple. The Masons believe that the sacred name sanctified the stone and that the name symbolized the Grand Architect of the Universe, the Builder who, upon the sacred foundation stone, built the world. The Mason's quest, through the passing of degrees, is his search for the Lost Word or truth, but until that wisdom is found, he must be content with the substitute signs and words to guide him to the ultimate truth. The goal is to cast aside the substitute and possess the actual truth. The stone symbolizes the Grand Architect, so the stone of foundation symbolizes divine truth; thus, the true meaning of Freemasonry is bound to the science of morality, a peculiar system of morality veiled in allegory and illustrated by symbols, and a truth upon which all

493

Freemasonry is built. In Brontë's allegory, the Freemasons have crushed morality.

Like the Freemasons, Brontë provides her readers with substitute signs and words to guide them to the ultimate truth. She leaves clues and anagrams to aid the search for the truth, especially with regards to the land theft and to her identity as the author of *Wuthering Heights*. She, too, derived poetic pleasure from the spirit of the allegory. Her narrator, therefore, is not a literal character from a story, but something deeper, an entity "difficult to meet," a spectre or spirit that resides inside the pages of *Wuthering Heights* like the spirit of Catherine resides inside Lockwood. She provides more clues in the following paragraph as she explains the narrator's birth:

"I came to consciousness at a moment within the rim of twilight. I came upward out of the earth—not downward from heaven, and what first welcomed and seemed to aid me to life was a large disk high over me, a globule, clear, cragged and desolate. I saw the moon before I could see the sky; but that too, night-veiled and star-inspired, soon opened for me. A sweet silence watched my birth-hour."

The narrator's awakening coincides with Brontë's explanation that the landscape at Widdop held the key to the origin of *Wuthering Heights*. She appears to be describing the spirit of the novel that grew from that initial viewing of the giant rock formations on the desolate moor that "came upward out of the earth." If Brontë rode through the area in the pre-dawn hours, her observation of the land in twilight would have been beautiful and unforgettable. The spirit of the book, therefore, arose from her imagination, fired up by the sight of the huge boulders. Christopher Heywood describes the geographical reasons for this particularly stunning land formation as surmised in the 1830s: "The limestone district was created by volcanic pressure which up-ended the underlying slate beds, thrusting skywards the deep layer of limestone and its upper mantle of gritstone." The glaciers later sculpted the caps on the peaks. A milder upheaval formed moorland hills in the south: "Among the relatively low-lying gritstone edges around Haworth, Halifax, Huddersfield and Hathersage, the gritstone mantle has remained" (33). The area deeply stirred Brontë's visionary powers, and her clues in the Willie Ellin fragment, as to the birth of the novel, continue to redirect the reader to this region.

(Brontë may also have been leaving clues as to the location of her stories when she used so many character names that begin with the letter "H." The number of towns and villages whose names begin with this letter suggest that strategy may have been the basis for her choice.)

The narrator in the Willie Ellin fragment wonders if he would ever have connected with humanity without the aid of "a certain vital, mortal essence." This essence, with her "great sorrows and strong feelings," is the author Currer Bell. Without her passion and "great labouring heart," he would never have come into existence. The book is published, and its spirit experiences a burst of humanity inside a "current of life flowing out after to towns and thickly peopled scenes, returning thence with accessions— life circulating in a free, ordinary channel . . . coursing parallel with populous highways." Brontë is describing the journey *Wuthering Heights* took as bookshops and libraries acquired copies: it circulated free through the circulating libraries, travelling along the roads from town to town. Brontë herself enjoyed the convenience of a circulating library that visited Haworth on a regular basis.

The final paragraph in this section returns to the image of an "individual human being" described as "a solitary old woman" who "became housekeeper of Ellin Balcony." This character could also be Brontë, caretaker of the Brontë myth and keeper of the truth. This woman reads and thinks: "I believe it was because she *did* think, however little, that I had the power to perceive her presence. Those who had lived here before her never thought, and into an existence all material I could not enter." Until Brontë formed her thoughts onto the page, no one had thought to tell this story. Without her mind, the story of *Wuthering Heights* would never have come into the material world as a book, and the spirit of the novel would never have been born. That spirit, the narrator, is "difficult to meet" because it exists solely in the pages of a fiction, but as the "surviving representative," it bears witness to the crimes.

Brontë had personified books before. In a letter to George Smith in 1851, she admits that she understands why her publisher has rejected *The Professor*. Nonetheless, she still loves the novel: "my feelings towards it can only be paralleled by those of a doting parent towards an idiot child."

When Smith suggests keeping the manuscript at his office, she declines the offer, once again personifying the book: "His modest merit shrinks at the thought of going alone and unbefriended to a spirited Publisher" (*Letters, Vol.II* 572). In an 1851 letter to the author Julia Kavanagh, Brontë thanks her for sending her a copy of her novel *Nathalie* and apologizes for not responding sooner, explaining that the book had only just arrived: "she has been waiting in London to come down in a parcel with some other books. At last however I have made her acquaintance, read her through from the title-page to 'Finis'" (558). The fragment of Willie Ellin supports this view that Brontë would imagine *Wuthering Heights* with its own spirit or soul, and used this creative device as the solution to her riddle.

The remaining clue in the Willie Ellin fragment can be found in the name itself. At the end of *Wuthering Heights*, Nelly Dean sings a child ballad called "Fairy Annie's Wedding" about a servant called Annie. She loves the master of the house who is about to marry Annie's sister Elinor, but when Elinor realizes that Annie loves the man, she leaves and Annie becomes the man's wife; consequently, the servant rises to the status of the master's wife. This, of course, is also the story behind *Jane Eyre*: Jane rises from the position of governess in Rochester's house to become the master's wife. Christopher Heywood suggests that Brontë includes this ballad of "Fair Annie" in *Wuthering Heights* to construct the story around "marriage prohibitions," especially those pertaining to cousins and "siblings by adoption," a theme that relates to the two young cousins, Hareton and Catherine who, by the end of the story, are planning to marry: *Nice end to heath mates*. The prohibition fails to affect their union but, in the case of Heathcliff and Catherine, it excludes them from marrying each other because the Earnshaws have adopted Heathcliff, thereby preventing him from marrying into the family. As Heywood states, "the entire story results from the prohibition." The "Fairy Annie" ballad seems to pertain more to Catherine's change in status than to a marriage prohibition and, based on the next clue, the importance of prohibition may be less about the law than about social convention (40-1).

Brontë relies on another child ballad called "Sweet Willie and Fair Annie," also known as "Lord Thomas and Annet," as the underlying condition for Catherine's rejection of Heathcliff. In the ballad, Willie loves Annie and wants to marry her, but he recognizes that, although she is pretty and he loves her, she lacks property and money. The less attractive brown girl, however, has money but lacks a place in his heart, so he goes to his father for advice and poses his question as a riddle: "Come riddle us, riddle us, father dear, / Yea both of us into one; / whether shall I marry Fair Annie / or bring the brown bride home?" The father is a practical man and advises his son to marry the woman who has houses, land, gold, and horses. His mother and sister agree, so Willie marries the brown girl. Sad Annie comes to the wedding, which provokes the brown bride to kill her, and Willie then kills his new bride. The two lovers are buried near each other, and where he lies grows a tree, and where she lies grows a rose bush: "And as they grew and as they drew, / until they two did meet; / and everyone that past them by / Said, 'Thae's been lovers sweet'" (Child Ballads).

Heathcliff and Catherine are buried beside each other as well, but Catherine's gravesite is "half buried in heath" while Heathcliff's recent grave is "bare," so no trees or rosebushes grow from their remains to link the two lovers, but a similar sentiment from the ballad is echoed in the novel.

The other child ballad that mirrors "Sweet Willie and Fair Annie," is "Lord Thomas and Fair Ellinor." In variations of this ballad, the lady's name is shortened to Ellin. This ballad tells the identical story and, in the end, they, too, are buried together: "Lord Thomas was buried in the church, / Fair Ellin in the choir; / And from her bosom there grew a rose / and out of Lord Thomas the briar. / They grew till they reached the church tip top, / When they could grow no higher; / And then they entwined like a true lover's knot / For all true lovers to admire."

In chapter nine of *Wuthering Heights*, Catherine sits with Nelly Dean and asks for her advice much like Willie asks for his father's. Catherine accepts Edgar's proposal but wonders if she made the right decision. Nelly asks if she loves Edgar, and Catherine says she does because he loves her, and because he is handsome, young, cheerful, and rich, but she admits that her decision has not made her happy. She strikes her breast and says, "In whichever place the soul lives—in my soul, and in my heart, I'm convinced I'm wrong!" She loves Heathcliff, but he is too poor and "low;" it would "degrade" her to marry him, and they would be forced to live as beggars. Her situation and choice resemble Willie's and Annie's, and her decision to marry Edgar sets in motion Heathcliff's revenge.

Like Sweet Willie who presents his case to his family in the form of a riddle, in the Willie Ellin fragment, Brontë's narrator poses his question to the reader as a riddle when he asks, "Who am I?" The solution arises from the number of clues that all point to the inspiration and origins of *Wuthering Heights*: Brontë directs the reader to the landscape with its stunning rock formations, to the fraud, to the Masons and their allegories and, finally, to the child ballads. The spirit of *Wuthering Heights* says: while others "never thought," the novel's essence was able to come into being precisely because Brontë "*did* think."

Wuthering Heights, neither a divine text nor a miraculous wonder, is a complex, extraordinary masterpiece from the pen of Charlotte Brontë. Few women have ever achieved so much in literature, and no writer, after concealing her identity, has ever gone to such intricate and profound lengths to reveal herself as the real author of that powerful story. Why else would she leave this riddle if not to tell us, "I was there, and *Wuthering Heights* is my book."

ANAGRAMS

<u>Letter to Heger</u>

"1) I must say one word to you in English—/ 2) I wish I could write to you more / 3) cheerful letters, 4) for when I read this over, / 5) I find it to be somewhat gloomy—/ 6) but forgive me my dear master / 7) do not be irritated at my sadness—/ 8) according to the words of the Bible: / 9) 'out of the fullness of the heart, / 10) the mouth speaketh' / 11) and truly I find it difficult / 12) to be cheerful / 13) so long as I think / 14) I shall never see you more. / 15) You will perceive by the / 16) defects in this letter / 17) that I am forgetting / 18) the French language—/ 19) yet I read all / 20) the French books I can get, / 21) and learn daily a portion by heart—/ 22) but I have never heard / 23) French spoken but once / 24) I left Brussels—/ 25) and then it sounded / 26) like music in my ears—/ 27) every word was most precious to me / 28) because it reminded me of you—/ 29) I love French for your sake / 30) with all my heart and soul. / 31) Farewell my dear master—/ 32) may God protect you with special care / 33) and crown you / 34) with peculiar blessings" (*Letters, Vol.I* 435).

Two lie. Hid our union's system. Agony. How idiotic is rule. Wore myself out. Cruel tether. Defer vow—one hair shirt. Beg, wait. Hid my fool emotions. Fate sum: Get bride, marry, move. Master distant, so beyond tirade. If together, Catholic bond—bed rows. Shut off, on shelf. Hate roulette. Hush meek poet that, if in city, did flirt—adult fun. Curb hotel fee: goal—inn. Share menu. Hot kiss. Lovely soiree. Bury vice sheets. Left whole pile, yet fight interdict—engulf heart. Time to grant a change. Relay detail: On thicket bench, fears go. I tarry. Lay idle hand on Bonaparte. Thrive. Beau had nerve. Beckon, confer, then sup. Free lust. Bliss. Eat, sin, end odd hunt. A cry, kiss, lie immune. Sweet sorrow verse put busy Romeo in mood. If meet dead cue, am icy. Warm fire. Fur cloak over shy one. Had hot lust in alley. Mates retry: defame wall. How to court? Eye a papist cycle diagram. Our own candy. Publish secrets wailing.

1) *Two lie hid our union's system agony* 2) *How idiotic is rule wore my out* 3) *self cruel tether* 10) *hush that meek poet* 11) *if in city did flirt adult fun* 12) *curb hotel fee* 13) *goal inn hot kiss* 14) *share menu lovely soiree* 15) *bury whole pile vice yet* 16) *left interdict sheets* 17) *fight time to grant a* 18) *change engulf heart* 19) *relay detail* 19) *fears go on thicket bench* 21) *thrive beau had nerve* 22) *beckon confer then sup* 23) *free lust bliss* 24) *eat sin end odd hunt* 25) *a cry kiss lie immune* 26) *sweet sorrow verse put mood am icy* 27) *busy if meet dead cue in Romeo.*

The remainder of the anagrams fit with their respective numbers in the letter above.

Final Letters

On or after February 21, 1855:

My dear Ellen:

"I must write one line / out of my weary bed. / The news of Mercy's / probable recovery / came like a ray of joy to me. / I am not going to talk about my sufferings / it would be useless and painful. / I want to give you an assurance / which I know will comfort you / and that is that I find in my husband / the tenderest nurse / the kindest support / the best earthly comfort / that ever woman had. / His patience never fails / and it is tried / by sad days and broken nights."

Remit fury. See union wilt. Wed a booty—me. Amoral men joke. Love robbery caper. Why free? Coy fee. Amity costs. Souse took tin fund. Mating buys off gaol is argument, but wed a plain Ellis. Navigate low court seas. How? Way, if lucky, with moronic union. Shy maid had abundant hints fit tin urn. Need three tests. Poke third test puns. Myth brother flees cot at a mad Haworth event. Finish. Did leave secret pain. Dying. Hobby ends as Titan tankards rise.

Remit see union wilt / fury wed a booty me / men costs why free / love robbery caper / joke amoral coy fee amity. / Took tin mating gaol / buys off is argument / souse but wed Ellis / a plain fund. / Navigate court seas way union / low if lucky how with moronic. / Shy maid had abundant hints fit tin / urn need three tests. / Poke third test puns. / Myth brother flees cot it /

a mad Haworth event. / Finish leave secret pain / Titan did rise / dying hobby ends as tankards.

Late February, 1855.

Dear Amelia:

"Let me speak the plain truth. / My sufferings are very great. / My nights indescribable. / Sickness with scarce a reprieve. / I strain until what I vomit is mixed with blood. / Medicine I have quite / discontinued. / If you can send me anything that will do good do. / As to my husband / My heart is knit to him. / He is so tender, so good helpful patient. Poor Joe! long has he to suffer. / May God soon send him, / you, all of us health strength—/ comfort."

He has kept up ill treatment. / Fear mystery fever is urn gag. / They end scribbling aims. / Wise, cheap trick. Serves arsenic. . / Twit tin ritual. Hoax—womb void. Limited his sin. / Hive quiet came. Induced to die in sin. / Doodling fund—high, easy, toady income. Want lot. / Do nasty ambush. / Shrink, maim tithe toy. / Pulpit fool. He needs hag to end stories. / Sons of heath group jeer fool. / Moody. Has me nod, sign. / On cot! Hush! Form—legal theft. Oust fly.

He has kept up ill treatment. / Fear mystery fever is urn gag. / They end scribbling aims. / Serves arsenic wise cheap trick / Tin ritual sin / hoax womb void limited his twit. / Hive quiet came die in / induced to sin. / Fund easy income / today want doodling high lot. / Shrink maim tithe toy. / Do nasty ambush. / End stories he / pulpit fool needs hag to. / Sons of heath group jeer fool. / Moody nod has me sign / on hush legal theft oust fly / form cot.

March, 1855.

Dear Amelia:

"1) I'll try to write a line myself. / 2) The medicines produced / 3) no perceptible effect on me / 4) but I thank you for them / 5) all the same. / 6) I would not let / 7) Arthur write to Dr. Henriquez. / 8) I knew it would be / 9) wholly useless. / 10) For 2 days I have been / 11) something better / 12) owing to the milder weather. / 13) We all grieve / 14) that there is no better news of Joe. / Oh for happier times. / My little grandchild / when shall I see her again? / God bless you."

Style will for maternity lie. / Did seem prudent choice. / Force pen. Complete benefit. / A future book myth hint: / a mate's hell. / Raze required. Do truth until throw in towel. / Yell woe, but like wind, uses howls. / Beware of avid honesty. Might not be reset. / Wrote eight with role named. / Legal review to see how rent rebates join theft. / Heath is prime proof. / Target: mill—did lynch. / An high healer was senile, / so busy Lodge.

Lines 6-9 are the only anagrams that require a small shift from one phrase to the other. Lines 13 and 14 meld perfectly.

6) *Do until towel* / 7) *rage required truth throw in.* / 8) *Woe but like wind* / 9) *uses howls yell.* / 13) *Legal review* / 14) *to see how rent rebates join theft.*

March 1855.

My dear Ellen:

"Thank you much for Mrs. Hewitt's / sensible clear letter. / Thank her too. / In much her case was / wonderfully like mine, / but I am reduced / to greater weakness. / The skeleton emaciation is the same / etc. etc. etc. / I cannot talk, / even to my dear / patient constant Arthur / I can say but few words / at once. / These last two days / I have been somewhat better, / and have taken some beef tea, / spoonsful of wine and water, / a mouthful of light pudding / at different times. / Dear Ellen / I realize full well / what you have gone through / and will have to go through / with poor Mercy. / Oh may you continue to be / supported and not sink / Sickness here has been / terribly rife. Papa is well now. / Kindest regards to / Mr. And Mrs. C your mother, / Mercy. / Write when you can. / Yours C.B. Nicholls."

Knew truth, so rich, famous Bell relates secret in myth. / Then hook rat. / If church men kill me now, as a wise rule—deny. / Audit curbed me. See strange tea work. / Tie to hemlock in a senate. Emit ashes etc. etc. etc. / Link not an act. / Eye venom dart. Snatch torn rat. Put in tea. / Two-faced act wins as bury one. / At stately sow shed the thieves beat beam owner. / Name, vote, shake, be neat, fade. / Awful red pawn fits noose on. / Lift up, hang. Tough feat if termites. Find old mud, / lean elder. / Then zeal will rule life. Who gave a rough youth a tough lad howl over night? Worm hypocrite. / Undo knot, auction drapes, buy pints. Yeomen hoot. / Banshees shriek. Try brier life scene. / Own law applies. / Gets dark. Den riots. Stormy murder march. No mercy. / Cue war. On they win. / Holy in cross club.

Knew myth truth so rich famous / Bell relates secret in / then hook rat. / Church men wise as a / rule kill if deny me now. / Audit curbed me / see strange tea work. / Tie to hemlock in a senate. Emit ashes. / Link not an act. / Eye venom dart. / Snatch torn rat put in tea. / Two-faced wins as bury / act one. / At stately sow shed / the thieves beat beam owner. / Even fake death. Emanate sob. / Red pawn fits awful noose on / lift up hang tough if old mud / termites fate find. / Lean elder / Zeal will rule life / then who gave a rough youth / a tough lad howl over night / worm hypocrite. / Auction yeomen hoot buy / undo knot drapes pints. / Banshees shriek scene. / Try brier life. / Own law applies. / Gets dark den riots / stormy murder march / no mercy. / On they win. Cue war. / Holy in cross club.

"In the name of God amen. / I, Charlotte Nicholls, of Haworth / in the parish of Bradford / And county of York, / being of sound / and disposing mind / memory and understanding, / but mindful of my own mortality, / do this seventeenth day / of February in the year of our Lord, / One thousand eight / hundred and fifty-five, / make this my last Will / and Testament / in manner and form / following, / that is to say. / In case I die without issue / I give and bequeath to my husband / all my property / to be his absolutely / and entirely, / but,/ In case I leave issue / I bequeath to my husband / the interest of my property / during his lifetime, / and at his death I desire / that the principal should go / to my surviving child / or children; / should there be more / than one child, / share and share alike. / And I do hereby / make and appoint / my said husband, / Arthur Bell Nicholls, /clerk, / sole executor of this / my last Will and Testament / In witness whereof I have to this / my last Will and Testament / subscribed my hand, / the day and year / first above written—/ Charlotte Nicholls."

None fathomed enigma. I halt chronicle. Lost. Crook bit hand. Funny day to rehash prior wrath. Off food. So begin odd spinning: found maid's money, so grand master did flout tidy wolf matrimony. Nun numb. Had to buy off thieves. Deny rare nets. Then find hairy fool, true drone. Said enough to verify fund death. Walk in, sit still, stand, mend, net mate. Wolf ran a mayhem log from inn. / That is to say, */ Who initiates suicide? Antique tin by bed had a use. Shove mug in lady. Enter, play merry plot. Obey lout. Lash bites. /* But /* Ease nut's vile cuisine as had baby; quiet home. Empty ruin, yet fight theft. Smile or die prisoner. Inherits the ideas. A cold pair haunt heights' plot. Add urn logic. Vivid myths enrich lord. Brothers ink a harsh deal. Elude cheat, hold inn, erase home. Inane papa in the dark bed. Moody. Sundays bad. Call brother ill. Shun him.* Clerk *cheers exit. Oust fool. Little madman wants style. Now finish hot tea. Thieves mad, want tin. Sly mate wiser. Tells sudden baby smirch. They fit a wit's banter over ill health corn. Yarn cost? Dead.*

None fathomed enigma /I /halt chronicle lost / Bit hand rehash prior wrath off food / crook funny to day. / So begin found / odd spinning maid's / money grand master did nun / flout tidy wolf matrimony numb. / Thieves had to deny nets / rare buy off. / Hairy fool, true drone / said enough to then / verify fund death find. / Walk sit still mayhem / stand net mate / mend a ran from inn / wolf in log. / That is to say, */ Initiates suicide who use / antique tin by bed had a shove mug / play merry plot / obey lout lash bites / enter in lady. /*but /* ease vile cuisine as / had baby quiet home nuts / empty yet or prisoner theft / smile fight die ruin. / Inherits the ideas add a / cold pair haunt heights plot / urn logic vivid myths / enrich lord / brothers elude home / cheat hold inn / ink a harsh deal erase. / Inane papa in the dark bed moody / bad Sundays him / call brother ill shun /*clerk /* cheers exit oust fool / little madman wants style. / Now finish hot tea wiser thieves/ mad want tin sly mate tells / sudden baby smirch/ they a dead yarn/ fit wit's banter over / ill health corn cost.*

WORKS CITED
AND
FREEMASONRY REFERENCES

Alexander, Christine (ed.). *An Edition of the Early Writings of Charlotte Brontë.* Oxford: Basil Blackwell, vol. I, 1987; vol. II, parts 1 and 2, 1991.

---.*Tales of Glass Town, Angria, and Gondal: Selected Early Writings.* Oxford UP, 2010.

Alexander, Christine and Margaret Smith (eds). *The Oxford Companion to the Brontës.* Oxford UP, 2003.

Allott, Miriam (ed.). *The Brontës: The Critical Heritage.* London: Routledge, 1974.

---. *Emily Brontë's Wuthering Heights* (Casebook), Revised ed. London: Macmillan, 1992.

---. *Charlotte Brontë Jane Eyre and Villette: A Casebook* London: Macmillan, 1973.

Babbage Report. Wright, Jeffrey, 'Babbage Report, Haworth 1850.' An Ancestry.com Community. Accessed June 2008 <http://freepages.genealogy.rootsweb.ancestry.com/ ~jeffreywright/Babbage%20Report>.

Barker, Juliet. *The Brontës.* New York: St. Martin's, 1994.

Beer, Frances (ed.). *The Juvenilia of Jane Austen and Charlotte Brontë.* London: Penguin Classics, 1986.

Benson, Edward. *Charlotte Brontë.* London: Edward Arnold, 1978.

Bentley, Phyllis. *The Brontës and Their World.* London: Thames and Hudson, 1969.

Bewick, Thomas. *A History of British Birds.* Vol. I. London: Longman and Co., 1826.

'Thomas Bewick' by Roger H. Boulet. 4 April 1997. The Edmonton Art Gallery. Accessed September 2009. <http://www.sharecom.ca/bewick>)

Bloom, Harold (ed.). *Emily Brontë's Wuthering Heights: Bloom's Notes.* With an Introduction by Harold Bloom. Broomall, PA: Chelsea House Publishers, 1996.

Brontë, Anne. *Agnes Grey.* Eds. Robert Inglesfield and Hilda Marsden, with an Introduction and Notes by Robert Inglesfield. Oxford: Oxford World's Classics, 1998.

---. *The Tenant of Wildfell Hall.* Ed. Stevie Davies, with an Introduction and Notes by Stevie Davies. London: Penguin Books, 1996.

Brontë, Charlotte, 'Biographical Notice of Ellis and Acton Bell' (1850),

Emily Brontë, *Wuthering Heights*. Penguin Classics Edition, 2003, pp xliii-xlix.

---. *Jane Eyre.* Ed. Margaret Smith, with an Introduction and Notes by Sally Shuttleworth. Oxford: Oxford World's Classics, 2000.

---. *Shirley.* Hertfordshire: Wordsworth, 1993.

---. 'Editor's Preface to the New (1850) Edition of *Wuthering Heights*,'

Emily Brontë, *Wuthering Heights*. Penguin Classics Edition, 2003, pp l-liv.

---. *The Professor.* Eds. Margaret Smith and Herbert Rosengarten, with an Introduction by Margaret Smith. Oxford: Oxford World's Classics, 1998.

---. *Villette.* Introduction by Susan Fromberg Schaeffer. London: Bantam Classic, 1986.

---. *Wuthering Heights.* Ed. Pauline Nestor, with an Introduction by Pauline Nestor, and a Preface by Lucasta Miller. London: Penguin, 2003.

---. *Wuthering Heights.* Introduction by Margaret Drabble. London: Everyman Ltd., 1978.

---. *Wuthering Heights.* Notes by Helen Small. Oxford UP, 2009.

Emily Brontë's *Wuthering Heights: Bloom's Notes.* Ed. Harold Bloom, with an Introduction by Harold Bloom. Broomall, PA: Chelsea House Publishers, 1996.

Brontë, Patrick Branwell. 'Branwell and Alexander Percy.' Accessed September 2010 <http://www.enotes.com/nineteenth-century-criticism/patrick-branwell-bronte>.
<http://www.incompetech.com/authors/bbronte>.

Brontë, Reverend Patrick. *Cottage Poems.* Halifax: P.K. Holden, 1811. 'Who Were the Brontës?' *The Brontë Parsonage Museum and Brontë Society.* Accessed March 2011 <http://www.bronte.org.uk>.

'The Miscellaneous and Unpublished Writings of Charlotte Brontë and Patrick Branwell Brontë.' 'Unpublished Writing.' Accessed January 2011 <http:ia300234.us.archive.org-2-texts>.

Brother in the Shadow: Stories and Sketches by Branwell Brontë. Eds. Mary Butterfield and R.J. Duckett. Bradford: Bradford Art Galleries & Museums, 1988.

Campbell, Marie. *Strange World of the Brontës.* Ammanford: Sigma Leisure, 2001.

Carlyle, Jane Welch. *Jane Carlyle: Newly Selected Letters.* Eds. Kenneth J. Fielding and David R. Sorensen. Aldershot England: Ashgate Pub.

Ltd., 2004.

Chapple, J.A.V. and Arthur Pollard. *The Letters of Mrs. Gaskell.* Manchester: Mandolin, 1997.

Child Ballads. 73B 'Lord Thomas and Annet' and 73D 'Lord Thomas and Annet' Accessed December 2009. <http://www.sacred-Texts.com/neu/eng/child/ch073.htm>.

Child Ballads 116. 'Adam Bell'. Accessed December 2009 <http://traditionalmusic.co.uk/child-ballads/ch116.htm>.

Chitham, Edward. *A Brontë Family Chronology.* Hampshire, N.Y.: Palgrave MacMillan, 2003.

---. *A Life of Emily Brontë.* Oxford: Blackwell, 1987.

---. "The Themes of *Wuthering Heights.*" *Critical Essays on Emily Brontë.* Ed. Thomas John Winnifrith. N.Y.: G.K. Hall, 1997.

Collins, Robert G. (ed.). *The Hand of the Arch-Sinner: Two Angrian Chronicles of Branwell Brontë.* Oxford: Clarendon Press, 1993.

Critical Essays on Emily Brontë. Thomas John Winnifrith (ed.). N.Y.: G.K. Hall, 1997.

Crosby, Dr. John. "Branwell Brontë's 'honest and kindly friend': Dr. John Crosby of Great Ouseburn." By Alice Barrigan. 22, April 2007. Accessed 15 January 2011 <http://jakesbarn.co/uk>.

Davies, Stevie (ed.). Anne Brontë. *The Tenant of Wildfell Hall.* London: Penguin Books, 1996.

Dinsdale, Ann. *The Brontës of Haworth.* London: Frances Lincoln, 2006.

---. Conversation of October 2006 with the author of *The Brontës of Haworth* and *Old Haworth.* Re: William and Enoch Thomas, at Haworth, West Yorkshire.

Dobell, Sydney. *The Life and Letters of Sydney Dobell.* Ed. Emily Jolly. Vol. I. London: Smith, Elder, 1878.

DuMaurier, Daphne. *The Infernal World of Branwell Brontë.* London: Virago, 2006.

Feather, John Waddington. 'The Dialect of Shirley.' Accessed January 2011 <http://www. Yorkshiredialect.com/conts.htm>.

Fermi, Sarah and Dorinda Kinghorn. "The Brontës and the Case of the Beaver Forgery." Vol. 21, Parts 1 and 2, pp.15-24 (1993) Brontë Society Transactions.

Fraser, Rebecca. *The Brontës.* London: Crown, 1988.

Freemasonry References can be found at the end of the 'Works Cited.'

Gaskell, Elizabeth Cleghorn, *The Life of Charlotte Brontë.* With an Introduction by Winifred Gerin. London, N.Y.: Dent, Dutton, 1971.

Gerin, Winifred. *Branwell Brontë.* London: T. Nelson, 1961.

---. *Charlotte Brontë: The Evolution of Genius.* Oxford UP, 1967.

---. *Emily Brontë: A Biography.* Oxford: Clarendon, 1971.

Gezari, Janet. 'Poems of Doubtful Authorship.' Accessed February 2011 <http://courses.wcupa.edu/fletcher/gezari.htm>.

Glen, Heather. *Charlotte Brontë: The Imagination in History.* Oxford UP, 2002.

---. (ed). *Charlotte Brontë: Tales of Angria.* London: Penguin, 2006.

Gordon, Lyndall. *Charlotte Brontë: A Passionate Life.* N.Y.: W.W. Norton, 1994.

Greenwood, R. (2005). *Who was Who in Haworth During the Brontë Era.* 1820-61, To date unpublished.

Hatfield, C.W. (ed.). *The Complete Poems of Emily Jane Brontë.* New York: Columbia UP. Reprint Edition, 1995.

Heywood, Christopher. 'The *Wuthering Heights* Landscape.' *Wuthering Heights.* Peterborough: Broadview Press, 2001.

Lathbury, Roger. 'The Avaricious and the Intransigent: A Match Made in London.' Re: Newby and Brontë. *English Matters.* Accessed January 2010 <http://englishmatters.gmu.edu/issue8/lathbury_body.htm>.

Lock, John, and Canon W.T. Dixon. *A Man of Sorrow.* London: Nelson, 1965.

Malham-Dembleby, John. *The Confessions of Charlotte Brontë.* Published privately.Bradford: Leah Malham-Dembleby, 1954.

Massington, Hugh. *The Great Victorians.* London: Iver Nicholson and Watson, 1932.

Moore, Virginia. *The Life and Eager Death of Emily Brontë.* London: Rich and Cowan, 1936.

Neufeldt, Victor (ed.). *The Works of Patrick Branwell Brontë:* An Edition, vol. I.N.Y.: Garland, 1997.

---. *The Works of Patrick Branwell Brontë.* Vol. III (1837-1848). N.Y. and London: Garland, 1999.

Oates, Joyce Carol. 'Emily Brontë's *Wuthering Heights.' Uncensored: Views and (Re)views.* N.Y.: Harper Collins, 2005.

Oxford Companion to the Brontës. Eds. Christine Alexander and Margaret Smith. Oxford UP, 2003.

Peeck-O'Toole, Maureen. *Aspects of Lyric in the Poetry of Emily Brontë.* Amsterdam:Editions Rodopi, 1989.

Peel, Robert. 'Robert Peel's Speech.' Accessed September 2008 <http://www.historyhome.co.uk/polspeech/catholic.htm>.

Reid, T. Wemyss. *Charlotte Brontë:* A Monograph. N.Y.: Haskell House, 1970.

Rigby, Elizabeth. '*Vanity Fair*--and *Jane Eyre.' Quarterly Review.*

84:167, (December 1848): 153-185. Date: 10/2/2000. Accessed
September 2010
<http://faculty.plattsburgh.edu/peter.friesen/default.asp?go=252>.

Robinson, A. Mary F. *Emily Brontë.* www.openlibrary.org. Accessed
February 2011
<http://www.readbooksonline.net/read/33969/71183>.

Shattock, Joanne (ed.). *The Cambridge Bibliography of English
Literature.* Vol. 4. 1800-1900. Cambridge UP, 1999.

Shorter, Clement K. *Charlotte Brontë and Her Circle.* London: Hodder
and Stoughton, 1896.

---. *Charlotte Brontë and Her Sisters.* London: Hodder and Stoughton,
1905.

---. (ed.). *The Complete Poems of Emily Brontë.* With an Introductory
Essay by W. Robertson Nicoll. New York and London: Hodder and
Stoughton, 1908.

Smith, George. *The Recollections of a Long and Busy Life.* (1895)
Unpublished autobiography. Adam Matthew Publications. Accessed
May 2006 <http://www.adam-matthew-
publications.co.uk/digital_guides/nineteenth_century_literary_
manuscripts_part_2/publishers-note.aspx>.

Smith, Margaret (ed.). *The Letters of Charlotte Brontë.* 3 Vols. Oxford:
Clarendon Press, 1995-2004.

The Cambridge Bibliography of English Literature. Ed. Joanne Shattock.
Vol. 4. 1800-1900. Cambridge UP, 1999.

The Oxford Companion to the Brontës. Eds. Christine Alexander and
Margaret Smith. Oxford UP, 2003.

The Vancouver Sun. 'Arsenic Linked to Adult-Onset Diabetes: Study."
20 August 2008, A5, *Reuters.*

Treffert, Dr. Darold A. and Dr. Daniel D. Christensen. 'The Mind of A
Savant.' *Scientific American Magazine.* Dated 2005. Accessed
March 2008 <http://scientificamerican.com/Article.cfm?id=inside-
the-mind>. See also 'Magic Trick' at
<http://www.wisconsinmedicalsociety.org/_Savant/_RES/_media/
video/treffert/video.html>.

Wellesley, Arthur. 'Duke of Wellington's Speech.'
<http:www.historyhome.co.uk/Polspeech/catholic.htm>. Accessed
September 2008.

Whitehead, S.R. *The Brontës' Haworth: The Place and the People the
Brontës Knew.* Haworth: Ashmount Press, 2006.

Wills. <www.archives.wyjs.org.uk> Re: Yorkshire wills before 1858 proved in courts of Archbishop of York. Now wills are at Borthwick. <http://www.mlfhs.org.uk/Infobase/Begin-Wills.php>. 'Although the majority of wills were proved within a few months of the testator's death, there was no pressure to do so within any particular time limit.'

Wilson, Romer. *All Alone: The Life and Private History of Emily Jane Brontë.* London: Chatto and Windus, 1928.

Winnifrith, Thomas John (ed.). 'Emily Brontë: The Latitude of Interpretation.' *Critical Essayson Emily Brontë.* N.Y.: G.K. Hall, 1997.

FREEMASONRY REFERENCES

'Alternative Religions.' Dated: 2011. About.com. Accessed March 2011 <http://altreligion.about.com/library/texts/bl_textindex.htm#masonry>.

'Ancient Landmarks of Freemasonry.' Dated: 1998. Geocities.yahoo.com Accessed December 2004 <http://www.geocities.com/Athens/oracle/1190/landmarks.html>.

Binns, S.H. (W.Bro.) *The History of Freemasonry in Haworth.* P.P.J.G.W. 1999.

Defoe, Stephen A. masonicdictionary.com. 'Consecration.' Dated 2005-2007.Accessed June 2009 <http://www.masonicdictionary.com>.

Dewar, James. *The Unlocked Secret: Freemasonry Examined.* London: William Kimber, 1966.

'Dictionary of Freemasonry.' Dated: 2005. The Masonic High Council. Accessed March 2009 <http://www.rgle.org.uk/Dictionary.htm>.

Feather, W. (Bro.) *History of the Three Graces Lodge No. 408 Haworth 1792-1931."*

'Freemasonry.' Dated: 1999-2002. Accessed September 2008 <http://freemasonry.bcy.ca/ritual/list.pdf> and <http://www.freemasonry.bcy.ca/grandlodge/landmarks.htm> and <http://www.freemasonry.bcy.ca/texts/gmd1999/pondering.htm>.

'Grand Lodge of Alberta, Ancient Free and Accepted Masons.' Dated 2004. freemasons.ab.ca. Accessed December 2004 <http://www.freemasons.ab.ca>.

'Grand Lodge of Canada in the Province of Ontario, Freemasonry.' Dated: 2004.grandlodge.on.ca. Accessed December 2004 <http://www.grandlodge.on.ca>.

'Historical Documents.' Dated 2011. freemasoncollection.com.
 Accessed February 2011 <http://freemasoncollection.com/9-
 MASONICBOOKS-AND-TEXTS-IN-ENGLISH/historical-
 documents-of-freemasonry.php>.

Jones, Bernard E. *Freemasons' Guide and Compendium.* With a forward
 by J. Heron Lepper. London: George G. Harrap, Revised Edition,
 1963.

Long Branch Lodge 632. 'Landmark 16.' Accessed June 2010
 <http://www.longbranchlodge.ca/history.htm>.

MacKenzie, Kenneth R.H. (ed.), *The Royal Masonic Cyclopedia.*
 Willingborough:The Acquarian Press, 1877, 1987.

Mackey, Albert G. M.D. *An Encyclopedia of Freemasonry and its Kindred
 Sciences* Vol. 1, The New and Revised Edition. N.Y. and London:
 The Masonic History Company, 1914.

---.*Symbolism of Freemasonry.* N.Y.: Clark and Maynard, 1882.

'Masonic Dictionary.' Dated: 2004. the lodgeroom.com. Accessed
 December 2004
 <http://www.thelodgeroom.com/dictionarya.html>. (Entries A-C).

'Masonic Grand Lodge of Oregon.' Dated September 2004. masonic-
 oregon.com. Accessed December 2004 <http://www.Masonic-
 oregon/whatis.htm>.

'Masons of California.' Dated 2004. freemason.org. Accessed December
 2004 <http://www.freemason.org/cfo/july_august_2001/>.

Moore, Charles Whillock. 'Encyclopedia of Freemasonry.' *The
 Freemasons' Monthly Magazine,* Vol. III. Boston: Tuttle and
 Dennett, 1844.

Pick, Fred. L. and G. Norman Knight. *The Pocket History of
 Freemasonry.* Revised by Frederick Smyth. 1898-1966. London:
 Frederick Muller, 1991.

'Phoenix Masonry.' Dated: 2007. Accessed December 2008
 <http://www.phoenixmasonry.org/genesis_of_freemasonry.htm> and
 <http://www.Phoenixmasonry.org/mackeys_encyclopedia/index.htm>

'Sacred Text Archive--Freemasonry.' 'The Rite of Intrusting, and the
 Symbolism of Light.' Ch. XXII. Dated 2011. AccessedMay2011
 <http://www.sacredtexts.com/mas/sof/sof24.htm>.

Scott, C.J. 'The Tradition of the Old York T.I Lodge of Mark Master
 Masons: An enquiry into early Freemasonry at Bradford and
 neighbourhood. 1713-1873. Accessed April 2011
 <http://www.brad.ac.uk/webofhiram/?section=York_rite&page=
 tradoldyork.html>.

'Signet Chapter No. 129.' Dated 200-2011. Accessed May 2011

<http://www.mastermason.com/Signet129_PA/oes_theme.htm>.

Springer, Joel H. 'The Ornaments of a Lodge.' themasonictrowel.com. Dated July 2007. Accessed March 2008 <http://www.themasonictrowel.com/Articles/Symbolism/ lodge_files/the_ornaments_of_a_lodge.htm>.

'The United Grand Lodge of England.' Dated: 2002. grandlodge-england.org. Accessed December 2004 <http://www.grandlodge-england.org/masonry/what-is-freemasonry.htm>.

Made in the USA
Charleston, SC
07 June 2013